Aśvaghoṣa's Gold

TRANSLATIONS OF

Buddhacarita and Saundarananda

by Mike Cross

Abbreviations:

BC: Buddhacarita
DN: Digha Nikāya (Collection of Long Discourses)
EBC: EB Cowell
EHJ: EH Johnston
LC: Linda Covill
MMK: Mūla-madhyamaka-kārikā ("The Middle" of Nāgārjuna)
MN: Majjhima Nikāya (Collection of Middle-Length Discourses)
PO: Patrick Olivelle
SamN: Samyutta Nikāya (Connected Discourses)
SED: The Monier-Williams Sanskrit Dictionary
SN: Saundarananda

First edition of these texts and translations in this format: Nov, 2015.

(Prepared in digital format for free distribution by Ānandajoti Bhikkhu.)

This revised edition prepared and published by Mike Luetchford
Windbell Publications May, 2023

Cover shows a detail from a Borobudur carving, depicting Siddhārtha's flight from Kapilavāstu on the horse Kanthaka.

"This royal war-horse, also, as he went, did not touch the ground, the tips of his hooves seeming to dangle separately in midair." (BC8.45)

Table of Contents

- Preface to Second Edition -

From going back to The Middle of Nāgārjuna (MMK), it becomes clear, in light of emptiness, that Sanskrit *smṛti* (Pali: *sati*) means remembering, or thinking, what one wants to happen. And happen is the operative word.

In the concluding section of the Rāhula Sutta in Pali (MN62; see Appendix), the Buddha advises Rāhula to let thinking happen, as a letting happen. *Ānāpāna-satiṁ Rāhula bhāvanaṁ bhāvehi* means "Let happen, Rāhula, as a letting happen, thinking in the activity of breathing in & out."

Eight years ago, before going back to The Middle of Nāgārjuna, I did not translate like that either *ānāpāna-satiṁ* (Sanskrit: *ānāpāna- smṛtiṁ*) or *bhāvanaṁ*.

Rather, in the first edition of this work I translated *smṛtiṁ* as if it were a state - a state of mindfulness, awareness, or vigilance. The emphasis that Nāgārjuna puts, not on things or states, but rather on action and other happenings, caused me to see that, as is often the case, the first definitions given in the Sanskrit dictionary had, after all, come closest to hitting the target. Those first definitions of *smṛti* are -ing words: remembering and thinking. Both those words describe a practitioner practising recollection in the active sense of remembering to think what he or she is doing, in the broader context of everything else that's happening. So *smṛti*, to me (I admit I borrowed the term from FM Alexander) is "thinking in activity." *Smṛti* is primarily an effort of prevention, which would be why the Buddha compared it to armour - *smṛti-varma* is the armour of thinking, or the armour of thinking in activity. *Ānāpāna-smṛti*, in Saundarananda 15.64, is not a state of being mindful of breathing but is rather - very literally - "remembering, while breathing in and out." *Ānāpāna-smṛti* is remembering what one wants to happen (and not to happen) while breathing in and out. That is, in other words, thinking in the activity of breathing in and out - as a letting happen.

In the first edition, again, I translated the instrumental *bhāvanayā* "by the means of mental development" or "by means of cultivation [of the mind]." But Nāgārjuna's emphasis on the primacy of what happens, again, caused me to see that *bhāvana* (or the feminine *bhāvanā* favoured by Aśvaghoṣa) is in most contexts best translated simply as "letting happen." So in, for example, SN16.5, the practitioner prevails over all pollutants *bhāvanayā*, by the practice of letting happen. That verse, tellingly, contains three words - *bhāvanayā* (by letting happen), *abhibhūya* (prevailing over), and *bhūyaḥ* (again) - all derived from the verbal root √*bhū*. This, I think, was Aśvaghoṣa hinting at the importance of a verb whose many meanings include to happen. That √*bhū* can mean not only to exist, or to be, but also to happen, I now see, was vital not only for Nāgārjuna's purposes but also for the purposes of Aśvaghoṣa before him. SN16.5 offered a big clue. SN12.9 offered an even bigger clue that I also missed. SN17.21 was another momentous one, certainly worth revisiting. SN12.43, 13.44 and 13.51 were just some of the other ones.

These were not trivial instances of missing the target on my part, since the whole point of every verse that Aśvaghoṣa and Nāgārjuna wrote, in the end, might be to put out the fires of thirsting and clinging, as Aśvaghoṣa put it, *bhāvanayā*, by the practice of letting happen - using *bhāvanā* like water (SN15.5). Equally, the whole point might be to stop the ignorance which is behind all our unwitting doings, as Nāgārjuna put it, *bhāvanāt*, through the practice of letting happen (MMK26.11). And, as a practice of letting happen, there might be no practice more effective, as the Buddha praised it at the end of the Rāhula Sutta, than *ānāpāna-satiṁ*; that is, in Sanskrit *ānāpāna-smṛtiṁ*, thinking in the activity of breathing in and out – as a non-doing practice, as a letting happen.

Another turning word derived from √*bhū* whose significance in Aśvaghoṣa's poetry I missed is *svabhāva*. Due again to the ambiguity of √*bhū*, *svabhāva* can literally be translated, in accordance with the truth of emptiness, as "spontaneous (*sva-*) happening (*bhāva*)," and can equally literally be translated as the very antithesis of emptiness, as "self- (*sva-*) existence (*bhāva*)." Thus the instrumental *svabhāvena* (or *svabhāva-* at the beginning of a compound), in the former sense, means happening by itself, spontaneously, naturally, and in the latter sense intrinsically, by its inherent nature, by its very self-existence. The opportunities these double meanings presented for playing with irony – in verses like BC8.70, SN6.12, SN13.30, SN15.30, SN16.15, SN16.46, SN17.15, SN17.38 – would not have been lost on Aśvaghoṣa. But eight years ago, before listening to Nāgārjuna's detailed critique of his realist opponent's conception of *svabhāva*, this irony was lost on me.

So I am very grateful to Michael Luetchford for making it possible to publish this second edition and for allowing these two translations in particular – of *smṛti* and of various derivatives of √*bhū* where √*bhū* can mean to happen – to be amended. Most of the editing of Aśvaghoṣa's poetry itself needed to happen, as it turned out, in Saundarananda Cantos 16 and 17, where *bhāvanā* is at the center of the Buddha's teaching and of Nanda's effort.

M.C. Spring 2023

- Introduction -

Convenient Fictions, Irreligious Irony, Golden Sitting

For the last seven years,[1] at the therapeutic snail's pace of one verse per day, I have been translating two works of Aśvaghoṣa known in Sanskrit as *mahā-kāvya*, epic poems or epic tales. They are not exactly works of fiction; they are based on historical fact, but only loosely. In any case, they are not to be taken too literally, because they are so full of metaphor and – in the gap between their ostensible and hidden meanings – so full of irony.

Some teachings, like the Buddha's four noble truths, are well represented both on and below the surface.

Those four noble truths are:

1. the truth of suffering,
2. the truth of the arising of suffering,
3. the truth of cessation of suffering, and
4. the truth of a practical means leading in the direction of the cessation of suffering.

Aśvaghoṣa records the Buddha's statement of the four noble truths, in brief, like this:

iti duḥkham etad
This is suffering.
iyam asya samudaya-latā pravartikā
This is the tangled mass of causes producing it.
śāntir iyam
This is cessation.
ayam upāya iti
Here is a means.[2]

Here the fourth noble truth is not expressed in terms of a metaphor. *Upāya* means that by which one reaches one's aim, an expedient of any kind, a means-whereby.

At the same time, the Buddha did use for the fourth noble truth the metaphor of a path (*mārga*). Hence:

> "This is suffering, which is constant and akin to trouble; this is the cause of suffering, akin to starting it; / This is cessation of suffering, akin to walking away. And this, akin to a refuge, is a peaceable path." // SN16.4 //

The Noble Eightfold Path, also known as the Middle Way, is a metaphor for the threefold practice of ignorance-destroying wisdom (*prajñā*), backed by twofold practice of meditative balance (*samādhi*), backed by the threefold practice of integrity (*śīla*).[3]

---

[1] This Introduction, prepared for the first edition at the end of 2015, has for this second edition been only very lightly edited, except for its concluding section – on the meaning of Golden Sitting – which has been rewritten in light of Nāgārjuna's clarification in MMK of the teaching of emptiness.

[2] See Saundarananda SN3.12.

[3] In the Mahā-parinibbāna-suttaṁ (DN16, see Appendix), the Buddha seems to emphasize this

In reality there *is* such a thing as practice of threefold *śīla*, twofold *samādhi*, and threefold *prajñā*, leading in the direction of ending of ignorance, but there is no such path as a Noble Eightfold Path. The Path is a kind of fiction. In the real world, there are real, non-fictional paths that can be walked, like the ancient Ridgeway running across England from Salisbury Plain to East Anglia. There are real roads that can be travelled, like the Pan-American highway linking many nations in Northern, Central and South America. But no Noble Eightfold Path or Middle Way is marked on any map.

So even such a core teaching as the Noble Eightfold Path is a metaphor, a fiction. It is something akin to the dream which, if we are lucky, helps our tired bodies and minds to recuperate during the night.

But Zen masters from the time of the Buddha, though invariably steeped in actual practice, have shown themselves to be skilled in the use of such dreamlike fictions – using their fingers, metaphorically, to point at the moon. And none has been more skilled in using metaphors, similes, parodies, et cetera, than Aśvaghoṣa.

Convenient Fictions

Speaking of putting fictions to practical use, in 1906, in a book titled The Integrative Action of the Nervous System, Sir Charles Sherrington wrote of "*the convenient fiction of the simple reflex.*"

The convenient fiction of the simple reflex.

A lot of irrational, fearful, unconscious human behavior can be explained with reference to a primitive fear reflex called (after the Austrian pediatrician Ernst Moro who identified it) "the Moro reflex." As a simple reflex, a thing unto itself, the Moro reflex is a convenient but empty fiction. Any simple reflex is an empty fiction because the human organism and its environment all work unfathomably together, in an integrated way, as a whole. And yet the Moro reflex, though a fiction, is convenient. When in Buddhacarita Canto 8 Aśvaghoṣa describes arms being thrown up and out in grief,[4] when in Saundarananda Canto 6 he describes Sundarī performing the same abduction of the arms while gasping and going red,[5] and when indeed in SN Canto 12 he describes the shocked Nanda seeming to go white,[6] I find it convenient to refer in my footnotes to the Moro reflex – as if there were such a thing, as a thing unto itself, as a Moro reflex.

The use of convenient fictions as a means to convey the real gist of the Buddha's teaching, as evidenced in the first instance by the Noble Eightfold Path, goes back all the way to Gautama Buddha himself. The Lotus Sūtra emphasizes how skilled the Buddha was in the use of expedient means (*upāya-kauśalya*), including the kind of metaphors and parables with which the Lotus Sūtra abounds.[7]

---

particular order – *śīla* (using voice and body well, making a clean living) supporting *samādhi* (true mindfulness, balanced stillness), supporting *prajñā* (seeing and thinking straight, true initiative) – while at the same time each element supports the others in a circular fashion. So it might be a case of "altogether, one after the other."

4 BC8.24, 8.37.

5 SN6.27.

6 SN12.8.

7 The second chapter of the Lotus Sutra is titled "Expedient Means," and the third chapter is titled "Parable" or "Metaphor."

The 14th Zen patriarch in India, Nāgārjuna, again, is known for the explicit distinction he makes between two levels of truth:

> The buddhas' teaching of dharma rests on two truths: the truth of the convenient fictions of the world, and ultimate truth. Those who do not know the distinction between these two truths do not know what it's really like deep in the Buddha's teaching. Ultimate truth is not taught without relying on the conventional. Without understanding of the ultimate truth, nirvāṇa is not realized.[8]

Twelve generations after Gautama Buddha, and two generations before Nāgārjuna, sits the 12th Zen patriarch in India. His name, Aśvaghoṣa - Horse (*aśva*) Whinny (*ghoṣa*) - is so far less well known than the name of his Dharma-grandson Nāgārjuna. This is despite the sterling efforts of EH Johnston, the Oxford professor who laid the foundations of Aśvaghoṣa study with his Sanskrit texts and English translations of Aśvaghoṣa's two epic poems, Buddhacarita ("Acts of the Buddha"; 1936) and Saundarananda ("Nanda the Fair"; 1932).[9]

Another Oxford University academic, Linda Covill, has more recently demonstrated in her book A Metaphorical Study of Saundara-nanda (2009) how very adept Aśvaghoṣa was, as a poet on a par with Kālidāsa, at dealing in convenient fictions.

What so far has not been well recognized is

(1) the extent of the irony which resides in the gap between the ostensible and hidden meaning of Aśvaghoṣa's fictions; and

(2) the extent to which Aśvaghoṣa, like the Buddha before him, and like Nāgārjuna after him, and no less than the Zen masters of China and Japan who followed Aśvaghoṣa and Nāgārjuna, was primarily concerned with the supremely practical matter of how (and how not) to sit.[10]

Investigating Aśvaghoṣa's Irony - Being Caused Constantly to Mind the Gap

The first of Aśvaghoṣa's two poems, Buddhacarita, ostensibly means "Acts of the Buddha" or "Life of the Buddha." Ostensibly, Buddhacarita is a biography, an epic poem that tells the life-story of Gautama Buddha. Below the surface, however, the Sanskrit word *buddha* is a past participle meaning "awakened." And *carita* is also a participle meaning "gone" or "going," and by extension "acting, action, practice." Below the surface, then, *buddha-carita* can be understood to mean "awakened action." Below the surface, *buddha-carita* is a word by which Aśvaghoṣa may have intended to point obliquely in the direction of sitting practice that is liberated from unconscious doing.

---

[8] *Mūla-madhyamaka-kārikā* (MMK) chapter 24, Exploring the Noble Truths (verses 8 - 10).

[9] Almost all of Aśvaghoṣa's original Sanskrit text of Saundarananda is extant, and largely for this reason I followed EHJ in translating it first. But I believe, for various reasons, that Aśvaghoṣa wrote Buddhacarita first. One reason is that Aśvaghoṣa covers the teaching of dependent arising in detail in BC Canto 14; then in Saundarananda he refers only lightly in passing to the 12-fold chain.

[10] Much academic debate has been devoted to the question of whether Aśvaghoṣa was primarily a poet or a monk. But that is a stale debate. Discussion of what Buddhist school Aśvaghoṣa belonged to has even less to recommend it. Aśvaghoṣa is better revered as a person who defied categorization, a person who was - in his own terms - *anya*, different.

The second poem, Saundarananda, ostensibly means "Nanda the Fair," as per EH Johnston, or "Handsome Nanda," as per Linda Covill. Ostensibly, Saundarananda is another biography, a poem that tells the story of the Buddha's younger brother Nanda, who is notably good-looking (*saundara*) and whose name (*nanda*) means "Joy." Below the surface, *saundarananda* can be understood to mean "beautiful joy" – in which case *saundarananda* is a word by which Aśvaghoṣa may have intended, again, to suggest the beauty and joy of just sitting.

Not only the titles of the two poems, but also the title of every canto, and turning words within each verse, all seem to invite investigation along these lines. Ostensibly, the meaning is this. But below the surface, the meaning is this, or – digging deeper – the meaning might also be this, or this, or maybe even this.

Here are a few examples to illustrate the point. In square brackets in the translation, and in the footnotes to each canto, you will find many more examples highlighted.

- the one, the seven, the five, the three and the two

In BC Canto 2 Aśvaghoṣa praises the King as follows:

> He gave direction to the one and guarded the seven; he shunned the seven and turned his attention to the five; / He experienced the three and minded the three; he knew the two and abandoned the two. //2.41//

This is a kind of riddle. I think it is designed to draw our attention to the fact that practically every verse can, like this one, be read on more than one level.

Ostensibly the King in question is Prince Siddhārtha's father, King Śuddhodana, in which case *the one* would seem to refer to the person of the King himself, or else his kingdom. Below the surface, *giving direction to the one* may be read as a suggestion of what Dōgen calls the secret of sitting-meditation – naturally becoming one piece.[11]

EH Johnston notes that the sevens are the seven constituents of a kingdom and the seven vices of kings. Patrick Olivelle[12] identifies the seven constituents of a kingdom as king, minister, countryside, fort, treasury, army and ally; and the seven vices of a king as three vices springing from anger (verbal abuse, physical assault, and plunder of property) and four vices springing from passion (hunting, gambling, women, and drink). In the hidden meaning, however, the seven could be the seven limbs of awakening – as, in the first instance, virtues to be developed; and in the second instance, antithetically, as idealistic concepts to be negated.[13]

EHJ notes that five refers to the five *upāyas*, means of success against an enemy. Olivelle traces these five back to the Mahā-bhārata, which lists the five policies as conciliation, giving gifts, fomenting dissension, war, and staying quiet. In the hidden meaning, however,

[11] In the original edition of his instructions for sitting-meditation (*Fukan-zazengi-shinpitsu-bon*), Dōgen expresses the secret of Zazen as 自成一片 (*ji-jō-ippen*), naturally/spontaneously becoming one piece.

[12] Life of Buddha (2008).

[13] The seven, mentioned in SN17.58, are investigation of happenings, energy, joy, confidence, equanimity, balanced stillness, and mindfulness.

the five might be the five senses, which the Buddha so often compared to dangerous enemies.

Ostensibly the three are the triple set of dharma, wealth, and pleasure, the three aims of a king's life. In the hidden meaning, the three to experience and the three to mind, might be greed, anger and delusion.

Ostensibly, again, the two a king should know are good and bad policy. But in the hidden meaning the two to know, as a prelude to abandoning that duality, are body and mind.

Why did Aśvaghoṣa write a verse as ambiguous as this? I think because he wanted to cause us to consider more than one possible meaning of each element. He wanted to cause us to dig below the surface of his convenient fictions, not only in a verse like this one, which looks like a riddle, but also in all his other verses which don't look like riddles, but each of which is in fact a riddle.[14]

- the lord of the earth

The lord of the earth (*bhūmi-patiḥ,* BC1.7) - also called the protector of men (*nṛpaḥ,* BC4.22), the best of men (*narendraḥ,* BC8.17), the king (*rājā,* BC9.7), et cetera - ostensibly means King Śuddhodana, ruler of Kapilavāstu and father of Prince Sarvārtha-siddhaḥ. In the hidden meaning, the King means a king of dharma. In the hidden meaning, every man and every woman who sits supported by the earth, dropping off body and mind in the earth's gravitational field, is a lord of the earth.

- the son of the best of men

The son of the best of men (*narendra-sūnuḥ,* BC3.60; *narendra-putraḥ,* BC8.10) - also called the self-begotten of a protector of men (*nṛpātmajaḥ,* BC3.29), the son of a protector of men (*nṛpa-sutaḥ;* BC12.4) et cetera - ostensibly means Prince Sarvārtha-siddha, son of King Śuddhodana. In the hidden meaning, every recipient of the Buddha's teaching - i.e. you and I who are endeavouring to get to the bottom of this teaching now - is a son or a daughter of the best of men.

- the royal seat of the best of men

The royal seat of the best of men (*narendra-sadmā;* BC3.47) - also called the palace (*bhavanam,* BC1.88) - ostensibly means King Śuddhodana's fortified palace in Kapilavāstu. In the hidden meaning, the samādhi which is king of samādhis, i.e. sitting upright in the full lotus posture, is just the royal seat of the best of men. Providing further potential for ironic wordplay, *bhavanam,* besides meaning a palace, has the secondary meanings of 1. coming into existence, and 2. the place where anything grows (BC3.88; BC12.5).

- the royal road

The royal road (*rāja-mārgaḥ,* BC3.4) - also called the road of the best of men (*narendra-mārgaḥ;* BC3.53) - ostensibly means the main street in the capital city, the royal highway, Kapilavāstu High St. In the hidden meaning the royal road is the process of practicing the practice that leads in the direction of cessation of suffering.

- the one who is different

In many places where Aśvaghoṣa describes individuals within a group, but especially in connection with women, he will talk about some women and then about another woman

[14] There are said to be many instance in the Pāli Suttas (e.g SamN 1) of the Buddha posing riddles in a similar way.

(*anyā*, BC3.17) or about several others (*anyāḥ*, BC4.35). In the hidden meaning, *anyā* is one who is different. In Shōbōgenzō such a person is given the ironic epithet of 非仏, a non-buddha.[15] A non-buddha means a real individual practicing buddha, as opposed to the ideal generic saint that we tend to expect a buddha to be.[16]

- the being without virtue

One of the adornments of the one who is different is the being-without virtue (*nairguṇyam*, BC6.24). When the Prince speaks of himself in terms of being without virtue, the hidden meaning has to do with the virtue of being without – for example, the virtue of being without anger, greed and delusion. Or the virtue of freedom from clinging to virtue.

- action in the zone of the gods

When the heavy gates barring the way out of Kapilavāstu spontaneously open up, the horse-master Chandaka describes it as *daivo vidhiḥ* (BC8.46), which ostensibly means something like "a divine accomplishment" or "an act of God." On the surface, *daivo vidhiḥ* suggests a miracle in the narrow religious sense of a happening, realized by divine intervention, that defies the law of cause and effect. But *vidhi* can mean any act or action, and *daivaḥ* means "coming from the gods" not only in a literal or religious sense, but also in the irreligious sense intended by a sportsman or an actor who speaks of the gods being on his or her side. In the hidden meaning, then, the seemingly miraculous happening is nothing more religious or supernatural – and nothing less valuable – than what happens when a performer is temporarily in the non-doing zone.

- the golden seat

The ostensible meaning of *kāñcanam āsanam* (BC5.44) is a golden seat, a seat made of gold – something solid and fixed. But *āsanam* is an *-na* neuter action noun whose original meaning is sitting. So the hidden meaning of *kāñcanam āsanam* is golden sitting. In which case, like the royal seat of the best of men, it suggests in its hidden meaning something less set, less weighty and less solid than what it seems to mean on the surface.

These are a small sample of the convenient fictions that Aśvaghoṣa uses in Buddhacarita as he continues, verse by verse, to play with verbal irony, dramatic irony, and – under the smiling eyes of the gods – cosmic irony. I haven't even mentioned Māra's army of demon throngs (*bhūta-gaṇāḥ*) in BC Canto 13, or the fire-colored molten metal (*agni-varṇam ayo-rasam*) that wrong-doers are caused to imbibe in BC Canto 14, or the fabulous birds and trees of Indra's paradise described in SN Canto 10.

But perhaps the best indication of how far Aśvaghoṣa can go in his use of irony – and especially in the use of what I have called his irreligious irony – is seen in his treatment of women.

---

[15] See Master Dōgen's Shōbōgenzō chap. 28, *Butsu-kojo-no-ji*, para [58]; trans. Gudo Nishijima, Chodo Cross.

[16] In a similar way Dōgen in his revised edition of his instructions for Zazen (*Fukan-zazengi-rufu-bon*) says that 非思量, non-thinking, is the secret of sitting-meditation. Non-thinking is usually understood to mean "what is different from thinking," i.e. action itself, the action of just sitting. But 非思量 can also be understood to mean true mindfulness, mindfulness that we remember to direct where it ought to be directed – in other words, mindfulness, but not what people generally think mindfulness to be. So 非思量 ostensibly means "action which is different from thinking"; but below the surface 非思量 might mean thinking, but not what people understand by thinking.

Sometimes when Aśvaghoṣa describes the behavior of a group known collectively as "the women" or "the girls" or "these fine ladies," he is simply parodying the behavior - which he evidently sees as beautiful even in its unenlightened barging about - of a group of monks in a *vihāra*, or place of practice. Thus, for example, in BC Canto 3:

> But some among these fine ladies, hurry though they might in their eagerness, / Were stopped in their tracks, by the heft of the mighty chariots of their hips and their corpulent breasts. //BC3.16//

This, I think, is a humorous parody of heavy-footed Friar Tuck types - monks who were unduly interested in their midday meals.

Another use of irony which I think is peculiar to Aśvaghoṣa appears in BC Canto 4. It is a kind of inverted double entendre whereby behavior that is overtly sexual is understood by the knowing reader to represent some aspect of the Buddha's teaching. For example:

> One girl, whose mouth with copper-red lower lip betrayed a whiff of distilled nectar, / Whispered in his ear, "Let the secret be revealed!" //4.31//

What is thus suggested, below the surface, might be a teacher's effort to transmit the secret of true mindfulness.

But use of this technique is at its most wickedly subversive in a series of verses in BC Canto 5 where Aśvaghoṣa describes "different" (i.e. enlightened) ones who are manifesting all kinds of unconventional postures, having totally dropped off. In the verse which concludes the series, we can't help worrying that Aśvaghoṣa might have gone too far, when he seems to paint a picture of a woman who is so deeply fallen into a drunken stupor that she is showing off her genitals:

> With her oral cavity open and her legs spreading out, so that she sprayed saliva, and made visible what normally remains secret, / One very different one had dropped off; rocking somewhat in her intoxication, she did not make a pretty sight, but filled an irregular frame. //BC5.61//

In the hidden meaning, the individual in question has not dropped off in the sense of having fallen asleep, but has totally dropped off body and mind. In that sense, she, or he, is manifesting the real secret of sitting practice - not by trying to conform to somebody's false conception of "correct posture," but on the contrary by having let go of all of that.

Champsecret, France; Aylesbury, England
September - October 2015

ERRATA: Golden Sitting Revisited

sabba-pāpassa akaraṇaṁ, kusalassa upasampadā /
sacitta-pariyodapanaṁ etaṁ buddhāna' sāsanaṁ //[17]

sarva-pāpasyākaraṇaṁ kuśalasyopasaṁpadaḥ /
svacitta-paryavadanam etad buddhasya śāsanam //[18]

諸惡莫作 衆善奉行
自淨其意 是諸佛教 [19]

The not doing of any wrong, undertaking what is good,
Cleansing one's own mind – this is the teaching of buddhas.

At the end of my Introduction eight years ago, I cited this as the original teaching of the Buddha, preserved in four languages. Then, ever slow on the uptake, I asked: But what did the Buddha mean, exactly, by cleansing one's mind?

The answer to that question was already there, clearly stated if I'd been able to notice, in Pali Suttas, like DN16 and SamN22.45 (see Appendix), where the Buddha often speaks of freeing the mind from polluting influences (*āsavehi*), by not clinging (*an-upādāya*).

In Saundarananda the Buddha expresses this negative "by not clinging" (*an-upādāya*) with the positive "by letting happen" (*bhāvanayā*).

I didn't understand eight years ago that the Zen masters of ancient China expressed exactly these means of freeing the mind with the characters 坐禅, "sitting-meditation."

I for one was misled by the Chinese character 禅 (Chinese: *cha'an*; Japanese: *zen*) representing the sound of the Sanskrit *dhyāna*, rather than *bhāvanā*. The Chinese character that came closest to translating *bhāvanā* seemed to be 修, cultivate, as in 修智慧, cultivating wisdom. On those grounds I formed the mistaken impression that there must be two kinds of meditative practice – as if working through the four *dhyānas* must have evolved into what the Chinese masters called just sitting, and then there must be this other kind of clinical method of mind-training, preserved in Tibet but not transmitted to Japan, involving the specific cultivation of various antidotes – like cultivating friendliness as the antidote to anger and cultivating joy as the antidote to discontent.

But no. When the penny dropped that *bhāvanā* can literally be translated "letting happen," it became obvious why in Aśvaghoṣa's metaphor there were not two golden seats.

---

[17] Pāḷi. *Dhammapāda* 183.
[18] Sanskrit. *Udānavarga* 28.1.
[19] Chinese. Quoted from Master Dōgen's Shōbōgenzō chap. 10, *Shoaku-makusa*.

The one golden seat turns out, after all, to be a metaphor for the non-doing practice of just sitting which, as a letting happen, is inherently friendly and joyful. And so, though of course the non-doing practice of letting happen is not always easy to practice truly, in a friendly and joyful way, the original practice couldn't be more simple. Golden sitting is as simple, and as difficult, in the end, as just letting it happen, not clinging.

Which is not to say that clinging, as the affliction that forms the ninth link in the 12-fold dependent arising of suffering, is to be targeted directly, as if clinging existed as a thing unto itself, as the one key link in the 12, which must be consigned to non-existence. A War on Clinging makes no more sense than a War on Unwittingness (the first link) or a War on Doings/Fabrications/Works of Conditioning (the second link). Without clarity in regard to emptiness, however, it can be hard for an enthusiastic practitioner not to proceed in an unwittingly war-like manner, fabricating objectives to be achieved, concocting things to be done, contriving targets to be taken out. And this must be why, in Saundarananda Canto 17, Aśvaghoṣa describes Nanda's practice of golden sitting really proving effective in freeing the mind from polluting influences only after Nanda's recognition, in SN17.21, of the real meaning of emptiness.

Kāñcanam āsanam, "golden sitting," in its hidden meaning, is a happening that is empty of self-existence – and that understanding makes all the difference.

Champsecret, France
Spring 2023

- Acknowledgements -

I would like here to express thanks and pay respects to teachers and fellow swimmers in four streams of practice – namely 1. the Zen/Mahāyāna tradition that spread from India in the west to Japan in the Far East, 2. the Theravāda tradition of Thailand, Sri Lanka, and South-east Asia, 3. the Nālandā tradition as preserved in Tibet, and 4. the more recent stream of non-doing practice which is the FM Alexander Technique.

Top of the list of teachers to whom I am indebted has to be the Zen teacher Gudo Nishijima, whom I met in Tokyo in June 1982, when I was 22 and he was 62. He firmly established all his students on the way of daily sitting-practice. At the same time he very much emphasized the importance of going back to ancient texts and, like archaeologists with spades and brushes, excavating their lost meanings. Always painting with broad and unworried strokes, he taught that sitting-meditation is something we practice for our own benefit, whereas translation work is to benefit others. That is not strictly accurate, of course, but as a starting point, it is not a bad approximation of the truth.

Gudo Nishijima practised and taught "just sitting" as championed by the 13th century Japanese Zen master Dōgen in his great work Shōbōgenzō. This practice of just sitting, it is clear from Shōbōgenzō, Dōgen regarded as thoroughly conducive to the cultivation of wisdom. Still, when from the age of 48 I began to read descriptions in Aśvaghoṣa's writing of the Buddha's teaching of *bhāvanā*, I seriously lacked wisdom in regard to what *bhāvanā* might really mean. As a word, *bhāvanā* means cultivation, or development of the mind, or mind training, or meditation. But what did it mean as a practice?

One could argue – especially with the benefit of hindsight – that the "just" of "just sitting" expresses the absence of doings (*saṁskārān*) born of ignorance (*avidyā*); therefore, truly just to sit is already to be cultivating the wisdom that puts an end to all doings born of ignorance. In which case, who needs other kinds of *bhāvanā*, beyond the cultivation of just this wisdom?

In Canto 16 of Saundarananda, however, the Buddha teaches Nanda to cultivate, when occasion demands it, not only wisdom in general but also, for example, friendliness (*maitrī*) as the particular antidote to ill-will (*vyāpāda*).

This kind of developing of the mind in certain directions, as a meditative practice, is not something I had become familiar with, during my years in Japan translating Shōbōgenzō into English and purporting to practice "just sitting." So translating Aśvaghoṣa forced me to turn to (a) the descriptions of different kinds of *bhāvanā* in original Pāḷi texts, like for example the Rāhula Sutta, translated in exemplary fashion by Ānandajoti Bhikkhu; and (b) the first-person testimony of Tibetan monks like the 14th Dalai Lama, as elucidated in particular by Matthieu Ricard, the French monk who has been famously burdened – through no fault of his own, but because of the measurable benefits of his own mind-training – with the title "the happiest man in the world."

Second on my list of teachers to acknowledge here, then, is the Theravāda monk Ānandajoti Bhikkhu. To him I am indebted not only for his exemplary translations from Pāḷi, all of which are made freely available at his website (www.ancient-buddhist-texts.net), but also for his unstinting guidance and encouragement along the way. The publication of this translation in its present form is very largely due to his example of how to go about making an ancient text one's own, through painstaking study of the variants (different ways in which an ancient manuscript can be read) and of the meter, and how then to go about making the ancient text, together with an English translation of it, easily and freely available.

Though I have not met Matthieu Ricard in person, thanks to the Internet I almost feel as if I have met him, along with the Dalai Lama whose teaching of mind-training Matthieu Ricard has done so much to clarify. So I would like to express a sincere debt of gratitude to all those many generations of teachers who kept the Nālandā tradition alive in Tibet, even after it had died out in its Indian birthplace. I see Aśvaghoṣa as very much belonging to that Nālandā tradition, as also to the Zen/Mahāyana tradition, and to the Theravāda tradition.

Or perhaps it is more accurate to say that these various traditions all belong originally to nobody but the Buddha, to whose non-sectarian teaching Aśvaghoṣa was entirely devoted.

In his efforts to establish the Zen tradition in Japan, Dōgen wrote at the very beginning of Shōbōgenzō that the buddha-tathāgatas possess a subtle method which is supreme and *free of doing* (無為). This *freedom from doing* (無為, Chinese: *wu-wei*; Japanese: *mu-i*) is a truth that seems to have emerged in China thousands of years ago, more or less independently from the Buddha's teaching. This same truth of freedom from doing emerged again, at the end of 19th century, in Tasmania when a young actor named FM Alexander stumbled upon it in his detailed investigations, using a three-way mirror, of how he was using himself. And so I have come to be indebted also to many teachers of the FM Alexander Technique who have given me glimpses of what freedom from doing might really be. Among these many Alexander teachers, I would like to express my gratitude to four teachers in particular, two men and two women.

I ended up training as an Alexander teacher at a school in Aylesbury run by Ray Evans and Ron Colyer. My family set up home in Aylesbury in order to be close to the training school, and my wife Chie trained as an Alexander teacher with Ray and Ron after I finished my three-year training.

The core principle of Alexander work is that if we stop doing the wrong thing, the right thing does itself. Sadly, how the right thing does itself remains a mystery beyond the greedy grasping of the intellect. But how, in spite of our best intentions, we end up doing the wrong thing, is something that our minds can become clearer about. That being so, I am indebted to Ray Evans for his singular insights into how, when a person goes directly for an end, wrong doing emerges out of what Alexander called "faulty sensory appreciation."

Ray led his trainees to understand how immature primitive reflexes (and especially a primitive fear reflex called the Moro reflex) can cause anybody (but especially a Zen practitioner with an emotional investment in sitting well) to become a slave to the feeling that he is sitting in the right posture. The feeling is delusory, because in fact there is no such thing as a right posture. As FM Alexander truly said, echoing Nāgārjuna, "There is no such thing as a right position.... but there *is* such a thing as a right direction."

If the late Ray Evans was a genius in this matter of unreliable feeling or "faulty sensory appreciation," Ray's fellow teacher-trainer Ron Colyer has remained in my eyes a master of allowing others to experience freedom from what Alexander called "end-gaining" - the emotional habit of going directly for a desired end.

End-gaining involves going for a desired end without paying due attention to intermediate steps in the process. Trying to be right – as one is invariably prone to try, as a would-be Alexander teacher (or, worse still, as a would-be Zen master) – is end-gaining itself. And stopping this end-gaining, it turns out, is not so easy.

On an Alexander teacher training course, then, as an antidote to end-gaining, it is vital that work is done in an atmosphere in which it is perfectly OK not to be right, where it is OK to be as wrong as ever one is. An Alexander lesson from Ron Colyer, everybody who has ever had such a lesson agrees, is an experience in being given limitless such freedom to go wrong. Nobody can keep taking himself too seriously in a room filled with the deep, warm, resonant laughter of a teacher who never fails to encourage the individual to be the individual he or she is, and who never fails to put the Constructive into *Constructive Conscious Control of the Individual.*[1]

After I finished Alexander teacher training with Ray and Ron, I continued for a number of years to have one-to-one Alexander lessons from two very experienced women teachers of the technique. One of these teachers was Nelly Ben-Or, who once described her efforts to teach me as costing her half her life! Nelly's teaching demands on a deep level "the giving up of what ordinarily governs us." I am afraid that, despite Nelly's best efforts, I have continued to hold on tightly – and sometimes incredibly aggressively – to what ordinarily governs me. So, to Nelly, both heartfelt thanks and shame-faced apologies. I am sorry Nelly, for being such a terrible student, and for being so rude and aggressive while you were only trying to help me! Please forgive me.

Next, my undying gratitude goes out to the late Marjory Barlow, the niece of FM Alexander, who taught me, while I was lying on her teaching table with my knees bent, to give up three ideas: (1) the idea of being right; (2) the idea of doing the process of undoing which is described by words like "back to lengthen and widen"; and (3) the idea of moving a leg – in order to be truly free to go ahead and move the leg.

I should not neglect to acknowledge the encouragement and support I received from readers of a daily blog, Mining Aśvaghoṣa's Gold, that I kept while working on these translations. Particular thanks go out to my brother Ian Cross, and Sanskrit pundits Karttikeya and Malcolm Markovitch. The late Michael Thaler (author of the blog One Foot In Front of the Other) offered encouragement and inspiration in my early days of blogging. Others who helped in various ways – in some cases simply by leaving me to get on with it – were Maggie Lamb, Nuria George, Gisela Wilson, Pierre Turlur, Laurie Blundell, Alex Gould, George Askounis, Denis Le Grand, Gustav Ericsson and David Essoyan. Special thanks are due to Jordan Fountain who in 2012 made a website for the audio recordings of Saundarananda, painstakingly linking each verse back to the corresponding page on Mining Aśvaghoṣa's Gold.

Last but by no means least I would like to say thank you to two staunch supporters I met while living in Japan. First, thank you to my wife Chie who has put up with me for more than 25 years now, and made many sacrifices along the way to allow me to continue tap, tap, tapping away on this keyboard. Second, I would like to thank for his generous support

[1] *Constructive Conscious Control of the Individual* is the title of the second of FM Alexander's four books. When simply "Constructive Conscious Control" was suggested as an alternative title, for a saving of three words, Alexander is said to have replied, "But don't you see? That would be to omit the most important part!"

over many years, a wise and kind Japanese economist named Tadashi Nakamae. After working fairly unhappily for four years in Japan as an English teacher and then as a copy editor, I decided in the summer of 1986 to give up work, shave my head, and devote myself whole-heartedly to just sitting. This needless to say, had perilous financial implications. But a few weeks into the 90-day sitting retreat that I had decided to practice in my Tokyo flat, I got a phone call quite out of the blue. An independent research company called Nakamae International Economic Research had just been established in the city. Would I be interested in attending an interview for a part-time job as English editor of the NIER Quarterly Report? I ended up working for NIER for the next 25 years, in Tokyo, where I was enabled not only to survive but actually to save some money, and when I returned to England, working remotely via the internet. The Zen gods were clearly on my side in the summer of 1986 when that phone call came in – as seemed to be confirmed when Mr Nakamae turned out to have a strong connection with the late Japanese Zen teacher Tsunemasa Abe. Tsunemasa Abe in turn, from an early age, was like a grandson to perhaps the most famous Zen teacher in Japan in the 20th century, Kodo Sawaki.

In conclusion, then, in writing these acknowledgments I am conscious of how much this translation owes itself, in countless unfathomable dependently-arisen ways, to the wisdom and compassion of many others. Since I received financial support from the Japan Foundation for the Shōbōgenzō translation, I feel in some sense indebted to the whole of Japanese society. Again, since my two sons received excellent educations at the expense of the British tax-payer, I feel similarly indebted to everybody in this great free country where I was born and to which I returned twenty years ago.

Over the course of those twenty years, the last seven of which have been spent with Aśvaghoṣa as guide and travelling companion, this translator has not had the smoothest of rides. This is largely due, I am sure, to the influence of what FM Alexander called "unduly excited fear reflexes and emotions." And yet somehow – even in spite of the translator continuing to carry with him his heavy baggage of fear and ignorance – this translation of two truly wonderful epic poems now seems, with the gods on its side, to have been allowed to arrive at its end. So thank you to all the many people not mentioned here by name who have allowed this work to come to what, I feel, is a satisfactory conclusion.

There again, feeling is ever prone to be unreliable.

ERRATA (ctd): Bhāvana Need Not Take an Object

In this second edition, as mentioned already, I have changed the translation of *bhāvanā* from "cultivation [of the mind]" or "[mental] development" to "the practice of letting happen" or simply "letting happen."

In the Rāhula Sutta, the Buddha repeatedly advises Rāhula *bhāvanaṃ bhāvehi*, so that both the imperative *bhāvehi* (let happen!) and the object *bhāvanaṃ* (letting happen) are formed from the causative of the verbal root √*bhū*, whose meanings include both to be and to happen. At some point, thanks to reciting the concluding section of Rāhula Sutta on a daily basis, the penny dropped that the translation "let letting happen happen!" worked remarkably well.

The Buddha's advice *Mettaṃ Rāhula bhāvanaṃ bhāvehi* started to translate itself "Let happen, Rāhula, the friendly practice of letting happen." Or "Let happen, Rāhula, the friendliness of letting happen." Either way, the point is not to cultivate friendliness per se. The point is to practice the practice of letting happen which, as a letting happen, is inherently friendly.

Letting happen, as opposed to doing, has to be friendly because, as FM Alexander taught, "we cannot do an undoing." We cannot, in a direct, aggressive manner, force release to happen. Rather, "You've got to talk to it nicely."

Translating *bhāvanā* like this, as letting happen, has felt like hitting the target. There again, feeling is still as prone as ever to be unreliable!

What I felt eight years ago to have been a satisfactory conclusion, at least in regard to the meaning and translation of *bhāvanā,* was in hindsight not at all a satisfactory conclusion. And so, again, I am grateful to Michael Luetchford for giving me the chance to clear up any confusion I caused, or added to.

I hope I have made the most of the opportunity by revising the translation of important verses in Saundarananda Cantos 16 and 17, centered on how to practice *bhāvanā.* I have also revised and rewritten many footnotes, especially in those two cantos. But I have not edited out what I got wrong above in my previous Acknowledgements, in the hope that showing my workings might help readers see for themselves where I went wrong. I went wrong primarily in a non-empty conception of consigning enemies to non-existence – as when a War is waged on Ignorance, or on Doings, or on Clinging... or on Drugs, or on Terror, or on Covid, or on Climate Change.

To see this now, at the age of 63 already, may be a case of better late than never. It might be the fundamental error of my ways. It might also be the fundamental error of the ways of many influential people who received an elite British education, as I did, in the 1970s. If I see the error more clearly now than I did when the first edition of Aśvaghoṣa's Gold was published in 2015, special acknowledgement for that must be due to Nāgārjuna.

M.C. Spring 2023

Buddhacarita
of
Aśvaghoṣa

Canto 1: bhagavat-prasūtiḥ
The Birth of Something Beautiful

Introduction

In the title of the present canto *bhagavat* is ostensibly a term of reverence applied to gods and saints – Lord, Glorious One, Divine One, Adorable One, Venerable One, Holy One. But *-vat* is a possessive suffix, and *bhaga* is from the root √*bhaj*, which means to share out, or to obtain as one's share, to enjoy. Meanings of *bhaga* given in the dictionary include good fortune, happiness, welfare, prosperity; dignity, majesty, distinction, excellence, beauty; love, sexual passion, amorous pleasure. So not all of these words necessarily carry a spiritual connotation.

The star of the present canto is a sage who stands apart from the run-of-the-mill brahmins – spiritual materialists – who were eager to receive the king's gifts of gold and cows. This singular sage's name was Asita, which means "the Not-White One" – the one who, unlike the others, did not purport to be so spiritual, but who was rather devoted to sitting (*āsana-stham*, verse 52). Asita's intuition, as events unfold, proves to be real. He hits the target.

Ostensibly, then, the present canto describes a birth that was miraculous in the religious sense. But in its subversive subtext the canto describes a birth that was miraculous in an irreligious sense. Hence in this translation, not "The Birth of the Holy One" but rather "The Birth of Something Beautiful."

aikṣvāka ikṣvāku-sama-prabhāvaḥ śākyeṣv aśakyeṣu viśuddha-vṛttaḥ /
priyaḥ śarac-candra iva prajābhyaḥ śuddhodano nāma babhūva rājā // 1.1 //
Among the unshakable[1] Śākyas there was a king, a descendant of Ikṣvāku who in might was the equal of Ikṣvāku, a man of well-cleansed conduct / Who was loved by those below him, like the autumn moon: Śuddhodana was his name – 'Possessed of Well-Cleansed Rice.' //1.1//

tasyendra-kalpasya babhūva patnī * * * * * * * * * * * /
padmeva lakṣmīḥ pṛthivīva dhīrā māyeti nāmnānupameva māyā // 1.2 //
That Indra-like king had a queen: - - - - - - - - - - - - / Like lotus-hued Padmā in her beauty and self-possessed as Mother Earth, she was Māyā by name and was like Māyā, the peerless goddess of beauty.[2] //1.2//

*** /**
tataś ca vidyeva samādhi-yuktā garbhaṁ dadhe pāpa-vivarjitā sā // 1.3 //
...Like knowledge conjoined with balance, she who was far removed from evil conceived a child. //1.3//

---

[1] *Aśakya*, lit. "not to be overcome, invincible" – a play on the clan name Śākya.
[2] Māyā ("Art") and Padmā ("The Lotus-Hued One") are aliases of the goddess of fortune and beauty most commonly known as Lakṣmī ("Beauty").

* /
* * * * * * * * * * * **na tan-nimittaṁ samavāpa tāpam // 1.4 //**
[Before she conceived, she saw in her sleep a white lord of elephants entering her body, but] she did not on that account incur any pain. //1.4//[3]

sā tasya deva-pratimasya devī garbheṇa vaṁśa-śriyam udvahantī /
*** * * vīta-śrama-śoka-māyā * * * * * * * * * * * *] // 1.5 //**
She, the queen of that god-like king, bearing in her womb the light of his royal line, / And being devoid of weariness, sorrow, and the *māyā* which is deceit,[4] [set her mind on the pristine forest.[5]] //1.5//

sā lumbinīṁ nāma vanānta-bhūmiṁ citra-drumāṁ caitrarathābhirāmām /
***] // 1.6 //**
For the grove called Lumbinī, which, with its manifold trees, would have pleased Citra-ratha,[6] / [She left the King, there to brood, in the wooded solitude].[7] //1.6//

āryāśayāṁ tāṁ * * * * * * vijñāya kautūhala-harṣa-pūrṇaḥ
śivāt purād bhūmi-patir jagāma tat-prītaye nāpi vihāra-hetoḥ // 1.7 //
Appreciating the nobility of her instinct...., and filled with joyful anticipation, / The master of the earth[8] departed from the blessed city at her pleasure – and not for the pleasure of an excursion.[9] //1.7//

---

3 The Sanskrit in these opening verses was reconstituted by EH Johnston from the Tibetan. Text in square brackets is based on EH Johnston's English translation, which he based mainly on Weller's Tibetan text and German translation but also partly on Beal's Chinese text and English translation. The Chinese 於彼象天后 降神而處胎, though it led Beal to a different reading (in which he translated 象 as "likeness" rather than as "elephant"), at least corroborates the reference to an elephant.

4 *Māyā* means "art," and by extension, "illusion, unreality, deception, fraud, trick, sorcery, witchcraft, magic."

5 Chinese: 樂處空閑林, "enjoying the empty forest."

6 Citra-ratha, "He of the Bright Chariot," is the king of the gandharvas who, along with the celestial nymphs, beautify Indra's heaven. *Citra* means bright or multifarious, manifold; hence the reference to manifold trees.

7 Chinese: 寂靜順禪思 啓王請遊彼, "[for] dhyāna/thinking, following peace and quiet, she asked the king for permission to pass time pleasantly there."

8 *Bhūmi-pati,* "master of the earth," here means the king. Often in his epic poetry, Aśvaghoṣa uses expressions like these in describing the dignified behavior of a buddha, i.e. a king of dharma, that is, one who is sovereign in the realm of what happens. (As a feminine noun, *bhū* means 1. happening, 2. the earth.)

9 *Vihāra* means walking for pleasure or exploring – as in the title of BC Canto 2. *Vihāra* was also used as the name of a place given over to practice of activities like walking, lying down, standing, and sitting.

tasmin vane śrīmati rāja-patnī prasūti-kālaṁ samavekṣamāṇā /
śayyāṁ vitānopahitāṁ prapede nārī-sahasrair abhinandyamānā // 1.8 //
In that glorious grove, perceiving that it was time for the birth, / The queen took to a bed covered over with an awning, being joyfully received into the bosom of thousands of fellow women. //1.8//

tataḥ prasannaś ca babhūva puṣyas tasyāś ca devyā vrata-saṁskṛtāyāḥ /
pārśvāt suto loka-hitāya jajñe nirvedanaṁ caiva nirāmayaṁ ca // 1.9 //
Then, as a propitious moon passed into the asterism of *Puṣya*, to that queen sanctified by the manner of her action – / Through her,[10] for the welfare of the world – a son was born, painlessly and healthily. //1.9//

ūror yathaurvasya pṛthoś ca hastān māndhātur indra-pratimasya mūrdhnaḥ /
kakṣīvataś caiva bhujāṁsa-deśāt tathāvidhaṁ tasya babhūva janma // 1.10 //
Just as Aurva was born from the thigh, Pṛthu from the hand, Indra-equalling Māndhātṛ from the head, / And Kakṣīvat from the armpit: of that same order was his birth. //1.10//

krameṇa garbhād abhiniḥsṛtaḥ san babhau cyutaḥ khād iva yony-ajātaḥ /
kalpeṣv anekeṣu ca bhāvitātmā yaḥ saṁprajānan suṣuve na mūḍhaḥ // 1.11 //
Having emerged from the womb gradually,[11] he whose position at birth was never fixed,[12] shone as if he had dropped from empty space. / Again, as one whose self had been developing over many eons, he was born with integral awareness, and not in a wrong position. //1.11//

dīptyā ca dhairyeṇa ca yo rarāja bālo ravir bhūmim ivāvatīrṇaḥ /
tathātidīpto 'pi nirīkṣyamāṇo jahāra cakṣūṁṣi yathā śaśāṅkaḥ // 1.12 //
With brightness he shone, and with constancy, like a newly-risen sun inundating the earth; / Thus he blazed too brightly to be gazed upon, and at the same time he stole the eyes, in the manner of the hare-marked moon. //1.12//

sa hi sva-gātra-prabhayojjvalantyā dīpa-prabhāṁ bhāskaravan mumoṣa /
mahārha-jāmbūnada-cāru-varṇo vidyotayām āsa diśaś ca sarvāḥ // 1.13 //
For with the blazing light of his body, he blotted out the light of lamps as does the sun; / And with his beautiful luster of precious gold, he enlightened all directions. //1.13//

---

[10] *Pārśva* means "the side"; therefore, ostensibly the ablative *pārśvāt* means "through her side." But *pārśvāt* sometimes simply means "by means of, through." So in this case the ostensible meaning requires a leap of the imagination, whereas the real or hidden meaning expresses the more everyday miracle of a natural birth.

[11] *Krameṇa* – the birth went well, being neither precipitous nor prolonged.

[12] *Yony-ajātaḥ* ostensibly means not born by a vaginal birth. The Chinese has 不由於生門 ("not through the birth gate"). But besides the birth canal, *yoni* has the secondary meaning of "the form of existence or station fixed by birth (e.g. that of a man, Brahman, animal)."

anākulāny ubja-samudgatāni niṣpeṣavad vyāyata-vikramāṇi /
tathaiva dhīrāṇi padāni sapta saptarṣi-tārā-sa-dṛśo jagāma // 1.14 //
With even footsteps, his feet rising up like water-born lotuses, and coming down in long stamping strides: / Seven such firm steps he took, looking like the Seven Seer cluster of stars.[13] //1.14//

bodhāya jāto 'smi jagadd-hitārtham antyā bhavotpattir iyaṁ mameti /
catur-diśaṁ siṁha-gatir vilokya vāṇīṁ ca bhavyārtha-karīm uvāca // 1.15 //
"For awakening I am born, for the welfare of the world; this for me is the ultimate coming into existence." / Surveying the four quarters, he of lion's gait voiced a sound that conveyed this gist of what would be.[14] //1.15//

khāt prasrute candra-marīci-śubhre dve vāri-dhāre śiśiroṣṇa-vīrye /
śarīra-saṁsparśa-sukhāntarāya nipetatur mūrdhani tasya saumye // 1.16 //
Flowing out of the emptiness, as radiant as moonbeams, two showers of raindrops, had a cooling and a heating effect / Conveying the ease that is conveyed through bodily contact, as they fell upon his cool, moist, moon-like head.[15] //1.16//

śrīmad-vitāne kanakojjvalāṅge vaiḍūrya-pāde śayane śayānam /
yad gauravāt kāñcana-padma-hastā yakṣādhipāḥ saṁparivārya tasthuḥ // 1.17 //
As he lay on a bed with a glorious royal canopy, a base of shining gold and legs of cats'-eye gems, / An honor guard of *yakṣa*-wranglers stood around him, with golden lotuses in hand. //1.17//

*** * * * * ś ca divaukasaḥ khe yasya prabhāvāt praṇataiḥ śirobhiḥ /**
ādhārayan pāṇḍaram ātapa-traṁ bodhāya jepuḥ paramāśiṣaś ca // 1.18 //
Heaven-dwellers who seemed to be concealed in the sky, with heads bowed down at his majesty, / Held up a white umbrella, and sang their best wishes for his awakening. //1.18//

mahoragā dharma-viśeṣa-tarṣād buddheṣv atīteṣu kṛtādhikārāḥ /
yam avyajan bhakti-viśiṣṭa-netrā mandāra-puṣpaiḥ samavākiraṁś ca // 1.19 //
Mighty serpents who, in their thirst for the choicest dharma, had watched over buddhas of the past, / Fanned him, their eyes exuding partiality, and covered him in a confetti of *mandāra* blossoms. //1.19//

---

[13] *Saptarṣi*, the Seven Seers: the constellation we call the Plough, or the Big Dipper, within the larger constellation of Ursa Major.

[14] In other words, we need not understand literally that the baby declared in polished Sanskrit meter, *antyā bhavotpattir iyaṁ mameti, "This for me is the ultimate coming into existence."* More likely, in exhibiting nothing more or less miraculous than the neo-nate stepping reflex and a newborn's unbridled cry, the baby forcefully announced his presence, as if to say, "I am here. This for me is it."

[15] Coolness, moistness, and mildness are characteristics attributed to the mildly intoxicating juice of the *soma* plant, collected under the moonlight and hence identified with the moon.

tathāgatotpāda-guṇena tuṣṭāḥ śuddhādhivāsāś ca viśuddha-sattvāḥ /
devā nanandur vigate 'pi rāge magnasya duḥkhe jagato hitāya // 1.20 //
Gladdened by a birth that went so well, those whose essence is pure and who dwell in the clear blue yonder, / The gods, though devoid of any red taint of passion, rejoiced for the welfare of a world steeped in sorrow. //1.20//

yasya prasūtau giri-rāja-kīlā vātāhatā naur iva bhūś cacāla /
sa-candanā cotpala-padma-garbhā papāta vṛṣṭir gaganād anabhrāt // 1.21 //
At his birth the earth, anchored by the king of mountains, shook like a ship being battered in a gale; / And a sandalwood-scented rain, containing lilies and lotuses, fell from the cloudless sky.[16] //1.21//

vātā vavuḥ sparśa-sukhā mano-jñā divyāni vāsāṁsy avapātayantaḥ /
sūryaḥ sa evābhyadhikaṁ cakāśe jajvāla saumyārcir anīrito 'gniḥ // 1.22 //
Breezes blew that were pleasant to the touch and agreeable to the mind, causing fancy clothing to fall off. / The sun shone with extra brightness, being nothing but itself. Fire, with a full, moon-like flame, burned without being stirred. //1.22//

prāg-uttare cāvasatha-pradeśe kūpaḥ svayaṁ prādur abhūt sitāmbuḥ /
antaḥ-purāṇy āgata-vismayāni yasmin kriyās-tīrtha iva pracakruḥ // 1.23 //
In the north-eastern corner of the residence a well of pure water spontaneously appeared;[17] / And there the royal householders, filled with wonder, performed bathing practices as if on the bank of a sacred stream. //1.23//

dharmārthibhir bhūta-gaṇaiś ca divyais tad-darśanārthaṁ vanam āpupūre /
kautūhalenaiva ca pāda-pebhyaḥ puṣpāny akāle 'pi * * * * * // 1.24 //
Hosts of divine, dharma-needy beings, being motivated to meet him, filled up the forest. / And such indeed was the zealous absorption, that blossoms, even out of season, were caused to fall from trees. //1.24//

*** /**
*** * * * * * * * * * * ayatnato * * * * * * * // 1.25 //**
[Diseases cleared up,] naturally. //1.25//[18]

---

[16] The falling of rain from a cloudless sky (*gaganād anabhrāt*) is ostensibly a miracle. But as Nāgārjuna would later explain in detail, in reality there is no such thing, as a thing existing unto itself, as a cloud. In this sense the sky is always empty.

[17] The ancient Indian sages apparently deemed the north-east to be the best direction for wells and water tanks.

[18] No Sanskrit is extant from BC1.25 through to the last line of BC1.40; and for these verses, unlike for the opening verses of the chapter, EH Johnston did not endeavor further to restore Aśvaghoṣa's original Sanskrit. EHJ's translation from the Tibetan for this verse was: "At that time the noxious creatures consorted together and did each other no hurt. Whatever diseases there were among mankind were cured too without effort." "Without effort" may well have been *ayatnatas* in Sanskrit, represented in the Chinese translation by 自, by itself, spontaneously, naturally (不療自然除).

*** /**
diśaḥ praseduḥ * * * * * * * * * * * * * * * * * // 1.26 //
Directions became clear... //1.26//[19]

*** /**
jagad-vimokṣāya guru-prasūtau * * * * * * * * * * * // 1.27 //
The guru had been born for the liberation of the world. [Only the God of Love did not rejoice.] //1.27//[20]

[On seeing the marvelous birth of his son, the king, steadfast though he was, was much disturbed, and from his affection a double stream of tears flowed, born of joy and apprehension. //1.28//][21]

[The queen also was filled with fear and joy. //1.29//][22]

[Superstitious old women... /...prayed to the gods for good fortune. //1.30//][23]

[Brahmins of learning and eloquence, and reputed good conduct... /... said to the king: //1.31//][24]

["Men born on earth, for their peace, desire above all else a son. Rejoice, for this is the lamp of your people. //1.32//][25]

---

[19] EHJ: "The birds and deer did not call aloud and the rivers flowed with calm waters. The quarters became clear (Tibetan: *phyogs rnams rab snaṅ*) and the sky shone cloudless; the drums of the gods resounded in the air."

[20] EHJ: "When the Guru was born for the salvation of all creatures, the world became exceeding peaceful, as though, being in a state of disorder, it had obtained a ruler. Kāmadeva alone did not rejoice." The Chinese translation has 唯彼魔天王 震動大憂惱, "Only he, the celestial king Māra, trembled and was greatly distressed." Māra, "the Destroyer," also known as Kāma-deva, "God of Love," is the subject of BC Canto 13.

[21] Six lines of Chinese correspond: 父王見生子 奇特未曾有 素性雖安重 驚駭改常容 二息交胸起 一喜復一懼.

[22] EHJ: "The queen was filled with fear and joy, like a stream of hot and cold water mixed, because the power of her son was other than human on the one hand, and because she had a mother's natural weakness on the other."

[23] EHJ: "The pious old women failed in penetration, seeing only the reasons for alarm; so, purifying themselves and performing luck-bringing rites, they prayed to the gods for good fortune." The Chinese has 互亂祈神明, "in mutual confusion praying to the divine intelligence."

[24] EHJ: "When the Brahmans, famed for conduct, learning and eloquence, had heard about these omens and considered them, then with beaming faces full of wonder and exultation they said to the king, who was both fearful and joyful:" The Chinese translation also mentions 高名稱, "lofty fame."

[25] EHJ: "'On earth men desire for their peace no excellence at all other than a son. As this lamp of yours is the lamp of your race, rejoice and make a feast to-day." The Chinese includes 人生於世間 唯求殊勝子, "people in the world only wish for an excellent son."

[Your son, among beings beset by suffering, will be a leader. //1.33//][26]

[Having the luster of gold, and the radiance of a lamp, /... he will be either a spiritual seer or an earthly king. //1.34//][27]

[Should he desire earthly sovereignty, he will stand above all kings, as the sun outshines all stars. //1.35//][28]

[Should he seek freedom in the forest, then he will stand on the earth transcending all teachings, as Mount Meru stands as king of all mountains. //1.36//][29]

[As gold is the best of metals, Meru of mountains, the ocean of waters, / And as the moon is the best of planets, he will be the best of men. //1.37//][30]

[His eyes are blazing and yet mild, deep blue with long black lashes. How will these eyes not see everything?" //1.38//][31]

[The king said to the brahmins: "Why should these signs be seen in him, when they were not seen in any former king? What is the cause?..." /... Then the brahmins said to him: //1.39//][32]

---

[26] EHJ: "Therefore in all steadfastness renounce anxiety and be merry; for your race will certainly flourish. He who has been born here as your son is the leader for those who are overcome by the suffering of the world." The Chinese includes 靈祥集家國, "spiritual fortune will be concentrated in your family and nation" and 必爲世間救 "he will surely be the world's salvation."

[27] EHJ: "According to the signs found on this excellent one, the brilliance of gold and the radiance of a lamp, he will certainly become either an enlightened seer or a Cakravartin monarch on earth among men." The Chinese translation includes 金色 "the color of gold."

[28] EHJ: " Should he desire earthly sovereignty, then by his might and law he will stand on earth at the head of all kings, as the light of the sun at the head of all constellations." The Chinese includes 猶如世光明 日光爲最勝, "just as, of brightness in the world, the light of the sun is best."

[29] EHJ: " Should he desire salvation and go to the forest, then by his knowledge and truth he will overcome all creeds and stand on the earth, like Meru king of mountains among all the heights." The Chinese includes 譬如須彌山 普爲諸山王, "just as Sumeru Mountain, among all mountains everywhere, is the king."

[30] EHJ: "As pure gold is the best of metals, Meru of mountains, the ocean of waters, the moon of planets and the sun of fires, so your son is the best of men." The Chinese includes 諸宿月爲最, "among constellations, the moon is best."

[31] EHJ: "His eyes gaze unwinkingly and are limpid and wide, blazing and yet mild, steady and with very long black eyelashes. How can he not have eyes that see everything?" The Chinese describes 淨目, his pure eye.

[32] EHJ: "Then the king said to the twice-born: "What is the cause that these excellent characteristics should be seen, as you say, in him, when they were not seen in previous great-souled kings?" Then the Brahmans said to him:" The Chinese includes 如此奇特相 以何因緣故, "special signs like these, are due to what causes and conditions?"

************************* /**
************* nidarśanāny atra ca no nibodha // 1.40 //**
["Some things, such as wisdom, glorious deeds, and a king's fame, are beyond former and latter. And yet every effect arises from a cause.] So listen to these examples [of unprecedented accomplishment:] //1.40//[33]

yad rāja-śāstraṁ bhṛgur aṅgirā vā na cakratur vaṁśa-karāv-ṛṣī tau /
tayoḥ sutau saumya sasarjatus tat kālena śukraś ca bṛhas-patiś ca // 1.41 //
That science of kingship which Bhṛgu[34] and Aṅgiras[35], those two lineage-founding seers, failed to formulate, / Was created in the course of time, O gentle sir!, by their sons Śukra[36] and Bṛhas-pati.[37] //1.41//

sārasvataś cāpi jagāda naṣṭaṁ vedaṁ punar yaṁ dadṛśur na pūrve /
vyāsas tathainaṁ bahudhā cakāra na yaṁ vasiṣṭhaḥ kṛtavān aśaktiḥ // 1.42 //
And Sārasvata[38] articulated again a lost Veda which forebears had never seen; / Vyāsa,[39] 'the Compiler,' likewise, arranged it into many sections, which Vasiṣṭha,[40] for lack of Capability, had not done. //1.42//

vālmīkir ādau ca sasarja padyaṁ jagrantha yan na cyavano maharṣiḥ /
cikitsitaṁ yac ca cakāra nātriḥ paścāt tad ātreya ṛṣir jagāda // 1.43 //
Vālmīki[41] invented a meter which the great seer Cyavana,[42] in his compositions, had never used; / And that treatise on healing which Atri failed to produce, the seer Ātreya[43] would later expound. //1.43//

---

[33] EHJ: "'In respect of wisdom, renowned deeds and fame of kings there is no question of former and latter. And, since in the nature of things there is a cause here for the effect, listen to our parallels thereto." The Chinese includes 物性之所生 各從因緣起, "That which in the nature of things is born/produced, in each case arises out of causes and conditions."

[34] Name of an ancient seer regarded as progenitor of the Bhṛgu tribe.

[35] Another ancient seer, regarded as the father of the fire-god Agni. Various hymns and law books are attributed to him.

[36] "The Bright One," a name of the planet Venus or its regent (regarded as the son of Bhṛgu). Also a name of Agni.

[37] "Lord of Prayer." EH Johnston notes that Śukra and Bṛhas-pati are regularly coupled together as the authors of the first treatises on political science

[38] See also SN Canto 7: *So too did brahma-begotten Aṅgiras, when his mind was seized by passion, have sex with Sarasvatī; To her was born his son Sarasvata, who gave voice again to missing Vedas. //SN7.31 //*

[39] Vyāsa, classifier of the Vedas, is also known as Dvaipāyana, "island-born," since he was born in a small island in the Ganges. Nanda also refers to him in SN Canto 7: *Dvaipāyana, equally, while having dharma as his primary object, enjoyed a woman at a brothel in Kāśi; Struck by her foot, with its trembling ankle bracelet, he was like a cloud being struck by a twist of lightning. // SN7.30 //*

[40] Vasiṣṭha was the owner of the cow of plenty mentioned in SN1.3. His son's name was Śakti, "Capability."

[41] Author of the *Rāmāyaṇa.*

[42] One of the authors of the *Ṛg Veda.*

[43] A famous physician whose name Ātreya means "descended from Atri."

yac ca dvijatvaṁ kuśiko na lebhe tad gādhinaḥ sūnur avāpa rājan /
velāṁ samudre sagaraś ca dadhre nekṣvākavo yāṁ prathamaṁ babandhuḥ // 1.44 //
That rank of twice-born brahmin[44] which "Squint-Eyed" Kuśika never won, O King!, the son of Gādhin did attain;[45] / And "Poison-Possessing" Sagara[46] gave the ocean a shoreline, a boundary which formerly the Ikṣvākus had failed to fix. //1.44//

ācāryakaṁ yoga-vidhau dvijānām aprāptam anyair janako jagāma /
khyātāni karmāṇi ca yāni śaureḥ śūrādayas teṣv abalā babhūvuḥ // 1.45 //
The status of teacher to twice-born brahmins of the method of yoga, a status that nobody but a brahmin had obtained, Janaka did attain;[47] / And the celebrated deeds of Śauri, "Descended from the Mighty," were beyond the power of Śūra, "the Mighty Man" himself, and his contemporaries. //1.45//

tasmāt pramāṇaṁ na vayo na vaṁśaḥ kaś-cit kva-cic chraiṣṭhyam upaiti loke /
rājñām ṛṣīṇāṁ ca hi tāni tāni kṛtāni putrair akṛtāni pūrvaiḥ // 1.46 //
The criterion, then, is neither age nor descent; anyone anywhere may attain pre-eminence in the world. / For, among kings and seers, sons have achieved various things that forebears failed to achieve." //1.46//

evaṁ nṛpaḥ pratyayitair dvijais tair āśvāsitaś cāpy abhinanditaś ca /
śaṅkām aniṣṭāṁ vijahau manastaḥ praharṣam evādhikam āruroha // 1.47 //
The king, being thus cheered and encouraged by those trusted twice-born provers, / Banished from his mind awkward doubt and rose to still greater heights of joy. //1.47//

prītaś ca tebhyo dvija-sattamebhyaḥ satkāra-pūrvaṁ pradadau dhanāni /
bhūyād ayaṁ bhūmi-patir yathokto yāyāj jarām etya vanāni ceti // 1.48 //
And so upon those truest of the twice-born,[48] he joyfully bestowed riches, along with hospitality, / Wishing "May the boy become a king as prophesied and retire to the forest in his old age." //1.48//

---

[44] In this verse, it is clear from the context that *dvi-ja-tvam*, lit. "twice-born-ness" means being a Brahman.

[45] Viśva-mitra "Friend of All," who was the son of Gādhin and the grandson of Kuśika, was born into the warrior caste of kṣatriyas but after enduring years of ascetic self-denial eventually earned the epithet *brahmarṣi*, "Brahman Seer" - only then to be captivated by the nymph Ghṛtācī. Nanda refers to the same story in SN7.35.

[46] So called because of poison given to his pregnant mother by the other wife of his father.

[47] King Janaka, as such, was a member of the kṣatriya cast of royal warriors. As such, again, he reversed the usual relationship in which brahmins would have taught yoga to kings.

[48] *Dvija-sattamebhyaḥ*, "to the truest of the twice-born," seems here to contain a pinch of irony. In later cantos (esp. BC Canto 7) *dvi-ja* (twice-born, born again) might be intended to carry a hidden, non-pejorative meaning. But here Aśvaghoṣa seems to suggest, below the surface, that the brahmins were self-seeking and not so true. The great seer Asita, who appears in the following verse, is not included among the twice-born [brahmins] - he is not called *dvi-jaḥ*; he, evidently, was one who was different (*anyaḥ*).

atho nimittaiś ca tapo-balāc ca taj-janma janmānta-karasya buddhvā /
śākyeśvarasyālayam ājagāma saddharma-tarṣād asito maharṣiḥ // 1.49 //
Then, awoken by dint of practice of austerities and alerted via signs to the birth of the one who would put an end to birth, / There appeared at the palace of the Śākya king, driven by a thirst for true dharma, the great seer Asita, "the Not White One."[49] //1.49//

taṁ brahmavid brahmavidāṁ jvalantaṁ brāhmyā śriyā caiva tapaḥ-śriyā ca /
rājño gurur gaurava-satkriyābhyām praveśayām āsa narendra-sadma // 1.50 //
The king's own guru, a knower of brahma among brahma-knowers,[50] ushered in him who was blazing with brahma-begotten brilliance and with the glowing heat of ascetic exertion – / The king's guru, with the gravity and hospitality due to a guru, ushered Asita into the king's royal seat. //1.50//

sa pārthivāntaḥ-pura-saṁnikarṣaṁ kumāra-janmāgata-harṣa-vegaḥ /
viveśa dhīro vana-saṁjñayaiva tapaḥ-prakarṣāc ca jarāśrayāc ca // 1.51 //
He entered the intimate surroundings of the women's quarters of the palace, bristling with a rush of joy at the prince's birth, / But steady, seeing the harem as if it were a forest, through his exceptional practice of austerities – and thanks also to old age. //1.51//

tato nṛpas taṁ munim āsana-sthaṁ pādyārghya-pūrvaṁ pratipūjya samyak /
nimantrayām āsa yathopacāraṁ purā vasiṣṭhaṁ sa ivāntidevaḥ // 1.52 //
Then that sage who was devoted to sitting,[51] the king fittingly honored, with foot-washing water and with welcoming water; / The king offered to him appropriate service, as once upon a time Antideva did to Vasiṣṭha.[52] //1.52//

dhanyo 'smy anugrāhyam idaṁ kulaṁ me yan māṁ didṛkṣur bhagavān upetaḥ /
ājñāpyatāṁ kiṁ karavāṇi saumya śiṣyo 'smi viśrambhitum arhasīti // 1.53 //
"Fortunate am I and favoured is my family in that you, beauty-possessed man!, have come to see me. / Let me know, O moonlike man of *soma*!, what I should do. Please believe in me, for I am ready to be taught." //1.53//

evaṁ nṛpeṇopamantritaḥ san sarveṇa bhāvena munir yathāvat /
sa vismayotphulla-viśāla-dṛṣṭir gambhīra-dhīrāṇi vacāṁsy uvāca // 1.54 //
Being bidden like this by a ruler of men, the sage, with his whole being, [responded] appropriately; / He whose expansive eye was, in his state of wonderment, wide open, voiced words whose sound was deep and sonorous: //1.54//

---

[49] Asita, "black, not white," is thought to be a back formation from *sita*, "white." Assuming that Aśvaghoṣa chose the name himself, the suggestion might be that Asita was different from brahmins who affected spiritual purity. Hence Asita's intuition was real, and it would hit the target.

[50] As discussed in connection with Arāḍa's teaching in BC Canto 12, *brahma* is derived from √*bṛh*, whose meanings include to grow, to develop, to get fat.

[51] The ostensible meaning of *āsana-sthaṁ* is "remaining seated" or simply "sitting down."

[52] The story of how Antideva went to heaven after serving warm water to Vasiṣṭha is contained in the *Mahā-bhārata*.

mahātmani tvayy upapannam etat priyātithau tyāgini dharma-kāme /
sattvānvaya-jñāna-vayo-'nurūpā snigdhā yad evaṁ mayi te matiḥ syāt // 1.55 //
"This befits you, great and noble soul that you are, hospitable, generous, and dharma-loving, / That you should show towards me, reflecting your character, family, wisdom and vitality, such affectionate appreciation. //1.55//

etac ca tad yena nṛpa-rṣayas te dharmeṇa sūkṣmeṇa dhanāny avāpya /
nityaṁ tyajanto vidhivad babhūvus tapobhir āḍhyā vibhavair daridrāḥ // 1.56 //
This, moreover, is that means whereby those seers who were rulers of men, on garnering riches, by the subtle method, / And constantly giving those riches away, in a principled manner, became flush with austerities and bereft of luxuries. //1.56//

prayojanaṁ yat tu mamopayāne tan me śṛṇu prītim upehi ca tvam /
divyā mayāditya-pathe śrutā vāg bodhāya jātas tanayas taveti // 1.57 //
But as to my own motive in coming here, hear it from me and be glad: / The cosmic word, I have heard – on Āditi's way, on the path of the sun – is that your son has been born for the sake of awakening. //1.57//

śrutvā vacas tac ca manaś ca yuktvā jñātvā nimittaiś ca tato 'smy upetaḥ /
didṛkṣayā śākya-kula-dhvajasya śakra-dhvajasyeva samucchritasya // 1.58 //
Listening for that directive,[53] applying the mind to it, and intuiting it by signs, on that basis I am arrived[54] / Desirous of seeing the banner of the Śākya clan held aloft like the flag of mighty Indra." //1.58//

ity etad evaṁ vacanaṁ niśamya praharṣa-saṁbhrānta-gatir narendraḥ /
ādāya dhātry-aṅka-gataṁ kumāraṁ saṁdarśayām āsa tapo-dhanāya // 1.59 //
Thus discerning this direction, the king, with a joyful spring in his step, / Took the prince, who was sitting on a nurse's lap, and showed him to austerity-rich [Asita]. //1.59//

cakrāṅka-pādaṁ sa tato mahārṣir jālāvanaddhāṅguli-pāṇi-pādam /
sorṇa-bhruvaṁ vāraṇa-vasti-kośaṁ savismayaṁ rāja-sutaṁ dadarśa // 1.60 //
Then the great seer observed the wheel-marked feet, the webbed fingers and toes, / The circle of hair between the eyebrows, and the testes drawn up like an elephant's: disbelievingly did he behold the son of the king. //1.60//

dhātry-aṅka-saṁviṣṭam avekṣya cainaṁ devy-aṅka-saṁviṣṭam ivāgni-sūnum /
babhūva pakṣmānta-vicañcitāśrur niśvasya caiva tridivonmukho 'bhūt // 1.61 //
As he watched [the prince] sitting in the lap of a nurse, like the son of Agni sitting in the lap of divine nymphs, / [Asita's] tears dangled on the ends of his eyelashes, and, taking a deep breath, he looked up towards the heavens. //1.61//

---

[53] *Vacas* like *vacanam* in the next verse ostensibly suggests a spoken word or act of speaking. At the same time, *vacas* and *vacanam* can also mean a teaching or direction.

[54] Ostensible meaning: "thus I have come to the palace." In the hidden meaning, "on the basis of that direction, here I am, happening here like this."

dṛṣṭvāsitaṁ tv aśru-pariplutākṣaṁ snehāt tanū-jasya nṛpaś cakampe /
sa-gadgadaṁ bāṣpa-kaṣāya-kaṅṭhaḥ papraccha sa prāñjalir ānatāṅgaḥ // 1.62 //
But when the ruler of men beheld [Asita] all teary-eyed, the king's attachment to his own flesh and blood caused him to shudder: / Stammering, choking back astringent tears, with his cupped hands held before him, and his body bent low, he asked: //1.62//

alpāntaraṁ yasya vapuḥ surebhyo bahv-adbhutaṁ yasya ca janma dīptam /
yasyottamaṁ bhāvinam āttha cārthaṁ taṁ prekṣya kasmāt tava dhīra bāṣpaḥ // 1.63 //
"On beholding him whose form is little different from the gods, whose shining birth was wonderful in many ways, / And whose purpose, you said, was destined to be of the highest order, why, O Steadfast Soul, would you shed tears? //1.63//

api sthirāyur bhagavan kumāraḥ kac-cin na śokāya mama prasūtaḥ /
labdhā kathaṁ-cit salilāñjalir me na khalv imaṁ pātum upaiti kālaḥ // 1.64 //
Will the prince, O one full of fortune![55], be blessed with long life? Heaven forfend that he was born for my sorrow! / Am I in my cupped hands somehow to have gained water, only for Death to come and drink it? //1.64//

apy akṣayaṁ me yaśaso nidhānaṁ kac-cid dhruvo me kula-hasta-sāraḥ /
api prayāsyāmi sukhaṁ paratra supto 'pi putre 'nimiṣaika-cakṣuḥ // 1.65 //
Again, will the repository of my glory be immune to decay? I hope the extending hand of my family is secure! / Shall I depart happily to the hereafter, keeping one eye open in my son, even while I sleep? //1.65//

kac-cin na me jātam aphullam eva kula-pravālaṁ pariśoṣa-bhāgi /
kṣipraṁ vibho brūhi na me 'sti śāntiḥ snehaṁ sute vetsi hi bāndhavānām // 1.66 //
Heaven forbid that my family's new shoot has budded only to wither away before opening. / Tell me quickly, O abundantly able one!; I have no peace, for you know the love that blood relatives invest in a child." //1.66//

ity āgatāvegam aniṣṭa-buddhyā buddhvā narendraṁ sa munir babhāṣe /
mā bhūn matis te nṛpa kā-cid anyā niḥsaṁśayaṁ tad yad avocam asmi // 1.67 //
Knowing the king to be thus agitated by a sense of foreboding, the sage said: / "Let not your mind, O protector of men, be in any way disturbed;[56] what I have said I have said beyond doubt. //1.67//

---

[55] "O one full of fortune" and "O beauty-possessed man" are translations of the vocative *bhagavan* – as is "O glorious one!" *Bhagavat*, as in the Canto title *bhagavat-prasutiḥ*, means one possessed of *bhaga*. The meanings of *bhaga* include fortune, happiness, welfare, and beauty.

[56] *Anyā*: more literally, "different."

nāsyānyathātvaṁ prati vikriyā me svāṁ vañcanāṁ tu prati viklavo 'smi /
kālo hi me yātum ayaṁ ca jāto jāti-kṣayasyāsulabhasya boddhā // 1.68 //
Worried I am not about a twist of fate for him; distressed I am, though, about missing out myself. / For the time is nigh for me to go, now that he is born, who will know the secret of putting birth to death. //1.68//

vihāya rājyaṁ viṣayeṣv anāsthas tīvraiḥ prayatnair adhigamya tattvam /
jagaty ayaṁ moha-tamo nihantuṁ jvaliṣyati jñāna-mayo hi sūryaḥ // 1.69 //
Indifferent to objects, he will give up his kingdom; then, through exacting and unrelenting effort, he will realize the truth; / And then, to dispel the darkness of delusion in the world, he will shine forth as a sun whose substance is knowing. //1.69//

duḥkhārṇavād vyādhi-vikīrṇa-phenāj jarā-taraṅgān maraṇogra-vegāt /
uttārayiṣyaty ayam uhyamānam ārtaṁ jagaj jñāna-mahā-plavena // 1.70 //
Out of the surging sea of suffering, whose scattered foam is sickness, whose waves are old age, and whose terrible tide is death, / He will deliver the afflicted world which is borne helplessly along, by means of the great raft of knowing. //1.70//

prajñāṁbu-vegāṁ sthira-śīla-vaprāṁ samādhi-śītāṁ vrata-cakravākām /
asyottamāṁ dharma-nadīṁ pravṛttāṁ tṛṣṇārditaḥ pāsyati jīva-lokaḥ // 1.71 //
The river whose flow is the water of wisdom, whose steep banks are sturdy integrity, whose coolness is balance, and whose greylag geese, calling and answering,[57] are acts of obedience - / That highest of rivers - the water of dharma flowing forth from him - the thirst-afflicted world of living beings will drink. //1.71//

duḥkhārditebhyo viṣayāvṛtebhyaḥ saṁsāra-kāntāra-patha-sthitebhyaḥ /
ākhyāsyati hy eṣa vimokṣa-mārgaṁ mārga-pranaṣṭebhya ivādhvagebhyaḥ // 1.72 //
To sorrow-afflicted, object-laden souls, stuck in the scrubby ruts of saṁsāra, / He will tell a way out, as if to travelers who have lost their way. //1.72//

vidahyamānāya janāya loke rāgāgnināyaṁ viṣayendhanena /
prahlādam ādhāsyati dharma-vṛṣṭyā vṛṣṭyā mahā-megha ivātapānte // 1.73 //
To people being burned in this world by a fire of passion whose fuel is objects, / He with a rain of dharma will bring joyous refreshment like a great cloud with rain at the end of sweltering heat. //1.73//

---

[57] Water birds - greylag geese, or in some translations ruddy ducks - called *cakra-vāka*, lit. "circular calling," were known to call mournfully - *ang, ang* - to each other when separated during the night. They feature prominently in Sanskrit romantic poetry.

tṛṣṇārgalaṁ moha-tamaḥ-kapāṭaṁ dvāraṁ prajānām apayāna-hetoḥ /
vipāṭayiṣyaty ayam uttamena saddharma-tāḍena dur-āsadena // 1.74 //
The door with panels of darkness and delusion, bolted shut by thirst, he will break open to let people out / By means of a thump of the highest order – the incontestable clout of true dharma, alongside which it is hard to sit. //1.74//

svair moha-pāśaiḥ pariveṣṭitasya duḥkhābhibhūtasya nirāśrayasya /
lokasya saṁbudhya ca dharma-rājaḥ kariṣyate bandhana-mokṣam eṣaḥ // 1.75 //
For folk entangled in the twisted fetters of their own delusion, for folk pulled down into their misery who lack the means to be lifted up, / He when he is fully awake, as a king of dharma, will undo the ties that bind. //1.75//

tan mā kṛthāḥ śokam imaṁ prati tvam asmin sa śocyo 'sti manuṣya-loke /
mohena vā kāma-sukhair madād vā yo naiṣṭhikaṁ śroṣyati nāsya dharmam // 1.76 //
Therefore do not sorrow for him; those who deserve sorrow are those in this human world who, / Whether through the delusion that stems from sensual desires, or because of fervent inspiration, will not learn his ultimate dharma. //1.76//

bhraṣṭasya tasmāc ca guṇād ato me dhyānāni labdhvāpy akṛtārthataiva /
dharmasya tasyāśravaṇād ahaṁ hi manye vipattiṁ tri-dive 'pi vāsam // 1.77 //
And since I have fallen short of that merit, in spite of having mastered the stages of meditation, I have failed. / Because of being a non-learner of his dharma, I deem it a misfortune to remain even in the highest heaven." //1.77//

iti śrutārthaḥ sasuhṛt-sadāras tyaktvā viṣādaṁ mumude narendraḥ /
evaṁ-vidho 'yaṁ tanayo mameti mene sa hi svām api sāravattām // 1.78 //
Thus informed, the king in the company of his wife and friends dismissed dejection and rejoiced; / For, thinking "Such is this son of mine," he saw his son's excellence as being also his own. //1.78//

ārṣeṇa mārgeṇa tu yāsyatīti cintā-vidheyaṁ hṛdayaṁ cakāra /
na khalv asau na-priya-dharma-pakṣaḥ saṁtāna-nāśāt tu bhayaṁ dadarśa // 1.79 //
But then it preyed upon his mind that his son might trace a seer's path: / Biased against dharma he surely was not, but dread he did foresee from the ending of his line. //1.79//

atha munir asito nivedya tattvaṁ suta-niyataṁ suta-viklavāya rājñe /
sa-bahu-matam udīkṣyamāṇa-rūpaḥ pavana-pathena yathāgataṁ jagāma // 1.80 //
And so the sage Asita went away, having let the reality be known, having caused the king, who was worried about his child, to know the inevitable reality tied to having a child. / While people, with varying degrees of appreciation, looked up at his excellent form, the Not White One went as he had come, on the way of the wind. //1.80 //

kṛta-mitir anujā-sutaṁ ca dṛṣṭvā muni-vacana-śravaṇe ca tan matau ca /
bahu-vidham anukampayā sa sādhuḥ priya-sutavad viniyojayāṁ cakāra // 1.81 //
[A royal relative] who, having beheld his younger sister's son, knew the score, saw to it that the sage's direction should be listened to and given thought; / [This uncle] in many different ways, with empathy, being himself straight and true, saw to this as if for his own beloved son. //1.81//

nara-patir api putra-janma-tuṣṭo viṣaya-gatāni vimucya bandhanāni /
kula-sadṛśam acīkarad yathāvat priya-tanayas tanayasya jāta-karma // 1.82 //
Even the king himself, delighted at the birth of a son, loosened his ties to worldly objects / Whereupon, in a manner befitting his nobility, he performed for his son, out of love for his son, a rite of birth. //1.82//

daśasu pariṇateṣv ahaḥsu caiva prayata-manāḥ parayā mudā parītaḥ /
akuruta japa-homa-maṅgalādyāḥ parama-bhavāya sutasya devatejyāḥ // 1.83 //
Again, when ten days were up, with a purified mind, and filled with the greatest gladness, / He performed mutterings, fire oblations, ritual movements and other acts of religious worship, with a view to the ultimate well-being of his son. //1.83//

api ca śata-sahasra-pūrṇa-saṁkhyāḥ sthira-balavat-tanayāḥ sahema-śṛṅgīḥ /
anupagata-jarāḥ payasvinīr gāḥ svayam adadāt suta-vṛddhaye dvijebhyaḥ // 1.84 //
Still more, cows numbering fully a hundred thousand, with strong, sturdy calves and gilded horns, / Unimpaired by age or infirmity, yielding milk in abundance, he freely gave to the twice-born brahmins, with a view to his son's advancement. //1.84//

bahu-vidha-viṣayās tato yatātmā sva-hṛdaya-toṣa-karīḥ kriyā vidhāya /
guṇavati divase śive muhūrte matim akaron muditaḥ pura-praveśe // 1.85 //
With his self reined in, then, on that basis - after performing sacrificial acts which were variously oriented towards his end and which made him feel gratified in his heart - / At an auspicious moment in a good day, he rejoicingly resolved to enter the city. //1.85//

dvi-rada-rada-mayīm atho mahārhāṁ sita-sita-puṣpa-bhṛtāṁ maṇi-pradīpām /
abhajata śivikāṁ śivāya devī tanayavatī praṇipatya devatābhyaḥ // 1.86 //
And then into a precious palanquin made from a tusker's two tusks, which was filled with the white flowers of the White Flower, the *sita*, and which had pearls for lamps, / The god-queen with her child repaired, having bowed down, for good fortune, before images of gods. //1.86//

puram atha purataḥ praveśya patnīṁ sthavira-janānugatām apatya-nāthām /
nṛ-patir api jagāma paura-saṁghair divam amarair maghavān ivārcyamānaḥ // 1.87 //
Now, having let his wife enter the city ahead of him – her with their offspring, and elders[58] trailing behind – / The king also approached, applauded by groups[59] of townsfolk, like gift-bestowing Indra entering heaven, applauded by the immortals. //1.87//

bhavanam atha vigāhya śākya-rājo bhava iva ṣaṇ-mukha-janmanā pratītaḥ /
idam idam iti harṣa-pūrṇa-vaktro bahu-vidha-puṣṭi-yaśas-karaṁ vyadhatta // 1.88 //
Headlong into his palace, then, dived the Śākya king, happy as Bhava at the birth of six-faced Kārttikeya.[60] / "Do this! Do that!" he commanded, his face brimming with joy, as he made arrangements for all sorts of lavishness and splendor. //1.88//

iti nara-pati-putra-janma-vṛddhyāṁ sa-jana-padaṁ kapilāhvayaṁ puraṁ tat /
dhana-da-puram ivāpsaro-'vakīrṇaṁ muditam abhūn nala-kūbara-prasūtau // 1.89 //
Thus at the happy development which was the birth of the king's son, that city named after Kapila,[61] along with surrounding settlements, / Showed its delight, just as the city of the Wealth-Giver, spilling over with celestial nymphs, became delighted at the birth of Nala-kūbara.[62] //1.89//

iti buddha-carite mahā-kāvye bhagavat prasūtir nāma prathamaḥ sargaḥ // 1 //
The first canto, titled "The Birth of Something Beautiful,"
in an epic story of awakened action.

---

[58] *Sthavira* means elder, as in *sthavira-vādins* or "Devotees of the Teaching of the Elders."
[59] *Saṁgha* means group or community. These two terms *sthavira* and *saṁgha* may have a hidden significance insofar as in the second general council held at Vaiśāli, one hundred years after the Buddha's death, a schism is said to have arisen between *Sthavira-vādins* (Pāli *Thera-vādī*) and *Mahā-saṁghikas* or "Members of the Great Community."
[60] Six-faced Kārttikeya was the son of the fire-god Agni, aka Bhava, mentioned above in BC1.61.
[61] Kapilavastu.
[62] Nāla-kubara was a son of Kubera, here called *dhāna-da,* "the Wealth-Giver." Usually depicted as a dwarfish figure with a large paunch, Kubera was nonetheless revered by many as the god of riches and treasure.

Canto 2: antaḥ-pura-vihāraḥ
Exploring within the Women's Quarters
[or Faring Well within the Battlements]

Introduction

Antar means within, and *pura* means 1. fortress, castle, city, town; 2. the female apartments. *Antaḥ-pura* is thus given in the dictionary as the king's palace, and the female apartments. *Vihāra* includes the meanings of travelling around for fun, exploring, and faring well.

The canto concludes by affirming the historical fact that the Śākya prince who would become the Buddha, in the period before he left the palace, enjoyed sensual pleasures with his wife and with other women in the royal palace. And ostensibly the canto title points to these sexual explorations with women within the women's apartments – hence, "Exploring within the Women's Quarters."

As with Saundarananda Canto 2 (A Portrait of the King), however, Aśvaghoṣa seems, below the surface, to be more interested in portraying King Śuddhodana as a paragon of the transcendent virtues of a buddha. Such virtues, called *pāramitās* – transcendent virtues, transcendent accomplishments, or perfections – are traditionally six in number:

> *śīla*, discipline, integrity, not doing wrong (see e.g. BC2.33; 2.34; 2.43; 2.44; 2.52)
> *prajñā*, wisdom (BC2.35; 2.52).
> *dāna*, free giving (BC2.36; 2.40)
> *vīrya*, strongly directed energy, heroic endeavor (BC2.40; 2.50)
> *kṣānti*, forbearance (BC2.42; 2.43)
> *dhyāna*, meditation (BC2.45)

To these six are sometimes added:

> *maitra*, friendship (BC2.6; 2.35)
> *adhisthāna*, steadfast resolution (BC2.34; 2.49)
> *satya*, truthfulness (BC2.38)
> *upekṣā*, equanimity (BC2.52)

But nowhere does Aśvaghoṣa enumerate the six or the ten pāramitās like this one by one. In fact nowhere in Aśvaghoṣa's two epic poems does the word *pāramitā* even appear. In the present canto, there is a reference to the steadfast integrity (*sthira-śīla*) of Yaśodharā's family in BC2.26, but none of the above pāramitās, by name, is ascribed to the king.

Nevertheless, the main point of this canto, below the surface, seems to be to describe how a lord of the earth, along with those below him, all fare well, within safe limits, when the protector of men manifests transcendent virtues. Hence, to convey this central hidden meaning, the canto title might better be rendered "Faring Well within the Battlements."

ā janmano janma-jarānta-gasya tasyātmajasyātma-jitaḥ sa rājā /
ahany ahany artha-gajāśva-mitrair vṛddhiṁ yayau sindhur ivāmbu-vegaiḥ // 2.1 //
Following the birth of his self-begotten son – following the birth of the self-conquering son who would get to the bottom of birth and aging – / The king day by day waxed mightier by dint of wealth, elephants, horses and allies, as a river develops by dint of its tributaries. //2.1//

dhanasya ratnasya ca tasya tasya kṛtākṛtasyaiva ca kāñcanasya /
tadā hi naikān sa nidhīn avāpa manorathasyāpy atibhāra-bhūtān // 2.2 //
The king obtained all sorts of money and treasure, of wrought gold, or unwrought bullion – / He obtained manifold reserves, loaded, as it were, even beyond the capacity of the chariot of his mind.[1] //2.2//

ye padma-kalpair api ca dvipendrair na maṇḍalaṁ śakyam ihābhinetum /
madotkaṭā haimavatā gajās te vināpi yatnād upatasthur enam // 2.3 //
And elephants surrounded him that none in this world, not even top tuskers of Padma's ilk,[2] Could lead around a circle – / Himālayan elephants massively in rut stationed themselves, without the making of any effort at all, about his circle. //2.3//

nānāṅka-cihnair nava-hema-bhāṇḍair vibhūṣitair lamba-saṭais tathānyaiḥ /
saṁcukṣubhe cāsya puraṁ turaṅgair balena maitryā ca dhanena cāptaiḥ // 2.4 //
[His city was traversed] by horses [or fast movers][3] of different strokes and distinctive characters, rigged out in new gold gear,[4] and [traversed] by other types too, adorned with long braided manes[5]; / Again, his city shook with [the stomping of] horses obtained by force, won through friendship, and bought with money.[6] //2.4//

puṣṭāś ca tuṣṭāś ca tathāsya rājye sādhvyo 'rajaskā guṇavat-payaskāḥ /
udagra-vatsaiḥ sahitā babhūvur bahvyo bahu-kṣīra-duhaś ca gāvaḥ // 2.5 //
Equally in his kingdom, well-fed and well-satisfied, well-disposed, dustless, and overflowing with goodness,[7] / There were, together with their lanky young, many cows,[8] which yielded abundant milk. //2.5//

---

[1] *Mano-ratha* generally means "heart's joy," but here as in several other places Aśvaghoṣa makes a play on *ratha* whose meanings include both joy and chariot.

[2] Padma is the southernmost of the elephants that support the earth.

[3] *Turaṁga* lit. "fast-going," ostensibly means a horse. So on the surface Aśvaghoṣa is talking about horses but below the surface he may have in mind those whose consciousness is quick.

[4] Ostensibly, new gold trappings. In the hidden meaning, instruments for newly producing what is golden, or for digging out for the first time gold itself. The meanings of *bhaṇḍa* include 1. a tool or instrument, and 2. a horse's harness of trappings.

[5] In the hidden meaning, generic ascetic strivers.

[6] Is this an example of *madhyamaka* logic of thesis, anti-thesis and synthesis – such that force is opposed to friendliness, and in the middle way is the practical mechanism of the market?

[7] The first half of the verse seems to invite us to expect that the subject will be good teachers.

[8] In the original Sanskrit the subject, cows (*gāvah*), comes at the very end of the verse.

madhya-sthatāṁ tasya ripur jagāma madhya-stha-bhāvaḥ prayayau suhṛttvam /
viśeṣato dārḍhyam iyāya mitraṁ dvāv asya pakṣāv aparas tu nāsa // 2.6 //
An enemy of his entered into neutrality; neutrality turned into friendship; / friendship became something exceptionally solid. For him, though he had two sides, "the other" did not exist. //2.6//

tathāsya mandānila-megha-śabdaḥ saudāminī-kuṇḍala-maṇḍitābhraḥ /
vināśma-varṣāśani-pāta-doṣaiḥ kāle ca deśe pravavarṣa devaḥ // 2.7 //
For him, equally, with whispers of rainclouds blown by lazy breezes, with clouds of thunder gilded by rings of lightning, / But without any flak from showers of stone missiles or falling thunderbolts, at the right time and place, it rained. //2.7//

ruroha sasyaṁ phalavad yathārtu tadākṛtenāpi kṛṣi-śrameṇa /
tā eva cāsyauṣadhayo rasena sāreṇa caivābhyadhikā babhūvuḥ // 2.8 //
Each crop developed fruitfully in accordance with its season, without toil at the plough being done then at all;[9] / And those same plants, for him, became herbs, only stronger, in taste and in efficacy. //2.8//

śarīra-saṁdeha-kare 'pi kāle saṁgrāma-saṁmarda iva pravṛtte /
svasthāḥ sukhaṁ caiva nirāmayaṁ ca prajajñire garbha-dharāś ca nāryaḥ // 2.9 //
In dealing with that circumstance which, like a clash between armies, spells danger for the body, / Remaining even then in their natural state, with ease and without disease, pregnant women gave birth. //2.9//

pṛthag vratibhyo vibhave 'pi garhye na prārthayanti sma narāḥ parebhyaḥ /
abhyarthitaḥ sūkṣma-dhano 'pi cāryas tadā na kaś-cid vimukho babhūva // 2.10 //
Save for those observing a vow, no man, however lacking in means, ever begged from others; / And no noble person, however scant his resources, turned away when asked to give. //2.10//

nāgauravo bandhuṣu nāpy adātā naivāvrato nānṛtiko na hiṁsraḥ /
āsīt tadā kaś-cana tasya rājye rājño yayāter iva nāhuṣasya // 2.11 //
No disrespect nor any stinginess towards kinsmen, nor any lawlessness at all, or untruthfulness or cruelty, / Was shown by anybody in his kingdom at that time, as in the realm of King Yayāti, son of Nahuṣa.[10] //2.11//

---

[9] Like *vināpi yatnād* (without any effort at all) in verse 3 above, the suggestion is of the effortlessness and spontaneity which we aspire to in the practice of non-doing. Ostensible meaning, then: no effort was made. Real meaning: effort emerged naturally, and work was done without undue stress.

[10] Yayāti represents somebody in ancient Indian mythology who recognized the error of his former ways, with beneficial subsequent results for his kingdom. As such he is praised twice in Saundarananda: *Those equals of Indra took charge of that city with noble ardour but without arrogance; / And they thus took on forever the fragrance of honor, like the celebrated sons of Yayāti.// SN1.59 // Bhūri-dyumna and Yayāti and other excellent kings, / Having bought heaven by their actions, gave it up again, after that karma ran out - // SN11.46 //*

udyāna-devāyatanāśramāṇāṁ kūpa-prapā-puṣkariṇī-vanānām /
cakruḥ kriyās tatra ca dharma-kāmāḥ pratyakṣataḥ svargam ivopalabhya // 2.12 //
Gardens, temples, and ashrams, wells and drinking fountains, lotus-ponds and woods, / Lovers of dharma established there as acts of religious sacrifice – almost as if they had seen heaven with their own eyes.[11] //2.12//

muktaś ca durbhikṣa-bhayāmayebhyo hṛṣṭo janaḥ svarga ivābhireme /
patnīṁ patir vā mahiṣī patiṁ vā parasparaṁ na vyabhiceratuś ca // 2.13 //
Exempt from famine, terror, and sickness, people dwelt there as gladly as if they were in heaven; / And neither husband against wife nor wife against husband did man and woman do each other wrong. //2.13//

kaś-cit siṣeve rataye na kāmaṁ kāmārtham arthaṁ na jugopa kaś-cit /
kaś-cid dhanārthaṁ na cacāra dharmaṁ dharmāya kaś-cin na cakāra hiṁsām // 2.14 //
Nobody served desire for pleasure; nobody, on account of desire, guarded wealth; / Nobody practiced dharma for a prize; nobody, in pursuit of dharma, did harm.[12] //2.14//

steyādibhiś cāpy aribhiś ca naṣṭaṁ svasthaṁ sva-cakraṁ para-cakra-muktam /
kṣemaṁ subhikṣaṁ ca babhūva tasya purānaraṇyasya yathaiva rāṣṭre // 2.15 //
Theft and suchlike were non-existent, as also were enemies; his realm was self-sufficient, immune to outside interference, / Pleasant to live in and plentifully provided – just as it was, once upon a time, in the kingdom of An-araṇya, "Nowhere Wild."[13] //2.15//

tadā hi taj-janmani tasya rājño manor ivāditya-sutasya rājye /
cacāra harṣaḥ praṇanāśa pāpmā jajvāla dharmaḥ kaluṣaṁ śaśāma // 2.16 //
For at that time, at the time of that birth, in that king's kingdom, as in the kingdom of Sun-begotten Manu, / Joy prevailed and wickedness was no more; dharma burned bright and foulness faded away. //2.16//

evaṁ-vidhā rāja-sutasya tasya sarvārtha-siddhiś ca yato babhūva /
tato nṛpas tasya sutasya nāma sarvārtha-siddho 'yam iti pracakre // 2.17 //
And since in that son begotten by the king such fulfillment of everything was realized / The ruler of men named that son of his accordingly, saying "He is Sarvārtha-siddha, Fulfilment of Everything." //2.17/

---

[11] *Pratyakṣataḥ... iva*: as if before their eyes. The ironic implication is that these worshippers of a religious dharma, involving religious rites, ceremonies and sacrifices (*kriyāḥ*), had not in fact seen what they aspired to with their own eyes.

[12] The three elements of this verse are the triple set of *kāma* (desire/love), *artha* (wealth), and *dharma* – identified in ancient India before the Buddha as three aims of human life. The verse suggests that the aims in themselves were not harmful, in a golden age, under enlightened sovereignty, when those aims were not pursued in a wrong way.

[13] A truly civilized place, in a mythical Golden Age?

devī tu māyā vibudharṣi-kalpaṁ dṛṣṭvā viśālaṁ tanaya-prabhāvam /
jātaṁ praharṣaṁ na śaśāka soḍhuṁ tato 'vināśāya divaṁ jagāma // 2.18 //
But having witnessed her offspring's mighty power, which could rival that of a divine seer, / Queen Māyā could not endure the extreme joy that arose in her; and so, rather than towards total oblivion, she 'went to heaven.'[14] //2.18//

tataḥ kumāraṁ sura-garbha-kalpaṁ snehena bhāvena ca nirviśeṣam /
mātṛ-ṣvasā mātṛ-sama-prabhāvā saṁvardhayām ātmajavad babhūva // 2.19 //
Then the prince whose peers were the progeny of gods, was brought up by the unconditional means of love and affection: / His mother's sister, who in her power was like his mother, caused him to grow as if he were her own son. //2.19//

tataḥ sa bālārka ivodaya-sthaḥ samīrito vahnir ivānilena /
krameṇa samyag vavṛdhe kumāras tārādhipaḥ pakṣa ivātamaske // 2.20 //
And so, like the early-morning sun on the way up, or like a fire being fanned by wafts of air, / Gradually, the child developed well - like the waxing moon in the bright fortnight. //2.20//

tato mahārhāṇi ca candanāni ratnāvaliś cauṣadhibhiḥ sagarbhā /
mṛga-prayuktā rathakāś ca haimā ācakrire 'smai suhṛd-ālayebhyaḥ // 2.21 //
Then precious preparations of sandalwood, and a string of jewels with herbs inside them, / And little golden carts drawn by deer, were brought to him, from the homes of good-hearts - //2.21//

vayo-'nurūpāṇi ca bhūṣaṇāni hiraṇ-mayā hasti-mṛgāśvakāś ca /
rathāś ca gavo vasana-prayuktā tantrīś ca cāmīkara-rūpya-citrā // 2.22 //
And ornaments appropriate for his age, toy elephants, deer and horses, made of gold, / And carts, and oxen[15] harnessed by finely woven fabric, with a tether for their calves, of gold and silver strands. //2.22//

evaṁ sa tais tair viṣayopacārair vayo-'nurūpair upacaryamāṇaḥ /
bālo 'py abāla-pratimo babhūva dhṛtyā ca śaucena dhiyā śriyā ca // 2.23 //
While thus indulged by various sense-stimulating gifts, of a sort appropriate for his age,[16] / Child though he was, he was not like a child in constancy, and in simplicity, sagacity and dignity. //2.23//

---

[14] In short, she died. But rather than forget her, people said that she had gone to heaven.
[15] Traditional symbol of bodhisattva-practice.
[16] With the repetition from the previous verse of description of toys as age-appropriate (*vayo-'nurūpa*), Aśvaghoṣa seems to wish to emphasize, wisely, the importance of playthings that give children the sense stimulation they need at different stages of their development.

vayaś ca kaumāram atītya madhyaṁ samprāpya bālaḥ sa hi rāja-sūnuḥ /
alpair ahobhir bahu-varṣa-gamyā jagrāha vidyāḥ sva-kulānurūpāḥ // 2.24 //
For, having passed through the early stage of life and arrived at the middle,[17] he, the young son of a king / Grasped in a few days subjects that took many years to master – fields of learning that befitted the house to which he belonged. //2.24//

naiḥśreyasaṁ tasya tu bhavyam arthaṁ śrutvā purastād asitān maharṣeḥ /
kāmeṣu saṅgaṁ janayāṁ babhūva vanāni yāyād iti śākya-rājaḥ // 2.25 //
But having heard before, from the great seer Asita, that the prince's future purpose would be transcendent bliss, / The Śākya king encouraged in his son attachment to sensual desires, so that he might not go to the forest. //2.25//

kulāt tato 'smai sthira-śīla-yuktāt sādhvīṁ vapur-hrī-vinayopapannām /
yaśodharāṁ nāma yaśo-viśālāṁ vāmābhidhānāṁ śriyam ājuhāva // 2.26 //
Then the king summoned for him, from a family of steadfast integrity, a true woman, the possessor of fine form, modesty and discipline, / A woman full of glory whose name was Yaśodharā, "Bearer of Glory" – in the shape of such a woman did the king invoke Śrī, goddess of fortune. //2.26//

vidyotamāno vapuṣā pareṇa sanatkumāra-pratimaḥ kumāraḥ /
sārdhaṁ tayā śākya-narendra-vadhvā śacyā sahasrākṣa ivābhireme // 2.27 //
The prince, with his supremely fine form shining forth, like "the Prince Who Was Forever Fresh," Sanat-kumāra,[18] / Enjoyed himself together with that Śākya princess as did mighty "All-Eyed" Indra,[19] mightily, with Śacī. //2.27//

kiṁ-cin manaḥ-kṣobha-karaṁ pratīpaṁ kathaṁ na paśyed iti so 'nucintya /
vāsaṁ nṛpo vyādiśati sma tasmai harmyodareṣv eva na bhū-pracāram // 2.28 //
[The king asked himself:] "How might he not see the slightest unpleasantness that could cause disturbance in his mind?" / Reflecting thus, the king assigned to the prince a residence up in the bowels of the palace, far away from the bustle on the ground. //2.28//

tataḥ śarat-toyada-pāṇḍareṣu bhūmau vimāneṣv iva rañjiteṣu /
harmyeṣu sarvartu-sukhāśrayeṣu strīṇām udārair vijahāra tūryaiḥ // 2.29 //
Then, in penthouse apartments painted white as autumn clouds – like the seven-story palaces of gods, only on the earth – / And appointed for comfort in every season, he roamed for fun among female players of the finest instruments. //2.29//

---

[17] *Madhyam*, the middle – the middle stage between childhood and adulthood, or, in the hidden meaning, the middle way between extremes, i.e. moderation or balance.

[18] Name of one of the four or seven sons of Brahmā. The name *sanat-kumāra* is sometimes given to any great saint who retains youthful purity.

[19] Indra being "all-eyed" (lit. "thousand-eyed") refers to the story of how Ahalya's aged husband Gautama punished Indra for seducing his wife by cursing Indra to carry his shame on his body in the form of a thousand vulvae. These female organs later turned to eyes when Indra worshipped the sun-god Surya.

kalair hi cāmīkara-baddha-kakṣair nārī-karāgrābhihatair mṛdaṅgaiḥ / varāpsaro-nṛtya-samaiś ca nṛtyaiḥ kailāsa-vat tad-bhavanaṁ rarāja // 2.30 //
For, with sounds of gold-studded tambourines being softly beaten by women's fingers, / And with dancing like the dancing of the choicest heavenly nymphs, that residence was as fabulous as Mount Kailāsa.[20] //2.30//

vāgbhiḥ kalābhir lalitaiś ca hāvair madaiḥ sakhelai madhuraiś ca hāsaiḥ / taṁ tatra nāryo ramayāṁ babhūvur bhrūvañcitair ardha-nirīkṣitaiś ca // 2.31 //
Using sweet nothings and playful gestures, accompanied by tipsy movements and charming chuckles, / The women there caressed him with secretly arched eyebrows, and sidelong glances. //2.31//

tataḥ sa kāmāśraya-paṇḍitābhiḥ strībhir gṛhīto rati-karkaśābhiḥ / vimāna-pṛṣṭhān na mahīṁ jagāma vimāna-pṛṣṭhād iva puṇya-karmā // 2.32 //
And so, embraced by experts in erotic addiction, by women who were unsagging in pursuit of pleasure, / He did not descend from high up in the palace down to earth – as a doer of good would not descend, from an upper carriage of gods on high. //2.32//

nṛpas tu tasyaiva vivṛddhi-hetos tad-bhāvinārthena ca codyamānaḥ / śame 'bhireme virarāma pāpād bheje damaṁ saṁvibabhāja sādhūn // 2.33 //
The king, meanwhile, having as his inner motive only his son's growth, while also being goaded by [Asita's] prediction of his son's future purpose, / Maintained himself in balance and restrained himself from evil; he did his share of self-regulation and he left their share to the good.[21] //2.33//

nādhīravat kāma-sukhe sasañje na saṁrarañje viṣamaṁ jananyām / dhṛtyendriyāśvāṁś capalān vijigye bandhūṁś ca paurāṁś ca guṇair jigāya // 2.34 //
He did not cling, like an irresolute type, to sensual pleasure; nor was he unduly enamored with a female agent of rebirth; / The restless horses of the senses he tamed through constancy. He surpassed by his virtues both royal relatives and townsfolk. //2.34//

nādhyaiṣṭa duḥkhāya parasya vidyāṁ jñānaṁ śivaṁ yat tu tad adhyagīṣṭa / svābhyaḥ prajābhyo hi yathā tathaiva sarva-prajābhyaḥ śivam āśaśaṁse // 2.35 //
He did not pursue learning to the detriment of the other but was steeped in that wisdom which is kindness; / For he wished all the best, in like manner, for his own offspring and for every offshoot. //2.35//

---

[20] Fabulous residence of Kubera, lord of wealth, and paradise of Śiva.

[21] The ostensible meaning may be as per EH Johnston's "he rewarded the good." The hidden meaning may reflect the principle of not doing wrong and letting the right thing do itself.

bhaṁ bhāsuraṁ cāṅgirasādhidevaṁ yathāvad ānarca tad-āyuṣe saḥ /
juhāva havyāny akṛśe kṛśānau dadau dvi-jebhyaḥ kṛśanaṁ ca gāś ca // 2.36 //
To the shining constellation whose regent is the planet Āṅgirasa,[22] he religiously recited a song of praise, for his son's long life. / In a fiery fire of Agni, he offered what was to be offered. And to the twice-born brahmins he gave both gold and cows.[23] //2.36//

sasnau śarīraṁ pavituṁ manaś ca tīrthāmbubhiś caiva guṇāmbubhiś ca /
vedopadiṣṭaṁ samam ātmajaṁ ca somaṁ papau śānti-sukhaṁ ca hārdam // 2.37 //
To cleanse body and mind, he bathed in the waters of sacred bathing places, and in the waters of merit; / And at one and the same time, he imbibed what is prescribed in the Vedas and what is produced from within: the *soma*-juice and the ease of a tranquil heart. //2.37//

sāntvaṁ babhāṣe na ca nārthavad yaj jajalpa tattvaṁ na ca vipriyaṁ yat /
sāntvaṁ hy atattvaṁ paruṣaṁ ca tattvaṁ hriyāśakann ātmana eva vaktum // 2.38 //
He spoke gently, and yet said nothing lacking in reality; he chatted the truth, and yet said nothing nasty; / For a gently spoken untruth, or a harshly told truth, modesty forbade him from voicing, even inwardly. //2.38//

iṣṭeṣv aniṣṭeṣu ca kārya-vatsu na rāga-doṣāśrayatāṁ prapede /
śivaṁ siṣeve 'vyavahāra-labdhaṁ yajñaṁ hi mene na tathā yathāvat // 2.39 //
When things pleasant and unpleasant called for action, he did not resort to reliance on raw desire, and faults; / He dwelt in the benign state which is won without fuss; for an act of devotion involving sacrifice[24] he valued not so highly. //2.39//

āśāvate cābhigatāya sadyo deyāmbubhis tarṣam acecchidiṣṭa /
yuddhād ṛte vṛtta-paraśvadhena dviḍ-darpam udvṛttam abebhidiṣṭa // 2.40 //
Again, when the expectant came up to him, there and then, using the waters of giving, he washed away thirst; / And without starting a war but using the battleaxe of action, the enemy's swollen pride[25] he burst. //2.40//

---

[22] Jupiter.

[23] The verse seems to express affirmation of service of dharma, and at the same time sardonic negation of superstitious or religious beliefs and customs.

[24] Ostensibly *yajñaṁ*, "sacrifice," refers to religious rituals like animal sacrifice, but the real meaning, in this context, might be performance of any task in a manner which places undue emphasis on ends over means. See also BC2.49.

[25] *Dviḍ-darpam.* Ostensible meaning: the enemy's swollen pride. Hidden meaning: the enemy, swollen pride.

ekaṁ vininye sa jugopa sapta saptaiva tatyāja rarakṣa pañca /
prāpa tri-vargaṁ bubudhe tri-vargaṁ jajñe dvi-vargaṁ prajahau dvi-vargam // 2.41 //
He gave direction to the one and guarded the seven; he shunned the seven[26] and turned his attention to the five;[27] / He experienced the three and minded the three;[28] he knew the two and abandoned the two.[29] //2.41//

kṛtāgaso 'pi pratipādya vadhyān nājīghanan nāpi ruṣā dadarśa /
babandha sāntvena phalena caitāṁs tyāgo 'pi teṣāṁ hy anayāya dṛṣṭaḥ // 2.42 //
Even those who had committed a capital offence he did not put to death, nor even looked upon with anger. / With gentleness, and by way of retribution, he held them confined - for letting go of them, obviously, was also to invite trouble. //2.42//

ārṣāṇy acārīt parama-vratāni vairāṇy ahāsīc cira-saṁbhṛtāni /
yaśāṁsi cāpad guṇa-gandhavanti rajāṁsy ahārsīn malinī-karāṇi // 2.43 //
Ultimate practices of the ancient seers, he repeated; long-harboured hostilities, he renounced; / And merit-scented feats of honor, he achieved. [But] the defiling dust of his passions, he did own. //2.43//

na cājihīrṣīd balim apravṛttaṁ na cācikīrṣīt para-vastv-abhidhyām /
na cāvivakṣīd dviṣatām adharmaṁ na cādidhakṣīdd hṛdayena manyum // 2.44 //
No inclination did he have to raise tax (or pay tribute)[30] that had not accrued, to covet what belonged to others, / To discuss the wrongness of hateful foes, or to ignite anger in his own heart. //2.44//

tasmiṁs tathā bhūmi-patau pravṛtte bhṛtyāś ca paurāś ca tathaiva ceruḥ /
śamātmake cetasi viprasanne prayukta-yogasya yathendriyāṇi // 2.45 //
While that earth-lord was acting thus, the mandarins and the townsfolk behaved likewise, / Like the senses of a person who is harnessed to practice, when the thinking mind is peaceful and clear.[31] //2.45//

---

[26] Ostensibly (as per EH Johnston's note), "The sevens are the constituents of a kingdom and the seven vices of kings." In the hidden meaning, the sevens would be the seven limbs of awakening and the seven underlying tendencies of the mind (see SN17.58).

[27] Five ostensibly refers to the five *upāyas* [means of success against an enemy]; in the hidden meaning, the five might be five senses.

[28] Ostensibly the three are the triple set of dharma, wealth, and sensual desire, the three aims of a king's life. In the hidden meaning, greed, anger and delusion might be the three to experience and mind.

[29] Ostensibly the two might be (as per EHJ's note) good and bad policy. In the hidden meaning, divided consciousness (third in the 12 links) is the casual grounds of psycho-physicality (fourth in the 12 links), and psycho-physicality is causal grounds of divided consciousness. See BC Canto 14, verses 74-76.

[30] Ostensibly, the king did not out of greed raise taxes unjustly. In the hidden meaning, a lord of the earth already has everything he needs, and so does not out of greed curry favor. *Baliṁ √hṛ* could mean to raise tax or to pay tribute.

[31] Ostensibly the second half of the verse illustrates the first half; in fact the real teaching - since our

kāle tataś cāru-payo-dharāyāṁ yaśodharāyāṁ sva-yaśo-dharāyām /
śauddhodane rāhu-sapatna-vaktro jajñe suto rāhula eva nāmnā // 2.46 //
Then in time to a bearer of lovely milk, to Yaśodharā, a bearer of glory by her own actions, / Was born a son who beamed like a rival of "Eclipsing" Rāhu,[32] and that moon-faced son of Śuddhodhana's son was named Rāhula. //2.46//

atheṣṭa-putraḥ parama-pratītaḥ kulasya vṛddhiṁ prati bhūmi-pālaḥ /
yathaiva putra-prasave nananda tathaiva pautra-prasave nananda // 2.47 //
And so having had the son he desired, and feeling satisfaction of the highest order at the extension of his house, a keeper of the earth, / Just as he had rejoiced at the delivery of a son, rejoiced equally at the delivery of a son of his son.[33] //2.47//

putrasya me putra-gato mamaiva snehaḥ kathaṁ syād iti jāta-harṣaḥ /
kāle sa taṁ taṁ vidhim ālalambe putra-priyaḥ svargam ivārurukṣan // 2.48 //
Joyfully he pondered: "By what means might there occur in my son this same attachment to a son as I have?" / With this in mind, the king devoted himself in good time to this and that prescribed practice, as if he were a *putra-priya,* an "offspring-loving" bird, aspiring to soar to heaven. //2.48//

sthitvā pathi prāthama-kalpikānāṁ rājarṣabhāṇāṁ yaśasānvitānām /
śuklāny amuktvāpi tapāṁsy atapta yajñaiś ca hiṁsā-rahitair ayaṣṭa // 2.49 //
Standing firmly on the path of primeval royal bulls steeped in glory, / He practiced austerities with his whites still on, and he worshipped with sacrificial acts that did no harm. //2.49//

ajājvaliṣṭātha sa puṇya-karmā nṛpa-śriyā caiva tapaḥ-śriyā ca /
kulena vṛttena dhiyā ca dīptas tejaḥ sahasrāṁśur ivotsisṛkṣuḥ // 2.50 //
And so this pious man of pure karma blazed with the majesty of a ruler of men, and with the glow of hot austerity. / Made brilliant by good family,[34] good conduct and good sense, he was like the thousand-rayed sun, desiring to emit its brightness. //2.50//

---

primary interest is in hierarchies in the brain and nervous system, and not in politics – is contained in the second half. This is a technique we will encounter repeatedly in figures of speech employed by Aśvaghoṣa.

[32] Rāhu, "the Seizer," is the name of a demon who is supposed to seize the sun and moon and thus cause eclipses.

[33] In the hidden meaning, a keeper of the earth (*bhūmi-pālaḥ*) is a buddha and delivery of a son (*putra-prasava*) might mean stimulating a student into action. *Prasava* can mean 1. begetting, procreation, birth, or 2. setting in motion, stimulation.

[34] *Kula* means good family or, in the hidden meaning, noble lineage.

svāyaṁbhuvaṁ cārcikam arcayitvā jajāpa putra-sthitaye sthita-śrīḥ /
cakāra karmāṇi ca duṣkarāṇi prajāḥ sisṛkṣuḥ ka ivādi-kāle // 2.51 //
Again, having devoutly caused to be chanted those chants of praise attributed to "Spontaneously Happening" Brahmā,[35] he of abiding majesty muttered a prayer for his son's safe abiding / And performed difficult karmic rites – like Ka,[36] in the beginning, desiring to create creatures. //2.51//

tatjyāja śastraṁ vimamarśa śāstraṁ śamaṁ siṣeve niyamaṁ viṣehe /
vaśīva kaṁ-cid viṣayaṁ na bheje piteva sarvān viṣayān dadarśa // 2.52 //
The hymn of praise he could set aside; dogmatic scripture he could scarce abide. He applied himself to equanimity; and subjected himself to restraint. / Into any sensory realm, he, like a master, did not slide. All realms, he, like a patriarch, did realize. //2.52//

babhāra rājyaṁ sa hi putra-hetoḥ putraṁ kulārthaṁ yaśase kulaṁ tu /
svargāya śabdaṁ divam ātma-hetor dharmārtham ātma-sthitim ācakāṅkṣa // 2.53 //
For he cherished his sovereignty on account of his son, his son for the sake of his noble house, his house as an expression of honor, / He cherished expression of truth as a way to heaven, and heaven as a function of the self. He desired the continued existence of the self for the sake of dharma. //2.53//

evaṁ sa dharmaṁ vividhaṁ cakāra sadbhir nipātaṁ śrutitaś ca siddham /
dṛṣṭvā kathaṁ putra-mukhaṁ suto me vanaṁ na yāyād iti nāthamānaḥ // 2.54 //
Thus he practiced the dharma of many strata which the good alight upon, and penetrate through listening, / All the time asking himself: "Now that my son has seen the face of his son, how might he be stopped from going to the forest?" //2.54//

rirakṣiṣantaḥ śriyam ātma-saṁsthāṁ rakṣanti putrān bhuvi bhūmi-pālāḥ /
putraṁ narendraḥ sa tu dharma-kāmo rarakṣa dharmād viṣayeṣu muñcan //2.55//
Desiring to preserve their own personal power, on this earth, keepers of the earth guard against their sons. / But this dharma-loving lord of men had guarded his son from dharma, by letting him loose among sensual objects. //2.55//

---

[35] Svayam-bhū is a name given to Brahmā and sometimes also to Śiva. Due to the ambiguity of *bhū*, *svayam-bhū* (like *sva-bhāva*, as discussed in the Preface to the second edition) can be literally translated in such a way as to represent one of two diametrically opposed concepts. At one extreme, *svayam-bhū* is a name that befits a god who is "Self-Existing" – i.e. Independent. At the other extreme, "Spontaneously Happening" describes what is dependently arisen. In the latter sense, could there be an allusion, for example, to the buddhas of the three times, to whom a verse is traditionally recited for the transference of merit?

[36] Ka is an alias of Prajā-pati, "lord of creatures," the creator deity. *Ka* is also the name of the first consonant of the Sanskrit alphabet. Does *duṣkarāṇi* (hard to do, difficult) in this context mean totally impossible to achieve?

vanam anupama-sattvā bodhisattvās tu sarve
viṣaya-sukha-rasa-jñā jagmur utpanna-putrāḥ /
ata upacita-karmā rūḍha-mūle 'pi hetau
sa ratim upasiṣeve bodhim āpan na yāvat // 2.56 //

To the forest, nonetheless, went all bodhisattvas, all matchless beings on the way to awakening, who had known the taste of sensuality and produced a son. / Thus did he who had heaped up ample karma, even while the cause [of his awakening] was a developing root, partake of sensual enjoyment in the period before he took possession of awakening. //2.56//

iti buddha-carite mahā-kāvye 'ntaḥ-pura-vihāro nāma dvitīyaḥ sargaḥ // 2 //

The 2nd canto, titled "Faring Well Within the Battlements,"
in an epic tale of awakened action.

Canto 3: saṁvegotpattiḥ
Arising of Nervous Excitement

Introduction

In this canto, depending on how one reads it, the prince is either appalled or inspired. Ostensibly he is appalled by visions, conjured by the gods, of (a) old age, (b) sickness and (c) death. In the hidden meaning, on entering the royal road he is inspired (a) by a mature person who has well-developed powers of forgetting; (b) by a person, rendered helpless by disabled senses, whose pride has been broken by multiple failures and disappointments; and (c) by one who has stopped trying mindfully to breath. Either way, whether by disgust or by enthusiasm, the prince's fear reflexes are stimulated, and his mind is perturbed – the *saṁvega* of the canto title, which means violent agitation or excitement, is from the root *saṁ-√vij,* which means to tremble or start with fear. *Utpatti* means arising.

tataḥ kadā-cin mṛdu-śādvalāni puṁs-kokilonnādita-pādapāni /
śuśrāva padmākara-maṇḍitāni gītair nibaddhāni sa kānanāni // 3.1 //
Then, one day, he went to places carpeted with tender grass where trees resounded with a cuckoo's calls, / To places adorned with profusions of lotuses – he went to forests fabricated in songs.[1] //3.1//

śrutvā tataḥ strī-jana-vallabhānāṁ mano-jña-bhāvaṁ pura-kānanānām /
bahiḥ-prayāṇāya cakāra buddhim antar-gṛhe nāga ivāvaruddhaḥ // 3.2 //
Thus having heard how agreeable were the city's forests, which the women loved so dearly, / He, like an elephant shut inside a house, made a decision to get out. //3.2//

tato nṛpas tasya niśamya bhāvaṁ putrābhidhānasya mano-rathasya /
snehasya lakṣmyā vayasaś ca yogyām ājñāpayām āsa vihāra-yātrām // 3.3 //
Then the king, catching the gist of the prince's expression of his heart's desire, / Convened a procession, commensurate with his affection and his wealth, and with a young man's energy – the ruler of men decreed a pleasure outing. //3.3//

nivartayām āsa ca rāja-mārge saṁpātam ārtasya pṛthag-janasya /
mā bhūt kumāraḥ su-kumāra-cittaḥ saṁvigna-cetā iti manyamānaḥ // 3.4 //
He decreed, again, that on the royal road no afflicted common person must be met, / So that the prince with his impressionable young mind would not be mentally perturbed – or so the king supposed. //3.4//

---

[1] *Gītair nibaddhāni* could also mean "covered with songs" or "furnished with songs." Also the old Nepalese manuscript has not *gītair* but *śīte* (in the cold; hence "to forests chained in the cold"). The Tibetan and Chinese translations, however, indicate that the prince heard about the forests in songs. Is the point to highlight how motivating nervous agitation can begin with nothing more substantial than an idea?

pratyaṅga-hīnān vikalendriyāṁś ca jīrṇāturādīn kṛpaṇāṁś ca dikṣu /
tataḥ samutsārya pareṇa sāmnā śobhāṁ parāṁ rāja-pathasya cakruḥ // 3.5 //
Those bereft of extremities,[2] with disabled organs of sense, along with pitiable people everywhere – the old, the infirm, and the like – / Were therefore caused, with great gentleness, to clear the area, so that the royal road was made to shine with great splendor. //3.5 //

tataḥ kṛte śrīmati rāja-mārge śrīmān vinītānucaraḥ kumāraḥ /
prāsāda-pṛṣṭhād avatīrya kāle kṛtābhyanujño nṛpam abhyagacchat // 3.6 //
And so in majestic action on the royal road, a majesty-possessing heir-apparent with an amenable assembly in his train, / Having alighted at the proper time from atop his elevated perch, approached, with his assent, a protector of men. //3.6//

atho narendraḥ sutam āgatāśruḥ śirasy upāghrāya ciraṁ nirīkṣya /
gaccheti cājñāpayati sma vācā snehān na cainaṁ manasā mumoca // 3.7 //
Then the king, tears welling, gazed long upon his son, kissed his head, / And issued his command, with the word "Go!" But with his heart, because of attachment, he did not let him go. //3.7//

tataḥ sa jāmbūnada-bhāṇḍa-bhṛdbhir yuktaṁ caturbhir nibhṛtais turaṅgaiḥ /
aklība-vidvac-chuci-raśmi-dhāraṁ hiraṇ-mayaṁ syandanam āruroha // 3.8 //
Yoked to four calm submissive horses bearing golden trappings, / With a complete man of knowledge and integrity holding the reins, was the golden carriage which he then ascended. //3.8//

tataḥ prakīrṇojjvala-puṣpa-jālaṁ viṣakta-mālyaṁ pracalat-patākam /
mārgaṁ prapede sadṛśānuyātraś candraḥ sanakṣatra ivāntarīkṣam // 3.9 //
And so a road bestrewn with masses of flowers in full bloom, along which wreaths hung down and flags fluttered fleetingly,[3] / He entered, with suitable backing, like the moon entering the sky in the company of stars. //3.9//

kautūhalāt sphītataraiś ca netrair nīlotpalārdhair iva kīryamāṇaḥ /
śanaiḥ śanai rāja-pathaṁ jagāhe pauraiḥ samantād abhivīkṣyamāṇaḥ // 3.10 //
And while eyes that bulged with curiosity, covered him, like so many halves of blue lotuses, / He travelled the royal road, quietly and calmly, viewed on all sides by the townsfolk. //3.10//

---

[2] The ostensible meaning is having missing limbs, but the ironic hidden meaning is being free of extreme views and habits. The ironic hidden meaning of the rest of this verse will emerge during the course of the canto, as the prince considers the meaning of growing old, not breathing, and so on.

[3] Ostensibly garlands and flags festooned the road as marks of joyful celebration. In a possible hidden meaning, wreaths and fluttering flags on the royal road which is the noble eightfold path, were marks of impermanence.

taṁ tuṣṭuvuḥ saumya-guṇena ke-cid vavandire dīptatayā tathānye /
saumukhyatas tu śriyam asya ke-cid vaipulyam āśaṁsiṣur āyuṣaś ca // 3.11 //
Some praised him for his gentle, moon-like quality; others celebrated his blazing brilliance. / But such was the brightness of his face, that some wished to make his majesty their own, and to attain the depth of his vital power.[4] //3.11//

niḥsṛtya kubjāś ca mahā-kulebhyo vyūhāś ca kairātaka-vāmanānām /
nāryaḥ kṛśebhyaś ca niveśanebhyo devānuyāna-dhvajavat praṇemuḥ // 3.12 //
Hunch-backed men from noble houses, and regiments of mountain-men and dwarves, / And women from homes of no consequence,[5] like hanging flags in the procession of a god, all came out and bowed. //3.12//

tataḥ kumāraḥ khalu gacchatīti śrutvā striyaḥ preṣya-janāt pravṛttim /
didṛkṣayā harmya-talāni jagmur janena mānyena kṛtābhyanujñāḥ // 3.13 //
Then the women, hearing from their servants the news that the prince was on his way, / Went, wishing to see him, onto the roofs and balconies - with assent from their masters.[6] //3.13//

tāḥ srasta-kāñcī-guṇa-vighnitāś ca supta-prabuddhākula-locanāś ca /
vṛttānta-vinyasta-vibhūṣaṇāś ca kautūhalenānibhṛtāḥ parīyuḥ // 3.14 //
Impeded by slipping girdles and strings, with the bleary eyes of those being roused from deep sleep,[7] / And having put on their unfolded splendour[8] as events unfolded, the girls, unabashed in their eager desire, circled around. //3.14//

prāsāda-sopāna-tala-praṇādaiḥ kāñcī-ravair nūpura-nisvanaiś ca /
vitrāsayantyo gṛha-pakṣi-saṅghān anyonya-vegāṁś ca samākṣipantyaḥ // 3.15 //
With the banging of feet on platform steps, with jingling of girdles and jangling of anklets, / They sent congregations[9] of house sparrows fluttering, and each derided the others for their haste.[10] //3.15//

---

[4] Thesis, antithesis, synthesis - two opposing views, and effort in the direction of abandoning all views?

[5] Ostensible meaning: low-status women. Hidden meaning: monks who have left home already? The three groups can be seen as following a dialectic progression to do with social status.

[6] Ostensibly this sounds chauvinistic. In a possible hidden meaning, however, again, the women with their various peculiarities represent individual practitioners practicing under the guidance of a teacher whose gender and personal background is of no consequence.

[7] In the hidden meaning, from unconscious behavior.

[8] In the hidden meaning, their unfolded ochre robes (*kaṣāyas*).

[9] This is one of several occasions where Aśvaghoṣa uses *saṅgha* as a collective noun. Nowhere does he use the word in the sense it is conventionally used in Buddhist circles, to mean a formal community or congregation.

[10] A parody of a group of practitioners barging unskillfully about.

kāsāṁ-cid āsāṁ tu varāṅganānāṁ jāta-tvarāṇām api sotsukānām /
gatiṁ gurutvāj jagṛhur viśālāḥ śroṇī-rathāḥ pīna-payo-dharāś ca // 3.16 //
But some among these fine ladies, hurry though they might in their eagerness, / Were stopped in their tracks, by the heft of the mighty chariots of their hips and their corpulent breasts. //3.16//

śīghraṁ samarthāpi tu gantum anyā gatiṁ nijagrāha yayau na tūrṇam /
hriyāpragalbhā viniqūhamānā rahaḥ-prayuktāni vibhūṣaṇāni // 3.17 //
An individual who was different,[11] meanwhile, though she was capable of going quickly, restrained her movement and went slowly, / Not showing off, but modestly keeping secret, splendid adornments connected to intimate practices.[12] //3.17//

paras-parotpīḍana-piṇḍitānāṁ saṁmarda-saṁkṣobhita-kuṇḍalānām /
tāsāṁ tadā sasvana-bhūṣaṇānāṁ vātāyaneṣv apraśamo babhūva // 3.18 //
At the windows at that time, the women pressed up against each other in squashed masses, their earrings colliding and ricocheting, / Their jewellery rattling, so that in each airy aperture there was a commotion. //3.18//

vātāyanebhyas tu viniḥsṛtāni paras-parāyāsita-kuṇḍalāni /
strīṇāṁ virejur mukha-paṅkajāni saktāni harmyeṣv iva paṅka-jāni // 3.19 //
And yet, as they emerged from the windows, ear-rings setting each other aflutter, / The women's lotus faces looked like flowers of mud-born lotuses that had attached themselves to the grand mansions.[13] //3.19//

tato vimānair yuvatī-karālaiḥ kautūhalodghāṭita-vātapānaiḥ /
śrīmat samantān nagaraṁ babhāse viyad vimānair iva sāpsarobhiḥ // 3.20 //
Thus, with its lofty mansions, whose gaping balconies young women lined, and whose shutters had been opened up out of curiosity, / The splendid city was wholly resplendent, like space, with its celestial chariots bearing celestial nymphs. //3.20//

vātāyanānām aviśāla-bhāvād anyonya-gaṇḍārpita-kuṇḍalānām /
mukhāni rejuḥ pramadottamānāṁ baddhāḥ kalāpā iva paṅka-jānām // 3.21 //
Through the narrowness of the windows, the women's ear-rings overlapped each other's cheeks, / So that the faces of those most gorgeous of girls seemed like tied-together bunches of lotus flowers.[14] //3.21//

---

[11] Ostensibly *anyā* simply means another woman; below the surface, an individual who was different is a non-buddha – i.e. a buddha who is different from ordinary people's stereotypical expectations of what a buddha might be.

[12] Ostensibly, for example, lacy under-garments. In the hidden meaning, for example, a certificate of transmission. *Rahas* means 1. privacy, a secret, a mystery; 2. sexual intercourse.

[13] Even as he parodies the barging about of individuals who have come together to practice, Aśvaghoṣa sees something very beautiful in that collective effort – though he never once speaks of a Buddhist *saṁgha*.

[14] A suggestion of individuals in a group harmonizing together – a suggestion that is antithetical to the description of the contrary individual in BC3.17?

taṁ tāḥ kumāraṁ pathi vīkṣamāṇāḥ striyo babhur gām iva gantu-kāmāḥ /
ūrdhvonmukhāś cainam udīkṣamāṇā narā babhur dyām iva gantu-kāmāḥ // 3.22 //
As down they gazed at the prince upon the road, the women seemed to wish to go to earth; / And the men, as up they looked at him, with upturned faces, seemed to wish to go to heaven. //3.22//

dṛṣṭvā ca taṁ rāja-sutaṁ striyas tā jājvalyamānaṁ vapuṣā śriyā ca /
dhanyāsya bhāryeti śanair avocañ śuddhair manobhiḥ khalu nānya-bhāvāt // 3.23 //
Seeing the king's son shining bright with beauty and majesty, those women said in a soft whisper, "Lucky is his wife!" - speaking with pure minds and out of no other sense at all.[15] //3.23//

ayaṁ kila vyāyata-pīna-bāhū rūpeṇa sākṣād iva puṣpa-ketuḥ /
tyaktvā śriyaṁ dharmam upaiṣyatīti tasmin hi tā gauravam eva cakruḥ // 3.24 //
"He of arms so lengthened and full, so they say, who is like a flower-bannered god of love in manifest form, / Will give up royal sovereignty and pursue dharma." Thus the women conferred on him the full weight of their estimation. //3.24//

kīrṇaṁ tathā rāja-pathaṁ kumāraḥ paurair vinītaiḥ śuci-dhīra-veṣaiḥ /
tat pūrvam-ālokya jaharṣa kiṁ-cin mene punar-bhāvam ivātmanaś ca // 3.25 //
On his first reading of the royal road, which was filled like this with obedient citizens ostensibly displaying purity and steadfastness,[16] / The prince was thrilled, and somewhat conscious of himself being as if reborn.[17] //3.25//

puraṁ tu tat svargam iva prahṛṣṭaṁ śuddhādhivāsāḥ samavekṣya devāḥ /
jīrṇaṁ naraṁ nirmamire prayātuṁ saṁcodanārthaṁ kṣitipātmajasya // 3.26 //
But when they saw that city all buoyed up, as if it were heaven, the gods whose perch is purity / Elicited an old man to wander by, for the purpose of provoking a prince who was an offspring of a protector of the earth. //3.26//

---

[15] What is ostensibly praise of purity is really tragicomic irony. The women in their innocence do not suppose what grief is about to come Yaśodharā's way. "Out of no other sense" is *nānya-bhāvāt* - a possible hidden meaning, then, might be "having no sense of irony."

[16] Meanings of *veṣa* include 1. dress, clothes, and 2. artificial exterior, assumed appearance. To add further ambiguity, the old Nepalese manuscript has *ceṣaiḥ*, which was most probably a corruption of *veṣaiḥ* but could possibly have been a corruption of *ceṣṭaiḥ* (gestures).

[17] *Punar-bhāva*, being born again, ostensibly carries a favorable meaning. But on the royal road, the suggestion may be (taking *veṣaiḥ* to mean assumed appearances), one should beware of first impressions. The truth, on the royal road, may be that the doings which the ignorant one does do, always lead, until such time as they are stopped, in the direction of repeated becoming (*punar-bhavāya*; see MMK26.1).

tataḥ kumāro jarayābhibhūtaṁ dṛṣṭvā narebhyaḥ pṛthag-ākṛtiṁ tam /
uvāca saṁgrāhakam āgatāsthas tatraiva niṣkampa-niviṣṭa-dṛṣṭiḥ // 3.27 //
And so the prince beheld that man humbled by growing old, who was of an order different to other men;[18] / He quizzed the gatherer of the reins,[19] being full of interest in that state, in which sole direction he rested his eyes, immovably.[20] //3.27//

ka eṣa bhoḥ sūta naro 'bhyupetaḥ keśaiḥ sitair yaṣṭi-viṣakta-hastaḥ /
bhrū-saṁvṛtākṣaḥ śithilānatāṅgaḥ kiṁ vikriyaiṣā prakṛtir yad-ṛcchā // 3.28 //
"Who is this man, O master of the horses, that has appeared with hair all white, hand firmly gripping a staff,[21] / Eyes concealed below his brow, limbs loose and bending: Is this strange transformation his original condition? Is it a chance occurrence?"//3.28//

ity evam uktaḥ sa ratha-praṇetā nivedayām āsa nṛpātmajāya /
saṁrakṣyam apy artham adoṣa-darśī tair eva devaiḥ kṛta-buddhi-mohaḥ // 3.29 //
Addressed thus, the driver of a chariot of joy divulged to the offspring of a ruler of men / The very information he was supposed to protect; failing to see the fault in this, under the influence of those same old gods, he was confounded by way of his own resolve.[22] //3.29//

rūpasya hantrī vyasanaṁ balasya śokasya yonir nidhanaṁ ratīnām /
nāśaḥ smṛtīnāṁ ripur indriyāṇām eṣā jarā nāma yayaiṣa bhagnaḥ // 3.30 //
"Ripping away of beautiful appearance, defeat of force, beginning of sorrow, ending of joys of passion, / And fading out of things remembered: an adversary of the senses is this process, called 'growing old,' by which the one here is being undone. //3.30//

pītaṁ hy anenāpi payaḥ śiśutve kālena bhūyaḥ parisarpam urvyām /
krameṇa bhūtvā ca yuvā vapuṣmān krameṇa tenaiva jarām upetaḥ // 3.31 //
For even such a man in infancy sucked milk and, in the course of time, again, he went on hands and knees upon the earth;[23] / Having become, step by step, an adult in possession of his body, by that same process, step by step, he has grown old." //3.31//

ity evam ukte calitaḥ sa kiṁ-cid rājātmajaḥ sūtam idaṁ babhāṣe /
kim eṣa doṣo bhavitā mamāpīty asmai tataḥ sārathir abhyuvāca // 3.32 //
Thrown somewhat off balance on being thus informed, he the fruit of a king's loins said to the master of the horses: / "Will I also have this fault in the future?" Then the driver of the chariot in which the two were riding said to him: //3.32//

---

[18] In the hidden meaning, one grown old means a fully developed person, a buddha.
[19] In the hidden meaning, *saṁgrāhakam* "a gatherer of the reins," might also mean a buddha.
[20] The object of the focused contemplation could be the old one or, equally, could be the state of one who holds the reins, having tamed the horses. A parallel phrase follows in verse 40, with reference to the one who has been broken.
[21] In the ostensible meaning, a sign of weakness. In the hidden meaning, a sign of firmness?
[22] The gods, as in Greek drama, are the masters of cosmic irony.
[23] In the hidden meaning, for example, during the act of making a prostration.

āyuṣmato 'py eṣa vayaḥ-prakarṣo niḥsaṁśayaṁ kāla-vaśena bhāvī /
evaṁ jarāṁ rūpa-vināśayitrīṁ jānāti caivecchati caiva lokaḥ // 3.33 //
The present span of life of you who are so full of life will also in future, through the power of time, surely run its course. / The world knows that growing old thus destroys beautiful appearances, and yet the world desires it." //3.33//

tataḥ sa pūrvāśaya-śuddha-buddhir vistīrṇa-kalpācita-puṇya-karmā /
śrutvā jarāṁ saṁvivije mahātmā mahāśaner ghoṣam ivāntike gauḥ // 3.34 //
And so he whose mind had been cleansed by good intentions, before the fact,[24] he who had heaped up piles of good karma, through long kalpas, by his acts, / When he heard about growing old, recoiled mightily, like a bull hearing the crash of a nearby thunderbolt. //3.34//

niḥśvasya dīrghaṁ sva-śiraḥ prakampya tasmiṁś ca jīrṇe viniveśya cakṣuḥ /
tāṁ caiva dṛṣṭvā janatāṁ saharṣāṁ vākyaṁ sa saṁvigna idaṁ jagāda // 3.35 //
He took an audible deep breath, then shook his head, then fixed his eye upon the old man,[25] / And then he took in the joyful throng; after that, still in a state of alarm, he uttered these words:[26] //3.35//

evaṁ jarā hanti ca nirviśeṣaṁ smṛtiṁ ca rūpaṁ ca parā-kramaṁ ca /
na caiva saṁvegam upaiti lokaḥ praty-akṣato 'pīdṛśam īkṣamāṇaḥ // 3.36 //
"Growing old like this demolishes - without discrimination - memory, beautiful appearance, and forcefulness; / And yet the world is not stirred, even as the world witnesses it so before its very eyes. //3.36//

evaṁ gate sūta nivartayāśvān śīghraṁ gṛhāṇy eva bhavān prayātu /
udyāna-bhūmau hi kuto ratir me jarā-bhave cetasi vartamāne // 3.37 //
Being so, O master of the horses, turn the horses back![27] Take us home, good sir, quickly! For what pleasure can there be for me in parkland while the reality of growing old is occupying my mind?"//3.37//

athājñayā bhartṛ-sutasya tasya nivartayām āsa rathaṁ niyantā /
tataḥ kumāro bhavanaṁ tad eva cintā-vaśaḥ śūnyam iva prapede // 3.38 //
And so at the behest of the child of his master, the tamer of horses turned the chariot around; / Then into the palace, that real piece of royal real estate,[28] the prince went, in the thrall of anxious thought, as if he were going into emptiness. //3.38//

---

[24] *Pūrva*, beforehand, in advance. A passing reminder that the secret is in the preparation, that the readiness is all?

[25] The verb *pra-√kamp* means to shake or to loosen. In the hidden meaning, does taking a deep breath, loosening the head (i.e. letting the head/neck be free), and fixing one's eye upon the Old Man (the Buddha), suggests meditative practice itself?

[26] An ironic description of giving a "dharma-talk" in front of a joyfully expectant audience?

[27] The hidden meaning of turning back is brought out in detail in BC Canto 6, *Chandaka / Turning Back.*

[28] *Bhavana* means a place of abode, a palace, and the place where anything grows. In the hidden meaning, turning back to the royal abode symbolizes coming back to just sitting in full lotus.

yadā tu tatraiva na śarma lebhe jarā jareti praparīkṣamāṇaḥ /
tato narendrānumataḥ sa bhūyaḥ krameṇa tenaiva bahir jagāma // 3.39 //
When actually there, however, he found no happiness, looking deeper and deeper into aging, and thinking, "growing old..., growing old..."; / Whereupon, with the king's approval, again, by the exact same procedure, he went outside. //3.39//

athāparaṁ vyādhi-parīta-dehaṁ ta eva devāḥ sasṛjur manuṣyam /
dṛṣṭvā ca taṁ sārathim ābabhāṣe śauddhodanis tad-gata-dṛṣṭir eva // 3.40 //
Then one whose body was encompassed by sickness,[29] a human being unlike any other, those same old gods conjured up; / And on seeing him the son of Śuddhodana addressed the driver of the chariot, with his eye directed squarely in that direction. //3.40//

sthūlodaraḥ śvāsa-calac-charīraḥ srastāṁsa-bāhuḥ kṛśa-pāṇḍu-gātraḥ /
ambeti vācaṁ karuṇaṁ bruvāṇaḥ paraṁ samāśritya naraḥ ka eṣaḥ // 3.41 //
"That individual with an expanded belly, whose body moves as he breathes, whose arms hang loose from his shoulders, whose limbs are wasted and pale, / And who, pathetically, keeps saying 'Mother!,' while leaning on others for support:[30] This man is Who?" //3.41//

tato 'bravīt sārathir asya saumya dhātu-prakopa-prabhavaḥ pravṛddhaḥ /
rogābhidhānaḥ sumahān anarthaḥ śakro 'pi yenaiṣa kṛto 'svatantraḥ // 3.42 //
Then spoke the leader who was in the same chariot as him[31]: "O gentle moon-like man! Stemming originally from excitement of primitive elements and now far advanced / Is the momentous reverse, known as a breakdown,[32] that has rendered even this strong man helpless."[33] //3.42//

ity ūcivān rāja-sutaḥ sa bhūyas taṁ sānukampo naram īkṣamāṇaḥ /
asyaiva jātaḥ pṛthag eṣa doṣaḥ sāmānyato roga-bhayaṁ prajānām // 3.43 //
The son of the king spoke again, being moved by pity as he looked at the man: / "Is this fault arisen specifically in the one here? Is the terror of breaking down common to all creatures?" //3.43//

---

[29] In the hidden meaning, a person steeped in the truth of suffering; a man of clouded eyes. *Vyādhi* means disorder, disease, sickness but also "any tormenting or vexatious thing."

[30] Ostensibly he leans on others because of being too sick to stand, and cries for his mother. In the hidden meaning he goes begging, addressing women he meets as *ambā*, "mother," a term of respect?

[31] *Sārathir asya* ostensibly means "his charioteer" or "his leader." But *sārathi* is from *sa-ratha*, which as an adverbial phrase means "on the same chariot with" or simply "together with." The phrase thus serves as a reminder that, whether drivers or passengers, we are all in the same chariot.

[32] *Roga*, disease, sickness, is from the root √*ruj*, to break or shatter - as when an illusion is shattered.

[33] *Asvatantraḥ*, lit. "not pulling his own strings" - an ironic suggestion of non-doing?

tato babhāṣe sa ratha-praṇetā kumāra sādhāraṇa eṣa doṣaḥ /
evaṁ hi rogaiḥ paripīḍyamāno rujāturo harṣam upaiti lokaḥ // 3.44 //
Then the driver of that vehicle of joy said: "This fault, O Prince, is common to all. / For, while thus pressed all around by forces of disintegration, people pained by disorder move towards pleasure."[34] //3.44//

iti śrutārthaḥ sa viṣaṇṇa-cetāḥ prāvepatāmbūrmi-gataḥ śaśīva /
idaṁ ca vākyaṁ karuṇāyamānaḥ provāca kiṁ-cin mṛdunā svareṇa // 3.45 //
Mentally dejected to listen to this truth, the prince trembled like the moon reflected in ripples of water; / And, emoting with compassion, he uttered these words, in a somewhat feeble voice: //3.45//

idaṁ ca roga-vyasanaṁ prajānāṁ paśyaṁś ca viśrambham upaiti lokaḥ /
vistīrṇam ajñānam aho narāṇāṁ hasanti ye roga-bhayair amuktāḥ // 3.46 //
"Seeing this for living creatures as 'the evil of disease,' still the world rests easy. / Vast, alas, is the ignorance of men who laugh and joke though not yet liberated from their fears of disease. //3.46//

nivartyatāṁ sūta bahiḥ-prayāṇān narendra-sadmaiva rathaḥ prayātu /
śrutvā ca me roga-bhayaṁ ratibhyaḥ pratyāhataṁ saṁkucatīva cetaḥ // 3.47 //
Let the chariot of joy, O master of the horse!, be turned back from going onward and outward. Let the chariot go back to the royal seat of the best of men.[35] / Having learned of the danger arising from disease, my mind, driven back from miscellaneous enjoyments, also seems to turn inward." //3.47//

tato nivṛttaḥ sa nivṛtta-harṣaḥ pradhyāna-yuktaḥ praviveśa veśma /
taṁ dvis tathā prekṣya ca saṁnivṛttaṁ paryeṣaṇaṁ bhūmi-patiś cakāra // 3.48 //
Then, having turned back, and having turned back exuberance, he deeply entered the royal abode, absorbed in deep reflection. / And, seeing him thus twice turned back, a possessor of the earth made an investigation. //3.48//

śrutvā nimittaṁ tu nivartanasya saṁtyaktam ātmānam anena mene /
mārgasya śaucādhikṛtāya caiva cukrośa ruṣṭo 'pi ca nogra-daṇḍaḥ // 3.49 //
On learning, then, a cause of turning back, he felt himself being totally abandoned by him.[36] / And though [the possessor of the earth] railed against the overseer who was charged with clearing the road,[37] however annoyed he was, he did not resort to cruelty with the cudgel. //3.49//

---

[34] In the hidden meaning, those struck by the truth of suffering direct their practice towards *nirvāṇa*. "Driver of the vehicle of joy," "master of the horse," "tamer of horses," et cetera, all indicate that the charioteer is, below the surface, thus teaching the teaching of a buddha.

[35] In the hidden meaning, again, the royal seat might be the act of sitting in the lotus posture.

[36] In the ostensible meaning, the king felt himself being abandoned by his son. In the hidden meaning, is a possessor of the earth aware of a process of being forgotten by himself?

[37] In the hidden meaning, a dharma-holder who (like Nanda in SN Canto 18) has been charged with

bhūyaś ca tasmai vidadhe sutāya viśeṣa-yuktaṁ viṣaya-pracāram /
calendriyatvād api nāma śakto nāsmān vijahyād iti nāthamānaḥ // 3.50 //
And once more he arranged for his son a special playground of sensual enjoyments, / All the time praying: "Though it be through the fickle power of the senses, would that he were unable to leave us!" //3.50//

yadā ca śabdādibhir indriyārthair antaḥpure naiva suto 'sya reme /
tato bahir vyādiśati sma yātrāṁ rasāntaraṁ syād iti manyamānaḥ // 3.51 //
And since his son had taken no delight in the sounds of voices, or in the other sensory stimuli, within the battlements of the women's apartments, / The king gave the order for a trip outside, thinking that this might be a different kind of enjoyment. //3.51//

snehāc ca bhāvaṁ tanayasya buddhvā saṁvega-doṣān avicintya kāṁś-cit /
yogyāḥ samājñāpayati sma tatra kalāsv abhijñā iti vāra-mukhyāḥ // 3.52 //
Attentive, out of attachment, to his son's state of mind, and heedless of any faults associated with nervous excitement,[38] / He summoned to be present there well-practiced women who, being adept in subtle skills, were mistresses of deferred pleasure.[39] //3.52//

tato viśeṣeṇa narendra-mārge svalaṁkṛte caiva parīkṣite ca /
vyatyasya sūtaṁ ca rathaṁ ca rājā prasthāpayām āsa bahiḥ kumāram // 3.53 //
Then, once the royal road had been adorned even more beautifully and had been inspected with even more care, / The king switched around the charioteer and the chariot, and urged the prince on his way, outwards.[40] //3.53//

tatas tathā gacchati rāja-putre tair eva devair vihito gatāsuḥ /
taṁ caiva mārge mṛtam uhyamānaṁ sūtaḥ kumāraś ca dadarśa nānyaḥ // 3.54 //
Consequently, as the son of the king thus went into movement, those same old gods conjured up one who had breathed his last;[41] / And as he, being dead, was borne along the road, nobody saw him but the charioteer and the prince. //3.54//

---

carrying the torch of that transmission which dispels all views and opinions?

[38] The point might be to emphasize the importance of establishing the will to the truth, without worrying about attendant faults. For example, Dōgen wrote that the bodhi-mind has been established in drunkenness.

[39] *Kalāsv abhijñā iti vāra-mukhyāḥ*. Ostensibly the best among skillful courtesans; in the hidden meaning (which will be brought out in the following canto), masters skilled in the use of expedient means, or indirect tactics.

[40] Symbolizing reciprocal efforts, to sit with mind, and to sit with body, in the direction of dropping off body and mind?

[41] In the hidden meaning, one who had stopped breathing, i.e. one who had given up trying to control his breath, or other vital processes, by direct means. One who had learned to let the right thing do itself.

athābravīd rāja-sutaḥ sa sūtaṁ naraiś caturbhir hriyate ka eṣaḥ /
dīnair manuṣyair anugamyamāno yo bhūṣito 'śvāsy avarudyate ca // 3.55 //
Then the son of the king said to the master of the horses: "This is Who, who is being carried by four people,[42] / Who is being followed by afflicted human beings, who is beautifully adorned, and yet, as one who does not breathe, inspires tears." //3.55//

tataḥ sa śuddhātmabhir eva devaiḥ śuddhādhivāsair abhibhūta-cetāḥ /
avācyam apy artham imaṁ niyantā pravyājahārārthavad īśvarāya // 3.56 //
Then the charioteer, while his mind was overpowered by the gods whose essence is purity itself, by the gods who sit upon pure perches, / He, in a voice full of meaning, as the tamer of the horses,[43] conveyed to the prince the unspeakable meaning in question. //3.56//

buddhīndriya-prāṇa-guṇair viyuktaḥ supto visaṁjñas tṛṇa-kāṣṭha-bhūtaḥ /
saṁvardhya saṁrakṣya ca yatnavadbhiḥ priya-priyais tyajyata eṣa ko 'pi // 3.57 //
"Dissevered from the strings of sense power and breathing, inactive and insensible, akin to straw and wood, / Having been nurtured and cherished, he is deliberately left alone by his dearest friends - this, indeed, is Who."[44] //3.57//

iti praṇetuḥ sa niśamya vākyaṁ saṁcukṣubhe kiṁ-cid uvāca cainam /
kiṁ kevalo' syaiva janasya dharmaḥ sarva-prajānām ayam īdṛśo 'ntaḥ // 3.58 //
On hearing the words of a guide he was somewhat agitated, and said to him: / "Is this a condition unique to this person here? Is such the end for all creatures?" //3.58//

tataḥ praṇetā vadati sma tasmai sarva-prajānām idam anta-karma /
hīnasya madhyasya mahātmano vā sarvasya loke niyato vināśaḥ // 3.59 //
Then the guide said to him: "This is the ultimate karma of all creatures: / For everybody in this world, whether low, middling, or mighty, utter loss is certain."[45] //3.59//

tataḥ sa dhīro 'pi narendra-sūnuḥ śrutvaiva mṛtyuṁ viṣasāda sadyaḥ /
aṁsena saṁśliṣya ca kūbarāgraṁ provāca nihrādavatā svareṇa // 3.60 //
Then, mild-mannered though he was, as a son of the best of men, on learning of dying, he sank back and down, instantly deflated, / And, bringing his shoulder into contact with the tip of the pole of the yoke of the chariot,[46] he asserted in a sonorous voice: //3.60//

---

[42] Four or more often five (= one who has breathed his last + four who support him or her?) is the traditional minimum number to form a community devoted to the practice of the Buddha's teaching.

[43] Again, in the hidden meaning, *niyantā*, restrainer, tamer of horses, may be taken as an epithet for a teacher of the Buddha's teaching.

[44] A person who is as one with the ineffable, the unspeakable, unbelievable truth.

[45] In the hidden meaning, emptiness is the most reliable thing there is?

[46] In the ostensible meaning, he reached the point of giving up, and rested back on the chariot. In the hidden meaning, he contacted the point at which he might begin to make effort to move the chariot.

iyaṁ ca niṣṭhā niyatā prajānāṁ pramādyati tyakta-bhayaś ca lokaḥ /
manāṁsi śaṅke kaṭhināni nṝṇāṁ svasthās tathā hy adhvani vartamānāḥ // 3.61 //
"This, for sentient creatures, is a certain conclusion, and yet the world barges heedlessly about, disregarding danger. / Stiffened, I venture, are the mental sinews of men, who so self-assuredly remain on such a path.[47] //3.61//

tasmād rathaḥ sūta nivartyatāṁ no vihāra-bhūmer na hi deśa-kālaḥ /
jānan vināśaṁ katham ārti-kāle sacetanaḥ syād iha hi pramattaḥ // 3.62 //
Therefore, O master of the horses, let our chariot of joy be turned back, for this is not the time or the place for roaming around: / Knowing utter loss, in the hour of pain, how could anybody possessed of consciousness be negligent in this area?" //3.62//

iti bruvāṇe 'pi narādhipātmaje nivartayām āsa sa naiva taṁ ratham /
viśeṣa-yuktaṁ tu narendra-śāsanāt sa-padma-ṣaṇḍaṁ vanam eva niryayau // 3.63 //
Even with an offspring of a ruler of men telling him so, assuredly he did not turn that chariot back; / Rather, following the order of the best of men, to a wood imbued with special distinction, to Sa-padma-ṣaṇda-vana, 'the Wood of the Liberated Bull among Lotuses,' he ventured farther out. //3.63//

tataḥ śivaṁ kusumita-bāla-pādapaṁ paribhramat-pramudita-matta-kokilam /
vimānavat-sa-kamala-cāru-dīrghikaṁ dadarśa tad vanam iva nandanaṁ vanam // 3.64 //
There with young trees in flower, lusty cuckoos roving joyously around, / And tiered pavilions in charming stretches of lotus-covered water, that happy glade he glimpsed, like Nandana-vana, 'the Gladdening Garden' of Indra. //3.64//

varāṅganā-gaṇa-kalilaṁ nṛpātmajas tato balād vanam atinīyate sma tat /
varāpsaro-vṛtam alakādhipālayaṁ nava-vrato munir iva vighna-kātaraḥ // 3.65 //
Most lushly wooded with beautiful women was that park, to which the offspring of a ruler of men was then forcibly led, / Like a sage to a palace populated by the choicest nymphs in Alaka,[48] when his practice is young and he is nervous about impediments. //3.65//

iti buddha-carite mahākāvye saṁvegotpattir nāma tṛtīyaḥ sargaḥ // 3 //
The 3rd canto, titled "Arising of Nervous Excitement"
in an epic tale of awakened action.

---

[47] A double-bluff – ostensibly the prince is being ironic, but in the hidden meaning bodhisattvas on the path are indeed steadfast.
[48] The capital city of the realm of Kubera, Lord of Wealth.

Canto 4: strī-vighātanaḥ
Warding 'Women' Away

Introduction

Aśvaghoṣa's teaching points resolutely in the direction of abandoning all -isms. That being so, it would be a mistake to see Aśvaghoṣa as a champion of feminism as an ideology. On the other hand, when in Saundarananda Canto 8 (titled A Tirade against Women), Aśvaghoṣa presents in detail the misogynist view of a certain Buddhist striver, it should be understood that he is satirizing that unenlightened view.

In a deeper reading of the present canto, then, the "warding away" (*vighātana*) of the canto title refers, not to the Prince's rebuffing of a gang of women who were ostensibly out to seduce him, but rather to the abandonment of the generic concept "woman" or "women" (*strī*). To this end, Aśvaghoṣa describes various individuals who are different (*anyā*) using various stratagems to capture the heart of the Prince. And these women are not only different from each other: they represent buddhas using skilful means, and as such are quite different from what we first thought, on a superficial reading of the canto title "Warding Women Away."

tatas tasmāt purodyānāt kautūhala-calekṣaṇāḥ /
pratyujjagmur nṛpa-sutaṁ prāptaṁ varam iva striyaḥ // 4.1 //
Then, out of that royal plot, their interested eyes darting, / The women advanced to meet the son of the king as if he were an arriving suitor. //4.1//

abhigamya ca tās tasmai vismayotphulla-locanāḥ /
cakrire samudācāraṁ padma-kośa-nibhaiḥ karaiḥ // 4.2 //
And having approached him, their peepers opened wide in wonderment, / They made their salutations with hands like lotus buds, //4.2//

tasthuś ca parivāryainaṁ manmathākṣipta-cetasaḥ /
niścalaiḥ prīti-vikacaiḥ pibantya iva locanaiḥ // 4.3 //
And keeping him in their midst they stationed themselves, their minds caught fast by ardour; / While, with motionless eyes that sparkled with relish, they seemed almost to be indulging in a feast. //4.3//

taṁ hi tā menire nāryaḥ kāmo vigrahavān iti /
śobhitaṁ lakṣaṇair dīptaiḥ saha-jair bhūṣaṇair iva // 4.4 //
For those women esteemed him as a god of love in physical form, / Made beautiful by brilliant attributes like the adornments one is born with.[1] //4.4//

---

[1] Ostensibly, *saha-jair-bhūṣaṇaiḥ* means "with ornaments born on him." But the real intention might be to suggest that nothing is more beautiful than what develops naturally.

saumyatvāc caiva dhairyāc ca kāś-cid enaṁ prajajñire /
avatīrṇo mahīṁ sākṣād gūḍhāṁśuś candramā iti // 4.5 //
Because of his *soma*-steeped mildness, and his constant gravity, some women intuited him to be, / Alighting on the earth in person, a moon whose beam is contained within. //4.5//

tasya tā vapuṣākṣiptā nigṛhītaṁ jajṛmbhire /
anyonyaṁ dṛṣṭibhir hatvā śanaiś ca viniśaśvasuḥ // 4.6 //
Entranced by his form, they inwardly opened out / And, killing each other with glances, exhaled deeply and quietly. //4.6//

evaṁ tā dṛṣṭi-mātreṇa nāryo dadṛśur eva tam /
na vyājahrur na jahasuḥ prabhāveṇāsya yantritāḥ // 4.7 //
Thus, with the full extent of their mind's eyes, the women did nothing but behold him: / They did not speak and did not laugh, held spellbound by his power.[2] //4.7//

tās tathā tu nir-ārambhā dṛṣṭvā praṇaya-viklavāḥ /
purohita-suto dhīmān udāyī vākyam abravīt // 4.8 //
But seeing them so disinclined to do, thinking them timid about displaying love, / The clever son of a family priest, 'Hurry-Up' Udāyin, spoke his piece: //4.8//

sarvāḥ sarva-kalā-jñāḥ stha bhāva-grahaṇa-paṇḍitāḥ /
rūpa-cāturya-saṁpannāḥ sva-guṇair mukhyatāṁ gatāḥ // 4.9 //
"Adept in all the subtle arts, expert in understanding the emotions, / Possessed of beautiful form and dexterity, by graces that are proper to you, you all have risen to pre-eminence.[3] //4.9//

śobhayeta guṇair ebhir api tān uttarān kurūn /
kuberasyāpi cākrīḍaṁ prāg eva vasu-dhām imām // 4.10 //
By the means of these graces you could cause to shine even that superior kingdom of the Northern Kurus, / And even the pleasure-grove of Kubera – all the more, then, this earthly acreage. //4.10//

śaktāś cālayituṁ yūyaṁ vīta-rāgān ṛṣīn api /
apsarobhiś ca kalitān grahītuṁ vibudhān api // 4.11 //
You are able to spur into movement even dispassionate seers; / And even gods enticed by heavenly nymphs you are able to hold transfixed. //4.11//

---

2 A long silent exhalation, followed by doing nothing but beholding him – like a moon whose beam is directed within. These descriptions may be taken in their hidden meaning as a suggestion of the practice of turning one's own light and letting it shine, by just sitting.

3 The irony here (and the challenge for the translator) is that Udāyin thinks he is describing pre-eminent courtesans, but his words equally well describe buddhas.

bhāva-jñānena hāvena rūpa-cāturya-saṁpadā /
strīṇām eva ca śaktāḥ stha saṁrāge kiṁ punar nṛṇām // 4.12 //
Again, through knowing the emotions, through challenging invitations, through possession of beautiful form and dexterity, / You are powerful agents in respect of passion in women, to say nothing of passion in men. //4.12//

tāsām evaṁ vidhānāṁ vo viyuktānāṁ sva-gocare /
iyam evaṁ-vidhā ceṣṭā na tuṣṭo 'smy ārjavena vaḥ // 4.13 //
You being as you are, like this, each set apart in her own sphere of activity, / This action of yours is like this - in you, I am not satisfied with innocence. //4.13//

idaṁ nava-vadhūnāṁ vo hrī-nikuñcita-cakṣuṣām /
sadṛśaṁ ceṣṭitaṁ hi syād api vā gopa-yoṣitām // 4.14 //
For women who have recently taken their vows[4] and who modestly turn the light of their eyes within, / This behavior of yours might be fitting - as also for the wives of cowherds![5] //4.14//

yad api syād ayaṁ dhīraḥ śrī-prabhāvān mahān iti /
strīṇām api mahat teja iti kāryo 'tra niścayaḥ // 4.15 //
Though this man may prove to be, by his majestic light, a mighty steadfast man, / Mighty also is the efficacy of women - in which matter verification is to be carried out: //4.15//

purā hi kāśi-sundaryā veśa-vadhvā mahān-ṛṣiḥ /
tāḍito 'bhūt padā vyāso dur-dharṣo devatair api // 4.16 //
For once upon a time the Beauty of Benares, Kāśi-sundarī, a common woman, / Beat with a flick of her foot the great seer Vyāsa whom even the gods could not conquer.[6] //4.16//

manthāla-gautamo bhikṣur jaṅghayā vāra-mukhyayā /
piprīṣuś ca tad-arthārthaṁ vyasūn niraharat purā // 4.17 //
The beggar Manthāla Gautama, wishing to please the royal courtesan 'Legs' Jaṅgā, / Again in olden times, with that aim in view, carried corpses out for burial.[7] //4.17//

gautamaṁ dīrgha-tapasaṁ maharṣiṁ dīrgha-jīvinam /
yoṣit saṁtoṣayām āsa varṇa-sthānāvarā satī // 4.18 //
The great seer Gautama Dīrgha-tapas was long on asceticism and in longevity, / But a girl pleasured him who was low in color and standing.[8] //4.18//

---

[4] Ostensibly, marriage vows. In the hidden meaning, bodhisattva vows.
[5] Ostensibly, this is Udayin's snobbery. In the hidden meaning, the principle might be that of Dōgen's *Fukan-zazengi* - Rules of Sitting-Meditation Recommended for Everybody.
[6] See also BC1.42 and SN7.30.
[7] EH Johnston suspected that this verse may have been an interpolation.
[8] A high-minded ascetic named Dīrgha-tapas is also mentioned at the beginning of Saundarananda (SN1.4).

ṛṣya-śṛṅgaṁ muni-sutaṁ tathaiva strīṣv apaṇḍitam /
upāyair vividhaiḥ śāntā jagrāha ca jahāra ca // 4.19 //
Ṛṣya-śṛṅga, 'Antelope Horn,' a sage's son, was similarly inexpert in regard to women; / Śāntā, 'Tranquility,' using various wiles, took him captive and carried him away.[9] //4.19//

viśvāmitro maharṣiś ca vigāḍho 'pi mahat-tapaḥ /
daśa-varṣāṇy ahar mene ghṛtācy āpsarasā hṛtaḥ // 4.20 //
And the great seer Viśvā-mitra, 'Friend of All,' though steeped in rigorous asceticism, / Deemed ten years to be a day, while captivated by the nymph Ghṛtācī.[10] //4.20//

evam-ādīn ṛṣīṁs tāṁs tān anayan vikriyāṁ striyaḥ /
lalitaṁ pūrva-vayasaṁ kiṁ punar nṛpateḥ sutam // 4.21 //
Various seers such as these have women brought down; / How much more then the son of the king, who is in the first flush of frolicsome youth? //4.21//

tad evaṁ sati viśrabdhaṁ prayatadhvaṁ tathā yathā /
iyaṁ nṛpasya vaṁśa-śrīr ito na syāt parāṅmukhī // 4.22 //
It being so, with calm confidence, apply yourselves in such a way, / That this light of the lineage of a protector of men might not be turned away from here.[11] //4.22//

yā hi kāś-cid yuvatayo haranti sadṛśaṁ janam /
nikṛṣṭotkṛṣṭayor bhāvaṁ yā gṛhṇanti tu tāḥ striyaḥ // 4.23 //
For any girl entrances those on her level, / But those who stop the heart of low and high: they are true women." //4.23//

ity udāyi-vacaḥ śrutvā tā viddhā iva yoṣitaḥ /
samāruruhur ātmānaṁ kumāra-grahaṇaṁ prati // 4.24 //
Having thus attended to the words of Udāyin, the women, as if they had been pricked, / Went up, rising above themselves, in the direction of apprehending the prince.[12] //4.24//

tā bhrūbhiḥ prekṣitair hāvair hasitair laḍitair gataiḥ /
cakrur ākṣepikāś ceṣṭā bhīta-bhītā ivāṅganāḥ // 4.25 //
Using their foreheads, using glimpsed enticements, using smiling artful dodges, / The women performed suggestive actions, like women wary of fear.[13] //4.25//

---

[9] See also SN7.34.
[10] Through his seduction by the nymph Ghṛtācī (also known as Menakā), Viśvā-mitra fathered Śakuntalā, who is the heroine of Kālidāsa's famous play "*The Recognition of Śakuntalā.*" See also SN7.35.
[11] This is a good example of the ironic use of the term "a protector of men" to describe, in the hidden meaning, the Buddha or a buddha-ancestor.
[12] Ostensibly, towards seduction of the prince. In the hidden meaning, towards their realization of the buddha-nature, or towards the prince's realization of his own buddha-nature?
[13] Ostensibly, they looked skittish. In the hidden meaning, they were alert to the terrors of sickness, aging and death.

rājñas tu viniyogena kumārasya ca mārdavāt /
jahuḥ kṣipram aviśraṁbhaṁ madena madanena ca // 4.26 //
But in view of the king's assignment, and thanks to a prince's mildness of manner, / They quickly shed their diffidence – through inspiration and through enchantment. //4.26//

atha nārī-jana-vṛtaḥ kumāro vyacarad vanam /
vāsitā-yūtha-sahitaḥ karīva himavad-vanam // 4.27 //
And so, surrounded by the women, the prince roved around the wood / Like a bull elephant accompanied by a herd of single females as he roves a Himālayan forest. //4.27//

sa tasmin kānane ramye jajvāla strī-puraḥsaraḥ /
ākrīḍa iva vibhrāje vivasvān apsaro-vṛtaḥ // 4.28 //
In that delightful forest, attended by the women, he shone / Like Vivasvat, the Shining Sun, in the Vibhrāja pleasure grove, surrounded by *apsarases.* //4.28//

madenāvarjitā nāma taṁ kāś-cit tatra yoṣitaḥ /
kaṭhinaiḥ paspṛśuḥ pīnaiḥ saṁhatair valgubhiḥ stanaiḥ // 4.29 //
Pretending to be tipsy, some girls there / Brushed him, with firm, round, closely set, beautiful breasts. //4.29//

srastāṁsa-komalālamba-mṛdu-bāhu-latābalā /
anṛtaṁ skhalitaṁ kā-cit kṛtvainaṁ sasvaje balāt // 4.30 //
One girl – from whose relaxed shoulders delicately dangled soft arms like tendrils – / Simulated a stumble, so that she could not help but cling to him.[14] //4.30//

kā-cit tāmrādharoṣṭhena mukhenāsava-gandhinā /
viniśaśvāsa karṇe 'sya rahasyaṁ śrūyatām iti // 4.31 //
One girl, whose mouth with copper-red lower lip betrayed a whiff of distilled nectar, / Whispered in his ear, "Let the secret be revealed!" //4.31//

kā-cid ājñāpayantīva provācārdrānulepanā /
iha bhaktiṁ kuruṣveti hastaṁ saṁśliṣya lipsayā // 4.32 //
As if she were giving an order, one girl who was moist with body oils insisted: / "Perform the act of devotion here!" as – wanting it – she closely attached herself to a hand.[15] //4.32//

muhur-muhur mada-vyāja-srasta-nīlāṁśukāparā /
ālakṣya-rasanā reje sphurad vidyud iva kṣapā // 4.33 //
A different girl, as she repeatedly simulated intoxication, and let her dark blue robe, made of fine cloth, slip down, / Showed scarcely observable glimmers of sensibility, like a night lit by lightning, in flashes.[16] //4.33//

---

[14] This verse has a play on *abalā*, "one who is weak (f.)" i.e. a girl, a so-called member of the weaker sex, and *balāt*, "perforce," "helplessly." The ironic subtext is that relaxed shoulders and soft arms are sometimes a mark of strength, and simulation of a stumble might be an expedient means.

[15] In the hidden meaning, wanting to attain the ineffable, she adhered to the Buddha's teaching.

kāś-cit kanaka-kāñcībhir mukharābhir itas tataḥ /
babhramur darśayantyo 'sya śroṇīs tanv aṁśukāvṛtāḥ // 4.34 //
Some women wobbled from here to there, their golden girdle-trinkets tinkling noisily, / As they exhibited to him swaying hips thinly veiled by a robe of fine cloth.[17] //4.34//

cūta-śākhāṁ kusumitāṁ pragṛhyānyā lalaṁbire /
su-varṇa-kalaśa-prakhyān darśayantyaḥ payodharān // 4.35 //
Ones who were different held and hung onto a flowering mango branch, / Causing others to see breasts, resembling golden jugs, which would bear milk. [Or clouds, set off by the golden pinnacles of stūpas, which would bear water.] [[Or containers, resembling golden jars, of the lifeblood.]][18] //4.35//

kā-cit padma-vanād etya sa-padmā padma-locanā /
padma-vaktrasya pārśve 'sya padma-śrīr iva tasthuṣī // 4.36 //
One girl, from out of a bed of lotuses, bearing a lotus and looking through lotus eyes, / Came and stood by the side of the lotus-faced one, like Śrī, the lotus-hued goddess of beauty. //4.36//

madhuraṁ gītam anv-arthaṁ kā-cit sābhinayaṁ jagau /
taṁ svasthaṁ codayantīva vañcito 'sīty avekṣitaiḥ // 4.37 //
A sweet song whose meaning was clear, one girl sang, with actions that suited the words, / As if she were goading the one who was self-assured with glimpses whose gist was, "You are cheating yourself!" //4.37//

śubhena vadanenānyā bhrū-kārmuka-vikarṣiṇā /
prāvṛtyānucakārāsya ceṣṭitaṁ dhīra-līlayā // 4.38 //
A different girl, with a bright countenance, the bows of her eyebrows being spread wide apart, / Put on his manner and did what he did - playfully replicating his seriousness [or having fun, with gravity]. //4.38//

pīna-valgu-stanī kā-cidd hāsāghūrṇita-kuṇḍalā /
uccair avajahāsainaṁ sa-māpnotu bhavān iti // 4.39 //
One girl, whose breasts were big and beautiful, and whose earrings whirled round as she laughed, / Taunted him from above, as if to say, "Catch up with me, mister!"[19] //4.39//

---

[16] In the hidden meaning, did Aśvaghoṣa see himself using words repeatedly, in flashes, to simulate intoxication?

[17] A parody of kaṣaya-clad practitioners barging heedlessly about?

[18] *Payo-dhara* literally means "fluid-bearers" and hence breasts (as containing milk), or clouds (as containing water), or even the women themselves (as containing vital spirit, or the lifeblood). *Kalaśa* means jug or jar, but it too has a secondary meaning: a round pinnacle on the top of a temple (especially the pinnacle crowning a Buddhist *caitya* or *stūpa*).

[19] A parody of a larger-than-life Zen master?

apayāntaṁ tathaivānyā babandhur mālya-dāmabhiḥ /
kāś-cit sākṣepa-madhurair jagṛhur vacanāṅkuśaiḥ // 4.40 //
Different ones in the same vein, as he wandered away, held him back with daisy chains;[20] / While some girls stopped him in his tracks with the elephant hooks of sweet words, barbed with irony. //4.40//

pratiyogārthinī kā-cid gṛhītvā cūta-vallarīm /
idaṁ puṣpaṁ tu kasyeti papraccha mada-viklavā // 4.41 //
One girl, wishing to be contrary, seized the branch of a mango tree - / "Now then! Whose flower is this?" she demanded, bewildered by blithe exuberance. //4.41//

kā-cit puruṣavat kṛtvā gatiṁ saṁsthānam eva ca /
uvācainaṁ jitaḥ strībhir jaya bho pṛthivīm imām // 4.42 //
One girl, acting like a man, in her way of moving and standing still, / Said to him: "Women have defeated you. Now you defeat this earth!" //4.42//

atha lolekṣaṇā kā-cij jighrantī nīlam utpalam /
kiṁ-cin mada-kalair vākyair nṛpātmajam abhāṣata // 4.43
Then a girl with avid eyes, who was smelling the flower of a blue lotus, / Said, with words that intoxication rendered somewhat indistinct, to the one begotten out of the selves of protectors of men: //4.43//

paśya bhartaś citaṁ cūtaṁ kusumair madhu-gandhibhiḥ /
hema-pañjara-ruddho vā kokilo yatra kūjati // 4.44 //
"Observe, master, the mango tree covered with honey-scented blossoms / Where, as if confined in a golden cage, the cuckoo keeps on calling. //4.44//

aśoko dṛśyatām eṣa kāmi-śoka-vivardhanaḥ /
ruvanti bhramarā yatra dahyamānā ivāgninā // 4.45 //
See [or realize] this: the sorrowless [state of an] *a-śoka*, augmenter [or expunger][21] of a lover's sorrow, / Where bumble bees buzz as if being singed by a fire.[22] //4.45//

cūta-yaṣṭyā samāśliṣṭo dṛśyatāṁ tilaka-drumaḥ /
śukla-vāsā iva naraḥ striyā pītāṅga-rāgayā // 4.46 //
Witness the *tilaka* tree, being closely embraced by the mango's branch, / Like a white-robed man[23] by a woman whose limbs are coated in scented yellow cosmetics. //4.46//

---

[20] By subtle, indirect means - not by brute force.
[21] *Vivardhana* could be derived from *vi-√vṛdh*, to augment, or from *vi-√vardh*, to cut off, expunge.
[22] In pain, or in a state of sincere action.
[23] In the hidden meaning, the intention may be to remind the reader of the difficulty of practicing as a lay practitioner (a wearer of white clothes).

phullaṁ kurubakaṁ paśya nirbhuktālaktaka-prabham /
yo nakha-prabhayā strīṇāṁ nirbhartsita ivānataḥ // 4.47 //
Look at the *kurubaka* plant, with its red flower-heads - It is luminous, like one that has yielded up every drop of red sap, / And yet, as if outshone, by the luminance of women's finger-nails, it is bowing down.[24] //4.47//

bālāśokaś ca nicito dṛśyatām eṣa pallavaiḥ /
yo 'smākaṁ hasta-śobhābhir lajjamāna iva sthitaḥ // 4.48 //
Again, see [or realize] this: [the state of] a young *a-śoka* - It is brimming with new shoots / And yet, as if abashed, at the hennaed loveliness of our hands, it remains modestly standing there. //4.48//

dīrghikāṁ prāvṛtāṁ paśya tīra-jaiḥ sinduvārakaiḥ /
pāṇḍurāṁśuka-saṁvītāṁ śayānāṁ pramadām iva // 4.49 //
Look at the stretch of still water, veiled by the *sindu-vāra* shrubs growing around its banks, / Like a woman, clad in fine white cloth, who is lying down.[25] //4.49//

dṛśyatāṁ strīṣu māhātmyaṁ cakravāko hy asau jale /
pṛṣṭhataḥ preṣyavad bhāryām anuvṛtyānugacchati // 4.50 //
Let it be realized, with reference to females of the species, what greatness is. That greylag gander in the water over there, for instance :- / Trailing behind his mate like a slave, he follows.[26] //4.50//

mattasya para-puṣṭasya ruvataḥ śrūyatāṁ dhvaniḥ /
aparaḥ kokilo 'nuktaḥ pratiśrutkeva kūjati // 4.51 //
Let the sound be heard of the intoxicated male who is calling - he who was nourished by one other than his mother![27] / Another male cuckoo, acting without scruple, makes a call like an echo. //4.51//

api nāma vihaṅ-gānāṁ vasantenāhṛto madaḥ /
na tu cintayataś cittam janasya prājña-māninaḥ // 4.52 //
Can spring deliver exuberant joy, to those that fly the skies, / But not the mind of a thinking man who thinks that he is wise?" //4.52//

---

[24] A suggestion of enlightenment as the manifestation of humility?

[25] Ostensibly the reclining woman is an erotically exciting image. In the hidden meaning, does a long stretch of still water suggest an expanse of time spent coming back to quiet?

[26] The ostensible point is that the goose is stronger than the gander. The real point might be that there is great strength in following.

[27] In the hidden meaning, a man or a woman who was caused to grow by his or her teacher, in the direction of totally letting himself or herself go.

ity evaṁ tā yuvatayo manmathoddāma-cetasaḥ /
kumāraṁ vividhais tais tair upacakramire nayaiḥ // 4.53 //
In this manner those girls, with hearts unbridled by love, / Approached the chosen One using many and various stratagems. //4.53//

evam ākṣipyamāṇo 'pi sa tu dhairyāvṛtendriyaḥ /
martavyam iti sodvego na jaharṣa na sismiye // 4.54 //
And even while, in such a manner, he was being put to shame, keeping his senses contained by constancy, / And still excited, by the prospect of dying, he neither bristled nor blushed. //4.54//

tāsāṁ tattve 'navasthānaṁ dṛṣṭvā sa puruṣottamaḥ /
samaṁ vignena dhīreṇa cintayām āsa cetasā // 4.55 //
He, an excellent man, considering those girls to have a loose foothold in reality, / Deliberated, with a mind that was agitated and at the same time resolute:[28] //4.55//

kiṁ vinā nāvagacchanti capalaṁ yauvanaṁ striyaḥ /
yato rūpeṇa saṁpannaṁ jarā yan nāśayiṣyati // 4.56 //
"What is missing in these women that they do not understand youthfulness to be fleeting? / Because, whatever is possessed of beauty, aging will destroy. //4.56//

nūnam etā na paśyanti kasya-cid roga-saṁplavam /
tathā hṛṣṭā bhayaṁ tyaktvā jagati vyādhi-dharmiṇi // 4.57 //
Surely they fail to foresee anybody finishing with dis-ease, / So joyful are they, having set fear aside, in a world that is subject to disease. //4.57//

anabhijñāś ca su-vyaktaṁ mṛtyoḥ sarvāpahāriṇaḥ /
tathā svasthā nirudvignāḥ krīḍanti ca hasanti ca // 4.58 //
Evidently, again, they are ignorant of the death that sweeps all away, / So easy in themselves are they, as, unstirred, they play and laugh. //4.58//

jarāṁ vyādhiṁ ca mṛtyuṁ ca ko hi jānan sa-cetanaḥ /
svasthas tiṣṭhen niṣīded vā suped vā kiṁ punar haset // 4.59 //
For what man in touch with his reason, who knows aging, sickness and death, / Could stand or sit at ease, or lie down - far less laugh? //4.59//

yas tu dṛṣṭvā paraṁ jīrṇaṁ vyādhitaṁ mṛtam eva ca /
svastho bhavati nodvigno yathācetās tathaiva saḥ // 4.60 //
Rather, when one man sees another who is worn out and riddled with sickness, not to mention dead, / And he remains at ease in himself, unstirred, he acts as though his reason were absent.[29] //4.60//

---

[28] The irony might be that the prince had established an excellent will to the truth, but it was the ones among the women who were different, if Aśvaghoṣa's irony is understood, that were truly living in reality.

viyujyamāne hi tarau puṣpair api phalair api /
patati cchidyamāne vā tarur anyo na śocate // 4.61 //
For at a tree's shedding of its flowers and fruits, / And at its falling, or at its felling, no other tree mourns."[30] //4.61//

iti dhyāna-paraṁ dṛṣṭvā viṣayebhyo gata-spṛham /
udāyī nīti-śāstra-jñas tam uvāca suhṛttayā // 4.62 //
Seeing the prince thus absorbed in thinking and without desire for objects, / Udāyin, knowing the rules of how to handle people, said to him, in a spirit of friendship: //4.62//

ahaṁ nṛ-patinā dattaḥ sakhā tubhyaṁ kṣamaḥ kila /
yasmāt tvayi vivakṣā me tayā praṇaya-vat-tayā // 4.63 //
"I am, by appointment to the King, fit, so he thinks, to be a friend to you; / On which grounds I am going to speak to you as frankly as this. //4.63//

ahitāt pṛatiṣedhaś ca hite cānupravartanam /
vyasane cāparityāgas trividhaṁ mitra-lakṣaṇam // 4.64 //
Keeping one out of harm's way, urging one on in the good, / and not deserting one in adversity, are the three marks of a friend. //4.64//

so 'haṁ maitrīṁ pratijñāya puruṣārthāt parāṅmukham /
yadi tvā samupekṣeya na bhaven mitratā mayi // 4.65 //
Now that I personally have promised my friendship to you, who is turning his back on an aim of human life, / If I then were to abandon you, there would be no friendship in me. //4.65//

tad bravīmi suhṛd-bhūtvā taruṇasya vapuṣmataḥ /
idaṁ na pratirūpaṁ te strīṣv adākṣiṇyam īdṛśam // 4.66 //
Speaking, therefore, as a friend, I must say that for a handsome young man / It does not become you to be so tactless towards women. //4.66//

anṛtenāpi nārīṇāṁ yuktaṁ samanuvartanam /
tad-vrīḍā-parihārārtham ātma-raty artham eva ca // 4.67 //
For women, even if the means are deceitful, obedience is appropriate, / To sweep away their diffidence, and purely for the purpose of enjoying oneself! //4.67//

---

[29] An ironic description of the transcendence of sitting-buddha – in which reason is not absent, but may appear to be absent?

[30] Ostensibly a criticism of the state in which reason does not appear to be operating. Below the surface, a pointer to the teaching that the non-emotional preaches dharma (see Shōbōgenzō chap. 53)?

saṁnatiś cānuvṛttiś ca strīṇāṁ hṛdaya-bandhanam /
snehasya hi guṇā yonir māna-kāmāś ca yoṣitaḥ // 4.68 //
Humility and submissive behaviour are, for women, what captures the heart – / Because excellent acts engender tender feelings, and women are lovers of honor. //4.68//

tad arhasi viśālākṣa hṛdaye 'pi parāṅ-mukhe /
rūpasyāsyānurūpeṇa dākṣiṇyenānuvartitum // 4.69 //
Therefore, O large-eyed one, though your heart be otherwise inclined, / With tact and delicacy that befit such a beautiful form, you should submit! //4.69//

dākṣiṇyam auṣadhaṁ strīṇāṁ dākṣiṇyaṁ bhūṣaṇaṁ param /
dākṣiṇya-rahitaṁ rūpaṁ niṣpuṣpam iva kānanam // 4.70 //
For women, tact and delicacy are medicine; tact and delicacy are the highest adornment; / Beautiful form without tact and delicacy is like a garden without flowers. //4.70//

kiṁ vā dākṣiṇya-mātreṇa bhāvenāstu parigrahaḥ /
viṣayān durlabhāṁ llabdhvā na hy avajñātum arhasi // 4.71 //
Equally, what good are tact and delicacy alone? Let all be bounded by what is real! / For, having gained objects that are hard to gain, you should not think light of such.[31] //4.71//

kāmaṁ param iti jñātvā devo 'pi hi puraṁdaraḥ /
gautamasya muneḥ patnīm ahalyāṁ cakame purā // 4.72 //
Knowing desire to be paramount, even the god Puraṁdara, 'Cleaver of Strongholds,' for example, / Made love in olden times to Ahalyā, the wife of the sage Gautama.[32] //4.72//

agastyaḥ prārthayām āsa soma-bhāryāṁ ca rohiṇīm /
tasmāt tat-sadṛśīṁ lebhe lopā-mudrām iti śrutiḥ // 4.73 //
And so much did Agastya desire Red Rohiṇī, the wife of moon-god Soma, / That he came to possess, tradition has it, a woman modelled after her, 'The Robber of Attributes,' Lopā-mudrā.[33] //4.73//

utathyasya ca bhāryāyāṁ mamatāyāṁ mahā-tapāḥ /
mārutyāṁ janayām āsa bharad-vājaṁ bṛhas-patiḥ // 4.74 //
Again, the great ascetic Bṛhas-pati, 'Lord of Prayer,' begat Bharad-vāja, 'Bearer of Velocity,' / In 'Self-Centred' Mama-tā, who was a daughter of the storm-gods and the wife of [his brother] Utathya.[34] //4.74//

---

[31] Thus, even Udāyin's argument, shallow though it sounds on the surface, can be read as pointing in its hidden meaning to the Buddha's teaching of skillful means, or expediency.

[32] Puraṁdara is an epithet of Indra, whose liaison with Ahalyā is also mentioned in SN7.25. See also note to BC2.27. The philosophical question Udāyin raises is how important desire is.

[33] Agastya is said to have fashioned Lopā-mudrā by taking her doe-eyes from deer, and other attractive attributes from other animals.

[34] In the Sanskrit original, the subject of the verse, Bṛhas-pati (see also BC1.41) comes at the end. The effect is to emphasize the hypocrisy, and the weakness in the face of sexual desire, of the oh-so-pious 'Lord of Prayer.'

bṛhas-pater mahiṣyāṁ ca juhvatyāṁ juhvatāṁ varaḥ /
budhaṁ vibudha-dharmāṇaṁ janayām āsa candramāḥ // 4.75 //
And the Moon, most eminent among oblation-offerers, begat 'The Learned' Budha, who was innately very learned, / In Bṛhas-pati's own esteemed wife, while she was offering an oblation. //4.75//

kālīm caiva purā kanyāṁ jala-prabhava-saṁbhavām /
jagāma yamunā-tīre jāta-rāgaḥ parāśaraḥ // 4.76 //
In olden times, again, the maiden Kālī whose birth had its origin in water, / Was pressed for sex on a bank of the Yamunā by lusting Parāśara, 'The Crusher.' [35]//4.76//

mātaṅgyām akṣamālāyāṁ garhitāyāṁ riraṁsayā /
kapiñjalādaṁ tanayaṁ vasiṣṭho 'janayan muniḥ // 4.77 //
The sage Vasiṣṭha[36] through desire for sexual enjoyment, / Begat his son Kapiñjalāda in the despised outcaste Akṣa-mālā. //4.77//

yayātiś caiva rājarṣir vayasy api vinirgate /
viśvācyāpsarasā sārdhaṁ reme caitra-rathe vane // 4.78 //
There again, the royal seer Yayāti,[37] though his best years were behind him, / Enjoyed a romp in Citra-ratha's woods with the celestial nymph Viśvācī //4.78//

strī-saṁsargaṁ vināśāntaṁ pāṇḍur jñātvāpi kauravaḥ /
mādrī-rūpa-guṇākṣiptaḥ siṣeve kāma-jaṁ sukham // 4.79 //
'The Pale' Pāṇḍu, a king in the Kuru line, knew that intercourse with his wife would end in death / And yet, bowled over by Mādrī's beautiful attributes, he indulged in pleasure born of desire.[38] //4.79//

karāla-janakaś caiva hṛtvā brāhmaṇa-kanyakām /
avāpa bhraṁśam apy evaṁ na tu seje na man-matham // 4.80 //
And 'the Dreadful Begetter' Karāla-janaka when he abducted a brahmin maiden, / Though he thus incurred ruin, never stopped attaching to his love. //4.80//

---

[35] Kalī was the mother of Vyāsa, 'the Compiler' (see BC1.42). See also SN7.29.

[36] Owner of the cow of plenty. See also BC1.42, BC1.52; SN7.28.

[37] Yayāti's kingdom is mentioned in a favourable light in BC2.11. See also SN1.59, SN11.46.

[38] As king of the Kurus, Pāṇḍu married the princess Mādrī along with another princess named Kuntī. While out hunting in the woods Pāṇḍu accidentally shot the sage Kindama while the latter had taken the form of a deer and was mating with a doe. The wounded sage Kindama placed a curse on Pāṇḍu to the effect that he would die if he ever again had sex. Pāṇḍu then remorsefully renounced his kingdom and lived with his wives as a celibate ascetic. After fifteen years of ascetic celibacy, however, when his second wife Kuntī was away, Pāṇḍu was irresistibly drawn to his first wife Mādrī, and so fulfilled the sage's curse and died. The story is also referenced in SN7.45.

evam ādīn mahātmāno viṣayān garhitān api /
rati-hetor bubhujire prāg eva guṇa-saṁhitān // 4.81 //
Great men, driven by pleasure, enjoyed objects such as these, / Even when those enjoyments were forbidden - how much more [to be enjoyed] are those that come with merit?[39] //4.81//

tvaṁ punar nyāyataḥ prāptān balavān rūpavān yuvā /
viṣayān avajānāsi yatra saktam idaṁ jagat // 4.82 //
And yet you disdain enjoyments that fittingly belong to you, a young man possessed of strength and handsome form; / You despise objects to which the whole world is attached." //4.82//

iti śrutvā vacas tasya ślakṣṇam āgama-saṁhitam /
megha-stanita-nirghoṣaḥ kumāraḥ pratyabhāṣata // 4.83 //
Having listened to these polished words of his, complete with scriptural references, / The prince in a voice resonant as thunder spoke back: //4.83//

upapannam idaṁ vākyaṁ sauhārda-vyañjakaṁ tvayi /
atra ca tvānuneṣyāmi yatra mā duṣṭhu manyase // 4.84 //
"This talk intimating friendship is fitting in you, / And I shall bring you round in the areas where you misjudge me. //4.84//

nāvajānāmi viṣayān jāne lokaṁ tad-ātmakam /
anityaṁ tu jagan matvā nātra me ramate manaḥ // 4.85 //
I do not despise objects. I know them to be at the heart of human affairs. / But seeing the world to be impermanent, my mind does not delight in them. //4.85//

jarā vyādhiś ca mṛtyuś ca yadi na syād idaṁ trayam /
mamāpi hi manojñeṣu viṣayeṣu ratir bhavet // 4.86 //
Aging, disease, and death - in the absence of these three, / Enjoyment might exist for me also in agreeable objects.[40] //4.86//

nityaṁ yady api hi strīṇām etad eva vapur bhavet /
doṣavatsv api kāmeṣu kāmaṁ rajyeta me manaḥ // 4.87 //
For if indeed the beauty that women have here and now could be eternal, / Then desires, however blemished by imperfection, might - it is true - please my mind. //4.87//

---

[39] Ostensibly Udāyin, despite his protestations of friendship, is trying to tempt the prince down the backslider's path. In the hidden meaning, he might be upholding a true friend's teaching of *alpecchu-saṁtuṣṭi*, wanting little and being content.

[40] Ironically, the prince is predicting how it will be for him in future.

yadā tu jarayā pītaṁ rūpam āsāṁ bhaviṣyati /
ātmano 'py anabhipretaṁ mohāt tatra ratir bhavet // 4.88 //
But since growing old will drain from them any semblance of beauty, / Enjoyment of such, on the grounds of ignorance, might be an occurrence that nobody - including the women themselves - should expect.[41] //4.88//

mṛtyu-vyādhi-jarā-dharmā mṛtyu-vyādhi-jarātmabhiḥ /
ramamāṇo hy asaṁvignaḥ samāno mṛga-pakṣibhiḥ // 4.89 //
A man whose substance is dying, being ill, and growing old, who remains unperturbed while playing / With others whose essence is dying, being ill, and growing old, is as one with the birds and beasts.[42] //4.89//

yad apy āttha mahātmānas te 'pi kāmātmakā iti /
saṁvego 'traiva kartavyo yadā teṣām api kṣayaḥ // 4.90 //
Although you say that even the greats are desirous by nature, / That is rather a cause to be nervous, since, for them also, ending is the rule. //4.90//

māhātmyaṁ na ca tan manye yatra sāmānyataḥ kṣayaḥ /
viṣayeṣu prasaktir vā yuktir vā nātmavattayā // 4.91 //
I fail to see greatness there, where ending is the general rule[43] - / Where there is, on the one side, adherence to objects, and, on the other, no union with the state of self-possession.[44] //4.91//

yad apy ātthānṛtenāpi strī-jane vartyatām iti /
an-ṛtaṁ nāvagacchāmi dākṣiṇyenāpi kiṁ-cana // 4.92 //
Although you say that even deception may be used as a means to deal with women, / I have no understanding at all of deception, even when used with tact and delicacy.[45] //4.92//

na cānuvartanaṁ tan me rucitaṁ yatra nārjavam /
sarva-bhāvena saṁparko yadi nāsti dhig astu tat // 4.93 //
Neither do I find submissive behavior to be agreeable, where sincerity is lacking; / If coming together is not with one's whole being, then out with it![46] //4.93//

---

[41] In the hidden meaning, enjoyment of growing older (i.e. becoming wiser) is a pleasant surprise.

[42] Ostensibly, his level is sub-human. In the hidden meaning he, together with other buddhas, is at one with nature.

[43] In the hidden meaning, the prince has yet to realize the truth of cessation.

[44] In the hidden meaning, adhering to objects might mean, e.g. diligently tending a crop of vegetables; and no union with the state of self-possession might be synonymous with body and mind dropping off.

[45] In the hidden meaning, the prince has yet to understand what he will later preach as "skillful means."

[46] Ostensibly, Aśvaghoṣa is celebrating the prince's idealism. Below the surface, he might be inviting the reader to notice how impractical idealism is, since it negates the possibility of starting from present doubt-ridden imperfection - aka polishing a tile.

anṛte śrad-dadhānasya saktasyādoṣa-darśinaḥ /
kiṁ hi vañcayitavyaṁ syāj jāta-rāgasya cetasaḥ // 4.94 //
If a person believes in, sticks to, and sees no fault in untruth, / What could there be worth deceiving in a soul so redly tainted?[47] //4.94//

vañcayanti ca yady eva jāta-rāgāḥ paras-param /
nanu naiva kṣamaṁ draṣṭuṁ narāḥ strīṇāṁ nṛṇām striyaḥ // 4.95 //
And if those tainted by redness do indeed deceive one another, / Then is it never appropriate for men to see women, or women men?[48] //4.95//

tad evaṁ sati duḥkhārtaṁ jarā-maraṇa-bhāginam /
na māṁ kāmeṣv anāryeṣu pratārayitum arhasi // 4.96 //
Since in this situation I am pained by suffering and am an heir to growing old and dying, / You should not try to persuade me to stray into ignoble desires.[49] //4.96//

aho 'tidhīraṁ balavac ca te manaś caleṣu kāmeṣu ca sāra-darśinaḥ /
bhaye 'pi tīvre viṣayeṣu sajjase nirīkṣamāṇo maraṇādhvani prajāḥ // 4.97 //
How extremely firm and strong is your mind if in transient desires you see what is essential – / If, even in the midst of acute terror, you stick to objects, while watching sentient creatures on the road to extinction![50] //4.97//

ahaṁ punar bhīrur atīva-viklavo jarā-vipad-vyādhi-bhayaṁ vicintayan /
labhe na śāntiṁ na dhṛtiṁ kuto ratiṁ niśāmayan dīptam ivāgninā jagat // 4.98 //
I, in contrast, am fearful – I am exceedingly agitated as I contemplate the terror of aging, death, and disease; / I know neither peace nor constancy, much less enjoyment, seeing the world blazing as if it were on fire. //4.98//

asaṁśayaṁ mṛtyur iti prajānato narasya rāgo hṛdi yasya jāyate /
ayo-mayīṁ tasya paraimi cetanāṁ mahā-bhaye rajyati yo na roditi // 4.99 //
When a man knows the certainty of death and yet the red taint of delight arises in his heart, / I venture that his consciousness must be made of steel, who does not weep but delights in the great terror."[51] //4.99//

---

[47] For the hidden meaning, see e.g. the story of Handsome Nanda, a redly-tainted soul in whom the Buddha clearly saw something worth deceiving.
[48] In the hidden meaning, the question calls into question the validity of the concepts "women" and "men" – hence the hidden meaning of the canto title *Warding 'Women' Away.*
[49] In the superficial meaning, "I am weak, so please don't tempt me." In the real meaning, "I am already established on the path, so don't waste your breath."
[50] In the hidden meaning, e.g. a brain surgeon, appreciating how transient human life is, nevertheless sticks to his decision to remove a brain tumor.
[51] In ostensibly mocking a libertine, the prince unwittingly praises buddha.

atho kumāraś ca viniścayātmikāṁ cakāra kāmāśraya-ghātinīṁ kathām /
janasya cakṣur gamanīya-maṇḍalo mahī-dharaṁ cāstam iyāya bhās-karaḥ // 4.100 //
And so, as the prince made a speech, that was tantamount to a decision, murdering any recourse to Love, / The disc that is plain for all to see went to meet the western mountain – light-producer meeting Earth-container. //4.100//

tato vṛthā-dhārita-bhūṣaṇa-srajaḥ kalā-guṇaiś ca praṇayaiś ca niṣphalaiḥ /
sva eva bhāve viniguhya manmathaṁ puraṁ yayur bhagna-mano-rathāḥ striyaḥ // 4.101 //
Then, their ornaments and garlands having been worn in vain, their graceful arts and displays of affection having proved fruitless, / Each enshrouding her love within her own heart, the women traipsed back to the city, for the chariots of their fancy had been rent apart. //4.101//

tataḥ purodyāna-gatāṁ jana-śriyaṁ nirīkṣya sāye pratisaṁhṛtāṁ punaḥ /
anityatāṁ sarva-gatāṁ vicintayan viveśa dhiṣṇyaṁ kṣiti-pālakātmajaḥ // 4.102 //
Then, having witnessed the beautiful women's brightness which had pervaded the park receding once more into the twilight, / The one begotten from a guardian of the earth, contemplating all-pervading impermanence, entered his earthen-hearthed dwelling. //4.102//

tataḥ śrutvā rājā viṣaya-vimukhaṁ tasya tu mano
na śiśye tāṁ rātriṁ hṛdaya-gata-śalyo gaja iva /
atha śrānto mantre bahu-vividha-mārge sa-sacivo
na so 'nyat-kāmebhyo niyamanam apaśyat suta-mateḥ // 4.103 //
Then, hearing that the prince's mind was turned away from objects, the king, like an elephant with an arrow in its heart, did not sleep that night; / Though he wearied himself further in all sorts of consultations with his ministers, he saw no other means, aside from desires, to control his offspring's mind. //4.103//

iti buddha-carite mahā-kāvye strī-vighātano nāma caturthaḥ sargaḥ // 4 //
The 4th canto, titled "Warding Women Away,"
in an epic tale of awakened action.

Canto 5: abhiniṣkramaṇaḥ
Getting Well & Truly Out

Introduction

Kramaṇa means stepping, walking, going. With the prefix *nis-* (out, forth, away), *niṣkramaṇa* means going out or going forth. And the additional prefix *abhi-* (over) adds emphasis and a sense of transcendence – as also in the title of Canto 14, *Abhisaṁbodhi*, The Total Transcendent Awakening.

Ostensibly the transcendence in question is the Prince's transcendence of family life, in going forth from Kapilavāstu.

At the same time, following on from the previous canto, there are further vivid descriptions of individual women who are different (*anyā*). And for a person steeped in the ignorant misconception of "correct posture," these descriptions are very challenging. They seem, below the surface, to ask: Whether or not you are a home-leaver, have you really, well and truly, got free of all the old conceptions that stopped you from being free?

sa tathā viṣayair vilobhyamānaḥ paramarhair api śākya-rāja-sūnuḥ /
na jagāma ratiṁ na śarma lebhe hṛdaye siṁha ivātidigdha-viddhaḥ // 5.1 //
Though enticed in this way by most costly sensual enjoyments [or by most worthy objects], the son of the Śākya king / Neither partook of pleasure nor obtained relief – like a lion pierced in its heart by a poisoned arrow. //5.1//

atha mantri-sutaiḥ kṣamaiḥ kadā-cit sakhibhiś citra-kathaiḥ kṛtānuyātraḥ /
vana-bhūmi-didṛkṣayā śamepsur nara-devānumato bahiḥ pratasthe // 5.2 //
Then one day, attended by sons of ministers whose diverse chatter would make them suitable companions, / Since, in his desire for tranquility, he wanted to visit the forest, with the king's permission he set off out. //5.2//

nava-rukma-khalīna-kiṅkiṇīkaṁ pracalac-cāmara-cāru-hema-bhāṇḍam /
abhiruhya sa kanthakaṁ sad-aśvaṁ prayayau ketum iva drumābja-ketuḥ // 5.3 //
Onto the good horse Kanthaka, decked with bridle-bit and small bells of new gold, with waving plume, and with lovely golden harness, / He climbed, and rode forth, like a star among trees, or a star among lotuses, on a shooting star.[1] //5.3//

---

[1] The simile can be understood in more than one way, due to the ambiguity of *ketu* (brightness, sign, flag, comet, etc.) and *drumābja* (tree + water-born). The suggestion in this translation is of stillness in movement.

sa vikṛṣṭatarāṁ vanānta-bhūmiṁ vana-lobhāc ca yayau mahī-guṇāc ca /
salilormi-vikāra-sīra-mārgāṁ vasu-dhāṁ caiva dadarśa kṛṣyamāṇām // 5.4 //
To the edge of a more distant forest, he rode, by dint of his impatient yearning for the woods, and on the grounds of the merit inherent in the Earth;[2] / And there indeed, where tracks of ploughs had turned the soil to waves, he saw the bountiful earth[3] being tilled. //5.4//

hala-bhinna-vikīrṇa-śaṣpa-darbhāṁ hata-sūkṣma-krimi-kīṭa-jantu-kīrṇām /
samavekṣya rasāṁ tathā-vidhāṁ tāṁ svajanasyeva vadhe bhṛśaṁ śuśoca // 5.5 //
As the ploughs tore and scattered tufts of young grass over the soil, and littered the soil with dead worms, insects, and other little creatures, / He saw that soil[4] like that, and felt intense sorrow, as if at the killing of his own human relatives. //5.5//

kṛṣataḥ puruṣāṁś ca vīkṣamāṇaḥ pavanārkāṁśu-rajo-vibhinna-varṇān /
vahana-klama-viklavāṁś ca dhuryān paramāryaḥ paramāṁ kṛpāṁ cakāra // 5.6 //
Again, seeing the men ploughing, their complexions riven by the wind, the sun's rays and the dust, / and seeing the oxen unsteady from the exhaustion of drawing, the most noble one felt extreme pity. //5.6//

avatīrya tatas turaṅga-pṛṣṭhāc chanakair gāṁ vyacarac chucā parītaḥ /
jagato janana-vyayaṁ vicinvan kṛpaṇaṁ khalv idam ityuvāca cārtaḥ // 5.7 //
Then, getting down off the back of his fleet-footed steed, he slowly moved over the ground,[5] overtaken by sorrow. / And as he reflected on how life comes into existence and perishes, hurting, he uttered, "How pitiful this is." //5.7//

manasā ca viviktatām abhīpsuḥ suhṛdas tān anuyāyino nivārya /
abhitaś cala-cāru-parṇavatyā vijane mūlam upeyivān sa jaṁbvāḥ // 5.8 //
Desiring to be alone with his thoughts, he fended away those amicable hangers on / And drew close to the root of a solitary rose-apple tree whose abundant plumage fluttered agreeably all around. //5.8//

niṣasāda sa yatra śaucavatyāṁ bhuvi vaidūrya-nikāśa-śādvalāyām /
jagataḥ prabhava-vyayau vicinvan manasaś ca sthiti-mārgam ālalambe // 5.9 //
There he sat upon the honest, verdant earth[6] whose horizons shimmered like emeralds; / And, while reflecting how the living world arises and perishes, he dangled on the path of standing firmly upright, which is of the mind.[7] //5.9//

---

[2] *Mahī* (lit. the great one [f.]) means the Earth, Mother Earth.
[3] *Vasu-dhā* (lit. wealth-giver [f]), the bountiful earth.
[4] *Rasā* (f) means soil or earth.
[5] *Gām* (f) means a cow, or the earth as the milk-cow of kings.
[6] *Bhū* (again, feminine) is the usual term for the earth. At the same time, *bhū* means happening.
[7] The juxtaposition of *ālalambe* (he hung, he dangled) and *sthiti* (standing upright or standing firm) seems to hint at the balancing act of letting sitting happen, resolutely but without fixity. *Bhuvi* (loc.) means "on the earth" and at the same time, "in an act of arising/happening."

samavāpta-manaḥ-sthitiś ca sadyo viṣayecchādibhir ādhibhiś ca muktaḥ /
sa-vitarka-vicāram āpa śāntaṁ prathamaṁ dhyānam anāsrava-prakāram // 5.10 //
In stumbling upon firm upstandingness of the mind, he was instantly released from worries, such as those associated with desires for objects; / He entered the first peaceful stage, in which there are ideas and thoughts, of the meditation whose essence is freedom from polluting influences.[8] //5.10//

adhigamya tato viveka-jaṁ tu parama-prīti-sukhaṁ manaḥ-samādhim /
idam eva tataḥ paraṁ pradadhyau manasā loka-gatiṁ niśamya samyak // 5.11 //
But then, having experienced that most excellent state of joy and ease, born of seclusion, which is integration of the mind, / He proceeded to give consideration to the following evident fact – since, by means of the mind, he had clearly seen the way of the world. //5.11//

kṛpaṇaṁ bata yaj janaḥ svayaṁ sann avaśo vyādhi-jarā-vināśa-dharmā /
jarayārditam āturaṁ mṛtaṁ vā param ajño vijugupsate madāndhaḥ // 5.12 //
"O how pitiable it is that human beings, while being ourselves at the mercy of sickness, aging and death, / Should tend, in our ignorance and wanton blindness, to disavow the other, who is afflicted by old age, or who is diseased or dying. //5.12//

iha ced aham īdṛśaḥ svayaṁ san vijugupseya paraṁ tathā-svabhāvam /
na bhavet sadṛśaṁ hi tat-kṣamaṁ vā paramaṁ dharmam imaṁ vijānato me // 5.13 //
For if I here, being like that myself, should disavow another in the same condition, / That would not be worthy of me, or conduce to my knowing this most excellent dharma." //5.13//

iti tasya vipaśyato yathāvaj jagato vyādhi-jarā-vipatti-doṣān /
bala-yauvana-jīvita-pravṛtto vijagāmātma-gato madaḥ kṣaṇena // 5.14 //
While he, for his part, was properly seeing through faults of the living associated with sickness, aging, and death, / The high spirits that had once intoxicated him, arising from his strength, youth and life, instantly evaporated. //5.14//

na jaharṣa na cāpi cānutepe vicikitsāṁ na yayau na tandri-nidre /
na ca kāma-guṇeṣu saṁrarañje na vididveṣa paraṁ na cāvamene // 5.15 //
He felt neither thrill nor pang; into intellectual striving, or lassitude and sleepiness, he did not fall; / He was not reddened by passion for sensual desires, and neither did he hate, or look down upon, the other. //5.15//

---

[8] The first *dhyāna* is also described in SN Canto 17 and BC Canto 12 as containing ideas and thoughts, and being born of seclusion.

iti buddhir iyaṁ ca nī-rajaskā vavṛdhe tasya mahātmano viśuddhā /
puruṣair aparair adṛśyamānaḥ puruṣaś copasasarpa bhikṣu-veṣaḥ // 5.16 //
Thus did this dustless mind, this mind which is cleansed, develop in him whose nature was great; / Whereupon, unseen by the other men, up crept a man who was dressed in beggar's garb. //5.16//

nara-deva-sutas tam abhyapṛcchad vada ko 'sīti śaśaṁsa so 'tha tasmai /
nara-puṁgava janma-mṛtyu-bhītaḥ śramaṇaḥ pravrajito 'smi mokṣa-hetoḥ // 5.17 //
The prince asked him: "Say! Who are you?," to which he replied: / "O bull among men! Alarmed by birth and death, I have gone forth as an ascetic striver, for the sake of liberation. //5.17//

jagati kṣaya-dharmake mumukṣur mṛgaye 'haṁ śivam akṣayaṁ padaṁ tat /
sva-jane 'nya-jane ca tulya-buddhir viṣayebhyo vinivṛtta-rāga-doṣaḥ // 5.18 //
Desiring liberation in a world marked by decay, I pursue that happy step which is immune to decay. / I am even-minded towards my own people and other people; turning back from objects, I have allowed the stain of redness to fade away. //5.18//

nivasan kva-cid eva vṛkṣa-mūle vijane vāyatane girau vane vā /
vicarāmy aparigraho nirāśaḥ paramārthāya yathopapanna-bhaikṣaḥ // 5.19 //
Dwelling anywhere – at the root of a tree, or in an abandoned house, or on a mountain, or in the forest, / I wander here and there, with no possessions and no expectations, subsisting, for the sake of ultimate riches, on whatever scraps I chance to get from begging." //5.19//

iti paśyata eva rāja-sūnor idam uktvā sa nabhaḥ samutpapāta /
sa hi tad-vapur-anya-buddhi-darśī smṛtaye tasya sameyivān divaukāḥ // 5.20 //
He uttered these words, while the son of the king looked powerlessly on, and then he vanished into the clouds; / For he was a sky-dweller who, peeping the prince's mind conflicting with his body, had come to help him towards mindfulness. //5.20//

gaganaṁ kha-ga-vad gate ca tasmin nṛ-varaḥ saṁjahṛṣe visismiye ca /
upalabhya tataś ca dharma-saṁjñam abhiniryāṇa-vidhau matiṁ cakāra // 5.21 //
When he had gone, like a bird into the sky, the foremost of men was full of gladness and wonder; / And having thus received a hint of dharma, he set his mind on the matter of marching forth. //5.21//

tata indra-samo jitendriyāśvaḥ pravivikṣuḥ param aśvam āruroha /
parivartya janaṁ tv avekṣamāṇas tata evābhimataṁ vanaṁ na bheje // 5.22 //
And so, powerful as Indra, with the powerful horses of his senses tamed, the prince mounted his highest of horses, wishing to get started. / But then, having regard for people, he turned [his horse] around again, and did not repair directly to the longed for forest. //5.22//

sa jarā-maraṇa-kṣayaṁ cikīrṣur vana-vāsāya matiṁ smṛtau nidhāya /
praviveśa punaḥ puraṁ na kāmād vana-bhūmer iva maṇḍalaṁ dvipendraḥ // 5.23 //
Desiring to put an end to aging and dying, he had – while remaining mindful – directed his thinking towards living in the forest, / And yet he reluctantly re-entered the city, like a mighty elephant from the jungle entering a ring. //5.23//

sukhitā bata nirvṛtā ca sā strī patir īdṛkśa ih' āyatākṣa yasyāḥ /
iti taṁ samudīkṣya rāja-kanyā praviśantaṁ pathi sāñjalir jagāda // 5.24 //
"Made happy, alas, and *nirvṛtā,* perfectly contented, is the woman whose husband is such as you are here, O one of lengthened eyes!" / Thus, on seeing him entering, did a young princess exclaim, as she watched by the road with her hollowed hands joined. //5.24//

atha ghoṣam imaṁ mahābhra-ghoṣaḥ pariśuśrāva śamaṁ paraṁ ca lebhe /
śrutavān sa hi nirvṛteti śabdaṁ parinirvāṇa-vidhau matiṁ cakāra // 5.25 //
Then, he of battle-cry like roaring thunder-cloud, listened to this cry of woe, and experienced a calmness most profound; / For as he heard the word *nirvṛtā,* "perfectly contented," he set his mind on the matter of *pari-nirvāṇa* – the happiness of complete extinction.[9] //5.25//

atha kāñcana-śaila-śṛṅga-varṣmā gaja-megha-rṣabha-bāhu-nisvanākṣaḥ /
kṣayam akṣaya-dharma-jāta-rāgaḥ śaśi-siṁhānana-vikramaḥ prapede // 5.26 //
Then, statuesque as a golden mountain peak, with the arms, voice, and eyes of an elephant, a cloud, and a bull, / Ardent desire having been aroused in him for [or by] something imperishable, he of moon-like faces and lion's paces entered the palace. //5.26//

mṛga-rāja-gatis-tato 'bhyagacchan nṛpatiṁ mantri-gaṇair upāsyamānam /
samitau marutām iva jvalantaṁ maghavantaṁ tri-dive sanat-kumāraḥ // 5.27 //
And so, going with the gait of a king of beasts, he approached the lord of men attended by his coveys of ministers, / Like "Fresh Prince" Sanat-kumāra in the third heaven approaching shining Indra among his retinue of storm-gods. //5.27//

praṇipatya ca sāñjalir babhāṣe diśa mahyaṁ nara-deva sādhv-anujñām /
parivivrajiṣāmi mokṣa-hetor niyato hy asya janasya viprayogaḥ // 5.28 //
Bowing down with hollowed hands joined, he said: "Grant me, O god among men, proper assent! / I desire to go wandering, for the sake of liberation, since, for a man such as I am, the invariable rule is separation." //5.28//

---

[9] *Nirvṛta* is from the root √*vṛ*, to stop, whereas *nirvāṇa* is from another root, for example, √*vā*, to blow; but in both words the prefix *nir-* suggests something having faded out. The prefix *pari-* adds the sense of completeness.

iti tasya vaco niśamya rājā kariṇevābhihato drumaś cacāla /
kamala-pratime 'ñjalau gṛhītvā vacanaṁ cedam uvāca bāṣpa-kaṇṭhaḥ // 5.29 //
The king, hearing these words of his, shook like a tree assaulted by an elephant; / He grasped the hands that were folded like a lotus and spoke, in a voice choked with tears, as follows: //5.29//

pratisaṁhara tāta buddhim etāṁ na hi kālas tava dharma-saṁśrayasya /
vayasi prathame matau calāyāṁ bahu-doṣāṁ hi vadanti dharma-caryām // 5.30 //
"Put off this idea, my son; it is not time for you to be united with your dharma. / For early in life when the mind is changeable there are, they say, many pitfalls in the practice of dharma. //5.30//

viṣayeṣu kutūhalendriyasya vrata-khedeṣv asamartha-niścayasya /
taruṇasya manaś calaty araṇyād anabhijñasya viśeṣato viveke // 5.31 //
When his curious senses reach out to objects, when in the face of wearying observances he lacks fixity of purpose, / When, above all, he is not accustomed to seclusion, the mind of one who is young veers away from the wasteland. //5.31//

mama tu priya-dharma dharma-kālas tvayi lakṣmīm avasṛjya lakṣa-bhūte /
sthira-vikrama vikrameṇa dharmas tava hitvā tu guruṁ bhaved adharmaḥ // 5.32 //
For me, O lover of dharma! it is time for religious dharma – after I have surrendered to you, the apple of my eye, the apple of my royal power. / But for you, O firmly striding force! After you have forcibly forsaken your own father, religious dharma might turn into irreligion. //5.32//

tad imaṁ vyavasāyam utsṛja tvaṁ bhava tāvan nirato gṛha-stha-dharme /
puruṣasya vayaḥ-sukhāni bhuktvā ramaṇīyo hi tapo-vana-praveśaḥ // 5.33 //
Therefore give up this fixity of purpose and be, for the present moment, devoted to the dharma that abides in living at home; / For when a man has already experienced the joys of vernal energy, his entry then into the ascetic's grove is something to delight in." //5.33//

iti vākyam idaṁ niśamya rājñaḥ kalaviṅka-svara uttaraṁ babhāṣe /
yadi me pratibhūś caturṣu rājan bhavasi tvaṁ na tapo-vanaṁ śrayiṣye // 5.34 //
Having heard these words of the king, he with the voice of a *kalaviṇka* bird[10] spoke his reply: / "If in four things, O king, you will be my guarantor, I will not go to the ascetic grove – //5.34//

na bhaven maraṇāya jīvitaṁ me viharet svāsthyam idaṁ ca me na rogaḥ /
na ca yauvanam ākṣipej jarā me na ca saṁpattim imām hared vipattiḥ // 5.35 //
My life shall not lead to death; no breakdown shall put asunder my present state of soundness; / Growing old shall not take away my youthfulness; and going wrong shall not impinge upon what presently goes well."[11] //5.35//

---

[10] Famed for its beautiful song.

iti dur-labham artham ūcivāṁsaṁ tanayaṁ vākyam uvāca śākya-rājaḥ /
tyaja buddhim imāṁ ati-pravṛttām avahāsyo 'ti-mano-ratha-kramaś ca // 5.36 //
To the son who had expressed such a difficult purport,[12] the Śākya king told his command: / "Abandon this idea, which goes too far! A way of high-flown fancy is ridiculous." //5.36//

atha meru-gurur guruṁ babhāṣe yadi nāsti krama eṣa nāsmi vāryaḥ /
śaraṇāj jvalanena dahyamānān na hi niścikramiṣum kṣamaṁ grahītum // 5.37 //
Then he who had the moment of Mount Meru addressed his momentous relative: "Whether or not this turns out to be a way, I ought not to be held back; / For when a house is being consumed by fire it is not right to stop a man who seeks a way out. //5.37//

jagataś ca yathā dhruvo viyogo nanu dharmāya varaṁ svayaṁ viyogaḥ /
avaśaṁ nanu viprayojayen mām akṛta-svārtham atṛptam eva mṛtyuḥ // 5.38 //
Again, since for the living world separation is the immutable constant, is it not better for the separation to be willingly done for dharma's sake? / Will not death, whether I like it or not, separate me, leaving me unsatisfied, the doing of my own thing being unfinished?" //5.38//

iti bhūmi-patir niśamya tasya vyavasāyaṁ tanayasya nirmumukṣoḥ /
abhidhāya na yāsyatīti bhūyo vidadhe rakṣaṇam uttamāṁś ca kāmān // 5.39 //
A lord of the earth, thus perceiving the fixity of purpose of his freedom-seeking son, / Declared "He shall not go!" And he provided him with an increased guard, along with the most exquisite objects of desire. //5.39//

sacivais tu nidarśito yathāvad bahu-mānāt praṇayāc ca śāstra-pūrvam /
guruṇā ca nivārito 'śru-pātaiḥ praviveśāvasathaṁ tataḥ sa śocan // 5.40 //
Apprised, following protocol, by ministers, with great respect and affection and with reference to sacred books; / While forbidden by his father, with falling tears, he went then into his lodging quarters, sorrowing. //5.40//

cala-kuṇḍala-cumbitānanābhir ghana-niśvāsa-vikampita-stanībhiḥ /
vanitābhir adhīra-locanābhir mṛga-śāvābhir ivābhyudīkṣyamāṇaḥ // 5.41 //
Women whose swaying ear-rings lightly kissed their mouths, and whose deep sighs caused their breasts[13] to tremble, / Watched him with skittish eyes, like young does, looking up. //5.41//

---

[11] On the surface, the prince is asking the king to guarantee what could never be, since all lives lead to death. Below the surface, the irony is that the Buddha would in fact obtain the nectar of immortality. And a deeper irony still might be that obtaining the nectar of immortality would itself be a kind of dying. Similarly for the other three conditions.

[12] Ostensibly *dur-labham artham* means a thing that is hard to do; below the surface *dur-labham artham* might be meaning that is hard to grasp.

[13] *Stana* means the female breast (either human or animal), teat, udder - a part of mammalian anatomy to which Aśvaghoṣa keeps coming back.

sa hi kāñcana-parvatāvadāto hṛdayonmāda-karo varāṅganānām /
śravaṇāṅga-vilocanātmabhāvān vacana-sparśa-vapur-guṇair jahāra // 5.42 //
For he with the luminance of a golden mountain, he who unhinged beautiful women's hearts, / Carried away their ears, bodies, eyes, and souls, with his speech, sensitivity, handsome form, and excellent qualities. //5.42//

vigate divase tato vimānaṁ vapuṣā sūrya iva pradīpyamānaḥ /
timiraṁ vijighāṁsur ātma-bhāsā ravir udyann iva merum āruroha // 5.43 //
Then, when day was done, blazing like the sun with his handsome form, / The one who would by his own brightness dispel darkness ascended the palace, like the rising sun ascending Mount Meru.[14] //5.43//

kanakojjvala-dīpta-dīpa-vṛkṣaṁ vara-kālāguru-dhūpa-pūrṇa-garbham /
adhiruhya sa vajra-bhakti-citraṁ pravaraṁ kāñcanam āsanaṁ siṣeve // 5.44 //
Rising above, [he sat seated within] a light-tree that blazed with golden brightness, a womb filled with the finest fragrance of *kālāguru*, 'impenetrable lightness,' / And streaked with dotted lines of diamonds - he occupied a most excellent seat [or practiced most excellent sitting], made of gold.[15] //5.44//

tata uttamam uttamāṅganās taṁ niśi tūryair upatasthur indra-kalpam /
himavac-chirasīva candra-gaure draviṇendrātmajam apsaro-gaṇaughāḥ // 5.45 //
Then the upmost of women, accompanied by musical instruments, waited in the night on him the upmost man, a man to rival Indra; / They waited on him like cumuli of celestial nymphs waiting on the son of the Lord of Wealth up upon a moon-white Himālayan peak. //5.45//

paramair api divya-tūrya-kalpaiḥ sa tu tair naiva ratiṁ yayau na harṣam /
paramārtha-sukhāya tasya sādhor abhiniścikramiṣā yato na reme // 5.46 //
But even those ultimate instruments, on a par with heavenly harps, gave him no pleasure nor any joy. / His desire, as a sincere man going straight for his goal, was to get out, in pursuit of the happiness of ultimate riches; and therefore he was not in the mood for play. //5.46//

---

[14] *Āruroha* means he ascended, he went up. The upward direction is given further emphasis by *adhiruhya* in the next verse, and *uttamam* in the next verse but one.

[15] *Kanaka*, *ujjvala*, and *dīpta* in the first pāda, and *kāñcana* in the fourth pāda, as nouns, can all mean gold. Ostensibly Aśvaghoṣa is describing a golden seat (*kāñcanam āsanam*), but *āsana* is originally an *-na* neuter action noun that means "sitting." A *dīpa-vṛkṣam* ("light-tree") ostensibly means a candlestick, but in the hidden meaning a tree of light and golden sitting might be synonymous. *Kālāguru* was the proper name for a kind of black aloe wood, but *kālāguru* (*kāla* + *a-guru*) literally means a lightness (*a-guru*) that is black or dark (*kāla*), i.e. difficult to see distinctly or impenetrable. Wrapping up the possible allusion to sitting practice itself are the streaks of dotted lines of diamonds (*vajra-bhakti-citra*) which may suggest the needlework on the kaṣāya of the one who is sitting.

atha tatra surais tapo-variṣṭhair akaniṣṭhair vyavasāyam asya buddhvā /
yugapat pramadā-janasya nidrā vihitāsīd vikṛtāś ca gātra-ceṣṭāḥ // 5.47 //
At that juncture, the *a-kaniṣṭha* gods, the doyens of asceticism 'of whom none is youngest,' being acquainted with his fixity of purpose, / Visited, upon all the young women at once, deep sleep, and upon the women's bodies and limbs, irregular poses.[16] //5.47//

abhavac chayitā hi tatra kā-cid viniveśya pracale kare kapolam /
dayitām api rukma-pattra-citrāṁ kupitevāṅka-gatāṁ vihāya vīṇām // 5.48 //
There was one girl there, for instance, who slept with her cheek resting on a precarious hand, / Her cherished lute, brightly decorated with gold-leaf, lying by her lap as if cast aside in anger.[17] //5.48//

vibabhau kara-lagna-veṇur anyā stana-visrasta-sitāṁśukā śayānā /
ṛju-ṣaṭ-pada-paṅkti-juṣṭa-padmā jala-phena-prahasat-taṭā nadīva // 5.49 //
Another individual,[18] clasping her bamboo flute in her hand, as she slept with a white robe slipping down from her breast, / Resembled a river where a line of orderly bees is visiting a lotus – a river where foam from the water is giving the shore a white smile.[19] //5.49//

nava-puṣkara-garbha-komalābhyāṁ tapanīyojjvala-saṁgatāṅgadābhyām /
svapiti sma tathāparā bhujābhyāṁ parirabhya priyavan mṛdaṅgam eva // 5.50 //
With her two arms as soft as the sepals of young lotuses, with her two arms whose blazing golden bands[20] had merged together, / Slept an individual who thus was different, embracing, as if it were a beloved friend, nothing more or less than a drum.[21] //5.50//

---

[16] *Vikṛta* means changed but especially changed for the worst – deformed, disfigured, abnormal. *Vikṛta* can also mean unnatural, strange, extraordinary. So the ostensible meaning is that the women were sleeping in grotesque forms. But in the hidden meaning which emerges from the following fourteen verses, each different individual was letting her own light shine, without trying to make herself meet any external or internal norm of "correct posture."

[17] A parody of a monk who has dropped off next to a begging bowl that resembles the body of a large-bellied lute?

[18] *Anyā*, one who is different. One who does not necessarily conform to expectations.

[19] To explain the simile: the woman resembles a flowing river; the line of bees correspond to the bamboo flute, and the lotus to the woman's hand; the white foam along the shore corresponds to the white robe. What is harder to understand, however, is the point of the metaphor – what connection is intended between a beautiful scene in nature and a pose that has been described as irregular, or grotesque (*vikṛta*)?

[20] For soft arms see also BC4.30. Golden cuffs or golden arm-bands are a recurring theme (see also verses 54 and 81). Is the suggestion of unhindered circulation when shoulders, elbows, and wrists are free?

[21] Like the expanded belly of a Happy Buddha? For expanded belly, see also BC3.41.

nava-hāṭaka-bhūṣaṇās tathānyā vasanaṁ pītam anuttamaṁ vasānāḥ /
avaśā vata nidrayā nipetur gaja-bhagnā iva karṇikāra-śākhāḥ // 5.51 //
Other individuals who, similarly, were different, who, wearing their peerless yellow garments, lent beauty to new-found gold from gold-rich Hāṭaka, / Dropped down helpless (alas!) under the influence of sleep, like Karṇikāra branches broken by an elephant.[22] //5.51//

avalaṁbya gavākṣa-pārśvam anyā śayitā cāpa-vibhugna-gātra-yaṣṭiḥ /
virarāja vilambi-cāru-hārā racitā toraṇa-śāla-bhañjikeva // 5.52 //
Another individual slept leaning against the side of a round window, her slender body curved like a bow; / She shone, entrancing in her pendulous splendour, like the breaker of a Śāla branch, sculpted in an arched gateway.[23] //5.52//

maṇi-kuṅḍala-daṣṭa-pattra-lekhaṁ mukha-padmaṁ vinataṁ tathāparasyāḥ /
śata-pattram ivārdha-vakra-nāḍaṁ sthita-kāraṇḍava-ghaṭṭitaṁ cakāśe // 5.53 //
With its streaks of scented make-up nibbled by jewelled ear-rings, the bowed lotus-face of one, again, who was different, / Looked a picture, like a lotus of many petals, with its stalk half rounded, that had been pecked and dunked by a perching duck.[24] //5.53//

aparāḥ śayitā yathopaviṣṭāḥ stana-bhārair avanamyamāna-gātrāḥ /
upaguhya parasparaṁ virejur bhuja-pāśais tapanīya-pārihāryaiḥ // 5.54 //
Other individuals, having dropped off as they sat, their bodies bowing down under the troy weight[25] of their breasts, / Shone forth, as they drew each other into a protective embrace, using the leashes of their arms, with golden cuffs. //5.54//

mahatīṁ parivādinīṁ ca kā-cid vanitāliṅgya sakhīm iva prasuptā /
vijughūrṇa calat-suvarṇa-sūtrā vadanenākula-yoktrakojjvalena // 5.55 //
One woman, who was far gone, embraced a large lute as if it were her confidante; / She rolled about, her golden strings trembling, and her face shining with the golden radiance of fastenings fallen into disarray.[26] //5.55//

---

[22] The suggestion is of sitting practitioners wearing ochre robes, all dropping off together body and mind.

[23] A particularly famous example of such a sculpture adorns an arched gateway to the great stupa commissioned by Aśoka at Sanchi. The point might be that it would be false always to associate beautiful form with symmetry. If when you sit, your right shoulder is lower than your left shoulder, don't fiddle about trying to put it right, you ignoramus – let it all be wrong!

[24] Neither should we strive, when sitting, to push and pull anything into what we feel to be upright alignment. The point is to drop off body and mind, not to simulate perfect physical form. Thus Aśvaghoṣa here might be praising the beauty of one who does not sit bolt upright but whose back is naturally somewhat rounded.

[25] *Bhāra* means weight in general, but a particular weight (20 *tulās*) of gold.

[26] A metaphor for coming undone, i.e. for the *undoing* of needless tensions?

paṇavaṁ yuvatir bhujāṁsa-deśād avavisraṁsita-cāru-pāśam anyā /
sa-vilāsa-ratānta-tāntam ūrvor vivare kāntam ivābhinīya śiśye // 5.56 //
Another young woman had close to her a portable drum, whose impeccable strap she had let slip down from her shoulder.[27] / As if the drum were her breathless beloved, at the end of playful enjoyment, she had brought it into the open space between her thighs, and dropped off. //5.56//

aparā na babhur nimīlitākṣyo vipulākṣyo 'pi śubha-bhruvo 'pi satyaḥ /
pratisaṁkucitāravinda-kośāḥ savitary astam ite yathā nalinyaḥ // 5.57 //
Different women, though truly they had large eyes and beautiful brows, did not make a pretty sight,[28] with their eyes closed, / Like lotus ponds with their lotus buds closed at the setting of the sun. //5.57//

śithilākula-mūrdhajā tathānyā jaghana-srasta-vibhūṣaṇāṁśu-kāntā /
aśayiṣṭa vikīrṇa-kaṇṭha-sūtrā gaja-bhagnā pratiyātan'-āṅganeva // 5.58 //
One adorable woman, similarly, was otherwise: decorative threads had fallen from her hips, and her hair was undone and dishevelled [or her thoughts were occupied with undoing].[29] / She had dropped off, sending her necklaces scattering [or propagating the Neck Sūtra], like a statue-woman, broken by elephants.[30] //5.58//

aparās tv avaśā hriyā viyuktā dhṛti-matyo 'pi vapur-guṇair upetāḥ /
viniśaśvasur ulbaṇaṁ śayānā vikṛtāḥ kṣipta-bhujā jajṛmbhire ca // 5.59 //
Contrary ones, meanwhile, helplessly and shamelessly – possessed though they were of self-command and personal graces – / Exhaled, in their repose, in a manner that was extra-ordinary and unreasonable; and, in irregular fashion, their arms moving impulsively, they stretched out.[31] //5.59//

vyapaviddha-vibhūṣaṇa-srajo 'nyā visṛtāgranthana-vāsaso visaṁjñāḥ /
animīlita-śukla-niścalākṣyo na virejuḥ śayitā gatāsu-kalpāḥ // 5.60 //
Different individuals, leaving trinkets jettisoned and garlands trashed, unconsciously, in robes of undone knots, / With their bright, motionless eyes open, displayed no beauty, reposing there like women who had breathed their last. //5.60//

---

[27] For a monk to carry his or her bowl using a shoulder strap is traditional behavior.

[28] *Na babhur* means they did not shine. The ostensible meaning is they looked bad. But the real meaning might be that they made no effort to look good – just as a beautiful lotus pond makes no effort, but looks fine whatever happens.

[29] Ostensibly *ākula* means "disheveled" but it can also mean "eagerly occupied." *Mūrdha-ja* (lit. "head-born" or "begotten from the head") ostensibly means the hair that grows on the head but its hidden meaning might be thinking that is conceived in the head.

[30] The original meaning of *sūtra* is string or thread, as in a string of pearls. The breaking of a statue might be a metaphor for breaking the fixed conception of correct posture – as preached in the Sūtra of Liberation of the Neck.

[31] What is spontaneous movement? The behavior of the ignorant who just do whatever they like, without self-restraint? Or the behavior of the enlightened who just do whatever they like, without self-restraint? The matter is discussed, with reference to the non-buddha, in Shōbōgenzō chap. 28, *Butsu-kojo-no-ji.*

vivṛtāsya-puṭā vivṛddha-gātrī prapatad-vaktra-jalā prakāśa-guhyā /
aparā mada-ghūrṇiteva śiśye na babhāse vikṛtaṁ vapuḥ pupoṣa // 5.61 //
With her oral cavity open and her legs spreading out, so that she sprayed saliva, and made visible what normally remains secret, / One very different one had dropped off; rocking somewhat in her intoxication, she did not make a pretty sight, but filled an irregular frame.[32] //5.61//

iti sattva-kulānvayānurūpaṁ vividhaṁ sa pramadā-janaḥ śayānaḥ /
sarasaḥ sadṛśaṁ babhāra rūpaṁ pavanāvarjita-rugna-puṣkarasya // 5.62 //
Thus, each in accordance with her nature and her lineage, that company of women – all reposing in diversity – / Bore the semblance of a lotus-pond whose lotuses had been bent down and broken by the wind. //5.62//

samavekṣya tathā tathā śayānā vikṛtās tā yuvatīr adhīra-ceṣṭāḥ /
guṇavad-vapuṣo 'pi valgu-bhāṣā nṛpa-sūnuḥ sa vigarhayāṁ babhūva // 5.63 //
Beholding them dropped off in irregular fashion, in this way and that, seeing the lack of constraint in the movement of their limbs, / Perfectly beautiful though those women were in their form, and beautifully dulcet in their speech, the son of the king was moved to scorn:[33] //5.63//

aśucir vikṛtaś ca jīva-loke vanitānām ayam īdṛśaḥ sva-bhāvaḥ /
vasanābharaṇais tu vañcyamānaḥ puruṣaḥ strī-viṣayeṣu rāgam eti // 5.64 //
"Impure and impaired – such, in the living world of men, is the nature of women. / And yet, deceived by clothes and accoutrements, a man is reddened with love for a woman's sensual charms.[34] //5.64//

vimṛśed yadi yoṣitāṁ manuṣyaḥ prakṛtiṁ svapna-vikāram īdṛśaṁ ca /
dhruvam atra na vardhayet pramādaṁ guṇa-saṁkalpa-hatas tu rāgam eti // 5.65 //
If a man reflected on women's original nature, and on how such change is wrought by sleep, / Surely by these means he would not be making intoxication grow. Smitten by a notion of excellence, however, he is moved to redness."[35] //5.65//

---

[32] In the last of these fourteen verses, the gap between ostensible and hidden meaning is stretched to the limit. Ostensibly the scene portrayed is disgusting: saliva is being sprayed out from the open mouth of an ignorant one who is asleep. In the hidden meaning, the spraying might be going on inside the oral cavity of a conspicuously healthy person who is free of undue tension. Ostensibly a woman is unconsciously revealing her private parts. In the hidden meaning, a buddha might be revealing secrets of the Buddha's teaching.

[33] The scorn, in a superficial reading, is directed towards women.

[34] On a deeper reading, the prince's scorn is directed towards men who are slaves to sensual desire for women who in their imperfect (impure and impaired) reality, really are beautiful.

[35] Ostensibly the allusion is to "impurity meditation." In a deeper reading, could the reflection in question be reflection on the buddha-nature?

iti tasya tad-antaraṁ viditvā niśi niścikramiṣā samudbabhūva /
avagamya manas tato 'sya devair bhavana-dvāram apāvṛtaṁ babhūva // 5.66 //
When he had seen this deficiency in the other,[36] the desire sprang up in him to escape in the night; / Whereupon, under the influence of gods, who were steeped in this mind,[37] the entrance of the palace was found to be wide open. [Or the way to freedom from existence was seen to be wide open.][38] //5.66//

atha so 'vatatāra harmya-pṛṣṭhād yuvatīs tāḥ śayitā vigarhamāṇaḥ /
avatīrya tataś ca nirviśaṅko gṛha-kakṣyāṁ prathamaṁ vinirjagāma // 5.67 //
And so he descended from the palace heights scorning those women who were asleep, / And thus, having descended, being quite without doubt, he went directly into the outer courtyard.[39] //5.67//

turagāvacaraṁ sa bodhayitvā javinaṁ chandakam ittham ity uvāca /
hayam ānaya kanthakaṁ tvarāvān amṛtaṁ prāptum ito 'dya me yiyāsā // 5.68 //
He woke that ready runner of the fleet of foot, the stableman Chandaka, and addressed him as follows: / "Bring me in haste the horse Kanthaka! I wish today to flee from here, in order to obtain the nectar of immortality. //5.68//

hṛdi yā mama tuṣṭir adya jātā vyavasāyaś ca yathā dhṛtau niviṣṭaḥ /
vijane 'pi ca nāthavān ivāsmi dhruvam artho 'bhimukhaḥ sa me ya iṣṭaḥ // 5.69 //
Since there has arisen today in my heart a certain satisfaction,[40] since strenuous fixity of purpose has settled down into a contented constancy, / And since even in solitude I feel as if I am in the presence of a protector, assuredly, the valuable object to which I aspire is smiling upon me. //5.69//

hriyam eva ca saṁnatiṁ ca hitvā śayitā mat-pramukhe yathā yuvatyaḥ /
vivṛte ca yathā svayaṁ kapāṭe niyataṁ yātum anāmayāya kālaḥ // 5.70 //
As the women, abandoning all shame and submission, relaxed in front of me; / And as the doors opened, spontaneously, it is doubtless time to depart, in pursuit of wellness." //5.70//

---

[36] Ostensibly the deficiency is the impurity of women; in the deeper meaning, the deficiency is in the attachment to sensual passion of men.

[37] In the hidden meaning, the gods are cosmic observers of irony. Therefore they are steeped in the mind which sees its own faults not in itself but in the other.

[38] A play on *bhavana*, whose meanings include "palace" and "place of growth" and "coming into existence"?

[39] In the hidden meaning, in being without doubt is the prince committing the sin of certainty? In scorning others who are asleep, is it the prince himself who is not yet awake?

[40] Ostensibly the prince is demonstrating the virtue of contentment, but in the hidden meaning he might still be demonstrating the sin of religious certainty.

pratigṛhya tataḥ sa bhartur ājñāṁ viditārtho 'pi narendra-śāsanasya /
manasīva pareṇa codyamānas tura-gasyānayane matiṁ cakāra // 5.71 //
Chandaka acquiesced, on those grounds, in his master's wisdom – though he knew the meaning of a king's command – / And he made the decision, as if his mind were being moved by another, to bring the horse. //5.71//

atha hema-khalīna-pūrṇa-vaktraṁ laghu-śayyāstaraṇopagūḍha-pṛṣṭham /
bala-sattva-javānvay'-opapannaṁ sa varāśvaṁ tam upāninAya bhartre // 5.72 //
And so one whose mouth was filled with a golden bit, one whose back was overspread by the instant refuge of a light covering of cloth,[41] / One endowed with strength, spirit, quickness and pedigree – a most excellent horse he brought out for the master. //5.72//

pratata-trika-puccha-mūla-pārṣṇiṁ nibhṛtaṁ hrasva-tanūja-pṛṣṭha-karṇam /
vinat'-onnata-pṛṣṭha-kukṣi-pārśvaṁ vipula-protha-lalāṭa-kaṭy-uraskam // 5.73 //
His tail, supports, and heels formed spreading triangles; the mane around his crown and ears was closely cropped, in an unassuming manner; / The curves of his back, belly and sides wound downward and wound upward; his horse's nostrils expanded, as did his forehead, hips and chest.[42] //5.73//

upagṛhya sa taṁ viśāla-vakṣāḥ kamalābhena ca sāntvayan kareṇa /
madhurākṣarayā girā śaśāsa dhvajinī-madhyam iva praveṣṭu-kāmaḥ // 5.74 //
He whose chest was broad reached up and drew him to himself; then, while comforting with a lotus-like hand, / He bade him with a song of soothing noises, as might a warrior when preparing to go, where banners fly, into the middle: //5.74//

bahuśaḥ kila śatravo nirastāḥ samare tvām adhiruhya pārthivena /
aham apy amṛtaṁ padaṁ yathāvat turaga-śreṣṭha labheya tat kuruṣva // 5.75 //
"Often indeed has a lord of the earth expelled enemies while riding in battle on you! / So that I too might realise the deathless step, please, O best of horses, act! //5.75//

su-labhāḥ khalu saṁyuge sahāyā viṣayāvāpta-sukhe dhanārjane vā /
puruṣasya tu dur-labhāḥ sahāyāḥ patitasyāpadi dharma-saṁśraye vā // 5.76 //
Readily indeed are companions found when the battle is joined, or in the happiness at the gaining of the end, when the booty is acquired; / But companions are hard for a man to find when he is getting into trouble – or when he is turning to dharma. //5.76//

iha caiva bhavanti ye sahāyāḥ kaluṣe karmaṇi dharma-saṁśraye vā /
avagacchati me yathāntar-ātmā niyataṁ te 'pi janās tad-aṁśa-bhājaḥ // 5.77 //
There again, all in this world who are companions, whether in tainted doing or in devotion to dharma, / Living beings without exception – as my inner self intuits – are entitled to their share of the prize. //5.77//

---

[41] In the hidden meaning, a *kaṣāya*, an ochre robe.
[42] Ostensibly, a description of the horse; in the hidden meaning, of a master.

tad idaṁ parigamya dharma-yuktaṁ mama niryāṇam ato jagadd-hitāya /
turagottama vega-vikramābhyāṁ prayatasv ātma-hite jagadd-hite ca // 5.78 //
Fully appreciate, then, this act of mine, yoked to dharma, of getting out, proceeding from here, for the welfare of the world; / And exert yourself, O best of horses, with quick and bold steps, for your own good and the good of the world." //5.78//

iti suhṛdam ivānuśiṣya kṛtye turaga-varaṁ nṛ-varo vanaṁ yiyāsuḥ /
sitam asita-gati-dyutir vapuṣmān ravir iva śāradam abhram āruroha // 5.79 //
Having thus exhorted the best of horses, as if exhorting a friend to his duty, and desiring to ride into the forest, / The best of men with his handsome form, bright as fire, climbed aboard the white horse, like the sun aboard an autumn cloud, up above. //5.79//

atha sa pariharan niśītha-caṇḍaṁ parijana-bodha-karaṁ dhvaniṁ sad-aśvaḥ /
vigata-hanu-ravaḥ praśānta-heṣaś-cakita-vimukta-pada-kramo jagāma // 5.80 //
And so, avoiding the noise that stridently attacks slumber, avoiding the noise that makes people all around wake up,[43] / Being through with sputtering, the fires of his neighing all extinguished, that good horse, with footsteps liberated from timidity, set off. //5.80//

kanaka-valaya-bhūṣita-prakoṣṭhaiḥ kamala-nibhaiḥ kamalān iva pravidhya /
avanata-tanavas tato 'sya yakṣāś cakita-gatair dadhire khurān karāgraiḥ // 5.81 //
Bowing *yakṣas*, their wrists adorned with golden bands, their lotus-like hands seeming to emit sprays of lotus flowers, / Their lotus-petal fingertips coyly trembling, then bore up that horse's hooves. //5.81//

guru-parigha-kapāṭa-saṁvṛtā yā na sukham api dvi-radair apāvriyante /
vrajati nṛpa-sute gata-svanās tāḥ svayam abhavan vivṛtāḥ puraḥ pratolyaḥ // 5.82 //
Primary pathways were blocked by gates with heavy bars [or by gates whose bars were gurus][44] – gates not easily opened, even by elephants – / But as the prince went into movement, those major arteries, noiselessly and spontaneously, became open. //5.82//

pitaram abhimukhaṁ sutaṁ ca bālaṁ janam anuraktam anuttamāṁ ca lakṣmīm /
kṛta-matir apahāya nir-vyapekṣaḥ pitṛ-nagarāt sa tato vinirjagāma // 5.83 //
The father who doted on him, a son who was still young; the people who loved him; and an incomparable fortune – / With his mind made up and without a care, he had left them all behind, and so, on that basis, from the city of his fathers, away he went. //5.83//

---

[43] In the hidden meaning what is denied might be the sense of compulsion – making people wake up in the sense of trying to force them to wake up, by direct, unskillful means.

[44] As an adjective, *guru* means heavy. As a noun it means a venerable or respectable person, like a father or a teacher, and especially a spiritual preceptor.

atha sa vikaja-paṅkajāyatākṣaḥ puram avalokya nanāda siṁha-nādam /
janana-maraṇayor adṛṣṭa pāro na punar ahaṁ kapilāhvayaṁ praveṣṭā // 5.84 //
Then he with the lengthened eyes of a lotus – one born of mud, not of water[45] – surveyed the city and roared a lion's roar: / "Until I have seen the far shore of birth and death I shall never again enter the city named after Kapila." //5.84//

iti vacanam idaṁ niśamya tasya draviṇa-pateḥ pariṣad-gaṇā nananduḥ /
pramudita-manasaś ca deva-saṅghā vyavasita-pāraṇam āśaśaṁsire 'smai // 5.85 //
Having heard this declaration of his, the yakṣa cohorts sitting around Kubera, Lord of Wealth, rejoiced; / And jubilant sanghas[46] of gods conveyed to him the expectation that a resolution must be carried through to the end. //5.85//

huta-vaha-vapuṣo divaukaso 'nye vyavasitam asya ca duṣkaraṁ viditvā /
akuruta tuhine pathi prakāśaṁ ghana-vivara-praṣṛtā ivendu-pādāḥ // 5.86 //
Sky-dwellers of a different ilk,[47] with fiery forms, knowing how difficult his resolution was to do, / Produced on his dewy path a brightness like moon-beams issuing through chinks in the clouds. //5.86//

hari-turaga-turaṅgavat-turaṅgaḥ sa tu vicaran manasīva codyamānaḥ /
aruṇa-paruṣa-tāram antar-ikṣaṁ sa ca su-bahūni jagāma yojanāni // 5.87 //
With the one in question, as quick as the bay horse of Indra, moving swiftly on, as if being spurred in his mind, / The one in question[48] rode into the dawn sky, where ruddy Aruṇa[49] tarnishes the stars, and a good many miles he went. //5.87//

iti buddha-carite mahā-kāvye 'bhiniṣkramaṇo nāma pañcamaḥ sargaḥ // 5 //
The 5th canto, titled "Getting Well & Truly Out,"
in an epic tale of awakened action.

---

[45] *Paṅkaja*, "mud-born," means a lotus. *Vikaja* can be read as not (*vi*) water (*ka*) born (*ja*) – in which case the point might be to emphasize that the bodhisattva was not only an ideal archetype but also a real human being.

[46] Here is one of several examples of Aśvaghoṣa using the word *saṁgha* to mean a group or a religious congregation. It is remarkable that Aśvaghoṣa never once uses the word saṁgha in the conventional sense of a community of devotees of the Buddha – though he does describe the Buddha leading Nanda to a *vihāra*.

[47] Once again *anye* indicates individuals who were different. The religious congregations of gods in heaven were one kind of sky-dweller, burdening the bodhisattva with their expectation. These were sky-dwellers of a different ilk – perhaps they were real fireflies?

[48] The subject of each line is *sa*, he, that one. But was the one in question the prince, Sarvārtha-siddha? Or was the one in question the horse, Kanthaka?

[49] Dawn personified.

Canto 6: chandaka-nivartanaḥ
Chandaka & Turning Back

Introduction

The ostensible title of the present canto is Turning Chandaka Back, so that it describes the Prince sending the horseman Chandaka back to Kapilavāstu.

Below the surface, however, the verb *ni-√vṛt*, to turn back, to stop, has deep meaning in the Buddha's teaching as Aśvaghoṣa records it. Hence in Saundarananda Canto 16, the Buddha tells Nanda:

Comprehend, therefore, that suffering is doing; witness the faults impelling it forward;
Realise its stopping as non-doing; and know the path as a turning back (*nivartakam*). // SN16.42 //

tato muhūrtābhyudite jagac-cakṣuṣi bhās-kare /
bhārgavasyāśrama-padaṁ sa dadarśa nṛṇāṁ varaḥ // 6.1 //
Then at the instant of the rising of the light-producing eye of the world, / The ashram of a son of Bhṛgu[1] he the best of men did see. //6.1//

supta-viśvasta-hariṇaṁ svastha-sthita-vihaṅgamam /
viśrānta iva yad dṛṣṭvā kṛtārtha iva cābhavat // 6.2 //
Deer there breathed easy, in unsuspecting sleep, and birds perched with self-assurance – / On seeing which he seemed reposed, like one who has been successful. //6.2//

sa vismaya-nivṛtty arthaṁ tapaḥ-pūjārtham eva ca /
svāṁ cānuvartitāṁ rakṣann aśva-pṛṣṭhād avātarat // 6.3 //
As an act of inhibition of pride, and out of respect, yes, for ascetic endeavour, / While guarding his own submission,[2] he got down off the back of the horse. //6.3//

avatīrya ca pasparśa nistīrṇam iti vājinam /
chandakaṁ cābravīt prītaḥ snāpayann iva cakṣuṣā // 6.4 //
Having got down he patted the war-horse, saying "Well done," / And said to Chandaka, with joyful appreciation, as if bathing him in his eyes: //6.4//

---

[1] Bhṛgu was the name of a prominent family of the brahman, or priestly, class. The seer regarded as the ancestor of the family was also called Bhṛgu.

[2] The concept of *anuvartitā*, submissiveness or compliance, featured in Udāyin's speech (BC4.50, 4.67, 4.69) and the prince's reply (BC4.93). In this verse the ostensible meaning is that the prince maintained his submissiveness, i.e. he was polite. A deeper and more skeptical reading is that he withheld submission. In fact, at this stage, the prince is not prepared to submit to the principle of asceticism – this doesn't happen until the end of BC Canto 12.

imaṁ tārkṣyopama-javaṁ turaṅgam anugacchatā /
darśitā saumya mad-bhaktir vikramaś cāyam ātmanaḥ // 6.5 //
"By following this horse as swift as Tārkṣya,[3] / O mellow man of soma, you have shown devotion to me. This, at the same time, is your own valiant doing. //6.5//

sarvathāsmy anya-kāryo 'pi gṛhīto bhavatā hṛdi /
bhartṛ-snehaś ca yasyāyam īdṛśī śaktir eva ca // 6.6 //
While altogether absorbed in alternative pursuit,[4] I am taken into the heart by you – / You who possess this allegiance to a master and at the same time such proactive power. //6.6//

a-snigdho 'pi samartho 'sti niḥ-sāmarthyo 'pi bhaktimān /
bhaktimāṁs caiva śaktaś ca durlabhas tvad-vidho bhuvi // 6.7 //
Some, while uncongenial, are capable; some, though ineffectual, are devoted; / One of your ilk, both devoted and able, is hard to find on this earth. //6.7//

tat prīto 'smi tavānena mahā-bhāgena karmaṇā /
dṛśyate mayi bhāvo 'yaṁ phalebhyo 'pi parāṅ-mukhe // 6.8 //
Therefore I am gladdened by this most magnificent action of yours. / This attitude towards me is conspicuous, turned away while I am from rewards.[5] //6.8//

ko janasya phala-sthasya na syād abhimukho janaḥ /
janī-bhavati bhūyiṣṭhaṁ sva-jano 'pi viparyaye // 6.9 //
What person would not tend to turn his face in the direction of a person who offers promise of reward? / Even one's own people become, on the whole, part of common humankind, in the event of a turnaround in the opposite direction.[6] //6.9//

kulārthaṁ dhāryate putraḥ poṣārthaṁ sevyate pitā /
āśayāc chliṣyati jagan nāsti niṣkāraṇāsvatā // 6.10 //
For the sake of continuing a line, a son is maintained; on account of his nurturing of growth, a father is served; / Living beings cohere because of an agenda – there is no unselfishness without a cause.[7] //6.10//

---

[3] Tārkṣya is described in the Ṛg-veda as a swift horse, but also taken to be a bird and later (e.g. in the Mahā-bhārata) identified with Garuda. Is the prince praising Chandaka for the kind of submissive following that co-exists with initiative – as the passive and active co-exist in the *samādhi* of accepting and using the self?

[4] Ostensibly by *anya-kārya* "other work," the prince is apologizing for his mind having been on other things. In the hidden meaning, *anya* might express the principle of truly alternative pursuit, as a thinking and non-thinking individual.

[5] Being *phalebhyaḥ parāṅ-mukhaḥ*, turned away from rewards, may be taken as an amplification of the meaning of *anya*, being different, in verse 6.

[6] A possible hidden meaning relates to the *turning back* of the canto title. Ostensibly, when things turn out badly for ordinary people (one of whom Chandaka is not), even members of one's own family become just anybody. Is the hidden meaning, e.g. that when a bodhisattva turns back towards her original nature, all human beings are already her own family?

[7] The ironic hidden meaning might be that having a true agenda liberates us from selfishness.

kim uktvā bahu saṁkṣepāt kṛtaṁ me sumahat-priyam /
nivartasvāśvam ādāya saṁprāpto 'smīpsitaṁ padam // 6.11 //
Why say much? It is a great kindness to me that you have, in a word, done. / Take the horse and turn back! I have arrived where I wanted to be." //6.11//

ity uktvā sa mahā-bāhur ānṛśaṁsa-cikīrṣayā /
bhūṣaṇāny avamucyāsmai saṁtapta-manase dadau // 6.12 //
Thus having spoken, he of mighty arm, desiring by his action to prevent what injures a man,[8] / Unloosened ornaments and gave them to him whose mind was inflamed with grief. //6.12//

mukuṭād dīpa-karmāṇaṁ maṇim ādāya bhāsvaram /
bruvan vākyam idaṁ tasthau sāditya iva mandaraḥ // 6.13 //
The shining pearl, which serves as a source of light, he took into his possession, from his crown, / And firmly he stood, speaking these words, like Mount Mandara[9] in the Aditi-begotten sun. //6.13//

anena maṇinā chanda praṇamya bahuśo nṛpaḥ /
vijñāpyo 'mukta-viśrambhaṁ saṁtāpa-vinivṛttaye // 6.14 //
"Using this pearl, Chanda, bow down repeatedly, / And, without loosening your grip on fearlessness,[10] commune with the protector of men[11] so that the fires of anguish may be turned back and extinguished. //6.14//

jarā-maraṇa-nāśārthaṁ praviṣṭo 'smi tapo-vanam /
na khalu svarga-tarṣeṇa nāsnehena na manyunā // 6.15 //
[Tell the king as follows:]
'For an end to aging and death, I have entered the ascetic woods; / Not out of any thirst for heaven, nor disaffectedly, nor with zealous ardour. //6.15//

tad evam abhiniṣkrāntaṁ na māṁ śocitum arhasi /
bhūtvāpi hi ciraṁ śleṣaḥ kālena na bhaviṣyati // 6.16 //
So you ought not to grieve for me who thus am well and truly gone; / Since any union, for however long it has existed, in time will cease to exist. //6.16//

---

[8] Ostensibly *ānṛśaṁsa-cikīrṣayā* means "desiring to do a kindness." But *a-nṛ-śaṁsa* (lit. not man-injuring) is originally negative, and brings to mind the preventive principle, which might be the true pearl.

[9] A sacred mountain said to have served the gods for a churning-stick with which to churn the ocean.

[10] *Viśrambha* means 1. loosening, relaxation; 2. confidence, trust; and 3. absence of restraint, familiarity. So *amukta-viśrambham* might be read as a paradoxical directive along the lines of *thinking the state of not-thinking* - e.g. "without loosening your grip on loosening" or "without letting go of coming undone."

[11] Ostensibly *vijñāpyaḥ* means "tell him" or "let him know." In the hidden meaning, the communication Aśvaghoṣa has in mind might be non-verbal.

dhruvo yasmāc ca viśleṣas tasmān mokṣāya me matiḥ /
viprayogaḥ kathaṁ na syād bhūyo 'pi sva-janād iti // 6.17 //
And since separation is certain therefore my mind is directed towards liberation / In order that, somehow, one might not be repeatedly dissevered from one's own people. //6.17//

śoka-tyāgāya niṣkrāntaṁ na māṁ śocitum arhasi /
śoka-hetuṣu kāmeṣu saktāḥ śocyās tu rāgiṇaḥ // 6.18 //
For me who has left, to leave sorrow behind, you ought not to sorrow. / Those stuck on sorrow-causing desires – those who carry the taint of redness – rather, are the ones to sorrow for. //6.18//

ayaṁ ca kila pūrveṣām asmākaṁ niścayaḥ sthiraḥ /
iti dāyādya-bhūtena na śocyo 'smi pathā vrajan // 6.19 //
And this, assuredly, was the firm resolve of our forebears! / Going, in this spirit, by a path akin to an inheritance, I am not to be sorrowed after. //6.19//

bhavanti hy artha-dāyādāḥ puruṣasya viparyaye /
pṛthivyāṁ dharma-dāyādāḥ durlabhās tu na santi vā // 6.20 //
For when a man experiences a reverse and comes to an end,[12] there are heirs to a thing of substance he possesses. / Dharma-heirs, however, on the earth, are hard to find, or else do not exist.[13] //6.20//

yad api syād asamaye yāto vanam asāv iti /
akālo nāsti dharmasya jīvite cañcale sati // 6.21 //
Though he might be said to have gone at a bad time to the forest, / In dharma, in truth, no bad time exists – life being as fickle as it is. //6.21//

tasmād adyaiva me śreyaś cetavyam iti niścayaḥ /
jīvite ko hi viśrambho mṛtyau praty-arthini sthite // 6.22 //
Therefore my conviction is that, this very day, the better state is there to be garnered in me. / For who can rely on lasting life while inimical death stands by?' //6.22//

evam-ādi tvayā saumya vijñāpyo vasudhādhipaḥ /
prayatethās tathā caiva yathā māṁ na smared api // 6.23 //
With words like these and otherwise,[14] my gentle friend, you are to commune with a ruler of the wealth-giving earth; / And may you endeavor further, so that he is not mindful of me at all.[15] //6.23//

---

[12] The meanings of *viparyaya* include turning round and coming to an end. The ostensible meaning here is coming to an end, i.e. dying. The hidden meaning may be as per verse 9.

[13] Ostensibly, the prince is thinking light of *artha*, wealth, things of substance, and assigning weight to religious dharma. Cf MMK24.8: *"The buddhas' teaching of dharma rests on two truths: the truth of the convenient fictions of the world, and ultimate truth (satyaṃ ca paramārthataḥ)."* But dharma-heirs on the ground are hard to find?

[14] In the hidden meaning, by both verbal and – more importantly – by non-verbal means.

[15] Ostensibly, so that he, the king, forgets about me, the prince. In a hidden meaning, so that he

api nairguṇyam asmākaṁ vācyaṁ nara-patau tvayā /
nairguṇyāt tyajyate snehaḥ sneha-tyāgān na śocyate // 6.24 //
Indeed, speak to the king of our being-without virtue.[16] / Because of the being-without virtue, attachment is abandoned.[17] Because of abandoning attachment, one does not suffer grief." //6.24//

iti vākyam idaṁ śrutvā chandaḥ saṁtāpa-viklavaḥ /
bāṣpa-grathitayā vācā pratyuvāca kṛtāñjaliḥ // 6.25 //
Having heard these words, the anguished Chanda, / With voice clogged with tears, as he stood with hands held together in a reverent posture, answered back: //6.25//

anena tava bhāvena bāndhavāyāsa-dāyinā /
bhartaḥ sīdati me ceto nadī-paṅka iva dvipaḥ // 6.26 //
"Because of this purport of yours, which so exercises those who are close to you,[18] / My heart, Master!, sinks, like an elephant into mud by a river. //6.26//

kasya notpādayed bāṣpaṁ niścayas te 'yam īdṛśaḥ /
ayo-maye 'pi hṛdaye kiṁ punaḥ sneha-viklave // 6.27 //
Who would not be moved to tears by a resolve such as this of yours, / Even with a heart made of iron? How much more with a heart befuddled by attachment? //6.27//

vimāna-śayanārhaṁ hi saukumāryam idaṁ kva ca /
khara-darbhāṅkuravatī tapo-vana-mahī kva ca // 6.28 //
For where could there co-exist this softness, fit for a bed in a palace, / And the ground of the ascetic forest, covered with hard blades of *darbha* grass?[19] //6.28//

śrutvā tu vyavasāyaṁ te yad aśvo 'yaṁ mayāhṛtaḥ /
balāt kāreṇa tan nātha daivenaivāsmi kāritaḥ // 6.29 //
But when I learned from you your purpose, Master, and I brought for you this horse, / I was caused to do it, inescapably, by a doing which really was divine. //6.29//

kathaṁ hy ātma-vaśo jānan vyavasāyam imaṁ tava /
upānayeyaṁ turagaṁ śokaṁ kapilavastunaḥ // 6.30 //
For how by my own will could I, knowing this purpose of yours, / Lead swift-going sorrow away from Kapilavastu[20]? //6.30//

---

drops off body and mind?

[16] Ostensibly, *nairguṇyam* means absence of virtue. The hidden meaning may be the virtue of being without – e.g. being without ignorance and associated doings, attachments, and so on.

[17] Ostensible meaning: when we see the faults in a loved one, attachment to that loved one diminishes. Is a hidden meaning related to fetter no. 3 of the ten fetters?

[18] *Āyāsa* mean 1. effort, exertion, 2. trouble, anguish. Ostensibly Chandaka means that what is in the prince's heart will cause anguish to his relatives. A hidden meaning may be that what is in the hearts and minds of buddhas and bodhisattvas encourages people around them to join in an effort.

[19] Ostensibly it is a rhetorical question. In the hidden meaning, is it a pointer to the condition in which hard and soft co-exist in harmony?

[20] In the ostensible meaning *kapilavastunaḥ* is genitive so that *turagaṁ śokaṁ kapilavastunaḥ* means

tan nārhasi mahā-bāho vihātuṁ putra-lālasam /
snigdhaṁ vṛddhaṁ ca rājānaṁ sad-dharmam iva nāstikaḥ // 6.31 //
Therefore, O man of mighty arm! The fond old king who is so devoted to his son / You should not forsake in the way that a nihilist forsakes true dharma.[21] //6.31//

saṁvardhana-pariśrāntāṁ dvitīyāṁ tāṁ ca mātaram
devīṁ nārhasi vismartuṁ kṛta-ghna iva sat-kriyām // 6.32 //
And the queen who exhausted herself bringing you up, your second mother – / You should not forget her in the way that an ingrate forgets the rendering of kindness.[22] //6.32//

bāla-putrāṁ guṇavatīṁ kula-ślāghyāṁ pati-vratām /
devīm arhasi na tyaktuṁ klībaḥ prāptām iva śriyam // 6.33 //
The princess, mother of your young son and possessor of her own virtues, who is laudable as a noble lady and loyal as a wife – / You should not leave her in the way that a sissy abdicates a high office he has assumed. //6.33//

putraṁ yāśodharaṁ ślāghyaṁ yaśo-dharma-bhṛtāṁ varam /
bālam arhasi na tyaktuṁ vyasanīvottamaṁ yaśaḥ // 6.34 //
The boy who is Yaśodhara's laudable son, a most excellent bearer of your glory and dharma – / You should not part from him in the way that a compulsive grafter forgoes ultimate glory. //6.34//

atha bandhuṁ ca rājyaṁ ca tyaktum eva kṛtā matiḥ /
māṁ nārhasi vibho tyaktuṁ tvat-pādau hi gatir mama // 6.35 //
Or else, if kith and kingdom you are determined to renounce, / Please, Master, do not abandon me – for your two feet are my refuge. //6.35//

nāsmi yātuṁ puraṁ śakto dahyamānena cetasā /
tvām araṇye parityajya sumantra iva rāghavam // 6.36 //
I am not able, with a mind that is burning, to go to the city, / Having left you behind in the woods – as Sumantra was unable to leave behind Raghu-descended Rāma.[23] //6.36//

"the horse, the bale/sorrow of Kapilavastu." In that case, Chandaka's question is "how could I have brought the horse to you?" In the hidden meaning, *kapilavastunaḥ* is ablative, so that *turagaṁ śokaṁ kapilavastunaḥ* means "swift-going sorrow from Kapilavastu." In that case Chandaka is asking about the means quickly to dispel sorrow. For example, is the means doing by one's own volition? Or is the means non-doing, in which the right thing seems to do itself?

[21] Ostensibly Chandaka is saying (falsely) that the prince should never leave the king at all. In a hidden meaning, is he saying (truly) that, when it comes to leaving home, the home-leaver should not leave in a misguided manner?

[22] Again, the hidden meaning may be that one *should* leave, but not like that.

[23] In the *Rāmāyaṇa*, Su-mantra (lit. 'Following Good Advice') is the name of a minister and charioteer of Rāma's father Daśa-ratha. In Canto 57 of the *Rāmāyaṇa*, titled The Return of Sumantra, the charioteer Sumantra does leave Rāma behind in the woods physically, but emotionally he does not.

kiṁ hi vakṣyati māṁ rājā tvad-ṛte nagaraṁ gatam /
vakṣyāmy ucita-darśitvāt kiṁ tavāntaḥ-purāṇi vā // 6.37 //
For what will the king express to me when I arrive in the city without you? / Again, what shall I express, based on seeing what is expedient, to the ones within the battlements, who belong to you?[24] //6.37//

yad apy ātthāpi nairguṇyaṁ vācyaṁ nara-patāv iti /
kiṁ tad vakṣyāmy abhūtaṁ te nir-doṣasya muner iva // 6.38 //
Though you have said that the being-without virtue is to be communicated to a ruler of men, / How am I to communicate what in you is absent – as is absent in a faultless sage?[25] //6.38//

hṛdayena sa-lajjena jihvayā sajjamānayā /
ahaṁ yady api vā brūyāṁ kas tac-chrad-dhātum arhati // 6.39 //
Or, even if, with shame-tinged heart and cleaving tongue, / I were to speak words, who is going to give credence to that?[26] //6.39//

yo hi candramasas taikṣṇyaṁ kathayec chrad-dadhīta vā /
sa doṣāṁs tava doṣa-jña kathayec chrad-dadhīta vā // 6.40 //
One who would tell of, or have confidence in, the fierceness of the mellow moon, / He would tell of faults in you, O knower of faults!, or would have confidence therein.[27] //6.40//

sānukrośasya satataṁ nityaṁ karuṇa-vedinaḥ /
snigdha-tyāgo na sadṛśo nivartasva prasīda me // 6.41 //
For one who is eternally compassionate, who is constantly steeped in kindness, / It is not befitting to abandon devoted friends. Turn back, please, for me.[28] //6.41//

---

[24] Again, ostensibly Chandaka is worrying about somehow finding a way out of a personal predicament. In a hidden meaning, a student might be asking about the expedient means whereby he might convey to other followers of the Buddha the Buddha's truth of non-doing.

[25] This is a question which, two generations after Aśvaghoṣa, Nāgārjuna famously picks up in his exposition of the absence, in everything that happens, of self-existence – the teaching known for short as śūnyatā, emptiness.

[26] Ostensibly Chandaka says, "Even if did tell such a lie, about your lack of virtue, who would believe me anyway?" In this case, the cause for shame, and the cause for the tongue getting tied, is the telling of a lie. Below the surface, the shame might be in having recourse to words – insofar as words are an inferior means of communicating the virtue of being without. (But this is never to affirm the fallacy of a separate transmission outside of the verbal teaching.)

[27] If we follow ancient Indian custom, the moon is inherently mild and mellow. In the ancient Indian view, therefore, the moon is not fierce. But the Buddha's teaching is in the direction of abandoning all views.

[28] Ostensibly Chandaka is exhorting the prince to turn back towards Kapilavastu. In a hidden meaning, to turn back might be to learn the backward step of turning light around and letting it shine – and in this way never to abandon all bodhisattvas and mahāsattvas.

iti śokābhibhūtasya śrutvā chandasya bhāṣitam /
svasthaḥ paramayā dhṛtyā jagāda vadatāṁ varaḥ // 6.42 //
Having listened to this speech of the grief-stricken Chanda, / Being at ease in himself, thanks to constancy of the highest order, the best of speakers spoke: //6.42//

mad-viyogaṁ prati chanda saṁtāpas tyajyatām ayam /
nānā-bhāvo hi niyataḥ pṛthag-jātiṣu dehiṣu // 6.43 //
"Let this distress at separation from me, Chanda, be abandoned. / Disparate existence is the rule, among singly-born beings who own a body.[29] //6.43//

sva-janaṁ yady api snehān na tyajeyaṁ mumukṣayā /
mṛtyur anyonyam avaśān asmān saṁtyājayiṣyati // 6.44 //
Even if, while retaining the desire to be free, I, through attachment, fail to abandon my own people, / Death, perforce, will cause us totally to abandon one another.[30] //6.44//

mahatyā tṛṣṇayā duḥkhair garbheṇāsmi yayā dhṛtaḥ /
tasyā niṣphala-yatnāyāḥ kvāhaṁ mātuḥ kva sā mama // 6.45 //
With a great desire, and attendant sufferings, she bore me in her womb: / When her effort's fruit is naught,[31] where will I be, for my mother? Where she, for me? //6.45//

vāsa-vṛkṣe samāgamya vigacchanti yathāṇḍa-jāḥ /
niyataṁ viprayogāntas tathā bhūta-samāgamaḥ // 6.46 //
Just as, on a roosting-tree, birds of an egg-born feather flock together and then go their separate ways, / So does an association of real beings always have separation as its end.[32] //6.46//

sametya ca yathā bhūyo vyapayānti balāhakāḥ /
saṁyogo viprayogaś ca tathā me prāṇināṁ mataḥ // 6.47 //
Just as clouds join together and then drift apart again, / So, as I see it, is the joining and separation of those who breathe. //6.47//

yasmād yāti ca loko 'yaṁ vipralabhya parasparam /
mamatvaṁ na kṣamaṁ tasmāt svapna-bhūte samāgame // 6.48 //
And since this world slips away, each side leaving the other disappointed, / The sense that it belongs to me is not fitting, in a coming together that's like a dream.[33] //6.48//

---

[29] In the hidden meaning, individuals, each of whom, in just sitting, is lord of the earth.
[30] In the hidden meaning, death might be the state of a practitioner who is through with breathing.
[31] In the hidden meaning, when the practitioner comes to quiet.
[32] In the hidden meaning, separation might mean, for example, the ending of attachment.
[33] In the hidden meaning, the suggestion might be the dropping away of divided consciousness of body and mind, self and external world.

sahajena viyujyante parṇa-rāgeṇa pāda-pāḥ /
anyenānyasya viśleṣaḥ kiṁ punar na bhaviṣyati // 6.49 //
Trees shed the redness of leaves generic to them; / How much surer is separation to come to pass between one individual and another one who is different.[34] //6.49//

tad evaṁ sati saṁtāpaṁ mā kārṣīḥ saumya gamyatām /
lambate yadi tu sneho gatvāpi punar āvraja // 6.50 //
It being so, O mellow man of *soma*, do not agonize! Let there be movement! / And if attachment lingers on, having gone away, then come again.[35] //6.50//

brūyāś cāsmāsu sāpekṣaṁ janaṁ kapilavastuni /
tyajyatāṁ tad-gataḥ snehaḥ śrūyatāṁ cāsya niścayaḥ // 6.51 //
And say to people in Kapilavastu who look to me with expectation: / 'Let attachment directed there be given up, and let this purpose here and now be heard.[36] //6.51//

kṣipram eṣyati vā kṛtvā jarā-mṛtyu-kṣayaṁ kila /
akṛtārtho nirārambho nidhanaṁ yāsyatīti vā // 6.52 //
Either he will come back quickly, I believe, having put an end to aging and death, / Or else deflated, his aim undone,[37] he will go to his own end.[38] //6.52//

iti tasya vacaḥ śrutvā kanthakas turagottamaḥ /
jihvayā lilihe pādau bāṣpam uṣṇaṁ mumoca ca // 6.53 //
Having listened to these words of his, Kanthaka, highest among swift-going horses, / Licked the prince's feet with his tongue and shed hot tears. //6.53//

jālinā svastikāṅkena cakra-madhyena pāṇinā /
āmamarśa kumāras taṁ babhāṣe ca vayasyavat // 6.54 //
Using a hand whose fingers formed a gapless web, a mark of well-being,[39] using a hand with a wheel in its middle,[40] / The prince stroked the horse and spoke to him like a friend equal in years[41]: //6.54//

---

[34] Ostensibly *anyenānyasya viśleṣaḥ* means "the separation *of* one thing *from* another thing which is different from it." This is supposed to be even surer than a tree's shedding of the leaves which originally belong to it. In the hidden meaning, the prince might be speaking of the one-to-one transmission of a letting go.

[35] Ostensible meaning: Go back to Kapilavastu! Hidden meaning: Practice meaningful repetition!

[36] Ostensible meaning: Listen to the following words! Hidden meaning: Mind here and now is buddha?

[37] Ostensibly *a-kṛtārthaḥ* means unsuccessful. Ironically, it might mean being successful in a negative matter, like un-doing or non-doing.

[38] He will come back to his original state.

[39] *Svastikāṅkena* means "with the swastika mark." The swastika is originally an auspicious sign or mark of well-being (*sv* = well; *asti* = being). Rather than understanding the swastika to be an extraneous symbol, I have taken the webbed fingers (i.e. fingers being without deformity, having no gaps between them) as the auspicious sign itself.

[40] Ostensibly, the hand carried not only swastika symbols but also a wheel sign on its palm. An alternative reading is that the prince in stroking his horse was conscious of his hand not only as a mechanical device but also as an energy center; and so he used his hand with a *cakra* (wheel) in its middle.

muñca kanthaka mā bāṣpaṁ darśiteyaṁ sad-aśvatā /
mṛṣyatāṁ sa-phalaḥ śīghraṁ śramas te 'yaṁ bhaviṣyati // 6.55 //
"Do not shed tears, Kanthaka! This the true horse-nature is proven.[42] / Let it be. This effort of yours will rapidly become fruitful." //6.55//

maṇi-tsaruṁ chandaka-hasta-saṁsthaṁ tataḥ kumāro niśitaṁ gṛhītvā /
kośād asiṁ kāñcana-bhakti-citraṁ bilād ivāśī-viṣam udbabarha // 6.56 //
The jeweled hilt in Chandaka's hand the prince then sharply grasped, / And from its sheath the gold-streaked sword, like a viper from its hole, he drew up and out. //6.56//

niṣkāsya taṁ cotpala-pattra-nīlaṁ ciccheda citraṁ mukuṭaṁ sa-keśam /
vikīryamāṇāṁśukam antar-īkṣe cikṣepa cainaṁ sarasīva haṁsam // 6.57 //
Unsheathing that dark blue blade - ushering out the darkness of the 'lotus petal' brand[43] - he cut off his patterned headdress, along with his hair, / And into the middle distance between earth and heaven, as the unravelling muslin spread softly shining wings,[44] he launched it, like a bar-headed goose towards a lake. //6.57//

pūjābhilāṣeṇa ca bāhu-mānyād divaukasas taṁ jagṛhuḥ praviddham /
yathāvad enaṁ divi deva-saṅghā divyair viśeṣair mahayāṁ ca cakruḥ // 6.58 //
With eager desire to worship it, because it was so greatly to be revered, the beings who dwell in heaven seized upon that jetsam; / And divine congregations in heaven,[45] with due ceremony, with special celestial honors,[46] exalted it. //6.58//

muktvā tv alaṁkāra-kalatravattāṁ śrī-vipravāsaṁ śirasaś ca kṛtvā /
dṛṣṭvāṁśukaṁ kāñcana-haṁsa-citram vanyaṁ sa dhīro 'bhicakāṅkṣa vāsaḥ // 6.59 //
He, however, having let go of being wedded to ornaments, having acted to banish the crowning glory from his head, / And having seen the softly shining light whose brightness is the best of gold,[47] he with firm steadfastness longed for clothing of the forest. //6.59//

---

[41] They *were* friends, but were *not* equal in years; hence "like."

[42] Does a horse have the buddha-nature? Aśvaghoṣa nowhere discusses buddha-nature (*buddhatā*). But here he has the prince speak of *sad-aśva-tā*, true-horse-nature.

[43] The meanings of *utpala-pattra* include 1. the leaf or petal of a blue lotus, 2. a *tilaka* (an auspicious or superstitious or religious mark on the forehead), and 3. a broad-bladed knife. *Nila* means dark blue or dark. *Utpala-pattra-nilam* ostensibly means a dark-blue blade, but below the surface is there also an indirect suggestion of dispensing with the darkness of ancient superstitions, like lucky marks?

[44] An unavoidably creative translation. *Vikīryamāṇāṁśukam* could equally well mean "its fine cloth being unravelled" or "its gentle light being diffused." *Aṁśuka* generally means fine white cloth, muslin, but the Apte dictionary also gives "a mild or gentle blaze of light." EH Johnston notes that the Tibetan translation also takes *aṁśu* in the sense of rays of light.

[45] *Divi deva-saṁghāh*, "divine congregations in heaven." Notice again that Aśvaghoṣa uses *saṁgha* as a collective noun for various beings in saṁsāra - like gods in heaven and applauding townsfolk (BC1.87) - but not for human individuals who in practice are following the Buddha. *Saṁgha* is nowhere used in Aśvaghoṣa's poems in the conventional sense of "a brotherhood of monks" or "a community of Buddhists."

[46] *Divyair viśeṣaiḥ* means "with divine specialities." At the same time a *viśeṣa*, or special mark, is another name for the lucky religious symbol painted on the forehead.

[47] *Kāñcana* means gold (as in *kāñcanam āsanam*, golden seat/sitting). *Haṁsa* means goose or swan, or,

tato mṛga-vyādha-vapur-divaukā bhāvaṁ viditvāsya viśuddha-bhāvaḥ /
kāṣāya-vastro 'bhiyayau samīpaṁ taṁ śākya-rāja-prabhavo 'bhyuvāca // 6.60 //
Then a sky dweller in the guise of a hunter of forest game, his heart being pure, knew what was in the other's heart / And he drew near, in his ochre-colored camouflage. The son of the Śākya king said to him: //6.60//

śivaṁ ca kāṣāyam ṛṣi-dhvajas te na yujyate hiṁsram idaṁ dhanuś ca /
tat saumya yady asti na saktir atra mahyaṁ prayacchedam idaṁ gṛhāṇa // 6.61 //
"Your propitious ochre robe, the banner of a seer, does not go with this deadly bow. / Therefore, my friend, should there be no attachment in this matter, give me that and you take this." //6.61//

vyādho 'bravīt kāma-da kāmam ārād anena viśvāsya mṛgān nihatya /
arthas tu śakropama yady anena hanta pratīcchānaya śuklam etat // 6.62 //
The hunter spoke: "This robe, O granter of desires, is the means whereby, from as far away as desired, I inspire trust in wild creatures, only to shoot them down....[48] / But if you have a use for this means, O man as mighty as Indra, here, accept it, and render here the white." //6.62//

pareṇa harṣeṇa tataḥ sa vanyaṁ jagrāha vāso 'ṁśukam utsasarja /
vyādhas tu divyaṁ vapur eva bibhrat tac-chuklam ādāya divaṁ jagāma // 6.63 //
Then, with joy of the highest order, he took the garment of the forest and gave away his linen finery; / But the hunter, wearing the very essence of the divine, went to heaven, taking that whiteness with him.[49] //6.63//

tataḥ kumāraś ca sa cāśva-gopas tasmiṁs tathā yāti visismiyāte /
āraṇyake vāsasi caiva bhūyas tasminn akārṣṭāṁ bahu-mānam āśu // 6.64 //
Then the prince and the horse-master (*aśva-gopa*),[50] marveled at his departing in such a manner; / And of that clothing of the forest all the more highly did they think. //6.64//

chandaṁ tataḥ sāśru-mukhaṁ visṛjya kāṣāya-saṁvid-dhṛti-kīrti-bhṛt saḥ /
yenāśramas tena yayau mahātmā saṁdhyābhra-saṁvīta ivoḍu-rājaḥ // 6.65 //
Then, having set the tear-faced Chanda free, clad in consciousness of the ochre robe and wearing constancy and honor, / He moved majestically in the direction of the ashram, like the moon – king among stars – veiled by a dusky cloud. //6.65//

---

in compounds, the best of anything. So ostensibly "the goose of gold" might refer to the muslin headdress which flew away like a bar-headed goose. But I think the real meaning which Aśvaghoṣa had in mind was to point to the practice of sitting in lotus as potentially the most valuable thing there is.

[48] Below the surface, this might be a suggestion of a function of the so-called "ritual robe," before it is realized as an emblem of what is real, not religious in the narrow sectarian sense.

[49] Is the suggestion, again, below the surface, that what is white, or spiritually pure, rightly belongs in heaven – a place that cannot really be witnessed, as a separate place? Cf Nāgārjuna's discussion of the divine in MMK ch. 27, where the emphasis is on continuity.

[50] Aśvaghoṣa calls Chandaka by many epithets in this canto. This one, *aśva-gopa* ('horse-keeper'), seems to be a play on his own name *aśva-ghoṣa* ('horse-whinny').

tatas tathā bhartari rājya-niḥspṛhe tapo-vanaṁ yāti vivarṇa-vāsasi /
bhujau samutkṣipya tataḥ sa vāji-bhṛd bhṛśaṁ vicukrośa papāta ca kṣitau // 6.66 //
And so, as his master was retiring like this into the ascetic woods, desiring nothing in the way of sovereignty[51] and wearing clothing of no distinction,[52] / The preserver of the war-horse, there and then, threw up his arms, cried out wildly, and fell upon the earth. //6.66//

vilokya bhūyaś ca ruroda sa-svaraṁ hayaṁ bhujābhyām upaguhya kanthakam /
tato nir-āśo vilapan muhur muhur yayau śarīreṇa puraṁ na cetasā // 6.67 //
Looking again, he bellowed in full voice and embraced the horse Kanthaka with both arms; / Thus, devoid of hope or expectation, and lamenting over and over, he journeyed back to the city with his body, not with his mind.[53] //6.67//

kva-cit pradadhyau vilalāpa ca kva-cit kva-cit pracaskhāla papāta ca kva-cit /
ato vrajan bhakti-vaśena duḥkhitaś cacāra bahvīr avaśaḥ pathi kriyāḥ // 6.68 //
Here he reflected,[54] there he lamented; here he stumbled, there he fell; / And so keeping on, suffering pain on account of devotion, he did without meaning to do many actions on the path. //6.68//

iti buddha-carite mahā-kāvye chandaka-nivartano nāma ṣaṣṭhaḥ sargaḥ // 6 //
The 6th canto, titled "Chandaka Turning Back,"
in an epic tale of awakened action.

---

[51] In the hidden meaning, is nothing (or the truth of emptiness) what confers true sovereignty?

[52] The meaning of *vivarṇa* is having no color or having no caste. Its ostensible meaning is pejorative – the dictionary gives "pale; low, vile; belonging to a mixed caste." Thus Aśvaghoṣa subverts those pejorative meanings in his ironic description of the kaṣāya as *vivarṇa-vāsas*, "clothing of no distinction."

[53] Ostensible meaning: Looking [at the prince] again, he wept out loud, and hugged the horse Kanthaka with both arms. / Then, hopelessly lamenting over and over again, he withdrew to the city with his body, though his heart was not in it.
Hidden meaning: Seeing [everything] with fresh eyes, he loudly roared [the lion's roar], having fully embraced the horse-power of Kanthaka. / On that basis, being without expectation and repeatedly sorrowing [for the clinging world], he journeyed to the city riding a wave of pure physical energy – nothing mental.

[54] √*dhyai*, the root from which *dhyāna* is derived, means to ponder or to brood, and also to meditate. Ostensibly Chandaka is described as a hapless emotional being, brooding as he goes on his miserable way. Below the surface, the verse might be Aśvaghoṣa's ironic description of his own life, centered on non-doing practice of letting happen.

Canto 7: tapo-vana-praveśaḥ
Entering the Woods of Painful Practice

Introduction

As a sweeping generalization, *tapas*, asceticism, is bad in Aśvaghoṣa's writing, in contrast to *yoga*, practice, which is good. There again, another general rule for a student of Aśvaghoṣa might be to forego sweeping generalizations, and to go beyond bad and good.

Ostensibly, then, the title of the present canto describes the Prince's entry (*praveśa*) into the "the ascetic grove" (*tapo-vana*). But in the hidden meaning, it may be up to each one of us individually to go metaphorically into the woods and investigate what the real meanings of *tapas* - beyond the straw doll of "asceticism" - might be. Before it defines *tapas* as "religious austerity," for example, SED defines *tapas* as 1. warmth, heat, and 2. pain, suffering.

tato visṛjyāśru-mukhaṁ rudantaṁ chandaṁ vana-cchandatayā nir-āsthaḥ /
sarvārthasiddho vapuṣābhibhūya tam āśramaṁ siddha iva prapede // 7.1 //
Then, having sent on his way the weeping tear-faced Chanda, and being interested in nothing,[1] through a *chanda* (a partiality) for the forest, / Sarvārtha-siddha, All Things Realized, overpowering the place by his physical presence, entered that ashram like a *siddha*, a realized man. //7.1//

sa rāja-sūnur mṛga-rāja-gāmī mṛgājiraṁ tan mṛgavat praviṣṭaḥ /
lakṣmī-viyukto 'pi śarīra-lakṣmyā cakṣūṁṣi sarvāśramiṇāṁ jahāra // 7.2 //
He the son of a king, moving like a lion-king, entered like a forest creature that arena of forest creatures; / By the majesty of his physical person, though bereft of the tokens of majesty, he stole the eyes of all the ashram-dwellers[2] - //7.2//

sthitā hi hasta-stha-yugās tathaiva kautūhalāc cakra-dharāḥ sa-dārāḥ /
tam indra-kalpaṁ dadṛśur na jagmur dhuryā ivārdhāvanataiḥ śirobhiḥ // 7.3 //
For standing in precisely that manner, rooted in their curiosity, with yoke in hand, were the wheel-bearers, with wives in tow; / They beheld him the equal of Indra, and did not move, like beasts of burden with their heads half bowed.[3] //7.3//

---

[1] *Nir-āsthaḥ* - ostensible meaning, not interested in anything; hidden meaning, interested in the possibility of *pari-nirvāṇa*, or emptiness, or other aspects of the truth of cessation.
[2] The next five verses expand on this generic description of *sarvāśramiṇām*, "all the ashram-dwellers," by considering in detail particular types.
[3] Was being accompanied by wives an indication of indecision? Or was having the head half bowed (in the middle way between being pulled back and falling too far forward) an indication that these individuals were originally buddhas, in the state of readiness to act?

viprāś ca gatvā bahir idhma-hetoḥ prāptāḥ samit-puṣpa-pavitra-hastāḥ /
tapaḥ-pradhānāḥ kṛta-buddhayo 'pi taṁ draṣṭum īyur na maṭhān abhīyuḥ // 7.4 //
And inspired brahmins, who had gone out for fuel to feed the sacred fire, and returned holding in their hands kindling, flowers, and *kuśa* grass,[4] / Though they were men of formed minds for whom ascetic practice was paramount, they went to see him. They did not go towards their huts. //7.4//

hṛṣṭāś ca kekā mumucur mayūrā dṛṣṭvāmbu-daṁ nīlam ivonnamantam /
śaṣpāṇi hitvābhimukhāś ca tasthur mṛgāś calākṣā mṛga-cāriṇaś ca // 7.5 //
Bristling with rapture also, the peacocks let loose their cries, as if they had seen a dark raincloud rising up;[5] / While, letting grass fall as they turned to face him, the deer stood still, along with the deer-imitators, with only their eyes moving. //7.5//

dṛṣṭvā tam ikṣvāku-kula-pradīpaṁ jvalantam udyantam ivāṁśumantam /
kṛte 'pi dohe janita-pramodāḥ prasusruvur homa-duhaś ca gāvaḥ // 7.6 //
Seeing him, the lamp of the Ikṣvāku tribe, shining like the rising sun, / The cows that were milked for offerings, though they had already been milked, were overjoyed, and flowed forth again.[6] //7.6//

kac-cid vasūnām ayam aṣṭamaḥ syāt syād aśvinor anyataraś cyuto ' tra /
uccerur uccair iti tatra vācas tad-darśanād vismaya-jā munīnām // 7.7 //
"Could this be the eighth of the *vasus*, the good gods, or one of the two *aśvins*, the charioteers, alighting here?" / Calls like this went up on high, born of the bewilderment of the sages there, at seeing him. //7.7//

lekharṣabhasyeva vapur-dvitīyaṁ dhāmeva lokasya carācarasya /
sa dyotayām āsa vanaṁ hi kṛtsnaṁ yad-ṛcchayā sūrya ivāvatīrṇaḥ // 7.8 //
For, like the physical double of Indra, bull of gods, like the glory of all that moves and is still in the world, / He lit up the whole forest – as if the Sun himself had dropped by. //7.8//

tataḥ sa tair āśramibhir yathāvad abhyarcitaś copanimantritaś ca /
pratyarcayāṁ dharma-bhṛto babhūva svareṇa sāmbho-'mbu-dharopamena // 7.9 //
Then, being honored and invited, with due courtesy, by those ashram-dwellers, / He in return, to the upholders of a dharma, paid his respects with a voice like rain-clouds full of rain. //7.9//

---

[4] *Samit* can mean war, as well as kindling. *Pavitra* can mean a means of purification, as well as *kuśa* grass. This makes possible the hidden meaning that they were "holding in their hands the means of purification which is a flower of war." The war, in that case, might be the war on sleep, and a means of purification might be a means of eliminating pollutants such as sensual desire, becoming, and unwittingness (see Appendix, DN16).

[5] In Sanskrit poems in general peacocks are described as bursting into joyous song at the coming of the rains. At the same time, in Saundarananda (SN1.11) Aśvaghoṣa poked fun at ascetic peacocks with their dreadlocks – *śikhin* means both peacock and having a lock or tuft of hair on top of the head.

[6] For the ironic hidden meaning of cows being milked, cf SN1.3.

kīrṇaṁ tathā puṇya-kṛtā janena svargābhikāmena vimokṣa-kāmaḥ /
tam āśramaṁ so 'nucacāra dhīras tapāṁsi citrāṇi nirīkṣamāṇaḥ // 7.10 //
Through the ashram that was filled in this manner with pious people having designs upon heaven, / He, being desirous of release, steadily walked, observing the various ascetic practices. //7.10//

tapo-vikārāṁś ca nirīkṣya saumyas tapo-vane tatra tapo-dhanānām /
tapasvinaṁ kaṁ-cid anuvrajantaṁ tattvaṁ vijijñāsur idaṁ babhāṣe // 7.11 //
And the moon-like man of soma-mildness, when he had observed there, in that forest of ascetic severity, the ascetic contortions of ascetics steeped in severity, / He spoke as follows, wanting to know the truth of it, to one of the ascetics who was walking along with him: //7.11//

tat-pūrvam-adyāśrama-darśanaṁ me yasmād imaṁ dharma-vidhiṁ na jāne /
tasmād bhavān arhati bhāṣituṁ me yo niścayo yat prati vaḥ pravṛttaḥ // 7.12 //
"Since today is my first visit to an ashram and I do not understand this method of dharma; / Therefore, kind sir, please tell me – you are all possessed of what intention, directed towards what."[7] //7.12//

tato dvi-jātiḥ sa tapo-vihāraḥ śākyarṣabhāyarṣabha-vikramāya /
krameṇa tasmai kathayāṁ cakāra tapo-viśeṣāṁs tapasaḥ phalaṁ ca // 7.13 //
And so the twice-born man,[8] an explorer of the pleasure of painful practice, spoke to the bull of the Śākyas, whose steps were the steps of a bull – / He spoke to him, in steps, about the varieties of painful practice and about the fruit of painful practice.[9] //7.13//

agrāmyam annaṁ salila-prarūḍhaṁ parṇāni toyaṁ phala-mūlam eva /
yathāgamaṁ vṛttir iyaṁ munīnāṁ bhinnās tu te te tapasāṁ vikalpāḥ // 7.14 //
"Unprocessed food – food that grows in the presence of water – leaves and water and fruits and roots: / This, according to tradition, is the fare of sages.[10] But in their painful practices there are alternative approaches, each being distinct. //7.14//

---

[7] Ostensibly a question; in the hidden meaning, a statement of ineffable reality?

[8] *Dvi-jātiḥ* or *dvi-jaḥ*, one twice-born, generally indicates a Brahman, re-born through investiture with the sacred thread. But these terms can also indicate a tooth and a bird. This particular twice-born individual is going to tell the truth on more than one level, and so in the hidden meaning *dvi-jātiḥ*, or "born again," may be taken to mean enlightened.

[9] Aśvaghoṣa generally uses *tapas* with a pejorative connotation (*tapas* = asceticism vs *yoga* = practice). Below the surface in the present canto, however, *tapas* (hard practice, painful practice) can be read as representing practice itself, which, even if it need not be painful in theory, so often tends to be painful in practice.

[10] EH Johnston amended the text to *salile prarūḍham* and translated accordingly "that which grows in the water." This conveys the ostensible meaning of very restrictive ascetic fare. But the real or hidden meaning might simply be to convey the general rule that sages (not only ascetic ones) eat food that is natural, not over-processed.

uñchena jīvanti kha-gā ivānye tṛṇāni ke-cin mṛgavac caranti /
ke-cid bhujaṅgaiḥ saha vartayanti valmīka-bhūtā iva mārutena // 7.15 //
Ones who are different live by gleaning crumbs, like movers in emptiness, or birds[11]; some graze on leaves of grass, like deer; / Some, together with sitters in coils, or snakes – as if they were ant-hills – subsist on thin air. //7.15//

aśma-prayatnārjita-vṛttayo 'nye ke-cit sva-dantāpahatānna-bhakṣāḥ /
kṛtvā parārthaṁ śrapaṇaṁ tathānye kurvanti kāryaṁ yadi śeṣam asti // 7.16 //
Ones who are different live by what is ground out through effort on a stone; some are sustained by breaking food down with their own teeth; / Ones, again, who are different, having done the cooking for others, do what is for them to do, if anything is left over.[12] //7.16//

ke-cij jala-klinna-jaṭā-kalāpā dviḥ pāvakaṁ juhvati mantra-pūrvam /
mīnaiḥ samaṁ ke-cid apo vigāhya vasanti kūrmollikhitaiḥ śarīraiḥ // 7.17 //
Some, their matted coils of hair dripping with water, twice pour butter into the fire, with mantras [or make offerings of two times three, using a mantra][13] / Some, like fishes, go deep into the water and there they abide, their bodies scratching the surface of the tortoise.[14] //7.17//

evaṁ-vidhaiḥ kāla-citais tapobhiḥ parair divaṁ yānty aparair nṛ-lokam /
duḥkhena mārgeṇa sukhaṁ kṣiyanti duḥkhaṁ hi dharmasya vadanti mūlam // 7.18 //
Through painful practices such as these, accumulated over time, they arrive, via superior practices, at heaven, and via lowlier ones at the world of human beings.[15] / By an arduous path they come to inhabit ease; for suffering, they say, is the starting point of dharma.[16] //7.18//

---

[11] Ostensibly *kha-gāḥ*, "movers in emptiness," means birds. Below the surface it suggests those who are free, i.e. those who have left home to live the wandering life.

[12] Ostensibly a twice-born brahmin ascetic is listing some rules for ascetic practice. In the hidden meaning, one who is born again is continuing to suggest the everyday life of buddhas, bodhisattvas and mahāsattvas.

[13] *Dvis* means twice or twice a day. *Pāvaka* means fire, but also, because fire is of three kinds, the number 3; *pāvaka* is also given in the dictionary as "a kind of *ṛṣi*, a saint, a person purified by religious abstraction or one who purified from sin." *Juhvati* means they make a sacrifice, especially by pouring butter into the fire. But *juhvati* can also simply mean they honor. A *mantra*, according to one explanation of its etymology, from the root √*man*, to think, literally means "an instrument of thought." Many possible hidden meanings, then, can be read into *dviḥ pāvakaṁ juhvati mantra-pūrvam.* For example: "twice [a day], using thought as an instrument, they honor a great seer."

[14] Ostensibly the brahmin ascetic is describing an ascetic practice involving holding the breath under water: "And there they abide, their bodies being scratched by turtles." In the hidden meaning, the suggestion might be that even the buddhas, with all their wisdom, cannot fathom the merit of just sitting, but are content at least to scratch the surface.

[15] The ironic hidden meaning might be that buddhas opt for the lowlier, or more humble, practice among fellow human beings.

[16] Again, the words apply equally to a dharma of asceticism and to the Buddha's dharma of four noble truths.

ity evam-ādi dvipadendra-vatsaḥ śrutvā vacas tasya tapo-dhanasya /
adṛṣṭa-tattvo 'pi na saṁtutoṣa śanair idaṁ cātma-gataṁ babhāṣe // 7.19 //
The son of a chief among two-footed beings, listened to words like these, and more, under that man steeped in painful practice / But he failed to see the truth of it, and was not satisfied. Silently he said to himself: //7.19//

duḥkhātmakaṁ naika-vidhaṁ tapaś ca svarga-pradhānaṁ tapasaḥ phalaṁ ca /
lokāś ca sarve pariṇāmavantaḥ sv-alpe śramaḥ khalv ayam āśramāṇām // 7.20 //
"Asceticism in its various forms has suffering at its core; at the same time, ascetic practice has heaven as its chief reward; / And yet every world is subject to change - all this toil in ashrams, for so very little! //7.20//

śriyam ca bandhūn viṣayāṁś ca hitvā ye svarga-hetor niyamaṁ caranti /
te viprayuktāḥ khalu gantu-kāmā mahattaraṁ bandhanam eva bhūyaḥ // 7.21 //
Those who abandon prestige, connections, and objects, to observe restrictions for the sake of heaven - / Evidently, when parted from there, are destined to go only into greater bondage. //7.21//

kāya-klamair yaś ca tapo 'bhidhānaiḥ pravṛttim ākāṅkṣati kāma-hetoḥ /
saṁsāra-doṣān aparīkṣamāṇo duḥkhena so 'nvicchati duḥkham eva // 7.22 //
And he who, by the bodily travails called ascetic practice, desires advancement for the sake of desire / While failing to attend to the faults that fuel saṁsāra - he by the means of suffering pursues nothing but suffering. //7.22//

trāsaś ca nityaṁ maraṇāt prajānāṁ yatnena cecchanti punaḥ prasūtim /
satyāṁ pravṛttau niyataś ca mṛtyus tatraiva magnā yata eva bhītāḥ // 7.23 //
Though people are ever afraid of dying, still actively they strive for re-birth, / And just in their doing, their death is assured - right there, where they are drowning, in fear itself. //7.23//

ihārtham eke praviśanti khedaṁ svargārtham anye śramam āpnuvanti /
sukhārtham āśā kṛpaṇo 'kṛtārthaḥ pataty an-arthe khalu jīva-lokaḥ // 7.24 //
Some individuals go through grim exhaustion for an end in this world, others suffer the ascetic grind for an end in heaven - / Pitifully expectant, having happiness as its end but failing to accomplish its end, humankind sinks into end-less disappointment. //7.24//

na khalv ayaṁ garhita eva yatno yo hīnam utsṛjya viśeṣa-gāmī /
prājñaiḥ samānena pariśrameṇa kāryaṁ tu tad yatra punar na kāryam // 7.25 //
Not to be blamed, certainly, is this effort which, casting aside the inferior, aims for distinction; / But the work wise men should do, exerting themselves as one, is that work wherein nothing further needs doing. //7.25//

śarīra-pīḍā tu yadīha dharmaḥ sukhaṁ śarīrasya bhavaty adharmaḥ /
dharmeṇa cāpnoti sukhaṁ paratra tasmād adharmaṁ phalatīha dharmaḥ // 7.26 //
If causing the body pain, in contrast, is the dharma here, the body being happy constitutes the opposite of dharma. / And yet by the dharma the body is [supposed] to obtain happiness in future. On those grounds, the dharma here results in the opposite of dharma. //7.26//

yataḥ śarīraṁ manaso vaśena pravartate vāpi nivartate vā /
yukto damaś-cetasa eva tasmāc cittād ṛte kāṣṭha-samaṁ śarīram // 7.27 //
Since the body, by the mind's command, either carries on or stops its doing, / Therefore what is appropriate is taming of the mind. Without the thinking mind, the body is like a wooden log. //7.27//

āhāra-śuddhyā yadi puṇyam iṣṭaṁ tasmān mṛgāṇām api puṇyam asti /
ye cāpi bāhyāḥ puruṣāḥ phalebhyo bhāgyāparādhena parāṅmukhārthāḥ // 7.28 //
If the good is to be got through purity of food, it follows that there is good in even the creatures of the forest; / As also there are human beings who, through the reaping of fruits, subsist as outsiders – human beings who, because of contravening destiny, are turned away from wealth.[17] //7.28//

duḥkhe 'bhisaṁdhis tv atha puṇya-hetuḥ sukhe 'pi kāryo nanu so 'bhisaṁdhiḥ /
atha pramāṇaṁ na sukhe 'bhisaṁdhir duḥkhe pramāṇaṁ nanu nābhisaṁdhiḥ // 7.29 //
But if the cause of good is the ability to handle hardship, then is not the same ability to be practiced with regard to happiness? / Or else, if being able to handle happiness is not the standard, then how can ability to handle hardship be the standard? //7.29//

tathaiva ye karma-viśuddhi-hetoḥ spṛśanty apas-tīrtham iti pravṛttāḥ /
tatrāpi toṣo hṛdi kevalo 'yaṁ na pāvayiṣyanti hi pāpam āpaḥ // 7.30 //
Those again who, with a view to purifying their karma, zealously sprinkle on themselves water which they feel to be sacred, / Are only, in so doing, pleasing their own heart, for wrong will never be washed away by waters. //7.30//

spṛṣṭaṁ hi yad yad guṇavadbhir ambhas tat tat pṛthivyāṁ yadi tīrtham iṣṭam /
tasmād guṇān eva paraimi tīrtham āpas tu niḥsaṁśayam āpa eva // 7.31 //
Whatever water has been touched by people steeped in good – that is sacred bathing water, if such on earth is sought. / Therefore, virtues, yes, I do see as a sacred ford. But water, without doubt, is water." //7.31//

---

[17] Ostensibly the prince is poking fun at the conception that religious merit (*puṇya*) is to be gained by eating pure food – because, if it were so, even deer and even outcasts could gain religious merit by living outside of human civilization. In the hidden meaning, forest monks (creatures of the forest) do indeed gain merit by transcending the will to fame and profit and living as outsiders.

iti sma tat tad bahu-yukti-yuktaṁ jagāda cāstaṁ ca yayau vivasvān /
tato havir-dhūma-vivarṇa-vṛkṣaṁ tapaḥ-praśāntaṁ sa vanaṁ viveśa // 7.32 //
Thus, employing many and various forms of reasoning, did he speak, as the Brilliant One set behind the Western Mountain. / Then he went where the trees, veiled by smoke from burnt offerings, were turning gray; the practicing of pain there having ceased, he went into the forest... //7.32//

abhyuddhṛta-prajvalitāgni-hotraṁ kṛtābhiṣekarṣi-janāvakīrṇam /
jāpya-svanākūjita-deva-koṣṭhaṁ dharmasya karmāntam iva pravṛttam // 7.33 //
... Into the flaring forest, where the sacrificial flame was passed from fire to blazing fire; into the bespattered forest, filled with seers performing their bathing rites; / Into the cooing forest, where shrines to gods resounded with muttered prayers; into the forest which was like a hive of dharma, all busy with doing. //7.33//

kāś-cin niśās tatra niśā-karābhaḥ parīkṣamāṇaś ca tapāṁsy uvāsa /
sarvaṁ parikṣepya tapaś ca matvā tasmāt tapaḥ-kṣetra-talāj jagāma // 7.34 //
For several nights, resembling the night-making moon, he dwelt there, investigating ascetic practices; / And, having embraced asceticism in the round and come to his own conclusion about it, he made to depart from that field of asceticism. //7.34//

anvavrajann āśramiṇas tatas taṁ tad-rūpa-māhātmya-gatair manobhiḥ /
deśād anāryair abhibhūyamānān maharṣayo dharmam ivāpayāntam // 7.35 //
Then the ashram-dwellers followed him, their minds directed on his beauty and dignity - / Like great seers following the dharma, when, from a land being overrun by uncivil people, the dharma is retreating.[18] //7.35//

tato jaṭā-valkala-cīra-khelāṁs tapo-dhanāṁś caiva sa tān dadarśa /
tapāṁsi caiṣām anurudhyamānas tasthau śive śrīmati vṛkṣa-mūle // 7.36 //
Then those men whose wealth was painful practice he beheld in their matted locks, strips of bark, and flapping rags; / So seeing, and yet feeling towards their austerities a fond respect, he remained there standing, at the foot of an auspicious and splendid tree. //7.36//

athopasṛtyāśrama-vāsinas taṁ manuṣya-varyaṁ parivārya tasthuḥ /
vṛddhaś ca teṣāṁ bahu-māna-pūrvaṁ kalena sāmnā giram ity uvāca // 7.37 //
And so the ashram-dwellers stepped near and stood surrounding that most excellent human being, / And the most mature among them, being full of respect, spoke in a soft voice these gentle words: //7.37//

---

[18] This could be another example in which the second half of a simile, ironically, carries the main gist of what Aśvaghoṣa seems to want to suggest - namely, that we should not attach to a geographical location, but should just follow the dharma.

tvayyāgate pūrṇa ivāśramo 'bhūt saṁpadyate śūnya iva prayāte /
tasmād imaṁ nārhasi tāta hātuṁ jijīviṣor deham iveṣṭam āyuḥ // 7.38 //
"At your coming the ashram seemed to become full; at your going, it seems to become empty. / Therefore, my son, you should desist from leaving this [place of painful exertion] – like the cherished life-force [not leaving] the body of a man who is fighting for his life.[19] //7.38//

brahmarṣi-rājarṣi-surarṣi-juṣṭaḥ puṇyaḥ samīpe himavān hi śailaḥ /
tapāṁsi tāny eva tapo-dhanānāṁ yat saṁnikarṣād bahulī bhavanti // 7.39 //
For near to us, inhabited by brahmin seers, king-seers, and god-seers, rises a holy Himālayan mountain[20] / Through whose closeness are augmented those very investments of painful effort of people whose capital is painful effort. //7.39//

tīrthāni puṇyāny abhitas tathaiva sopāna-bhūtāni nabhas-talasya /
juṣṭāni dharmātmabhir ātmavadbhir devarṣibhiś caiva nṛparṣibhiś ca // 7.40 //
All around us, likewise, are holy bathing places, which are akin to stairways to heaven;[21] / They are frequented by seers whose essence of themselves is dharma, and by seers possessed of themselves – by divine seers and by seers who are protectors of men. //7.40//

itaś ca bhūyaḥ kṣamam uttaraiva dik sevituṁ dharma-viśeṣa-hetoḥ /
na tu kṣamaṁ dakṣiṇato budhena padaṁ bhaved ekam api prayātum // 7.41 //
And going further, from here, the direction is northward that deserves to be cultivated, for the sake of distinction in dharma; / It ill befits a wise man to take, contrarily, even one step that might lead southward.[22] //7.41//

tapo-vane 'sminn atha niṣkriyo vā saṁkīrṇa-dharme patito 'śucir vā /
dṛṣṭas tvayā yena na te vivatsā tad brūhi yāvad rucito 'stu vāsaḥ // 7.42 //
Or else, in this forest of painful practice, you have seen one who neglects rites; or you have seen one who is not pure, one who, in a commingled dharma, has fallen / And for this reason there is in you no desire to dwell – then say as much, and be pleased to stay! [or express as much, in which act of abiding, let light be shone!][23] //7.42//

---

[19] Again, when A is like B, ostensibly the point of B is to illustrate A, but really A is the convenient fiction and the real message is in B.

[20] Alternate reading of *puṇyaḥ... himavān*: a pleasant snow-clad peak. "A holy Himālayan mountain" sounds religious, but this spiritual reading is undermined by the hidden reading.

[21] Alternate reading: "All around us, likewise, are wholesome bathing places which, at the level of the air, consist of steps." Again the hidden reading undermines the holiness of bathing places which are esteemed as stairways to a spiritual place.

[22] Ostensibly, northward means towards the Himālayas; in the hidden meaning, north means up and south means down?

[23] In the hidden meaning, one who neglects rites is a non-buddha, who expresses his or her true nature in the backward step of turning light and letting it shine. *Rucita* means shone upon (by the sun &c), and hence pleasant. *Astu* means "let it be." So *rucito 'stu* ostensibly means "be pleased to...," but the hidden meaning might be "let [light] be shone."

ime hi vāñchanti tapaḥ-sahāyaṁ tapo-nidhāna-pratimaṁ bhavantam /
vāsas tvayā hīndra-samena sārdhaṁ bṛhas-pater apy udayāvahaḥ syāt // 7.43 //

For these want as their companion in ascetic practice you who resemble a repository of ascetic practice[24] – / Because abiding with you, the equal of Indra, would be a means of lifting up even Bṛhas-pati, 'the Lord of Spiritual Growth.'" //7.43//

ity evam ukte sa tapasvi-madhye tapasvi-mukhyena manīṣi-mukhyaḥ /
bhava-praṇāśāya kṛta-pratijñaḥ svaṁ bhāvam antar-gatam ācacakṣe // 7.44 //

When he, in the midst of the ascetics, was thus addressed by the first ascetic, he the first in perspicacity, / Since he had vowed to end the *bhava* which is becoming, disclosed the *bhāva* of his own real inner feelings and thoughts: //7.44//

ṛjv-ātmanāṁ dharma-bhṛtāṁ munīnām iṣṭātithitvāt sva-janopamānām /
evaṁ-vidhair māṁ prati bhāva-jātaiḥ prītiḥ parā me janitaś ca mārgaḥ // 7.45 //

"Under dharma-upholding sages who tend in their core towards uprightness, and who are, in their willing hospitality, like family, / To have had shown towards me such manifestations of sincerity has filled me with great joy, and has opened for me a way. //7.45//

snigdhābhir ābhir hṛdayaṁ gamābhiḥ samāsataḥ snāta ivāsmi vāgbhiḥ /
ratiś ca me dharma-nava-grahasya vispanditā saṁprati bhūya eva // 7.46 //

By these emollient words of yours, which seep through to the heart, I am as if smeared all over; / And the enjoyment a beginner feels, at newly laying hands on dharma, is now pulsing through me all over again. //7.46//

evaṁ pravṛttān bhavataḥ śaraṇyān atīva saṁdarśita-pakṣapātān /
yāsyāmi hitveti mamāpi duḥkhaṁ yathaiva bandhūṁs tyajatas tathaiva // 7.47 //

To leave you all like this, so devoted to all you do and so hospitable, to leave you who have shown me such excessive kindness – / It pains me that I will leave you like this and depart, even as it pained me to leave my kith and kin. //7.47//

svargāya yuṣmākam ayaṁ tu dharmo mamābhilāṣas tv apunar-bhavāya /
asmin vane yena na me vivatsā bhinnaḥ pravṛttyā hi nivṛtti-dharmaḥ // 7.48 //

But this dharma of yours aims at heaven, whereas my desire is for no more becoming; / Which is why I do not wish to dwell in this wood: for a non-doing dharma is different from doing.[25] //7.48//

---

[24] Alternate reading of *tapo-nidhāna-pratimaṁ bhavantam*: "you who represent the laying aside of asceticism."

[25] Other possible readings of *bhinnaḥ pravṛttyā hi nivṛtti-dharmaḥ* include: 1. "A non-doing dharma is destroyed by doing;" 2. "The dharma of non-doing is mixed in with doing." Besides the ostensible meaning of "different from," *bhinna* can mean 1. split or destroyed; and 2. mixed or mingled with. The ambiguity may have been intentional on Aśvaghoṣa's part, inviting us to ask ourselves what the relation is between non-doing and doing, in practice and in theory.

tan nāratir me na parāpacāro vanād ito yena parivrajāmi /
dharme sthitāḥ pūrva-yugānurūpe sarve bhavanto hi mahārṣi-kalpāḥ // 7.49 //
So it is neither displeasure in me nor wrong conduct by another that causes me to walk away from this wood; / For, standing firm in a dharma adapted to the first age of the world, all of you bear the semblance of great sages.[26]//7.49//

tato vacaḥ sūnṛtam arthavac ca su-ślakṣṇam ojasvi ca garvitaṁ ca /
śrutvā kumārasya tapasvinas te viśeṣa-yuktaṁ bahu-mānam īyuḥ // 7.50 //
Then, having listened to the prince's speech, which was both friendly and full of real meaning, / Thoroughly gracious and yet strong and proud, those ascetics held him in especially high regard. //7.50//

kaś-cid dvijas tatra tu bhasma-śāyī prāṁśuḥ śikhī dārava-cīra-vāsāḥ /
ā-piṅgalākṣas tanu-dīrgha-ghoṇaḥ kuṇḍaika-hasto giram ity uvāca // 7.51 //
But up spoke one twice-born individual there, whose practice was to lay in ashes; standing tall, clothed in bark strips and wearing his hair in a top-knot, / His eyes dark red, his nose long and thin, holding in one hand a bowl-shaped container, he said these words:[27] //7.51//

dhīmann udāraḥ khalu niścayas te yas tvaṁ yuvā janmani dṛṣṭa-doṣaḥ /
svargāpavargau hi vicārya samyag yasyāpavarge matir asti so 'sti // 7.52 //
"O man of understanding! High indeed is the purpose of one who, young as you are, has seen the faults in rebirth; / For the man who, having properly thought about heaven and about ending rebirth, is minded towards ending rebirth – he *is* the man! //7.52//

yajñais tapobhir niyamaiś ca tais taiḥ svargaṁ yiyāsanti hi rāgavantaḥ /
rāgeṇa sārdhaṁ ripuṇeva yuddhvā mokṣaṁ parīpsanti tu sattvavantaḥ // 7.53 //
For those who are colored by desire's red taint, desire by various austerities, restrictions, and acts of devotion, to go to heaven; / Whereas, having battled with red desire as if with an enemy, those who are animated by the true essence, desire to arrive at liberation. //7.53//

tad buddhir eṣā yadi niścitā te tūrṇaṁ bhavān gacchatu vindhya-koṣṭham /
asau munis tatra vasaty arāḍo yo naiṣṭhike śreyasi labdha-cakṣuḥ // 7.54 //
Therefore if this is your settled purpose, go quickly to the region of the Vindhya Hills; / There lives the sage Arāḍa, who has gained insight into the ultimate good. //7.54//

---

[26] The suffix *kalpa* means having the form of, resembling, like but with a degree of inferiority. On one level, then, the prince is praising those who are devoted to hard practice. But below the surface, the affirmation is by no means unreserved.

[27] Being tall (*prāṁśuḥ*) and holding a bowl-shaped vessel (*kuṇḍa*) could be marks of a forest bhikṣu. But could laying in ashes also be such a mark?

tasmād bhavāñ chroṣyati tattva-mārgaṁ satyāṁ rucau saṁpratipatsyate ca /
yathā tu paśyāmi matis tathaisā tasyāpi yāsyaty avadhūya buddhim // 7.55 //
From him you will hear the method of the *tattvas* (or the path of reality)[28] and will follow it as far as you like; / But since this mind of yours is such you will, I am sure, progress on, after shaking off the *buddhi*, or intelligence, of even that sage. //7.55//

spaṣṭocca-ghoṇaṁ vipulāyatākṣaṁ tāmrādharauṣṭhaṁ sita-tīkṣṇa-daṁṣṭram /
idaṁ hi vaktraṁ tanu-rakta-jihvaṁ jñeyārṇavaṁ pāsyati kṛtsnam eva // 7.56 //
For, beneath a straight and high nose, and lengthened and widened eyes, with its lower lip the color of copper, and its large teeth, sharp and white, / This mouth, with its thin red tongue, will drink up the whole ocean of what is to be known. //7.56//

gambhīratā yā bhavatas tv agādhā yā dīptatā yāni ca lakṣaṇāni /
ācāryakaṁ prāpsyasi tat pṛthivyāṁ yan narṣibhiḥ pūrva-yuge 'py avāptam // 7.57 //
Moreover, in view of this unfathomable depth which you have,[29] in light of this brilliance, and judging by these signs, / You will realize on earth that seat of a teacher which was obtained not even by seers of the first age." //7.57//

paramam iti tato nṛpātmajas tam ṛṣi-janaṁ pratinandya niryayau /
vidhivad anuvidhāya te 'pi taṁ praviviśur āśramiṇas tapo-vanam // 7.58 //
"Very well," said the son of a protector of men; then, bidding a glad farewell to that group of seers, he went out. / For their part, having duly seen him off, the ashram-dwellers entered anew the woods of painful practice. //7.58//

iti buddha-carite mahā-kāvye tapo-vana-praveśo nāma saptamaḥ sargaḥ // 7 //
The 7th canto, titled "Entering the Woods of Painful Practice,"
in an epic tale of awakened action.

---

[28] *Tattva* (truth, reality) and *buddhi* (intellect, view) were concepts in Sāṁkhya philosophy, wherein 20-odd *tattvas*, or truths, were enumerated. In fact Arāḍa in BC Canto 12 does not enumerate *tattvas*, though he does speak of *tattva-jñāḥ*, those who know the truth / the *tattvas* (BC12.65). And he cites *buddhi* ("the intelligent") in the category of *prakṛti*, Primary Matter (BC12.18).

[29] Or "to which you belong" - the genitive *bhavatas* leaves open both subjective and objective readings.

Canto 8: antaḥ-pura-vilāpaḥ
Lamenting within the Women's Quarters
[or Lamenting from within the Battlements]

Introduction

As discussed in the introduction to Canto 2, the ostensible meaning of *antaḥ-pura* is "the women's apartments," but literally *antaḥ-pura* means within (*antar*) a fortress, city or other fortified area (*pura*). Hence *antaḥ-pura* can mean not only the women's quarters within a palace complex but also, more widely, a king's palace - and, in the hidden meaning, the area that falls within the sphere of protection of a protector of men, i.e. the sphere of influence of a buddha.

The other element of the canto title, *vilāpa*, ostensibly means unconscious expression of grief, as when a cow moos through the night for a calf that has been taken away to satisfy the market for veal. But in verse 70, the actions of a lamenting queen are described as *ruroda dadhyau vilalāpa*, "she wept, she reflected/meditated, she lamented." In the hidden meaning, then, *vilāpa* might suggest not unconscious expression of grief but rather conscious teaching on suffering that emerges, via reflection and meditation, out of suffering. In this sense, the Buddha's turning of the Dharma-wheel, in which he taught the four noble truths, was just lamenting from within the battlements.

Ironically, then, below the surface this canto is a kind of celebration. It is a celebration of the truths of suffering, arising of suffering, cessation of suffering, and practice leading towards cessation of suffering. The ironic subtext of celebration is there, for example, when Chanda describes non-doing action seeming spontaneously to do itself, in the zone of the gods.

tatas turaṅgāvacaraḥ sa dur-manās tathā vanaṁ bhartari nirmame gate /
cakāra yatnaṁ pathi śoka-nigrahe tathāpi caivāśru na tasya cikṣipe // 8.1 //
In low spirits, meanwhile - with his master gone thus,[1] with no sense of me and mine, to the forest - / He whose sphere was horses made on the road an effort to suppress his sorrow. And surely enough, he, while also being thus, failed to banish his tears. //8.1//

yam eka-rātreṇa tu bhartur ājñayā jagāma mārgaṁ saha tena vājinā /
iyāya bhartur virahaṁ vicintayaṁs tam eva panthānam ahobhir aṣṭabhiḥ // 8.2 //
But the road which at his master's behest he with that warhorse had travelled in one night - / That same road, pondering the master's desertion, [or reflecting on the separateness of a master,] he now travelled in eight days.[2] //8.2//

---

[1] *tathā.... gate*, "thus... gone," suggests one meaning of *tathāgata*, "the Thus-Gone," as an epithet of the Buddha.
[2] Ostensibly he travelled slowly because of being in a bad state. The alternative reading is that Chandaka - representing the more mental aspect of a psycho-physical unity - was in a reflective or meditative state.

hayaś ca saujasvi cacāra kanthakas tatāma bhāvena babhūva nirmadaḥ /
alaṁkṛtaś cāpi tathaiva bhūṣaṇair abhūd gata-śrīr iva tena varjitaḥ // 8.3 //
And the horse Kanthaka moved himself by an effort of physical strength; he panted; he was, through his whole being, devoid of ebullience;[3] / Again, decked though he was in decorative trappings, he seemed, without the one in question, to lack luster. //8.3//

nivṛtya caivābhimukhas tapo-vanaṁ bhṛśaṁ jiheṣe karuṇaṁ muhur muhuḥ /
kṣudhānvito 'py adhvani śaṣpam ambu vā yathā purā nābhinananda nādade // 8.4 //
And yet, having turned back, so that he was fronting the woods of painful practice, loudly he neighed, pitifully,[4] again and again. / However hungry he was, he neither rejoiced at nor partook of, as before, grass or water on the road.[5] //8.4//

tato vihīnaṁ kapilāhvayaṁ puraṁ mahātmanā tena jagadd-hitātmanā /
krameṇa tau śūnyam ivopajagmatur divākareṇeva vinā-kṛtaṁ nabhaḥ // 8.5 //
And so, the city called after Kapila, the city forsaken by that mighty soul whose soul was given to the welfare of the world, / The two approached, step by gradual step, as if approaching emptiness – an emptiness like the sky bereft of the day-making sun. //8.5//

sa-puṇḍarīkair api śobhitaṁ jalair alaṁkṛtaṁ puṣpa-dharair nagair api /
tad eva tasyopavanaṁ vanopamaṁ gata-praharṣair na rarāja nāgaraiḥ // 8.6 //
The city's park, though graced by lotus-covered waters, though adorned by flower-bearing plants, / Being nothing but that park itself, was like the woods – it no longer exuded lordly splendor[6] now that the citizens' exuberant joy was gone. //8.6//

tato bhramadbhir diśi dīna-mānasair anujjvalair bāṣpa-hatekṣaṇair naraiḥ /
nivāryamāṇāv iva tāv ubhau puraṁ śanair apasnātam ivābhijagmatuḥ // 8.7 //
Thus, as though being slowed down, by men wandering in their direction, men with dispirited minds, men no longer blazing, men whose eyes tears had knocked out,[7] / The two together approached the city – as silently as if going to a funeral bath. //8.7//

---

[3] Ostensibly, again, *nirmada* suggests being at a low psycho-physical ebb. But *mada* has connotations of being puffed up with pride or intoxication or wantonness. So in its hidden meaning *nirmada* also points to a reflective or meditative state. Cf. SN12.11: "Trembling went he of mighty arm, like a top bull elephant, through with rut (*nirmadaḥ*)."

[4] *Karuṇam* can mean either deserving or showing compassion. Ostensibly the meaning here is pitifully in the sense of deserving pity; the hidden meaning may be that the neighing was pitiful in the archaic sense of pitiful – i.e. being full of pity.

[5] Ostensibly the horse also had changed for the worse. But in the ironic hidden meaning, something in Kanthaka – representing greater physical prowess in a psycho-physical unity – had changed for the better.

[6] *Na rarāja*; in the hidden meaning, there is no pejorative sense: the park was as it was. See also note to verse 13.

[7] In the ironic hidden meaning, men who no longer have any illusions – non-buddhas.

niśamya ca srasta-śarīra-gāminau vināgatau śākya-kularṣabheṇa tau
mumoca bāṣpaṁ pathi nāgaro janaḥ purā rathe dāśarather ivāgate // 8.8 //
And seeing the pair with disjointed gaits, their bodies hanging loosely,[8] coming back without the bull of the Śākya herd, / The people of the city let their tears fall on the road – like in ancient times when the chariot of Rāma, son of 'Ten Chariots' Daśa-ratha, came back [without Rāma]. //8.8//

atha bruvantaḥ samupeta-manyavo janāḥ pathi chandakam āgatāsravaḥ /
kva rāja-putraḥ pura-rāṣṭra-nandano hṛtas tvayāsāv iti pṛṣṭhato 'nvayuḥ // 8.9 //
There again, speaking tensely, common folk afflicted by distress[9] addressed Chandaka on the road – / "Where is the Child of the King, the joy of the city and of the kingdom? You have stolen away that child!" they said, from the rear, following behind.[10] //8.9//

tataḥ sa tān bhaktimato 'bravīj janān narendra-putraṁ na parityajāmy aham /
rudann-ahaṁ tena tu nirjane vane gṛha-stha-veśaś ca visarjitāv iti // 8.10 //
Then he said to those devout folk: "No neglecter am I of the child of a lord among men. / On the contrary, by that child in the folk-free forest, the weeping I, and the clothes of a householder, are both cast off together."[11] //8.10//

idaṁ vacas tasya niśamya te janāḥ su-duṣkaraṁ khalv iti vismayam yayuḥ /
patadd hi jahruḥ salilaṁ na netra-jaṁ mano nininduś ca phalārtham ātmanaḥ // 8.11 //
When those common folk heard this utterance of his, because of its very great difficulty, they were dismayed; / For the eye-born flood of falling tears they had not averted, and their own minds, taking account of karmic retribution, they did blame.[12] //8.11//

athocur adyaiva viśāma tad vanaṁ gataḥ sa yatra dvipa-rāja-vikramaḥ /
jijīviṣā nāsti hi tena no vinā yathendriyāṇāṁ vigame śarīriṇām // 8.12 //
Or else they said: "Right now let us go into that forest,[13] where he is, whose stride is the stride of a king of elephants; / For without him we have no wish to live on, like embodied beings when the power of the senses has departed. //8.12//

---

[8] Cf BC3.28 *śithilānatāṅgaḥ*, "limbs loose and bending."

[9] Amendment to *āgatāśravaḥ*, would give "visited by tears." But *āgatāsravaḥ* or "afflicted by the pollutants [namely, desire (*kāmāsrava*), becoming (*bhavāsrava*), and ignorance (*avidyāsrava*)]," as per the Old Nepalese manuscript, also has meaning.

[10] A suggestion of a lack of initiative which tends to be shown by religious followers? In the hidden meaning, are the devout expecting some kind of outside intervention, so that their own buddha-nature might be restored to them?

[11] In the hidden meaning, Chandaka is (1) emphasizing the importance of each individual regularly not neglecting (atop a round black cushion) his or her own buddha-nature; and (2) suggesting how, ultimately, it is not I who abandons *the weeping I* so much as it is the buddha-nature which casts off *the weeping I.*

[12] In short, this group of devout believers, not being awake to the four noble truths, wallowed in self-reproach.

[13] Or else they rushed too hastily into action.

idaṁ puraṁ tena vivarjitaṁ vanaṁ vanaṁ ca tat tena samanvitaṁ puram /
na śobhate tena hi no vinā puraṁ marutvatā vṛtra-vadhe yathā divam // 8.13 //
This city without him is the woods, and those woods in his presence are a city. / For in his absence our city does not shine - like heaven without *marut*-attended Indra, at the slaying of Vṛtra [Or like the sky, without the Almighty and his storm-gods, at the break-up of a thunder-cloud]."[14] //8.13//

punaḥ kumāro vinivṛtta ity atho gavākṣa-mālāḥ pratipedire 'ṅganāḥ /
vivikta-pṛṣṭhaṁ ca niśamya vājinaṁ punar gavākṣāṇi pidhāya cukruśuḥ // 8.14 //
"The prince has come back again!" said the women, as now they appeared in the rows of round windows. / But seeing the horse's empty back, they closed the windows again and wailed. //8.14//

praviṣṭa-dīkṣas tu sutopalabdhaye vratena śokena ca khinna-mānasaḥ /
jajāpa devāyatane narādhipaś cakāra tās tāś ca yathāśrayāḥ kriyāḥ // 8.15 //
Whereas, having undertaken complete dedication, with a view to getting a son, his mind exhausted by observance and by sorrow, / The ruler of men spoke in whispers in the temple, and performed, as he felt fit, various actions.[15] //8.15//

tataḥ sa bāṣpa-pratipūrṇa-locanas turaṅgam ādāya turaṅgamānugaḥ /
viveśa śokābhihato nṛpa-kṣayaṁ yudhāpinīte ripuṇeva bhartari // 8.16 //
Then, with eyes filled with tears, the horse-servant betook to himself the horse[16] / And, beaten by sorrow, he entered the abode of a protector of men[17] - as though his master had been spirited away by an enemy warrior [or like when a master has been reeled in by a deceitful combatant].[18] //8.16//

---

[14] According to a myth recorded in the *Ṛg-veda*, having killed the demon Vṛtra, Indra went to the ends of the earth to conceal himself. Ostensibly *vṛta* means this demon, who was supposed to be in possession of the clouds. But *vṛta* also means a non-fictional thunder-cloud.

[15] In the hidden meaning, the ruler of men might represent one who, having dedicated himself completely (*praviṣṭa-dīkṣaḥ*), with a view to gaining Dharma-heirs (*sutopalabdhaye*), exhausts himself by grieving for a suffering world and by practice - he is able to convey his teaching by secret whispers in a temple, or by acting in his everyday life just as he pleases.

[16] A suggestion of sitting with body and with mind?

[17] *Nṛpa-kṣayam*, the abode of a protector of men, the seat of a king, carries, as in so many similar instances, the hidden meaning of sitting-meditation, as dropping off of body and mind.

[18] Ostensibly Chanda was downcast, in a bad state, like one whose master has been spirited away *yudhā ripunā*, by an enemy warrior. For a possible hidden meaning: one master is reeled in, or led astray, by another master - and thus something transcendent is celebrated, as in so many of the famous koans recorded in Tang China.

vigāhamānaś ca narendra-mandiraṁ vilokayann aśru-vahena cakṣuṣā /
svareṇa puṣṭena rurāva kanthako janāya duḥkhaṁ prativedayann iva // 8.17 //
Also entering the royal stable, while looking through tearful eyes, Kanthaka roared in a full-sounding voice, as if making his suffering known to the people. //8.17// [Alternative translation] Immersing himself in the place of stillness of the best of men,[19] while looking, with an eye containing tears,[20] Kanthaka roared in a full-sounding voice, as if, for the benefit of humanity, causing suffering to be known. //8.17//

tataḥ kha-gāś ca kṣaya-madhya-gocarāḥ samīpa-baddhās turagāś ca sat-kṛtāḥ /
hayasya tasya pratisasvanuḥ svanaṁ narendra-sūnor upayāna-śaṅkitāḥ // 8.18 //
Then the birds whose feeding place was in the middle of the dwelling, and the well-treated horses tethered nearby, / Echoed the sound of that horse, in anticipation of the prince's approach. //8.18// [Alternative translation] Then those movers in empty space[21] whose range, in loss,[22] is the middle, and those venerated[23] movers in readiness[24] who are bound to immediacy,[25] / Echoed the sound of that horse, with the intuitive sense of getting close which belongs to a son or a daughter of the best of men[26]. //8.18//

janāś ca harṣātiśayena vañcitā janādhipāntaḥ-pura-saṁnikarṣa-gāḥ /
yathā hayaḥ kanthaka eṣa heṣate dhruvaṁ kumāro viśatīti menire // 8.19 //
Over-exuberance, again, deceived people who were moving in the vicinity of the battlements of their lord.[27] / "Since the horse Kanthaka is here neighing," they thought, "It must be that the prince is on his way!" //8.19//

ati-praharṣād atha śoka-mūrchitāḥ kumāra-saṁdarśana-lola-locanāḥ /
gṛhād viniścakramur āśayā striyaḥ śarat-payodād iva vidyutaś calāḥ // 8.20 //
And so in their exuberant joy, the women who had been insensible with grief, their darting eyes now eager for a sight of the prince, / Stepped forth from their homes full of hope – like flashes of lightning from an autumn cloud.[28] //8.20//

---

[19] *Mandira* is from the root √*mand*, to stand still, to abide. It means a place of abiding, e.g. a waiting room, or a stable for horses. So *narendra-mandiram* ostensibly means the royal stable, but again a hidden meaning might be sitting-meditation as a place of calm abiding.

[20] In a possible hidden meaning, insight informed by the four noble truths.

[21] *Kha-gāḥ*, "goers in empty space," means birds, and, in a possible hidden meaning, those whose practice is emptiness.

[22] The meanings of *kṣaya* include 1. abode, dwelling-place and 2. loss, destruction.

[23] The meanings of *sat-kṛta* include 1. well-treated and 2. venerated, worshipped.

[24] *Tura-gāḥ*, "fast goers," means horses, and, in a possible hidden meaning, those whose consciousness is quick, people who are awake.

[25] *Samīpa-baddha*: 1. tethered (*baddha*) nearby (*samīpa*); 2. bound (*baddha*) to nearness (*samīpa*). In a hidden meaning, then, this might be a phrase equivalent to Dōgen's 被礙兀地 (*gocchi ni saeraru*), "bound to the still state." Cf also *nidrayā hṛta*, "seized by repose," in verse 47 below.

[26] *Narendra-sūnoḥ*, "of the son of best of men," means the prince's, and in a possible hidden meaning, belonging to a follower of the Buddha.

[27] The deceitful combatant of BC8.16 may be relevant here – a hidden sense being that we are, via a state of nervous excitement, brought by expedient means into the sphere of influence of buddhas, as e.g. Nanda was in the story of Handsome Nanda.

[28] In the hidden meaning, the women's eager interest mirrors the curiosity of those who have

vilamba-veṣyo malināṁśukāmbarā nirañjanair bāṣpa-hatekṣaṇair mukhaiḥ /
kṛṣṇā vivarṇā mṛjayā vinā-kṛtā divīva tārā rajanī-kṣayāruṇāḥ // 8.21 //
Their hair having dropped down, wearing garments of dirty cloth,[29] with unrouged faces whose eyes had been marred by tears,[30] / Bereft of cosmetic embellishment, they manifested themselves as colorless – like stars in the sky when red dawn is dispelling dark night. //8.21//

arakta-tāmraiś caraṇair anūpurair akuṇḍalair ārjava-karṇikair mukhaiḥ /
svabhāva-pīnair jaghanair amekhalair a-hāra-yoktrair muṣitair iva stanaiḥ // 8.22 //
Their feet were without ornaments and not painted red; their faces were flanked by plain ears, ears without ear-rings; / Their hips and thighs, without girdles, were naturally full; their female breasts, without their ropes of pearls, seemed to have been stripped naked. //8.22// [Alternative translation] Their unembellished practices[31] were not reddened by passion; their mouths[32] were connected with ears of frankness, unfettered ears; / Their hips and thighs, ungirt of the belts that signified social rank,[33] expanded by themselves; their breasts, without any attachment to stripping away,[34] seemed to have been laid bare. //8.22//

nirīkṣya tā bāṣpa-parīta-locanā nir-āśrayaṁ chandakam aśvam eva ca /
viṣaṇṇa-vaktrā rurudur varāṅganā vanāntare gāva iva ṛṣabhojjhitāḥ // 8.23 //
Looking through tearful eyes at the destitute Chandaka-and-horse,[35] having nothing to depend upon, / Those beautiful women wept, with downcast faces, like cows in the woods abandoned by the bull. //8.23//

tataḥ sa-bāṣpā mahiṣī mahī-pateḥ pranaṣṭa-vatsā mahiṣīva vatsalā /
pragṛhya bāhū nipapāta gautamī vilola-parṇā kadalīva kāñcanī // 8.24 //
Then the king's queen, Gautamī, tearful as a doting water buffalo that had lost her calf, / Abducted her arms[36] and fell, fronds shuddering, like a golden banana plant. //8.24//

---

established the will to the truth, in regard to what a buddha's enlightenment might be.

[29] In the hidden meaning, a reference to the filthy rags (Jap: *funzo-e*) traditionally regarded as the best and purest material out of which to patch together a kaṣāya.

[30] *Bāṣpa-hatekṣaṇaiḥ*, as in verse 7 above.

[31] *Caraṇa* means foot and, in the hidden meaning, practice.

[32] *Mukha* means face or mouth.

[33] *Mekhala* means a girdle or belt, but (according to SED) "especially one worn by men of the first three classes."

[34] The many meanings of *hāra* include a necklace, and taking away. In the hidden meaning, is Aśvaghoṣa praising the attitude of Zen practitioners who let body and mind drop away naturally, without being tempted to do anything to try to help the process along?

[35] In the hidden meaning, they realized not only the mental but also the physical. Ostensibly Chandaka and the horse were destitute (*nir-āśrayam*); in the hidden meaning, those who saw realized emptiness, having no self-existing thing to depend upon (*nir-āśrayam*).

[36] Cf the description of palaces seeming to fling out their arms in verse 37.

hata-tviṣo 'nyāḥ śithilātma-bāhavaḥ striyo viṣādena vicetanā iva /
na cukruśur nāśru jahur na śaśvasur na celur āsur likhitā iva sthitāḥ // 8.25 //
Other women, being bereft of sparkle, being flaccid in their core and in their arms, women who seemed by their languor to be almost insensible, / Neither cried out, nor shed tears; they neither audibly breathed, nor moved a muscle: As if in a painting, they stayed still. //8.25// [Alternative translation] Individual women, being different, being free of fury, being relaxed in their souls and loose in their arms, women who seemed by their languor to be almost insensible, / Neither cried out, nor shed tears; they neither audibly breathed, nor moved a muscle: As if in a painting, they stayed still.[37] //8.25//

adhīram anyāḥ pati-śoka-mūrchitā vilocana-prasravaṇair mukhaiḥ striyaḥ /
siṣiñcire proṣita-candanān stanān dharā-dharāḥ prasravaṇair ivopalān // 8.26 //
Other women, losing control, dizzied by sorrow for their lord, with streaming faces, whose wellsprings were eyes, / Wetted bare breasts bereft of sandal paste - like mountains with their wellsprings wetting rocks. //8.26// [Alternative translation] Those women, as individuals who were different, not in a fixed manner,[38] but as masters caused through sorrow to grow,[39] with streaming faces, whose wellsprings were eyes, / Wetted bare breasts bereft of sandal paste - like mountains with their wellsprings wetting rocks. //8.26//

mukhaiś ca tāsāṁ nayanāmbu-tāḍitaiḥ rarāja tad-rāja-niveśanaṁ tadā /
navāmbu-kāle 'mbu-da-vṛṣṭi-tāḍitaiḥ sravaj-jalais tāma-rasair yathā saraḥ // 8.27 //
And in the presence of the tear stricken faces of those individuals, that lair of kings, in that moment, was bathed in splendor - / Like a lake at the time of the first rains when clouds with their raindrops are striking its dripping lotuses.[40] //8.27//

su-vṛtta-pīnāṅgulibhir nir-antarair abhūṣaṇair gūḍha-sirair varāṅganāḥ /
urāṁsi jaghnuḥ kamalopamaiḥ karaiḥ sva-pallavair vāta-calā latā iva // 8.28 //
With hands whose gapless fingers were beautifully round and full, with unadorned hands whose blood-vessels were invisible, / With their hands resembling lotuses, the most beautiful of women beat their breasts - like wind-blown creepers beating themselves with their own tendrils. //8.28//

---

[37] As also in BC Canto 5, "the women" in the hidden meaning represent practitioners sitting still in a meditation hall. Ostensibly their arms were flaccid, lacking muscle tone; in the hidden meaning, their joints were free of undue tension. Ostensibly their lifeless state made their breathing unduly shallow and barely perceptible; in the hidden meaning, there was no restriction in their breathing, which was therefore as silent as a winter breeze in a forest without leaves.

[38] *Adhīra* means "deficient in calm self-command," excitable; in the hidden meaning, it means not fixed, adaptable.

[39] In the compound *pati-śoka-mūrchitāḥ*, *pati-śoka* ostensibly means "sorrow for their lord/master" but can equally mean "the sorrow of a master." The meanings of √*murch* include 1. to become solid, thicken, and, by extension, to stupefy; and 2. to expand, increase, grow. Hence *mūrchitāḥ* could be describing the women as 1. stupefied, fainting, dizzied [by sorrow for their lost lord]; or, in the hidden meaning, 2. caused to grow [through the experience of sorrow as a master].

[40] Here as in several previous verses, by comparing grieving women with rain-soaked lotuses Aśvaghoṣa hints at the possibility of there being profound beauty, even in bitter-sweet investigation of the noble truth of suffering.

kara-prahāra-pracalaiś ca tā babhur yathāpi nāryaḥ sahitonnataiḥ stanaiḥ /
vanānilāghūrṇita-padma-kampitaiḥ rathāṅga-nāmnāṁ mithunair ivāpagāḥ // 8.29 //
Again, as their conjoined and upturned breasts trembled under the barrage from their hands, those women also resembled rivers / Whose lotuses, sent whirling by the forest wind, shook into movement pairs of *rathaṅga* geese – geese called after a wheel.[41] //8.29//

yathā ca vakṣāṁsi karair apīḍayaṁs tathaiva vakṣobhir apīḍayan karān /
akārayaṁs tatra paras paraṁ vyathāḥ karāgra-vakṣāṁsy abalā dayālasāḥ // 8.30 //
Insofar as they goaded their bosoms with their hands, to that same degree they goaded their hands with their bosoms; / Those in that loop[42] whose strength was not in strength, their compassion being inactive,[43] made bosoms, and the tips of doing hands, antagonize each other.[44] //8.30//

tatas tu roṣa-pravirakta-locanā viṣāda-sambandha-kaṣāya-gadgadam /
uvāca niśvāsa-calat-payodharā vigāḍha-śokāśru-dharā yaśodharā // 8.31 //
But then, with eyes reddened by fury, stammering with the emotion that belongs to despondent love, / Up spoke a bearer of glory, whose milk-bearers[45] heaved as she sighed – bearing tears of grief running deep as the Earth, Yaśodharā said: //8.31//

niśi prasuptām avaśāṁ vihāya māṁ gataḥ kva sa chandaka man-mano-rathaḥ /
upāgate ca tvayi kanthake ca me samaṁ gateṣu triṣu kampate manaḥ // 8.32 //
"Leaving me helplessly asleep in the night, where, Chandaka, has the joy of my heart gone? / Seeing you and Kanthaka come back, when three departed,[46] my mind, in all honesty, wavers. //8.32//

---

[41] For more on *rathaṇga* geese, aka *cakravāka* ducks, see note to verse 60 below. Here women's breasts are compared to pairs of these birds being shaken into movement beneath lotus faces. On the surface, Aśvaghoṣa may seem to be unduly interested in beautiful women's breasts. Below the surface his point may be to stimulate us to reflect what it really is, whether we are a man or a woman, to be a mammal. For example, to what extent is the course of a life of a human being born on the earth, as a mammal, determined by emotion, and to what extent by reason?

[42] *Tatra* means there, or in that state, in that loop.

[43] The subject is *abalā dayālasāḥ*. Ostensibly *abalāh* means "those who are weak (f.)," i.e. women as the so-called weaker sex; and *dayālasāḥ* means "disinclined to pity" (*dayā* = pity, compassion; *a-lasa* = inactive, lazy, faint). In the hidden meaning, Aśvaghoṣa seems to be suggesting that true compassion tends to be manifested subtly, by indirect means, and not so much by brute force.

[44] A *kara*, a hand, is literally "a doer," from the root √*kṛ*, to do or make. Goading bosoms with hands might be a metaphor for stimulating the lazy heart and mind by doing something. Conversely, goading hands with bosoms can be understood as a metaphor for stimulating the lazy body by thinking something. The relation between bosoms and hands thus mirrors the relation already suggested between Kanthaka and Chanda, horse and groom.

[45] *Payodhara* means bearer or container of liquid, i.e. a cloud or a breast. The use of *payodhara* here is partly poetic, since Yaśodharā means Bearer of Glory. But it is also a further reminder of the mammalian nature of human grief.

[46] If Kanthaka is body and Chanda is mind, do Yaśodharā's words suggest that the missing third element is [her] heart?

anāryam asnidgham amitra-karma me nṛśaṁsa kṛtvā kim ihādya rodiṣi /
niyaccha bāṣpaṁ bhava tuṣṭa-mānaso na saṁvadaty aśru ca tac ca karma te // 8.33 //
It is an ignoble and ungentle action, the action of a non-friend,[47] that you, O dealer in others' pain,[48] have done to me. Why now do you weep? / Stop the tears! Let your mind be satisfied! Tears, and that action of yours, do not chime well together. //8.33//

priyeṇa vaśyena hitena sādhunā tvayā sahāyena yathārtha-kāriṇā /
gato 'rya-putro hy apunar nivṛttaye ramasva diṣṭyā sa-phalaḥ śramas tava // 8.34 //
For, thanks to you, a devoted friend – willing, well-meaning, and straight, a doer of what was necessary – / That noble son is gone, never to return. Be glad! How wonderful for you, that your effort was fruitful![49] //8.34//

varaṁ manuṣyasya vicakṣaṇo ripur na mitram aprājñam ayoga-peśalam /
suhṛd-bruveṇa hy avipaścitā tvayā kṛtaḥ kulasyāsya mahān upaplavaḥ // 8.35 //
It is better for a man to have an insightful enemy, rather than a friend of no wisdom, skilled in no method;[50] / For thanks to you, one versed in nothing who calls himself a friend,[51] great misfortune has befallen this noble house. //8.35//

imā hi śocyā vyavamukta-bhūṣaṇāḥ prasakta-bāṣpāvila-rakta-locanāḥ /
sthite 'pi patyau himavan-mahī-same pranaṣṭa-śobhā vidhavā iva striyaḥ // 8.36 //
These women are deeply to be commiserated, who have shed embellishments, whose bloodshot eyes are clouded by tears of lasting devotion, / Who are like widows who lost their former luster – though their master is still there, standing firm on those flat Himālayan uplands [or being as even as the snow-clad earth].[52] //8.36//

---

[47] *A-mitra,* a non-friend, in its hidden meaning might be a true friend – as a non-buddha is a true buddha, not one who necessarily conforms to expectations.

[48] *Nṛ-śaṁsa* lit. means "injuring men;" hence, cruel. In the hidden meaning, an ironic epithet for one steeped in the wisdom of the four noble truths?

[49] A double bluff – Yaśodharā intends her words to be ironic, not true. The real irony, below the surface, is that her words *are* true.

[50] *Aprājñam ayoga-peśalam. A-prājñam* ostensibly means unlearned, having no wisdom, but in the hidden meaning, having the wisdom of no, the wisdom of going without. *Ayoga-peśalam* ostensibly means skilful (*peśalam*) only in the wrong way *(ayoga)*" but, in the hidden meaning, skilful (*peśalam*) in the way (*yoga*) of no (*a-*).

[51] In the hidden meaning, again, the horse-tamer is a person of wisdom and compassion. *A-vipaś-cit* ostensibly means not (*a-*) knowing (*-cit*) enlightenment (*vipas*); hence unwise, ignorant; but in the ironic hidden meaning knowing (*-cit*) the enlightenment (*vipas*) of non- (*a-*).

[52] *Himavan-mahī-same* could be read "remaining as constant as the Himālayas or the Earth," or "being the same as the Himālayas and the earth," or "being as even as the ground in the Himālayas." In the hidden meaning, again, the women are Zen practitioners. The object of their devotion is constantly in balance.

imāś ca vikṣipta-viṭaṅka-bāhavaḥ prasakta-pārāvata-dīrgha-nisvanāḥ /
vinā-kṛtās tena sahāvarodhanair bhṛśaṁ rudantīva vimāna-paṅktayaḥ // 8.37 //
These rows of palaces too, flinging the dove-cots of their arms up and out,[53] their long calls being the cooing of devoted doves, / Seem when bereft of him, along with the women of the inner apartments, mightily to weep and wail. //8.37//

anartha-kāmo 'sya janasya sarvathā turaṅgamo 'pi dhruvam eṣa kanthakaḥ /
jahāra sarvasvam itas tathā hi me jane prasupte niśi ratna-cauravat // 8.38 //
This here horse Kanthaka, also, is constantly desirous that I, in every way, should come to naught.[54] / For thus, from here, he took away my everything – like a jewel thief who steals in the night, while people are fast asleep. //8.38//

yadā samarthaḥ khalu soḍhum āgatān iṣu-prahārān api kiṁ punaḥ kaśāḥ /
gataḥ kaśā-yāta-bhayāt kathaṁ nv ayaṁ śriyaṁ gṛhītvā hṛdayaṁ ca me samam // 8.39 //
When he is well able to defy even incoming arrows, to say nothing of whips, / How could fear[55] of a whip's goading have caused this [fast-goer] to go, snatching away, in equal measure, my royal pomp and my heart? //8.39//

anārya-karmā bhṛśam adya heṣate narendra-dhiṣṇyaṁ pratipūrayann iva /
yadā tu nirvāhayati sma me priyaṁ tadā hi mūkas turagādhamo 'bhavat // 8.40 //
Now the doer of un-āryan deeds is neighing loudly, as if filling with sound the seat of a first among men; / But when he carried away my love, then the low-down donkey was dumb.[56] //8.40//

yadi hy aheṣiṣyata bodhayan janaṁ khuraiḥ kṣitau vāpy akariṣyata dhvanim /
hanu-svanaṁ vājanayiṣyad uttamaṁ na cābhaviṣyan mama duḥkham īdṛśam // 8.41 //
For if he had whinnied, waking people up, or else had made a noise with his hoofs on the ground, / – Or had he made the loudest sound he could with his jaws [had he sounded the ultimate warning of death and disease[57]] – I would not have experienced suffering like this."[58] //8.41//

---

[53] An allusion to the infantile panic reflex (the so-called Moro reflex)? See also BC8.24 above, and the description of Sundarī in SN Canto 6 (SN6.24-27).

[54] In the hidden meaning, a suggestion of the fact that in the natural world all energy tends to dissipate? Kanthaka in general stands for the power of nature, or the physical body harnessed to the mind of Chanda. (Chandaka's name originally means Liking, Volition, Desire, Will.)

[55] *Bhayāt* means "because of fear." Below the surface Yaśodharā's question seems to ask whether what goes readily in nature can be forced to go through intimidatory tactics.

[56] Below the surface, is an auto-biographical element discernible? Is Aśvaghoṣa (the Horse-Whinny) mindful of his own loud efforts in the Dharma Hall and silent efforts in the Meditation Hall?

[57] *Hanu* means 1. (fr. √*han*, to destroy) "anything which destroys or injures life," death, disease; and 2. (not fr. √*han*) a jaw. Thus *hanu-svanam* ostensibly means "the sound of his jaws," but a hidden meaning might be "a sound [warning] of death and disease."

[58] Ostensible meaning: I would not have experienced such terrible suffering. Hidden meaning: I would not have experienced, in this manner, the purport of the four noble truths.

itīha devyāḥ paridevitāśrayaṁ niśamya bāṣpa-grathitākṣaraṁ vacaḥ /
adho-mukhaḥ sāśru-kalaḥ kṛtāñjaliḥ śanair idaṁ chandaka uttaraṁ jagau // 8.42 //
When thus he had heard, here in this world, the lament-laden words of the queen, whose every syllable had been punctuated with a tear, / Chandaka, face turned down, tongue-tied by his own tearfulness, and hands held like a beggar's, softly voiced the following response: //8.42//

vigarhituṁ nārhasi devi kanthakaṁ na cāpi roṣaṁ mayi kartum arhasi /
anāgasau svaḥ samavehi sarvaśo gato nṛ-devaḥ sa hi devi devavat // 8.43 //
"Please do not blame Kanthaka, O godly queen, nor show anger towards me. / Know us both as blameless in every way, for that god among men, O royal goddess, departed like a god. //8.43//

ahaṁ hi jānann api rāja-śāsanaṁ balāt kṛtaḥ kair api daivatair iva /
upānayaṁ tūrṇam imaṁ turaṅgamaṁ tathānvagacchaṁ vigata-śramo 'dhvani // 8.44 //
For, knowing full-well the instruction of the king,[59] I, as though I were compelled by gods of some description, / Swiftly brought this swift horse, and in that effortless manner I followed, on the road.[60] //8.44//

vrajann ayaṁ vāji-varo 'pi nāspṛśan mahīṁ khurāgrair vidhṛtair ivāntarā /
tathaiva daivād iva saṁyatānano hanu-svanaṁ nākṛta nāpy aheṣata // 8.45 //
This royal war-horse, also, as he went, did not touch the ground, the tips of his hooves seeming to dangle separately in midair. / His mouth was sealed as if, again, by a divine force; he neither neighed nor made a sound with his jaws [neither neighed nor sounded the warning of death and disease].[61] //8.45//

yadā bahir gacchati pārthivātmaje tadābhavad dvāram apāvṛtaṁ svayam /
tamaś ca naiśaṁ raviṇeva pāṭitaṁ tato 'pi daivo vidhir eṣa gṛhyatām // 8.46 //
The moment that the prince moved outwards, the way out spontaneously became open / And the darkness of night was broken as if by the sun – hence, again, let this be grasped as action in the presence of the gods. //8.46//

---

[59] *Rāja-śāsanam.* Ostensible meaning: King Śuddhodana's command. Hidden meaning: the teaching of the king of dharma.

[60] A suggestion of action – non-doing action – that seems effortlessly to do itself, when the gods are on our side?

[61] A suggestion of action that does itself in the Meditation Hall (as opposed to preaching that does itself in the Dharma Hall)?

yad apramatto 'pi narendra-śāsanād gṛhe pure caiva sahasraśo janaḥ /
tadā sa nābudhyata nidrayā hṛtas tato 'pi daivo vidhir eṣa gṛhyatām // 8.47 //
In accordance with the instruction of the best of men, people in their thousands, in house and town, were leaving nothing unattended;[62] / In that moment all were seized by repose and not roused to wakefulness[63] - hence, again, let this be grasped as action in the zone of the gods. //8.47//

yataś ca vāso vana-vāsa-saṁmataṁ nisṛṣṭam asmai samaye divaukasā /
divi praviddhaṁ mukuṭaṁ ca tadd hṛtaṁ tato 'pi daivo vidhir eṣa gṛhyatām // 8.48 //
And since, in that most opportune of moments, the robe approved for living the forest life was bestowed on him by a sky dweller, / And that headdress which he launched into the sky was borne away - hence, again, let this be grasped as action in the lap of the gods. //8.48//

tad evam āvāṁ nara-devi doṣato na tat-prayātaṁ prati-gantum arhasi /
na kāma-kāro mama nāsya vājinaḥ kṛtānuyātraḥ sa hi daivatair gataḥ // 8.49 //
Therefore, O royal goddess!, do not blame the two of us for his departure. / It was neither my nor this horse's own doing; for he went with the gods in his train."[64] //8.49//

iti prayāṇaṁ bahudhaivam adbhutaṁ niśamya tās tasya mahātmanaḥ striyaḥ /
pranaṣṭa-śokā iva vismayaṁ yayur mano-jvaraṁ pravrajanāt tu lebhire // 8.50 //
When thus the women heard of the starting out, which was in so many ways miraculous, of that mighty man, / They felt such amazement that the flame of sorrow seemed to go out. And yet they conceived, following on from the going forth, fever of the mind.[65] //8.50//

viṣāda-pāriplava-locanā tataḥ pranaṣṭa-potā kurarīva duḥkhitā /
vihāya dhairyaṁ virurāva gautamī tatāma caivāśru-mukhī jagāda ca // 8.51 //
Then, her eyes swimming in despondency, the grief-stricken Gautamī, like an osprey who had lost her chicks, / Gave up all semblance of composure and squealed. Tearful-faced, she gasped for the breath in which she said: //8.51//

---

[62] Ostensible meaning: at King Śuddhodana's behest, everybody was on guard. Hidden meaning: in accordance with the Buddha's teaching, many individuals devoted themselves to mindful practice - wherein body and mind dropped off naturally.

[63] *Abudhyata* is imperfect (woke up) or imperfect passive (was awakened). In looking for the hidden meaning, we are caused to question how or whether anybody wakes up or is woken up, with or without outside intervention.

[64] In the hidden meaning, a reminder that non-doing action is beyond psycho-physical duality?

[65] *Mano-jvaram*, "fever of the mind," ostensibly means grief, mental pain, heartache, following the prince's going forth. The hidden meaning might be that, following their own transcendence of grief, they became zealous in practice.

mahormimanto mṛdavo 'sitāḥ śubhāḥ pṛthak-pṛthaṅ mūla-ruhāḥ samudgatāḥ /
praveritās te bhuvi tasya mūrdha-jā narendra-maulī-pariveṣṭana-kṣamāḥ // 8.52 //
"Flowing in great waves, soft, black and beautiful, each hair rising up singly, growing from its own root: / Have those locks of his, born from his head, been cast upon the ground? – locks of hair which are fit to be encircled by a king's crown! //8.52// [Alternative translation] Flowing in great waves, soft, beautiful, and not white,[66] those thoughts of his, born from the summit,[67] have been cast upon the act of becoming[68] – / Each thought emerging singly, springing up from the fundamental: thoughts which are fit to encase the cranium of the best of men! //8.52//

pralamba-bāhur mṛga-rāja-vikramo maharṣabhākṣaḥ kanakojjvala-dyutiḥ /
viśāla-vakṣā ghana-dundubhi-svanas tathā-vidho 'py āśrama-vāsam arhati // 8.53 //
Does he with his long hanging arms and lion's stride, with his great bull-like eyes, and his splendid golden luster, / With his broad chest and thunderous resonance – does such a man deserve a life in an ashram? //8.53//

abhāginī nūnam iyaṁ vasuṁ-dharā tam ārya-karmāṇam anuttamaṁ patim /
tatas tato 'sau guṇavān hi tādṛśo nṛpaḥ prajā-bhāgya-guṇaiḥ prasūyate // 8.54 //
Shall this treasure-bearing earth not claim as her possessor that peerless man of noble action? / For such a protector of men, endowed as that one is in all respects with virtues, is born to her by the merits that her offspring accrue.[69] //8.54//

[66] *Asita*, "not-white," means black. The word is thought to be a back formation from *sita*, white. In its hidden meaning, as in connection with the sage Asita in BC Canto 1, *asita* suggests what is real as negation of idealistic purity.

[67] *Mūrdha-jāḥ*, lit. "born from the head," ostensibly means hairs; but in the hidden meaning, thoughts. At the same time, *mūrdhan* can mean the top or summit of anything. So there may be an added meaning of transcendent thoughts, thoughts of a higher order.

[68] The meanings of *bhū* include 1. the act of becoming or arising, 2. the earth.

[69] Ostensibly Queen Gautamī is expressing a doubt about whether the law of cause and effect will hold – the Earth deserves to be possessed by such a man as Siddhārtha, but he has abandoned his inheritance. Below the surface, the Queen's question represents ironic affirmation of cause and effect, since beneath the bodhi tree he will make the earth into his own possession.

sujāta-jālāvatatāṅgulī mṛdū nigūḍha-gulphau viṣa-puṣpa-komalau / vanānta-bhūmiṁ kaṭhināṁ kathaṁ nu tau sa-cakra-madhyau caraṇau gamiṣyataḥ // 8.55 //

How will his soft feet, with the web of the perfectly formed spreading between the toes - feet which, with their ankles concealed, have the tincture of the blue lotus[70] - / How will those feet tread the hard forest ground? Those two feet, bearing a wheel in the middle: how will they go? //8.55//

vimāna-pṛṣṭhe śayanāsanocitaṁ mahārha-vastrāguru-candanārcitam / kathaṁ nu śītoṣṇajalāgameṣu tac-charīram ojasvi vane bhaviṣyati // 8.56 //

How will his body, a body used to lying down and sitting up in the palace heights [or sitting in a state risen above disrespect][71] - a body honored with the most valuable of garments[72] and with the finest *a-guru* fragrance[73] - / How will his body subsist when cold and heat and rain come in? That body so possessed of vitality: how, in the forest, will it be? //8.56//

kulena sattvena balena varcasā śrutena lakṣmyā vayasā ca garvitaḥ / pradātum evābhyudito na yācituṁ kathaṁ sa bhikṣāṁ parataś cariṣyati // 8.57 //

How will a man so proud of his family, character, strength and shining splendour - so proud of his learning, prosperity, and power - / A man so up for giving, not for taking: how will he go around begging from others? //8.57//

śucau śayitvā śayane hiraṇ-maye prabodhyamāno niśi tūrya-nisvanaiḥ / kathaṁ bata svapsyati so 'dya me vratī paṭaikadeśāntarite mahī-tale // 8.58 //

How will he who, having slept on a pure golden bed, is awakened in the night by sounds of musical instruments, / How now will my vow-keeper drop off, on the surface of the earth, with a single piece of cloth in between?" //8.58// [Alternative translation] How will he who, after lying down in a pure golden act of lying down,[74] is caused to expand[75] in the night by sounds in the fourth state:[76] / How now will my vow-keeper[77] drop off, on the surface of the earth, with a single piece of cloth[78] in between?" //8.58//

---

[70] As it stands the second pāda is enigmatic, leading EH Johnston to amend *viṣa-puṣpa* ("the poisonous flower" = the blue lotus) to *bisa-puṣpa* ("[as tender as] a lotus-fibre or a flower"). *Bisa* means shoot, or fibre of the lotus. *Puṣpa* means flower. And *komala* means 1. tender, and 2. of like colour. With EHJ's amendment to *bisa-puṣpa-komalau,* then, the second pāda carries on from the first pāda describing the softness of the prince's feet. If the original was *viṣa-puṣpa-komalau,* its sense may in fact have been antithetical to the first pada, subverting idealism with the suggestion of a flower that on the surface looks as beautiful as a blue lotus but whose name suggests another, different dimension.

[71] *Vimāna* means 1. disrespect, 2. a palace.

[72] Ostensibly, golden brocade; in the hidden meaning, a bhikṣu's robe sewn from discarded cloth.

[73] *Aguru* means aloe incense; at the same time *a-guru* literally means "not heavy." So in the hidden meaning the suggestion is of a body lifted up by lightness.

[74] *Śayana* means bed; but originally it is an *-na* neuter action noun which means lying down, reclining - one of the four kinds of action, along with *āsana*, sitting.

[75] The meanings of *pra-√budh* include 1. to awaken (trans.), and 2. to cause to expand or bloom.

[76] *Tūrya* means 1. a musical instrument, but 2. (= *turya*) the fourth, forming a fourth part, the fourth state.

imaṁ pralāpaṁ karuṇaṁ niśamya tā bhujaiḥ pariṣvajya paras-paraṁ striyaḥ / vilocanebhyaḥ salilāni tatyajur madhūni puṣpebhya iveritā latāḥ // 8.59 //
Having heard this pitiful[79] lament, the women entwined each other with their arms / And let the tears drop from their eyes – like shaken creepers dropping beads of nectar from their flowers.[80] //8.59//

tato dharāyām apatad yaśodharā vicakravākeva rathāṅga-sāhvayā / śanaiś ca tat tad vilalāpa viklavā muhur muhur gadgada-ruddhayā girā // 8.60 //
Then Yaśodharā, "Bearer of Glory," dropped to the all-bearing earth like a goose named, for her circular call, *rathāṅgā*,[81] but without the circle-making gander.[82] / In dismay, she stuttered bit by bit this and that lament, her voice by sobbing gagged and gagged again. //8.60//

sa mām anāthāṁ saha-dharma-cāriṇīm apāsya dharmaṁ yadi kartum icchati / kuto 'sya dharmaḥ saha-dharma-cāriṇīṁ vinā tapo yaḥ paribhoktum icchati // 8.61 //
"If he wishes to perform dharma, the Law, having left me widowed, having cast aside his partner in dharma, his lawful wife, / Then where is his dharma? Where is the dharma of one who, without his partner in dharma, wishes to go ahead before her and taste ascetic practice? //8.61//

śṛṇoti nūnaṁ sa na pūrva-pārthivān mahāsudarśa-prabhṛtīn pitā-mahān / vanāni patnī-sahitān upeyuṣas tathā hi dharmaṁ mad ṛte cikīrṣati // 8.62 //
He surely has never heard of the earth-lords of ancient times, such as 'Very Beautiful to Behold' Mahā-su-darśa and other ancestors, / Who went into the woods accompanied by their wives – since thus he wishes, without me, to perform dharma. //8.62//

makheṣu vā veda-vidhāna-saṁskṛtau na daṁpatī paśyati dīkṣitāv ubhau / samaṁ bubhukṣū parato 'pi tat-phalaṁ tato 'sya jāto mayi dharma-matsaraḥ // 8.63 //
Or else he fails to see that, during sacrificial oblations, both husband and wife are consecrated, both being sanctified through Vedic rites, / And both wishing thereafter to enjoy together the fruit of that sanctification – out of such blindness is born the besotted stinginess with dharma that he has shown towards me. //8.63//

---

[77] With *me vratī*, "my vow-observing [husband]," Yaśodharā is ostensibly being sarcastic. Below the surface, however, *vratī* accurately describes the prince as one who will keep his vow (see BC5.84) to reach the far shore.

[78] *Paṭaika* ostensibly means what passes as an ascetic's bedding, for sleeping; in the hidden meaning, a prostration cloth, for bowing.

[79] *Karuṇam.* See note to verse 4 above.

[80] Again, the suggestion below the surface is of a group of individuals touched by the teaching of the truth of suffering. Though the emotion in question is grief, Aśvaghoṣa sees beauty in it.

[81] *Rathāṅga-sāhvayā* (feminine) literally means "[the female goose] named 'chariot wheel.'" *Ratha* = chariot; *aṅga* = limb, part; *sāhvaya* = named.

[82] *Cakravāka* (masculine) means a male of the same species – *rathāṅga* and *cakravāka* are two names for the water-bird, variously identified as the greylag goose, or ruddy goose, or Brahmini duck, couples of which species are known in Sanskrit poetry to call out for each other mournfully during the night in a circular fashion – *aṇg, aṇg.* Both *rathāṅga* and *cakra* convey the meaning of a wheel or circle. See also verse 29.

dhruvaṁ sa jānan mama dharma-vallabho manaḥ priyerṣyā-kalahaṁ muhur mithaḥ /
sukhaṁ vibhīr mām apahāya rosaṇāṁ mahendra-loke 'psaraso jighṛkṣati // 8.64 //
Evidently, as dharma's beloved, he left me suddenly and in secret, knowing that my mind would be violently jealous where he, my own darling, was concerned. / Having so easily and fearlessly deserted me in my anger, he is wishing to obtain heavenly nymphs in the world of Great Indra! //8.64//

iyaṁ tu cintā mama kīdṛśaṁ nu tā vapur-guṇaṁ bibhrati tatra yoṣitaḥ /
vane yad arthaṁ sa tapāṁsi tapyate śriyaṁ ca hitvā mama bhaktim eva ca // 8.65 //
But this concern I do have – what kind of physical excellence do those women possess who are there? / On which account he undergoes austerities in the forest, having abandoned not only royal power but also my loving devotion. //8.65//

na khalv iyaṁ svarga-sukhāya me spṛhā na taj janasyātmavato 'pi dur-labham /
sa tu priyo mām iha vā paratra vā kathaṁ na jahyād iti me mano-rathaḥ // 8.66 //
This longing in me is truly not for the happiness of paradise (Nor is that happiness hard to achieve for a man possessed of himself), / But how might I never be deserted by what I hold most dear? – That is the chariot of my mind.[83] //8.66//

abhāginī yady aham āyatekṣaṇaṁ śuci-smitaṁ bhartur udīkṣituṁ mukham /
na manda-bhāgyo 'rhati rāhulo 'py ayaṁ kadā-cid aṅke parivartituṁ pituḥ // 8.67 //
Even if I am not to be blessed with the good fortune to behold the brightly smiling face, with its long eyes, of my husband; / Does this poor unfortunate Rāhula deserve never to roll around in his father's lap? //8.67// [Alternative translation] Even if I am not to be blessed with the good fortune to look up to the brightly smiling face, with its long eyes, of a master;[84] / Does this poor unfortunate Rāhula deserve never to be reborn in the lap of the ancestors[85]? //8.67//

aho nṛ-śaṁsaṁ su-kumāra-varcasaḥ su-dāruṇaṁ tasya manasvino manaḥ /
kala-pralāpaṁ dviṣato 'pi harṣaṇaṁ śiśuṁ sutaṁ yas tyajatīdṛśaṁ svataḥ // 8.68 //
O how terribly hard and cruel is the mind of him, so full of mind, whose light is so gentle! / An infant son, whose burbling would gladden even an enemy, he leaves in such a manner, just as he likes. //8.68//

---

[83] *Ratha* means 1. chariot, 2. joy. Therefore *mano-ratha* can mean 1. the chariot of the mind, the mind as a chariot; and 2. a heart's joy. The hidden meaning might be that the chariot of every human mind is truly driven not by desire for what can be taken away, but rather by desire for what cannot be taken away.

[84] *Bhartṛ*, depending on context, means a husband or a master.

[85] *Pitṛ*, depending on context, means a father or an ancestor.

mamāpi kāmaṁ hṛdayaṁ su-dāruṇaṁ śilā-mayaṁ vāpy ayaso 'pi vā kṛtam /
anāthavac chrī-rahite sukhocite vanaṁ gate bhartari yan na dīryate // 8.69 //
My heart too must be very hard - made of stone or else wrought of iron - / In that it does not split apart, when left like an orphan, now that its protector, who was accustomed to comfort, has gone, shorn of his royal glory, to the forest." //8.69//

itīha devī pati-śoka-mūrchitā ruroda dadhyau vilalāpa cāsakṛt /
svabhāva-dhīrāpi hi sā satī śucā dhṛtiṁ na sasmāra cakāra no hriyam // 8.70 //
Thus did a goddess here in this world, being insensible with grief on account of her husband [or being caused by grief to grow, on account of a master],[86] repeatedly weep, reflect, and lament. / For, steadfast as she was by nature, she in her pain was not mindful of constancy and made no show of modesty.[87] //8.70//

tatas tathā śoka-vilāpa-viklavāṁ yaśodharāṁ prekṣya vasuṁ-dharā-gatām /
mahāravindair iva vṛṣṭi-tāḍitair mukhaiḥ sa-bāṣpair vanitā vicukruśuḥ // 8.71 //
Then, seeing her thus undone by grief and lamentation, seeing Yaśodharā alighting on the ground[88] - the Bearer of Glory on the treasure-bearing Earth - / The women, with tearful faces like big lotuses battered by raindrops, vented their sorrow. //8.71//

samāpta-jāpyaḥ kṛta-homa-maṅgalo nṛ-pas tu devāyatanād viniryayau /
janasya tenārta-raveṇa cāhataś cacāla vajra-dhvanineva vāraṇaḥ // 8.72 //
The protector of men, meanwhile, having finished with muttering of prayers, being through with oblations and benedictions, had got out from the temple, the abode of gods;[89] / And yet, struck by that sound of people suffering, still he trembled, like an elephant struck by the sound of a thunderbolt. //8.72//

niśāmya ca chandaka-kanthakāv ubhau sutasya saṁśrutya ca niścayaṁ sthiram /
papāta śokābhihato mahī-patiḥ śacī-pater vṛtta ivotsave dhvajaḥ // 8.73 //
Having observed the two, Chandaka and Kanthaka, while being well informed as to the steadfast unity of purpose of a son, / A lord of the earth had fallen down, toppled by sorrow,[90] like the flag of Indra, Lord of Might, when the carnival is over. //8.73//

---

[86] *Pati-śoka-mūrchitā,* as in verse 26. The meanings of *pati* include lord, husband, and master. Again, *mūrchitā* ostensibly describes Yaśodharā as insensible, but the hidden meaning of *mūrchitā* is "caused to grow."

[87] In the hidden meaning, she was naturally constant, without trying to be mindful about it, and naturally modest without making any show of it. In this, she was like the beautiful women in BC5.57 who did not make a pretty sight. Digging still deeper for hidden meaning, is there a suggestion in *svabhāva-dhīrā* that the true grounds for steadfastness is *bhāvanā* - the natural practice of letting happen?

[88] In the hidden meaning, seeing her enlightened, awake to harsh reality.

[89] In the hidden meaning, a true protector of men (a buddha) is like somebody who has already used a raft to cross over a river and therefore no longer needs a raft - nor indeed a fabrication falsely purporting to be a raft.

[90] In the hidden meaning, body and mind had dropped off, under the influence of the teaching of the four noble truths.

tato muhūrtaṁ suta-śoka-mohito janena tulyābhijanena dhāritaḥ /
nirīkṣya dṛṣṭyā jala-pūrṇayā hayaṁ mahī-tala-stho vilalāpa pārthivaḥ // 8.74 //
And so, momentarily stupefied in filial grief,[91] buttressed by people of like ancestry,[92] / A lord of the earth, with a view that was full to overflowing,[93] eyeballed a horse,[94] whereupon, standing on the surface of the earth, the earth-lord lamented:[95] //8.74//

bahūni kṛtvā samare priyāṇi me mahat tvayā kanthaka vipriyaṁ kṛtam /
guṇa-priyo yena vane sa me priyaḥ priyo 'pi sann apriyavat praveritaḥ // 8.75 //
"After doing for me in battle many acts of love, you, Kanthaka, have done one great act of non-love; / For the lover of merit whom I love, your beloved friend though he is, you have cast - lovelessly - into the woods. //8.75//

tad adya māṁ vā naya tatra yatra sa vraja drutaṁ vā punar enam ānaya /
ṛte hi tasmān mama nāsti jīvitaṁ vigāḍha-rogasya sad-auṣadhād iva // 8.76 //
Therefore either take me today to the place where he is, or else go quickly and bring him back here; / For without him there is no life for me, as for a gravely ill man without good medicine.[96] //8.76//

suvarṇa-niṣṭhīvini mṛtyunā hṛte su-duṣkaraṁ yan na mamāra saṁjayaḥ /
ahaṁ punar dharma-ratau sute gate mumukṣur ātmānam anātmavān iva // 8.77 //
When 'Gold-Spitting' Suvarṇa-niṣṭhīvin was borne away by death, it was a miracle that Saṁjaya 'The Victorious' did not die. / I, however, am wishing, with the passing of a dharma-loving son, to be rid of myself, as if I were not in possession of myself.[97] //8.77//

vibhor daśa-kṣatra-kṛtaḥ prajāpateḥ parāpara-jñasya vivasvad-ātmanaḥ /
priyeṇa putreṇa satā vinā-kṛtaṁ kathaṁ na muhyed dhi mano manor api // 8.78 //
For, though Manu is the mighty lord of living creatures, maker of ten dominions, knower of former and latter things, son of the shining Sun, / When dispossessed of a beloved true son, how could the mind of even Manu not be bewildered?[98] //8.78//

---

[91] *Suta-śoka* could equally mean grief for a son, or the grief of a son. *Muhūrtaṁ... mohitaḥ*, "momentarily stupefied," might be an ironic expression of a moment of forgetting oneself.

[92] Ostensibly the king was so weak that he needed to be propped up by family members to enable him to walk. In the hidden meaning, the buddhas of the three times are on the side of one who sits as a lord of the earth.

[93] *Dṛṣṭyā jala-pūrṇayā* ostensibly means "with eyes filled with tears." In its hidden meaning "with a view filled to overflowing" might be an ironic description of a person who has abandoned all views in dealing with reality.

[94] The eye, or more concretely, the eyeball represents the mind as an instrument of practice. Eyeballing the horse suggests no disunity in the psycho-physical.

[95] In the hidden meaning, an earth-lord's lament is a buddha's preaching of the four noble truths.

[96] Good medicine - effective medicine without harmful side-effects - is a metaphor for the Buddha's dharma.

[97] The grief of Saṁjaya (or Sṛñjaya) when his son Suvarṇa-niṣṭhīvin was borne away by death, is mentioned twice in the Mahā-bhārata. Ostensibly King Śuddhodana is saying his grief is greater even than that, so that he wishes to die. In the hidden meaning, a king of dharma is inclined to forget himself in sitting, dropping off body and mind?

[98] Ostensibly the king is discussing Manu's loss of a son. But exactly thinking, the subject that is

ajasya rājñas tanayāya dhīmate narādhipāyendra-sakhāya me spṛhā /
gate vanaṁ yas tanaye divaṁ gato na mogha-bāṣpaḥ kṛpaṇaṁ jijīva ha // 8.79 //
That wise son of King A-ja,[99] ruler of men and friend of Indra: I envy him, / Who, when his son [Rāma] went to the forest, went himself to heaven. He did not live a miserable life of shedding tears in vain. //8.79// [Alternative translation] I envy a wise son of a non-hereditary king,[100] a son who was sovereign among men, and a friend of Indra – / A son who, when a son retired to the forest, was in heaven, a son who did not live a pitiable life of shedding tears in vain.[101] //8.79//

pracakṣva me bhadra tad āśramājiraṁ hṛtas tvayā yatra sa me jalāñjaliḥ /
ime parīpsanti hi te pipāsavo mamāsavaḥ preta-gatiṁ yiyāsavaḥ // 8.80 //
Describe for me, O friend of benign nature, the hermit's arena, that place where you have taken him who is my cupped hands for the fluid of forefathers.[102] / For these life-breaths of mine are thirsty, wishing to gain their end, wishing to go the way of the departed."[103] //8.80//

iti tanaya-viyoga-jāta-duḥkham kṣiti-sadṛśaṁ saha-jaṁ vihāya dhairyam /
daśaratha iva rāma-śoka-vaśyo bahu vilalāpa nṛ-po vi-saṁjña-kalpaḥ // 8.81 //
Thus, suffering the pain born of a son's loss,[104] a protector of men threw away the constancy, akin to the earth, which was his natural birth-right;[105] / And like Daśaratha in the grip of grief for Rāma – like he was unconscious[106] – he lamented profusely. //8.81//

---

dispossessed is not Manu but the mind of Manu. In that case the king's question causes us to ask about bewilderment of a mind – for example, should we endeavor in the direction of non-bewilderment of mind, by developing constancy like the earth (see verse 81 below)? Or should we welcome the bewilderment that follows from the falsification of a long-cherished view?

99 *Ajasya rājñas tanaya* ostensibly means King Daśa-ratha ('Ten Chariots'), who was the son of King A-ja ('Not Born') and the father of Rāma.

100 *A-ja*, "not born," in the hidden meaning, describes a king who was not born into a royal line. And a non-hereditary king means, for example, a lord of the earth in sitting, who has become a lord of the earth by his or her own efforts and thanks to the teaching of a teacher who is not necessarily a blood relative. Implicit in the verse, then, is the principle that the earth-lord who is father of such a son is also, invariably, the son of such a son.

101 *Na mogha-bāṣpaḥ*, lit. "not being one of vain tears," ostensibly means not shedding tears, which are in vain (i.e. not enduring vain suffering), but there may be a suggestion below the surface of not letting one's endurance of suffering be in vain. We can't avoid shedding tears. But those tears should not be shed in vain.

102 *Jalāñjali* means the hollowed palms filled with water offered to ancestors. In the hidden meaning it may represent the means of transmission of that teaching which, metaphorically speaking, is the ancestors' lifeblood.

103 In the hidden meaning, an ironic expression of desire to walk the path of forgetting the self?

104 The ostensible meaning of *tanaya-viyoga* is losing a son, or separation from a son; a hidden meaning is a son's losing – as when a Zen student forgets himself. In that case "suffering born of a son's losing," might describe, for example, legs becoming painful during sitting practice.

105 *Kṣiti-sadṛśaṁ saha-jaṁ... dhairyam* ostensibly means the gravity (*dhairyam*) which is innate (*saha-jam*) in a hereditary earth-lord such as Śuddhodana. In the hidden meaning *dhairyam* suggests the earth-like virtues of constancy, calmness, and bearing up, which are everybody's birth-right – i.e. the buddha-nature. In the hidden meaning, to throw away such virtue might mean to kill the Buddha, if one should meet him on the road.

106 *Vi-saṁjña-kalpaḥ*, "as if unconscious," ostensibly describes a person who remains in the grip of

śruta-vinaya-guṇānvitas tatas taṁ mati-sacivaḥ pravayāḥ puro-hitaś ca /
sama-dhṛtam idam ūcatur yathāvan na ca paritapta-mukhau na cāpy aśokau // 8.82 //
Then he was addressed by a counsellor, a knowing friend possessed of learning, discipline and virtue, and by the family priest, a man advanced in years; / The two spoke fittingly these equally-weighted[107] words, neither showing agonized faces nor being nonchalant. //8.82//

tyaja nara-vara śokam ehi dhairyaṁ ku-dhṛtir ivārhasi dhīra nāśru moktum /
srajam iva mṛditām apāsya lakṣmīṁ bhuvi bahavo hi nṛ-pā vanāny atīyuḥ // 8.83 //
"Abandon sorrow, O best of men, and come back to constancy; you should not shed tears, O stout soul, like a man who lacked grit.[108] / For, flinging away their fortune like a crushed garland, many rulers of men on this earth have gone into the forests. //8.83//

api ca niyata eṣa tasya bhāvaḥ smara vacanaṁ tad ṛṣeḥ purāsitasya /
na hi sa divi na cakra-varti-rājye kṣaṇam api vāsayituṁ sukhena śakyaḥ // 8.84 //
Moreover, this orientation of mind was predestined in him – remember those words long ago of the seer Asita, 'the Not White One.' / For neither in heaven nor in the domain of a wheel-rolling king could he, even for a moment, be made happily to dwell. //8.84//

yadi tu nṛ-vara kārya eva yatnas tvaritam udāhara yāvad atra yāvaḥ /
bahu-vidham iha yuddham astu tāvat tava tanayasya vidheś ca tasya tasya // 8.85 //
But if, O best of men, an effort is emphatically to be made, quickly say the word, and we two will go to it at once. / Let the battle take place, right here right now, on many fronts, between a son of yours and the various prescriptions of fate [or between a son of yours and miscellaneous rules].[109] //8.85//

nara-patir atha tau śaśāsa tasmād drutam ita eva yuvām abhiprayātam /
na hi mama hṛdayaṁ prayāti śāntiṁ vana-śakuner iva putra-lālasasya // 8.86 //
"On those grounds," the lord of men then ordered them, "go quickly you two to battle, starting right here; / For my heart no more goes to quiet, than does the heart of a bird of the forest when it longs for a missing nestling." //8.86//

---

unconscious reaction. But exactly thinking "as if unconscious" implies being conscious. Ironically, then, the compound suggests the condition of an enlightened being who is holding up a mirror, as it were, to Nature.

[107] A suggestion of reason/intelligence co-existing with experience? The two servants of the king seem to represent dual aspects of wisdom, in the same way that Kanthaka and Chandaka seem to represent the physical and the mental.

[108] In the hidden meaning, you should shed tears, but not in the manner of a man who lacked grit.

[109] *Vidher... tasya tasya.* The many meanings of *vidhi* include a rule, injunction, precept, law; method, standard; manner of acting; and fate, destiny. This same counsellor seems to use *vidhi* in BC9.66-67 in the sense of a rule, standard, or manner of proceeding.

paramam iti narendra-śāsanāt tau yayatur amātya-purohitau vanaṁ tat /
kṛtam iti sa-vadhū-janaḥ sa-dāro nṛpatir api pracakāra śeṣa-kāryam // 8.87 //
"Agreed!" the two said, in accordance with the order of the first among men.[110] And to that forest went the two of them, close advisor and family priest. / "Enough said!" said the lord of men. And along with daughters and queen, he got on and did what remained to be done. //8.87//

iti buddha-carite mahā-kāvye 'ntaḥ-pura-vilāpo nāmāṣṭamaḥ sargaḥ // 8 //
The 8th canto, titled "Lamenting from within the Battlements,"
in an epic tale of awakened action.

---

[110] In the hidden meaning, to show an attitude of obedience, or submission to something outside oneself, is, in the final analysis, to be in accordance with the Buddha's teaching.

Canto 9: kumārānveṣaṇaḥ
The Seeking of a Prince

Introduction

The canto title *kumārānveṣaṇaḥ* ostensibly describes the efforts of King Śuddhodana's two emissaries to track down his son, the Prince (*kumāra*). The alternative reading is that the seeking (*anveṣaṇa*) in question is the investigation which the Prince is determined to do by himself for himself, not taking anybody else's word for anything.

Still another possibility is to read *kumāra*, which means not only prince but also child, as both the subject and the object of the seeking – as in the famous story from ancient China where a Zen master describes real sincerity as "a child of fire coming looking for fire."

tatas tadā mantri-purohitau tau bāṣpa-pratodābhihatau nṛpeṇa /
viddhau sad-aśvāv iva sarva-yatnāt sauhārda-śīghraṁ yayatur vanaṁ tat // 9.1 //
Then the two,[1] knowing informant and veteran priest, smitten by a protector of men, prodded with a goad of tears,[2] / Making every effort, like two good horses spurred into action, went with good-hearted swiftness[3] to that forest. //9.1//

tam āśramam jāta-pariśramau tāv upetya kāle sadṛśānuyātrau /
rājarddhim utsṛjya vinīta-ceṣṭāv upeyatur bhārgava-dhiṣṇyam eva // 9.2 //
The two arrived, tired and weary, at that abode of tiring exertion. Having arrived at a favorable moment, with what was appropriate for the journey, / The two abandoned royal pomp and, in a modest manner, arrived at the hearth of a son of Bhṛgu – they arrived at the very place of fire of a son of fire.[4] //9.2//

tau nyāyatas taṁ pratipūjya vipraṁ tenārcitau tāv api cānurūpam /
kṛtāsanau bhārgavam āsana-sthaṁ chittvā kathām ūcatur ātma-kṛtyam // 9.3 //
They honored that inspired sage, following the standard, and were saluted by him accordingly. / As two who had sat,[5] they spoke to one who abode in the act of sitting[6] – cutting out chat, they told the son of Bhṛgu their private business. //9.3//

---

[1] The two may be taken as representing every kind of duality that is spurred into action when one gets moving in the right direction.

[2] In the hidden meaning, a long whip, or goad, of tears (*bāṣpa-pratoda*) might be a metaphor for the four noble truths, whose effect is to stimulate us, by means of suffering, into practice leading towards cessation of suffering.

[3] *Sauhārda-śīghram*, with the quickness, or readiness to act, associated with the compassion of a friend, or "good-heart" (*su-hṛd*).

[4] BC6.1 also says that the ashram in question was that of a son of Bhṛgu. The Bhṛgus are said to be closely connected with fire. *Dhiṣṇya* means a place or abode, or a home where a hearth is. One of its meanings is a side altar consisting of earth heaped up beside a fire.

[5] Ostensibly *kṛtāsanau* (fr. *kṛta* doing, having done + *āsana*, sitting) simply means "seated."

[6] As in the description of Asita in BC1.52, the ostensible meaning of *āsana-stham* is "remaining seated" or simply "sitting down." Here, as again in BC1.52, the hidden meaning may be to praise a sage as being devoted to sitting and as abiding in the act of sitting – having cut out idle chatter (*chittvā kathām*).

śuddhaujasaḥ śuddha-viśāla-kīrter ikṣvāku-vaṁśa-prabhavasya rājñaḥ /
imaṁ janaṁ vettu bhavān adhīraṁ śruta-grahe mantra-parigrahe ca // 9.4 //
"Though we belong to a king in the line of Ikṣvāku who is pure in his bodily energy and pure in his wide renown, / Know, good sir, that the men before you are not sure of ourselves[7] in apprehending what truth is taught[8] and in comprehending the art of thought.[9] //9.4//

tasyendra-kalpasya jayanta-kalpaḥ putro jarā-mṛtyu-bhayaṁ titīrṣuḥ /
ihābhyupetaḥ kila tasya hetor āvām upetau bhagavān avaitu // 9.5 //
A son, like 'Victorious' Jayanta, of that Indra-like king, wishing to transcend the terror of aging and dying, / Has, it is said, come here. May you, venerable one, see us two as having arrived[10] because of him." //9.5//

tau so 'bravīd asti sa dīrgha-bāhuḥ prāptaḥ kumāro na tu nāvabuddhaḥ /
dharmo 'yam āvartaka ity avetya yātas tv arāḍābhimukho mumukṣuḥ // 9.6 //
[The sage] told them: "Indeed! The young prince, he of long arms, did arrive, but not as an unwitting youth.[11] / On the contrary, seeing that this dharma practiced here involves repeatedly coming back,[12] he set out towards Arāḍa, seeking freedom." //9.6//

tasmāt tatas tāv upalabhya tattvaṁ taṁ vipram āmantrya tadaiva sadyaḥ /
khinnāvakhinnāv iva rāja-bhaktyā prasasratus tena yataḥ sa yātaḥ // 9.7 //
Thus, on those grounds, the two of them grasped the truth,[13] and said goodbye at once to that inspired sage, / Whereon, as if tired and yet tireless, through their royal devotion,[14] they staunchly went in that direction in which the other had gone. //9.7//

---

7 The meanings of *adhīra* include not fixed, deficient in calm self-command, weak-minded. It is ostensibly self-deprecating but in the hidden meaning could suggest freedom from the sin of certainty. See also note to BC8.26.

8 *Śruta-graha*, lit. "grasping what is listened to," suggests the work of a veteran priest.

9 *Mantra-parigraha*, lit. "comprehending consultation / the instrument of thought," suggests the work of a king's counsellor.

10 In the hidden meaning, *upeta* may be synonymous with *tathāgata* in the sense of arrived at reality.

11 *Kumāraḥ* means a prince or a child or youth. The canto title *kumārānveṣanaḥ*, ostensibly describes a prince being sought, but it could equally mean a prince doing the seeking. And, in a still deeper hidden meaning, the suggestion might be of seeking out child-mind i.e. open-mindedness – investigating the buddha-nature with beginner's mind.

12 *Āvartakaḥ,* from the root *ā-√vṛt*, to turn around or turn back. Ostensibly, *āvartakaḥ* refers to repeated re-birth in saṁsāra. In the hidden meaning, does a dharma practiced here and now involve repeatedly coming back?

13 *Upalabhya tattvam*, similarly, ostensibly means "understanding the fact of the matter," but in the hidden meaning suggests realization of reality here and now.

14 *Rāja-bhaktyā* ostensibly means "because of devotion to the king." Below the surface, the suggestion is that being on the royal road (of sitting-meditation) caused them to be born along by the truth of non-doing.

yāntau tatas tau mṛjayā vihīnam apaśyatāṁ taṁ vapuṣā jvalantam /
nṛpopaviṣṭaṁ pathi vṛkṣa-mūle sūryaṁ ghanābhogam iva praviṣṭam // 9.8 //
As thus on those grounds they were going, they saw him, who had totally neglected purification,[15] shining with handsome form, / On the road, royally seated at the foot of a tree - like the sun when it has entered a canopy of cloud. //9.8//

yānaṁ vihāyopayayau tatas taṁ purohito mantra-dhareṇa sārdham /
yathā vana-sthaṁ saha-vāmadevo rāmaṁ didṛkṣur munir aurvaśeyaḥ // 9.9 //
Thus on those grounds the veteran, abandoning a vehicle, went in his direction, joined by the keeper of the compass of thought - / As, when Rāma was in the forest, the sage Aurvaśeya, 'Dawn's Descendant,' along with the minister Vāmadeva, went to Rāma, wishing to see him.[16] //9.9//

tāv arcayām āsatur arhatas taṁ divīva śukrāṅgirasau mahendram /
pratyarcayām āsa sa cārhatas tau divīva śukrāṅgirasau mahendraḥ // 9.10 //
The two fittingly honored him, as in heaven 'Shining' Śukra and Āṅgirasa caused great Indra to shine; / And he in return fittingly honored those two, as in heaven great Indra caused Śukra and Āṅgirasa to shine.[17] //9.10//

kṛtābhyanujñāv abhitas tatas tau niṣīdatuḥ śākya-kula-dhvajasya /
virejatus tasya ca saṁnikarṣe punar-vasū yoga-gatāv ivendoḥ // 9.11 //
Having thus on these grounds been allowed, the two, in the presence of the flag of the Śākya family,[18] sat; / And in his vicinity they shone - like the twin stars of Punar-vasu in conjunction with the moon.[19] //9.11//

taṁ vṛkṣa-mūla-stham abhijvalantaṁ puro-hito rāja-sutaṁ babhāṣe /
yathopaviṣṭaṁ divi pārijāte bṛhas-patiḥ śakra-sutaṁ jayantam // 9.12 //
The veteran priest addressed that son of a king who abode at the foot of the tree, shining, / As in heaven 'Lord of Prayer' Bṛhas-pati addressed 'Victorious' Jayanta, son of Mighty Indra, sitting under the celestial coral tree: //9.12//

---

[15] *Mṛjayā vihīnam* ostensibly means that the prince had gone without washing; in the hidden meaning, the suggestion may be that in sitting naturally, he had already gone beyond religious rites of purification.

[16] The ostensible point of this verse seems to be to draw a parallel between the story of Sarvārtha-siddha and the story of Rāma as told in the Rāmāyaṇa. Below the surface, Aśvaghoṣa may have intended to convey more important meaning with the words *yānaṁ vihāya*, "abandoning a vehicle."

[17] Śukra (fr. *√śuc,* to glow), "The Shining One," is a name of Agni, god of fire; and Agni is regarded as the chief son of Aṅgiras. So Śukra ("the Shining One") and Āṅgirasa ("son of Aṅgiras") can be understood to be two names for one entity - and in this sense representative of all dualities, like body and mind, which we are required to shine light upon, and shake off.

[18] *Śākya-kula-dhvaja* ostensibly means the Śākya prince himself, but in the hidden meaning "the banner of the house of Śākya[muni]," suggests a traditionally-sewn kaṣāya.

[19] Ostensibly Aśvaghoṣa is picking up a simile in the Rāmāyaṇa about Punarvasu and the moon. Below the surface, the intention, again, may be to cause us to investigate what psycho-physicality is, since some understand Punarvasu to be an asterism consisting of two stars (the alpha and beta Geminorum), while some understand Punar and Vasu to be two stars forming an asterism. Punarvasu literally means "Restoring Goods" or "Restoring Wealth," but grammatically, as here, is dual.

tvac-choka-śalye hṛdayāvagāḍhe mohaṁ gato bhūmi-tale muhūrtam /
kumāra rājā nayanāmbu-varṣo yat tvām avocat tad idaṁ nibodha // 9.13 //
"Learn of the moment when a king, losing consciousness,[20] is on the ground, the arrow of your sorrow having penetrated his core[21] – / To these words which the king, O child!, his eyes raining tears, said to you, listen well: //9.13//

jānāmi dharmaṁ prati niścayaṁ te paraimi te bhāvinam etam artham /
ahaṁ tv akāle vana-saṁśrayāt te śokāgnināgni-pratimena dahye // 9.14 //
'I know your resolve with regard to dharma. I realize that this will be your goal. But at your going to the forest at the wrong time, I am consumed with a fire of sorrow that burns like a fire. //9.14//

tad ehi dharma-priya mat-priyārthaṁ dharmārtham eva tyaja buddhim etām /
ayaṁ hi mā śoka-rayaḥ pravṛddho nadī-rayaḥ kūlam ivābhihanti // 9.15 //
So come back, you who holds dharma dear, because of what is dear to me. For no reason but dharma itself, abandon this idea of yours. / For this swollen stream of sorrow eats away at me as the flow of a river eats away its bank. //9.15//

meghāmbu-kakṣādriṣu yā hi vṛttiḥ samīraṇārkāgni-mahāśanīnām /
tāṁ vṛttim asmāsu karoti śoko vikarṣaṇocchoṣaṇa-dāha-bhedaiḥ // 9.16 //
For the action which on clouds, water, brushwood and mountains, is exerted by wind, sun, fire and the mighty thunderbolt: / Sorrow exerts that action on us – tearing us apart, causing us to become dry, burning us out and demolishing us.[22] //9.16//

tad bhuṅkṣva tāvad vasudhādhipatyaṁ kāle vanaṁ yāsyasi śāstra-dṛṣṭe /
an-iṣṭa-bandhau kuru māpy upekṣāṁ sarveṣu bhūteṣu dayā hi dharmaḥ // 9.17 //
So enjoy for the present sovereignty over the earth. You will return to the forest at the right moment, as per the *śāstras*, or temporal sciences. / Never show disregard for your less fortunate kin. For dharma is compassion directed towards all beings.[23] //9.17//

---

[20] *Mohaṁ gataḥ* lit. means "gone/going to loss of consciousness," i.e. being in a state of deluded bewilderment. In the hidden meaning, forgetting oneself, dropping off body and mind?

[21] Ostensibly the veteran priest is referring to the King, Śuddhodana, but in the hidden meaning *rājā*, a king, might mean one who is lord of the earth in sitting, being struck by the teaching of the four noble truths.

[22] In the hidden meaning, being dismantled and becoming dry might be an ironic suggestion of what it is really to understand the four noble truths. See also SN Canto 17: *The action which on fire, trees, ghee and water is exerted by rainclouds, wind, a flame and the sun, / Nanda exerted that action on the faults, quenching, uprooting, burning, and drying them up. //SN17.59//*

[23] Below the surface an earth-lord is preaching the Buddha's teaching in a four-phased progression – covering subjective sovereignty, objective knowledge, not doing wrong, and realization of the Buddha's dharma.

na caiṣa dharmo vana eva siddhaḥ pure 'pi siddhir niyatā yatīnām /
buddhiś ca yatnaś ca nimittam atra vanaṁ ca liṅgaṁ ca hi bhīru-cihnam // 9.18 //
Neither is this dharma realized only in the woods: Its realization is assured in the city too, for those who make the effort. / Intention and energy are what count in this arena. For the forest and the uniform are a mark of fearfulness.[24] //9.18//

maulī-dharair aṁsa-viṣakta-hāraiḥ keyūra-viṣṭabdha-bhujair narendraiḥ /
lakṣmy-aṅka-madhye parivartamānaiḥ prāpto gṛha-sthair api mokṣa-dharmaḥ // 9.19 //
By kings bearing crowns, by kings with strings of pearls hanging over their shoulders, and their arms fortified by bands, / By kings lying cradled in Lakṣmi's lap – even by those who did remain in family life – the dharma of liberation has been attained. //9.19// [Alternative translation] Realized by kings who possess the earth,[25] by kings for whom battle is directed towards their own shoulders,[26] and whose arms are fortified by bands, / By kings acting in the middle, between the dual flanks of fortune[27] – and realized also by those who stay at home – is the dharma of liberation. //9.19//

dhruvānujau yau bali-vajrabāhū vaibhrājam āṣāḍham athāntidevam /
videha-rājaṁ janakaṁ tathaiva [pāka]-drumaṁ sena-jitaś ca rājñaḥ // 9.20 //
'Oblation-Offering' Bali and 'Thunderbolt-Armed' Vajra-bāhu, who were the younger brothers of 'The Immutable' Dhruva; 'Born of Brightness' Vaibhrāja, 'Born of the Midsummer Month' Āṣāḍha, and 'Close to the Gods' Antideva; / Likewise the Videha King Janaka, 'The Producer'; '[Ripening] Tree' [Pāka]-druma, and 'Army Vanquishing' King Senajit – //9.20//

etān gṛha-sthān nṛpatīn avehi naiḥśreyase dharma-vidhau vinītān /
ubhe 'pi tasmād yugapad bhajasva vittādhipatyaṁ ca nṛpa-śriyaṁ ca // 9.21 //
These men who remained at home as kings, you should know, were steeped in the dharma-practice that leads to the highest happiness; / Therefore, enjoy both together sovereignty over what is acquired and the glory of a protector of men.[28] //9.21//

---

[24] Ostensibly Śuddhodana is mocking solitude and the robe as marks of a coward. In the hidden meaning, he might be praising them as refuges of one rightly afraid of the terrors of aging, sickness and death.

[25] The meanings of *mauli/maulī* include 1. crown, and 2. earth.

[26] The meanings of *hāra* include 1. string of pearls, and 2. war, battle.

[27] *Lakṣmi:* 1. name of the Goddess of Fortune; 2. fortune. *Aṅka:* 1. lap; 2. side, flank. *Madhye*: 1. in the middle, 2. standing between two.

[28] Below the surface, a lord of the earth is giving good advice – not to put cart before horse or horse before cart.

icchāmi hi tvām upaguhya gāḍhaṁ kṛtābhiṣekaṁ salilārdram eva /
dhṛtātapatraṁ samudīkṣamāṇas tenaiva harṣeṇa vanaṁ praveṣṭum // 9.22 //
Having contained you in a close embrace, you being besprinkled, wet with nothing but water,[29] / Then seeing you in possession of the *ā-tapa-tra* (the big umbrella, the instrument of protection from the heat of *tapas*)[30] – I desire, only in that state of happiness, to enter the forest.'[31] //9.22//

ity abravīd bhūmi-patir bhavantaṁ vākyena bāṣpa-grathitākṣareṇa /
śrutvā bhavān arhati tat-priyārthaṁ snehena tat-sneham anuprayātum // 9.23 //
Thus did the king speak to you, with words punctuated by tears; / Having listened well, for the sake of his love, you should return his affection with affection. //9.23// [Alternative translation] Thus did a possessor of the earth speak to you, with words punctuated by tears; / Having listened well, on account of valuing that,[32] you should follow with attachment his attachment to that.[33] //9.23//

śokāmbhasi tvat-prabhave hy agādhe duḥkhārṇave majjati śākya-rājaḥ /
tasmāt tam uttāraya nātha-hīnaṁ nir-āśrayaṁ magnam ivārṇave nauḥ // 9.24 //
For in the deep sea whose water is sorrow and which has its origin in you – in the foaming sea of suffering – the Śākya king[34] submerses himself; / On that basis you should allow him, who has no protector, to cross to his destination, as a boat allows one to cross who, with nothing to hold onto, is submersed in a flood. //9.24//

bhīṣmeṇa gaṅgodara-saṁbhavena rāmeṇa rāmeṇa ca bhārgaveṇa /
śrutvā kṛtaṁ karma pituḥ priyārthaṁ pitus tvam apy arhasi kartum iṣṭam // 9.25 //
The action of Bhīṣma 'The Terrible,' who was born from the womb of Gaṅgā,[35] the action of Rāma,[36] and the action of Rāma the son of Bhṛgu[37] – / That action they did for the sake of what their fathers valued. Having studied that action, you also should do a father's desire.[38] //9.25//

---

[29] Ostensible meaning: when you have been anointed as my successor. Hidden meaning: when water has become for you nothing but water.

[30] Ostensible meaning: seeing you in possession of the royal umbrella. Hidden meaning: seeing you impervious to all forms of extremism, starting with asceticism.

[31] *Icchāmi... vanaṁ praveṣṭum*, "I wish/desire... to enter the forest," can be read below the surface as a buddha's pointing back to nature.

[32] *Tat-priyārtham:* 1. For the sake of his love (*tat* = the king); 2. because of valuing that (*tat* = that dharma / that forest).

[33] *Tat-sneham*: 1. His affection; 2. attachment to that.

[34] In the hidden meaning, a king [of dharma], in Śākyamuni's line, immerses himself in the four noble truths.

[35] Bhīṣma was the first son of King Śan-tanu by his first wife Gaṅga, but Bhīṣma relinquished his claim to his father's throne to honor his father's promise to his second wife, the fisherman's daughter Kāḷī. See SN7.41, SN7.44.

[36] Rāma, the hero of the Rāmāyaṇa, also gave up his claim to his father's throne, going voluntarily into exile in the forest. These two examples, then, undermine the case which the king is ostensibly making.

[37] Rāma son of Bhṛgu means Paraśu-rāma (Rāma with the Axe), who pleased his father by slaying Kārtavīrya. See SN9.17.

[38] *Pitṛ*: 1. father, 2, deceased ancestor. In the hidden meaning, you should act in accordance with the

saṁvardhayitrīṁ samavehi devīm agastya-juṣṭāṁ diśam aprayātām /
pranaṣṭa-vatsām iva vatsalāṁ gām ajasram ārtāṁ karuṇaṁ rudantīm // 9.26 //
Have regard for the queen who fostered you, and who has yet to go south, into the region inhabited by Agastya,[39] / Have regard for her who, like a loving mother-cow that lost her calf, is constantly and piteously wailing in distress. //9.26//

haṁsena haṁsīm iva viprayuktāṁ tyaktāṁ gajeneva vane kareṇum /
ārtāṁ sa-nāthām api nātha-hīnāṁ trātuṁ vadhūm arhasi darśanena // 9.27 //
[Rescue also your wife] who is like a goose separated from the gander, who is like a cow elephant deserted in the forest by the bull; / Your unhappy young wife, who is widowed though her husband lives - you should rescue her, by your presence.[40] //9.27//

ekaṁ sutaṁ bālam an-arha-duḥkhaṁ saṁtāpam antar-gatam udvahantam /
taṁ rāhulaṁ mokṣaya bandhu-śokād rāhūpasargād iva pūrṇa-candram // 9.28 //
Your only son, a young boy not deserving of hurt, who is bearing in secret the burning heat of anguish - / Release him, Rāhula, from his grief for his own flesh and blood [or from the sorrow of family ties][41]; release him like the full moon from Rāhu's eclipsing grasp. //9.28//

śokāgninā tvad virahendhanena niḥśvāsa-dhūmena tamaḥ-śikhena /
tvad-darśanāmbv icchati dahyamānam antaḥpuraṁ caiva puraṁ ca kṛtsnam // 9.29 //
Burning with a fire of grief whose fuel is your absence, burning with a fire whose fumes are sighs, and whose flames are hell, / While it seeks the water of your presence, is not only the royalty within the battlements but the whole city."[42] //9.29//

sa bodhisattvaḥ paripūrṇa-sattvaḥ śrutvā vacas tasya purohitasya /
dhyātvā muhūrtaṁ guṇavad guṇa-jñaḥ pratyuttaraṁ praśritam ity uvāca // 9.30 //
He the bodhisattva, the buddha-to-be, the one whose essence of being was awakening, he who in his essential being was perfect, having listened to the words of that veteran, / Meditated a moment and, as a knower of excellence, humbly spoke this excellent response: [or spoke this excellent response, full of secret meaning:][43] //9.30//

---

mind of eternal buddhas.

[39] The southern region inhabited by Agastya means the region of death; or, in the hidden meaning, the area where body and mind have dropped off.

[40] In the hidden meaning, you should deliver all sentient beings, by your state of awakening.

[41] *Bandhu-śoka* could mean 1. grief for his relative, or 2. grief from being related. Cf *pati-śoka* in the previous canto.

[42] The ostensible intention of the veteran's appeal is that the prince should extinguish the fires of people's grief by giving up and going home. The irony is that the bodhisattva will truly accomplish that task, on the contrary, by not going back to Kapilavastu yet.

[43] The meanings of *praśrita* include 1. leaning forward deferentially, humble, modest; and 2. hidden, obscure.

avaimi bhāvaṁ tanaye pitṛṇāṁ viśeṣato yo mayi bhūmi-pasya /
jānann api vyādhi-jarā-vipadbhyo bhītas tv agatyā sva-janaṁ tyajāmi // 9.31 //
"I understand the feelings of fathers towards a son, particularly the king's towards me, / And yet, even so knowing, afraid as I am of sickness, aging and death, there is nothing for it but that I abandon my kith and kin. //9.31//

draṣṭuṁ priyaṁ kaḥ sva-janaṁ hi necchen nānte yadi syāt priya-viprayogaḥ /
yadā tu bhūtvāpi ciram viyogas tato guruṁ snigdham api tyajāmi // 9.32 //
For who would not wish to see his nearest and dearest if, in the end, there were no separation from loved ones? / But since separation, however long delayed, happens, on those grounds the guru, however sticky he is with affection, I abandon. //9.32//

madd-hetukaṁ yat tu narādhipasya śokaṁ bhavān āha na tat priyaṁ me /
yat svapna-bhūteṣu samāgameṣu saṁtapyate bhāvini viprayoge // 9.33 //
If, however, the gentleman present viewed me as the cause of the king's sorrow, that view would not be near and dear to me / When, in comings together which are like a dream, he is suffering,[44] amid inevitable separation. //9.33//

evaṁ ca te niścayam etu buddhir dṛṣṭvā vicitraṁ jagataḥ pracāram /
saṁtāpa-hetur na suto na bandhur ajñāna-naimittika eṣa tāpaḥ // 9.34 //
After observing the world, in its manifold diversity, manifesting itself, you should let your mind go towards certainty, like this: / Neither the son nor a relative is the cause of suffering. This pain has its cause in ignorance. //9.34//

yadādhvagānām iva saṁgatānāṁ kāle viyogo niyataḥ prajānām /
prājño janaḥ ko nu bhajeta śokaṁ bandhu-pratijñāta-janair vihīnaḥ // 9.35 //
Since separation, as for travelers meeting on a road, is, in time, inevitable for living beings, / What wise man would wallow in sorrow when rid of people with whom he was purported to be related? //9.35//

ihaiti hitvā svajanaṁ paratra pralabhya cehāpi punaḥ prayāti /
gatvāpi tatrāpy aparatra gacchety evaṁ jane tyāgini ko 'nurodhaḥ // 9.36 //
Here a quitter comes, having left relations elsewhere. Eluding them here as well, off he goes again. / Even after going there, again he goes, to yet another place. What attachment can there be towards such a serial deserter?[45] //9.36//

---

[44] Since the bodhisattva addresses the veteran as *bhavān* (the gentleman present), which takes the third person singular, *saṁtapyate* (he is suffering) could refer to the king or equally to the veteran himself. Either way, a wrong view is being negated in which the cause of suffering is seen as residing in others.

[45] Ironic affirmation of the wandering life?

yadā ca garbhāt prabhṛti pravṛttaḥ sarvāsv avasthāsu vadhāya mṛtyuḥ /
kasmād akāle vana-saṁśrayaṁ me putra-priyas tatra bhavān avocat // 9.37 //
And since from the womb onwards, death in every situation is poised to strike, / How could his majesty who holds his son dear, being there present, say that my giving myself to the forest was ill-timed? //9.37//

bhavaty akālo viṣayābhipattau kālas tathaivārtha-vidhau pradiṣṭaḥ /
kālo jagat karṣati sarva-kālān arcārhakaḥ śreyasi sarva-kālaḥ // 9.38 //
In devotion to worldly objects, wrong time exists. In business, equally, a right time is indicated. / Away from mankind and unto itself, time is dragging all moments of time. In a happier state of higher good, all time is deserving of adoration.[46] //9.38//

rājyaṁ mumukṣur mayi yac ca rājā tad apy udāraṁ sadṛśaṁ pituś ca /
pratigrahītuṁ mama na kṣamaṁ tu lobhād apathyānnam ivāturasya // 9.39 //
That the king wishes to cede his kingdom to me – that indeed is noble, and worthy of a father; / But it would be no more fitting for me to accept, than for a sick man, out of greed, to accept food that is bad for him. //9.39//

kathaṁ nu mohāyatanaṁ nṛ-patvaṁ kṣamaṁ prapattuṁ viduṣā nareṇa /
sodvegatā yatra madaḥ śramaś ca parāpacāreṇa ca dharma-pīḍā // 9.40 //
How can kingship, as the dwelling place of delusion, be fit to be entered by a man of wisdom? / For there reside perturbation, intemperance, and exhaustion; and transgression against dharma through harsh treatment of others. //9.40//

jāmbūnadaṁ harmyam iva pradīptaṁ viṣeṇa saṁyuktam ivottamānnam /
grāhākulaṁ cāmbv iva sāravindaṁ rājyaṁ hi ramyaṁ vyasanāśrayaṁ ca // 9.41 //
For, like a golden palace on fire, like the finest food laced with poison, / And like a lotus pond full of crocodiles, kingship is attractive but it harbours calamities. //9.41//

itthaṁ ca rājyaṁ na sukhaṁ na dharmaḥ pūrve yathā jāta-ghṛṇā narendrāḥ /
vayaḥ-prakarṣe 'parihārya-duḥkhe rājyāni muktvā vanam eva jagmuḥ // 9.42 //
No comfort, then, is kingship; nor is it an inabdicable dharma – so that ancient kings who felt disgust, / As the drag of getting old brought forth inevitable suffering, ceded their kingdoms and retired nowhere else but to the forest. //9.42//

varaṁ hi bhuktāni tṛṇāny araṇye toṣaṁ paraṁ ratnam ivopaguhya /
sahoṣitaṁ śrī-sulabhair na caiva doṣair adṛśyair iva kṛṣṇa-sarpaiḥ // 9.43 //
For foraging herbs, out in the wilds, while clasping the highest contentment to one's breast like a hidden jewel, / Is much better than living with the faults that tend easily to go, like unseen black snakes, with royal glory. //9.43//

---

[46] Progression through four phases is again evident here in four pādas touching on 1. devotion, 2. worldly business, 3. relentless passing of moments of time, and 4. Time as synonymous with real life happening.

ślāghyaṁ hi rājyāni vihāya rājñāṁ dharmābhilāṣeṇa vanaṁ praveṣṭum /
bhagna-pratijñasya na tūpapannaṁ vanaṁ parityajya gṛhaṁ praveṣṭum // 9.44 //
For it is praiseworthy for kings to leave their kingdoms behind them and, in their desire for dharma, to betake themselves back to the forest. / But it is not fitting for a vow-breaker to shun the forest and betake himself back to the family. //9.44//

jātaḥ kule ko hi naraḥ sa-sattvo dharmābhilāṣeṇa vanaṁ praviṣṭaḥ /
kāṣāyam utsṛjya vimukta-lajjaḥ puraṁdarasyāpi puraṁ śrayeta // 9.45 //
For what man of character born into a good family, having betaken himself, in his desire for dharma, to the forest, / Would cast off the red-brown robe and, dead to shame, make for the city – even if the city were that of Indra, "Breaker Down of City Walls," himself? //9.45//

lobhādd hi mohād atha vā bhayena yo vāntam annaṁ punar ādadīta /
lobhāt sa mohād atha vā bhayena saṁtyajya kāmān punar ādadīta // 9.46 //
For he who, out of greed, out of ignorance, or else in fear, would take back the food he has vomited, / He, out of greed, out of ignorance, or else in fear,[47] would take back the desires he has renounced. //9.46//

yaś ca pradīptāc charaṇāt kathaṁ-cin niṣkramya bhūyaḥ praviśet tad eva /
gārhasthyam utsṛjya sa dṛṣṭa-doṣo mohena bhūyo 'bhilaṣed grahītum // 9.47 //
Again, he who, after barely escaping from a burning house, would go back again into that inferno – / He, after leaving family life, having seen the faults attendant on it, would desire in his ignorance to embrace it again. //9.47//

vahneś ca toyasya ca nāsti saṁdhiḥ śaṭhasya satyasya ca nāsti saṁdhiḥ /
āryasya pāpasya ca nāsti saṁdhiḥ śamasya daṇḍasya ca nāsti saṁdhiḥ // 9.47(b) //
There is no combining fire and water. Nor can falsity and truthfulness co-exist. / There is no compatibility between what is noble and what is wicked. Nor are pacification and punishment reconcilable. //9.47 (b)//[48]

yā ca śrutir mokṣam avāptavanto nṛpā gṛha-sthā iti naitad asti /
śama-pradhānaḥ kva ca mokṣa-dharmo daṇḍa-pradhānaḥ kva ca rāja-dharmaḥ // 9.48 //
Again, as for the tradition that rulers of men realized liberation while maintaining their status in the royal family – that is not so. / How can the dharma of liberation, in which peace is paramount, be reconciled with the dharma of a king, in which the rod is paramount? //9.48//

---

[47] The repeated phrase *atha vā bhavena*, "or else in fear," sets the bodhisattva's thinking apart from that of the striver in SN Canto 8: *"Greedy and untrained, devoid of decency and intelligence, / Truly, a wretched dog is wishing to eat again some food that he himself has vomited." // SN8.21 //*

[48] EHJ omitted this verse from his translation, partly on stylistic grounds and partly because it is absent from the Chinese translation. In the Tibetan translation this verse comes after verse 49.

śame ratiś cec chithilaṁ ca rājyaṁ rājye matiś cec chama-viplavaś ca /
śamaś ca taikṣṇyaṁ ca hi nopapannaṁ śītoṣṇayor aikyam ivodakāgnyoḥ // 9.49 //
When he delights in peace and quiet, his kingship is lax; when his mind turns to kingship, the peace and quiet is spoilt. / For peacefulness and severity are incompatible – as a unity is impossible of the cold and the hot, in water and fire. //9.49//

tan niścayād vā vasudhādhipās te rājyāni muktvā śamam āptavantaḥ /
rājyād mitā vā nibhṛtendriyatvād anaiṣṭhike mokṣa-kṛtābhidhānāḥ // 9.50 //
Resolutely, therefore, those rulers of the wealth-giving earth abandoned their kingdoms and obtained peace; / Or else, firmly anchored, on the grounds of sovereign power, on the grounds of subdued senses, they affixed the name 'liberation' to what was not the ultimate. //9.50//

teṣāṁ ca rājye 'stu śamo yathāvat prāpto vanaṁ nāham aniścayena /
chittvā hi pāśaṁ gṛha-bandhu-saṁjñaṁ muktaḥ punar na praviviksur asmi // 9.51 //
Or if any of those kings during his kingship did properly realize peace, be that as it may! I, for my part, have not come to the forest with any lack of conviction. / For, having cut the snare called kith and kin, I am free, and not about to enter [that snare] again." //9.51//

ity ātma-vijñāna-guṇānurūpaṁ mukta-spṛhaṁ hetumad ūrjitaṁ ca /
śrutvā narendrātmajam uktavantaṁ pratyuttaraṁ mantra-dharo 'py uvāca // 9.52 //
Words that reflected his facility for knowing the self, words free of eager desire, reasonable, yet powerful, / The son of the king thus spoke. Having listened, the counsellor[49] also spoke his piece: //9.52//

yo niścayo mantra-dharo tavāyaṁ nāyaṁ na yukto na tu kāla-yuktaḥ /
śokāya dattvā pitaraṁ vayaḥ-sthaṁ syād dharma-kāmasya hi te na dharmaḥ // 9.53 //
"This mantra-containing resolve[50] of yours is not improper; but neither is it suited to the present time. / For, to deliver your father in his old age into sorrow, for one who loves dharma as you do, might not be your dharma. //9.53//

nūnaṁ ca buddhis tava nāti-sūkṣmā dharmārthakāmeṣv avicakṣaṇā vā /
hetor adṛṣṭasya phalasya yas tvaṁ pratyakṣam arthaṁ paribhūya yāsi // 9.54 //
Assuredly, again, your judgement is not very acute, or else is dull, with regard to dharma, wealth and desires,[51] / In that, for the sake of an unseen result, you pass over conspicuous wealth. //9.54//

---

[49] *Mantra-dharaḥ*, counsellor, lit. means the bearer of *mantra*, or upholder of wise counsel.
[50] If the reading *mantra-dhara* is accepted here (neither EB Cowell nor EH Johnston accepted the reading), the compound is used as an adjective – *mantra*-containing. The meanings of mantra include 1. "instrument of thought," 2. sacred speech, 3. counsel, 4. secret.
[51] *Dharmārtha-kāma*, dharma, wealth and desires/pleasure – the triple set of worthy aims, according to an influential strand of ancient Indian thought.

punar-bhavo 'stīti ca ke-cid āhur nāstīti ke-cin niyata-pratijñāḥ /
evaṁ yadā saṁśayito 'yam arthas tasmāt kṣamaṁ bhoktum upasthitā śrīḥ // 9.55 //
Some say, moreover, that there is rebirth; others assert with conviction that there is not. / While this matter remains thus open to doubt, it is only natural to enjoy whatever royal rank has come our way. //9.55//

bhūyaḥ pravṛttir yadi kā-cid asti raṁsyāmahe tatra yathopapattau /
atha pravṛttiḥ parato na kā-cit siddho 'prayatnāj jagato 'sya mokṣaḥ // 9.56 //
If we do carry on hereafter in some form, we will enjoy ourselves in that life as befits our birth; / Or else, if there is no carrying on in any form beyond this life, release is already a given for this world, without any effort on our part. //9.56//

astīti ke-cit para-lokam āhur mokṣasya yogaṁ na tu varṇayanti /
agner yathā hy auṣṇyam apāṁ dravatvaṁ tadvat pravṛttau prakṛtiṁ vadanti // 9.57 //
Some say that the next world does exist but they do not affirm a means of exemption [from life carrying on there]; / For, just as heat belongs to fire and wetness belongs to water, nature,[52] so they say, is there in the carrying on. //9.57//

ke-cit svabhāvād iti varṇayanti śubhāśubhaṁ caiva bhavābhavau ca /
svābhāvikaṁ sarvam idaṁ ca yasmād ato 'pi mogho bhavati prayatnaḥ // 9.58 //
Others explain that it is on the grounds of *svabhāva*, existence of things as things unto themselves,[53] that there arise the good and the ugly, being and non-being. / And since this whole world is naturally arisen from things existing unto themselves, again therefore effort is all in vain. //9.58//

yad indriyāṇāṁ niyataḥ pracāraḥ priyāpriyatvaṁ viṣayeṣu caiva /
saṁyujyate yaj jarayārttibhiś ca kas tatra yatno nanu sa svabhāvaḥ // 9.59 //
When the working of the senses is circumscribed, and pleasantness and unpleasantness reside in the objects of the senses, / And when all is bound up with old age and infirmities, what place in that has effort? Is all of that not simply the existence, as things unto themselves, of things? //9.59//

adbhir hutāśaḥ śamam abhyupaiti tejāṁsi cāpo gamayanti śoṣam /
bhinnāni bhūtāni śarīra-saṁsthāny aikyaṁ ca dattvā jagad udvahanti // 9.60 //
The oblation-eating fire is stilled by water, and fiery flames cause water to dry up; / The disparate elements, when contained in a body, confer unity and so bear up the world. //9.60//

---

[52] *Prakṛti*, nature, or primal stuff, or the Primary Matter. See e.g. the description of the Sage Araḍa in BC12.17.

[53] *Svabhāva*, "existence of things as things unto themselves," or simply "self-existence," will be refuted at length, two generations after Aśvaghoṣa, by Nāgārjuna in his Mūla-madhyamaka-kārikā.

yat pāṇi-pādodara-pṛṣṭha-mūrdhnā nirvartate garbha-gatasya bhāvaḥ /
yad ātmanas tasya ca tena yogaḥ svābhāvikaṁ tat-kathayanti taj-jñāḥ // 9.61 //
When, with hands, feet, belly, back and head, a being develops in the womb, / And when there is union of that being with its soul – those who know those things describe it as a natural arising out of things unto themselves.[54] //9.61//

kaḥ kaṇṭakasya prakaroti taikṣṇyaṁ vicitra-bhāvaṁ mṛga-pakṣiṇāṁ vā /
svabhāvataḥ sarvam idaṁ pravṛttaṁ na kāma-kāro 'sti kutaḥ prayatnaḥ // 9.62 //
Who produces the sharpness of a thorn or the birds' and the beasts' diversity of being? / All this is brought about naturally, out of things that exist unto themselves. There is no such thing as free will. Where are the grounds, then, for making an effort? //9.62//

sargaṁ vadantīśvaratas tathānye tatra prayatne puruṣaṣya ko 'rthaḥ /
ya eva hetur jagataḥ pravṛttau hetur nivṛttau niyataḥ sa eva // 9.63 //
Others say, in a similar way, that creation arises from Īśvara, the Almighty. What meaning is there, in that case, in a person's effort, / When what causes the world's carrying on is the same immutable agency that causes cessation? //9.63//

ke-cid vadanty ātma-nimittam eva prādur-bhavaṁ caiva bhava-kṣayaṁ ca /
prādur-bhavaṁ tu pravadanty ayatnād yatnena mokṣādhigamaṁ bruvanti // 9.64 //
There are others who say that the individual soul is the cause of both coming into being and being no more; / But whereas coming into being happens, they say, without effort, only by strenuous effort, they assert, is release attained.[55] //9.64//

naraḥ pitṝṇām anṛṇaḥ prajābhir vedair ṛṣīṇāṁ kratubhiḥ surāṇām /
utpadyate sārdham ṛṇais tribhis tair yasyāsti mokṣaḥ kila tasya mokṣaḥ // 9.65 //
A man becomes free of his debt to the ancestors through his offspring, to the ancient sages through the Vedas, and to the gods through acts of sacrifice. / He is born with these three debts and when from these three he is released, there, so they say, in him, is release. //9.65//

ity evam etena vidhi-krameṇa mokṣaṁ sa-yatnasya vadanti taj-jñāḥ /
prayatnavanto 'pi hi vikrameṇa mumukṣavaḥ khedam avāpnuvanti // 9.66 //
In this way, say experts in the matter, by this order of proceeding, is release assured, to one who makes effort. / For if their effort, however persevering, is disorderly, seekers of release obtain only exhaustion. //9.66//

---

[54] *Svābhāvika*, here used as an adjective, is a name given to a so-called "school of Buddhism." Neither Aśvaghoṣa nor Nāgārjuna, however, recognized the existence of any such school. For them the Buddha's teaching would not have been subject to analysis on sectarian lines.

[55] Having stated the case against bothering to make any effort, the counsellor now proceeds to hedge his bet and state the opposite case for making strenuous goal-oriented effort.

tat saumya mokṣe yadi bhaktir asti nyāyena sevasva vidhiṁ yathoktam /
evaṁ bhaviṣyaty upapattir asya saṁtāpa-nāśaś ca narādhipasya // 9.67 //
Therefore, O mild-mannered man of the *soma*, if you are devoted to release, honor the standard, in the proper manner, as prescribed. / Thus will come about the realization of [the release] and the ending of the anguish of the lord of men. //9.67//

yā ca pravṛttā tava doṣa-buddhis tapo-vanebhyo bhavanaṁ praveṣṭum /
tatrāpi cintā tava tāta mā bhūt pūrve 'pi jagmuḥ sva-gṛhān vanebhyaḥ // 9.68 //
Again, as for your thinking it a fault to re-enter the palace from the ascetic woods, / Have no worry in that regard, dear son – people even in ancient times left the forests and went back home. //9.68//

tapo-vana-stho 'pi vṛtaḥ prajābhir jagāma rājā puram ambarīṣaḥ /
tathā mahīṁ viprakṛtām anāryais tapovanād etya rarakṣa rāmaḥ // 9.69 //
When he was petitioned by his subjects, though he had been abiding in the ascetic forest, King Ambarīṣa went to the city. / So too, when the Great Earth was being abused by ignoble people, did Rāma return from the ascetic forest and reign over her.[56] //9.69//

tathaiva śālvādhipatir drumākhyo vanāt sasūnur nagaraṁ viveśa /
brahmarṣi-bhūtaś ca muner vasiṣṭhād dadhre śriyaṁ sāṁkṛtir antidevaḥ // 9.70 //
So again did Druma, the Śālva king whose name means Tree, in the company of his son, enter the city from the forest. / And, having become a *brahmarṣi*, a brahman seer, Antideva the Sāṁkṛti received the royal insignia from the sage Vasiṣṭha. //9.70//

evaṁ-vidhā dharma-yaśaḥ-pradīpā vanāni hitvā bhavanāny atīyuḥ /
tasmān na doṣo 'sti gṛhaṁ prayātuṁ tapo-vanād dharma-nimittam eva // 9.71 //
Such lanterns as these of the splendor of dharma quit the forests and returned to their houses. / There is no fault in going home, therefore, away from the ascetic forest, when the reason is dharma itself!" //9.71//

tato vacas tasya niśamya mantriṇaḥ priyaṁ hitaṁ caiva nṛpasya cakṣuṣaḥ /
anūnam avyastam asaktam adrutaṁ dhṛtau sthito rāja-suto 'bravīd vacaḥ // 9.72 //
Then, after he had listened to the fond and well-meaning words of a counsellor who was the eye of a ruler of men, / Leaving nothing omitted and nothing garbled, neither getting stuck nor getting carried away, standing firm in his resolve, the son of a king said: //9.72//

---

[56] Cf. Nanda's apology in SN Canto 7: *"For the Śālva king, along with his son; and likewise Ambarīṣa and Rāma and Andha, and Rantideva, son of Sāṅkṛti / Cast off their rags and clothed themselves again in finest fabrics; they cut their twisted dreadlocks off and put their crowns back on." // SN7.51 //*

ihāsti nāstīti ya eṣa saṁśayaḥ parasya vākyair na mamātra niścayaḥ /
avetya tattvaṁ tapasā śamena vā svayaṁ grahīṣyāmi yad atra niścitam // 9.73 //
"As to the doubt you raise, about existence in this world and non-existence, I shall arrive at conviction in this matter not by way of another's words. / Seeing the truth by the heat of asceticism, or else by cooling tranquility, I will grasp for myself what, in this matter, is to be ascertained. //9.73//

na me kṣamaṁ saṁśaya-jaṁ hi darśanaṁ grahītum avyakta-paras-parāhatam /
budhaḥ para-pratyayato hi ko vrajej jano 'ndhakāre 'ndha ivāndha-deśikaḥ // 9.74 //
For it would ill befit me to accept a worldview born of doubt, unintelligible and beset with internal contradictions. / For what wise person would proceed on the grounds of another person's grounds – like a blind man in the darkness, whose guide is blind? //9.74//

adṛṣṭa-tattvasya sato 'pi kiṁ tu me śubhāśubhe saṁśayite śubhe matiḥ /
vṛthāpi khedo hi varaṁ śubhātmanaḥ sukhaṁ na tattve 'pi vigarhitātmanaḥ // 9.75 //
Even in my present state of not having realized the truth, yet still, though good and bad be in doubt, my inclination is to the good. / For better the toil, though the toil was in vain, of a soul given over to the good, than the gratification of one, though onto the truth, whose attitude was reprehensible. //9.75//

imaṁ tu dṛṣṭvāgamam avyavasthitaṁ yad uktam āptais tad avehi sādhv iti /
prahīṇa-doṣa-tvam avehi cāptatāṁ prahīṇa-doṣo hy anṛtaṁ na vakṣyati // 9.76 //
Notice, pray!, that this tradition you describe is not exactly determined, and know to be truly unerring that which is spoken by true people. / Again, know the state of a true person to be freedom from faults, for one without faults will never speak an untruth. //9.76//

gṛha-praveśaṁ prati yac ca me bhavān uvāca rāma-prabhṛtīn nidarśanam /
na te pramāṇaṁ na hi dharma-niścayeṣv alaṁ pramāṇāya parikṣata-vratāḥ // 9.77 //
And as for what you said to me about going home, citing as an example Rāma and the rest, / They are not the standard. For, in no way, as a standard for decisions in dharma, do vow-breakers measure up. //9.77//

tad evam apy eva ravir mahīṁ pated api sthiratvaṁ himavān giris tyajet /
adṛṣṭa-tattvo viṣayonmukhendriyaḥ śrayeya na tv eva gṛhān pṛthag-janaḥ // 9.78 //
That being so, even the sun may fall to the earth, even a Himālayan mountain may relinquish its firmness, / But never would I, not having realized the truth, my senses oriented expectantly towards objects, go back home as a common man. //9.78//

ahaṁ viśeyaṁ jvalitaṁ hutāśanaṁ na cākṛtārthaḥ praviśeyam ālayam /
iti pratijñāṁ sa cakāra garvito yatheṣṭam utthāya ca nirmamo yayau // 9.79 //
I would go into the oblation-eating fire when it is blazing, but I would not, with my task unaccomplished, go back home." / Thus did he declare, with pride but with no sense of me and mine, as he stood up and, as per his declared intent, went on his way. //9.79//

tataḥ sa-bāṣpau saciva-dvijāv ubhau niśamya tasya sthiram eva niścayam /
viṣaṇṇa-vaktrāv anugamya duḥkhitau śanair agatyā puram eva jagmatuḥ // 9.80 //
Then the counsellor and the twice-born veteran, both in tears, having perceived his unshakeable resolve, / Tagged along, in the grip of suffering, with despondent faces; and then meekly, having no other course, the two of them went back to the city in question. //9.80//

tat-snehād atha nṛpateś ca bhaktitas tau sāpekṣaṁ pratiyayatuś ca tasthatuś ca /
dur-dharṣaṁ ravim iva dīptam ātma-bhāsā taṁ draṣṭuṁ na hi pathi śekatur na moktum // 9.81 //
Out of affection for him, and out of devotion to the king, the two went worriedly on their way, and then the two stood still; / For, as he blazed with his own light, like the blinding sun, they were able neither to behold him on the road nor to let him go. //9.81//

tau jñātuṁ parama-gater gatiṁ tu tasya pracchannāṁś cara-puruṣāñ chucīn vidhāya /
rājānaṁ priya-suta-lālasaṁ nu gatvā drakṣyāvaḥ katham iti jagmatuḥ kathaṁ-cit // 9.82 //
In order to monitor the progress, however, of him whose progress was of the highest order, those two appointed honest men to spy for them in secret. / "How on earth are we to go and see the king, who is so devoted to his beloved son?," they fretted, as somehow, with difficulty, the two of them progressed. //9.82//

iti buddha-carite mahā-kāvye kumārānveṣaṇo nāma navamaḥ sargaḥ // 9 //
The 9th canto, titled "The Seeking of a Prince,"
in an epic tale of awakened action.

Canto 10: śreṇyābhigamanaḥ
Śreṇya Drawing Near

Introduction

Once again the title is a person and a verb, and this time the person is ostensibly the subject of the verb. The person is Śreṇya, also known as King Bimbisāra, ruler of the ancient kingdom of Magadha. The verb *abhigamana* ostensibly describes Śrenya approaching the Prince with a view to persuading him to change his mind.

One alternative reading of the canto title is as a co-ordinative (*dvandva*) compound of two elements: 1. Śreṇya and 2. Drawing Near. In this reading, Śreṇya is Śreṇya, and the one getting closer is the bodhisattva who, as in Canto 13, simply sits in lotus, as immovably as Mount Kailāsa.

At the same time there is a sense in which, below the surface, ironically, the words of Śreṇya himself get closer and closer to the truth, so that by the closing verses of the Canto Śreṇya is describing how people who have, in the true sense, grown old, as if they have crossed beyond a wasteland, finally breathe easy.

sa rāja-vatsaḥ pṛthu-pīna-vakṣās tau havya-mantrādhikṛtau vihāya /
uttīrya gangāṁ pracalat taraṅgāṁ śrīmad-gṛhaṁ rājagṛhaṁ jagāma // 10.1 //
The king's beloved boy, whose chest was broad and full, after he had got rid of those two, the heads of *havya* and of *mantra*, oblations and machinations, / Crossed the billowing Ganges and went to Rāja-gṛha, "Kingsbury," with its splendid residences.[1] // 10.1//

śailaiḥ su-guptaṁ ca vibhūṣitaṁ ca dhṛtaṁ ca pūtaṁ ca śivais tapodaiḥ /
pañcācalāṅkaṁ nagaraṁ prapede śāntaḥ svayambhūr iva nāka-pṛṣṭham // 10.2 //
Well guarded, and beautified, by mountains; preserved, and purified, by healing hot springs; / In the hook of five hills, stood the city he entered – like 'Spontaneously Happening' Brahmā,[2] unperturbed, entering the heights of heaven. //10.2//

gāmbhīryam ojaś ca niśāmya tasya vapuś ca dīptaṁ puruṣān atītya /
visismaye tatra janas tadānīṁ sthāṇu-vratasyeva vṛṣa-dhvajasya // 10.3 //
Perceiving the depth and strength of that man, and the shining form which outshone men, / The people there at that time were filled with wonder – as if [perceiving the depth and strength and shining form] of the one, unmoving in his vow of practice, whose emblem is the bull.[3] //10.3//

---

[1] Rāja-gṛha was the capital of Magadha, the kingdom ruled at that time by Śreṇya, also known as Bimbi-sāra.

[2] Conventionally Svayam-bhū means either Brahmā or Śiva – or sometimes the other of the three gods in the Hindu triad, Viṣṇu. See also note to BC2.51.

[3] The god whose emblem is the bull most probably means Śiva.

taṁ prekṣya yo 'nyena yayau sa tasthau yas tatra tasthau pathi so 'nvagacchat /
drutaṁ yayau yaḥ sa jagāma dhīraṁ yaḥ kaś-cid āste sma sa cotpapāta // 10.4 //
On seeing him, whoever was going the other way stood still; whoever was there in the road standing still, followed along; / whoever was going hurriedly, went steadily; and anybody who was sitting, sprang up.[4] //10.4//

kaś-cit tam ānarca janaḥ karābhyāṁ sat-kṛtya kaś-cic chirasā vavande /
snigdhena kaś-cid vacasābhyananda naivaṁ jagāmāpratipūjya kaś-cit // 10.5 //
Some people honored him with joined hands; some properly paid homage, using their head;[5] / some sang his praises with devoted words. Nobody, in this way, went without showing religious reverence.[6] //10.5//

taṁ jihriyuḥ prekṣya vicitra-veṣāḥ prakīrṇa-vācaḥ pathi maunam īyuḥ /
dharmasya sākṣād iva saṁnikarṣe na kaś-cid anyāya-matir babhūva // 10.6 //
Fancy dressers when they saw him felt ashamed. Random chatterers on the road fell silent. / As when in the physical presence of dharma,[7] nobody had an irregular thought. //10.6//

anya-kriyāṇām api rāja-mārge strīṇāṁ nṛṇāṁ vā bahu-māna-pūrvam /
taṁ deva-kalpaṁ nara-deva-sūnuṁ nirīkṣamāṇā na tatarpa dṛṣṭiḥ // 10.7 //
Though on the royal road they were engaged in different work,[8] adoring women and men beheld him, / The god-like son of a man-god, but satisfaction was not realized by their admiring gaze. //10.7//

bhruvau lalāṭaṁ mukham īkṣaṇe vā vapuḥ karau vā caraṇau gatiṁ vā /
yad eva yas tasya dadarśa tatra tad eva tasyātha babandha cakṣuḥ // 10.8 //
Eyebrows, forehead, mouth, or organs of seeing; body or hands; feet or manner of going – / Whatever aspect of him any of them looked at, to that very target her or his eye was bound. //10.8//

---

[4] Ostensible meaning: they stopped sitting and got up. Hidden meaning: they carried on sitting, and went up more.

[5] They prostrated themselves, bowing their head to the floor; and/or they used their head (for something other than a hat-rack) and paid attention to what they were doing.

[6] Ostensibly Aśvaghoṣa is praising all the townsfolk for the attitude of religious devotion. Below the surface, is he ironically bemoaning the absence of any individual who was different (*anyaḥ* or *anyā*)?

[7] The ostensible meaning of *sākṣāt* (ablative of *sa* [possessing] + *akṣa* [eye]) is "before one's own eyes." Below the surface, *dharmasya sākṣāt* could suggest realizing the dharma not only on the outside, but as one's own practice of sitting upright.

[8] Ostensibly they were otherwise occupied, engaged in miscellaneous tasks. *Anya-kriyāṇām* ostensibly means "other tasks," but in the hidden meaning, the labors of an individual who is different, the actions of a non-buddha.

dṛṣṭvā ca sorṇa-bhruvam āyatākṣaṁ jvalac-charīraṁ śubha-jāla-hastam /
taṁ bhikṣu-veṣaṁ kṣiti-pālanārhaṁ saṁcukṣubhe rājagṛhasya lakṣmīḥ // 10.9 //
On seeing him, moreover, with the circle of hair between his eyebrows and with his widely extending eyes, with his shining body and beautiful webbed hands, / On seeing in a beggar's garb him who was fit to rule the earth, the Royal Grace of Rājagṛha[9] was ruffled. //10.9//

śreṇyo 'tha bhartā magadhājirasya bāhyād vimānād vipulaṁ janaugham /
dadarśa papraccha ca tasya hetuṁ tatas tam asmai puruṣaḥ śaśaṁsa // 10.10 //
And so Śreṇya,[10] master of the Magadha domain, from an outer palace turret, saw the great throng, / And inquired into the motive behind it. Then a man conveyed that [motive] to him - //10.10//

jñānaṁ paraṁ vā pṛthivī-śriyaṁ vā viprair ya ukto 'dhigamiṣyatīti /
sa eṣa śākyādhipates-tanū-jo nirīkṣyate pravrajito janena // 10.11 //
"Ultimate knowing, or else earthly power, inspired sages said he would realize: / It is he, the son of the Śākya ruler, who, having gone forth, is being admired by the people." //10.11//

tataḥ śrutārtho manasāgatārtho rājā babhāṣe puruṣaṁ tam eva /
vijñāyatāṁ kva pratigacchatīti tathety athainaṁ puruṣo 'nvagacchat // 10.12 //
Then, having learned the motive, having been motivated in his own mind, the king told that same man: / "Let me know in what direction he is going!"[11] The man said "So be it!" and followed him. //10.12//

a-lola-cakṣur yuga-mātra-darśī nivṛtta-vāg yantrita-manda-gāmī /
cacāra bhikṣāṁ sa tu bhikṣu-varyo nidhāya gātrāṇi calaṁ ca cetaḥ // 10.13 //
Looking, with eyes that did not dance, a yoke's length ahead; not speaking; moving slowly and with restraint, / He the best of beggars, however, went begging - placing within limits his limbs and the inconstant mind. //10.13//

ādāya bhaikṣaṁ ca yathopapannaṁ yayau gireḥ prasravaṇaṁ viviktam /
nyāyena tatrābhyavahṛtya cainan mahī-dharaṁ pāṇḍavam āruroha // 10.14 //
Having accepted whatever food was offered, he went to a solitary mountain spring, / And there, according to principle, that food he did eat, and the hill of the Pāṇḍavas he did ascend.[12] //10.14//

---

[9] *Rājagṛhasya lakṣmīh* (f.) is enigmatic. Among the meanings of *lakṣmī* are 1. grace, and 2. the Good Genius or Fortune of a king personified (and often regarded as a rival of his queen). Simply thinking, the appearance of the bodhisattva-prince created a stir.

[10] The ruler of the kingdom of Magadha, also known as Bimbi-sāra.

[11] Below the surface, the suggestion is that the bodhisattva, even before his realization of the truth, was able to stimulate Śreṇya's will to the truth - there being, for bodhisattvas and buddhas alike, such a thing as a right direction. That direction, verses 14 and 15, implicitly suggest, is primarily upward.

[12] *Āruroha*, from *ā-√ruh*, to rise up.

tasminn avau lodhra-vanopagūḍhe mayūra-nāda-pratipūrṇa-kuñje /
kāṣāya-vāsāḥ sa babhau nṛ-sūryo yathodayasyopari bāla-sūryaḥ // 10.15 //
On that hill covered with *lodhra*[13] groves, its thickets filled with the crying of peacocks, / Wearing the ochre robe, that human sun shone forth like the morning sun up above the eastern mountain.[14] //10.15//

tatrainam ālokya sa rāja-bhṛtyaḥ śreṇyāya rājñe kathayāṁ cakāra /
saṁśrutya rājā sa ca bāhumānyāt tatra pratasthe nibhṛtānuyātraḥ // 10.16 //
That servant of the king, having seen him there, reported back to King Śreṇya. / And the king, having listened, out of great respect, set off in that direction, with only a modest retinue. //10.16//

sa pāṇḍavaṁ pāṇḍava-tulya-vīryaḥ śailottamaṁ śaila-samāna-varṣmā /
maulī-dharaḥ siṁha-gatir nṛ-siṁhaś calat-saṭaḥ siṁha ivāruroha // 10.17 //
The hill of the Pāṇḍavas, that most exalted of rocks, he of rock-like stature and heroic power on a par with the Pāṇḍavas,[15] / A human lion, wearing the royal headdress and going with a lion's gait, like a lion with bouncing mane – that hill [King Śreṇya also] did ascend.[16] //10.17//

tataḥ sma tasyopari śṛṅga-bhūtaṁ śāntendriyaṁ paśyati bodhisattvam /
paryaṅkam āsthāya virocamānaṁ śaśāṅkam udyantam ivābhra-kūñjāt // 10.18 //
Then he saw, up above[17] that hill, being in the nature of a peak, the bodhisattva, the power of his senses quieted, / Coming back to sitting with legs fully crossed, and shining forth, like the moon rising[18] out of a thicket of clouds. //10.18//

taṁ rūpa-lakṣmyā ca śamena caiva dharmasya nirmāṇam ivopadiṣṭam /
sa-vismayaḥ praśrayavān narendraḥ svayambhuvaṁ śakra ivopatasthe // 10.19 //
To him who, with his wealth of handsome form and his calmness, was like a work of dharma built to specification, / The first among men, filled with wonder, respectfully drew near, as to 'Spontaneously-Happening' Brahmā the mighty Indra drew near.[19] //10.19//

---

[13] A tree (Symplocos Racemosa) that has yellow flowers. So the hill was yellow, like a mountain with the morning sun on it, while the bodhisattva in his yellow-red robe was like the sun.

[14] *Udaya*, which means the eastern mountain (behind which the sun rises), is lit. "going up" (*ud-* = up, *aya* = going). *Upari* means upward, up above.

[15] The story of the epic battle between the Pāṇḍavas (descended from Paṇḍu) and their cousins the Kauravas (descended from Kuru) is told in the *Mahā-bhārata* and also in the *Bhagavad-gita.*

[16] *Āruroha*, again, from *ā-√ruh*, to rise up

[17] *Upari,* again, means upward, up above.

[18] *Udyantam*, again, is from *ud-√i,* to go up.

[19] *Upa-√sthā* means to place oneself near, to bring oneself into the presence of. There is a dual sense of Śreṇya (1) following the bodhisattva, relatively speaking, in the right direction (upward); and (2) being near to the center of energetic action, like the sun (verse 15), the moon (verse 18), and Svayam-bhū, "Spontaneous Happening" himself (verses 2, 19).

taṁ nyāyato nyāya-vidāṁ variṣṭhaṁ sametya papraccha ca dhātu-sāmyam /
sa cāpy avocat sadṛśena sāmnā nṛ-paṁ manaḥ-svāsthyam an-āmayaṁ ca // 10.20 //
Having come, in a proper way, into the presence of the best of knowers of a proper way, the king asked after the balance of his bodily humors; / And he also, in a suitably equable manner, spoke to a protector of men, of mental well-being and freedom from disease. //10.20//

tataḥ śucau vāraṇa-karṇa-nīle śilā-tale saṁniṣasāda rājā /
nṛpopaviśyānumataś ca tasya bhāvaṁ vijijñāsur idaṁ babhāṣe // 10.21 //
Then, on a rock as grey as an elephant's ear, on a clean slab of rock, the king sat down; / And, while sitting as a protector of men, being allowed by the other,[20] and wanting to know the reality of that other,[21] he spoke as follows: //10.21//

prītiḥ parā me bhavataḥ kulena kramāgatā caiva parīkṣitā ca /
jātā vivakṣā suta yā yato me tasmād idaṁ sneha-vaco nibodha // 10.22 //
"I have, in connection with your noble house, a love of the highest order, transmitted from offspring to offspring, and tested well.[22] / Hence the desire, O offspring, which is born in me to speak. Therefore, to this expression of loving devotion, give your attention.[23] //10.22//

āditya-pūrvaṁ vipulaṁ kulaṁ te navaṁ vayo dīptam idaṁ vapuś ca /
kasmād iyaṁ te matir akrameṇa bhaikṣāka evābhiratā na rājye // 10.23 //
Mighty is your house, with a son of 'The Infinite' Aditi as its founder;[24] young is your life; and shining is this your handsome form – / From where came this will of yours which, all of a sudden, is set not on kingship but on abject begging?[25] //10.23//

gātraṁ hi te lohita-candanārhaṁ kāṣāya-saṁśleṣam an-arham etat /
hastaḥ prajā-pālana-yogya eṣa bhoktuṁ na cārhaḥ para-dattam annam // 10.24 //
For your body is worthy of red sandal unguents, not of contact with reddish-brown cloth. / This hand is fitted for the protection of subjects, and not for the eating of food given by others. //10.24//

---

[20] *Anumatas tasya.* Ostensible meaning: with his permission. Hidden meaning: letting *it* do it.

[21] *Tasya bhāvam.* Ostensible meaning: his intention/disposition. Hidden meaning: the reality of *it* happening.

[22] In the hidden meaning, is Śreṇya presaging devotion to a one-to-one transmission in the lineage of Zen ancestors?

[23] Ostensible meaning: Listen to these affectionate words! Hidden meaning: Attend to the practice of sitting-meditation – as the Buddha, putting compassion into practice, taught it.

[24] The Śākyas were said to be descended from Īkṣvāku, the first king of the solar dynasty. Here *āditya* (son of Aditi) means the sun.

[25] Ostensibly Śreṇya's question is a rhetorical one, expressing surprise. Below the surface, he might be drawing our attention to the unfathomable nature of something ineffable.

tat saumya rājyaṁ yadi paitṛkaṁ tvaṁ snehāt pitur necchasi vikrameṇa /
na ca kramaṁ marṣayituṁ matis te bhuṇkṣvārdham asmad-viṣayasya śīghram // 10.25 //
So if, my friend, out of love for your father, you do not wish by forcible means to inherit your father's kingdom, / But you have no mind to hold out for a regular succession, then enjoy possession of half of my realm, right away! //10.25//

evaṁ hi na syāt svajanāvamardaḥ kāla-krameṇāpi śama-śrayā śrīḥ /
tasmāt kuruṣva praṇayaṁ mayi tvaṁ sadbhiḥ sahīyā hi satāṁ samṛddhiḥ // 10.26 //
For in this way there will be no inflicting of pain on your own kin, and royal power will come peacefully and in a timely and orderly manner. / Do me this kindness, therefore, because in association with the good is there growth of the good. //10.26//

atha tv idānīṁ kula-garvitatvād asmāsu viśrambha-guṇo na te 'sti /
vyūḍhāny anīkāni vigāhya bāṇair mayā sahāyena parān jigīṣa // 10.27 //
Or if, for the present, pride in your own noble house precludes you from placing your trust in ours, / Then piercing with arrows the massed ranks of armies, seek, with me as an ally, to conquer foreign foes. //10.27//

tad buddhim atrānyatarāṁ vṛṇīṣva dharmārtha-kāmān vidhivad bhajasva /
vyatyasya rāgād iha hi tri-vargaṁ pretyeha ca bhraṁśam avāpnuvanti // 10.28 //
So decide, in respect of these two options, between one and the other, and pursue dharma, wealth, and pleasure in a principled manner - / For when men in this world, because of passion, overdo [any one of] the triple set, in both this world and the next they suffer ruination. //10.28//

yo hy artha-dharmau paripīḍya kāmaḥ[26] syād dharma-kāmau paribhūya cārthaḥ /
kāmārthayoś coparameṇa dharmas tyājyaḥ sa kṛtsno yadi kāṅkṣito 'rthaḥ // 10.29 //
For when pleasure overwhelms wealth and dharma, or wealth overpowers dharma and pleasure, / Or dharma spells the death of pleasure and wealth - we must abandon it, if we aspire to meaning in the round. //10.29//

tasmāt tri-vargasya niṣevaṇena tvaṁ rūpam etat saphalaṁ kuruṣva /
dharmārtha-kāmādhigamaṁ hy an-ūnaṁ nṛṇām an-ūnaṁ puruṣārtham āhuḥ // 10.30 //
Therefore by devotion to the triple set let this splendid frame of yours bear fruit. / For the integral attainment of dharma, wealth and pleasure is for mankind, they say, the whole meaning of a human life. //10.30//

[26] *Kāmah* is nominative singular of *kāma*, whose meanings include 1. desire, 2. pleasure, and 3. sensual love. See also note to verse 33 below.

tan niṣphalau nārhasi kartum etau pīnau bhujau cāpa-vikarṣaṇārhau /
māndhātṛvaj jetum imau hi yogyau lokān api trīn iha kiṁ punar gām // 10.31 //
So do not render fruitless these muscular arms that were meant to draw a bow; / For, like Māndhātṛ, these two [arms] are capable of conquering even the three worlds here and now, let alone the earth.[27] //10.31//

snehena khalv etad ahaṁ bravīmi naiśvarya-rāgeṇa na vismayena /
imaṁ hi dṛṣṭvā tava bhikṣu-veṣaṁ jātānukampo 'smy api cāgatāśruḥ // 10.32 //
I say this with sheer affection - not with eager desire for dominion and not with doubt. / For, seeing this beggar's clothing of yours, I am moved to compassion and visited by tears. //10.32//

yāvat sva-vaṁśa-pratirūpa-rūpaṁ na te jarābhyety abhibhūya bhūyaḥ /
tad bhuṇkṣva bhikṣāśrama-kāma kāmān kāle 'si kartā priya-dharma dharmam // 10.33 //
Therefore, before the beauty that befits your noble house is overpowered by the onset of ageing, / Enjoy desires,[28] O desirer of the beggar's stage, and in due time, O devotee of dharma, you will practice dharma. //10.33//

śaknoti jīrṇaḥ khalu dharmam āptuṁ kāmopabhogeṣv agatir jarāyāḥ /
ataś ca yūnaḥ kathayanti kāmān madhyasya vittaṁ sthavirasya dharmam // 10.34 //
One who is old, assuredly, is able to realize dharma. In old age the drive is absent for enjoyment of sensual pleasures. / And so pleasures, they say, belong to the young; acquisition of substance to one in the middle; dharma to a mature elder.[29] //10.34//

dharmasya cārthasya ca jīva-loke pratyarthi-bhūtāni hi yauvanāni /
saṁrakṣyamāṇāny api dur-grahāṇi kāmā yatas tena yathā haranti // 10.35 //
For, in the world of the living, youthful indiscretions are the enemy of dharma and of wealth. / However well we guard against those immature acts, to get a grip on them is hard, for which reason desires duly prevail. //10.35//

vayāṁsi jīrṇāni vimarśavanti dhīrāṇy avasthāna-parāyaṇāni /
alpena yatnena śamātmakāni bhavanty agatyaiva ca lajjayā ca // 10.36 //
The old are contemplative, steady, intent on stability; / They become peaceful with little bother - through sheer helplessness, and humbleness.[30] //10.36//

---

[27] Cf. the bodhisattva's reply in the next canto: *Even as heaven rained down upon him golden rain after he had conquered all four continents / And obtained half of Mighty Indra's throne, there was for Māndhātṛ in outer realms only dissatisfaction. //BC11.13//*

[28] *Kāmān* is accusative plural of *kāma*, translated in this canto, as one of the triple set, as "pleasure."

[29] Ostensibly *madhyasya vittam* (wealth of the middle) and *sthavirasya dharmam* (dharma of the elder) are two different things belonging to two different age-groups. But there is no particle *ca*. So the ironic intention might be that a true elder (Sanskrit: *sthavira*; Pāli: *thera*) is of the middle, and his or her dharma is not only abstract teaching, but something really to be acquired.

[30] Ostensibly Śreṇya is describing people rendered impotent and timid by old age. Ironically, he is also describing those whose practice is mature, in which case *agati*, being helpless, is an expression of non-doing; and *lajjā*, modesty, is absence of pride and awareness of faults.

ataś ca lolaṁ viṣaya-pradhānaṁ pramattam akṣāntam adīrgha-darśi /
bahu-cchalaṁ yauvanam abhyatītya nistīrya kāntāram ivāśvasanti // 10.37 //
And so, having outgrown the fickle years whose main concern is objects, having got over heedless, impatient, short-sighted immaturity, / Having passed beyond pretense-filled adolescence, they breathe again, as if having crossed a wasteland.[31] //10.37//

tasmād adhīraṁ capala-pramādi navaṁ vayas tāvad idaṁ vyapaitu /
kāmasya pūrvaṁ hi vayaḥ śaravyaṁ na śakyate rakṣitum indriyebhyaḥ // 10.38 //
Just let pass, therefore, this irresolute phase, this fickle and heedless phase of juvenility; / For the first flush is the target of Desire and cannot be protected from the power of the senses.[32] //10.38//

atho cikīrṣā tava dharma eva yajasva yajñaṁ kula-dharma eṣaḥ /
yajñair adhiṣṭhāya hi nāka-pṛṣṭhaṁ yayau marutvān api nāka-pṛṣṭham // 10.39 //
Now if your desire is to practice nothing but dharma, then offer up the act of offering,[33] as is the dharma of your noble house; / For, having gone, by means of acts of offering, up to the upper reaches of heaven, even 'Marut-attended' Indra, by means of acts of offering, reached those uppermost reaches. //10.39//

suvarṇa-keyūra-vidaṣṭa-bāhavo maṇi-pradīpojjvala-citra-maulayaḥ /
nṛparṣayas tāṁ hi gatiṁ gatā makhaiḥ śrameṇa yām eva mahārṣayo yayuḥ // 10.40 //
For, with arms hugged by golden bands, with conspicuous crowns blazing with the light of gems,[34] / Seers who were protectors of men have walked that same path, by their sacrifices, which the *maharishis*, the great seers, reached by their hard practice." //10.40//

---

[31] Ostensibly Śreṇya is describing old folk in retirement homes, but in the hidden meaning buddhas who have crossed beyond the suffering of saṁsāra.

[32] The hidden meaning might be the practical injunction not to do the wrong thing, here and now, by letting a momentary impulse pass, and not acting on it – the principle of free won't. In this sense, then, Śreṇya, has drawn very near – without recognizing just how close he has drawn to the Buddha's truth. In this sense, we can understand the canto title, below the surface, as suggesting not only Śreṇya's misguided proposal to the prince, but also Śreṇya's drawing near to the truth.

[33] *Yajasva yajñam.* Ostensible meaning: offer sacrifices! Hidden meaning: offer up acts of offering! Ostensibly Śreṇya is urging the bodhisattva, as a prince, to offer up oblations into the sacred fire. But verb and object from the same root, *yaj*, could also suggest the goalless offering of acting for the sake of acting.

[34] Golden bands, as previously (see e.g. BC5.50; 5.81) seem in the hidden meaning to suggest vital energy; similarly for illuminated crowns.

ity evaṁ magadha-patir vaco babhāṣe yaḥ samyag valabhid iva dhruvam babhāṣe /
tac-chrutvā na sa vicacāla rāja-sūnuḥ kailāso girir iva naika-citra-sānuḥ // 10.41 //
Thus spoke the ruler of the Magadhas, who talked straight, like "Force-destroying" Indra addressing "Immovable" Brahmā.[35] / Having heard that speech, the son of the king was not moved, like Mount Kailāsa[36] with its many conspicuous summits. //10.41//

iti buddha-carite mahā-kāvye 'śvaghoṣa-kṛte
śreṇyābhigamano nāma daśamaḥ sargaḥ // 10 //
The 10th canto, titled "Śreṇya Drawing Near,"
in this epic tale of awakened action.

---

[35] Dhruvam, "the Immovable," like Svayaṁ-bhū, "the Self-Existent" (or "the Spontaneously Happening"), is a name applied to Brahmā but also sometimes to Śiva and Viṣṇu.

[36] Kailāsa is thought to be derived from *kelāsa*, meaning crystal. In ancient Indian mythology, Kailāsa is the fabulous residence of Kubera, Lord of Wealth. As an actual mountain (Mount Kailash), it is a peak in the Kailash Range (Gangdisê Mountains), forming part of the Transhimalaya in Tibet, where it does seem to protrude from the earth like a giant crystal.

Canto 11: kāma-vigarhaṇaḥ
Blaming Desires

Introduction

When something goes wrong in life, it is often because we have been unduly eager to go directly for a desired result without paying due attention to the means. This undue eagerness to get a result is called in Sanskrit *tṛṣṇā*, thirsting (see verse 55). Thirsting is the eighth of the 12 links in the chain of dependent arising of suffering, as will be described in Canto 14. But *tṛṣṇā*, thirsting, is a particular manifestation of *kāma*, whose meanings include volition or desire in general. *Kāma* also means pleasure, and love – especially sexual love or sensuality. In the plural, moreover, like the English "desires," or "loves," *kāmāḥ* can mean the objects of desire or love.

Again, among the three pollutants whose influence prevents us from seeing the truth, along with *bhavāsrava*, the pollutant of becoming, and *avidyāsrava*, the pollutant of ignorance, there is *kāmāsrava*, the pollutant of desire, or of love, or of sensuality.

Ostensibly then the title of the present canto describes the bodhisattva, with righteous indignation, blaming desires. And the content of the canto, on a superficial reading, supports that understanding.

On a deeper reading, however, the bodhisattva repeatedly asks the question: "Who in possession of himself would delight in those desires?" Thus the bodhisattva, implicitly, does not put the blame on desires per se – at least not from verse 20 onwards. He rather puts the blame on failure to remain in possession of oneself.

Remaining self-possessed in Sanskrit is *ātmavat*, lit. having (*vat*) self (*ātma*). The bodhisattva's emphasis on such self-possession might be seen as valid at the level of conventional truth, as opposed to ultimate truth. After Canto 14, we can guess, the Buddha would go on to connect the convenient fiction of possession of a self with the deeper truth of emptiness. This progression is observable, for example, in the Rāhula Sutta (see Appendix) where the Buddha advises Rāhula first to think "Witnessing the whole body, I will breathe...," and then to think "Dropping off the fiction of a body, I will breathe...."

Even at the level of conventional truth, it is demonstrably true that a desire which could lead us into trouble, in fact turns out to be harmless, so long as, remaining in possession of ourselves, we do not act on it. And at the level of ultimate truth, there is neither a self-existent self that any of us can possess, nor a self-existent desire that we can get free of or get rid of or drive away.

Thus, Blaming Desires, or The Blaming of Desire – whether or not Aśvaghoṣa himself formulated the title – is another canto title that challenges us to keep digging deeper in our explorations of what the Buddha thought as a bodhisattva, and what he taught as the Buddha.

athaivam ukto magadhādhipena suhṛn-mukhena pratikūlam artham /
svastho 'vikāraḥ kula-śauca-śuddhaḥ śauddhodanir vākyam idaṁ jagāda // 11.1 //
Now when the monarch of the Magadhas, with friendly face, had addressed him thus, with contrary purport, / He whose noble house and personal integrity were pure, the son of 'Pure Mush' Śuddhodana, being well in himself and unperturbed, spoke this reply: //11.1//

nāścaryam etad bhavato 'bhidhānam jātasya haryaṅka-kule viśāle /
yan mitra-pakṣe tava mitra-kāma syād vṛttir eṣā pariśuddha-vṛtteḥ // 11.2 //
"This speech of yours is no surprise, born as you are into the illustrious line whose emblem is the lion[1] – / That you, O desirer of friendship,[2] whose course of action is pure should show towards a friend this considerate course of action. //11.2//

a-satsu maitrī sva-kulānurūpā na tiṣṭhati śrīr iva viklaveṣu /
pūrvaiḥ kṛtāṁ prīti-paraṁparābhis tām eva santas tu vivardhayanti // 11.3 //
Among the untrue, friendship formed by each in keeping with his tribe does not last – like sovereign power among the faint-hearted. / But friendship forged by repeated past favours, is just that benevolence which the true cause to grow. //11.3//

ye cārtha-kṛcchreṣu bhavanti loke samāna-kāryāḥ suhṛdāṁ manuṣyāḥ /
mitrāṇi tānīti paraimi buddhyā sva-sthasya vṛddhiṣv iha ko hi na syāt // 11.4 //
Those in the world who, for the good-hearted in hard times are there as human beings, helping with work to be done – / Those friends I esteem, advisedly, as friends indeed. For who would not be present around one going well in a period of vigorous prosperity? //11.4//

evaṁ ca ye dravyam avāpya loke mitreṣu dharme ca niyojayanti /
avāpta-sārāṇi dhanāni teṣāṁ bhraṣṭāni nānte janayanti tāpam // 11.5 //
And, having obtained riches in the world, those who in this way commit their riches to friends and to dharma, / Have made the most of their resources – whose dissipation, in the end, generates no grief. //11.5//

suhṛttayā cāryatayā ca rājan khalv eṣa yo mām prati niścayas te /
atrānuneṣyāmi suhṛttayaiva brūyām ahaṁ nottaram anyad atra // 11.6 //
With nothing but friendship and nobility, O king! comes this resolution of yours towards me. / Conciliation, in this situation, I too shall express with friendship plain and simple. No other response, in this situation, could I express. //11.6//

---

1 When his words are read like this, the Prince is returning the compliment that Śreṇya paid him in BC10.23, since the lion was an emblem of the solar race to which both kings, of Kapilavastu and Magadha, belonged. EHJ took Haryaṅka to be the same as Haryaṅga, a Bṛhad-ratha king whose name suggests the lion-legend of the Bṛhad-rathas, which is referred to in SN8.44 (*And Bṛhad-rathā, 'the Burly Heroine,' loved a lion: there is nothing women will not do.*). EHJ adds that fragmentary remains of the Buddhist dramas mention the Bṛhad-rathas' foundation of a city which seems to be Rājāgṛha.

2 *Mitra-kāma* means "O desirer of friendship" or "O lover of friendship." The *kāma* is as per the canto title.

ahaṁ jarā-mṛtyu-bhayaṁ viditvā mumukṣayā dharmam imaṁ prapannaḥ /
bandhūn priyān aśru-mukhān vihāya prāg eva kāmān aśubhasya hetūn // 11.7 //
Having become aware of the terror of aging and dying, I with desire for release[3] have taken to this dharma, / Leaving behind beloved tear-faced relatives – still more have I left behind desires, the causes of mischief! //11.7//

nāśīviṣebhyo hi tathā bibhemi naivāśanibhyo gaganāc cyutebhyaḥ /
na pāvakebhyo 'nila-saṁhitebhyo yathā bhayaṁ me viṣayebhya eva // 11.8 //
For I am not so afraid of venomous snakes, or of thunderbolts falling from the sky, / Or of fires supplied with air, as I am fearful of objects in the realm of the senses.[4] //11.8//

kāmā hy anityāḥ kuśalārtha-caurā riktāś ca māyā-sadṛśāś ca loke /
āśāsyamānā api mohayanti cittaṁ nṛṇāṁ kiṁ punar ātma-saṁsthāḥ // 11.9 //
For transient desires are robbers of the stuff of happiness. They are hollow, and resemble phantoms in the world. / Even in their anticipation, they delude the mind of men. How much more in their physical consummation? //11.9//

kāmābhibhūtā hi na yānti śarma tri-piṣṭape kiṁ bata martya-loke /
kāmaiḥ sa-tṛṣṇasya hi nāsti tṛptir yathendhanair vāta-sakhasya vahneḥ // 11.10 //
For those in thrall to desires arrive at happiness not in triple heaven, much less in the mortal world. / A man possessed of thirst is no more satisfied by desires than wind-befriended fire is satisfied by fuel. //11.10//

jagaty an-artho na samo 'sti kāmair mohāc ca teṣv eva janaḥ prasaktaḥ /
tattvaṁ viditvaivam an-artha-bhīruḥ prājñaḥ svayaṁ ko 'bhilaṣed an-artham // 11.11 //
There is nothing in the world as troublesome as desires, and yet it is to them that people, out of ignorance, are attached. / Knowing the truth to be so, what trouble-wary man of wisdom would willfully covet trouble? //11.11//

samudra-vastrām api gām avāpya pāraṁ jigīṣanti mahārṇavasya /
lokasya kāmair na vitṛptir asti patadbhir ambhobhir ivārṇavasya // 11.12 //
Even having taken possession of the sea-girt earth, men desire to conquer what lies beyond the great ocean. / The world is no more sated by desires than the ocean is sated by waters descending into it. //11.12//

devena vṛṣṭe 'pi hiraṇya-varṣe dvīpān samagrāṁś caturo 'pi jitvā /
śakrasya cārdhāsanam apy avāpya māndhātur āsīd viṣayeṣv atṛptiḥ // 11.13 //
Even as heaven rained down upon him golden rain after he had conquered all four continents / And obtained half of Mighty Indra's throne, there was for Māndhātṛ in outer realms only dissatisfaction. //11.13//

---

[3] *Mumukṣayā* is a desiderative form of √*muc*, to release.
[4] The bodhisattva here appears to identify *kāmāh*, desires in the plural, with *viṣayāḥ*, objects of the senses, sensual enjoyments.

bhuktvāpi rājyaṁ divi devatānāṁ śatakratau vṛtra-bhayāt pranaṣṭe /
darpān mahārṣīn api vāhayitvā kāmeṣv atṛpto nahuṣaḥ papāta // 11.14 //
Even having enjoyed kingship over the gods in heaven (after Indra, through fear of Vṛta, had fled), / And even, out of pride, having caused the Mahārishis to carry him, Nahuṣa, unsatisfied among desires, fell down.[5] //11.14//

aiḍaś ca rājā tri-divaṁ vigāhya nītvāpi devīṁ vaśam urvaśīṁ tām /
lobhād ṛṣibhyaḥ kanakaṁ jihīrṣur jagāma nāśaṁ viṣayeṣv atṛptaḥ // 11.15 //
Again, King Purū-ravas, son of Iḍā, having penetrated triple heaven and even brought into his thrall that goddess Dawn, Urvaśī, / Was still desirous, in his greed, of carrying off the Rishis' gold – unsatisfied, among all his possessions in sensory realms, he went to his end.[6] //11.15//

baler mahendraṁ nahuṣaṁ mahendrād indraṁ punar ye nahuṣād upeyuḥ /
svarge kṣitau vā viṣayeṣu teṣu ko viśvased bhāgya-kulākuleṣu // 11.16 //
From Bali[7] those realms passed to great Indra; from great Indra to Nahuṣa; and from Nahuṣa back again to Indra:/ Who, whether in heaven or on the earth, could breathe easy in realms so subject to the graces and indignities of fate? //11.16//

cīrāmbarā mūla-phalāmbu-bhakṣā jaṭā vahanto 'pi bhujaṅga-dīrghāḥ /
yair nanya-kāryā munayo 'pi bhagnāḥ kaḥ kāma-saṁjñān mṛgayeta śatrūn // 11.17 //
Despite being clothed in strips of bark or rags and subsisting on roots, fruit and water; despite wearing dreadlocks as long as snakes; / Despite having no extraneous duty, sages have still been defeated by them – Who would pursue those enemies called desires? //11.17//

ugrāyudhaś cogra-dhṛtāyudho 'pi yeṣāṁ kṛte mṛtyum avāpa bhīṣmāt /
cintāpi teṣām aśivā vadhāya tad vṛttināṁ kiṁ punar avratānām // 11.18 //
Again, 'Powerfully Armed' Ugrāyudha, though armed with a powerful weapon, on account of desires suffered death at the hands of Bhīṣma 'The Terrible.'[8] / Even the thought of those desires is pernicious, leading to their death men empowered with such practice – to say nothing of those who go unprotected by the vow of practice. //11.18//

---

[5] Nahuṣa was elected to replace Indra as top god, when Indra hid himself away after his slaying of Vṛtra (which is also referenced in BC8.13). Nahuṣa was not satisfied only with Indra's position but craved Indra's wife as well. As a result he was cursed to become a snake on earth, regaining his original form only after the Pāṇḍavas discovered him as a snake.

[6] The story of the love affair between Purūravas and Urvaśī is told in Kālidāsa's drama *Vikramorvaśī*, which means Urvaśī [Won] by Vikrama, or Dawn [Won] by Valour.

[7] Bali was the leader of the *asuras*, the enemies of the gods. He also was anointed as the king of gods, by Śukra (mentioned in BC1.41). After Bali's defeat by Viṣṇu, Indra was able to resume the role of king.

[8] In SN Canto 7, it is Jana-mejaya who, as a suitor of Bhīṣma's mother-in-law Kālī (aka Satyavatī), incurs the wrath of Bhīṣma the Terrible – see SN7.44. But the reference to Bhiṣma's killing of Ugrāyudha is corroborated in *Harivaṁsa* as well as in the *Mahā-bhārata.*

āsvādam alpaṁ viṣayeṣu matvā saṁyojanotkarṣam atṛptim eva /
sadbhyaś ca garhāṁ niyataṁ ca pāpaṁ kaḥ kāma-saṁjñaṁ viṣam ādadīta // 11.19 //
Knowing enjoyment of its taste, among objects in the sensory realm, to be petty; knowing it to be highly addictive; knowing it to be dissatisfaction itself; / Knowing it to be what disgusts the good; and knowing it to be invariably bad, who would administer to himself the pernicious drug called desires? //11.19//

kṛṣyādibhir dharmabhir anvitānāṁ kāmātmakānāṁ ca niśamya duḥkham /
svāsthyaṁ ca kāmeṣv akutūhalānāṁ kāmān vihātuṁ kṣamam ātmavadbhiḥ // 11.20 //
After they have seen the suffering of desire-driven men who are chained to duties such as ploughing and the rest / And have seen the well-being of men who are not unduly interested in desires, it is natural for people in possession of themselves to give desires up. //11.20//

jñeyā vipat kāmini kāma-saṁpat siddheṣu kāmeṣu madaṁ hy upaiti /
madād akāryaṁ kurute na kāryaṁ yena kṣato dur-gatim abhyupaiti // 11.21 //
To be known as a setback, when a man is desirous, is consummation of desires; for in realizing desires he tends to become intemperate. / Being intemperate leads him to do what should not be done, not what should be done. Thus diminished, he passes in the direction of difficulty. //11.21//

yatnena labdhāḥ parirakṣitāś ca ye vipralabhya pratiyānti bhūyaḥ /
teṣv ātmavān yācitakopameṣu kāmeṣu vidvān iha ko rameta // 11.22 //
Secured and maintained with much trouble, they cheat the trouble-taker, and go back whence they came. / When desires are like loans, who, being in possession of himself, being wise, being here and now, would delight in those desires?[9] //11.22//

anviṣya cādāya ca jāta-tarṣā yān atyajantaḥ pariyānti duḥkham /
loke tṛṇolkā-sadṛśeṣu teṣu kāmeṣu kasyātmavato ratiḥ syāt // 11.23 //
Those who thirst after desires, having wished for them and grasped them, in failing to let go of them, maintain their grip on suffering. / When desires are like a torch of blazing straw, who in the world in possession of himself would delight in those desires? //11.23//

---

[9] This apparently rhetorical question, the gist of which is repeated eleven times in the coming eleven verses, can be read as marking the transition to the second phase of this canto – a phase of ironic subversion of ostensible idealism. Ostensibly, the point of a rhetorical question is that no self-possessed person would delight in desires. In the hidden meaning, the question invites exploration of emptiness, in light of which there is no self-existing self to possess, and no self-existing desire to objectify and blame.

an-ātmavanto hṛdi yair vidaṣṭā vināśam archanti na yānti śarma /
kruddhogra-sarpa-pratimeṣu teṣu kāmeṣu kasyātmavato ratiḥ syāt // 11.24 //
People not possessed of themselves, being bitten in the heart by them, veer in the direction of utter loss and do not secure happiness. / When desires are like fierce angry snakes, who in possession of himself would delight in those desires? //11.24//

asthi kṣudhārtā iva sārameyā bhuktvāpi yān naiva bhavanti tṛptāḥ /
jīrṇāsthi-kaṅkāla-sameṣu teṣu kāmeṣu kasyātmavato ratiḥ syāt // 11.25 //
People afflicted by hunger, like dogs with a bone, however much they chew on them, never become satisfied. / When desires are like skeletons of dry bones, who in possession of himself would delight in those desires? //11.25//

ye rāja-caurodaka-pāvakebhyaḥ sādhāraṇatvāj janayanti duḥkham /
teṣu praviddhāmiṣa-saṁnibheṣu kāmeṣu kasyātmavato ratiḥ syāt // 11.26 //
Because of what they have in common with kings, thieves, water and fire, they engender suffering. / When desires are like lures hurled [by the hunter], who in possession of himself would delight in those desires? //11.26//

yatra sthitānām abhito vipattiḥ śatroḥ sakāśād api bāndhavebhyaḥ /
hiṁsreṣu teṣv āyatanopameṣu kāmeṣu kasyātmavato ratiḥ syāt // 11.27 //
People abiding in them are surrounded on all sides by adversity - adversity from friends and family even as from a sworn enemy. / When desires are as hazardous as a hazardous abode, who in possession of himself would delight in those desires? //11.27//

girau vane cāpsu ca sāgare ca yān bhraṁśam archanty abhilaṅghamānāḥ /
teṣu druma-prāgra-phalopameṣu kāmeṣu kasyātmavato ratiḥ syāt // 11.28 //
On a mountain; in the forest; in still waters; and in the ocean - leaping the extra inch as they reach for them, people veer in the direction of falling off. / When desires are like the fruit at the top of the tree, who in possession of himself would delight in those desires? //11.28//

tīvraiḥ prayatnair vividhair avāptāḥ kṣaṇena ye nāśam iha prayānti /
svapnopabhoga-pratimeṣu teṣu kāmeṣu kasyātmavato ratiḥ syāt // 11.29 //
Gained by bitter struggles on many fronts, here, in an instant, they go to nought. / When desires are like enjoyments in a dream, who in possession of himself would delight in those desires? //11.29//

yān arcayitvāpi na yānti śarma vivardhayitvā paripālayitvā /
aṅgāra-karṣū-pratimeṣu teṣu kāmeṣu kasyātmavato ratiḥ syāt // 11.30 //
People do not secure happiness, however much they kindle them, augment them, and tend them. / When desires are like fires of charcoal in a pit, who in possession of himself would delight in those desires? //11.30//

vināśam īyuḥ kuravo yad arthaṁ vṛṣṇy-andhakā mekhala-daṇḍakāś ca /
sūnāsi-kāṣṭha-pratimeṣu teṣu kāmeṣu kasyātmavato ratiḥ syāt // 11.31 //
For their sake, the Kurus went to their end, as did the Vṛṣṇi-Andhakas, and the Mekhala-Daṇḍakas.[10] / When desires are like a butcher's knife and slaughter bench, who in possession of himself would delight in those desires? //11.31//

sundopasundāv asurau yad artham anyonya-vaira-prasṛtau vinaṣṭau /
sauhārda-viśleṣa-kareṣu teṣu kāmeṣu kasyātmavato ratiḥ syāt // 11.32 //
For their sake, the *asura* duo Sunda and Upasunda destroyed each other, macho hostility having prevailed. / When desires cause the break-up of friendships, who in possession of himself would delight in those desires? //11.32//

yeṣāṁ kṛte vāriṇi pāvake ca kravyātsu cātmānam ihotsṛjanti /
sapatna-bhūteṣv aśiveṣu teṣu kāmeṣu kasyātmavato ratiḥ syāt // 11.33 //
To water, to fire and to flesh-eaters, for the sake of desires, men in this world deliver up their bodies. / When desires are the enemy happening,[11] who in possession of himself would delight in those unkind desires? //11.33//

kāmārtham ajñaḥ kṛpaṇaṁ karoti prāpnoti duḥkhaṁ vadha-bandhanādi /
kāmārtham āśā-kṛpaṇas tapasvī mṛtyuṁ śramaṁ cārchati jīvalokaḥ // 11.34 //
With desires in view the ignorant one acts pitiably; he brings on himself the suffering of lethal wounds, captivity and the rest; / With desires in view the world of the living, being pitiable in its aspirations, veers wretchedly towards death and exhaustion. //11.34//

gītair hriyante hi mṛgā vadhāya rūpārtham agnau śalabhāḥ patanti /
matsyo giraty āyasam āmiṣārthī tasmād anarthaṁ viṣayāḥ phalanti // 11.35 //
For deer are lured to their death by songs; moths fly into the fire on account of its bright appearance; / And the bait-hungry fish swallows the iron hook. Thus do objects of desire result in trouble. //11.35//

---

[10] EH Johnston notes that of the seven vices peculiar to kings four are known as *kāma-ja* [born of desire] – namely, dicing, wining, hunting and women. These four vices are illustrated in the examples from the slaughter-bench of history cited in this and the next verse. The vice of the Kurus was dicing; the vice of the Vṛṣṇi-Andhakas was drinking. The vice of the Mekhala-Daṇḍakas is assumed to be hunting (some textual uncertainty surrounds their name – the old Nepalese manuscript has *maithila-daṇḍakāḥ*). And Sunda and Upasunda were brought down by fighting over a woman.

[11] *Sa-patna* means rival, adversary, enemy. As the second element (B) in a compound (A-B), *bhūta* means 1. being like A, or 2. actually being A, or happening as A. Is there a hidden sense in which a person in possession of himself or herself deals with desires with confidence and with enjoyment, like a sportsman or sportswoman doing battle with an opponent? If so, the irony seems to climax here, with the last in the series of ostensibly rhetorical questions.

kāmās tu bhogā iti yan matiḥ syād bhogyā na ke-cit parigaṇyamānāḥ /
vastrādayo dravya-guṇā hi loke duḥkha-pratīkāra iti pradhāryāḥ // 11.36 //
As for the view "But desires are enjoyments!," no desire is to be reckoned as "to be enjoyed." / Clothes and other such material goods in the world, are rather to be seen in terms of counteracting pain. //11.36//

iṣṭaṁ hi tarṣa-praśamāya toyaṁ kṣun-nāśa-hetor aśanaṁ tathaiva /
vātātapāmbv-āvaraṇāya veśma kaupīna-śītāvaraṇāya vāsaḥ // 11.37 //
For water is good for the purpose of allaying thirst; food, in a very similar way, for staving off hunger; / A dwelling for protection against wind, the heat of the sun, and rain; clothing for covering the private parts and protecting against cold;[12] //11.37//

nidrā-vighātāya tathaiva śayyā yānaṁ tathādhva-śrama-nāśanāya /
tathāsanaṁ sthāna-vinodanāya snānaṁ mṛjārogya-balāśrayāya // 11.38 //
A place to lie down [or the act of lying down],[13] likewise, for striking a blow against sleep; a vehicle [or the act of going],[14] again, for taking the strain out of a journey; / A seat [or the act of sitting],[15] again, for reveling in the act of abiding; and a bath [or the act of bathing],[16] as a means for cleansing, and for health and strength. //11.38//

duḥkha-pratīkāra-nimitta-bhūtās tasmāt prajānāṁ viṣayā na bhogāḥ /
aśnāmi bhogān iti ko 'bhyupeyāt prājñaḥ pratīkāra-vidhau pravṛttaḥ // 11.39 //
For living creatures, therefore, objects in the sensory realm are factors in counteracting pain and suffering, and not enjoyments. / What wise one would admit "I am relishing enjoyments," while engaged in the counteraction? //11.39//

yaḥ pitta-dāhena vidahyamānaḥ śīta-kriyāṁ bhoga iti vyavasyet /
duḥkha-pratīkāra-vidhau pravṛttaḥ kāmeṣu kuryāt sa hi bhoga-saṁjñām // 11.40 //
For he who, when burning with a bilious fever, would consider a cooling action[17] to be an enjoyment – / He is the one who, while engaged in counteracting suffering, might call desires an enjoyment. //11.40//

---

[12] EH Johnston adds a cross-reference to a section in MN 2 titled *Sabbāsava-sutta*. In Sanskrit the title would be *Sarvāsrava-sūtra* (The Sūtra of All the Polluting Influences). With respect to clothing, for example, the sutta says: *"Here a bhikkhu, reflecting wisely, uses the robe only for protection from cold, for protection from heat, for protection from contact with gadflies, mosquitoes, wind, the sun, and creeping things, and only for the purpose of concealing the private parts."*

[13] *Śayyā.*

[14] *Yānam.*

[15] *Āsanam.*

[16] *Snānam.* Thus three of the four elements are *-na* neuter action nouns with the dual meanings of 1. the action, and 2. the thing used for the action. *Śayyā*, similarly, means both the act of sleeping and a bed.

[17] One of the meanings of *kriyā* is a medical treatment or the application of a remedy. *Śīta-kriyām*, therefore, ostensibly means a cooling medical treatment, i.e. a remedy employed to counteract a fever. The first definition of *kriyā* given in the dictionary, however, is simply action. Is a hidden meaning intended in which action itself is a cooling activity?

kāmeṣv anaikāntikatā ca yasmād ato 'pi me teṣu na bhoga-saṁjñā /
ya eva bhāvā hi sukhaṁ diśanti ta eva duḥkhaṁ punar āvahanti // 11.41 //
Again, since there is nothing absolute about desires, for that reason also, I do not call those desires an enjoyment. / For the very states of being that confer pleasure, also bring, in their turn, pain. //11.41//

gurūṇi vāsāṁsy agurūṇi caiva sukhāya śīte hy asukhāya gharme /
candrāṁśavaś candanam eva coṣṇe sukhāya duḥkhāya bhavanti śīte // 11.42 //
For garments which are heavy (*guru*), and sticks of fragrant aloe wood (*aguru*), are agreeable in the cold but not so in the summer heat; / While moonbeams and fragrant sandalwood are agreeable in the heat but disagreeable in the cold. //11.42//

dvandvāni sarvasya yataḥ prasaktāny alābha-lābha-prabhṛtīni loke /
ato 'pi naikānta-sukho 'sti kaś-cin naikānta-duḥkhaḥ puruṣaḥ pṛthivyām // 11.43 //
Since pairs of opposites – gain and loss, and the like – are attached to everything in the world, / For that reason, again, nobody exclusively has pleasure, nor does any man on the earth exclusively have pain. //11.43//

dṛṣṭvā ca miśrāṁ sukha-duḥkatāṁ me rājyaṁ ca dāsyaṁ ca mataṁ samānam /
nityaṁ hasaty eva hi naiva rājā na cāpi saṁtapyata eva dāsaḥ // 11.44 //
Again, seeing how interconnected are pleasure and pain, I deem kingship and slavery to amount to the same; / For a king does not always smile, nor does a slave always hurt. //11.44//

ājñā nṛ-patye 'bhyadhiketi yat syān mahānti duḥkhāny ata eva rājñaḥ /
āsaṅga-kāṣṭha-pratimo hi rājā lokasya hetoḥ parikhedam eti // 11.45 //
As for the point that to a protector of men accrues pre-eminent power, for that very reason are a king's sufferings great; / For a king is like a wooden peg – he becomes worn down, for the sake of the world. //11.45//

rājye nṛpas tyāgini bahv-a-mitre viśvāsam āgacchati ced vipannaḥ /
athāpi viśraṁbham upaiti neha kiṁ nāma saukhyaṁ cakitasya rājñaḥ // 11.46 //
Sovereignty is fleeting and faced with many enemies: when a protector of men believes in it and breathes easy, he is come to naught;[18] / Or else, if he cannot be confident in this present realm and rest easy, where does happiness lie, for a timorous king? //11.46//

---

[18] When Aśvaghoṣa writes of the coming to naught of a protector of men, there is generally an ironic subtext in which a practitioner is sitting on the royal road, totally forgetting himself.

yadā ca jitvāpi mahīṁ samagrāṁ vāsāya dṛṣṭaṁ puram ekam eva /
tatrāpi caikaṁ bhavanaṁ niṣevyaṁ śramaḥ parārthe nanu rāja-bhāvaḥ // 11.47 //
Even after a king has conquered the whole earth, only one city can serve as the royal seat – / And in that city, again, only one palace can be lived in [or only one field can be cultivated].[19] When this has been realized, is not the royal state[20] the exhausting of oneself for others? //11.47//

rājño 'pi vāso-yugam ekam eva kṣut-saṁnirodhāya tathānna-mātrā /
śayyā tathaikāsanam ekam eva śeṣā viśeṣā nṛpater madāya // 11.48 //
Enough, even for a king, is one set of clothes; for staving off hunger, similarly, the requisite measure of food; / Likewise one bed [or one act of lying down], and one seat [or one act of sitting].[21] All the other special things in the possession of a protector of men, serve the purpose of mental intoxication.[22] //11.48//

tuṣṭy-artham etac ca phalaṁ yadīṣṭam ṛte 'pi rājyān mama tuṣṭir asti /
tuṣṭau ca satyāṁ puruṣasya loke sarve viśeṣā nanu nir-viśeṣāḥ // 11.49 //
Again, if this fruit of which you speak is approved on account of contentment, even without kingship there is contentment for me. / And when contentment exists for a human being in this world, are not all special things nothing special? //11.49//

tan nāsmi kāmān prati saṁpratāryaḥ kṣemaṁ śivaṁ mārgam anuprapannaḥ /
smṛtvā su-hṛttvaṁ tu punaḥ punar māṁ brūhi pratijñāṁ khalu pālay' eti // 11.50 //
So not to be persuaded am I in the direction of desires, since I have entered on the peaceful, wholesome path. / But with friendship in mind, please tell me again and again: "Hold firm to your promise!" //11.50//

na hy asmy amarṣeṇa vanaṁ praviṣṭo na śatru-bāṇair avadhūta-mauliḥ /
kṛta-spṛho nāpi phalādhikebhyo gṛhṇāmi naitad vacanaṁ yatas te // 11.51 //
For not because of impatience have I entered the forest; nor did enemy arrows cause me to cast away a crown. / Nor is it because I aspire to superior fruits that I decline this offer of yours. //11.51//

yo dandaśūkaṁ kupitaṁ bhujaṅ-gaṁ muktvā vyavasyedd hi punar grahītum /
dāhātmikāṁ vā jvalitāṁ tṛṇolkāṁ saṁtyajya kāmān sa punar bhajeta // 11.52 //
For he who, having once let go, would resolve to grasp again, an angry snake with avid fangs, / Or a fiery torch of burning hay – he, having abandoned desires, would seek them out again. //11.52//

---

[19] The meanings of *bhavanam* include 1. a palace, and 2. the place where something grows, a field. The meanings of *niṣevyam* include 1. to be inhabited, and 2. to be practiced or cultivated.

[20] *Rāja-bhāva* ostensibly means existence as a king, but in the hidden meaning real sovereignty happening, for a king of dharma?

[21] *Āsanam*.

[22] In the ironic hidden meaning, an epic poem, for example, might serve as a needle for sitting-meditation.

andhāya yaś ca spṛhayed an-andho baddhāya mukto vidhanāya cāḍhyaḥ /
unmatta-cittāya ca kalya-cittaḥ spṛhāṁ sa kuryād viṣayātmakāya // 11.53 //
Again, the sighted man who envies a blind man, the free man who envies a prisoner, the rich man who envies a pauper; / And the sane man who envies the madman - he would feel envy towards the devotee of objects. //11.53//

bhaikṣopabhogīti ca nānukaṁpyaḥ kṛtī jarā-mṛtyu-bhayaṁ titīrṣuḥ /
ihottamaṁ śānti-sukhaṁ ca yasya paratra duḥkhāni ca saṁvṛtāni // 11.54 //
Not to be pitied, just because the food he enjoys is begged, is the man of action who intends to cross beyond the terror of aging and dying; / For him the highest happiness, the happiness of peace, is here and now, and miseries hereafter are rescinded. //11.54//

lakṣmyāṁ mahatyām api vartamānas tṛṣṇābhibhūtas tv anukaṁpitavyaḥ /
prāpnoti yaḥ śānti-sukhaṁ na ceha paratra duḥkhaiḥ pratigṛhyate ca // 11.55 //
But he is to be pitied who, though dwelling in the midst of great riches, is defeated by thirsting; / He fails to realize the happiness of peace here and now and is held in the grip of sufferings to come. //11.55//

evaṁ tu vaktuṁ bhavato 'nurūpaṁ sattvasya vṛttasya kulasya caiva /
mamāpi voḍhuṁ sadṛśaṁ pratijñāṁ sattvasya vṛttasya kulasya caiva // 11.56 //
For you to speak like this, in any event, befits your character, conduct, and noble house; / And for me also, to keep my promise is in conformity with my character, conduct, and noble house.[23] //11.56//

ahaṁ hi saṁsāra-rasena viddho viniḥsṛtaḥ śāntim avāptu-kāmaḥ /
neccheyam āptuṁ tri-dive 'pi rājyaṁ nir-āmayaṁ kiṁ bata mānuṣeṣu // 11.57 //
For I, stung by saṁsāra's sting, have gone forth desiring to obtain peace[24]; / Not even infallible sovereignty in triple heaven would I wish to win: how much less a kingdom among men? //11.57//

tri-varga-sevāṁ nṛpa yat tu kṛtsnataḥ paro manuṣyārtha iti tvam āttha mām /
an-artha ity eva mamārtha-darśanaṁ kṣayī tri-vargo hi na cāpi tarpakaḥ // 11.58 //
As for you, O king!, saying to me that devotion in the round to the three things is the highest human aim, / Those three, in my estimation of value, are an aim without value, for the three things are subject to decay and are not satisfying at all. //11.58//

---

[23] *Kula*, "noble house," includes the meanings of a family and a lineage.

[24] *Śāntim avāptu-kāmaḥ*. Notice again the paradox of seeming to blame desire in general, while being motivated by desire for peace and freedom. Cf Gudo Nishijima: "*In general, what we desire we should have.*"

pade tu yasmin na jarā na bhīr na ruṇ na janma naivoparamo na cādhayaḥ /
tam eva manye puruṣārtham uttamaṁ na vidyate yatra punaḥ punaḥ kriyā // 11.59 //
Whereas that step in which there is no aging, no fear, no disease, no birth, no death, and no worries – / That alone I consider to be the highest human aim, wherein the same activity does not keep happening, again and again. //11.59//

yad apy avocaḥ paripālyatāṁ jarā navaṁ vayo gacchati vikriyām iti /
a-niścayo 'yaṁ capalaṁ hi dṛśyate jarāpy adhīrā dhṛtimac ca yauvanam // 11.60 //
As for you saying, "Wait for old age, for youth tends to loss of strength of mind," / That is no sure thing; its precariousness is demonstrable – old age also can be irresolute and youth can be possessed of constancy. //11.60//

sva-karma-dakṣaś ca yadāntiko jagad vayaḥsu sarveṣv a-vaśaṁ vikarṣati /
vināśa-kāle katham avyavasthite jarā pratīkṣyā viduṣā śamepsunā // 11.61 //
And when Death who is so skilled at his work drags mankind, in all stages of life, helplessly to our end, / How, when the time of his demise is not subject to orderly arrangement, shall the wise man who seeks quiet look forward to old age? //11.61//

jarāyudho vyādhi-vikīrṇa-sāyako yadāntiko vyādha ivāśivaḥ sthitaḥ /
prajā-mṛgān bhāgya-vanāśritāṁs tudan vayaḥ-prakarṣaṁ prati ko mano-rathaḥ // 11.62 //
When Death, with old age as his weapon and diseases as his strewn projectiles, stands by like an implacable hunter, / Striking down the man-deer that seek refuge in the forest of good fortune, who can relish the prospect of a ripe old age? //11.62//

ato yuvā vā sthaviro 'tha vā śiśus tathā tvarāvān iha kartum arhati /
yathā bhaved dharmavataḥ kṛtātmanaḥ pravṛttir iṣṭā vinivṛttir eva vā // 11.63 //
So, whether as a young blood or as a venerable elder – or else as a child[25] – one should act quickly, here and now, in such a way that / Being possessed of dharma, and realizing oneself, one might lead the life approved as good, the life of progressive activity[26] – or indeed of cessation of activity.[27] //11.63//

yad āttha cādīpta-phalāṁ kulocitāṁ kuruṣva dharmāya makha-kriyām iti /
namo makhebhyo na hi kāmaye sukhaṁ parasya duḥkha-kriyayā yad iṣyate // 11.64 //
Again, as for you telling me, for the sake of dharma, to carry out a sacrificial act which is proper to my noble house and which will bring a brilliant result – / All hail and farewell to sacrifices! For I do not desire the happiness which is sought by an act that causes others suffering. //11.64//

---

[25] In the hidden meaning the suggestion may be of practice, at any age, with beginner's mind – or in the spirit of a child of fire who comes looking for fire.

[26] *Pravṛttiḥ*, or doing.

[27] *Vinivṛttiḥ*, or non-doing. Cf SN Canto 16: *Comprehend, therefore, that suffering is doing (pravṛttim) witness the faults impelling it forward; /Realise its stopping as non-doing (nivṛttim); and know the path as a turning back.//SN16.42//*

paraṁ hi hantuṁ vi-vaśaṁ phalepsayā na yukta-rūpaṁ karuṇātmanaḥ sataḥ /
kratoḥ phalaṁ yady api śāśvataṁ bhavet tathāpi kṛtvā kim-u yat kṣayātmakam // 11.65 //
For, to kill the helpless other in the desire to gain a reward would be ill becoming of a good man who was compassionate at heart, / Even if the result of the sacrifice were an everlasting reward – How much less is acting like that becoming when the essence of it is destructiveness? //11.65//

bhavec ca dharmo yadi nāparo vidhir vratena śīlena manaḥ-śamena vā /
tathāpi naivārhati sevituṁ kratuṁ viśasya yasmin param ucyate phalam // 11.66 //
And even without dharma as an alternative code of conduct involving a vow of practice, moral discipline, or calming of the mind, / Still it would never be right to carry out a sacrifice in which a reward is said to follow from slaughtering another creature. //11.66//

ihāpi tāvat puruṣasya tiṣṭhataḥ pravartate yat para-hiṁsayā sukham /
tad apy aniṣṭaṁ saghṛṇasya dhīmato bhavāntare kiṁ bata yan na dṛśyate // 11.67 //
So long as a person is continuing to be present right here in this world, if any happiness accrues to him through harm inflicted on others, / That happiness, for one who is compassionate and wise, is unwanted: How much more unwanted is unseen happiness in another existence? //11.67//

na ca pratāryo 'smi phala-pravṛttaye bhaveṣu rājan ramate na me manaḥ /
latā ivāmbho-dhara-vṛṣṭi-tāḍitāḥ pravṛttayaḥ sarva-gatā hi cañcalāḥ // 11.68 //
I am not to be swayed in the direction of going for results. My mind, O king!, does not delight in continuities of becoming.[28] / For, like creepers beaten down under a cloudburst, end-gaining actions[29] waver haphazardly in every direction. //11.68//

ihāgataś cāham ito didṛkṣayā muner arāḍasya vimokṣa-vādinaḥ /
prayāmi cādyaiva nṛpāstu te śivaṁ vacaḥ kṣamethāḥ mama tattva-niṣṭhuram // 11.69 //
And so here I am, having come desiring to see the sage Arāḍa, who speaks of liberation, / And there I shall go this very day. O protector of men, may you be well! Bear with words of mine which have been as harsh as reality. //11.69//

---

[28] *Bhaveṣu*, locative plural of *bhava* – the tenth of the 12 links in the causal chain of dependent arising. See BC Canto 14.

[29] *Pravṛttayaḥ* is plural of *pravṛtti*, translated in the singular in verse 63 above as "the life of progressive activity" and in SN16.42 as "doing." Cf the plural *saṁskārās*, "fabrications" (the second in the 12 links; see BC Canto 14), which can also be translated as "doings" or "works of conditioning." Because of their strong volitional (or end-gaining) aspect, which the Buddha seemed sometimes to emphasize, *saṁskārās* are translated by some translators as "volitions."

avendravad divy ava śaśvad arkavad guṇair ava śreya ihāva gām ava /
avāyur āryair ava sat-sutān ava śriyaś ca rājann ava dharmam ātmanaḥ // 11.70 //
Keep rejoicing like Indra in heaven. Keep shining forever like the sun. Keep on, by way of virtues. Keep, here in this world, to the higher good. Keep watch over the earth. / Keep your good health. Keep company with noble ones. Keep safe the sons and daughters of the good. Keep your royal power, O King, and your own dharma.[30] //11.70//

himāri-ketūdbhava-saṁbhavāntare yathā dvijo yāti vimokṣayaṁs tanum /
himāri-śatru-kṣaya-śatru-ghātane tathāntare yāhi vimocayan manaḥ // 11.71 //
Just as, inside the union of cold's enemy and the birth-place of a flame, twice-born [fire] gets going, releasing its physical self, / So, inside the act of slaying the enemy of the evaporation of the enemy of cold's enemy,[31] you are to get going, allowing to release, in the direction of coming undone, your mind.[32]" //11.71//

nṛpo 'bravīt sāñjalir āgata-spṛho yatheṣṭam āpnotu bhavān avighnataḥ /
avāpya kāle kṛta-kṛtyatām imāṁ mamāpi kāryo bhavatā tv anugrahaḥ // 11.72 //
With hands joined as if in prayer, the protector of men spoke, inspired: "May you gain your end without hindrance, just as you desire. / But when in time you have accomplished this task, please show favor towards me too."[33] //11.72//

---

[30] This verse features multiple plays on the imperative *ava*, from the root √*av* whose eighteen senses are said to include: to drive, impel, animate (as a car or horse); to promote, favor, to satisfy, refresh; to offer (as a hymn to the gods); to lead or bring to; (said of the gods) to be pleased with, like, accept favorably (as sacrifices, prayers or hymns); (chiefly said of kings or princes) to guard, defend, protect, govern.

[31] One solution to this riddle is as follows: The enemy of cold (*himāri*) is fire; the enemy of the enemy of cold (*himāri-śatru*) is water, whose evaporation is described as *himāri-śatru-kṣaya*, "the evaporation of the enemy of cold's enemy." This evaporation takes place in the heat of the sun. The enemy of evaporation (*himāri-śatru-kṣaya-śatru*) is the darkness that blots out the sun. And the act of slaying that darkness is an act of knowing by which ignorance is destroyed, e.g. just sitting. The riddle thus presages the Buddha's discovery at the end of BC Canto 14 that to destroy ignorance is to demolish the whole edifice of suffering.

[32] *Yāhi vimocayan manaḥ*, lit. "Go! unloosening the mind." Ostensibly the difficult riddle resolves itself into a short imperative which is not difficult to understand. Ironically, it turns out that the verbal riddle is no more difficult to solve than a cryptic crossword clue. But how many years of painful struggle are required to understand in practice the real meaning of *yāhi vimocayan manaḥ* ?

[33] In the missing second half of Buddhacarita, Aśvaghoṣa relates how the Buddha does indeed return to Rāja-gṛha to demonstrate to Śreṇya what he has realized.

sthiraṁ pratijñāya tatheti pārthive tataḥ sa vaiśvaṁtaram āśramaṁ yayau /
parivrajantaṁ tam udīkṣya vismito nṛpo 'pi vavrāja purim girivrajam // 11.73 //
Having steadfastly promised to a lord of the earth, "So be it!," [the bodhisattva] then proceeded to the ashram of an 'all-conquering' Viśvaṁtara.[34] / After watching him with amazement as he went wandering off, the protector of men also went on his way, to his 'mountain-fenced' fortress, Giri-vraja.[35] //11.73//

iti buddha-carite mahā-kāvye kāma-vigarhaṇo nāmaikā-daśaḥ sargaḥ // 11 //
The 11th canto, titled "Blaming Desires,"[36]
in an epic tale of awakened action.

[34] Viśvaṁtara (*viśva* = all; *tara* = surpassing) is generally an epithet for a buddha, but here it refers to the sage Arāḍa.

[35] Giri-vraja ("Mountain-Fenced") is another name for Rāja-gṛha, the capital of Magadha.

[36] It is not known with certainty whether the canto title was chosen by Aśvaghoṣa himself or not. If it was, then the irony of the canto is that what is truly blamed, below the surface, is not being *ātmavān*, in possession of oneself.

Canto 12: arāḍa-darśanaḥ
Seeing Arāḍa

Introduction

The length of the present canto – 121 verses – is perhaps indicative of how important the Zen master Arāḍa was in the education of the Buddha-to-be.

Once again the two-word compound of the title allows plenty of ambiguity. *Darśana*, as an *-na* neuter action noun from the root √*dṛś*, to see, means showing or seeing. Other meanings of *darśana* include eye-sight; visiting, meeting with; experiencing, realizing; view, doctrine, philosophical system; and becoming visible or known.

Ostensibly in the canto title *arāḍa* is the object of *darśana*; hence EH Johnston translated "Visit to Arāḍa." The obvious alternative translation – since the bulk of the canto is given over to Arāda's setting out of his system in his own words – is "Arāḍa's Doctrine" or "Arāḍa's Philosophical System."

The most important *darśana*, or realization, that the present canto describes, however, comes towards the end of the canto when the bodhisattva sees that sitting-meditation, on the basis of a healthy diet, is a true means to a true end, whereas ascetic self-denial is not. A canto title that better conveyed this hidden meaning might be "Arāḍa / Seeing," or "Arāḍa, and Realization."

tataḥ śama-vihārasya muner ikṣvāku-candramāḥ /
arāḍasyāśramaṁ bheje vapuṣā pūrayann iva // 12.1 //
Then to the *vihāra* of a sage whose recreation ground was peace, the moon of the Ikṣvākus betook himself – / To the ashram of Arāḍa he went, as if filling it with his shining form. //12.1//

sa kālāma-sa-gotreṇa tenālokyaiva dūrataḥ /
uccaiḥ svāgatam ity uktaḥ samīpam upajagmivān // 12.2 //
Seen from afar by that distant kinsman of Kālāma,[1] / And greeted immediately with a welcome that resounded up on high, he drew near. //12.2//

tāv ubhau nyāyataḥ pṛṣṭvā dhātu-sāmyaṁ paras-param /
dāravyor medhyayor vṛṣyoḥ śucau deśe niṣedatuḥ // 12.3 //
After each had asked, as was the rule, after the other's good health, / On two spotless wooden seats, at a clean place, the two of them sat. //12.3//

---

[1] Arāḍa Kālāma was the name of the only person that the Buddha would later recognize as his teacher. Though this canto also records his visit to Udraka Rāmaputra, the Buddha did not recognize that Udraka had been his teacher. (See *Ariyapariyesana-suttaṁ*, MN 26; The Discourse about the Noble Search. Trans. Ānandajoti Bhikkhu. See also note to verse 84 below.)

tam āsīnaṁ nṛpa-sutaṁ so 'bravīn muni-sattamaḥ /
bahumāna-viśālābhyāṁ darśanābhyāṁ pibann iva // 12.4 //
That son of a protector of men, sitting![2] The best of sages sang his praises, / Eyes with admiration opened wide, as if drinking him in: //12.4//

viditaṁ me yathā saumya niṣkrānto bhavanād asi /
chittvā sneha-mayaṁ pāśaṁ pāśaṁ dṛpta iva dvipaḥ // 12.5 //
"It is clear to me, O moony man of *soma*, how you have come forth from a palace,[3] / Cutting the snare of affection like a wild elephant breaking free of a fetter. //12.5//

sarvathā dhṛtimac caiva prājñaṁ caiva manas tava /
yas tvaṁ prāptaḥ śriyaṁ tyaktvā latāṁ viṣa-phalām iva // 12.6 //
Altogether steadfast, and wise, is your mind; / In that you have come here abandoning royal power as if it were a creeper bearing poison fruit. //12.6//

nāścaryaṁ jīrṇa-vayaso yaj jagmuḥ pārthivā vanam /
apatyebhyaḥ śriyaṁ dattvā bhuktocchiṣṭām iva srajam // 12.7 //
No wonder is it that, in their old age, lords of the earth have gone to the forest, / Handing to their offspring royal power, like what is left of a used garland. //12.7//

idaṁ me matam āścaryaṁ nave vayasi yad bhavān /
abhuktvaiva śriyaṁ prāptaḥ sthito viṣaya-gocare // 12.8 //
This I deem a wonder: that you in the flush of youth, / Without ever taking the reins of royal power, have come here, in the very thick of sense-objects. //12.8//

tad vijñātum imaṁ dharmaṁ paramaṁ bhājanaṁ bhavān /
jñāna-plavam adhiṣṭhāya śīghraṁ duḥkhārṇavaṁ tara // 12.9 //
To investigate this dharma, therefore, you are a supremely fit person. / Climbing aboard the raft of knowing, may you swiftly cross over the foaming sea of suffering. //12.9//

śiṣye yady api vijñāte śāstraṁ kālena varṇyate /
gāmbhīryād vyavasāyāc ca na parīkṣyo bhavān mama // 12.10 //
Although the teaching [as a rule] is elucidated after some time, when the student has been investigated, / From the depth of your sincerity, and the strength of your resolve, there is no need for me to examine you." //12.10//

iti vākyam arāḍasya vijñāya sa nararṣabhaḥ /
babhūva parama-prītaḥ provācottaram eva ca // 12.11 //
As Arāḍa said these words, that bull among men, investigating his words, / Was highly delighted and in response, emphatically, up he spoke: //12.11//

---

2 In the hidden meaning, did Aśvaghoṣa picture a student of a king of dharma, sitting in full lotus?

3 As in many previous instances, *bhavanam* ostensibly means a palace, but in the hidden meaning can mean a place where growth happens - and hence in its augmented (vṛddhi) form *bhāvanam*, the practice of letting happen.

viraktasyāpi yad idaṁ saumukhyaṁ bhavataḥ param /
akṛtārtho 'py anenāsmi kṛtārtha iva saṁprati // 12.12 //
"Though untainted by emotion, you show this extreme good grace, / Because of which, although I have yet to realize the aim, I feel like I am just realizing the aim here and now. //12.12//

didṛkṣur iva hi jyotir yiyāsur iva daiśikam /
tvad-darśanam ahaṁ manye titīrṣur iva ca plavam // 12.13 //
For, as one who wishes to see esteems a light, as one who wishes to travel esteems a guide, / I esteem your way of seeing[4] – as, again, one who wishes to cross a river esteems a boat. //12.13//

tasmād arhasi tad vaktuṁ vaktavyaṁ yadi manyase /
jarā-maraṇa-rogebhyo yathāyaṁ parimucyate // 12.14 //
So please explain it, if you deem it apt to be explained, / So that, from aging, dying and disease, this being may be released." //12.14//

ity arāḍaḥ kumārasya māhātmyād eva coditaḥ /
saṁkṣiptaṁ kathayāṁ cakre svasya śāstrasya niścayam // 12.15 //
Arāḍa, thus spurred by the prince's very great sincerity, / Related in brief the purport of his own teaching.[5] //12.15//

śrūyatām ayam asmākaṁ siddhāntaḥ śṛṇvatāṁ vara /
yathā bhavati saṁsāro yathā caiva nivartate // 12.16 //
"Let this be learned, O best of listeners, as our ultimate purpose: / How saṁsāra comes into being, and how it ceases to be. //12.16//

prakṛtiś ca vikāraś ca janma mṛtyur jaraiva ca /
tat tāvat sattvam ity uktaṁ sthira-sattva parehi tat // 12.17 //
Prakṛti, the Primary Matter, and *Vikāra*, its Transformation; birth, death, and old age: / All that is called *Sattva*, Being. May you, O one whose being is steadfast, comprehend it! //12.17//

tatra tu prakṛtir nāma viddhi prakṛti-kovida /
pañca bhūtāny ahaṁ-kāraṁ buddhim avyaktam eva ca // 12.18 //
But what therein is called *Prakṛti*, the Primary Matter, know, O knower of what is primary! / As the five elements,[6] self-consciousness, the intelligent, and *Avyaktam*, the Not Manifest. //12.18//

---

[4] *Darśanam* sometimes means a view, an opinion; but in this context, as the three similes make clear, the meaning is more practical.

[5] *Svasya śāstrasya niścayam.* Some commentators have taken Arāḍa as a teacher of saṁkhya philosophy, but this phrase indicates that what Arāḍa taught is what he had worked out for himself and made his own.

[6] *Pañca bhūtāni,* the five elements: ether, air, fire, water, earth.

vikāra iti budhyasva viṣayān indriyāṇi ca /
pāṇi-pādaṁ ca vādaṁ ca pāyūpasthaṁ tathā manaḥ // 12.19 //
See as *Vikāra*, Transformation, the sense-objects and the senses, / The hands and feet, the [organ of] speech, the anus and reproductive organs – equally the mind. //12.19//

asya kṣetrasya vijñānāt kṣetra-jña iti saṁjñi ca /
kṣetra-jña iti cātmānaṁ kathayanty ātma-cintakāḥ // 12.20 //
Because it knows this field, the conscious is called *Kṣetra-jña*, 'Knower of the Field.' / At the same time, those who contemplate the *ātman*, the self,[7] speak of the self as the knower of the field. //12.20//

sa-śiṣyaḥ kapilaś ceha pratibuddhir iti smṛtaḥ /
sa-putro '-pratibuddhas tu prajāpatir ihocyate // 12.21 //
Kapila,[8] the one studied by students, is known here as *Pratibuddhi*, the Awake; / Whereas Prajāpati,[9] the one endowed with progeny, is called here *Apratibuddha*, the Not Awake.[10] //12.21//

jāyate jīryate caiva bādhyate mriyate ca yat /
tad vyaktam iti vijñeyam avyaktaṁ tu viparyayāt // 12.22 //
What is born, what grows old, what is bound, what dies: / That is to be known as *Vyaktam*, the Manifest; otherwise it is *Avyaktam*, the Not Manifest. //12.22//

a-jñānaṁ karma tṛṣṇā ca jñeyāḥ saṁsāra-hetavaḥ /
sthito 'smiṁs tritaye jantus tat sattvaṁ nātivartate // 12.23 //
Ignorance, karma, and thirsting are to be known as the causes of saṁsāra; / A creature set in these three ways fails to transcend the aforementioned *Sattva*, Being – //12.23//

vipratyayād ahaṁ-kārāt saṁdehād abhisaṁplavāt /
aviśeṣānupāyābhyāṁ saṅgād abhyavapātataḥ // 12.24 //
[It fails] because of wrong grounding, because of 'I-doing' self-consciousness, because of blurring of sight, because of blurring of boundaries, / Because of lack of discrimination and wrong means, because of attachment, and because of pulling down.[11] //12.24//

---

7 The meanings of *ātman* include 1. the self, as used in everyday speech in such statements as "I see myself in the mirror," 2. the soul. Arāḍa's use of *ātman* is open to be read in either way.

8 "Kapila was the most eminent of the ancient Indian philosophers. His philosophical approach was unique and known as the *Saṁkhya* system. According to him truth must be supported by proof, i.e. perception or inference. Kapila denied the theory of creation of the universe by a being or God. He said the empircal universe consists of things evolved (*vyakta*) and things that are not evolved (*avyakta*). Kapila taught the two fundamentals of self or entity (*puruṣa*) and nature (*prakṛti*), or subject and object. All experience is based on the duality of knowing subject (*puruṣa*) and the known object (*prakṛti*)." From *The First Sermon of the Buddha*; 1994 (under "Kapila, the Rationalist" pp.15), by Ven. Dr. Rewata Dhamma

9 Prajāpati, lit. "lord of creatures," was revered as creator of the material universe having as his sons the five elements of ether, air, fire, water, and earth.

10 The opposition between Kapila and Prajāpati, then, as suggested by Arāda's description of the former as *sa-śisyaḥ* (with student/s) and the latter as *sa-putraḥ* (with his sons [= the elements]), may be seen as the opposition between the immaterial (especially the rational) and the material.

tatra vipratyayo nāma viparītaṁ pravartate /
anyathā kurute kāryaṁ mantavyaṁ manyate 'nyathā // 12.25 //
Among those, 'wrong grounding' keeps setting movement in the wrong direction – / It causes to be done wrongly what is to be done; and causes to be thought wrongly what has to be thought. //12.25//

bravīmy aham ahaṁ vedmi gacchāmy aham ahaṁ sthitaḥ /
itīhaivam ahaṁ-kāras tv anahaṁ-kāra vartate // 12.26 //
I speak, I know, I go, I stand firm – / It is thus that here, O unselfconscious one!, the self-consciousness of 'I-doing' carries on. //12.26//

yas tu bhāvān a-saṁdigdhān ekī-bhāvena paśyati /
mṛt-piṇḍavad asaṁdeha saṁdehaḥ sa ihocyate // 12.27 //
But what sees not blurred things as coalesced into one mass, / Like a ball of mud – O one who is free of blur! – here that is called blurring of sight. //12.27//

ya evāhaṁ sa evedaṁ mano buddhiś ca karma ca /
yaś caivaiṣa gaṇaḥ so 'ham iti yaḥ so 'bhisaṁplavaḥ // 12.28 //
'What I am is just this – this mind, this intelligence, this occupation. / Again, what this present group is, I am.' That is blurring of boundaries. //12.28//

aviśeṣaṁ viśeṣa-jña pratibuddhāprabuddhayoḥ /
prakṛtīnāṁ ca yo veda so 'viśeṣa iti smṛtaḥ // 12.29 //
What knows no distinction – O knower of distinctions! – between the Awake and the Not Awake, / Or among the constituent parts of the Primary Matter, is known as 'lack of discrimination.' //12.29//

namas-kāra-vaṣaṭ-kārau prokṣaṇābhyukṣaṇādayaḥ /
an-upāya iti prājñair upāya-jña praveditaḥ // 12.30 //
Calling out *namas,* 'Homage!'; calling out *vaṣat,* 'Into the flame!'; and sacrificial pre-sprinkling, over-sprinkling, and the rest, / Are declared by the wise – O knower of means! – to be wrong means. //12.30//

sajjate yena dur-medhā mano-vāg-buddhi-karmabhiḥ /
viṣayeṣv anabhiṣvaṅga so 'bhiṣvaṅga iti smṛtaḥ // 12.31 //
That by which the dull-witted, using mind, voice, intent and actions, / Are tied fast to objects – O one who is free of over-attachment! – that is known as over-attachment. //12.31//

[11] These eight are taken one by one in the following eight verses.

mamedam aham asyeti yad duḥkham abhimanyate /
vijñeyo 'bhyavapātaḥ sa saṁsāre yena pātyate // 12.32 //
The suffering of 'This is mine,' 'I belong to this,' – the suffering which one invents – / Know, as that suffering, the pulling down by which one is flung back into saṁsāra. //12.32//

ity avidyām hi vidvān sa pañca-parvāṁ samīhate /
tamo mohaṁ mahā-mohaṁ tāmisra-dvayam eva ca // 12.33 //
Thus does the wise one, then, targeting ignorance, think of ignorance as fivefold: / As obscuration, as delusion, as the Big Delusion, and as the two kinds of darkness. //12.33//

tatrālasyaṁ tamo viddhi mohaṁ mṛtyuṁ ca janma ca /
mahā-mohas tv asaṁmoha kāma ity eva gamyatām // 12.34 //
Among these, know obscuration to be sloth, and delusion to be dying and being born; / But the Big Delusion – O undeluded one! – understand to mean Love. //12.34//

yasmād atra ca bhūtāni pramuhyanti mahānty api /
tasmād eṣa mahā-bāho mahā-moha iti smṛtaḥ // 12.35 //
And since in Love even mighty beings swoon, / Therefore – O man of mighty arm! – it is known as the Big Delusion. //12.35//

tāmisram iti cākrodha krodham evādhikurvate /
viṣādaṁ cāndha-tāmisram aviṣāda pracakṣate // 12.36 //
With the word 'darkness' – O one without anger! – they refer to anger. / And depression – O irrepressible one! – they call 'blind darkness.' //12.36//

anayāvidyayā bālaḥ saṁyuktaḥ paṇca-parvayā /
saṁsāre duḥkha-bhūyiṣṭhe janmasv abhiniṣicyate // 12.37 //
The immature person who is possessed of this fivefold ignorance / Into saṁsāra, where suffering prevails, in birth after birth is swept.[12] //12.37//

draṣṭā śrotā ca mantā ca kārya-karaṇam eva ca /
aham ity evam āgamya saṁsāre parivartate // 12.38 //
'The seer, the hearer, the thinker, and the very act of doing what is to be done – / All that is I.' Having fallen into such thoughts, around and round he goes in saṁsāra. //12.38//

ity ebhir hetubhir dhīman janma-srotaḥ pravartate /
hetv abhāvāt phalābhāva iti vijñātum arhasi // 12.39 //
Thus – O perspicacious one! – in the presence of these causes, the stream of births starts flowing. / In the absence of causes, there is no effect, as you are to investigate. //12.39//

---

[12] *Abhiniṣicyate*, lit. "is effused." The root √*sic* has a liquid connotation, meaning to pour out, infuse, sprinkle, or irrigate. Nāgārjuna uses the passive *niṣicyate* in MMK26.2 – *nāma-rūpaṁ niṣicyate*, "psycho-physicality seeps in" (lit "name-and-form is infused/instilled").

tatra samyaṅ-matir vidyān mokṣa-kāma catuṣṭayam /
pratibuddhāprabuddhau ca vyaktam avyaktam eva ca // 12.40 //
In that absence – O desirer of release! – a right-minded man may know the four: / The Awake and the Not Awake; the Manifest and the Not Manifest.[13] //12.40//

yathāvad etad vijñāya kṣetra-jño hi catuṣṭayam /
ājavaṁjavatāṁ hitvā prāpnoti padam akṣaram // 12.41 //
For having properly fathomed this four, the knower of the field / Abandons the rushing torrent of births and deaths and realizes the undying step. //12.41//

ity arthaṁ brāhmaṇā loke parama-brahma-vādinaḥ /
brahma-caryaṁ carantīha brāhmaṇān vāsayanti ca // 12.42 //
For this purpose brahmins[14] here on earth, giving voice to the highest brahma[15], / Practise here and now brahma-practice,[16] and cause brahmins to dwell in it."[17] //12.42//

iti vākyam idaṁ śrutvā munes tasya nṛpātmajaḥ /
abhyupāyaṁ ca papraccha padam eva ca naiṣṭhikam // 12.43 //
The prince, having listened to these words of that sage, / Asked about the means; and about the step, yes,[18] which represents the end. //12.43//

brahma-caryam idaṁ caryaṁ yathā yāvac ca yatra ca /
dharmasyāsya ca paryantaṁ bhavān vyākhyātum arhati // 12.44 //
"How is this brahma-practice to be practiced? And to what lengths? And where? / Again, what is the end-point of this dharma? Will you please explain in detail." //12.44//

---

[13] Cf. the Buddha, quoted in Shōbōgenzō chap. 61, Kembutsu, Meeting Buddha: *"If we see [both] the many forms and [their] non-form, we at once meet the Tathāgata."*

[14] In a pejorative sense a *brāḥmaṇa*, or brahmin, is a man of the priestly caste responsible for divine knowledge of the supreme Spirit (*brahma*) or of the personal god (*brahmā*). In this sense, the Brahmanism of a brahmin in the Buddha's teaching is just another view to be abandoned. But, for example, in the final chapter of *Udāna-varga*, titled *Brahmāṇa-varga*, the Buddha seems to have used the term *brāhmanaṁ* in an affirmative sense, for a person devoted to pyscho-physical growth and development.

[15] *Parama-brahma-vādinaḥ* ostensibly means "speaking of the Supreme Spirit, Brahma." But *brahma* (from the root √*bṛh*, to become fat, to grow) has many possible meanings, including a pious effusion; a mantra, especially the sacred syllable Om; and the spiritual or celibate life (see following note).

[16] *Brahma-carya,* "brahma-practice," narrowly means celibacy – see e.g. SN11.25 where Nanda is ridiculed for practicing devout abstinence (*brahma-caryam*) for the sake of non-abstinence (*a-brahma-caryāya*) with heavenly nymphs. More broadly, cf MMK17.23 where *abrahmacarya-vāsa* is translated "a life not conducive to spiritual growth."

[17] Below the surface, the suggestion may be that promoting growth in others is the highest thing we can aspire to.

[18] The emphatic *eva* seems designed to remind us that in the final analysis, the point of polishing a tile might be – abandoning a Soto Zen view – to make a mirror.

ity arāḍo yathā-śāstraṁ vispaṣṭārthaṁ samāsataḥ /
tam evānyena kalpena dharmam asmai vyabhāṣata // 12.45 //
And so Arāḍa, by the book, succinctly, making his meaning plain, / Tried again, in a different way, to explain to him that same dharma. //12.45//

ayam ādau gṛhān muktvā bhaikṣākaṁ liṅgam āśritaḥ /
samudācāra-vistīrṇaṁ śīlam ādāya vartate // 12.46 //
"First, having left home and adopted the beggar's emblem, / Having taken to the way of integrity which is riveted with acts done well, the one in question carries on. //12.46//

saṁtoṣaṁ param āsthāya yena tena yatas tataḥ /
viviktaṁ sevate vāsaṁ nir-dvandvaḥ śāstra-vit kṛtī // 12.47 //
Staying close to the deepest contentment, with whatever, from wherever, / He abides in seclusion, free from dichotomies: a knower of the teaching, a man of action.[19] //12.47//

tato rāgād bhayaṁ dṛṣṭvā vairāgyāc ca paraṁ śivam /
nigṛhṇann indriya-grāmaṁ yatate manasaḥ śame // 12.48 //
He sees, on these grounds, how horror arises out of redness, but the highest happiness out of its absence, / And he mobilizes himself – curbing the senses – in the direction of quieting of the mind. //12.48//

atho viviktaṁ kāmebhyo vyāpādādibhya eva ca /
viveka-jam avāpnoti pūrva-dhyānaṁ vitarkavat // 12.49 //
Then he arrives at a stage secluded from desires, and also from things like malice; / He reaches the stage born of seclusion – the first dhyāna, in which there is thinking.[20] //12.49//

tac ca dhyāna-sukhaṁ prāpya tat tad eva vitarkayan /
apūrva-sukha-lābhena hriyate bāliśo janaḥ // 12.50 //
Experiencing this state of meditative ease, while thinking various things – this but also that – / The immature person is carried away by enjoyment of the new-found happiness. //12.50//

śamenaivaṁ vidhenāyaṁ kāma-dveṣa-vigarhiṇā /
brahma-lokam avāpnoti paritoṣeṇa vañcitaḥ // 12.51 //
Via tranquility of this order, which is the renouncing of loves and of hates, / At a brahma-world[21] this [youngster] arrives – if, by feeling fully satisfied, he is taken in. //12.51//

---

[19] The real meaning of this line was totally lost on those in China who spoke of "a separate transmission outside of the teaching." For them, Zen was all about being a man of action, while thinking light of verbal teaching.

[20] Arāḍa's description of the four dhyānas tallies very well with the description in SN Canto 17 of Nanda's practice and experience, viz: *Distanced from desires and tainted happenings, containing ideas and containing thoughts / Born of seclusion and possessed of joy and ease, is the first stage of meditation, which he then entered. // SN17.42 //*

jñātvā vidvān vitarkāṁs tu manaḥ-saṁkṣobha-kārakān /
tad-viyuktam avāpnoti dhyānaṁ prīti-sukhānvitam // 12.52 //
The wise one, in contrast, knowing thoughts to cause agitation of the mind, / Arrives at a stage divorced from that, a dhyāna containing its own joy and ease.[22] //12.52//

hriyamāṇas tayā prītyā yo viśeṣaṁ na paśyati /
sthānaṁ bhāsvaram āpnoti deveṣv ābhāsureṣu saḥ // 12.53 //
If, carried away by this joy, he sees no higher distinction, / He occupies a resplendent station among Ābhāsura deities, the Shining Gods.[23] //12.53//

yas tu prīti-sukhāt tasmād vivecayati mānasam /
tṛtīyaṁ labhate dhyānaṁ sukhaṁ prīti-vivarjitam // 12.54 //
The one, in contrast, who separates his mind from this joy and ease, / Obtains the third dhyāna - which has the ease without the joy.[24] //12.54//

yas tu tasmin sukhe magno na viśeṣāya yatnavān /
śubha-kṛtsnaiḥ sa sāmānyaṁ sukhaṁ prāpnoti daivataiḥ // 12.55 //
He who, immersed in this ease, has no will to higher distinction, / Experiences ease as one with Śubha-kṛtsna deities, the Gods of Resplendent Wholeness.[25] //12.55//

tādṛśaṁ sukham āsādya yo na rajyaty upekṣakaḥ /
caturthaṁ dhyānam āpnoti sukha-duḥkha-vivarjitam // 12.56 //
The one who, sitting in the presence of such ease, is not enamored of it but is indifferent - / He reaches the fourth dhyāna, beyond ease and suffering.[26] //12.56//

---

[21] A spiritual state.

[22] Cf SN Canto 17: *Even in that, he realized, ideas about aforesaid things, and thoughts about what is or is not good, / Are something not quieted, causing disturbance in the mind, and so he decided to cut them out. // SN17.44 //...And so gradually bereft of idea and thought, his mind tranquil from one-pointedness, / He realized the joy and ease born of balanced stillness - that inner wellbeing which is the second stage of meditation. // SN17.47 //*

[23] A state of intense spiritual ecstasy. Ibid: *And on reaching that stage, in which the mind is silent, he experienced an intense joy that he had never experienced before. / But here too he found a fault, in joy, just as he had in ideas. // SN17.48 //*

[24] Ibid: *For when a man finds intense joy in anything, paradoxically, suffering for him is right there. / Hence, seeing the faults there in joy, he kept going up, into practice that goes beyond joy. // SN17.49 // And so experiencing the ease enjoyed by the noble ones, from non-attachment to joy, knowing it totally, with his body, / He remained indifferent, fully aware, and, having realized the third stage of meditation, steady. // SN17.50 //*

[25] Ibid: *Since the ease here is beyond any ease, and there is no progression of ease beyond it, / Therefore, as a knower of higher and lower, he realized it as a condition of resplendent wholeness which he deemed - in a friendly way - to be superlative. // SN17.51 //*

[26] Ibid: *Then, having already transcended ease and suffering, and emotional reactivity, / He realized the lucidity in which there is indifference and full awareness: thus, beyond suffering and ease, is the fourth stage of meditation. // 17.54 //*

tatra ke-cid vyavasyanti mokṣa ity abhimāninaḥ /
sukha-duḥkha-parityāgād avyāpārāc ca cetasaḥ // 12.57 //
Some settle for that stage, thinking it, in their conceit, to be liberation – / Because of the giving up of ease and suffering, and because of the inactivity of the mind. //12.57//

asya dhyānasya tu phalaṁ samaṁ devair bṛhat-phalaiḥ /
kathayanti bṛhat-kālaṁ bṛhat-prajñā-parīkṣakāḥ // 12.58 //
Whereas, truly, the fruit of this act of meditating, like the abundant[27] fruit of the Bṛhat-phala deities, the Gods of Fat Profit, / Is immensely long-lasting – say those who investigate the vast real wisdom.[28] //12.58//

samādher vyutthitas tasmād dṛṣṭvā doṣāṁś charīriṇām /
jñānam ārohati prājñaḥ śarīra-vinivṛttaye // 12.59 //
The man of wisdom, giving up the balancing act of that samādhi, having seen the faults of people possessed of bodies,[29] / Rises to the challenge which is the act of knowing – he rises up, in the direction of bodily extinction.[30] //12.59//

tatas tad-dhyānam utsṛjya viśeṣe kṛta-niścayaḥ /
kāmebhya iva sat-prājño rūpād api virajyate // 12.60 //
Having thus let go of that meditation, and with his mind set on higher distinction, / The one who really understands what is real – like he lost interest in desires – loses interest in form.[31] //12.60//

śarīre khāni yāny asya tāny ādau parikalpayan /
ghaneṣv api tato dravyeṣv ākāśam adhimucyate // 12.61 //
Of spaces which are openings in his body, first he forms a picture; / Then in solid masses also, he affirms space. //12.61//

ākāśa-gatam ātmānaṁ saṁkṣipya tv aparo budhaḥ /
tad evānantataḥ paśyan viśeṣam adhigacchati // 12.62 //
Another one who is wise, in contrast, condenses into the center the self that permeates space, / And, seeing even that as unbounded, he thereby attains distinction.[32] //12.62//

---

[27] Abundant, Fat, immensely and vast, are all translations of *bṛhat*, from the root √*bṛh* which is discussed above in connection with *brahma.*

[28] Ibid. *Consequently, relying on the fourth stage of meditation, he made up his mind to win the worthy state, / Like a king joining forces with a strong and noble ally and then aspiring to conquer unconquered lands. // SN17.56 //*

[29] *Śarīriṇām,* embodied beings. Ostensibly, all earthly creatures. In the ironic hidden meaning, the unduly body-conscious?

[30] With this verse Arāḍa's description appears on the surface to depart from what the Buddha will later teach. Below the surface, however, throwing away concern about feeling balanced in one's being and looking good in one's form, might be a true step on the way of dropping off body and mind. Cf: *Then he cut the five upper fetters: with the sword of wisdom which is wielded by letting it happen, / He completely severed the five aspirational fetters, which are bound up with superiority, and tied to the first person. // SN17.57 //*

[31] Like the women sleeping in odd postures in Canto 5.

adhyātma-kuśalaṣ tv anyo nivartyātmānam ātmanā /
kiṁ-cin nāstīti saṁpaśyann ākiṁcanya iti smṛtaḥ // 12.63 //
But one who is different, one who is skillful in regard to his own self, having dropped off the self by means of the self, / In realizing that there is nothing there, is known as a man of being without anything.[33] //12.63//

tato muñjād iṣīkeva śakuniḥ pañjarād iva /
kṣetra-jño niḥsṛto dehān mukta ity abhidhīyate // 12.64 //
Thus, like the stalk from a sheath of *muñja* grass,[34] like a big bird from its cage, / The Knower of the Field, escaped from the body, is said to be liberated.[35] //12.64//

etat tat paramaṁ brahma nirliṅgaṁ dhruvam akṣaram /
yan mokṣa iti tattva-jñāḥ kathayanti manīṣiṇaḥ // 12.65 //
This is that supreme Brahma, beyond emblematic representation, constant, imperishable, / Which those who know the truth, learned brahmins, call 'Liberation.'[36] //12.65//

ity upāyaś ca mokṣaś ca mayā saṁdarśitas tava /
yadi jñātaṁ yadi rucir yathāvat pratipadyatām // 12.66 //
Thus the means, and the liberation, I have revealed to you; / If you have understood it, and if it pleases you, undertake it properly. //12.66//

jaigīṣavyo 'tha janako vṛddhaś caiva parāśaraḥ /
imaṁ panthānam āsādya muktā hy anye ca mokṣiṇaḥ // 12.67 //
For Jaigīṣavya, 'Son of Ambition,' and Janaka, 'The Begetter,' as well as Vṛddha Parāśara, 'The Old Crusher,' / By realizing this path in their sitting,[37] were liberated – as were other liberation-seekers, being different.[38]" //12.67//

---

[32] Cf what the Buddha tells Nanda in SN Canto 16: "*It may not be possible, following a single method, to kill off bad ideas that habit has so deeply entrenched; / In that case, one should commit to a second course but never give up the good work." // SN16.70 //*

[33] Ostensibly Arāḍa is describing a man with peculiar insight into the *ātman*, the self, or the individual vs. the universal soul. In the hidden meaning, *anyaḥ* again points to one beyond conventional understanding. He or she realizes what is to be realized simply in being without anything.

[34] *Saccharum bengalense* is a species of grass that grows very tall – Arāḍa seems to be indicating a conspicuous happening of some sort.

[35] If we accept the irony of the preceding verses, in which, below the surface, Arāḍa's teaching is a perfect mirror of what the Buddha himself will later teach, then this verse may be taken as the one that flags up the essential difference between Arāḍa's teaching and the dharma that the Buddha will teach.

[36] Arāḍa in the final analysis veers from the middle way in believing in a Supreme Brahma, whose existence is absolute, above and beyond the material world.

[37] Meanings of *ā-√sad* include 1. to meet with, reach, realize; and 2. to sit, sit near.

[38] As in so many previous instances, *anye* (others) in its hidden meaning suggests real individuals, who do not conform to easy assumptions or idealistic expectations.

iti tasya sa tad-vākyaṁ gṛhītvā tu vicārya ca /
pūrva-hetu-bala-prāptaḥ pratyuttaram uvāca ha // 12.68 //
But [the bodhisattva], having taken in these words of the other, and reflected on them this way and that, / Being possessed of the power of previous causes, spoke up in reply: //12.68//

śrutaṁ jñānam idaṁ sūkṣmaṁ parataḥ parataḥ śivam /
kṣetra-jñasyāparityāgād avaimy etad anaiṣṭhikam // 12.69 //
"I have listened to this wisdom of yours, which grows more subtle stage by stage, and more wholesome, / But insofar as the Knower of the Field is not abandoned, I see this wisdom as short of the ultimate. //12.69//

vikāra-prakṛtibhyo hi kṣetra-jñaṁ muktam apy aham /
manye prasava-dharmāṇaṁ bīja-dharmāṇam eva ca // 12.70 //
For, I consider 'the Knower of the Field,' even when freed from 'the Transformed and the Primary,' / To be engendering in nature and to be, in its very nature, a seed. //12.70//

viśuddho yady api hy ātmā nirmukta iti kalpyate /
bhūyaḥ pratyaya-sad-bhāvād amuktaḥ sa bhaviṣyati // 12.71 //
For even if the pure self[39] – 'the soul' – is declared to have been released, / Once again, as long as the grounds exist, it will become not released. //12.71//

ṛtu-bhūmy-ambu-virahād yathā bījaṁ na rohati /
rohati pratyayais tais tais tadvat so 'pi mato mama // 12.72 //
Just as, in the absence of season, soil and water, a seed does not grow, / But does rise up when those various causal grounds are present, so also, as I see it, does ['the soul'].[40] //12.72//

yat karmājñāna-tṛṣṇānāṁ tyāgān mokṣaś ca kalpyate /
atyantas tat-parityāgaḥ saty ātmani na vidyate // 12.73 //
And as for liberation being brought about through letting go of karma, ignorance and thirsting, / There is no complete abandonment of these three so long as the soul persists. //12.73//

hitvā hitvā trayam idaṁ viśeṣas tūpalabhyate /
ātmanas tu sthitir yatra tatra sūkṣmam idaṁ trayam // 12.74 //
By deeper and deeper abandoning of these three, higher distinction is obtained, / But where the soul prevails, there – subtly – these three are. //12.74//

---

[39] By *viśuddhaḥ... ātmā*, the pure self, the bodhisattva indicates that he has in view not the self we refer to in everyday speech but the self as philosophical or religious abstraction, the soul.
[40] The bodhisattva thus recognizes the existence of a soul but, presaging the teaching of dependent arising, he does not believe in a soul that exists absolutely as a thing unto itself.

sūkṣmatvāc caiva doṣāṇām avyāpārāc ca cetasaḥ /
dīrghatvād āyuṣaś caiva mokṣas tu parikalpyate // 12.75 //
And yet, because of the subtlety of the faults, because of the inactivity of the mind, / And because of the length of a lifetime, liberation is posited. //12.75//

ahaṁ-kāra-parityāgo yaś caiṣa parikalpyate /
saty ātmani parityāgo nāhaṁ-kārasya vidyate // 12.76 //
As for this abandonment of the self-consciousness of 'I-doing' which, again, is posited – / So long as the soul persists there has been no abandonment of 'I-doing.' //12.76//

saṁkhyādibhir amuktaś ca nir-guṇo na bhavaty ayam /
tasmād asati nairguṇye nāsya mokṣo 'bhidhīyate // 12.77 //
Again, when not freed from intellectual efforts like enumeration, this [abandoning] does not become free of defining features; / Therefore, in the absence of freedom from defining features,[41] there is said to be no freedom in it. //12.77//

guṇino hi guṇānāṁ ca vyatireko na vidyate /
rūpoṣṇābhyāṁ virahito na hy agnir upalabhyate // 12.78 //
For between things defined by features and the defining features there is no gap – / Bereft of form and heat, no fire, for example, is realized. //12.78//

prāg dehān na bhaved dehī prāg guṇebhyas tathā guṇī /
tasmād ādau vimuktaḥ san śarīrī badhyate punaḥ // 12.79 //
Prior to the body, no owner of a body can exist; prior to defining features, likewise, nothing defined by features can exist. / On this basis does the possessor of a body, having been free from the beginning, become bound again.[42] //12.79//

kṣetra-jño vi-śarīraś ca jño vā syād ajña eva vā /
yadi jño jñeyam asyāsti jñeye sati na mucyate // 12.80 //
Again, a disembodied knower of the field must be either a knower or else unknowing. / If he is a knower, something remains that he should know, and in something remaining that he should know, he is not liberated. //12.80//

athājña iti siddho vaḥ kalpitena kim ātmanā /
vināpi hy ātmanājñānaṁ prasiddhaṁ kāṣṭha-kuḍyavat // 12.81 //
Or else, if it's your conclusion that he is unknowing, then what is the point of inventing a soul? / For even when the soul is absent, not knowing is well established [or realizing is realized] – as in the case of a log or a wall. //12.81//[43]

---

[41] "Freedom from defining features" is *nairguṇya*, translated in BC Canto 6 as "the being-without virtue." See BC6.24.
[42] An ironic expression of donkey business arriving, in the everyday life of a Zen practitioner?
[43] The second half of this verse can be read in a number of ways, partly because of the ambiguity of *ātmanājñānam*, which could be *ātmanā* + *jñānam* (knowing) or *ātmanā* + *ajñānam* (not knowing) or *ātmanā* + *ājñānam* (realizing, noticing).

parataḥ paratas tyāgo yasmāt tu guṇavān smṛtaḥ /
tasmāt sarva-parityāgān manye kṛtsnāṁ kṛtārthatām // 12.82 //
But since abandonment that goes further and further back, is known, according to tradition, to be excellent, / Therefore I suppose that from abandoning all follows complete accomplishment of the task." //12.82//

iti dharmam arāḍasya viditvā na tutoṣa saḥ /
akṛtsnam iti vijñāya tata pratijagāma ha // 12.83 //
Thus, having understood the dharma of Arāḍa, he was not satisfied. / Knowing it to be incomplete, back he went from there. //12.83//

viśeṣam atha śuśrūṣur udrakasyāśramaṁ yayau /
ātma-grāhāc ca tasyāpi jagṛhe na sa darśanam // 12.84 //
So, desiring to learn of deeper distinction, he went to the ashram of Udraka.[44] / And his doctrine,[45] which was grounded in the notion of a soul, he also did not accept. //12.84//

saṁjñāsaṁjñitvayor doṣaṁ jñātvā hi munir udrakaḥ /
ākiṁcanyāt paraṁ lebhe saṁjñāsaṁjñātmikāṁ gatim // 12.85 //
For, knowing the fault in the duality of consciousness and unconsciousness, the sage Udraka had glimpsed, / Beyond being without anything, the [single] realm made up of consciousness and unconsciousness. //12.85//

yasmāc cālaṁbane sūkṣme saṁjñāsaṁjñe tataḥ param /
nāsaṁjñī naiva saṁjñeti tasmāt tatra gata-spṛhaḥ // 12.86 //
Since, again, there are subtle dual underpinnings in consciousness and in unconsciousness, [Udraka understood] that beyond that duality / There was neither the unconscious nor consciousness, on which grounds, being there, one was free of aspiring. //12.86//

---

[44] In *The First Sermon of the Buddha*, as quoted above, Ven. Rewata Dhamma noted that Udraka himself had not attained the realm of neither perception nor non-perception. He told the Bodhisattva only what the ascetic Rāma had achieved. So when the Bodhisattva proved himself to be the equal of his master [Rāma], he offered the Bodhisattva the leadership, and practicing under the Bodhisattva's guidance, he himself attained the highest jhānic state of neither perception nor non-perception.
Again, Ānandajoti Bhikkhu has pointed out, based on his translations of Ariyapariyesanasuttaṁ (MN 26) and Bodhirājakumārasuttaṁ (MN 85), that the Buddha did not refer to Udraka as having been his teacher. He rather described Udraka as having been a friend in brahma-practice (Pāli: *sabrahmacārī*).
Thus Arāḍa seems to have been the only one that the Buddha recognized as having been his teacher, and this is reflected in the relatively detailed attention given to Arāḍa's own words in this canto.

[45] *Darśanam*, view, doctrine, translated earlier (with reference to Arāḍa in verse 13) as "way of seeing"; and in the canto title – where *darśana* could carry several possible meanings – simply as "Seeing."

yataś ca buddhis tatraiva sthitānyatrāpracāriṇī /
sūkṣmāpaṭvī tatas tatra nāsaṁjñitvaṁ na saṁjñitā // 12.87 //
Again, because the mind, being right there, stood still, not wandering elsewhere, / Therefore in that state – that subtle, not intellectual, state of the mind – there was neither unconsciousness nor consciousness. //12.87//

yasmāc ca tad api prāpya punar āvartate jagat /
bodhi-sattvaḥ paraṁ prepsus tasmād udrakam atyajat // 12.88 //
But since, again, even having reached that state, [the mind] returns to the jostling world, / Therefore, desiring to reach the ultimate, the bodhisattva left Udraka. //12.88//

tato hitvāśramaṁ tasya śreyo 'rthī kṛta-niścayaḥ /
bheje gayasya rājarṣer nagarī-saṁjñam āśramam // 12.89 //
Thus having abandoned the ashram of that sage, seeking better, with determination, / He betook himself to the hermitage of the royal seer Gaya – to the ashram known as Nagarī. //12.89//

atha nairaṇjanā-tīre śucau śuci-parākramaḥ /
cakāra vāsam ekānta-vihārābhiratir muniḥ // 12.90 //
And so, on a pure bank of the Nairaṇjanā, he whose heroic endeavor was pure / Took up his dwelling as a sage who delighted in a solitary *vihāra* – a lonely practice-place, and the pleasure ground of devotion to a single end.[46] //12.90//

[* * *] tat-pūrvam pañcendriya-vaśoddhatān /
tapaḥ [* *] vratino bhikṣūn pañca niraikṣata // 12.91 //
Then he saw the five who had retreated there before him, raised up by their dominion over the five senses / As they upheld their vows of ascetic practice – he saw the five ascetic mendicants. //12.91//

te copatasthur dṛṣṭvātra bhikṣavas taṁ mumukṣavaḥ /
puṇyārjita-dhanārogyam indriyārthā iveśvaram // 12.92 //
Those bhikṣus saw him there and, desiring liberation, came up to him / As sensory objects answer to the capable one whose material riches, and freedom from disease, are earned on merit.[47] //12.92//

saṁpūjyamānas taiḥ prahvair vinayād anuvartibhiḥ /
tad-vaśa-sthāyibhiḥ śiṣyair lolair mana ivendriyaiḥ // 12.93 //
He was greatly honored by those [five] humble followers. Being obedient, because of training, they deferred to him, / Abiding as disciples under his dominion, like the restless senses deferring to the mind.[48] //12.93//

---

[46] The meanings of *ekānta* (*eka* = one + *anta* = end, border) include 1. a lonely or secret place, and 2. devotion to one object.

[47] The teaching point seems to be that in the real world – as opposed to the realm of human ideologies – hierarchies naturally exist.

mṛtyu-janmānta-karaṇe syād upāyo 'yam ity atha /
duṣkarāṇi samārebhe tapāṁsy anaśanena saḥ // 12.94 //
He intuited that here might be a means to end death and birth[49] / Whereupon he undertook harsh austerities, going without food. //12.94//

upavāsa-vidhīn naikān kurvan nara-durācarān /
varṣāṇi ṣaṭ śama-prepsur akarot kārśyam ātmanaḥ // 12.95 //
Doing many kinds of fasting that were difficult for a man to do, / For six years, in the quest for peace, he wasted himself away. //12.95//

anna-kāleṣu caikaikaiḥ sa kola-tila-taṇḍulaiḥ /
apāra-pāra-saṁsāra-pāraṁ prepsur apārayat // 12.96 //
At mealtimes, with jujube fruits, sesame seeds, and grains of rice, one by one, / In his quest for the far end of saṁsāra, where there is no end to ends, he kept himself alive. //12.96//

dehād apacayas tena tapasā tasya yaḥ kṛtaḥ /
sa evopacayo bhūyas tejasāsya kṛto 'bhavat // 12.97 //
Whatever was taken out of his body by that ascetic practice, / Was made up for by his amazing energy. //12.97//

kṛśo 'py akṛśa-kīrti-śrīr hlādaṁ cakre 'nya-cakṣuṣām /
kumudānām iva śarac-chukla-pakṣādi-candramāḥ // 12.98 //
Pared down as he was, yet with his glory and majesty unimpaired, he gladdened other eyes,[50] / As the hairy moon-lilies are gladdened,[51] at the beginning of the bright fortnight,[52] by the autumn moon. //12.98//

tvag-asthi-śeṣo niḥśeṣair medaḥ-piśita-śoṇitaiḥ /
kṣīṇo 'py akṣīṇa-gāmbhīryaḥ samudra iva sa vyabhāt // 12.99 //
Reduced to skin and bone, with no reserves remaining of fat or flesh or blood, / Diminished, and yet undiminished in his inner depths, like the sea, he sparkled. //12.99//

---

[48] The simile ostensibly says something about the relation between the five bhikṣus and the bodhisattva, but again Aśvaghoṣa may be more interested, below the surface, in describing subordination of the senses to the mind.

[49] Ostensibly he wrongly intuited that ascetic austerities might be a means. In the hidden meaning, he rightly intuited that subordination of the senses to the mind might be a means.

[50] *Anya-cakṣuṣām*: ostensible meaning: to the eyes of others; hidden meaning: to eyes which were different, to eyes that were contrarian, to eyes not bound to conventional ways of seeing.

[51] The *kumada* (= *Nymphaea pubescens*, the white water lily or hairy water lily) is seen in Sanskrit poetry as having a particularly strong connection with the moon. Hence *kaumudī* (of the hairy water lily) is another word for moonlight; and the moon is variously known as *kumuda-pati* (master of the hairy water lily), *kumada-suhṛd* (friend of the hairy water lily), and so on. In Kālidāsa's famous poem *Vikramorvāśīya*, the king will only revive at the touch of Urvāśī's hand, just as the hairy water lily blooms only under the moon's rays.

[52] *Śuklá-pakṣa* means the bright half of a month, the fifteen days when the moon is waxing.

atha kaṣṭa-tapaḥ-spaṣṭa-vyartha-kliṣṭa-tanur muniḥ /
bhava-bhīrur imāṁ cakre buddhiṁ buddhatva-kāṅkṣayā // 12.100 //
And so the sage whose body was evidently being tormented, to no avail, by pernicious austerities, / Formed – while being wary of becoming – the following resolve, in his longing for buddhahood. //12.100//

nāyaṁ dharmo virāgāya na bodhāya na muktaye /
jambu-mūle mayā prāpto yas tadā sa vidhir dhruvaḥ // 12.101 //
"This dharma is good neither for detachment, nor for awakening, nor for liberation. / What I realized back then, at the foot of the rose-apple tree – that is a sure method.[53] //12.101//

na cāsau durbalenāptuṁ śakyam ity āgatādaraḥ /
śarīra-bala-vṛddhy-artham idaṁ bhūyo 'nvacintayat // 12.102 //
But that cannot be realized by one who is weak." Thus did he reflect. / Still more, with a view to increasing his bodily strength, on this did he meditate further: //12.102//

kṣut-pipāsā-śrama-klāntaḥ śramād asvastha-mānasaḥ /
prāpnuyān manasāvāpyaṁ phalaṁ katham anirvṛtaḥ // 12.103 //
"Worn out by hunger, thirst and fatigue, with a mind that, from fatigue, is not well in itself, / How can one obtain the result which is to be realized by the mind – when one is not contented? //12.103//

nirvṛtiḥ prāpyate samyak satatendriya-tarpaṇāt /
saṁtarpitendriyatayā manaḥ-svāsthyam avāpyate // 12.104 //
Contentment is properly obtained through keeping the senses constantly appeased; / By full appeasement of the senses, wellness of the mind is realized. //12.104//

svastha-prasanna-manasaḥ samādhir upapadyate /
samādhi-yukta-cittasya dhyāna-yogaḥ pravartate // 12.105 //
In one whose mind is well and tranquil, *samādhi*, balanced stillness, sets in. / In one whose mind is possessed of samādhi, *dhyāna*, meditative practice, progresses. //12.105//

dhyāna-pravartanād dharmāḥ prāpyante yair avāpyate /
durlabhaṁ śāntam ajaraṁ paraṁ tad amṛtaṁ padam // 12.106 //
Through meditation's progress are obtained *dharmas*, timeless teachings, by which is realized the deathless – / That hard-won, quieted, unageing, ultimate immortal step." //12.106//

---

[53] See description of the prince naturally entering the first dhyāna, BC5.8-5.10.

tasmād āhāra-mūlo 'yam upāya iti niścayaḥ /
āhāra-karaṇe dhīraḥ kṛtvāmita-matir matim // 12.107 //
Having therefore decided that eating food is the foundation of this means to an end, / He, the firm and constant one, whose resolve was beyond measure, resolving to take food... //12.107//

snāto nairañjanā-tīrād uttatāra śanaiḥ kṛśaḥ /
bhaktyāvanata-śākhāgrair datta-hastas taṭa-drumaiḥ // 12.108 //
... had got out of the water – Having bathed, he climbed up the bank of the Nairañjanā, ascending, in his wizened state, gradually, / While, lowering the tips of their branches in devotion, the trees on the shore lent him a hand. //12.108//

atha gopādhipa-sutā daivatair abhicoditā /
udbhūta-hṛdayānandā tatra nandabalāgamat // 12.109 //
Just then a dairy farmer's daughter, impelled by the gods, came by, / With joy swelling up in her heart – there came Nanda-balā, 'Power of Joy.' //12.109//

sita-śaṅkhojjvala-bhujā nīla-kambala-vāsinī /
sa-phena-mālā-nīlāmbur yamuneva sarid-varā // 12.110 //
She wore a dark-blue shawl, and her arms were all lit up with white shells, / So that she seemed like the Yamunā, best of rivers, when its dark-blue waters are wreathed with foam. //12.110//

sā śraddhā-vardhita-prītir vikasal-locanotpalā /
śirasā praṇipatyainaṁ grāhayām āsa pāyasam // 12.111 //
She with a gladness bolstered by trust, with the lotuses of her eyes beaming, / Bowed her head respectfully to him and made him accept milk rice. //12.111//

kṛtvā tad-upabhogena prāpta-janma-phalāṁ sa tām /
bodhi-prāptau samartho 'bhūt saṁtarpita-ṣaḍ-indriyaḥ // 12.112 //
He, by eating that food, caused her to attain the fruit of her birth, / And he became capable of attainment of awakening, his six senses now being fully appeased. //12.112//

paryāptāpyāna-mūrtiś ca sārdhaṁ sva-yaśasā muniḥ /
kānti-dhairye babhāraikaḥ śaśāṅkārṇavayor dvayoḥ // 12.113 //
His physical body having realized fullness, along with the glory of his person, / The sage, as one, bore the radiant charm and the deep, constant calm of the moon and of the ocean. //12.113//

āvṛtta iti vijñāya taṁ jahuḥ paṇca-bhikṣavaḥ /
manīṣiṇam ivātmānaṁ nirmuktaṁ pañca-dhātavaḥ // 12.114 //
Knowing that he had turned back, the five bhikṣus left him / Like the five elements departing when a thinking self has been set free.[54] //12.114//

vyavasāya-dvitīyo 'tha śādvalāstīrṇa-bhūtalam /
so 'śvattha-mūlaṁ prayayau bodhāya kṛta-niścayaḥ // 12.115 //
And so with resolve as his companion, to where the earth was covered with fresh green grass, / To the foot of a fig-tree – an *aśvattha*, 'under which horses stand,'[55] – he went, setting his heart firmly in the direction of awakening. //12.115//

tatas tadānīṁ gaja-rāja-vikramaḥ pada-svanenānupamena bodhitaḥ /
mahā-muner āgata-bodhi-niścayo jagāda kālo bhujagottamaḥ stutim // 12.116 //
Just then the snake with the spirit of an elephant-king was awakened by the peerless sound of the sage's feet; / Realizing that the great sage was set on awakening, the black cobra Kāla, most excellent of serpents, sang the sage's praises: //12.116//

yathā mune tvac-caraṇāvapīḍitā muhur-muhur niṣṭanatīva medinī /
yathā ca te rājati sūryavat prabhā dhruvaṁ tvam iṣṭaṁ phalam adya bhokṣyase // 12.117 //
"As surely as the earth, O sage!, pressed down under your footsteps, rolls like thunder, / And as surely as the light of you shines forth like the sun, you today will enjoy the longed-for fruit. //12.117//

yathā bhramantyo divi cāṣa-paṅktayaḥ pradakṣiṇaṁ tvāṁ kamalākṣa kurvate /
yathā ca saumyā divi vānti vāyavas tvam adya buddho niyataṁ bhaviṣyasi // 12.118 //
As surely as flocks of blue jays wheeling through the sky keep you – O lotus-eyed one! – on their right wing, / And as surely as in the sky gentle breezes blow, you today will be an awakened one, a buddha." //12.118//

tato bhujaṅga-pravareṇa saṁstutas tṛṇāny upādāya śucīni lāvakāt /
kṛta-pratijño niṣasāda bodhaye mahā-taror mūlam upāśritaḥ śuceḥ // 12.119 //
Then, his praises having been sung by the best of serpents, [the sage] accepted from a grass-cutter some pristine grass, / And making a vow in the direction of awakening, he sat at the foot of the great tree, placing himself in the compass of the great pristine tree. //12.119//

---

[54] Ostensibly, they wrongly opined that he had given up, and went away in disgust. In a deeper reading, they truly grasped the real situation, and naturally left him alone, without any effort on his part to get rid of them.

[55] The tree in question (*Ficus Religiosa*) was so called because mature fig trees of that genus afforded horses plentiful shade from the sun.

tataḥ sa paryaṅkam akampyam uttamaṁ babandha suptoraga-bhoga-piṇḍitam /
bhinadmi tāvad bhuvi naitad āsanaṁ na yāmi yāvat kṛta-kṛtyatām iti // 12.120 //
Then the supreme, unshakeable cross-legged posture – in which sleeping serpents' coils are rolled into a ball – he took up, / As if to say, "I shall not break this sitting posture on the earth until I have done completely what is to be done." //12.120//

tato yayur mudam atulāṁ divaukaso vavāśire na mṛga-gaṇāḥ na pakṣiṇaḥ /
na sasvanur vana-taravo 'nilāhatāḥ kṛtāsane bhagavati niścitātmani // 12.121 //
Then the denizens of heaven felt unequalled joy; no sound did any beast make, nor any bird; / Though buffeted by the wind, no forest tree did creak, when the Glorious One took his sitting posture, resolute to the core. //12.121//

iti buddha-carite mahā-kāvye 'rāḍa-darśano nāma dvādaśaḥ sargaḥ // 12 //
The 12th canto, titled "Seeing Arāḍa,"
in an epic tale of awakened action.

Canto 13: māra-vijayaḥ
Victory Over Māra

Introduction

Māra, from the root √*mṛ*, to die, means the Killer, the Destroyer, the Evil One. *Vijaya* is from *vi-√ji*, to conquer or to emerge victorious.

And just as Chandaka is ostensibly the object of turning back in Canto 6, and Arāḍa is ostensibly the object of seeing in Canto 12, Māra is ostensibly the object against whom the bodhisattva emerges victorious in the present canto.

In attaining this victory, however, the bodhisattva does not engage with Māra directly at all. Rather, under the bodhi tree, the bodhisattva just sits there, letting Māra be as wrong as he likes.

An alternative canto title that more accurately conveyed this sense, then, would be "Māra, and Emerging Victorious."

tasmin vimokṣāya kṛta-pratijñe rājarṣi-vaṁśa-prabhave mahārṣau /
tatropaviṣṭe prajaharṣa lokas tatrāsa saddharma-ripus tu māraḥ // 13.1 //
As there he sat, having formed his vow, in the direction of freedom – as that great seer, sprung from a line of royal seers, / Sat right there – the world rejoiced. But Māra, the enemy of true dharma, trembled. //13.1//

yaṁ kāma-devaṁ pravadanti loke citrāyudhaṁ puṣpa-śaraṁ tathaiva /
kāma-pracārādhipatiṁ tam eva mokṣa-dviṣaṁ māram udāharanti // 13.2 //
Kāma-deva, "God of Love," they call him in the world, the bearer of the brightly-colored bow and bearer, equally, of flower-arrows; / That same despot in his playground of desire, the hater of liberation, they call Māra[1]. //13.2//

tasyātmajā vibhrama-harṣa-darpās tisro rati-prīti-tṛṣaś ca kanyāḥ /
papracchur enaṁ manaso vikāraṁ sa tāṁś ca tāś caiva vaco 'bhyuvāca // 13.3 //
His own sons, Hurry, Thrill and Pride, and his three girls, Fun, Pleasure and Thirst, / Asked him what was troubling his mind; and he said this to those boys and girls: //13.3//

asau munir niścaya-varma bibhrat sattvāyudhaṁ buddhi-śaraṁ vikṛṣya /
jigīṣur āste viṣayān madīyān tasmād ayaṁ me manaso viṣādaḥ // 13.4 //
"Over there a certain sage, wearing the armor of resolve, and drawing the bow of strength of mind, with its arrow of sharpness, / Is sitting, with the intention to conquer realms that belong to me – that is the reason for this despondency of my mind. //13.4//

---

[1] Māra, from the root √*mṛ*, to die, means "the Destroyer."

yadi hy asau mām abhibhūya yāti lokāya cākhyāty apavarga-mārgam /
śūnyas tato 'yaṁ viṣayo mamādya vṛttāc cyutasyeva videha-bhartuḥ // 13.5 //
For if he succeeds in overpowering me, and expounds to the world the path of disentanglement, / Then today this realm of mine is empty, like the defunct domain of an errant lord.[2] //13.5//

tad yāvad evaiṣa na labdha-cakṣur mad-gocare tiṣṭhati yāvad eva /
yāsyāmi tāvad vratam asya bhettuṁ setuṁ nadī-vega ivātivṛddhaḥ // 13.6 //
So, while he has yet to attain the Eye, while he remains within my range, / I shall go to destroy his vow, like the swollen torrent of a river breaking through a dike." //13.6//

tato dhanuḥ puṣpa-mayaṁ gṛhītvā śarān jagan-moha-karāṁś ca pañca /
so 'śvattha-mūlaṁ sa-suto 'bhyagacchad asvāsthya-kārī manasaḥ prajānām // 13.7 //
Then, grabbing his bow made of flowers and his five world-deluding arrows, / He with his offspring in tow approached the foot of the *aśvattha* tree – to the fig tree where a horse rests easy, went he who causes people's minds to be uneasy.[3] //13.7//

atha praśāntaṁ munim āsana-sthaṁ pāraṁ titīrṣuṁ bhava-sāgarasya /
viṣajya savyaṁ karam āyudhāgre krīḍan śareṇ' edam uvāca māraḥ // 13.8 //
And so Māra addressed the sage, who was quietly sitting, still,[4] wishing to cross beyond the ocean of becoming. / Keeping his left hand on the tip of his weapon, while playing with an arrow, Māra said this: //13.8//

uttiṣṭha bhoḥ kṣatriya mṛtyu-bhīta cara sva-dharmaṁ tyaja mokṣa-dharmam /
bāṇaiś ca yajñaiś ca vinīya lokaṁ lokāt padaṁ prāpnuhi vāsavasya // 13.9 //
"Up, up! You death-fearing kṣatriya warrior! Follow your own dharma. Set aside the dharma of liberation. / Subjugate the world, using arrows and sacrifices, and from the world obtain the position of an Indra, highest among the bright ones. //13.9//

---

[2] *Vṛttāc cyutasyeva videha-bhartuḥ*. More literally, "Like [the realm/domain] of a *videha*-lord who has fallen from good conduct." The literal meaning of *videha* is without (*vi-*) a body (*deha*), hence deceased, defunct. But Videha is also the name of a country, of the capital city of that country (Mithilā), and of the king of that country (especially Janaka). EHJ noted that the Videha king is presumably the Karāla-janaka mentioned in BC Canto 4: *And 'the Dreadful Begetter' Karāla-janaka when he abducted a brahmin maiden, / Though he thus incurred ruin, never stopped attaching to his love. //BC4.80//* Perhaps it was Aśvaghoṣa's intention to allude to this downfall of Janaka on the surface. But the line as translated suggests that Māra, despite his bluster, knew what a bubble his empire was – one false move and it would be gone.

[3] A play on *aśvattha* ("Where a Horse Rests Easy"; name of a genus of fig tree) and *asvāsthya*, being uneasy, being not well in oneself.

[4] *Āsana-stham* ostensibly means "remaining seated" but (as in the case of Asita in BC1.52) it carries the hidden meaning of being devoted to sitting in stillness.

panthā hi niryātum ayaṁ yaśasyo yo vāhitaḥ pūrvatamair narendraiḥ /
jātasya rājarṣi-kule viśāle bhaikṣākam aślāghyam idaṁ prapattum // 13.10 //
For this path is a glorious path to travel, forged by the most ancient of Indras among men; / Whereas, for one born into an illustrious house of royal seers, this way of a beggar is not a praiseworthy way to go. //13.10//

athādya nottiṣṭhasi niścitātman bhava sthiro mā vimucaḥ pratijñām /
mayodyato hy eṣa śaraḥ sa eva yaḥ sūrpake mīna-ripau vimuktaḥ // 13.11 //
Or if today you will not stand up, O determined man! then be rigid! Loosen not your vow! / For this arrow that I am holding up, is the very arrow that I let loose at Sūrpaka, the fishes' foe.[5] //13.11//

spṛṣṭaḥ sa cānena kathaṁ-cid aiḍaḥ somasya naptāpy abhavad vicittaḥ /
sa cābhavac chantanur asvatantraḥ kṣīṇe yuge kiṁ bata durbalo 'nyaḥ // 13.12 //
And barely touched by this arrow, [Purū-ravas,] the son of Iḍā, though he was the grandson of the moon-god Soma, lost his mind; / And 'Good Body' Śan-tanu also became out of control – what, then, will become in a degenerate age, of someone other, who is not so forceful?[6] //13.12//

tat kṣipram uttiṣṭha labhasva saṁjñāṁ bāṇo hy ayaṁ tiṣṭhati lelihānaḥ /
priya-vidheyeṣu rati-priyeṣu yaṁ cakravākeṣv iva notsṛjāmi // 13.13 //
Up! Up!, therefore! Quickly stand up! Come to consciousness! For here stands ready, with darting tongue, this arrow / Which, at fun-loving lovers who are head over heels in love, any more than at greylag geese,[7] I do not unleash!" //13.13//

ity evam ukto 'pi yadā nir-āstho naivāsanaṁ śākyamunir bibheda /
śaraṁ tato 'smai visasarja māraḥ kanyāś ca kṛtvā purataḥ sutāṁś ca // 13.14 //
Not interested, even when spoken to like this, Śākyamuni, the Śākya sage, never broke his sitting posture at all, / And so Māra shot the arrow at him having sent to the fore his daughters and sons. //13.14//

---

5 Sūrpaka, aka Śūrpaka seems to be identified here with the *mīna-ripu* "Fishes' Foe" mentioned by the striver in SN Canto 8, as part of his tirade against women: *The daughter of Sena-jit the Conqueror, so they say, coupled with a cooker of dogs; Kumud-vatī, 'the Lilly Pool,' paired up with Mīna-ripu, 'the Foe of Fishes'; / And Bṛhad-rathā, 'the Burly Heroine,' loved a lion: there is nothing women will not do. //SN8.44//* In SN Canto 10, Nanda, in describing his own torment, appears to refer to the incident Māra has in mind: *Therefore pour on me the water of your voice, before I am burned, as was The Fishes' Foe; / For a fire of passion is going now to burn me up, like a fire rising up to burn both undergrowth and treetops. //SN10.53//*

6 *Durbalo 'nyaḥ.* Ostensible meaning: a weakling (*durbalaḥ*) who is different (*anyaḥ*) from those mighty ancients. Hidden meaning: one who, being different (*anyaḥ*) from what people think, eschews compulsion and uses expedient means which are indirect and not forceful (*durbalaḥ*).

7 Greylag geese, or cakravāka ducks, like swans, are famous for naturally forming strong emotional bonds for life – so Māra sees them as not requiring the intervention of his bow and arrow.

tasmiṁs tu bāṇe 'pi sa vipramukte cakāra nāsthāṁ na dhṛteś cacāla /
dṛṣṭvā tathainaṁ viṣasāda māraś cintā-parītaś ca śanair jagāda // 13.15 //
But even when the arrow was unleashed at him, [the sage] thought nothing of it; from constancy, he did not budge. / Seeing him like this, Māra sank down into despondency and, filled with anxious thought, he said in a low voice: //13.15//

śailendra-putrīṁ prati yena viddho devo 'pi śambhuś calito babhūva /
na cintayaty eṣa tam eva bāṇaṁ kiṁ syād acitto na śaraḥ sa eṣaḥ // 13.16 //
"When Benevolent [Śiva] - god though he was - was pierced by the arrow, he toppled into the lap of the Mountain-King's daughter.[8] / This man gives not a second thought to the very same arrow! Does he maybe not have a heart? Or is it maybe not the same arrow? //13.16//

tasmād ayaṁ nārhati puṣpa-bāṇaṁ na harṣaṇaṁ nāpi rater niyogam /
arhaty ayaṁ bhūta-gaṇair asaumyaiḥ saṁtrāsanātarjana-tāḍanāni // 13.17 //
Therefore this one calls not for the flower-arrow, nor for a Thrilling, nor for the deployment of Fun; / This man merits, at the unlovely hands of demon throngs,[9] frights, rebukes, and beatings." //13.17//

sasmāra māraś ca tataḥ sva-sainyaṁ vighnam śame śākya-muneś cikīrṣan /
nānāśrayāś cānucarāḥ parīyuḥ śala-druma-prāsa-gadāsi-hastāḥ // 13.18 //
No sooner then had Māra called to mind his personal army, in his wish to form for the Śākya sage an impediment to peace, / Than multifarious followers had gathered round, carrying in their hands spears, trees, javelins, bludgeons and swords. //13.18//

varāha-mīnāśva-kharoṣṭra-vaktrā vyāghrarkṣa-siṁha-dviradānanāś ca /
ekekṣaṇā naika-mukhās tri-śīrṣā lambodarāś caiva pṛthūdarāś ca // 13.19 //
Having the faces of pigs, fish, horses, donkeys, and camels;[10] having the snouts of tigers, bears, lions, and two-tuskers;[11] / One-eyed, many-mouthed, three-headed;[12] with big bellies, just hanging, and with broad bellies, expanding;[13] //13.19//

---

[8] The Mountain-King's daughter means Pārvatī who, as told in Kālidāsa's epic poem *Kumāra-saṁbhava,* "Birth of the Prince," made up her mind to win the love of the theretofore ascetic and aloof Śiva. The prince in Kālidāsa's title is Kārttikeya, the god of war, son of Pārvatī and Śiva.

[9] *Bhūta-gaṇa* is given in the dictionary as 1. the host of living beings, and 2. a multitude of spirits or ghosts. The latter definition is the ostensible meaning here - "demon throngs." But in the hidden meaning Aśvaghoṣa is going to describe a number (*gaṇa*) of real individual beings (*bhūta*), inviting us to investigate the reality of each individual on a case by case basis. We may thereby be reminded that our initial impressions are ever liable to be false.

[10] In the hidden meaning, the line reminds us, with our two eyes, two ears and a mouth, of our shared inheritance. In our faces, human beings and the animals cited are the same. This corresponds to the universal, idealistic thesis.

[11] In support of the anti-thesis, the second line causes us to question whether our human noses are the same as elephants' trunks?

[12] In the hidden meaning, a description of being limited in one's view, speaking unreliable or changeable words, and being indecisive or subject to various emotional states? Hence an ironic description of everyday human life?

[13] In the hidden meaning, a description that makes one think of a happy buddha, with big pot-belly.

a-jānu-sakthā ghaṭa-jānavaś ca daṁṣṭrāyudhāś caiva nakhāyudhāś ca /
kabandha-hastā bahu-mūrtayaś ca bhagnārdha-vaktrāś ca mahā-mukhāś ca // 13.20 //
Having no knees and thighs, or having jars for knees;[14] equipped with large teeth and equipped with nails;[15] / Having big-bellied barrels for hands,[16] and many embodiments; with faces split in half, and mouths of epic dimensions;[17] //13.20//

bhasmāruṇā lohita-bindu-citrāḥ khaṭvāṅga-hastā hari-dhūmra-keśāḥ /
lamba-sphico vāraṇa-lamba-karṇāś carmāmbarāś caiva nirambarāś ca // 13.21 //
Grey as an ashen dawn, spotted with red marks; carrying their skulls-and-backbones in their hands [or in their elephants' trunks[18]]; having the smoky-colored hair of monkeys; / With pendulous hips and pendulous elephant-ears; clothed in hides and with nothing on; //13.21//

śvetārdha-vaktrā haritārdha-kāyās tāmrāś ca dhūmrā harayo 'sitāś ca /
vyālottarāsaṅga-bhujās tathaiva praghuṣṭa-ghaṇṭākula-mekhalāś ca // 13.22 //
With half their faces white; with half their bodies green [or with half their tree-trunks green][19]; some colored also coppery-red; or smoky-grey or reddish-brown or black; / Some, again, with their upper limbs[20] cloaked by snakes, and with girths fully girdled by sounding bells; //13.22//

tāla-pramāṇāś ca gṛhīta-śūlā daṁṣṭrā-karālāś ca śiśu-pramāṇāḥ /
urabhra-vaktrāś ca vihaṁgamākṣā mārjāra-vaktrāś ca manuṣya-kāyāḥ // 13.23 //
[Having the stature of palm-trees, while grasping stakes, or the stature of children, with mouths open wide and teeth sticking out; / Or having sheep's faces and birds' eyes, or cats' faces and human bodies. //13.23//][21]

---

[14] Below the surface, an ironic suggestion of what it feels like after a long spell sitting in lotus?

[15] *Daṁṣṭrāyudhāś caiva nakhāyudhāś ca* ostensibly describes monsters armed with tusks and armed with claws. But *daṁṣṭra* can also mean a human tooth, and *nakha* can also mean a human nail.

[16] A suggestion of hands that are totally free from undue tension, lying in the lap of a person who is sitting?

[17] A suggestion of the many forms in which a buddha manifests himself or herself for the purpose of preaching the Dharma in which two-sidedness is investigated and transcended?

[18] At the end of a compound *-hasta* means 1. holding in the hand, and 2. (of an elephant) holding in the trunk. Ostensibly Aśvaghoṣa is describing terrible monsters holding in their hand the skulls and spines of others, but the ironic intention may be to describe nothing more or less fantastic than real elephants, using their trunks to point their own skulls and spines in the direction they want to go. (Elephants were decorated in India since ancient times with the *tilaka*, or red spot painted on the forehead.) What is the teaching point? Again, it may be to remind us that first impressions can be misleading, especially in demonizing the seemingly monstrous other. Cf. Praise for "a rest from objectification" (*prapañcopaśamaṁ*) in MMK Dedicatory Verses.

[19] *Kāya* means 1. the body, 2. the trunk of a tree.

[20] The meanings of *bhuja*, similarly, include 1. the arm, of a human body, or of a terrible monster, and 2. the branch of a not-at-all-monstrous tree.

[21] This verse is probably an interpolation.

prakīrṇa-keśāḥ śikhino 'rdha-muṇḍā rajjvambarā vyākula-veṣṭanāś ca /
prahṛṣṭa-vaktrā bhṛkuṭī-mukhāś ca tejo-harāś caiva mano-harāś ca // 13.24 //
With hair strewn about, with topknots, with half-shaved heads[22]; encompassed in lines of thread,[23] and with their headdresses lying in disorder; / With delighted faces, and with grimaces, carrying off vital energy and carrying off hearts and minds.[24] //13.24//

ke-cid vrajanto bhṛśam āvavalgur anyonyam āpupluvire tathānye /
cikrīḍur ākāśa-gatāś ca ke-cit ke-cic ca cerus taru-mastakeṣu // 13.25 //
Some as they progressed sprang wildly into action; ones who were different, again, sprang up, each towards the others; / Some played in emptiness,[25] while some roamed about on the tops of trees.[26] //13.25//

nanarta kaś-cid bhramayaṁs triśūlaṁ kaś-cid vipusphūrja gadāṁ vikarṣan /
harṣeṇa kaś-cid vṛṣavan nanarda kaś-cit prajajvāla tanū-ruhebhyaḥ // 13.26 //
One, brandishing a three-pronged weapon, danced[27]; one, tearing to pieces a bludgeon [or a string of sentences],[28] thundered; / One, in his aroused state, moved like a bull; one, from the body-grown,[29] blazed forth. //13.26//

evaṁ-vidhā bhūta-gaṇāḥ samantāt taṁ bodhi-mūlaṁ parivārya tasthuḥ /
jighṛkṣavaś caiva jighāṁsavaś ca bhartur niyogaṁ paripālayantaḥ // 13.27 //
Such were the 'demon throngs' which, on all sides, stood surrounding him who was the root of bodhi,[30] / Wanting to capture, and wanting to destroy,[31] letting be done the will of the master.[32] //13.27//

---

[22] As when a monk is in the process of shaving his head.
[23] As when clothed in a kaṣāya.
[24] The meanings of *hṛ* include 1. to carry off, to rob, and 2. to capture or captivate.
[25] *Ākāśa*: 1. free or open space, emptiness ; 2. the sky.
[26] In the hidden meaning, when the Buddha sat on Vulture Peak he might have roamed over the tops of trees with his eyes.
[27] In the hidden meaning, he or she moved freely and joyfully, being in possession of the means which is the noble eightfold path, with its three prongs of *śila*, *samādhi* and *prajñā*?
[28] The meanings of *gadā* include 1. a series of sentences (as analysed by teachers of the Buddha's teaching), and 2. a club or bludgeon (as targeted by enemy fighters).
[29] The meanings *of tanū-ruha* listed in the dictionary include 1. hair, 2. feather, 3. wing, 4. son. But *tanū-ruha* literally means "body-grown" i.e. "grown on a body" (like hair or feather) or "grown out of a body" (like a son) or "developed by means of a body" (like wisdom?).
[30] The old Nepalese manuscript has *tam bodhi-mūlam*, which refers to him (*tam*; masculine), the bodhisattva, as the root of bodhi. EH Johnston amended to *tad bodhi-mūlam*. Since *tad* is neuter, the phrase thus refers to the root (*mūlam*; neuter). The Tibetan translator evidently read the original as *taṁ bodhisattvam*. See also verses 32 and 42.
[31] In the hidden meaning, wanting to grasp the true purport of the Buddha's teaching, and wanting to destroy ignorance.
[32] Ostensibly *bhartṛ*, the master, means Māra – but not, of course, in the hidden meaning.

taṁ prekṣya mārasya ca pūrva-rātre śākyarṣabhasyaiva ca yuddha-kālam /
na dyauś cakāśe pṛthivī cakampe prajajvaluś caiva diśaḥ saśabdāḥ // 13.28 //
Beholding, in the beginning of the night, that hour of the battle between Māra and the Śākya bull, / The sky did not shimmer but the earth did shake, and the four quarters did blaze forth resoundingly. //13.28//

viṣvag vavau vāyur udīrṇa-vegas tārā na rejur na babhau śaśāṅkaḥ /
tamaś ca bhūyo vitatāna rātriḥ sarve ca saṁcukṣubhire samudrāḥ // 13.29 //
From every direction the wind blew in wild gusts. The stars did not shine, the hare-marked moon did not show itself, /And Dark Night covered herself in an extra layer of darkness. While all the oceans churned. //13.29//

mahībhṛto dharma-parāś ca nāgā mahā-muner vighnam amṛṣyamāṇāḥ /
māraṁ prati krodha-vivṛtta-netrā niḥśaśvasuś caiva jajṛṁbhire ca // 13.30 //
The *nāgas*, as bearers of the Earth and committed supporters of dharma, not looking kindly on the hindrance to the great sage, / Their eyes rolling angrily in Māra's direction, hissed and snorted, and came unwound. //13.30//

śuddhādhivāsā vibudharṣayas tu sad-dharma-siddhy-artham iva pravṛttāḥ /
māre 'nukaṁpāṁ manasā pracakrur virāga-bhāvāt tu na roṣam īyuḥ // 13.31 //
But the divine sages of the Pure Abodes who are devoted, it seems, to the aim of perfectly attaining the True Dharma, / In their minds, out of dispassion, produced sympathy for Māra, so that they, in contrast, did not become angry. //13.31//

tad bodhi-mūlaṁ samavekṣya kīrṇaṁ hiṁsātmanā māra-balena tena /
dharmātmabhir loka-vimokṣa-kāmair babhūva hāhā-kṛtam antarīkṣe // 13.32 //
When they beheld that root of bodhi beset by that army of Māra, whose essence was desire to do harm, / Those whose essence was dharma, desiring the liberation of the world, whispered "Hā!... Hā!..." into the middle space between heaven and earth.[33] //13.32//

upaplavaṁ dharma-vidhes tu tasya dṛṣṭvā sthitaṁ māra-balaṁ mahārṣiḥ /
na cukṣubhe nāpi yayau vikāraṁ madhye gavāṁ siṁha ivopaviṣṭaḥ // 13.33 //
But when the great seer saw, as an affront to that method of dharma, Māra's army standing by, / He did not budge, nor was he bothered at all – he was like a lion among cows, sitting there in the middle.[34] //13.33//

---

[33] *Antarīkṣe*, "into the intermediate space between heaven and earth," seems to suggest finding somewhere between the wild spontaneity of the earth-bearing nāgas and the holier-than-thou attitude of divine sages.

[34] *Madhye... upaviṣṭaḥ*, "sitting in the middle," reinforces the sense of finding somewhere between two extremes.

māras tato bhūta-camūm udīrṇām ājñāpayām āsa bhayāya tasya /
svaiḥ svaiḥ prabhāvair atha sāsya senā tad-dhairya-bhedāya matiṁ cakāra // 13.34 //
Then Māra, to the phantom army he had mobilized, gave the order to strike fear into the sage; / And so that war machine of Māra's making – in which each was possessed of his own power – made up its mind to break the sage's composure. //13.34//

ke-cic calan-naika-vilambi-jihvās tīkṣṇogra-daṁṣṭrā hari-maṇḍalākṣāḥ /
vidāritāsyāḥ sthira-śaṅku-karṇāḥ saṁtrāsayantaḥ kila nāma tasthuḥ // 13.35 //
Some, with more than one tongue trembling and hanging down [or wagging and then wavering], with acutely savage bites, and yellow-red orbs for their jaundiced eyes, / With jaws gaping apart, and ears as solid as pegs, stood there purporting to be terrifying. //13.35//

tebhyaḥ sthitebhyaḥ sa tathā-vidhebhyaḥ rūpeṇa bhāvena ca dāruṇebhyaḥ /
na vivyathe nodvivije mahārṣiḥ krīḍat-subālebhya ivoddhatebhyaḥ // 13.36 //
From them, as they stood there like that, so horrid in their appearance and in their hearts, / The great seer did not flinch and did not shrink – any more than from naughty infants at play.[35] //13.36//

kaś-cit tato roṣa-vivṛtta-dṛṣṭis tasmai gadām udyamayāṁ cakāra /
tastambha bāhuḥ sagadas tato 'sya puraṁdarasyeva purā sa-vajraḥ // 13.37 //
Then one of them, turning his angry gaze upon [the sage], raised a club in his direction, / Whereupon his arm with the club became immovable – as in ancient times did the arm of Indra, 'Destroyer of Strongholds,' with the thunderbolt.[36] //13.37//

ke-cit samudyamya śilās tarūṁś ca viṣehire naiva munau vimoktum /
petuḥ sa-vṛkṣāḥ sa-śilās tathaiva vajrāvabhagnā iva vindhya-pādāḥ // 13.38 //
Some, having lifted up rocks and trees, were quite unable to unleash them at the sage; / With their trees and likewise with their rocks, down they fell – like the Vindhya foot-hills when smashed by the thunderbolt. //13.38//

kaiś-cit samutpatya nabho vimuktāḥ śilāś ca vṛkṣāś ca paraśvadhāś ca /
tasthur nabhasy eva na cāvapetuḥ saṁdhyābhra-pādā iva naika-varṇāḥ // 13.39 //
Rocks and trees and axes unleashed by some who had sprung up into the clouds, / Stayed up there in the clouds and did not fall down – like the many-hued foot-beams of a twilight nimbus. //13.39//

---

[35] The descriptions that follow, then, illustrate the power of the means of simply sitting still, without flinching or shrinking.

[36] The Mahā-bhārata relates several such instances of Indra finding himself temporarily incapable of movement. In perhaps similar vein, Dōgen wrote in *Fukan-zazengi* of Zen ancestors being "caught by the still state."

cikṣepa tasyopari dīptam anyaḥ kaḍaṅgaraṁ parvata-śṛṅga-mātram /
yan mukta-mātraṁ gagana-stham eva tasyānubhāvāc chata-dhā paphāla // 13.40 //
One who was different put above himself a blazing mass of straw, as high as the mountains' peaks; / As soon as he released it, it just hung there in the emptiness, then shattered, at his suggestion, into a hundred pieces. //13.40//

kaś-cij jvalann arka ivoditaḥ khād aṅgāra-varṣaṁ mahad utsasarja /
cūrṇāni cāmīkara-kandarāṇāṁ kalpātyaye merur iva pradīptaḥ // 13.41 //
One of them, burning brightly as the risen sun, unloosed from the sky a great shower of embers, / Like blazing Meru at the end of a kalpa spewing clouds of ash out of golden vents. //13.41//

tad bodhi-mūle pravikīryamāṇam aṅgāra-varṣaṁ tu sa-visphuliṅgam /
maitrī-vihārād ṛṣi-sattamasya babhūva raktotpala-pattra-varṣaḥ // 13.42 //
As it scattered around the root of bodhi,[37] however, that cinder-shower so full of fiery sparks / Became, through the supreme seer's exercise of friendliness, a rain of red lotus petals. //13.42//

śarīra-citta-vyasanātapais tair evaṁ-vidhais taiś ca nipātyamānaḥ /
naivāsanāc chākya-muniś cacāla sva-niścayaṁ bandhum ivopaguhya // 13.43 //
While being assailed by these various causes of trouble and pain for body and mind, / The Śākya sage never budged from sitting – for he had embraced his own resolve like a friend. //13.43//

athāpare nirjigilur mukhebhyaḥ sarpān vijīrṇebhya iva drumebhyaḥ /
te mantra-baddhā iva tat-samīpe na śaśvasur notsasṛpur na celuḥ // 13.44 //
Others, meanwhile, spat out snakes from their mouths as from rotten tree trunks. / Those [snakes], as if spellbound in his presence, neither hissed nor reared up nor travelled around.[38] //13.44//

bhūtvāpare vāri-dharā bṛhantaḥ sa-vidyutaḥ sāśani-caṇḍa-ghoṣāḥ /
tasmin drume tatyajur aśma-varṣaṁ tat puṣpa-varṣaṁ ruciraṁ babhūva // 13.45 //
Others became massive rain-clouds, with lightning and fierce crashing of thunder; / They dropped on that tree a shower of stones which turned into a pleasant rain of flowers. //13.45//

cāpe 'tha bāṇo nihito 'pareṇa jajvāla tatraiva na niṣpapāta /
anīśvarasyātmani dhūyamāṇo durmarṣaṇasyeva narasya manyuḥ // 13.46 //
An arrow placed in a bow by yet another, burned right where it was; it did not go – / Like anger being kindled, ineffectually, in the soul an unforgiving man. //13.46//

---

[37] *Bodhi-mūla*, "the bodhi-root," ostensibly means the root or foot of the bodhi tree. A hidden meaning, however, may be that the bodhisattva's exercise of friendliness was the root of bodhi.

[38] Cf SN16.35: *The faults do not attack a man who is standing firm in balanced stillness: like charmed snakes, they are spellbound.*

pañceṣavo 'nyena tu vipramuktās tasthur viyaty eva munau na petuḥ /
saṁsāra-bhīror viṣaya-pravṛttau pañcendriyāṇīva parīkṣakasya // 13.47 //
But five arrows that one who was different did shoot stayed up there in mid-air, and did not impinge upon the sage – / Like the five senses, during pursuit of objects, when those senses belong to a saṁsāra-fearing scrutinizer. //13.47//

jighāṁsayānyaḥ prasasāra ruṣṭo gadāṁ gṛhītvābhimukho mahārṣeḥ /
so prāpta-kālo vivaśaḥ papāta doṣeṣv ivānartha-kareṣu lokaḥ // 13.48 //
Bent on destruction, one who was different furiously sprang forth, wielding a bludgeon [or a string of sentences], while facing in the great seer's direction; / His time having come, into free fall he went, helplessly[39] – as helplessly as the world falling into calamitous faults. //13.48//

strī megha-kālī tu kapāla-hastā kartuṁ mahārṣeḥ kila citta-moham /
babhrāma tatrāniyataṁ na tasthau calātmano buddhir ivāgameṣu // 13.49 //
A woman, in contrast – Megha-kālī, "the One as Black as a Cloud" – bore in her hand a skull [or a bowl][40], in order to delude the mind of the truly great seer [or the mind of a would-be mahā-rishi][41]; / She flitted about there unrestrainedly, never standing still – like the intellect of a flibbertigibbet flitting through ancient scriptures. //13.49//

kaś-cit pradīptaṁ praṇidhāya cakṣur netrāgnināśī-viṣavad didhakṣuḥ /
tatraiva nāsīnam ṛṣiṁ dadarśa kāmātmakaḥ śreya ivopadiṣṭam // 13.50 //
One of them directed a blazing eye, desiring with the fire of his glare, like a venomous snake, to burn [his object] up; / He was blind to the seer sitting right there – as a sensualist is blind to a better way that has been pointed out. //13.50//

gurvīṁ śilām udyamayaṁs tathānyaḥ śaśrāma moghaṁ vihata-prayatnaḥ /
niḥśreyasaṁ jñāna-samādhi-gamyaṁ kāya-klamair dharmam ivāptu-kāmaḥ // 13.51 //
One who, again, was different, lifting up a heavy millstone, exerted himself for nothing, his efforts coming to naught; / He was like one seeking to obtain, through toilsome physical doings, the peerless dharma that is to be realized by the act of knowing and by the balanced stillness of samādhi. //13.51//

tarakṣu-siṁhākṛtayas tathānye praṇedur uccair mahataḥ praṇādān /
sattvāni yaiḥ saṁcukucuḥ samantād vajrāhatā dyauḥ phalatīti matvā // 13.52 //
Others who, likewise, were different, having the semblance of hyenas and of lions, howled with loud laughter and roared mighty roars, / At which beings on all sides made themselves small, deeming heaven, struck by the thunderbolt, to be bursting.[42] //13.52//

---

[39] *Vivaśaḥ*, being helpless, might suggest in its hidden meaning body and mind dropping off naturally and spontaneously, not because of my doing, but because of the right thing doing itself (*tattva-darśanāt*; MMK26.10).

[40] *Kapāla*: 1. a cup, jar; 2. the alms-bowl of a beggar; 3. the skull, cranium.

[41] *Kila*: 1. indeed, truly (a particle of asservation); 2. "so said," "so reported," pretendedly.

[42] An ironic suggestion of irony itself – whereby loud laughter is induced, and the bubble of religious pomposity is popped?

mṛgā gajāś cārta-ravān sṛjanto vidudruvuś caiva nililyire ca /
rātrau ca tasyām ahanīva digbhyaḥ khagā ruvantaḥ paripetur ārtāḥ // 13.53 //
Wandering creatures of the forest,[43] and elephants,[44] letting out calls of suffering,[45] dispersed in all directions and hid themselves away. / Again, on that night, as if it were day, from every quarter singing sky-goers[46] dropped down to earth, struck by suffering. //13.53//

teṣāṁ praṇādais tu tathā-vidhais taiḥ sarveṣu bhūteṣv api kampiteṣu /
munir na tatrāsa na saṁcukoca ravair garutmān iva vāyasānām // 13.54 //
But even as those individuals, by such sonorous expressions of themselves, were causing all beings to tremble, / The sage did not wobble, and did not make himself small,[47] any more than would Garuḍa,[48] at the cawing of crows. //13.54//

bhayāvahebhyaḥ pariṣad-gaṇebhyo yathā yathā naiva munir bibhāya /
tathā tathā dharma-bhṛtāṁ sapatnaḥ śokāc ca roṣāc ca sasāra māraḥ // 13.55 //
The less the sage was afraid of the fear-inducing mobs assembled there, / The more did Māra, the enemy of upholders of dharma, out of sorrow and out of rage, attack. //13.55//

bhūtaṁ tataḥ kiṁ-cid adṛśya-rūpaṁ viśiṣṭa-bhūtaṁ gagana-stham eva /
dṛṣṭvarṣaye drugdham a-vaira-ruṣṭaṁ māraṁ babhāṣe mahatā svareṇa // 13.56 //
Then a certain being, being of great distinction, but having no discernible form, just hanging there in the emptiness,[49] / Saw Māra seeking to do the seer harm and, without vengefulness or fury, boomed at Māra in a mighty voice: //13.56//

moghaṁ śramaṁ nārhasi māra kartuṁ hiṁsrātmatām utsṛja gaccha śarma /
naiṣa tvayā kampayituṁ hi śakyo mahā-girir merur ivānilena // 13.57 //
"Do not do, O Māra, work that is empty! Let go of hurtfulness! Come to quiet! / For this man can no more be shaken by you than the great mountain Meru can be shaken by the wind. //13.57//

---

[43] *Mṛgāḥ*. Ostensible meaning: deer. Ironic meaning: forest bhikṣus.
[44] *Gajāḥ*. Ostensible meaning: elephants. Ironic meaning: big beasts in the arena of the Buddha's teaching.
[45] In the hidden meaning, preaching the four noble truths.
[46] *Khagāḥ*. Ostensible meaning: birds. Ironic meaning: meditators who move in emptiness.
[47] *Saṁ-√kuc* means to contract, shrink, close (as a flower). In verse 52, in its hidden meaning, *saṁcukucuḥ* suggests self-restraint, or modesty, in a good sense – like excellent monks in a culture where the Buddha's teaching is strong, seeing themselves as only small fish in a big pond? Here *na saṁcukuca* means he did not shrink, he was not diminished in the face of trying circumstances.
[48] Garuḍa, "The Devourer," mighty chief of feathered beings.
[49] *Gagana* (like the *khā* of the sky-going birds) is another word which ostensibly means the sky but in its hidden meaning suggests a condition of absence of, for example, attachment to good posture, and absence of associated effort to hold oneself up. One who is "just hanging there in emptiness" (*gagana-stham eva*) is free of such effort.

apy uṣṇa-bhāvaṁ jvalanaḥ prajahyād āpo dravatvaṁ pṛthivī sthiratvam /
aneka-kalpācita-puṇya-karmā na tv eva jahyād vyavasāyam eṣaḥ // 13.58 //
Even if fire were to give up being hot, water its wetness and earth its solidity, / With the good karma he has heaped up over many kalpas, this one could never abandon his resolve. //13.58//

yo niścayo hy asya parākramaś ca tejaś ca yad yā ca dayā prajāsu /
aprāpya notthāsyati tattvam eṣa tamāṁsy ahatveva sahasra-raśmiḥ // 13.59 //
For, such is his firmness of will, and his courage, such is his fire, and such is his compassion for living creatures, / That this one will not rise up without having realized the truth – just as the thousand-rayed sun does not rise without dispelling darkness. //13.59//

kāṣṭhaṁ hi mathnan labhate hutāśaṁ bhūmiṁ khanan vindati cāpi toyam /
nirbandhinaḥ kiṁ-cana nāsty asādhyaṁ nyāyena yuktaṁ ca kṛtaṁ ca sarvam // 13.60 //
For, by twirling the fire-stick one obtains the oblation-eating flame. Again, by digging the earth one finds water. / For one who persists, nothing is impossible. Done according to principle, everything is truly done. //13.60//

tal lokam ārtaṁ karuṇāyamāno rogeṣu rāgādiṣu vartamānam /
mahā-bhiṣaṅ nārhati vighnam eṣa jñānauṣadhārthaṁ parikhidyamānaḥ // 13.61 //
Therefore, in his compassion for the afflicted world, as it twists and turns, through illnesses and through emotions like red passion – through breakdowns and booms – / This great man of healing deserves no impediment, as he wears himself out, in his quest for the medicine of knowing. //13.61//

hṛte ca loke bahubhiḥ ku-mārgaiḥ san-mārgam anvicchati yaḥ śrameṇa /
sa daiśikaḥ kṣobhayituṁ na yuktaṁ su-deśikaḥ sārtha iva pranaṣṭe // 13.62 //
And when, by many wrong byways, the world is being carried away, he who, with effort, is willing the right path, / He who knows the terrain, should no more be harassed than should an experienced guide when a caravan has got lost. //13.62//

sattveṣu naṣṭeṣu mahāndha-kāre jñāna-pradīpaḥ kriyamāṇa eṣaḥ /
āryasya nirvāpayituṁ na sādhu prajvālyamānas tamasīva dīpaḥ // 13.63 //
While living beings are lost in a great darkness, he is being made into a lantern of knowing – / It is no more right for a noble Āryan to snuff him out than to snuff out a light being kindled in the dark. //13.63//

dṛṣṭvā ca saṁsāra-maye mahaughe magnaṁ jagat pāram avindamānam /
yaś cedam uttārayituṁ pravṛttaḥ kaś cintayet tasya tu pāpam āryaḥ // 13.64 //
Again, seeing the world sunk in the great flood of saṁsāra and unable to find the far shore, / He has committed to ferry this world across – what man of honor would think evil upon him? //13.64//

kṣamā-śipho dhairya-vigāḍha-mūlaś cāritra-puṣpaḥ smṛti-buddhi-śākhaḥ /
jñāna-drumo dharma-phala-pradātā notpāṭanaṁ hy arhati vardhamānaḥ // 13.65 //
For the tree, deeply rooted in constancy, whose fibers are forbearance, whose blossom is good conduct, whose branches are awareness and good judgement, / The bestower of dharma-fruit, the tree of knowing, does not deserve to be uprooted, now that it is growing. //13.65//

baddhāṁ dṛḍhaiś cetasi moha-pāśair yasya prajāṁ mokṣayituṁ manīṣā /
tasmin jighāṁsā tava nopapannā śrānte jagad-bandhana-mokṣa-hetoḥ // 13.66 //
His purpose is to free living creatures who are bound in mind by the tightly gripping fetters of foolishness; / Your murderous intent towards him is not appropriate when he is exhausting himself to undo the ties that bind the world. //13.66//

bodhāya karmāṇi hi yāny anena kṛtāni teṣāṁ niyato 'dya kālaḥ /
sthāne tathāsminn upaviṣṭa eṣa yathaiva pūrve munayas tathaiva // 13.67 //
For now is the time circumscribed by those actions which he did for the sake of awakening; / Thus, in this act of firm abiding, this one is sitting, in exactly the manner of the sages of the past. //13.67//

eṣā hi nābhir vasudhā-talasya kṛtsnena yuktā parameṇa dhāmnā /
bhūmer ato 'nyo 'sti hi na pradeśo vegaṁ samādher viṣaheta yo 'sya // 13.68 //
For this place here is a navel in the surface of the earth, wholly possessed of deepest-seated core power; / For there is no other place on earth that could absorb the shock waves from the coming back into balance of this one here. //13.68//

tan mā kṛthāḥ śokam upehi śāntiṁ mā bhūn mahimnā tava māra mānaḥ /
viśrambhituṁ na kṣamam adhruvā śrīś cale pade kiṁ madam abhyupaiṣi // 13.69 //
So do not grieve; come to quietness. Do not be proud, Māra, of your greatness. / High rank is precarious and not apt to be relied upon. Why would you, on shaky footing, get above yourself?" //13.69//

tataḥ sa saṁśrutya ca tasya tad vaco mahā-muneḥ prekṣya ca niṣprakaṁpatām /
jagāma māro vimano hatodyamaḥ śarair jagac cetasi yair vihanyate // 13.70 //
And so, having listened to that speech of the other, and having witnessed the unshakability of a great sage, / Māra, deflated, his bubble pricked, went on his way, taking with him the arrows by which, in its heart and mind, the world is struck. //13.70//

gata-praharṣā viphalī-kṛta-śramā praviddha-pāṣāṇa-kaḍaṅgara-drumā /
diśaḥ pradudrāva tato 'sya sā camūr hatāśrayeva dviṣatā dviṣac-camūḥ // 13.71 //
All exuberance gone, its effort rendered fruitless, its stones, straw fire-bombs, and trees, all strewn about, / That army of his fled then in all directions, like a hostile army when hostility itself has done for the chain of command. //13.71//

dravati sapariṣakte nirjite puṣpa-ketau jayati jita-tamaske nīrajaske maharṣau / yuvatir iva sahāsā dyauś cakāśe sa-candrā surabhi ca jala-garbhaṁ puṣpa-varṣaṁ papāta // 13.72 //

As the Flower-Bannered One surrounded by his acolytes, melted away, defeated, leaving victorious the great seer, the passion-free vanquisher of darkness, / The moonlit sky shone like a smiling girl, and a rain of fragrant flowers, containing water, fell down. //13.72//

iti buddha-carite mahā-kāvye 'śvaghoṣa-kṛte
māra-vijayo nāma trayodaśaḥ sargaḥ // 13 //

The 13th canto, titled "Victory Over Māra,"
in this epic tale of awakened action, composed by Aśvaghoṣa.

Canto 14: abhisambodhiḥ
The Transcendent Total Awakening

Introduction

Cantos 15 to 28 of Buddhacarita, though preserved in Tibetan and Chinese translations, are lost in the original Sanskrit. There is no extant Sanskrit, either, for the present canto beyond verse 31. The Sanskrit colophon is therefore missing, but the canto title can be inferred from the Chinese translation in which the five Chinese characters 阿惟三菩提 represent phonetically the Sanskrit *abhisambodhi.*

Bodhi, from the root √*budh*, to wake, means awakening or enlightenment. The prefix *sam-* adds a sense of completeness or totality. And the prefix *abhi-* adds a sense of overarching transcendence.

tato māra-balaṁ jitvā dhairyeṇa ca śamena ca /
paramārthaṁ vijijñāsuḥ sa dadhyau dhyāna-kovidaḥ // 14.1 //
And so, having conquered Māra's army by the means of constancy and quietness, / Wanting to know the ultimate, he who was skilled in meditation meditated. //14.1//

sarveṣu dhyāna-vidhiṣu prāpya caiśvaryam uttamam /
sasmāra prathame yāme pūrva-janma-paraṁparām // 14.2 //
And having obtained utmost mastery over all ways of meditating, / He called to mind in the first watch of the night the succession of his previous births. //14.2//

amutrāham ayaṁ nāma cyutas tasmād ihāgataḥ /
iti janma-sahasrāṇi sasmārānubhavann iva // 14.3 //
"There I had this name; passing from there, I arrived here" – / Thus, thousands of births he recalled as if reliving them. //14.3//

smṛtvā janma ca mṛtyuṁ ca tāsu tāsūpapattiṣu /
tataḥ sattveṣu kāruṇyaṁ cakāra karuṇātmakaḥ // 14.4 //
Having remembered [his own] birth and death in those various existences, / Compassion towards all beings, on that basis, felt he whose very essence was compassion – //14.4//

kṛtveha sva-janotsargaṁ punar anyatra ca kriyāḥ /
atrāṇaḥ khalu loko 'yaṁ paribhramati cakravat // 14.5
"Abandoning kinsfolk here, only to carry on at the next place, doing its performances, / This world is vulnerable indeed, as it rolls round and around like a wheel." //14.5//

ity evaṁ smaratas tasya babhūva niyatātmanaḥ /
kadalī-garbha-niḥsāraḥ saṁsāra iti niścayaḥ // 14.6 //
While he was recollecting thus, there grew in him, who was resolute to the core, / The conviction that saṁsāra was no more durable than the fragile heart of a banana plant. //14.6//

dvitīye tv āgate yāme so 'dvitīya-parākramaḥ /
divyaṁ lebhe paraṁ cakṣuḥ sarva-cakṣuṣmatāṁ varaḥ // 14.7 //
But with the coming of the second watch, he who in valiant effort was second to none / He who was most excellent among all possessed of eyes, realized the divine act of seeing, the ultimate eye. //14.7//

tatas tena sa divyena pariśuddhena cakṣuṣā /
dadarśa nikhilaṁ lokam ādarśa iva nirmale // 14.8 //
On that basis, by the means of that divine seeing, that fully cleansed organ of sight, / He saw the whole Universe as if in a spotless mirror. //14.8//

sattvānāṁ paśyatas tasya nikṛṣṭotkṛṣṭa-karmaṇām /
pracyutiṁ copapattiṁ ca vavṛdhe karuṇātmatā // 14.9 //
As he observed the relegation and promotion of living beings possessed of the karma / Of pulling down or pulling up, his inherent compassion waxed greater. //14.9//

ime duṣkṛta-karmāṇaḥ prāṇino yānti durgatim /
ime 'nye śubha-karmāṇaḥ pratiṣṭhante tri-piṣṭape // 14.10 //
"These creatures of deeds badly done go to a bad place; / These others, good-doers, abide in the triple heaven. //14.10//

upapannāḥ pratibhaye narake bhṛśa-dāruṇe /
amī duḥkhair bahu-vidhaiḥ pīḍyante kṛpaṇaṁ bata // 14.11 //
Deservedly finding themselves[1] in a horrible and terribly harsh hell, / The former individuals are with many kinds of sufferings lamentably oppressed – alas![2] //14.11//

pāyyante kvathitaṁ ke-cid agni-varṇam ayo-rasam /
āropyante ruvanto 'nye niṣṭapta-stambham āyasam // 14.12 //
Some are caused to imbibe a potion, brought to the boil, of smelted fire-colored metal[3]; / Ones who are different[4] are planted up a molten column of the metal – there, roaring, they are caused to grow.[5] //14.12//

---

[1] *Upa-√pad* means to come to, arrive at, enter, and at the same time (with locative) to be fit for. So the past participle *upapanna*, which is used in this verse and in connection with the other realms of saṁsāra, too, can be read as including an affirmation of karma – as wrong-doers, as do-gooders, or as ones in the middle, we pass through saṁsāra as befits our karma.

[2] From here to verse 20, the description is of experience in hell, the first of the five saṁsāric realms under investigation.

[3] In the hidden meaning, the fire-colored metal might be gold – symbolizing what is most valuable.

pacyante piṣṭavat ke-cid ayas-kumbhīṣv avāṅ-mukhāḥ /
dahyante karuṇaṁ ke-cid dīpteṣv aṅgāra-rāśiṣu // 14.13 //
Some are cooked like paste in cauldrons of the metal, their faces looking down;[6] / Some are consumed, piteously, on heaps of flaming coals.[7] //14.13//

ke-cit tīkṣṇair ayo-daṁṣṭrair bhakṣyante dāruṇaiḥ śvabhiḥ /
ke-cid dhṛṣṭair ayas-tuṇḍair vāyasair āyasair iva // 14.14 //
Some are chewed up, harshly, by keen hounds with teeth made of the metal, / Some are scavenged by the crowing *ayas-tuṇḍas*, 'Metal-Beaks' – as if by carrion crows, made of the metal.[8] //14.14//

ke-cid dāha-pariśrāntāḥ śīta-cchāyābhikāṅkṣiṇaḥ /
asi-pattra-vanaṁ nīlaṁ baddhā iva viśanty amī // 14.15 //
Some, tired of burning, go hankering after cool shade; / The dark forest, where leaves are swords, like slaves in chains these enter.[9] //14.15//

pāṭyante dāruvat ke-cit kuṭhārair baddha-bāhavaḥ /
duḥkhe 'pi na vipacyante karmabhir dhāritāsavaḥ // 14.16 //
Some, their arms in chains, are split, like wood by axes. / Even in such hardship the ripening of their karma is not completed; by dint of their actions, their life-breath is preserved. //14.16//

sukhaṁ syād iti yat karma kṛtaṁ duḥkha-nivṛttaye /
phalaṁ tasyedam avaśair duḥkham evopabhujyate // 14.17 //
The action taken with the thought that it might bring happiness, the deed that was done with a view to cessation of suffering, / Now has as its result, this, suffering itself, experienced by the helpless.[10] //14.17//

---

4 Ostensibly *anye* means "others" – some are caused to imbibe the metal, others are caused to mount a column of the metal. In the hidden meaning, all of us are caused to suffer, and ones among us who are different are caused to grow?

5 The causative of *ā-√ruh* can mean: 1. to cause to mount or ascend ; 2. to cause to grow, and hence, to plant. Thus, whereas ostensibly *āropyante* means "they were caused to mount" [the column] or "they were planted" [up the column], ironically *āropyante* might also mean "they were caused to grow."

6 In the hidden meaning, as the face looks down during sitting-meditation?

7 In the hidden meaning, like beginners in a meditation hall whose legs seem to be on fire?

8 In the hidden meaning, some bodhisattvas, when they are pecked at by harsh criticism, are able to turn that negative experience into something valuable?

9 In the hidden meaning, the dark forest might represent the Buddha's unfathomable dharma, and entering like a slave in chains might be the attitude of a practitioner beginning a 90-day retreat.

10 In the hidden meaning, the deed that was done, shortly after hearing of the Buddha's teaching of four noble truths, with an idealistic agenda, now has its result real understanding of the four noble truths, by those who are helpless – by those know what it means not to do?

sukhārtham aśubhaṁ kṛtvā ya ete bhṛśa-duḥkhitāḥ /
āsvādaḥ sa kim eteṣāṁ karoti sukham anv api // 14.18 //
These who, with a view to happiness, have acted impurely and are greatly pained: / Does that enjoyment do anything for them, even slightly, in the way of happiness?[11] //14.18//

hasadbhir yat kṛtaṁ karma kaluṣaṁ kaluṣātmabhiḥ /
etat pariṇate kāle krośadbhir anubhūyate // 14.19 //
That cruddy deed that was done, while laughing, by those whose nature was crud-encrusted,[12] / Is in the fullness of time relived by them while lamenting. //14.19//

yady eva pāpa-karmāṇaḥ paśyeyuḥ karmaṇāṁ phalam /
vameyur uṣṇaṁ rudhiraṁ marmasv abhihatā iva // 14.20 //
If only wrong-doers could see the result of their actions, / They might vomit warm blood as if they had been struck in a vital part. //14.20//

ime 'nye karmabhiś citraiś citta-vispanda-saṁbhavaiḥ /
tiryag-yonau vicitrāyām upapannās tapasvinaḥ // 14.21 //
These different ones, by various actions stemming from palpitations of the mind, / Fittingly find themselves, poor penitent wretches, in some form or other of non-upright, animal existence.[13] //14.21//

māṁsa-tvag-vāla-dantārthaṁ vairād api madād api /
hanyante kṛpaṇaṁ yatra bandhūnāṁ paśyatām api // 14.22 //
On account of their flesh, skin, hair and teeth, out of sheer aggression and also just for fun, / Here they are slaughtered, lamentably - even as their kind look on.[14] //14.22//

a-śaknuvanto 'py avaśāḥ kṣut-tarṣa-śrama-pīḍitāḥ /
go-'śva-bhūtāś ca vāhyante pratoda-kṣata-mūrtayaḥ // 14.23 //
Powerless and helpless, oppressed by hunger, thirst, and exhaustion, / As oxen and horses,[15] they are driven along, while goads injure their bodies. //14.23//

---

[11] Ostensibly the question is whether past indulgence in sensual pleasure led to lasting happiness or not? In the deeper meaning, is it possible truly to understand the four noble truths without passing, at least somewhat, through suffering rooted in self-existence?

[12] *Kaluṣātman* ostensibly means "those whose essence/nature is foul." But as the second half of a compound, *ātman* (essence, nature) can also mean the understanding, intellect or mind. The latter reading is more in line with the principle that nobody is inherently evil, though everybody is capable of doing evil deeds.

[13] From here to verse 26, the description is of experience in the world of animals, the second of the five saṁsāric realms under investigation. *Tiryag-yoni*, lit. "the womb/birth of one going horizontally," ostensibly means "born as an animal," but in the hidden meaning might ironically suggest bodhisattva-actions practiced in the horizontal plane, e.g. lying down, and performing prostrations.

[14] Ostensibly the description is of a scene during a hunt or animal sacrifice; in the hidden meaning, the scene might be a school playground.

[15] At the end of a compound *-bhūta* means 1. being, or 2. being like. Ostensibly Aśvaghoṣa is describing those who are oxen and horses; in the deeper reading, he might be describing bodhisattvas passing through a phase of being driven like an ox or a workhorse under a whip.

vāhyante gaja-bhūtāś ca balīyāṁso 'pi dur-balaiḥ /
aṅkuśa-kliṣṭa-mūrdhānas tāḍitāḥ pāda-pārṣṇibhiḥ // 14.24 //
As elephants, again, they are driven, though they are the mighty ones, by the weak / Who torment their heads with hooks, and beat them, with foot and heel. //14.24//

satsv apy anyeṣu duḥkheṣu duḥkhaṁ yatra viśeṣataḥ /
paraspara-virodhāc ca parādhīnatayaiva ca // 14.25 //
Though there are other sufferings too, suffering here arises especially / From competing with each other while in the very thick of subjection to the enemy.[16] //14.25//

kha-sthāḥ kha-sthair hi bādhyante jala-sthā jala-cāribhiḥ /
sthala-sthāḥ sthala-saṁsthais ca prāpya caivetaretaraiḥ // 14.26 //
For dwellers in emptiness are jostled by dwellers in emptiness,[17] dwellers in water are jostled by those for whom water is life, / And dwellers on land are jostled by those who stand with them on firm ground - even as they push one another forward. //14.26//

upapannās tathā ceme mātsaryākrānta-cetasaḥ /
pitṛ-loke nir-āloke kṛpaṇaṁ bhuñjate phalam // 14.27 //
And so these ones, likewise, find themselves fittingly[18] - with minds given over to dissatisfaction - / In the murky world of deceased ancestors, where, lamentably, they reap their reward.[19] //14.27//

sūcī-chidropama-mukhāḥ parvatopama-kukṣayaḥ /
kṣut-tarṣa-janitair duḥkhaiḥ pīḍyante duḥkha-bhāginaḥ // 14.28 //
With mouths like the eye of a needle and mountainous bellies,[20] / By sufferings born of hunger and thirst they are pained - suffering being their lot. //14.28//

puruṣo yadi jānīta mātsaryasyedṛśaṁ phalam /
sarvathā śibi-vad dadyāc charīrāvayavān api // 14.29 //
If a man knew that such was the result of dissatisfaction,[21] / He would by all means, like Śibi, yield up the limbs from his body as well.[22] //14.29//

---

[16] In the hidden meaning, the enemy might be ignorance.

[17] *Kha-sthāḥ*. Ostensible meaning: birds: Hidden meaning: Those who abide in practice of non-doing.

[18] *Upapannāḥ*. Again, the ostensible connotation is *deservedly* - hungry ghosts are born in a dark world as retribution for bad karma. In the less pessimistic hidden meaning, any of the five realms is a *fitting* place to atone for bad karma and to heap up good karma.

[19] From here to verse 31, the description is of experience in the world of the deceased ancestors (*pitṛ-loke*). "Deceased ancestors" ostensibly means hungry ghosts, or *pretas*, in the third of the five saṁsāric realms under investigation. In the hidden meaning, a deceased ancestor might mean a Zen patriarch, who is steeped in the noble truths of suffering which are so hard to fathom; hence the world is described as murky (*nir-āloke*).

[20] In the hidden meaning, with mouths (in a meditation hall) closed, and with well-developed centres.

[21] *Mātsarya*: 1. envy, jealousy (and hence selfishness or stinginess); 2. displeasure, dissatisfaction. The ostensible meaning is that people are reborn as hungry ghosts as a result of faults like envy, jealousy, or stinginess. In the hidden meaning, do we enter the world of Zen patriarchs by investigating, in the first instance, the first noble truth?

[22] The story of Śibi, as recounted in the Mahā-bhārata and the Rāmāyaṇa, is that the gods tested Śibi

āśayā samatikrāntā dhāryamāṇāḥ sva-karmabhiḥ /
labhante na hy amī bhoktum praviddhāny aśucīny api // 14.30 //
For, totally exceeded by expectation,[23] and constrained by their own actions,[24] / These ones are not permitted to eat any impure droppings at all.[25] //14.30//

ime 'nye naraka-prakhye garbha-saṁjñe 'śuci-hrade /
upapannā manuṣyeṣu duḥkham archanti jantavaḥ // 14.31 //
These different ones find themselves in a place that seems like hell,[26] a pool of impurity called "the insides";[27] / Fittingly, among human beings, they find themselves[28] as lowly creatures experiencing suffering.[29] //14.31//

32.[30] At first, even at the moment of birth, they are gripped by sharp hands, as if sharp swords were piercing them, at which they weep bitterly.

33. They are loved and cherished and guarded by their kindred who bring them up with every care, only to be defiled by their own various deeds as they pass from suffering to greater suffering.

34. And in this state the fools, obsessed with desire, are borne along in the ever-flowing stream, thinking all the more, 'this is to be done and this is to be done.'

---

by taking the form of a hawk and a pigeon. Chased by the hawk, the pigeon fell into the lap of King Śibi. Then the King proved his generosity by offering to let the hawk eat his own flesh, rather than eating the pigeon. In SN Canto 11, Ānanda refers to the story: "*Through tender love for living creatures Śibi gave his own flesh to a hawk./ He fell back from heaven, even after doing such a difficult deed.*" // *SN11.42* // In the hidden meaning, does yielding up one's limbs suggest undoing of undue muscular tension around the hips and shoulders?

[23] EHJ regarded this wording as suspect, given "the sense clearly being that they reach the extreme limit of starvation." Hence EHJ translated "*Reaching the limit of longing....*" Being totally surpassed (*samatikrāntāḥ*) by hope or by expectation (*āśayā*), however, seems to convey an ironic hidden sense of the contentment of mendicants who are able to find satisfaction in not much.

[24] Ostensible meaning: held back in the realm of hungry ghosts as a consequence of their own bad karma. Ironic meaning: being masters of self-regulation – as symbolized in Shōbōgenzō by a ring through the nose.

[25] Ostensibly this refers to the tradition that some hungry ghosts are cursed with an insatiable desire to feed on human excreta, but are unable to do so due to their small mouths and narrow throats. In the hidden meaning "impure droppings" (*praviddhāny aśucīni*) might refer, for example, to an offering of food that is impure because of not having been freely given.

[26] *Naraka-prakhye.* A place that seems like hell is not in fact hell – it just sometimes seems that way.

[27] *Garbha:* 1. a womb; 2. the inside, middle, interior of anything. The ostensible meaning is that we are born as human beings into the filthy pool which is our mother's womb. The hidden meaning might be that this human life, when we are truly inside of it (rather than aspiring, say, to the Pure Land of Akṣobhya Buddha), is not so pure.

[28] "Fittingly... they find themselves," again translates *upapannāḥ*.

[29] From here to verse 34, the description is of experience in the human world, the fourth in the five saṁsāric realms under investigation.

[30] From here we no longer have the original Sanskrit. The text which follows is based mainly on the English version which EH Johnston produced, referring to the Tibetan translation from the Sanskrit. It is based also – to a lesser extent – on the Chinese translation.

35. These others, who have accumulated merit, are born in heaven, and are terribly burned by the flames of sensual passion, as by a fire.[31]

36. And from there they fall, still not satiated with the objects of sense, with eyes turned upwards, their brilliance gone, and wretched at the fading of their garlands.

37. And as their lovers fall helplessly, the celestial nymphs regard them pitifully and catch their clothes with their hands.

38. Some nymphs look as if they were falling to earth with their ropes of pearls swaying, as they try to hold up their lovers falling miserably from the pavilions.

39. Others, wearing ornaments and garlands of many kinds and grieved at their fall into suffering, follow them with eyes unsteady with sympathy.

40. In their love for those who are falling, the troops of celestial nymphs beat their breasts with their hands and, distressed, as it were, with great affliction, remain attached to them.

41. The dwellers in Paradise fall distressed to earth, lamenting, "Alas, grove of Citraratha[32]! Alas, heavenly lake! Alas, Mandākinī[33]! Alas, beloved!"

42. Paradise, obtained by many labours, is uncertain and transitory, and such suffering as this is caused by separation from it.

43. Alas, inexorably this is the law of action in the world; this is the nature of the world, and yet they do not see it to be such.

44. Others, who have disjoined themselves from sensual passion, conclude in their minds that their station is eternal; yet they too fall miserably from heaven.

45. In the hells is excessive torture; among animals, eating each other; among the pretas, the suffering of hunger and thirst; among human beings, the suffering of longings;

46. But in the heavens also, when one is separated from what one loves, the suffering of rebirth is excessive. For the ever-wandering world of living beings, there is no place to settle in peace.

47. This stream of the cycle of existence has no support and is ever subject to death. Living beings, thus beset on all sides, find no resting-place."

---

[31] From here to verse 44, the description is of experience as a god in heaven, the fifth in the five saṁsāric realms under investigation.

[32] Citraratha, "Bright Chariot," is the name of the chief of the gandharvas who dwell, together with the celestial nymphs, in Indra's paradise.

[33] Mandākinī, (from *manda* + *añc*) "going or streaming slowly," is the name of an arm of the earthly Ganges but especially of the Ganges which is supposed to flow through heaven.

48. Thus with the divine eye he examined the five spheres of life and found in saṁsāra no essential core, just as no heartwood is found in a banana plant when it is cut open.

49. Then as the third watch of that night drew on, the best of those who understand meditation meditated on the real nature of this world:

50. "Alas! Living creatures obtain but toil; over and over again they are born, grow old, die, pass on and are reborn.

51. Further man's sight is veiled by passion and by the darkness of delusion, and from the excess of his blindness he does not know the way out of this great suffering."

52. After thus considering, he reflected in his mind, "What is it, truly, whose existence causes the approach of the suffering of old age and death[34]?"

53. Penetrating the truth to its core, he understood that old age and death are produced, when there is birth.[35]

54. He saw that head-ache is only possible when the head is already in existence; for when the birth of a tree has come to pass, only then can the felling of the tree take place.[36]

55. Then the thought again arose in him, "What does this birth proceed from?" Then he saw rightly that birth arises out of becoming.[37]

56. With his divine eyesight he saw becoming arising from karma – not from a Creator or from Nature or from a self or without a cause.

57. Just as, if the first knot in a bamboo is wisely cut, everything quickly comes into order, so his knowing advanced in proper order.

58. Thereon the sage applied his mind to determining the origin of becoming. Then he saw that the origin of becoming was in taking hold.[38]

59. This taking hold is taking hold in the areas of rules and rituals,[39] of desires,[40] of narratives of self,[41] and of views[42] – as when fire and fuel have taken hold.

---

[34] *Jarā-maraṇa-duḥkha:* the suffering of aging and death; link no. 12. Cf MMK26.8.
[35] *Jati:* birth; link no. 11. Cf MMK26.8.
[36] Cf. SN16.10: *Even when violent winds blow, trees do not shake that never sprouted.*
[37] *Bhava:* becoming, coming into existence; link no. 10. Cf MMK26.7.
[38] *Upādāna:* taking hold, clinging, attachment; link no. 9. Cf. MMK26.6.
[39] *Śila-vratopādāna:* clinging to good conduct and vows of practice, to virtue and vows.
[40] *Kāmopādāna:* clinging to sensual love or to desires.
[41] *Ātma-vādopādāna*: clinging to talk of self, to a doctrine based on self, to a personal narrative (as in post-modernism?). Clinging to one's own story.
[42] *Dṛṣṭy-upādāna*: clinging to a view. Cf. MMK26.6.

60. Then the thought occurred to him, "From what cause comes taking hold?" Thereon he recognized the causal grounds of taking hold to be thirsting.[43]

61. Just as the forest is set ablaze by a little fire, when the wind fans it, so thirsting gives rise to the vast faults of sensual passion and the rest.

62. Then he reflected, "From what does thirsting arise?" Thereon he concluded that the cause of thirsting is feeling.[44]

63. Overwhelmed by feelings, the world thirsts for the means of satisfying those feelings; for in the absence of physical thirst nobody would take pleasure in drinking water.

64. Then he again meditated, "What is the source of feeling?" He, who had transcended feeling, saw the cause of feeling to be in contact.[45]

65. Contact is explained as the uniting of the object, the sense and consciousness, whence feeling is produced – just as fire is produced from the uniting of the two rubbing sticks and fuel.

66. Next he considered that contact has a cause. Thereon he recognized the cause to lie in six senses.[46]

67. The blind man does not see physical forms, since his eye does not connect them with consciousness; if sight exists, the connection takes place. Therefore there is contact, when a sense exists.

68. Further he made up his mind to understand the origin of six senses. Thereon the knower of causes knew the cause to be psycho-physicality.[47]

69. Just as the leaf and the stalk are only said to exist when there is a shoot in existence, so six senses only arise where psycho-physicality has arisen.

70. Then the thought occurred to him, "What is the cause of psycho-physicality?" Thereon he, who had passed to the further side of knowledge, knew its origin to lie in divided consciousness.[48]

---

[43] *Tṛṣṇā:* thirsting; link no. 8. Cf MMK26.6.
[44] *Vedanā:* feeling; link no. 7. Cf MMK26.5.
[45] *Sparśa* or *saṁsparśaḥ:* contact; link no. 6. Cf MMK26.3.
[46] *Ṣaḍ-āyatana:* six senses; link no. 5. Cf MMK26.3.
[47] *Nāma-rūpa:* psycho-physicality, or (more literally but less usefully) "name and form"; link no. 4. Cf MMK26.2.
[48] *Vijñāna:* consciousness, or divided consciousness; link no. 3. *Vi-√jñā* means to distinguish, discern, or discriminate. The prefix *vi-* is thought to derive from *dvi*, meaning "in two parts" as opposed to *sam-*, which expresses wholeness or union – as for example in *samādhi.* Cf MMK26.2.

71. When divided consciousness arises, psycho-physicality is produced. When the development of the seed is completed, the sprout assumes a bodily form.

72. Next he considered, "From what does divided consciousness come into being?" Then he knew that divided consciousness is produced by supporting itself on psycho-physicality."[49]

73. And so, having understood the order of causality, he thought it over; his mind turned it over this way and that way and did not turn aside to other thoughts.

74. Divided consciousness is the causal grounds from which arises psycho-physicality. Psycho-physicality, again, is the basis of divided consciousness.

75. Just as the coracle carries the bloke who carries the coracle, so divided consciousness and psycho-physicality are causes of each other.

76. Just as a red-hot iron causes grass to blaze and just as blazing grass makes an iron red-hot, of such a kind is their mutual causality.

77. Thus he understood that from divided consciousness arises psycho-physicality, from which originate senses, and from senses arises contact.

78. But out of contact, he knew feeling to be born; out of feeling, thirsting; out of thirsting, taking hold; out of taking hold, again, becoming.

79. From becoming arises birth, from birth he knew aging and death to arise. He truly realized that the birth of living beings, in new spheres in the cycle of saṁsāra, arises from causal grounds.

80. Then this conclusion came firmly on him, that from the ending of birth, old age and death are ended; that from the ending of becoming, birth itself is ended; and that becoming ends through the ending of taking hold.

81. Further, taking hold is ended through the ending of thirsting; when there is no such thing as feeling, there is no such thing as thirsting; if contact is ended, feeling does not come about; from the non-existence of six senses, contact is ended.

82. Similarly, if psycho-physicality is well and truly ended, six senses everywhere are ended too; but psycho-physicality is ended through the ending of divided consciousness, and divided consciousness is ended through the ending of doings.[50]

---

[49] This investigation of the circularity around links 3 and 4, divided consciousness and psycho-physicality, is also seen in Nāgārjuna's version in MMK chap. 26 (see MMK26.2-4). Except that Aśvaghoṣa has first gone back against the grain but now goes forwards with the grain, whereas Nāgārjuna starts going with the grain and then doubles back.

[50] *Saṁskārāḥ*; link no. 2. Cf MMK26.1 and 26.10. MMK26.10 provides a key to the translation of *saṁskārāḥ*, which for many hundreds of years has been a stumbling block in China and Japan. In

83. Again, the great seer understood that doings are inhibited by the complete absence of ignorance.[51] Therefore he knew properly what was to be known and stood out before the world as the Awakened One, the Buddha.[52]

Nāgārjuna's statement *saṁsāra-mūlaṁ saṁskārān avidvān saṁskaroty ataḥ* ("Thus rooted in saṁsāra the ignorant one does do doings"), both *saṁskārān* (doings) and *saṁskaroti* (does do) are from *saṁ-s-√kṛ*, which means to do, to make or put together, to confect, to concoct, to fabricate. In short, *saṁ-s-√kṛ* means to do, and *saṁskārān* does not mean (as the Chinese translation 行 indicates) "action" in general. Saṁskāras are doings, or fabrications, i.e. not spontaneous and natural actions, but works of conditioning fabricated out of ignorance.

[51] *Avidyā:* ignorance, unwittingness; link no. 1. Cf MMK26.1.

[52] For reference, here in full is ch. 26 of Nāgārjuna's mūla-madhyamaka-kārikā:
punar-bhavāya saṁskārān avidyā-nivṛtas tridhā |
abhisaṁskurute yāṁs tair gatiṁ gacchati karmabhiḥ ||MMK26.1||
vijñānaṁ saṁniviśate saṁskāra-pratyayaṁ gatau |
saṁniviṣṭe 'tha vijñāne nāma-rūpaṁ niṣicyate ||2||
niṣikte nāma-rūpe tu ṣaḍāyatana-saṁbhavaḥ |
ṣaḍāyatanam āgamya saṁsparśaḥ saṁpravartate ||3||
cakṣuḥ pratītya rūpaṁ ca samanvāhāram eva ca |
nāma-rūpaṁ pratītyaivaṁ vijñānaṁ saṁpravartate ||4||
saṁnipātas trayāṇāṁ yo rūpa-vijñāna-cakṣuṣām |
sparśaḥ saḥ tasmāt sparśāc ca vedanā saṁpravartate ||5||
vedanā-pratyayā tṛṣṇā vedanārthaṁ hi tṛṣyate |
tṛṣyamāṇa upādānam upādatte catur-vidham ||6||
upādāne sati bhava upādātuḥ pravartate |
syād dhi yady anupādāno mucyeta na bhaved bhavaḥ ||7||
pañca skandhāḥ sa ca bhavaḥ bhavāj jātiḥ pravartate |
jarā-maraṇa-duḥkhādi śokāḥ sa-paridevanāḥ ||8||
daurmanasyam upāyāsā jāter etat pravartate |
kevalasyaivam etasya duḥkha-skandhasya saṁbhavaḥ ||9||
saṁsāra-mūlaṁ saṁskārān avidvān saṁskaroty ataḥ |
avidvān kārakas tasmān na vidvāṁs tattva-darśanāt ||10||
avidyāyāṁ niruddhāyāṁ saṁskārāṇām asaṁbhavaḥ |
avidyāyā nirodhas tu jñānasyāsyaiva bhāvanāt ||11||
tasya tasya nirodhena tat tan nābhipravartate |
duḥkha-skandhaḥ kevalo 'yam evaṁ samyaṅ nirudhyate ||12||

[The original canto continues to verse 108]*

The 14th canto, titled "The Transcendent Total Awakening," in an epic tale of awakened action.

* [English translation updated Spring 2023, with *saṁskārān* translated as "fabrications"] Fabrications (2), on the way to further becoming (10), one impeded by unwittingness (1) re-fabricates (2) in three ways and by these doings does go to a painful destination. || Into the painful realm, conditioned by fabrications (2), settles divided consciousness (3). Then, where divided consciousness (3) has settled, psycho-physicality (4) seeps in. || But where psycho-physicality (4) has seeped in, there is the coming into being of six sense spheres (5). Six sense spheres (5) having arrived, there occurs contact (6).|| Depending on eye (5), on physicality (4), and on the bringing of the two together – depending in other words on psycho-physicality (4) – divided consciousness (3) occurs.|| Whatever conjunction there is of the three – physicality (4), consciousness (3) and eye (5) -- that is contact (6); and from that contact (6) there occurs feeling (7). || Conditioned by feeling (7), there is thirsting (8) – for the object of feeling (7) is thirsted after (8). While thirsting (8) is going on, clinging (9) takes hold (9) in the four ways. || Where there is clinging (9), the becoming (10) arises of the clinger (9), for if free of clinging (9) he would be liberated, and becoming (10) would not come into being (10). || The five aggregates are just being (10). Grounded in being (10), rebirth (11) happens. The suffering and suchlike of ageing and death – sorrows, accompanied by bewailing and complaining; || downheartedness, troubles (12) – because of rebirth (11), all this happens. Thus there is the coming into being of this whole aggregate of suffering. || In this way the one who fails to witness, rooted in cyclic existence, fabricates fabrications. || The unwitting one is thus the doer; the one who witnesses, thanks to the realising of reality, is not. || Where unwittingness is being stopped, fabrications do not happen. But stopping of unwittingness is thanks to practice, which belongs to just this understanding, of letting happen. || With the stopping of each, the others no longer carry on. This whole aggregate of suffering in this way is well and truly stopped.

Saundarananda
of
Aśvaghoṣa

Canto 1: kapilavāstu-varṇanaḥ
A Portrait of Kapilavāstu

// om namo buddhāya //

Om! Homage to the Buddha

Introduction

The opening canto of Saundarananda parallels the opening canto of Buddhacarita; both cantos reflect a certain ambivalence on Aśvaghoṣa's part towards the ancient Indian society into which the Buddha and his brother Nanda were born. On the one hand, being born into an aristocratic family of the kṣatriya cast, in a thriving city, was very advantageous for the development of the two princes. On the other hand, whenever Aśvaghoṣa writes of the views and practices of brahmins and ascetics, an ironic subtext is discernible not far below the surface. Ostensibly, then, the present canto presents an idealized portrait of the city of Kapilavāstu. But when we dig for hidden meaning, there is evidence also that Aśvaghoṣa saw ancient Indian culture and society as leaving much to be desired in terms of its irrational beliefs, immoderate practices, social injustice, and so on.

gautamaḥ kapilo nāma munir dharma-bhṛtāṁ varaḥ /
babhūva tapasi śrāntaḥ kākṣīvān iva gautamaḥ // 1.1 //
A sage named Kapila Gautama, an outstanding upholder of dharma, / Became as consumed in ascetic practice as was Kākṣīvat Gautama.[1] // 1.1 //

aśiśriyad yaḥ satataṁ dīptaṁ kāśyapavat tapaḥ /
āśiśrāya ca tad-vṛddhau siddhiṁ kāśyapavat parām // 1.2 //
Ceaselessly he shone his light, like Kāśyapa the sun, on blazing asceticism; / And in promoting that asceticism he pushed himself, like Kāśyapa the sage,[2] to extreme achievement. // 1.2 //

havīṁṣi yaś ca svātmārthaṁ gām adhukṣad vasiṣṭhavat /
tapaḥ-śiṣṭeṣu śiṣyeṣu gām adhukṣad vasiṣṭhavat // 1.3 //
For the offerings he served himself, he milked a cow, like Vasiṣṭha. / In schooling his disciples in asceticism, he milked a cow, like Vasiṣṭha.[3] // 1.3 //

---

[1] Kākṣīvat Gautama was an ancient Indian exemplar of ascetic practice – the kind of practice from which the Buddha turned away (see SN3.2).

[2] Kāśyapa is a patronym from *kaśyapa*, 'having black teeth,' which is (1) a name of the sun, and (2) the name of one of the seven great seers of ancient India, supposed author of several hymns of the Ṛg-veda.

[3] Vasiṣṭha, 'the most wealthy,' is the name of another ancient Indian seer, celebrated in the vedas as the owner of the mythical cow of plenty. *Gām* means a cow, and at the same time the earth, as the milk-cow of kings. The verse sounds like praise but is ambiguous – suggesting either that Vasiṣṭha's practice was "self-serving" in that it seemed to do itself, naturally, spontaneously, effortlessly; or else "self-serving" in that he served himself, and exploited others in the process. Aśvaghoṣa's real intention may be the latter, but in his undermining of Brahminical and Buddhist views, he is always circumspect, relying on irony rather than polemics.

māhātmyād dīrghatapaso yo dvitīya ivābhavat /
tṛtīya iva yaś cābhūt kāvyāṅgirasayor dhiyā // 1.4 //
In high-mindedness, he was like a second Dīrgha-tapas;[4] / And he was like a third in the mould of Kāvya[5] and Āṅgiras,[6] in religious thought. // 1.4 //

tasya vistīrṇa-tapasaḥ pārśve himavataḥ śubhe /
kṣetraṁ cāyatanaṁ caiva tapasām āśramo 'bhavat // 1.5 //
On a bright slope of the Himālayas this man steeped in ascetic practice / Had his ashram, the domain and the very seat of ascetic practices. // 1.5 //

cāru-vīrut-taru-vanaḥ prasnigdha-mṛdu-śadvalaḥ /
havir-dhūma-vitānena yaḥ sadābhra ivābabhau // 1.6 //
Wooded with charming shrubs and trees and abounding in lush, soft grass, / It was so thick[7] with sacrificial smoke that it constantly resembled a raincloud. // 1.6 //

mṛdubhiḥ saikataiḥ snigdhaiḥ kesarāstara-pāṇḍubhiḥ /
bhūmi-bhāgair asaṁkīrṇaiḥ sāṅgarāga ivābhavat // 1.7 //
With soft, sandy, and smooth soil, made yellowish white by a covering of *kesara* blossoms, / And divided into areas, with no commingling,[8] it was like a body painted with cosmetic pigments. // 1.7 //

śucibhis tīrtha-saṁkhyātaiḥ pāvanair bhāvanair api /
bandhumān iva yas tasthau sarobhiḥ sasaroruhaiḥ // 1.8 //
Pure, esteemed for their sacred presence,[9] edifying and promoting welfare,[10] / Like friends, were the lakes it stood among – fluent and bearing lotuses. // 1.8 //

---

[4] Dīrgha-tapas, 'performing long penances,' is the name of several ancient Indian seers.

[5] Kāvya is the patronymic of the ancient sage Uśanas, teacher of the *asuras*, who presides over the planet Venus.

[6] Another of the seven great seers, author of the hymns of the *Ṛg-veda*.

[7] A play on the word *vitāna*, which means (1) 'out of tune,' dejected, empty, dull; (2) great extent, heap, abundance; (3) an oblation, sacrifice.

[8] *Asaṁkīrṇaiḥ* means not mixed, not adulterated, not polluted, not impure, not born of a mixed marriage. Beneath a camouflage of *kesara* flowers, Aśvaghoṣa may be alluding, always with due circumspection, to traditional Bhramanical conceptions around caste.

[9] EH Johnston translated *tīrtha-saṁkhyātaiḥ* "famed as places of pilgrimage." *Tīrtha* means a passage, way, ford, stairs for landing or for descent into a river, bathing-place, place of pilgrimage on the banks of sacred streams. Is there a hidden connotation of the *tīrthika*, the "way-maker" or sectarian? In the Discourse that Set the Dharma-Wheel Rolling, the Buddha says "*There is no room here for those who have gone forth as sectarians*" (*bhūmir na cātra para-tīrthika niḥsṛtānāṁ; Lalita-vistara*).

[10] The description of the lakes as *bhāvana*, used as an adjective (lit. "causing [an effect] to happen," hence "promoting welfare") presages the Buddha's exhortation, in SN Cantos 15 & 16, that Nanda should cause pollutants to come out in the wash, by the means of *bhāvanā*, used as a verbal noun ("practice of letting happen"). See SN15.5 and 16.5. It might be a strong early hint of the teaching of Buddha that Aśvaghoṣa wants to emphasize.

paryāpta-phala-puṣpābhiḥ sarvato vana-rājibhiḥ /
śuśubhe vavṛdhe caiva naraḥ sādhanavān iva // 1.9 //
With abundant flowers and fruits beautifying the forests all around it, / It shone and it flourished, like a man furnished with a means. // 1.9 //

nīvāra-phala-saṁtuṣṭaiḥ svasthaiḥ śāntair anutsukaiḥ /
ākīrṇo 'pi tapo-bhṛdbhiḥ śūnyaśūnya ivābhavat // 1.10 //
Content to feed on wild rice and fruit, the ascetics were self-abiding, inhibited, and retiring. / Though the ashram was full of them, it seemed to be utterly empty. // 1.10 //

agnīnāṁ hūyamānānāṁ śikhināṁ kūjatām api /
tīrthānāṁ cābhiṣekeṣu śuśruve tatra nisvanaḥ // 1.11 //
The sound of the fires receiving offerings, of the peacocks with their crested heads uttering their repetitive cry,[11] / And of the sacred bathing places, during ablutions,[12] was all that one heard there. // 1.11 //

virejur hariṇā yatra suptā medhyāsu vediṣu /
salājair mādhavī-puṣpair upahārāḥ kṛtā iva // 1.12 //
The stags there, their manes beautifully braided,[13] on undefiled elevations fit to be sacrificial altars, / Seemed as though, complete with puffy rice and *mādhavi* flowers, they had been prepared as religious offerings. // 1.12 //

api kṣudra-mṛgā yatra śāntāś ceruḥ samaṁ mṛgaiḥ /
śaraṇyebhyas tapasvibhyo vinayaṁ śikṣitā iva // 1.13 //
Even lesser creatures moved there in the same subdued[14] manner as the stags, / As if from their ascetic protectors they had learned the rules of discipline. // 1.13 //

saṁdigdhe 'py apunar-bhāve viruddheṣv āgameṣv api /
pratyakṣiṇa ivākurvaṁs tapo yatra tapodhanāḥ // 1.14 //
Even in the face of a precarious immunity to rebirth and notwithstanding inconsistencies in their time-honored texts, / There and then, as if seeing with their own eyes,[15] the great ascetics practiced asceticism. // 1.14 //

---

[11] A sardonic allusion to the chanting of the ascetics with their dreadlocked hair-dos.

[12] Or did one hear, in a hidden meaning, the noise of sectarianism, being expressed during religious bathing? See note to verse 8, on *tīrtha*. The meanings of *abhiṣeka* include consecrating (by sprinkling water), religious bathing, and bathing of a divinity to whom worship is offered.

[13] The ostensible meaning of *suptāḥ* is asleep. At the same time SED gives *supta* (fr. *su + ptā*) as "having beautiful braids of hair." So on the surface Aśvaghoṣa is describing a peaceful scene (EHJ: "*the spotted deer, asleep in the enclosures sacred to worship...*"). But below the surface, Aśvaghoṣa is maybe continuing to poke fun at ascetic stags with their big hair.

[14] *Śāntāḥ*, "pacified" or "subdued," means in other words stilted. Aśvaghoṣa seems to be making fun of unduly careful practice – the result of trying to be mindful.

[15] The key word is *iva*, "as if." Aśvaghoṣa may be damning the great ascetics with faint praise.

yatra sma mīyate brahma kaiś-cit kaiś-cin na mīyate /
kāle nimīyate somo na cākāle pramīyate // 1.15 //
There some prayed to Brahma; none suffered the frustration of losing his way; / The *soma*,[16] at the right moment, was measured out; and nobody, at a random moment, came to nothing.[17] // 1.15 //

nirapekṣāḥ śarīreṣu dharme yatra sva-buddhayaḥ/
saṁhṛṣṭā iva yatnena tāpasās tepire tapaḥ // 1.16 //
There, each disregarding his body, but having his own view with regard to dharma, / And almost bristling with zeal, the ascetics set about their ascetic practice of asceticism. // 1.16 //

śrāmyanto munayo yatra svargāyodyukta-cetasaḥ /
tapo-rāgeṇa dharmasya vilopam iva cakrire // 1.17 //
There the toiling sages, hearts straining heavenward, / Seemed by their passion for asceticism almost to do dharma a mischief. // 1.17 //

atha tejasvi-sadanaṁ tapaḥ-kṣetraṁ tam āśramam /
ke-cid ikṣvākavo jagmū rājaputrā vivatsavaḥ // 1.18 //
Now, to that ashram, that seat of intensity, that domain of austerity, / There came certain sons of Ikṣvāku,[18] royal princes, wishing to stay. // 1.18 //

suvarṇa-stambha-varṣmāṇaḥ siṁhoreskā mahābhujāḥ /
pātraṁ śabdasya mahataḥ śriyāṁ ca vinayasya ca // 1.19 //
Tall they were like golden columns, lion-chested, strong-armed, / Worthy of their great name and royal insignia and good upbringing. // 1.19 //

arharūpā hy anarhasya mahātmānaś calātmanaḥ /
prājñāḥ prajñā-vimuktasya bhrātṛvyasya yavīyasaḥ // 1.20 //
For deserving were they, where undeserving was he. Big-minded were they, where fickle-minded was he. / And bright were they, where brainless was he: their younger half-brother. // 1.20 //

mātṛ-śulkād upagatāṁ te śriyaṁ na viṣehire
rarakṣuś ca pituḥ satyaṁ, yasmāc chiśriyire vanam // 1.21 //
The royal authority that had come to him, as his mother's bride-price, they had not usurped;[19] / Rather, keeping their father's promise, they had retreated to the forest. // 1.21 //

---

[16] *Soma* is an intoxicating liquor, squeezed from the stalks of the climbing *soma* plant, and offered in libations to ancient Hindu gods. See also SN2.31.

[17] Each line contains a play on the ambiguity of *mīyate*, which is one passive form from two different roots: *√mī* (lose one's way, perish, come to nothing) and *√ma* (measure out, pray). Randomly coming to nothing may be understood as an ironic expression of nirvāṇa.

[18] Ikṣvāku, from *ikṣu* 'sugar cane,' was the first king of the solar dynasty which bears his name. Many royal families in India, including the Buddha's family, traced their lineages back to him.

teṣaṁ munir upādhyāyo gautamaḥ kapilo 'bhavat /
guru-gotrād ataḥ kautsās te bhavanti sma gautamāḥ // 1.22 //
The sage Kapila Gautama became their preceptor; / And so, from the guru's surname, those Kautsas became Gautamas[20] – // 1.22 //

eka-pitror yathā bhrātroḥ pṛthag-guru-parigrahāt /
rāma evābhavad gārgyo vāsubhadro 'pi gautamaḥ // 1.23 //
Just as, though they were brothers born of one father, because they had different gurus / Rāma became a Gārgya and Vāsubhadra a Gautama. // 1.23 //

śākavṛkṣa-praticchannaṁ vāsaṁ yasmāc ca cakrire /
tasmād ikṣvāku-vaṁsyās te bhuvi śākyā iti smṛtāḥ // 1.24 //
And since they made a dwelling concealed among *śāka* trees, / Therefore those descendants of Ikṣvāku were known on earth as Śākyas.[21] // 1.24 //

sa teṣāṁ gautamaś cakre sva-vaṁsa-sadṛsīḥ kriyāḥ /
munir ūrdhvaṁ kumārasya sagarasyeva bhārgavaḥ // 1.25 //
Gautama performed services for them as for his own sons, / Like the Bhārgava sage later did for the child-prince Sagara;[22] // 1.25 //

kaṇvaḥ śākuntalasyeva bharatasya tarasvinaḥ /
vālmīkir iva dhīmāṁś ca dhīmator maithileyayoḥ // 1.26 //
Like Kaṇva did for Śākuntala's son, the intrepid Bharata;[23] / And like the inspired Vālmīki did for the inspired twin sons of Maithili.[24] // 1.26 //

tad vanaṁ muninā tena taiś ca kṣatriya-puṁgavaiḥ /
śāntāṁ guptāṁ ca yugapad brahma-kṣatra-śriyaṁ dadhe // 1.27 //
That forest, through the sage, and through those warrior heroes, / Radiated tranquility and security – the majesty of the *brahmin* and of the *kṣatriya*, in one yoke. // 1.27 //

---

[19] *Vi-ṣah* means (1) to overpower, and (2) to endure. Either meaning could apply here: they did not overthrow him, or they could not endure his sovereignty.

[20] I.e. the original surname of the Buddha's ancestors was Kautsa.

[21] Hence the Buddha's name Śākyamuni, "Sage of the Śākyas."

[22] Sa-gara, literally "With Poison," is the name of a great solar dynasty king brought up in the ashram of a Bhārgava sage named Aurva, who intervened after Sagara's mother was poisoned by a rival queen. The story is told in Book 3 of the *Mahā-bhārata.*

[23] The story of how Kanva brought up in his ashram Bharata (the son of King Duṣyanta and his wife Śākuntala) is originally told in the *Mahā-bhārata.* But the story is best known through Kālidāsa's play *The Recognition of Śākuntala.* See also verse 36.

[24] Along with the *Mahā-bhārata*, the other great Sanskrit epic of ancient Indian history is the *Rāmāyaṇa*, *Rāma's Journey*, the authorship of which is attributed to Vālmīki. Maithili, or the princess of Mithila, refers to Sita, Rāma's wife, esteemed in India as a standard-setter for wifely and womanly virtues. The final book of the *Rāmāyaṇa* describes how Rāma, bowing to public opinion, banishes Maithili to the forest, where the sage Vālmīki takes her into his ashram. Here the princess gives birth to twin boys, Lava and Kuśa, who become pupils of Vālmīki and are brought up in ignorance of their royal identity. Vālmīki composes the *Rāmāyaṇa* and teaches Lava and Kuśa to sing it.

ath' oda-kalaśaṁ gṛhya teṣāṁ vṛddhi-cikīrṣayā /
muniḥ sa viyad utpatya tān uvāca nṛpātmajān // 1.28 //
One day, while holding a jug of water, in his desire to nurture the princes' growth / The sage went up, into the air. Then he said to them: // 1.28 //

yā patet kalaśād asmād akṣayya-salilān mahīm /
dhārā tām anatikramya mām anveta yathā kramam // 1.29 //
"There will fall to earth from this flowing jug, whose flowing is unbreakable, / A line of drops: Do not overstep this mark, as in step you follow me." // 1.29 //

tataḥ paramam ity uktvā śirobhiḥ praṇipatya ca /
rathān āruruhuḥ sarve śīghra-vāhān alaṁkṛtān // 1.30 //
"Yes!" they said to this, and respectfully bowed, letting their heads fall forward. / Then all went up, onto chariots that were swiftly drawn, and well prepared. // 1.30 //

tataḥ sa tair anugataḥ syandana-sthair nabho-gataḥ /
tad āśrama-mahī-prāntaṁ paricikṣepa vāriṇā // 1.31 //
So they followed him in the flow,[25] while, walking on air, / The ends of the earth of that ashram he sprinkled with water. // 1.31 //

aṣṭāpadam ivālikhya nimittaiḥ surabhī-kṛtam /
tān uvāca muniḥ sthitvā bhūmi-pāla-sutān idam // 1.32 //
He set out a plan like a chessboard, like an eightfold plan, revealed by signs;[26] / Then the sage, standing still, spoke thus to those offspring of the guardians of the earth: // 1.32 //

asmin dhārā-parikṣipte nemi-cihnita-lakṣaṇe /
nirmimīdhvaṁ puraṁ yūyaṁ mayi yāte triviṣṭapam // 1.33 //
"Within this sprinkled line of drops, wherein your wheels have left a mark, / You are to build a city, when I am gone to heaven." // 1.33 //

---

[25] *Syandana-sthaiḥ*, translated here as "in the flow," ostensibly means "remaining in their chariots." But *syandana* is originally an *-na* neuter action noun meaning "moving on swiftly, running (as a chariot)" and hence a chariot. *Syandana* can also carry a liquid connotation, meaning liquefying or dissolving, which goes with the sense of water flowing drop by drop. The whole description is ostensibly of a fantastic or miraculous episode. In the hidden meaning, the suggestion is of action, moment by moment, that seems spontaneously to do itself.

[26] "Sign" is the first of several senses of *nimitta* used by Aśvaghoṣa in Saundara-nanda. *Nimitta* is a key word in Canto 16, where the Buddha uses it in the context of describing sitting practice as "letting happen" (*bhāvanā*). This sitting practice is the embodiment of the threefold *śīla*, twofold *samādhi*, and threefold *prajñā* which constitute the noble eightfold path. In some sense, then, this verse can be read as autobiographical on Aśvaghoṣa's part – his intention may be to reveal to us, not so directly but by indirect prompting via clues and signs, a way of practice that leads towards the cessation of suffering.

tataḥ kadā-cit te vīrās tasmin pratigate munau /
babhramur yauvanoddāmā gajā iva niraṅkuśaḥ // 1.34 //
Thereafter those lads, when in time the sage passed away, / Roamed about in their unbridled youth like elephants unchecked by a driver's hook. // 1.34 //

baddha-godhāṅgulī-vāṇā hasta-viṣṭhita-kārmukāḥ /
śar-ādhmāta-mahā-tūṇā vyāyatābaddha-vāsasaḥ // 1.35 //
[They roamed about] with bows in hand and leather-clad fingers on arrows, / Shafts causing sizeable quivers to swell, feathers preened and fastened on.[27] // 1.35 //

jijñāsamānā nāgeṣu kauśalaṁ śvāpadeṣu ca /
anucakrur vana-sthasya dauṣmanter deva-karmaṇaḥ // 1.36 //
Wishing to test their mettle among the elephants and big cats, / They emulated the god-like deeds of the forest-dwelling son of Duṣyanta.[28] // 1.36 //

tān dṛṣṭvā prakṛtiṁ yātān vṛddhān vyāghra-śiśūn iva /
tāpasās tad-vanaṁ hitvā himavantaṁ siṣevire // 1.37 //
Seeing their natural character emerge as those lads grew, like tiger cubs, / The ascetics abandoned that forest and retreated to the Himālayas. // 1.37 //

tatas tad-āśrama-sthānaṁ śūnyaṁ taiḥ śūnya-cetasaḥ /
paśyanto manyunā taptā vyālā iva niśaśvasuḥ // 1.38 //
Then, seeing the ashram [without ascetics,] desolate, the princes were desolate in their hearts. / In the red-hot anger of their indignation, they hissed like snakes. // 1.38 //

atha te puṇya-karmāṇaḥ pratyupasthita-vṛddhayaḥ /
tatra taj-jñair upākhyātān avāpur mahato nidhīn // 1.39 //
In time, through good conduct, they came to a maturity / In which they could obtain the great treasures that are disclosed through acts of knowing them. // 1.39 //

alaṁ dharmārtha-kāmānāṁ nikhilānām avāptaye /
nidhayo naika-vidhayo bhūrayas te gatārayaḥ // 1.40 //
Sufficient for full enjoyment of dharma, wealth, and pleasure;[29] / Abundant; and of many kinds: these were treasures beyond the reach of enemies. // 1.40 //

---

[27] *Vāsas* means (1) clothes, and (2) [in compounds] the feathers of an arrow.

[28] The son of Duṣyanta means Bharata, legendary founder of the Indian nation and chief protagonist of the *Mahā-bhārata* – the same intrepid Bharata mentioned in verse 26. Act 7 of Kālidāsa's play *The Recognition of Śakuntala* has the boy playing roughly with a baby lion, commanding the lion to open its jaws because he wishes to count its teeth.

[29] Dharma, wealth, and pleasure are three of the four aims of human existence (*puruṣārtha*) originally discussed in Book 12 of the *Mahā-bhārata*. The fourth aim is the aim that Aśvaghoṣa himself considered paramount: liberation or release (*mokṣa*) – see SN18.63.

tatas tat-pratilambhāc ca pariṇāmāc ca karmaṇaḥ /
tasmin vāstuni vāstu-jñāḥ puraṁ śrīman nyaveśayan // 1.41 //
On the grounds of what they thus acquired, and of the fading influence of their past karma, / They who knew building, at that site, founded a splendid city. // 1.41 //

sarid-vistīrṇa-parikhaṁ spaṣṭāñcita-mahāpatham /
śaila-kalpa-mahā-vapraṁ girivrajam ivāparam // 1.42 //
It had a moat as broad as a river, a main street that straightened and curved, / And great ramparts rising like mountains, as if it were another Giri-vraja.[30] // 1.42 //

pāṇḍurāṭṭāla-sumukhaṁ suvibhaktāntar-āpaṇam /
harmya-mālā-parikṣiptaṁ kukṣiṁ himagirer iva // 1.43 //
With its fine frontage of white watchtowers, and a well-apportioned central market / Overlooked by crescents of large houses, it was like a Himālayan valley. // 1.43 //

veda-vedāṅga-viduṣas tasthuṣaḥ ṣaṭsu karmasu /
śāntaye vṛddhaye caiva yatra viprān ajījapan // 1.44 //
Brahmins versed in the Vedas and Vedāṅgas,[31] and engaged in the six occupations,[32] / There they caused to pray, for peace and for prosperity. // 1.44 //

tad-bhūmer abhiyoktṝṇāṁ prayuktān vinivṛttaye /
yatra svena prabhāvena bhṛtya-daṇḍān ajījapan // 1.45 //
The regular soldiers[33] they employed there to repel assailants from their territory / They caused, with their sovereign power, to be victorious in battle. // 1.45 //

cāritra-dhana-saṁpannān salajjān dīrgha-darśinaḥ /
arhato 'tiṣṭhipan yatra śūrān dakṣān kuṭumbinaḥ // 1.46 //
Householders of character and means, who were modest, far-sighted, / Worthy, stout and able, they caused to settle there. // 1.46 //

vyastais tais-tair guṇair yuktān mati-vāg-vikramādibhiḥ /
karmasu pratirūpeṣu sacivāṁs tān nyayūyujan // 1.47 //
Individuals possessed of particular strong points such as thinking, talking, and taking steps, / They installed in corresponding offices as counsellors and ministers. // 1.47 //

---

[30] Giri-vraja was the capital of the ancient kingdom of Magadha. The city, which is also mentioned in SN3.15 as a place the enlightened Buddha frequented, is located in a valley surrounded by five rocky hills; hence the name Giri-vraja, or "Mountain-Fenced." It was also known in Sanskrit as Rāja-gṛha, "King's House," which is thought to be the derivation of the name of the city of Rajgir in the modern Indian state of Bihar (= Land of Vihāras).

[31] Vedāṅgas, "limbs of the Vedas," are teachings auxiliary to original works like the *Ṛg-veda* which go back to before, or at least to the very beginning of, Āryan migrations into northern India.

[32] In India's ancient caste system, six occupations were reserved for brahmins of the priestly caste: (1) teaching and (2) studying the Vedas; (3) offering and (4) officiating at sacrifices; (5) giving and (6) accepting gifts.

[33] *Bhṛtya-daṇḍān. Bhṛtya* means to be maintained, a servant (see also note to SN2.33). *Daṇḍa* means rod, embodied power, army. EHJ: *"their military forces."*

vasumadbhir avibhrāntair alaṁ-vidyair avismitaiḥ /
yad babhāse naraiḥ kīrṇaṁ mandaraḥ kinnarair iva // 1.48 //
Thronged by men who were wealthy but not wanton, and cultured but not conceited, / [The city] seemed like Mt. Mandara,[34] thronged by *kiṁnaras*.[35] // 1.48 //

yatra te hṛṣṭa-manasaḥ paura-prīti-cikīrṣayā /
śrīmanty udyāna-saṁjñāni yaśo-dhāmāny acīkaran // 1.49 //
There with glad hearts, desiring to bring joy to the citizens, / They commissioned those glorious abodes of beauty that we call 'gardens.' // 1.49 //

śivāḥ puṣkariṇīś caiva paramāgrya-guṇāmbhasaḥ /
nājñayā cetanotkarṣād dikṣu sarvāsv acīkhanan // 1.50 //
And lovely lotus pools of finest quality water, / Not at anybody's behest,[36] but because of being uplifted, they had dug in all directions. // 1.50 //

manojñāḥ śrīmatīḥ praṣṭhīḥ pathiṣūpavaneṣu ca /
sabhāḥ kūpavatīś caiva samantāt pratyatiṣṭhipan // 1.51 //
Rest-houses of the first rank, welcoming and splendid, on the roads and in the woods, / And complete even with wells, they caused to go up on all sides. // 1.51 //

hasty-aśva-ratha-saṁkīrṇam asaṁkīrṇa-janākulam /
anigūḍhārthi-vibhavaṁ nigūḍha-jñāna-pauruṣam // 1.52 //
Crowded with elephants, horses, and chariots,[37] [the city[38]] was crammed with people who did not crowd each other. / Material wealth was available to the needy, not secreted; but learning and spirit ran secret and deep. // 1.52 //

---

[34] Mandara, lit. "a pearl chain consisting of 8 or 16 strings," is the name of a sacred mountain where various deities and mythical beings were thought to reside. When the gods and *asuras* were in need of a large object with which to churn the ocean and recover the deathless nectar, the story goes, they used Mt. Mandara as a churning stick.

[35] *Kiṁnara* is lit. "what sort of man?" *Kiṁnaras* are mythical beings with a human figure and the head of a horse (or with a horse's body and the head of a man) in later times reckoned among the *gandharvas* or celestial choristers, and celebrated as musicians. *Kiṁnara* virtues are said to include possession of jewels, prowess in mountain climbing and the musical arts, and possession of charming smiles. Aśvaghoṣa seems to be referring here to this cultured aspect of *kiṁnara* society. *Kiṁnaras*, and their female counterparts *kiṁnarīs*, are also depicted in Saundarananda as deeply romantic and sexual beings. In SN8.12, for example, Nanda compares himself to a *kiṁnara* without his lover, roaming about, his semen ready, over mountain peaks.

[36] *Ājñā*, here used in the sense of "order" or "behest," appears in the title of Canto 18, *ājñā-vyākaraṇaḥ*, in which context its meaning is ambiguous, perhaps intentionally so. *Ājñā* can also mean "deep or liberating knowledge," and "unlimited power or full autonomy."

[37] "Crowded with elephants, horses, and chariots," is an epic tag – i.e. a stock phrase that frequently recurs in epic poetry. EHJ points out that contrary to conventional use of epic tags in older models of *kāvya* writing like the *Rāmāyaṇa*, Aśvaghoṣa, instead of unthinkingly repeating the tag, examines meaning to be found in its elements. Thus, in Aśvaghoṣa's writing the tag is not repeated – though a similar tag appears in SN3.1.

[38] The subject *tat puram* is contained in verse 55.

saṁnidhānam ivārthānām ādhānam iva tejasām /
niketam iva vidyānāṁ saṁketam iva saṁpadām // 1.53 //
Like a place where goals converge, where energies are focused, / Where learning activities are housed together, and where achievements come together, // 1.53 //

vāsa-vṛkṣaṁ guṇavatām āśrayaṁ śaraṇaiṣiṇām /
ānartaṁ kṛta-śāstrāṇām ālānaṁ bāhu-śālinām // 1.54 //
It was a homing tree for high flyers, a refuge for those seeking a place of rest, / An arena for those skilled in scientific endeavor, and a tethering post for the mighty.[39] // 1.54 //

samājair utsavair dāyaiḥ kriyā-vidhibhir eva ca /
alaṁcakrur alaṁ-vīryās te jagad-dhāma tat-puram // 1.55 //
By means of meetings, festivals, and acts of giving, and by means of traditional observances, / The heroes brought that city, the light of the world, to a glorious readiness. // 1.55 //

yasmād anyāyatas te ca kaṁ-cin nācīkaran karam /
tasmād alpena kālena tat tadāpūpuran puram // 1.56 //
Since they never levied any tax that was not just, / Therefore in a short time they caused the city to be full. // 1.56 //

kapilasya ca tasya ṛṣes tasminn āśrama-vāstuni /
yasmāt te tat-puraṁ cakrus tasmāt kapilavāstu tat // 1.57 //
And since, on the site of the ashram of the seer Kapila, / They had built that city, therefore it was called Kapilavāstu. // 1.57 //

kakandasya makandasya kuśāmbasyeva cāśrame /
puryo yathā hi śrūyante tathaiva kapilasya tat // 1.58 //
Just as cities sited on the ashrams of Kakanda, Makanda and Kuśāmba[40] / Were called after them, so that city was called after Kapila. // 1.58 //

āpuḥ puraṁ tat puruhūta-kalpās te tejasāryeṇa na vismayena /
āpur yaśo-gandham ataś ca śaśvat sutā yayāter iva kīrtimantaḥ // 1.59 //
Those equals of Indra[41] took charge of that city with noble ardor but without arrogance; / And they thus took on forever the fragrance of honor, like the celebrated sons of Yayāti.[42] // 1.59 //

---

[39] The four elements of this verse mirror the four elements of the previous verse, having to do with 1. goals, 2. energy, 3. learning, and 4. integral realization.

[40] Kakanda, which means "gold," is given in SED as the name of a king. Kuśāmba, son of Kuśa (a different Kuśa from the Kuśa referred to in verse 26), was the founder of the ancient city of Kauśāmbī (now the village of Kosam, on the Jumna, near Allahabad).

[41] Puru-hūta, lit. "invoked by many," is a name of Indra.

[42] Aśvaghoṣa would seem to be referring to the sons of Yayāti as good examples on account of the modesty, or lack of personal ambition, which four of King Yayāti's five sons demonstrated when they refused his request to trade their youth with him. The fifth son, Puru, agreed to Yayāti's bargain and became the King's successor. See also SN11.46.

tan nātha-vṛttair api rāja-putrair arājakaṁ naiva rarāja rāṣṭram /
tārā-sahasrair api dīpyamānair anutthite candra ivāntarīkṣam // 1.60 //
But under the sons of kings, active though they were as protectors, that kingless kingdom lacked kingly luster – / Like the sky, though stars are shining in their thousands, before the moon has risen. // 1.60 //

yo jyāyān atha vayasā guṇaiś ca teṣāṁ bhrātṝṇāṁ vṛṣabha ivaujasā vṛṣāṇām /
te tatra priya-guravas tam abhyaṣiñcann ādityā daśaśata-locanaṁ divīva // 1.61 //
So the senior among those brothers, in age and in merits, like the bull which is chief among bulls in bodily power, / They anointed there, attaching to the important, like the Ādityas in heaven anointing thousand-eyed Indra. // 1.61 //

ācāravān vinayavān nayavān kriyāvān ¦ dharmāya nendriya-sukhāya dhṛtātapatraḥ / tad bhrātṛbhiḥ parivṛtaḥ sa jugopa rāṣṭraṁ ¦ saṁkrandano divam ivānusṛto marudbhiḥ // 1.62 //
Possessed of good conduct, discipline, prudence and industry, / Bearing the big umbrella for duty's sake, not to pander to the power of the senses, / He guarded that realm, surrounded by his brothers, / Like roaring Indra[43] guarding heaven with his retinue of storm-gods. // 1.62 //

saundaranande mahākāvye kapilavāstu-varṇano nāma prathamaḥ sargaḥ //1//
The 1st Canto in the epic poem Handsome Nanda,[44] titled "A Portrait of Kapilavāstu."

[43] *Saṁkrandana*, "roaring," is another name of Indra.
[44] *Saundaranande mahākāvye* may also be read "in an epic tale of beautiful joy."

Canto 2: rāja-varṇanaḥ
A Portrait of the King

Introduction

The second canto of Saundarananda, like the second canto of Buddhacarita, paints an idealized picture of King Śuddhodana. In painting this picture of a non-Buddhist, or pre-Buddhist, king, Aśvaghoṣa seems to wish to inspire us to reflect on and to practise transcendent accomplishments like free giving, forbearance, valour, moral integrity, contemplativeness, and wisdom. Buddhists know these six virtues as six *pāramitā* – six transcendental virtues or six perfections. But by presenting them in connection with a king who, by biological necessity, pre-dated the prince who would be Buddha, Aśvaghoṣa seems to underline the truth that these virtues are universal. So if, as Buddhists, we believe in these virtues with a religious or sectarian attitude, revering these virtues as something special in Buddhism, we might be missing the implicit point of the present canto.

tataḥ kadā-cit kālena tad avāpa kula-kramāt /
rājā śuddhodhano nāma śuddha-karmā jitendriyaḥ // 2.1 //
Some time thereafter that [realm] passed, through familial succession, / To a king named Śuddodhana who, being pure in his actions,[1] had conquered the power of the senses.[2] // 2.1 //

yaḥ sasañje na kāmeṣu śrī-prāptau na visismiye /
nāvamene parān ṛddhyā parebhyo nāpi vivyathe // 2.2 //
Neither stuck in his desires nor conceited about gaining sovereignty, / He did not, as he grew, look down on others, and nor did he shrink from others in fear.[3] // 2.2 //

balīyān sattva-sampannaḥ śrutavān buddhimān api /
vikrānto nayavāṁś caiva dhīraḥ sumukha eva ca // 2.3 //
Strong and strong-minded; learned as well as intelligent; / Daring and yet prudent; determined, and cheerful with it; // 2.3 //

vapuṣmāṁś ca na ca stabdho dakṣiṇo na ca nārjavaḥ /
tejasvī na ca na kṣantaḥ kartā ca na ca vismitaḥ // 2.4 //
He had a fine form without being stiff; was dexterous but not dishonest; / Was energetic but not impatient; and active but never flustered. // 2.4 //

---

1 The *śuddha* ("pure") of *śuddha-karmāḥ* ("pure in his actions") is a play on the name Śuddhodana.

2 *Jitendriyaḥ*, which sometimes means an ascetic, as "one with conquered senses," is almost as per the title of Canto 13, *Śīlendriya-jayaḥ*, "Defeating the Power of the Senses through Good Conduct." Hence *śīla*, integrity, or pure conduct, keeping the precepts (1), is the first of the six transcendent accomplishments (*pāramitā*) which the idealized portrait of King Śuddhodana seems to present.

3 King Śuddhodana was thus also an exemplar of the transcendent accomplishment of *vīrya*, heroic endeavor, energy, valor (2). See also verse 15, in which *vīrya* is cited by name.

ākṣiptaḥ śatrubhiḥ saṁkhye suhṛdbhiś ca vyapāśritaḥ /
abhavad yo na vimukhas tejasā ditsayaiva ca // 2.5 //
Challenged by his enemies in battle, and petitioned by friends, / He was not backward in responding with an intense energy, and with a willingness to give.[4] // 2.5 //

yaḥ pūrvai rājabhir yātāṁ yiyāsur dharma-paddhatim /
rājyaṁ dīkṣām iva vahan vṛttenānvagamat pitṝn // 2.6 //
Wishing to tread the dutiful path of dharma trodden by previous kings, / And bearing his kingship like a call to total dedication, he emulated the ancestors through his conduct. // 2.6 //

yasya su-vyavahārāc ca rakṣaṇāc ca sukhaṁ prajāḥ /
śiśyire vigatodvegāḥ pitur-aṅka-gatā iva // 2.7 //
Due to his good governance, and under his protection, his subjects rested at ease, / Free from anxiety, as if in a father's lap. // 2.7 //

kṛtaśastraḥ kṛtāstro vā jāto vā vipule kule /
akṛtārtho na dadṛse yasya darśanam eyivān // 2.8 //
Whether skilled in use of book, or in use of sword; whether born into an eminent family, or not; / Anybody who came into his presence was seen to be useful.[5] // 2.8 //

hitaṁ vipriyam apy ukto yaḥ śuśrāva na cukṣubhe /
duś-kṛtaṁ bahv api tyaktvā sasmāra kṛtam aṇv api // 2.9 //
When given good advice, however disagreeable, he listened and did not react; / He let go of a wrong done to him, however great,[6] and remembered a service rendered, however small. // 2.9 //

praṇatān anujagrāha vijagrāha kula-dviṣaḥ
āpānnān parijagrāha nijagrāhāsthitān pathi // 2.10 //
The meek and mild he befriended; tribal foes he apprehended; / Sufferers he comprehended; waverers he reprehended. // 2.10 //

prāyeṇa viṣaye yasya tac-chīlam anuvartinaḥ /
arjayanto dadṛsire dhanānīva guṇān api // 2.11 //
As the general rule in his dominion, those influenced by his integrity / Seemed to take possession of virtues as if they were securing treasures.[7] // 2.11 //

---

[4] This represents the transcendent accomplishment of *dāna*, giving, generosity (3).

[5] The emphatic double negative has been translated as a positive. *Akṛtārthah* lit. "purpose not achieved," more accurately means "not successful," but there is a play on the word *kṛta*, translated in the first line as "skilled in use of."

[6] This represents the transcendent accomplishment of *kṣanti*, forbearance (4).

[7] Linda Covill: "they looked as though they were earning virtues like money."

Adhyaiṣṭa yaḥ paraṁ brahma na vyaiṣṭa satatam dhṛteḥ /
dānāny adita pātrebhyaḥ pāpaṁ nākṛta kiṁ-cana // 2.12 //
He minded the supreme sacred word; in fortitude, he never failed; / He gave fitting gifts to deserving recipients; and no evil did he do at all. // 2.12 //

dhṛtyāvākṣīt pratijṇāṁ sa sad-vājīvodyatāṁ dhuram /
na hy avāñcīc cyutaḥ satyān muhūrtam api jīvitam // 2.13 //
A promise undertaken he resolutely carried out, like a good horse carrying a load; / For he did not desire, apart from truthfulness, even a moment of life. // 2.13 //

viduṣaḥ paryupāsiṣṭa vyakāśiṣṭātmavattayā /
vyarociṣṭa ca śiṣṭebhyo māsīṣe candramā iva // 2.14 //
For the intellectually bright, he was there; with his own self-containment, he shone;[8] / And on people in the directed state, he positively beamed – like the moon in the last month of the rains. // 2.14 //

avedīd buddhi-śāstrābhyām iha cāmutra ca kṣamam /
arakṣīd dhairya-vīryābhyām indriyāṇy api ca prajāḥ // 2.15 //
Through intelligence and learning, he knew what was fitting,[9] both in here and out there; / He guarded, with constancy and energy, both his senses and his subjects. // 2.15 //

ahārṣīd duḥkham ārtānāṁ dviṣatāṁ corjitaṁ yaśaḥ /
acaiṣīc ca nayair bhūmiṁ bhūyasā yaśasaiva ca // 2.16 //
He bore away the suffering of the oppressed and the boastful fame of the cruel, / And covered the earth with guiding principles and a much greater glory. // 2.16 //

apyāsīd duḥkhitān paśyan prakṛtyā karuṇātamakaḥ /
nādhauṣīc ca yaśo lobhād anyāyādhigatair dhanaiḥ // 2.17 //
Seeing people suffering he overflowed with his original emotion as a man of compassion; / But he did not, through eager desire, undermine his honor by unprincipled acquisition of treasured objects. // 2.17 //

sauhārda-dṛḍha-bhaktitvān maitreṣu viguṇeṣv api /
nādidāsīd aditsīt tu saumukhyāt svaṁ svam arthavat // 2.18 //
In his kind-hearted iron devotion even to imperfect friends, / He had no will to take, but willingly gave, cheerful-faced, to each according to his need. // 2.18 //

---

[8] This represents the transcendent accomplishment of *dhyāna*, meditation (5). For deeper consideration of the virtue of *ātmavat*, "self-containment," or "being in possession of oneself," see BC Canto 11 where it is discussed in connection with desires.
[9] This represents the transcendent accomplishment of *prajñā*, wisdom (6).

anivedyāgram arhadbhyo nālikṣat kiṁ-cid aplutaḥ /
gām adharmeṇa nādhukṣat kṣīra-tarṣeṇa gām iva // 2.19 //
Without offering the first portion to revered beings, and without bathing, he did not eat anything; / Neither did he milk the earth unjustly, as a cow is milked by a man thirsting for milk. // 2.19 //

nāsṛkṣad balim aprāptaṁ nārukṣan mānam aiśvaram /
āgamair buddhim ādhikṣad dharmāya na tu kīrtaye // 2.20 //
He never scattered the food offering except when due; he never developed lordly arrogance; / Committing of the scriptures to his mind, he did for dharma, not for praise. // 2.20 //

kleśārhān api kāṁś-cit tu nākliṣṭa kliṣṭa-karmaṇaḥ /
ārya-bhāvāc ca nāghukṣad dviṣato 'pi sato guṇān // 2.21 //
A few doers of harsh deeds, though they deserved harsh treatment, he did not treat harshly; / And due to his noble nature he never cast a veil over the virtues of a true man, even one who defied him. // 2.21 //

ākṛkṣad vapuṣā dṛṣṭīḥ prajānāṁ candramā iva /
parasvaṁ bhuvi nāmṛkṣan mahāviṣam ivoragam // 2.22 //
With his fine form he ripped away, as does the moon, people's views; / He never touched, in an act of becoming, what belonged to others, any more than he would touch a venomous snake slithering on the earth.[10] // 2.22 //

nākrukṣad viṣaye tasya kaś-cit kaiś-cit kva-cit kṣataḥ /
adikṣat tasya hasta-stham ārtebhyo hy abhayaṁ dhanuḥ // 2.23 //
Nowhere in his dominion did anyone hurt by anyone lament; / For the bow in his hand bestowed peace upon the afflicted. // 2.23 //

kṛtāgaso 'pi praṇatān prāg eva priya-kāriṇaḥ /
adarśat snigdhayā dṛṣṭyā ślakṣṇena vacasāsicat // 2.24 //
Even those who transgressed, if they were submissive (and before them, of course, those who acted agreeably), / He surveyed with an affectionate eye, and steeped in loving speech. // 2.24 //

---

[10] *Bhuvi* is the locative of *bhū*, whose meanings include 1. the act of becoming (or happening), 2. the earth. To take account of this ambiguity *bhuvi* is here translated twice. The verbal root √*bhū*, from which *bhāvanā* is derived, covers a wide array of meanings from to exist (non-emptily) through to become, to be, and to happen (emptily). So the ambiguous use of *bhū* in this verse may be taken as another early invitation, like the use of *bhāvana* as an adjective in verse 1.8, to start pondering whether the causative verbal noun *bhāvanā*, with its earthy connotations, could mean cultivating in the sense of "causing to exist" or "bringing into being"? Or could *bhāvanā* simply mean, less actively, "letting be"? Again, might *bhāvanā* mean "making happen"? And could *bhāvanā* be usefully translated "letting happen"?

bahvīr adhyagamad vidyā viṣayeṣv akutūhalaḥ /
sthitaḥ kārtayuge dharme dharmāt kṛcchre 'pi nāsrasat // 2.25 //
He studied many subjects, without being interested in objects; / Abiding in dharma as it was in the golden age, he did not drift, even in a predicament, from dharma. // 2.25 //

avardhiṣṭa guṇaiḥ śaśvad avṛdhan mitra-sampadā /
avartiṣṭa ca vṛddheṣu nāvṛtad garhite pathi // 2.26 //
Because of his virtues, he continually grew; in his joy at the success of friends, he kept growing; / In the stream of forebears long since grown old, again he kept going... but go he did not, on a blameworthy path. // 2.26 //

śarair aśīśamac chatrūn guṇair bandhūn arīramat /
randhrair nācūcudad bhṛtyān karair nāpīpiḍat prajāḥ // 2.27 //
He quietened his enemies, using arrows; he gladdened his friends, using virtues; / His servants, when there were faults, he did not goad; the offshoots who were his subjects he did not, with doing hands, overtax.[11] // 2.27 //

rakṣanāc caiva śauryāc ca nikhilāṁ gām avīvapat
spaṣṭayā daṇḍa-nītyā ca rātri-sattrān avīvapat // 2.28 //
Under his protection, and because of his heroism, seeds were planted over the whole earth; / And by the transparent working of his judicial system, sessions were sat into the dark stillness of night.[12] // 2.28 //

kulaṁ rājarṣi-vṛttena yaśo-gandham avīvapat /
dīptyā tama ivādityas tejasārīn avīvapat // 2.29 //
By the conduct of a royal seer, he propagated through his house the fragrance of honor. / Like the son of Aditi[13] shining light into darkness, he with the intensity of his energy caused the enemies to scatter.[14] // 2.29 //

---

[11] *Karaiḥ* is the instrumental plural of *kara*, whose meanings include 1. the act of doing, 2. "the doer" = the hand, and 3. tax. In the hidden meaning, was the King an exemplar of how to transmit the truth of non-doing?

[12] The second and fourth pādas of this (and the following) verse include the same causative aorist form, *avīvapat*, from the root √*vap*, which means (1) to strew, scatter, or procreate; or (2) to shear, shave, cut off, mow down. In its causative usage √*vap* means (1) to put or plant in the ground; or (2) to cause to be shorn or cut back. Ostensibly the description is of a well-functioning judicial system, in which case *avīvapat* could mean that "night-sessions" (*rātri-sattrān*) were 1. prolonged, out of due diligence, or 2. cut short, thanks to decisiveness. In the hidden meaning, "night sittings" suggests sitting-meditation practiced at night.

[13] Āditya, or "son of Aditi," is a name of the sun.

[14] Again, "propagated" in the second pāda and "caused to scatter" in the fourth pāda are translations of *avīvapat*. The use of the same verb in four different contexts may be taken as a signal to the reader, or as a reminder, not to take what is written at face value.

apaprathat pitṝṁs caiva satputra-sadṛsair gunaiḥ /
salileneva cāmbhodo vṛttenājihladat prajāḥ // 2.30 //
Using virtues that befitted a good son, he caused the ancestors, again, to disseminate their light; / And, like a raincloud using rain, he enlivened his offshoots, his subjects, using conduct. // 2.30 //

dānair ajasra-vipulaiḥ somaṁ viprān asūṣavat /
rāja-dharma-sthitatvāc ca kāle sasyam asūṣavat // 2.31 //
With inexhaustible and great acts of giving, he caused the brahmins[15] to press out their *soma*[16]; / And by dutifully adhering to his kingly dharma, he caused corn,[17] at the right moment, to ripen.[18] // 2.31 //

adharmiṣṭhām acakathan na kathām akathaṁkathaḥ/
cakravartīva ca parān dharmāyābhyudasīṣahat // 2.32 //
He talked no talk that went against dharma, being free in himself of doubts and questions; / And, like a wheel-rolling king, he caused others to be courageous in service of dharma. // 2.32 //

rāṣṭram anyatra ca baler na sa kiṁ-cid adīdapat /
bhṛtyair eva ca sodyogaṁ dviṣad-darpam adīdapat // 2.33 //
No special tribute did he cause the kingdom to pay him; / But with sustained endeavour, and using only regulars,[19] he caused enemy pride to be cut down. // 2.33 //

svair evādīdapac cāpi bhūyo bhūyo guṇaiḥ kulam /
prajā nādīdapac caiva sarva-dharma-vyavasthayā // 2.34 //
Again and again, he caused his own house to be pure, using just his own virtues;[20] / At the same time, he did not let his offshoots decay,[21] for all were established in all dharmas.[22] // 2.34 //

---

[15] *Vipra* as an adjective means stirred or inwardly excited, inspired, wise. As a noun it can mean any inspired sage, seer, singer, or poet, but ostensibly here it means a brahmin priest.

[16] *Soma* literally means "what is pressed out." In the hidden meaning is there an autobiographical element? Did Aśvaghoṣa see himself to be a kind of *vipra* (a sage/singer/poet) out of whom epic poetry was being squeezed out?

[17] *Sasya* means 1. corn, and 2. virtue, merit.

[18] "Caused to press out" and "caused to ripen" are both translations of *asūṣavat.*

[19] *Bhṛtya* means one who is to be maintained, a dependent, servant; hence in this context the ostensible meaning is troops already on the payroll, regular troops (LC: "*using just his regular troops*"). In the hidden meaning, is there a suggestion that particular defilements, like hatred and pride, can all be defeated by the regular practice of letting happen (*bhāvanā*), which, as such, is inherently friendly and free of conceit?

[20] Cf. the Universal Precept of the Seven Buddhas: [Pali] *sabbapāpassa akaraṇaṁ, kusalassa upasampadā, sacittapariyodapanaṁ etaṁ buddhāna' sāsanaṁ.* [Chinese] 諸惡莫作 衆善奉行 自淨其意 是諸佛教. The not doing of any wrong, Undertaking what is good, Cleansing one's own mind – This is the teaching of buddhas.

[21] "Caused to pay" and "caused to be cut down" in verse 33, and "caused to be pure" and "let decay" in verse 34, are all translations of the same word *adīdapat,* derived from the roots √*dā* (to cause to pay), or √*dā* = √*do* (to cause to be cut down), or √*dā* = √*dai* (to cause to be pure), or √*dī* (to shine forth), or √*dī* (to cause to decay).

aśrāntaḥ samaye yajvā yajña-bhūmim amīmapat /
pālanāc ca dvijān brahma nirudvignān amīmapat // 2.35 //
A man of tireless sacrifice when the time was right, he caused sacrificial ground to be measured out; / And he enabled twice-born men,[23] who under his protection were unburdened by anxiety, to know the weight of the sacred word.[24] // 2.35 //

gurubhir vidhivat kāle saumyaḥ somam amīmapat /
tapasā tejasā caiva dviṣat-sainyam amīmapat // 2.36 //
In the presence of gurus, and obeying the rule, he caused the *soma* to be measured out on time, as a cool, mild man of *soma*,[25] / And yet, with intense ardor, with fiery energy, he saw the enemy army cut down to size.[26] // 2.36 //

prajāḥ parama-dharma-jñaḥ sūkṣmaṁ dharmam avīvasat /
darśanāc caiva dharmasya kāle svargam avīvasat //2.37 //
As knower of the dharma that is paramount, he caused his offshoots to abide in dharma in a small way, / And yet caused them, because of experiencing dharma, to let heaven wait.[27] //2.37 //

vyaktam apy artha-kṛcchreṣu nādharmiṣṭham atiṣṭhipat /
priya ity eva cāśaktaṁ na saṁrāgād avīvṛdhat // 2.38 //
Even the obvious candidate in a crisis, he did not appoint if it went against dharma; / Nor, out of nothing more than fondness, did he dotingly promote incompetence. // 2.38 //

---

[22] *Sarva-dharma-vyavasthayā* ("being established in all dharmas") may mean being grounded in the teaching which is the central teaching of the Lotus Sutra, namely, "all dharmas are real form," or "all happenings are reality." (Chinese/Japanese: 諸法実相 *shohō-jissō*.)

[23] *Dvi-ja*, "twice born," generally means a brahmin, considered to have been born again at his initiation ceremony. Aśvaghoṣa might equally have in mind the kind of re-birth that Nanda manifests at the beginning of SN Canto 12, when he begins to demonstrate real confidence in the Buddha's teaching of a better way (i.e. a way that is better than both hedonism and Brahmanism).

[24] *Brahma... amīmapat* could mean to know the weight of the sacred word, or could mean to anchor the sacred word (*brahma*) in the ground – see note on *amīmapat* appended to the following verse.

[25] In later cantos, the Buddha frequently addresses Nanda in the vocative case as *saumya*, which is generally translated "my friend!" but which literally means "man of the *soma*!" This is because the qualities attributed to the *soma*, and to the moon-god with whom sacrificial drinking of the *soma* was associated, are those of being in the first instance cool and moist; and by extension placid, gentle, mild, happy, pleasant, cheerful. In this verse, therefore, *saumyaḥ*, "man of *soma*," has connotations that are diametrically opposed to intense ardour and fiery energy.

[26] "Caused to be measured out" and "enabled to know the weight" in verse 36, and "caused to be measured out" and "saw cut down to size" in verse 37, are all translations of the same word, *amīmapat*, a causative aorist form which can be derived from at least four roots: √*mā* (to measure, build, erect), √*mi* (to know, to fix in the ground), √*mā* (to reap) and √*mī* (to diminish). The resulting ambiguity may be intended, again, to alert the reader to the ambiguity and irony which run through the whole of Saundarananda.

[27] "Caused to abide" and "caused to let wait" are translations of the same word *avīvasat*, derived from the root √*vas* (to cause to stay or wait). The wording invites the reader to understand that the king caused his subjects to dwell in heaven in future, while simultaneously allowing – for the more practically inclined – an alternative reading.

tejasā ca tviṣā caiva ripūn dṛptān abībhasat /
yaśo-dīpena dīptena pṛthivīṁ ca vyabībhasat // 2.39 //
With intense energy and with light he exposed to view his enemies, the conceited; / And with a blazing lantern of brightness, he caused the world to shine. // 2.39 //

ānṛsaṁsyān na yaśase tenādāyi sadārthine /
dravyaṁ mahad api tyaktvā na caivākīrti kiṁ-cana // 2.40 //
He gave out of kindness, not for his glorification, and always to meet a need; / Giving up even a thing of great substance, he mentioned nothing of it. // 2.40 //

tenārir api duḥkhārto nātyāji śaraṇāgataḥ /
jitvā dṛptān api ripūn na tenākāri vismayaḥ // 2.41 //
He did not shun one afflicted by suffering, even an enemy, who had taken refuge; / And having conquered his enemies, the conceited, he did not become proud on that account. // 2.41 //

na tenābhedi māryādā kāmād dveṣād bhayād api //
tena satsv api bhogeṣu nāsevīndriya-vṛttitā // 2.42 //
No rule did he break, out of love, hate, or fear; / Even while abiding in pleasurable circumstances, he did not remain in thrall to the power of the senses. // 2.42 //

na tenādarśi viṣamaṁ kāryaṁ kva-cana kiṁ-cana //
vipriya-priyayoḥ kṛtye na tenāgāmi nikriyāḥ // 2.43 //
He was never seen to do shoddily anything anywhere that needed to be done; / When required by friend and non-friend to act, he did not fall into inaction. // 2.43 //

tenāpāyi yathā-kalpaṁ somaś ca yaśa eva ca /
vedaś cāmnāyi satataṁ vedokto dharma eva ca // 2.44 //
He drank and guarded,[28] as prescribed, the *soma* and his honor; / And he was constantly mindful of the Vedas, as well as the dharma proclaimed in the Vedas.[29] // 2.44 //

evam-ādibhir atyakto babhūvāsulabhair guṇaiḥ /
aśakya-śakya-sāmantaḥ śākyarājaḥ sa śakravat // 2.45 //
Not eschewed by such uncommon virtues as these / Was he who on no side could be vanquished – the unshakable Śākya King, like Śakra.[30] // 2.45 //

---

[28] *Apāyi* is aorist passive from the root √*pā*, which means: (1) to drink; (2) to watch, keep, preserve. So one verb is used in two meanings for two objects. The implicit teaching point might be that context is everything.

[29] Again, the implicit teaching point might be, with respect to ancient wisdom, that its practical application is everything. Intellectual knowledge of ancient wisdom, on its own, is useless.

[30] *Śakra-vat*, "like the Mighty One," means like Indra, king of the gods in ancient Indian mythology. But the sound of the word might be more important than the meaning in this verse, whose primary function seems to be to round off, in a poetically pleasing manner, the long list of the king's virtues. Hence the euphonic combination of *a-śakya* (impossible), *śakya* (to be subdued or shackled), *Śākya* (name of the people of whom the Buddha's father was king), and *Śakra* (Mighty

atha tasmin tathā kāle dharma-kāmā divaukasaḥ /
vicerur diśi lokasya dharma-caryā didṛkṣavaḥ // 2.46 //
Now at that time dharma-loving denizens of the heavens / Moved into the orbit of the human world, wishing to investigate dharma movements. // 2.46 //

dharmātmānaś carantas te dharma-jijñāsayā jagat /
dadṛśus taṁ viśeṣeṇa dharmātmānaṁ narādhipam // 2.47 //
Those essences of dharma, moving, with the desire to know dharma, over the earth, / Saw that leader of men whose essence was particularly given over to dharma. // 2.47 //

devebhyas tuṣitebhyo 'tha bodhisattvaḥ kṣitiṁ vrajan /
upapattiṁ praṇidadhe kule tasya mahīpateḥ // 2.48 //
Then the bodhisattva came down to earth, and rather than among Tuṣita gods, / He put down birth-roots in the family of that earth-lord. // 2.48 //

tasya devī nṛdevasya māyā nāma tad ābhavat /
vīta-krodha-tamo-māyā māyeva divi devatā // 2.49 //
That man-god at that time had a goddess, a queen whose name was Māyā; / She was as devoid of anger, darkness and the *māyā* which is deceit as was the goddess Māyā in heaven. // 2.49 //

svapne 'tha samaye garbham āviśantaṁ dadarśa sā /
ṣaḍ-dantaṁ vāraṇaṁ śvetam airāvatam ivaujasā // 2.50 //
In a dream during that period she saw entering her womb / A white six-tusked elephant, mighty as Airāvata.[31] // 2.50 //

taṁ vinirdidiśuḥ śrutvā svapnaṁ svapna-vido dvijāḥ /
tasya janma kumārasya lakṣmī-dharma-yaśo-bhṛtaḥ //2.51 //
When they heard this dream, brahmins[32] who knew dreams predicted / The birth of a prince who would bring honor, through wealth or through dharma. //2.51 //

tasya sattva-viśeṣasya jātau jāti-kṣayaiṣiṇaḥ /
sācalā pracacālorvī taraṅgābhihateva nauḥ // 2.52 //
At the birth of this exceptional being whose mission was the end of re-birth / The earth with its immoveable mountains moved, like a boat being battered by waves. // 2.52 //

Indra). *Samantaḥ* means "on all sides," but can also be read as "a vassal, a feudatory prince." Thus, reading the 3rd pāda as *aśakyaḥ śakya-sāmantaḥ*, EHJ translated: *"This invincible king of the Shakyas, to whom the vassal princes were submissive, was endowed like Shakra with these and other rare virtues."*

[31] Airāvata, "produced from the ocean," is the name of Indra's elephant, who holds up the eastern quarter.

[32] *Dvijāḥ*, lit. "the twice-born."

sūrya-raśmibhir akliṣṭaṁ puṣpa-varṣaṁ papāta khāt /
dig-vāraṇa-karādhūtād vanāc caitrarathād iva // 2.53 //
A rain of flowers, unwilted by the sun's rays, fell from the sky / As if shaken from the trees of Citra-ratha's forest by the trunks of the elephants of the four quarters.[33] // 2.53 //

divi dundubhayo nedur dīvyatāṁ marutām iva/
didīpe ' bhyadhikaṁ sūryaḥ śivaś ca pavano vavau // 2.54 //
Drums sounded in heaven, as though the storm-gods were rolling dice; / The sun blazed inestimably, and the wind blew benignly. // 2.54 //

tutuṣus tuṣitāś caiva śuddhāvāsāś ca devatāḥ /
saddharma-bahumānena sattvānāṁ cānukampayā // 2.55 //
Gods in Tuṣita Heaven became calm and content, as did gods of the clear blue Śuddhāvāsa yonder,[34] / Through thinking highly of true dharma, and through fellow feeling among sentient beings. // 2.55 //

samāyayau yaśaḥ-ketuṁ śreyaḥ-ketu-karaḥ paraḥ/
babhrāje śāntayā lakṣmyā dharmo vigrahavān iva // 2.56 //
To one who was a lamp of honor came a supreme bringer of the brightness of betterment:[35] / He shone with tranquil splendor like dharma in a separate bodily form. // 2.56 //

devyām api yavīyasyām araṇyām iva pāvakaḥ/
nando nāma suto jajñe nityānanda-karaḥ kule // 2.57 //
To the king's younger queen, also, like fire in the notch of a fire-board, / A son was born named Nanda, Joy, a bringer of constant joy to his family. // 2.57 //

dīrgha-bāhur mahā-vakṣāḥ siṁhāṁso vṛṣabhekṣaṇaḥ
vapuṣāgryeṇa yo nāma sundaropapadaṁ dadhe // 2.58 //
Long in the arm, broad in the chest, with shoulders of a lion and eyes of a bull, / He because of his superlative looks bore the epithet "handsome." // 2.58 //

---

[33] Citra-ratha, "having a bright chariot," is the name of the king of the *gandharvas* - the heavenly guardians of *soma*.

[34] Śuddhāvāsa, "the pure abode," is the name of a region of the sky in the realm of form/matter. Gods who live there would therefore tend to be on the other side of the science vs religion debate from the Tuṣita gods, who belong to a heaven in the realm of desire/volition/spirit. So it may be that Aśvaghoṣa mentioned the Śuddhāvāsa gods for the sake of balance. In a similar way the first pāda of the previous verse seems to relate to a spiritual happening in heaven, whereas the second pāda has a less religious mood, describing storm-gods playing (against Albert Einstein's expectations) dice.

[35] *Śreyas* means the better state, better, a better way. EHJ translated "the highest good" and LC "Excellence." See also SN5.49, and several verses in SN Canto 12, where the Buddha encourages Nanda to have confidence in a better way.

madhumāsa iva prāptaś candro nava ivoditaḥ /
aṅgavān iva cānaṅgaḥ sa babhau kāntayā śriyā // 2.59 //
Like a first month in spring having arrived; like a new moon having risen; / Again, like the non-physical[36] having taken a physical form, he radiated sheer loveliness. // 2.59 //

sa tau saṁvardhayām āsa narendraḥ parayā mudā
arthaḥ sajjana-hastastho dharma-kāmau mahān iva // 2.60 //
The king with exceeding gladness brought up the two of them, / As great wealth in the hands of a good man promotes dharma and pleasure. // 2.60 //

tasya kālena sat-putrau vavṛdhāte bhavāya tau
āryasyārambha-mahato dharmārthāv iva bhūtaye // 2.61 //
Those two good sons, in time, grew up to do the king proud, / Just as, when his investment is great, dharma and wealth pay a noble person well. // 2.61 //

tayoḥ sat-putrayor madhye śākya-rājo rarāja saḥ /
madhya-deśa iva vyakto himavat-pāripātrayoḥ // 2.62 //
Being in the middle, with regard to those two good sons, the Śākya king reigned resplendent, / Like the Madhya-deśa, the Middle Region, adorned by the Himālaya and Pāriyātra mountains.[37] // 2.62 //

tatas tayoḥ saṁskṛtayo krameṇa narendra-sūnvoḥ kṛta-vidyayoś ca /
kāmeṣv ajasraṁ pramamāda nandaḥ sarvārtha-siddhas tu na saṁrarañja // 2.63 //
Then, gradually, those two sons of the king became educated, in practical arts and in learning. / Nanda frittered all his time on idle pleasures; but Sarvārtha-siddha, Accomplisher of Every Aim, was not mottled by the redness of passions. // 2.63 //

sa prekṣyaiva hi jīrṇam āturaṁ ca mṛtaṁ ca
vimṛśan jagad anabhijñam ārtacittaḥ /
hṛdaya-gata-para-ghṛṇo na viṣaya-ratim agamaj
janana-maraṇa-bhayam abhito vijighāṁsuḥ // 2.64 //
For he had seen for himself an old man, a sick man, and a corpse, / After which, as with a wounded mind he witnessed the unwitting world, / He was disgusted to the core and found no pleasure in objects / But wished totally to terminate the terror of being born and dying. // 2.64 //

---

[36] *Anaṅga,* "the non-physical" or "the bodiless," is an epithet of Kāma-deva, the god of love, whom Śiva rendered bodiless as a punishment, after a cupid's arrow had caused Śiva to fall out of love with ascetic practice and into love with the beautiful Pārvatī.

[37] The Pāriyātra is another name for the Vindhya mountains that lie to the south of the Ganges basin.

udvegād apunar-bhave manaḥ praṇidhāya
sa yayau śayita-varāṅganād anāsthaḥ /
niśi nṛpati-nilayanād vana-gamana-kṛtamanāḥ
sarasa iva mathita-nalināt kala-haṁsaḥ // 2.65 //
Having focused his agitated mind on the end of becoming, / He fled the king's palace, indifferent to the most beautiful of women sleeping there; / Determined to go to the forest, he fled in the night, / Like a goose from a lake of ruined lotuses. // 2.65 //

saundaranande mahā-kāvye rāja-varṇano nāma dvitīyaḥ sargaḥ // 2 //
The 2nd canto in the epic poem Handsome Nanda, titled "A Portrait of the King."

Canto 3: tathāgata-varṇanaḥ
A Portrait of the Tathāgata

Introduction

The forty-two verses of this short canto give as full an answer as can be given in forty-two verses to the questions: How did the bodhisattva Gautama become the Tathāgata, the Realized One? And what thereafter did he teach? The answer to the second question is presented not only in the abstract but also in a description of how the citizens of Kapilavāstu, under the Buddha's guiding influence, all lived in peace, exemplifying in their lives what it means to keep ten precepts.

tapase tataḥ kapilavāstu haya-gaja-rath'-augha-saṁkulaṁ /
śrīmad abhayam anurakta-janaṁ sa vihāya niścita-manā vanaṁ yayau // 3.1 //
For ascetic practice, then, he left Kapilavāstu – a teeming mass of horses, elephants and chariots, / Majestic, safe, and loved by its citizens. Leaving the city, he started resolutely for the forest. // 3.1 //

vividhāgamāṁs tapasi tāṁś ca vividha-niyamāśrayān munīn /
prekṣya sa viṣaya-tṛṣā-kṛpaṇān anavasthitam tapa iti nyavartata // 3.2 //
In the approach to ascetic practice of the various traditions, and in the attachment of sages to various restraints, / He observed the miseries of thirsting after an object. Seeing asceticism to be unreliable, he turned away from it. // 3.2 //

atha mokṣa-vādinam arāḍam upaśama-matiṁ tathoḍrakaṁ /
tattva-kṛta-matir upāsya jahāv ayam apy amārga iti mārga-kovidhaḥ // 3.3 //
Then Arāḍa, who spoke of freedom, and likewise Uḍraka, who inclined towards quietness, / He served, his heart set on truth, and he left. He who intuited the path intuited: "This also is not it." // 3.3 //

sa vicārayan jagati kiṁ nu paramam iti taṁ tam āgamaṁ /
niścayam anadhigataḥparataḥ paramaṁ cacāra tapa eva duṣ-karaṁ // 3.4 //
Of the different traditions in the world, he asked himself, which one was the best? / Not obtaining certainty elsewhere, he entered after all into ascetic practice that was most severe. // 3.4 //

atha naiṣa mārga iti vīkṣya tad api vipulaṁ jahau tapaḥ /
dhyāna-viṣayam avagamya paraṁ bubhuje varānnam amṛtatva-buddhaye // 3.5 //
Then, having seen that it was not the path, he also abandoned that extreme asceticism. / Understanding the realm of meditation to be supreme, he ate good food in readiness to realise the deathless. // 3.5 //

sa suvarṇa-pīna-yuga-bāhur ṛṣabha-gatir āyatekṣaṇaḥ /
plakṣam avaniruham abhyagamat paramasya niścaya-vidher bubhutsayā // 3.6 //
With golden arms fully expanded and as if in a yoke, with lengthened eyes, and bull-like gait, / He came to a fig tree, growing up from the earth, with the will to awakening that belongs to the supreme method of investigation. // 3.6 //

upaviśya tatra kṛta-buddhir acala-dhṛtir adri-rājavat /
māra-balam ajayad ugram atho bubudhe padaṁ śivam ahāryam avyayaṁ // 3.7 //
Sitting there, mind made up, as unmovingly stable as the king of mountains, / He overcame the grim army of Māra and awoke to the step which is happy, irremovable, and irreducible. // 3.7 //

avagamya taṁ ca kṛta-kāryam amṛta-manaso divaukasaḥ /
harṣam atulam agaman muditā vimukhī tu māra-pariṣat pracukṣubhe // 3.8 //
Sensing the completion of his task, the denizens of heaven whose heart's desire is the deathless nectar / Buzzed with unbridled joy. But Māra's crew was downcast and trembled. // 3.8 //

sa-nagā ca bhūḥ pravicacāla huta-vaha-sakhaḥ śivo vavau /
nedur api ca sura-dundubhayaḥ pravavarṣa cāmbu-dhara-varjitaṁ nabhaḥ // 3.9 //
The earth with its mountains shook, that which feeds the fire blew benignly, / The drums of the gods resounded, and from the cloudless sky rain fell.[1] // 3.9 //

avabudhya caiva paramārtham ajaram anukampayā vibhuḥ /
nityam amṛtam upadarśayituṁ sa varāṇasī-parikarām ayāt purīm // 3.10 //
Awake to the one great ageless purpose, and universal in his compassion, / He proceeded, in order to display the eternal deathless nectar, to the city sustained by the waters of the Varaṇā and the Asī – to Vārāṇasī. // 3.10 //

atha dharma-cakram ṛta-nābhi dhṛti-mati-samādhi-nemimat /
tatra vinaya-niyamāram ṛṣir jagato hitāya pariṣady avartayat // 3.11 //
And so the wheel of dharma – whose hub is uprightness, whose rim is constancy, determination, and balanced stillness, / And whose spokes are the rules of discipline – there the Seer turned, in that assembly, for the welfare of the world. // 3.11 //

iti duḥkham etad iyam asya samudaya-latā pravartikā /
śāntir iyam ayam upāya iti pravibhāgaśaḥ param idaṁ catuṣṭayam // 3.12 //
"This is suffering; this is the tangled mass of causes producing it; / This is cessation; and here is a means." Thus, one by one, this supreme set of four, // 3.12 //

---

[1] Ostensibly rain falling from the cloudless sky is something fantastic, a miracle. In the hidden meaning, it might be a suggestion of the dependently-arisen reality (see e.g. SN17.20-21) in which clouds can happen in abundance but there is never any such thing, as a thing unto itself, as a cloud.

abhidhāya ca tri-parivartam atulam anivartyam uttamaṁ /
dvādaśa-niyata-vikalpam ṛśir vininlāya kauṇḍina-sagotram āditaḥ // 3.13 //
The seer set out, with its three divisions[2] of the unequalled, the incontrovertible, the ultimate; / And with its combination of twelve causal connections;[3] after which he instructed, as the first follower, him of the Kauṇḍinya clan.[4] // 3.13 //

sa hi doṣa-sāgaram agādham upadhi-jalam ādhi-jantukaṁ /
krodha-mada-bhaya-taraṅga-calaṁ pratatāra lokam api ca vyatārayat // 3.14 //
For the fathomless sea of faults, whose water is falsity, where fish are cares, / And which is disturbed by waves of anger, lust, and fear; he had crossed, and he took the world across too. // 3.14 //

sa vinīya kāśiṣu gayeṣu bahu-janam atho giri-vraje /
pitryam api parama-kāruṇiko nagaraṁ yayāv anujighṛkṣayā tadā // 3.15 //
Having instructed many people at Kāśi and at Gaya as also at Giri-vraja, / He made his way then to the city of his fathers, in his deeply compassionate desire to include it. // 3.15 //

viṣayātmakasya hi janasya bahu-vividha-mārga-sevinaḥ /
sūrya-sadṛśa-vapur abhyudito vijahāra sūrya iva gautamas tamaḥ // 3.16 //
To people possessed by ends, serving many and various paths, / Splendor had arisen that seemed like the sun: Gautama was like the sun, dispelling darkness. // 3.16 //

abhitas tataḥ kapilavāstu parama-śubha-vāstu-saṁstutaṁ /
vastu-mati-śuci śivopavanaṁ sa dadarśa niḥspṛhatayā yathā vanaṁ // 3.17 //
Seeing then all sides of Kapilavāstu - which was famed for its most beautiful properties, / And was pure and clean in substance and design, and pleasantly wooded - he looked without longing, as though at a forest. // 3.17 //

aparigrahaḥ sa hi babhūva niyata-matir ātmanīśvaraḥ /
naika-vidha-bhaya-kareśu kim-u svajana-svadeśajana-mitra-vastuśu // 3.18 //
For he had become free of belonging: he was sure in his thinking, the master of himself. / How much less did he belong to those causes of manifold worry - family, countrymen, friends and property? // 3.18 //

---

[2] The three divisions of the noble eightfold path, as clarified in SN16.30-33, are 1. the threefold discipline of integrity (*śīla*; using the voice and body well, and earning a living well); 2. threefold wisdom (*prajñā*; insight into the four noble truths, thinking straight, and initiative); and 3. twofold tranquility (*samādhi*; thinking in activity and practicing balanced stillness).

[3] *Dvādaśa-niyata-vikalpam* refers to to the twelvefold teaching of dependent arising described in detail in BC Canto 14 and in MMK ch. 26.

[4] Kauṇḍinya is cited first in the long list of names of courageous individual practitioners that the Buddha holds up, from SN16.87, as examples for Nanda to emulate. Kauṇḍinya is also known as Ājñāta Kauṇḍinya, "Kauṇḍinya Who Knows" (Pali: Aññā Koṇḍañña), because at the end of the first turning of the Dharma-wheel, the Buddha is said to have declared, "Kauṇḍinya surely knows! Kauṇḍinya surely knows!"

pratipūjayā na sa jaharṣa na ca śucam avajñayāgamat /
niscita-matir asi-candanayor na jagāma duḥkha-sukhayoś ca vikriyāṁ // 3.19 //
Being revered gave him no thrill, and neither did disrespect cause him any grief. / His direction was decided, come sword or sandalwood, and whether the going was tough or easy he was not diminished. // 3.19 //

atha pārthivaḥ samupalabhya sutam upagataṁ tathāgataṁ /
tūrṇam abahu-turagānugataḥ suta-darśanotsukatayābhiniryayau // 3.20 //
And so the king learned that his son had arrived as the *Tathāgata*, the One Arrived Thus; / With but a few horses straggling behind him,[5] out the king charged, in his eagerness to see his son. // 3.20 //

sugatas tathāgatam avekṣya nara-patim adhīram āśayā /
śeṣam api ca janam aśru-mukhaṁ vininīṣayā gaganam utpapāta ha // 3.21 //
The *Sugata*, the One Gone Well, saw the king coming thus,[6] composure lost in expectation, / And saw the rest of the people too, with tearful faces; wishing to direct them, up he took himself, into the sky. // 3.21 //

sa vicakrame divi bhuvīva punar upaviveśa tasthivān /
niścala-matir aśayiṣṭa punar bahudhābhavat punar abhūt tathaikadhā // 3.22 //
He strode over heaven as if over the earth; and sat again, in the stillness of having stopped. / Without changing his direction, he lay down; he showed many changing forms[7] while remaining, in this manner, all of one piece. // 3.22 //

salile kṣitāv iva cacāra jalam iva viveśa medinīṁ /
megha iva divi vavarṣa punaḥ punar ajvalan nava ivodito raviḥ // 3.23 //
He walked over water as if on dry land, immersed himself in the soil as though it were water, / Rained as a cloud in the sky, and shone like the newly-risen sun. // 3.23 //

yugapaj jvalan jvalanavac ca jalam avasṛjaṁś ca meghavat /
tapta-kanaka-sadṛśa-prabhayā sa babhau pradīpta iva sandhyayā ghanaḥ // 3.24 //
Simultaneously glowing like a fire and passing water like a cloud,[8] / He gave off a light resembling molten gold, like a cloud set aglow by daybreak or by dusk. // 3.24 //

---

[5] In BC10.16, King Śreṇya is described as *nibhṛtānuyātraḥ*, "having only a modest retinue." The implication here, similarly, seems to be that going with a retinue of only a few horses was a mark of modesty.

[6] "Coming thus," is *tathāgatam*, a play on *tathāgata* which, as an epithet of the Buddha, is open to very many readings.

[7] *Bahudhābhavat* can quite literally be translated as nothing more supernatural than "he manifested himself (*abhavat*) in many ways (*bahudhā*)." At the same time with these descriptions Aśvaghoṣa seems to be inviting the supernaturally-inclined to invent their own more unlikely scenarios. Hence EHJ: "*He divided Himself into many forms and then became one again.*"

[8] The second of four pādas often harbours subversive content, as the element opposed to the innocence of idealism in a four-phased dialectic progression. *Jalam ava-√sṛj* literally means "to let loose water." Hence EHJ translated "*shedding water like a cloud.*" But in the hidden meaning (just as Jesus wept) did the Buddha piss?

tam udīkṣya hema-maṇi-jāla-valayinam ivotthitaṁ dhvajaṁ /
prītim agamad atulāṁ nṛpatir janatā natāś ca bahumānam abhyayuḥ // 3.25 //
Looking up at him in the network of gold and pearls that seemed to wrap around him like an upraised flag,[9] / The king became joyful beyond measure and the assembled people, bowing down, felt deep appreciation. // 3.25 //

atha bhājanī-kṛtam avekṣya manuja-patim ṛddhi-sampadā /
paura-janam api ca tat-pravaṇaṁ nijagāda dharma-vinayam vināyakaḥ // 3.26 //
And so, seeing that he had made a vessel of the ruler of men, through the wealth of his accomplishments, / And that the townsfolk also were amenable, the Guide gave voice to the dharma and the discipline. // 3.26 //

nṛpatis tataḥ prathamam āpa phalam amṛta-dharma-siddhaye /
dharmam atulam adhigamya muner munaye nanāma sa yato gurāv iva // 3.27 //
Then the royal hero reaped the first fruit for the fulfilment of the deathless dharma. / Having obtained unthinkable dharma from the sage, he bowed accordingly in the sage's direction, as to a guru. // 3.27 //

bahavaḥ prasanna-manaso 'tha janana-maraṇārti-bhīravaḥ /
śākya-tanaya-vṛṣabhāḥ kṛtino vṛṣabhā ivānala-bhayāt pravavrajuḥ // 3.28 //
Many then who were clear in mind – alert to the agony of birth and death – / Among mighty Śākya-born men of action, went forth into the wandering life, like bulls that had been startled by fire. // 3.28 //

vijahus tu ye 'pi na gṛhāni tanaya-pitṛ-mātr-apekṣayā /
te 'pi niyama-vidhim ā-maraṇāj jagṛhuś ca yukta-manasaś ca dadhrire // 3.29 //
But even those who did not leave home, out of regard for children or father or mother: / They also, until their death, embraced the preventive rule and, with ready minds, they held to it:[10] // 3.29 //

na jihiṁsa sūkṣmam api jantum api para-vadhopajīvanaḥ /
kiṁ bata vipula-guṇaḥ kula-jaḥ sadayaḥ sadā kim-u muner upāsakaḥ // 3.30 //
No living creature, no matter how small, was subjected to violence, even by a person who killed for a living, / Still less by a man of great virtue, good family and unfailing gentleness – and how much less by a servant of the Sage?[11] // 3.30 //

---

[9] This is the first of several verses in Saundarananda in which Aśvaghoṣa alludes to the color of the buddha-robe (see e.g. SN18.20). It is described as being yellow-red, and therefore, in the right light, having a golden hue. The robe is comparable to a net in that it is a patchwork of panels, stitched together in back-stitches whose heads sometimes look like little pearls.

[10] The final word can also be read as *dadhyire,* in which case *yukta-manasaś ca dadhyire* means "And, with ready minds, they meditated." EHJ's rejection of this reading, on the grounds that meditation is not suitable for householders, is not well founded. The context, however, which is observance of the ten precepts, does seem to point to *dadhrire* (they held to it) rather than *dadhyire* (they meditated*).*

[11] Precept one: not to inflict needless harm on living beings.

akṛśodyamaḥ kṛśadhano 'pi para-paribhavāsaho 'pi san /
nānya-dhanam apajahāra tathā bhujagād ivānya-vibhavādd hi vivyathe // 3.31 //
The man not shy of hard work and yet still short of money, though he could not bear the other's slights, / Did not, even so, carry off the other's goods; for he shrank from others' riches as from a snake.[12] // 3.31 //

vibhavānvito 'pi taruṇo 'pi viṣaya-capalendriyo 'pi san /
naiva ca para-yuvatīr agamat paramaṁ hi tā dahanato 'py amanyata // 3.32 //
Even the man of money and youth with senses excited by objects of his affection – / Even he never approached others' wives, for he deemed them to be more dangerous than a burning fire.[13] // 3.32 //

anṛtam jagāda na ca kaś-cid ṛtam api jajalpa nāpriyaṁ /
ślakṣṇam api ca na jagāv ahitaṁ hitam apy uvāca na ca paiśunāya yat // 3.33 //
Nobody told an untruth, nor made true but nasty gossip, / Nor crooned slick but malicious words, nor spoke kindly words that had a backbiting motive.[14] // 3.33 //

manasā lulobha na ca jātu para-vasuṣu gṛddha-mānasaḥ /
kāma-sukham asukhato vimṛśan vijahāra tṛpta iva tatra saj-janaḥ // 3.34 //
No greedy-minded person, in his heart, had any designs on the treasures of others; / Seeing sensual happiness to be no happiness, the wise went freely on their way, as if satisfied in that area already.[15] // 3.34 //

na parasya kaś-cid apaghātam api ca sa-ghṛṇo vyacintayat /
mātṛ-pitṛ-suta-suhṛt-sadṛśam sa dadarśa tatra hi parasparaṁ janaḥ // 3.35 //
Nobody showed any hostility towards the other; rather, they looked on others with positive warmth, / As mother, father, child or friend: for each person there saw in the other himself.[16] // 3.35 //

niyatam bhaviṣyati paratra bhavad api ca bhūtam apy atho /
karma-phalam api ca loka-gatir niyateti darśanam avāpa sādhu ca // 3.36 //
That the fruit of conduct, inevitably, will be realized in the future, is being realized now, and has been realized in the past; / And that thus is determined how one fares in the world: this is an insight that, again, each experienced unerringly.[17] // 3.36 //

---

[12] Precept two: not to steal.
[13] Precept three: not to engage in illicit sexual relations.
[14] Precepts four, five, six and seven: not to engage in four kinds of false speech.
[15] Precept eight: not to covet.
[16] Precept nine: not to show hostility.
[17] Precept ten: not to have any doubt about cause and effect.

iti karmaṇā daśa-vidhena parama-kuśalena bhūriṇā /
bhraṁśini śithila-guṇo 'pi yuge vijahāra tatra muni-saṁśrayāj janaḥ // 3.37 //
By this most skillful and powerful tenfold means, by the means of their conduct, / Although virtue was lax in a declining age, the people there, with the Sage's help, fared well. // 3.37 //

na ca tatra kaś-cid upapatti-sukham abhilalāṣa tair guṇaiḥ /
sarvam aśivam avagamya bhavaṁ bhava-saṁkṣayāya vavṛte na janmane // 3.38 //
But nobody there, because of his virtues, expected happiness in a resulting birth; / Having learned that all becoming is pernicious, people worked to eradicate becoming, not to become something. // 3.38 //

akathaṁkathā gṛhiṇa eva parama-pariśuddha-dṛṣṭayaḥ /
srotasi hi vavṛtire bahavo rajasas tanutvam api cakrire pare // 3.39 //
Even householders were free from endless doubting, their views washed spotlessly away: / For many had entered the stream,[18] and others[19] had reduced the passions to a trickle.[20] // 3.39 //

vavṛte 'tra yo 'pi viṣayeṣu vibhava-sadṛśeṣu kaś-cana /
tyāga-vinaya-niyamābhirato vijahāra so 'pi na cacāla sat-pathāt // 3.40 //
Even one there who had been given over to ends like wealth[21] / Was now content with free giving, discipline, and restraint: he also fared well, not straying from the true path. // 3.40 //

---

[18] *Srotasi hi vavṛtire.* √*vṛt* with locative more literally means to advance in, to flow along in. Stream-entry is the first of four levels of awakening, or fruits of dharma, that Nanda is described as realizing in Canto 17, "having shaken off every vestige of the personality view" (SN17.27). The personality view is the first of ten fetters, viz: 1. personality view, 2. doubting, 3. clinging to good conduct and vows of practice, 4. sensual desire, 5, ill will; 6. desire for form, 7. desire for the formless or immaterial, 8. conceit, 9. restlessness, 10. ignorance. One who is free from fetters 1-3 is a stream-winner, having entered the stream to nirvāna.

[19] Alternate translation: "Afterwards they reduced the passions to a trickle" – *pare* means 1. "others" and 2. "afterwards."

[20] *Rajasas*, "the passions" here suggests sensual desire and ill will, the fourth and fifth of the ten fetters. One who, besides the first three fetters, has overcome fetters 4-5 in their grosser form, is a "once-returner." He or she has attained the second fruit of dharma but, not yet being completely free of fetters 4-5, is still subject to one more return to the sensuous world. One who is fully freed from fetters 1-5 has attained the third fruit as a "non-returner." The first five fetters are called "lower fetters," since they tie us to sensuous realms, whereas the five upper fetters (see SN17.57) tie us to spiritual or aspirational realms. One who has cut all ten fetters, ending with ignorance, has attained the fourth fruit of arhathood (see SN17.57; 17.72).

[21] Cf. SN2.60 and 2.61. Aśvaghoṣa's attitude to wealth at first glance seems contradictory. But on closer investigation, there is no contradiction: as a means, wealth can be useful; but pursuit of wealth as an end is errant behavior.

api ca svato 'pi parato 'pi na bhayam abhavan na daivataḥ /
tatra ca susukha-subhikṣa-guṇair jahṛṣuḥ prajāḥ kṛta-yuge manor iva // 3.41 //
Neither from within the self, nor from without, did any terror arise; nor from fate. / By dint of their true happiness and material plenty and practical merits, the citizens there rejoiced as in the golden age of Manu.[22] // 3.41 //

iti muditam anāmayaṁ nirāpat kuru-raghu-pūru-puropamaṁ puraṁ tat /
abhavad abhaya-daiśike mahārṣau viharati tatra śivāya vīta-rāge // 3.42 //
Thus exulting in freedom from disease and calamity, that city was the equal of Kuru,[23] Raghu and Pūru, / With the great dispassionate Seer serving there, for the good of all, as a guide to peace.[24] // 3.42 //

iti saundaranande mahākāvye tathāgata-varṇano nāma tṛtīyaḥ sargaḥ //3//
The 3rd Canto in the epic poem Handsome Nanda, titled "A Portrait of the Tathāgata."

---

[22] Manu means archetypal Man, progenitor of the human race.
[23] Kuru was the name of an ancient Indo-Aryan tribe, and of their kingdom (see also SN9.17 and 9.20).
[24] *Abhaya*, peace, or absence of fear, is opposed to *bhayam* ("terror") in the previous verse. *Vi-hṛ*, translated previously as "to fare well," has a sense of freedom of movement, or carefree adventure, which has been lost in the translation of this verse (see also SN5.20).

Canto 4: bhāryā-yācitakaḥ
A Wife's Appeal

Introduction

Bhāryā, the feminine of *bhārya*, from the root *√bhṛ*, to bear, literally means a woman to be borne or supported or cherished or nourished or maintained; hence, a wife. *Yācitaka*, which as an adjective means borrowed and as a noun means something borrowed, is from the root *√yāc*, which means to ask or beg.

When we examine the content of the canto so as to understand the meaning of *bhāryā-yācitaka* in context, we find the scent of sensuality thick in the air, until Nanda sets out, hesitantly, to catch up with the Buddha on the road. In order to make this transition – in order to be released from his wife's loving embrace – Nanda makes a bargain with his wife Sundarī that he will be back before her make-up is dried. Hence, in EH Johnston's translation, *bhāryā-yācitakaḥ* is "The Wife's Bargain." Reflecting the original meaning of *√yāc*, Linda Covill translates *bhāryā-yācitakaḥ* "His Wife's Request," taking Sundarī to be the subject who begs Nanda to come back. In verse 32, however, it is rather Nanda who begs Sundarī to allow him to go and see the Buddha – as if he were asking to borrow some time away, a leave of absence. In this context, the inelegant "What He Begged His Wife for" would fit.

As in many other canto titles, then, the noun-verb combination of this canto title is open to numerous readings. What is not in doubt, in the overall context of the epic tale of Handsome Nanda, is that Nanda's wife was very beautiful, and that the love between Nanda and Sundarī was not only platonic but was also conspicuously sensual. Thus the memory of Sundarī continued to exert a strong pull on Nanda's body and mind long after he had left home to take to the wandering life. If we ever thought that a celibate life in the modern world has become a harder path to follow than it would have been in a more innocent antiquity, then the descriptions of love in the present canto vividly challenge that view.

munau bruvāṇe 'pi tu tatra dharmaṁ dharmaṁ prati jñātiṣu cādṛteṣu /
prāsāda-saṁstho madanaika-kāryaḥ priyā-sahāyo vijahāra nandaḥ // 4.1 //
But even when the Sage was there speaking the dharma, and even though other family members heeded the dharma, / Nanda passed the time in the company of his wife, staying in the palace penthouse, solely occupied with love. // 4.1 //

sa cakravākyeva hi cakravākas tayā sametaḥ priyayā priyārhaḥ /
nācintayad vaiśramaṇaṁ na śakraṁ tat-sthāna-hetoḥ kuta eva dharmam // 4.2 //
For joined with his wife like a greylag gander with a greylag goose,[1] and fitted for love, / He turned his thoughts neither to Vaiśravaṇa nor to Śakra: how much less, in that state, did he think about dharma? // 4.2 //

---

[1] Male and female greylag geese feature prominently in Sanskrit romantic literature. Their Sanskrit name, *cakravāka*, arises from the way they call to each other, the male gently honking, the female responding, the male replying, and so on; a cycle or 'wheel' (*cakra*) of song. Their gentle, musical '*aang aang aang*' is said to be one of the most enchanting calls in the natural world.

lakṣmyā ca rūpeṇa ca sundarīti stambhena garveṇa ca māninīti /
dīptyā ca mānena ca bhāminīti yāto babhāṣe trividhena nāmnā // 4.3 //
For her grace and beauty, she was called Lovely Sundarī; for her headstrong pride, Sulky Māninī; / And for her sparkle and spirit, Beautiful Bhāminī. So that she was called by three names. // 4.3 //

sā hāsa-haṁsā nayana-dvirephā pīna-stanātyunnata-padma-kośā /
bhūyo babhāse sva-kuloditena strī-padminī nanda-divākareṇa // 4.4 //
She of smiles like the bars of a bar-headed-goose, of eyes like black bees, and swelling breasts like the upward jutting buds of a lotus, / Shimmered all the more, a lotus-pool in female form, with the rising of a kindred luminary, the sun-like Nanda.[2] // 4.4 //

rūpeṇa cātyanta-manohareṇa rūpānurūpeṇa ca ceṣṭitena /
manuṣya-loke hi tadā babhūva sā sundarī strīṣu nareṣu nandaḥ // 4.5 //
For, with inordinately good looks, and moves to match those heart-stealing looks, / There was in the human world at that time, among women, [only] Sundarī, and among men, Nanda. // 4.5 //

sā devatā nandana-cāriṇīva kulasya nandī-jananaś ca nandaḥ /
atītya martyān anupetya devān sṛṣṭāv abhūtām iva bhūta-dhātrā // 4.6 //
She, like a goddess wandering in Indra's Gardens of Gladness,[3] and Nanda, the bringer of joy to his kin, / Seemed, having gone beyond mortals, and yet not become gods, to be happening in a production by the Orderer of Happenings.[4] // 4.6 //

tāṁ sundarīṁ cen na labheta nandaḥ sā vā niṣeveta na taṁ nata-bhrūḥ /
dvandvaṁ dhruvaṁ tad vikalaṁ na śobhetānyonya-hīnāv iva rātri-candrau // 4.7 //
If Nanda had not won Sundarī, or if she of the arched eyebrows had not gone to him, / Then, deprived of each other, the two would surely have seemed impaired, like the night and the moon.[5] // 4.7 //

---

[2] "Sun-like Nanda" alludes to Nanda's heritage as a descendant of Ikṣvāku, founder of the solar dynasty (see SN1.18).

[3] Nandana, lit. "Gladdening" is the name of Indra's paradise. This is the setting for Canto 10, where the Buddha introduces the gob-smacked Nanda to the all-surpassing beauty of the celestial nymphs, the *apsarases*.

[4] *Bhūta-dhātṛ* ostensibly means Brahmā as "the Creator of what Exists." The use of *abhūtām* and *bhūta,* two words from the verbal root √*bhū*, however, may suggest an emptier sub-text, in the middle way between existing and not existing.

[5] In Sanskrit the night (*ratrī*) is feminine and the moon (*candra*) is masculine.

kandarpa-ratyor iva lakṣya-bhūtaṁ pramoda-nāndyor iva nīḍa-bhūtam / praharṣa-tuṣṭyor iva pātra-bhūtaṁ dvandvaṁ sahāraṁsta tad andha-bhūtam // 4.8 //

As though a target[6] of the god of Love and his mistress Pleasure; as though a nest of Ecstasy and Joy; / As though a bowl of Excitement and Contentment; blindly the couple took their pleasure together.[7] // 4.8 //

parasparodvīkṣaṇa-tat-parākṣaṁ paraspara-vyāhṛta-sakta-cittam / parasparāśleṣa-hṛtāṅgarāgaṁ parasparaṁ tan-mithunaṁ jahāra // 4.9 //

Having eyes only for each other's eyes, minds hanging on each other's words, / Mutual embraces rubbing away the pigments that scented their bodies, the couple carried each other away. // 4.9 //

bhāvānuraktau giri-nirjhara-sthau tau kiṁnarī-kiṁpuruṣāv ivobhau / cikrīḍatuś cābhivirejatuś ca rūpa-śriyānyonyam ivākṣipantau // 4.10 //

Like a kiṁnara meeting a kiṁnarī by a cascading mountain torrent, loving love happening,[8] / The two of them flirted and shone, as if vying to outdo one another in alluring radiance. // 4.10 //

anyonya-saṁrāga-vivardhanena tad-dvandvam anyonyam arīramac ca / klamāntare 'nyonya-vinodanena salīlam anyonyam amīmadac ca // 4.11 //

By building up each other's passion, the pair gave each other sensual satisfaction; / And by playfully teasing each other during languid intervals, they gladdened each other again. // 4.11 //

vibhūṣayām āsa tataḥ priyāṁ sa siṣeviṣus tāṁ na mṛjāvahārtham / svenaiva rūpeṇa vibhūṣitā hi vibhūṣaṇānām api bhūṣaṇaṁ sā // 4.12 //

Wishing to cherish his beloved, he bedecked her there in finery, but not with the aim of making her beautiful – / For she was so graced already by her own loveliness that she was rather the adorner of her adornments.[9] // 4.12 //

---

6 The paper manuscript has *lakṣma* (= *deva-lakṣma*, "divine characteristic") rather than *lakṣya* ("target"); in a note to his English translation EHJ thought perhaps the former reading should be retained. Either reading fits with a four-phased interpretation of the verse along the lines of (1) something divine/spiritual/romantic/idealized, or a target, (2) a concrete place of refuge free from pursuit of targets, (3) a practical utensil like a bhikṣu's bowl, having both spiritual meaning and actual substance, and (4) a meeting of subject and object.

7 Each of the three dual compounds is a masculine-feminine combination: *kandarpa* (Love) is masculine, *rati* (Pleasure) is feminine; *pramoda* (Ecstasy) is masculine, *nāndī* (Joy) is feminine. *praharṣa* (Excitement) is masculine, *tuṣṭi* (Contentment) is feminine.

8 *Bhāva* is a word pregnant with many meanings, including "what happens" as well as the ostensible meanings here of love, passion, etc. Could *bhāvānuraktau*, in a hidden meaning, describe teacher and student enjoying the friendly practice of letting happen (*mettaṃ bhāvanaṃ*)? Cf MMK25.9: "*Whatever is going on, due to clinging or due to conditioning, that, without the clinging and conditioning, is taught as nirvāṇa.*" In the same vein, MMK25.19-20: "*Saṁsāra has nothing to distinguish it from nirvāṇa. Nirvāṇa has nothing to distinguish it from saṁsāra. Whatever upper edge nirvāṇa has is also the upper edge of saṁsāra. Between those two, not the slightest gap is witnessed.*"

dattvātha sā darpaṇam asya haste mamāgrato dhāraya tāvad enam /
viśeṣakaṁ yāvad ahaṁ karomīty uvāca kāntaṁ sa ca taṁ babhāra // 4.13 //
She put a mirror in his hand; "Just hold this in front of me / While I do my face," she said to her lover, and up he held it. // 4.13 //

bhartus tataḥ śmaśru nirīkṣamāṇā viśeṣakaṁ sāpi cakāra tādṛk /
niśvāsa-vātena ca darpaṇasya cikitsayitvā nijaghāna nandaḥ // 4.14 //
Then, beholding her husband's stubble she began to paint her face just like it, / But, with a breath on the mirror, Nanda soon took care of that. // 4.14 //

sā tena ceṣṭā-lalitena bhartuḥ śāṭhyena cāntar-manasā jahāsa /
bhavec ca ruṣṭā kila nāma tasmai lalāṭa-jihmāṁ bhru-kuṭiṁ cakāra // 4.15 //
At this wanton gesture of her husband, and at his wickedness, she inwardly laughed; / But, pretending to be furious with him, she cocked her eyebrows and frowned. // 4.15 //

cikṣepa karṇotpalam asya cāṁse kareṇa savyena madālasena /
pattrāṅguliṁ cārdha-nimīlitākṣe vaktre 'sya tām eva vinirdudhāva // 4.16 //
With a left hand made languid by love, she took a flower from behind her ear and threw it at his shoulder; / Again, as he kept his eyes half-shut, she sprinkled over his face the scented make-up she had been using to powder herself.[10] // 4.16 //

tataś calan nūpura-yoktritābhyām nakha-prabhodbhāsitarāṅgulibhyām /
padbhyāṁ priyāyā nalinopamābhyām mūrdhnā bhayān nāma nanāma nandaḥ // 4.17 //
Then, at his wife's lotus like feet, which were girt in trembling ankle bracelets, / Their toes sparkling with nail gloss, Nanda bowed his head, in mock terror.[11] // 4.17 //

sa mukta-puṣponmiṣitena mūrdhnā tataḥ priyāyāḥ priya-kṛd babhāse /
suvarṇa-vedyām anilāvabhagnaḥ puṣpātibhārād iva nāga-vṛkṣaḥ // 4.18 //
As his head emerged from beneath the discarded flower, he made as if to regain his lover's affections; / He looked like an ornamental nāga tree, overburdened with blossoms, that had toppled in the wind onto its golden pedestal. // 4.18 //

---

[9] LC: "for she was so adorned by her own beauty that it was she who lent loveliness to her jewels."

[10] "The scented make-up she had been using to powder herself" represents *pattrāṅgulim*, given in SED as "a decoration consisting in lines or streaks drawn on the face and body with musk and other fragrant substances." *Aṅguli* means finger. And *pattra*, leaf, would seem to allude to *tamāla-pattra* (see verse 20 below) which means 1. a leaf of the *tamāla* plant (Xanthochymus pictorius), and hence 2. a mark on the forehead made with the juice of this plant.

[11] Note the euphony, totally lost in translation, of *nāma nanāma nandaḥ*.

sā taṁ stanodvartita-hāra-yaṣṭir utthāpayām āsa nipīḍya dorbhyām /
kathaṁ kṛto 'sīti jahāsa coccair mukhena sācī-kṛta-kuṇḍalena // 4.19 //
Pressing him so close in her arms that her pearls lifted off from her swelling breasts, she raised him up; / "What are you doing!?" she cried laughingly, as her earrings dangled across her face. // 4.19 //

patyus tato darpaṇa-sakta-pāṇer muhur-muhur vaktram avekṣamāṇā /
tamāla-pattrārdra-tale kapole samāpayām āsa viśeṣakaṁ tat // 4.20 //
Then, looking repeatedly at the face of her husband, whose hand had clung to the mirror, / She completed her face-painting, so that the surface of her cheeks was wet with *tamāla* juice.[12] // 4.20 //

tasyā mukhaṁ tat sa-tamāla-pattraṁ tāmrādharauṣṭhaṁ cikurāyatākṣam /
raktādhikāgraṁ patita-dvirephaṁ sa-śaivalaṁ padmam ivābabhāse // 4.21 //
Framed by the tamāla smudges, her face with its cherry red lips, and wide eyes extending to her hair, / Seemed like a lotus framed by duck-weed, with crimson tips, and two big bees settled on it. // 4.21 //

nandas tato darpaṇam ādareṇa bibhrat tadā maṇḍana-sākṣi-bhūtaṁ /
viśeṣakāvekṣaṇa-kekarākṣo laḍat-priyāyā vadanaṁ dadarśa // 4.22 //
Attentively now, Nanda held the mirror, which was bearing witness to a work of beauty. / Squinting to see the flecks she had painted, he beheld the face of his impish lover. // 4.22 //

tat-kuṇḍalādaṣṭa-viśeṣakāntaṁ kāraṇḍava-kliṣṭam ivāravindam /
nandaḥ priyāyā mukham īkṣamāṇo bhūyaḥ priyānanda-karo babhūva // 4.23 //
The make-up was nibbled away at its edges by her earrings so that her face was like a lotus that had suffered the attentions of a *kāraṇḍava* duck. / Nanda, by gazing upon that face, became all the more the cause of his wife's happiness. // 4.23 //

vimāna-kalpe sa vimāna-garbhe tatas tathā caiva nananda nandaḥ /
tathāgataś cāgata-bhaikṣa-kālo bhaikṣāya tasya praviveśa veśma // 4.24 //
While Nanda, inside the palace, in what almost amounted to a dishonor,[13] was thus enjoying himself, / The Tathāgata, the One Thus Come, come begging time, had entered the palace, for the purpose of begging. // 4.24 //

avāṅmukho niṣpraṇayaś ca tasthau bhrātur gṛhe 'nyasya gṛhe yathaiva /
tasmād atho preṣya-jana-pramādād bhikṣām alabdhvaiva punar jagāma // 4.25 //
With face turned down, he stood, in his brother's house as in any other house, not expecting anything; / And then, since due to the servants' oversight, he received no alms, he went again on his way. // 4.25 //

[12] Lit. "She finished face-painting on the cheek with its surface wet with *tamāla* leaf."
[13] This can be read as a play on the word *vimāna*, which means 1. disrespect, dishonor, and 2. palace.

kā-cit pipeṣānuvilepanaṁ hi vāso 'ṅganā kā-cid avāsayac ca /
ayojayat snāna-vidhiṁ tathānyā jagranthur anyāḥ surabhīḥ srajaś ca // 4.26 //
For one woman was grinding fragrant body oils; another was perfuming clothes; / Another, likewise, was preparing a bath; while other women strung together sweet-smelling garlands. // 4.26 //

tasmin gṛhe bhartur ataś carantyaḥ krīḍānurūpaṁ lalitaṁ niyogam /
kāś-cin na buddhaṁ dadṛśur yuvatyo buddhasya vaiṣā niyataṁ manīṣā // 4.27 //
The girls in that house were thus so busy doing work to promote their master's romantic play / That none of them had seen the Buddha – or so the Buddha inevitably concluded. // 4.27 //

kā-cit sthitā tatra tu harmya-pṛṣṭhe gavākṣa-pakṣe praṇidhāya cakṣuḥ /
viniṣpatantaṁ sugataṁ dadarśa payoda-garbhād iva dīptam arkam // 4.28 //
One woman there, however, on glancing through a round side-window on the upper story of the palace, / Had seen the Sugata, the One Gone Well, going away – like the blazing sun emerging from a cloud. // 4.28 //

sā gauravaṁ tatra vicārya bhartuḥ svayā ca bhaktyārhatayārhataś ca /
nandasya tasthau purato vivakṣus tad-ājñayā ceti tadā cacakṣe // 4.29 //
Thinking in that moment of the importance of the Worthy One to the master of the house, and through her own devotion to the Worthy One, / She stood before Nanda, intending to speak. And then, with his permission,[14] up she spoke: // 4.29 //

anugrahāyāsya janasya śaṅke gurur gṛhaṁ no bhagavān praviṣṭaḥ /
bhikṣām alabdhvā giram āsanaṁ vā śūnyād araṇyād iva yāti bhūyaḥ // 4.30 //
"To show favor to us, I suppose, the Glorious One, the Guru, came into our house; / Having received neither alms, nor welcoming words, nor a place to sit, he is going away, as if from an empty forest." // 4.30 //

śrutvā maharṣeḥ sa gṛha-praveśaṁ satkāra-hīnaṁ ca punaḥ prayāṇam /
cacāla citrābharaṇāmbara-srak kalpa-drumo dhūta ivānilena // 4.31 //
When he heard that the great Seer had entered his house and departed again without receiving a welcome, / [Nanda] in his brightly-colored gems and garments and garlands, flinched, like a tree in Indra's paradise shaken by a gust of wind. // 4.31 //

kṛtvāñjaliṁ mūrdhani padma-kalpaṁ tataḥ sa kāntāṁ gamanaṁ yayāce /
kartuṁ gamiṣyāmi gurau praṇāmaṁ mām abhyanujñātum ihārhasīti // 4.32 //
He brought to his forehead hands joined in the shape of a lotus bud, and then he begged[15] his beloved to be allowed to go: / "I would like to go and pay my respects to the Guru. Please permit me, this once." // 4.32 //

---

[14] *Ājñā* here means permission or consent. Elsewhere in Saundarananda *ājñā* means deep or liberating knowledge. Its use in the title of the final canto may be a final instance of deliberate ambiguity.

sā vepamānā parisasvaje taṁ śālaṁ latā vāta-samīriteva /
dadarśa cāśru-pluta-lola-netrā dīrghaṁ ca niśvasya vaco 'bhyuvāca // 4.33 //
Shivering, she twined herself around him, like a wind-stirred creeper around a teak tree; / She looked at him through unsteady tear-filled eyes, took a deep breath, and told him: // 4.33 //

nāhaṁ yiyāsor guru-darśanārtham arhāmi kartum tava dharma-pīḍām /
gacchārya-putraihi ca śīghram eva viśeṣako yāvad ayaṁ na śuṣkaḥ // 4.34 //
"Since you wish to go and see the Guru, I shall not stand in the way of your dharma-duty. / Go, noble husband! But come quickly back, before this paint on my face is dry. // 4.34 //

saced bhaves tvaṁ khalu dīrgha-sūtro daṇḍaṁ mahāntaṁ tvayi pātayeyam /
muhur-muhus tvāṁ śayitaṁ kucābhyāṁ vibodhayeyaṁ ca na cālapeyam // 4.35 //
If you dawdle, I will punish you severely: / As you sleep I shall with my breasts, repeatedly wake you, and then not respond. // 4.35 //

athāpy anāśyāna-viśeṣakāyāṁ mayyeṣyasi tvaṁ tvaritaṁ tatas tvām /
nipīḍayiṣyāmi bhuja-dvayena nirbhūṣaṇenārdra-vilepanena // 4.36 //
But if you hurry back to me before my face-paint is dry, / Then I will hold you close in my arms with nothing on except fragrant oils." // 4.36 //

ity evam uktaś ca nipīḍitaś ca tayāsavarṇa-svanayā jagāda /
evaṁ kariṣyāmi vimuñca caṇḍe yāvad gurur dūra-gato na me saḥ // 4.37 //
Thus implored, and squeezed, by a dissonant-sounding [Sundarī], [Nanda] said: / "I will, my little vixen. Now let me go, before the Guru has gone too far." // 4.37 //

tataḥ stanodvartitata-candanābhyāṁ mukto bhujābhyāṁ na tu mānasena /
vihāya veṣaṁ madanānurūpaṁ tat-kārya-yogyam sa vapur babhāra // 4.38 //
And so, with arms made fragrant by her swollen sandal-scented breasts, she let him go – but not with her heart. / He took off clothes that were suited to love and took on a form that befitted his task. // 4.38 //

sā taṁ prayāntaṁ ramaṇaṁ pradadhyau pradhyāna-śūnya-sthita-niścalākṣī /
sthitocca-karṇā vyapaviddha-śaṣpā bhrāntaṁ mṛgaṁ bhrānta-mukhī mṛgīva // 4.39 //
She contemplated her lover leaving with brooding, empty, unmoving eyes, / Like a doe standing with ears pricked up as she lets grass drop down; and as, with a perplexed expression, she contemplates the stag wandering away. // 4.39 //

---

[15] *Yayāce*, "he begged," like the *yācita* of the canto title, is from the root √*yāc*.

didṛkṣayākṣīpta-manā munes tu nandaḥ prayāṇaṁ prati tatvare ca /
vivṛtta-dṛṣṭiś ca śanair yayau tāṁ karīva paśyan sa laḍat-kareṇum // 4.40 //
With his mind gripped by desire to set eyes upon the Sage, Nanda hurried his exit; / But then he went ponderously, and with backward glances – like an elephant looking back at a playful she-elephant. // 4.40 //

chātodarīṁ pīna-payodharoruṁ sa sundarīṁ rukma-darīm ivādreḥ /
kākṣeṇa paśyan na tatarpa nandaḥ pibann ivaikena jalaṁ kareṇa // 4.41 //
Between her swelling cloud-like breasts[16] and [the buttresses] of her full thighs, Sundarī's lean abdomen was like a golden fissure in a rock formation: / Looking at her could satisfy Nanda no better than drinking water out of one hand. // 4.41 //

taṁ gauravaṁ buddha-gataṁ cakarṣa bhāryānurāgaḥ punar ācakarṣa /
so 'niścayān nāpi yayau na tasthau turaṁs taraṅgeṣv iva rāja-haṁsaḥ // 4.42 //
Reverence for the Buddha drew him on; love for his wife drew him back: / Irresolute, he neither stayed nor went, like a king-goose pushing forwards against the waves. // 4.42 //

adarśanaṁ tūpagataś ca tasyā harmyāt tataś cāvatatāra tūrṇam /
śrutvā tato nūpura-nisvanaṁ sa punar lalambe hṛdaye gṛhītaḥ // 4.43 //
Once she was out of sight, he descended from the palace quickly – / Then he heard the sound of ankle bracelets, and back he hung, gripped in his heart again. // 4.43 //

sa kāma-rāgeṇa nigṛhyamāṇo dharmānurāgeṇa ca kṛṣyamāṇaḥ /
jagāma duḥkhena vivartyamānaḥ plavaḥ pratisrota ivāpagāyāḥ // 4.44 //
Held back by his love of love, and drawn forward by his love for dharma, / He struggled on, being turned about[17] like a boat on a river going against the stream. // 4.44 //

tataḥ kramair dīrghatamaiḥ pracakrame kathaṁ nu yāto na gurur bhaved iti /
svajeya tāṁ caiva viśeṣaka-priyāṁ kathaṁ priyām ārdra-viśeṣakām iti // 4.45 //
Then his strides became longer, as he thought to himself, "Maybe the Guru is no longer there!" / "Might I after all embrace my love, who is so especially loveable, while her face-paint is still wet?" // 4.45 //

---

[16] *Payo-dhara,* "containing water or milk," means 1. a cloud, and 2. a woman's breast.

[17] Gawronski suggested amendment to *nivartyamāmaḥ* ("being turned back"), as opposed to *vivartyamāmaḥ* ("being turned round"). For his Sanskrit text, EH Johnston retained *vivartyamāmaḥ* and in a note to his English translation several years later EHJ asserted "I still think my explanation correct; for it is based on the way a boat behaves when propelled against the stream." Subsequently, a fragment of manuscript was found in Central Asia by Friedrich Weller, showing *vivartyamāmaḥ* and thus tending to confirm that EHJ's intuition had indeed been correct.

atha sa pathi dadarśa mukta-mānaṁ pitṛ-nagare 'pi tathā gatābhimānam /
daśa-balam abhito vilambamānaṁ dhvajam anuyāna ivaindram arcyamānam // 4.46 //
And so on the road [Nanda] saw the One in Whom Absence Was Thus, the Tathāgata,[18] devoid of pride and – even in his father's city – haughtiness thus absent; / Seeing the Possessor of Ten Powers stopping and being honored on all sides, [Nanda] felt as if he were following Indra's flag.[19] // 4.46 //

saudaranande mahā-kāvye bhāryā-yācitako nāma caturthaḥ sargaḥ //4//
The 4th canto in the epic poem Handsome Nanda, titled "A Wife's Appeal."

---

[18] *Tathāgata* is not explicitly used here as an epipthet of the Buddha, but the description of the Buddha as being "similarly free" of haughtiness is a play on the meaning of the words *tathā* (similarly) and *gata* (gone, absent). When combined in the epithet *tathāgata*, these words *tathā* and *gata* (or *tathā* and *āgata*) can mean the Thus-Come, or the One Who Arrived Like This, or the One Who Arrived at Reality, or the Realized One. These are translations that suggest in the Buddha the presence of something ineffable. The use of *tathāgata* in today's verse, on the contrary, seems to point not to the presence of something but rather to the absence of something – the One in Whom Absence Was Like This.

[19] Weller's fragment has parts of an additional closing verse, numbered 45. So the Nepalese manuscripts had two earlier verses which Weller's Central Asian manuscript lacked, and the Central Asian manuscript had a final verse which the Nepalese manuscript lacked.

Canto 5: nanda-pravrājanaḥ
Nanda Is Caused to Go Forth.

Introduction

In the title of the present canto *pravrājana*, which means banishment or exile, is derived from the causative of *pra-√vraj*, which means to go forth, i.e. to leave home and take to the life of a wandering mendicant. So *nanda-pravrājanaḥ* means "Nanda Is Caused to Go Forth [as a Bhikkhu]."[1]

At the same time, Nanda means joy or happiness; and so the ironic hidden meaning of the canto title – ironic insofar as the title of the whole poem can be read as "An Epic Tale of Beautiful Happiness" (*Saundara-nanda mahā-kāvya*) – is "The Banishment of Joy."

There is beauty in Aśvaghoṣa's description of the shaven-headed Nanda, whom he compares to a rain-sodden lotus protruding limply from a pond, but for Nanda the shaving of his head does indeed represent the banishment of all joy. For Nanda, there is no happiness in it. Rather great joy and ultimate happiness follow much later in the process when, as described in Cantos 17 and 18, Nanda succeeds in gaining mastery over the Buddha's teaching of the four noble truths.

athāvatīryāśva-ratha-dvipebhyaḥ śākyā yathā-sva-rddhi-gṛhīta-veṣāḥ /
mahā-paṇebhyo vyavahāriṇaś ca mahā-munau bhakti-vaśāt praṇemuḥ // 5.1 //
Then the Śākyas, each clothed in accordance with his wealth and accomplishments, got down from their horses, chariots, and elephants, / And the traders came out of their big shops: by dint of their devotion, they bowed down before the great Sage. // 5.1 //

ke-cit praṇamyānuyayur muhūrtaṁ ke-cit praṇamyārtha-vaśena jagmuḥ /
ke-cit svayaivāyatane tu tasthuḥ kṛtvāñjalīn vīkṣaṇa-tat-parākṣāḥ // 5.2 //
Some bowed and then followed for a while; some bowed and went, being compelled to work. / But some remained still at their own dwelling-places,[2] their hands joined and eyes observing him in the distance. // 5.2 //

buddhas tatas tatra narendra-mārge sroto mahad-bhaktimato janasya /
jagāma duḥkhena vigāhamāno jalāgame srota ivāpagāyāḥ // 5.3 //
The Buddha then, and there, on the royal road, struggled on / Into the gushing throng of the greatly devoted, as if entering the torrent of a river in the rains. // 5.3 //

---

[1] EH Johnston translated "The Initiation of Nanda" and Linda Covill "Nanda is Made to Ordain."

[2] The Nepalese manuscripts have *ke-cit svakeṣv āvasatheṣu tasthuḥ* "Some stood/remained still at their own dwelling-places." Weller's fragment has *ke-cit svayaivāyatane tu tasthuḥ*. This might be translated "But some remained still at their very own (*svaya + eva*) seats (*āyatane*)," thus being even more suggestive, in its hidden meaning, of sitting-meditation itself. SED gives *āvasatha* as dwelling-place, abode, habitation, and *āyatana* as resting-place, support, seat, place, home, house.

atho mahadbhiḥ pathi saṁpatadbhiḥ saṁpūjyamānāya tathāgatāya /
kartuṁ praṇāmaṁ na śaśāka nandas tenābhireme tu guror mahimnā // 5.4 //
And so, with the great and the good rapidly converging on the road, to honor the Tathāgata, / Nanda was unable to make a bow; but still he could delight in the Guru's greatness. // 5.4 //

svaṁ cāvasaṅgaṁ pathi nirmumukṣur bhaktiṁ janasyānya-mateś ca rakṣan /
nandaṁ ca gehābhimukhaṁ jighṛkṣan mārgaṁ tato 'nyaṁ sugataḥ prapede // 5.5 //
Wishing to shake off adherents[3] to him on the road, while tending the devotion of people who were differently minded,[4] / And wishing to take Nanda in hand, who was turning for home, the One Gone Well therefore took a different[5] path. // 5.5 //

tato viviktaṁ ca vivikta-cetāḥ sanmārga-vin mārgam abhipratasthe /
gatvāgrataś cāgryatamāya tasmai nāndī-vimuktāya nanāma nandaḥ // 5.6 //
He of the solitary and separate mind, a knower of the true path, took a solitary and separate path; / And Nanda whose name was Joy, going out in front, could bow to him, the One gone beyond joy, who was furthest out in front. // 5.6 //

śanair vrajann eva sa gauraveṇa paṭāvṛtāṁso vinatārdha-kāyaḥ /
adho-nibaddhāñjalir ūrdhva-netraḥ sagadgadaṁ vākyam idaṁ babhāṣe // 5.7 //
Walking forward meekly, with respectful seriousness, with cloak over one shoulder, body half-stooped, / Hands held down and eyes raised up, Nanda stuttered these words: // 5.7 //

prāsāda-saṁstho bhagavantam antaḥ-praviṣṭam aśrauṣam anugrahāya /
atas tvarāvān aham abhyupeto gṛhasya kakṣyā mahato 'bhyasūyan // 5.8 //
"While I was in the palace penthouse, Glorious One, I learned that you came in for our benefit; / And so I have come in a hurry, indignant with the many members of the palace household. // 5.8 //

tat sādhu sādhu-priya mat-priyārtham tatrāstu bhikṣūttama bhaikṣa-kālaḥ /
asau hi madhyaṁ nabhaso yiyāsuḥ kālaṁ pratismārayatīva sūryaḥ // 5.9 //
Therefore, rightly, O Favorer of the Righteous, and as a favor to me, be there [at the palace], O Supreme Seeker of Alms, at the time for eating alms, / For the sun is about to reach the middle of the sky, as if to remind us of the time." // 5.9 //

---

[3] Or more literally "adherence" – *avasaṅgam* is singular.

[4] *Anya-mateḥ*, "other-minded," on the surface means heretical, non-Buddhist, skeptical, disbelieving, in a pejorative sense, but Aśvaghoṣa's real intention may be that the Buddha discouraged blind belief and valued the efforts of individuals to think his teaching out for themselves.

[5] For further examples in Saundarananda of this use of *anya*, which means not only "other" or "different" but also "odd, individual, singular, alternative, unconventional," see especially SN Canto 10.

ity evam uktaḥ praṇatena tena snehābhimānonmukha-locanena /
tādṛṅ nimittaṁ sugataś cakāra nāhāra-kṛtyaṁ sa yathā viveda // 5.10 //
Thus addressed by the bowing [Nanda], whose expectant eyes looked up with tender affection, / The One Gone Well made a sign such that Nanda knew he would not be taking a meal. // 5.10 //

tataḥ sa kṛtvā munaye praṇāmaṁ gṛha-prayāṇāya matiṁ cakāra /
anugrahārthaṁ sugatas tu tasmai pātraṁ dadau puṣkara-pattra-netraḥ // 5.11 //
Then, having made his bow to the Sage, he made up his mind to head home; / But, as a favor, the One Gone Well, with lotus petal eyes, handed him his bowl. // 5.11 //

tataḥ sa loke dadataḥ phalārthaṁ pātrasya tasyāpratimasya pātram /
jagrāha cāpa-grahaṇa-kṣamābhyāṁ padmopamābhyāṁ prayataḥ karābhyām // 5.12 //
The Incomparable Vessel was offering his own vessel, to reap a fruit in the human world, / And so Nanda, outstretched, held the bowl with lotus-like hands, which were better suited to the holding of a bow. // 5.12 //

parāṅmukhas tv anya-manaskam ārād vijñāya nandaḥ sugataṁ gatāstham /
hasta-stha-pātro 'pi gṛhaṁ yiyāsuḥ sasāra mārgān munim īkṣamāṇaḥ // 5.13 //
But as soon as he sensed that the mind of the One Gone Well had gone elsewhere and was not on him, Nanda backtracked[6]; / Wanting, even with the bowl in his hands, to go home, he sidled away from the path - while keeping his eye on the Sage. // 5.13 //

bhāryānurāgeṇa yadā gṛhaṁ sa pātraṁ gṛhītvāpi yiyāsur eva /
vimohayām āsa munis tatas taṁ rathyā-mukhasyāvaraṇena tasya // 5.14 //
Then, at the moment that he in his yearning for his wife, despite holding the bowl, was about to head for home, / Just then the Sage bamboozled him, by blocking his entrance to the highway. // 5.14 //

nirmokṣa-bījaṁ hi dadarśa tasya jñānaṁ mṛdu kleśa-rajaś ca tīvram /
kleśānukūlaṁ viṣayātmakaṁ ca nandaṁ yatas taṁ munir ācakarṣa // 5.15 //
For he saw that in Nanda the seed of liberation, which is wisdom, was tenuous; while the fog of the afflictions was terribly thick; / And since he was susceptible to the afflictions and sensual by nature, therefore the Sage reined him in. // 5.15 //

---

[6] *Parāṅmukha* means 1. having the face turned away or averted, turning the back upon; 2. being averse from, hostile to. Since the relevant portion of the text is missing or illegible in both palm-leaf and paper manuscripts, the ending could be *parāṅmukhaḥ* or *parāṅmukhaṁ* (as per Shastri's conjecture). EHJ notes that (a) Shastri's *parāṅmukhaṁ* may be correct; and (b) *parāṅmukhaḥ* (read here as "turning the back upon" i.e. back-tracking) might also mean "averse from following the Buddha."

saṁkleśa-pakṣo dvividhaś ca dṛṣṭas tathā dvikalpo vyavadāna-pakṣaḥ /
ātmāśrayo hetu-balādhikasya bāhyāśrayaḥ pratyaya-gauravasya // 5.16 //
There are understood to be two aspects to defilement; correspondingly, there are two approaches to purification:[7] / In one with stronger motivation from within, there is self-reliance; in one who assigns weight to conditions, there is outer-dependence. // 5.16 //

ayatnato hetu-balādhikas tu nirmucyate ghaṭṭita-mātra eva /
yatnena tu pratyaya-neya-buddhir vimokṣam āpnoti parāśrayeṇa // 5.17 //
The one who is more strongly self-motivated loosens ties[8] without even trying, on receipt of the slightest stimulus; / Whereas the one whose mind is led by conditions struggles to find freedom, because of his dependence on others. // 5.17 //

nandaḥ sa ca pratyaya-neya-cetā yaṁ śiśriye tan-mayatām avāpa /
yasmād imaṁ tatra cakāra yatnaṁ taṁ sneha-paṅkān munir ujjihīrṣan // 5.18 //
And Nanda, whose mind was led by conditions, became absorbed into whomever he depended on; / The Sage, therefore, made this effort in his case, wishing to lift him out of the mire of love. // 5.18 //

nandas tu duḥkhena viceṣṭamānaḥ śanair agatyā gurum anvagacchat /
bhāryā-mukhaṁ vīkṣaṇa-lola-netraṁ vicintayann ārdra-viśeṣakaṁ tat // 5.19 //
But Nanda followed the Guru meekly and helplessly, squirming with discomfort, / As he thought of his wife's face, her eyes looking out restlessly, and the painted marks still moist. // 5.19 //

tato munis taṁ priya-mālya-hāraṁ vasanta-māsena kṛtābhihāram /
nināya bhagna-pramadā-vihāraṁ vidyā-vihārābhimataṁ vihāram // 5.20 //
And so the Sage led him, lover of garlands of pearls and flowers, whom the month of Spring, [Love's friend,][9] had appropriated, / To a playground where women were a broken amusement – to the *vihāra*,[10] beloved as a pleasure-ground of learning. // 5.20 //

---

[7] *Vyavadāna*, "purification," is from the root *ava-√do*, which means to cut off or cut out. Cf. Udānavarga 28.1: *sarva-pāpasyākaraṇaṁ kuśalasyopasaṁpadaḥ / svacitta-paryavadanam etad buddhasya śāsanam //* The corresponding Pali (Dhammapāda 183) is *sabbapāpassa akaraṇaṁ, kusalassa upasampadā / sacittapariyodapanaṁ etaṁ buddhāna' sāsanaṁ //* In Chinese: 諸惡莫作 衆善奉行 自淨其意 是諸佛教. SED gives the Sanskrit *paryavadāna* as "complete destruction or disappearance." The Pali *pariyodapanaṁ* and the Chinese 淨, however, both mean purification or cleansing.
The not doing of any wrong,
Undertaking what is good,
Cleansing one's own mind –
This is the teaching of buddhas.

[8] *Nirmucyate* is originally passive – he is easily freed, he naturally comes undone.

[9] *Vasanta*, lit. "the brilliant (season)," Spring, is often personified and considered as a friend or attendant of Kāma-deva, god of Love.

[10] *Vihāra*, which means walking for pleasure or amusement, and hence a place of recreation or pleasure-ground, was the name given to a hall where monks met or walked about. It came to mean the grounds of a monastery or temple.

dīnaṁ mahā-kāruṇikas tatas taṁ dṛṣṭvā muhūrtaṁ karuṇāyamānaḥ /
kareṇa cakrāṅka-talena mūrdhni pasparśa caivedam uvāca cainam // 5.21 //
Then the Greatly Compassionate One, watching him in his moment of misery and pitying him, / Put a hand, with wheel-marked palm, on his head and spoke to him thus: // 5.21 //

yāvan na hiṁsraḥ samupaiti kālaḥ śamāya tāvat kuru saumya buddhim /
sarvāvavasthāsu hi vartamānaḥ sarvābhisāreṇa nihanti mṛtyuḥ // 5.22 //
"While murderous Time has yet to come calling, set your mind, my friend, in the direction of peace. / For operating in all situations, using all manner of attacks, Death kills. // 5.22 //

sādhāraṇāt svapna-nibhād asārāl lolaṁ manaḥ kāma-sukhān niyaccha /
havyair ivāgneḥ pavaneritasya lokasya kāmair na hi tṛptir asti // 5.23 //
Restrain the restless mind from sensual pleasures, which are common, dream-like, and insubstantial; / For no more than a wind-fanned fire is sated by offerings are men satisfied by pleasures. // 5.23 //

śraddhā-dhanaṁ śreṣṭhatamaṁ dhanebhyaḥ prajñā-rasas tṛpti-karo rasebhyaḥ /
pradhānam adhyātma-sukhaṁ sukhebhyo 'vidyā-ratir duḥkhatamā ratibhyaḥ // 5.24 //
Most excellent among gifts is the gift of confidence. Most satisfying of tastes is the taste of real wisdom. / Foremost among comforts is being comfortable in oneself. The bliss of ignorance is the sorriest bliss.[11] // 5.24 //

hitasya vaktā pravaraḥ suhṛdbhyo dharmāya khedo guṇavān śramebhyaḥ /
jñānāya kṛtyaṁ paramaṁ kriyābhyaḥ kim indriyāṇām upagamya dāsyam // 5.25 //
The kindest-hearted friend is he who tells one what is truly salutary. The most meritorious effort is to exhaust oneself in pursuit of the truth. / Supreme among labours is to work towards true understanding. Why would one enter into service of the senses? // 5.25 //

tan niścitaṁ bhī-klama-śug-viyuktaṁ pareṣv anāyattam ahāryam anyaiḥ /
nityaṁ śivaṁ śānti-sukhaṁ vṛṇīṣva kim indriyārthārtham anartham ūḍhvā // 5.26 //
Select then that which is conclusive, which is beyond fear, fatigue and sorrow, and which is neither dependent on others nor removable by others: / Select the lasting and benign happiness of extinction. What is the point of enduring disappointment, by making an object of sense-objects? // 5.26 //

---

[11] The alternative reading *vidyā-ratir duḥkhatamā ratibhyaḥ* means "delight in [intellectual] knowledge is the sorriest delight." So, if *'vidya* is read, with the silent prefix *a-*, then the sentence means that ignorance is the sorriest bliss; but without the silent prefix, the sentence means that knowledge is the sorriest bliss. The ambiguity may well be intentional.

jarā-samā nāsty amṛjā prajānāṁ vyādheḥ samo nāsti jagaty anarthaḥ /
mṛtyoḥ samaṁ nāsti bhayaṁ pṛthivyām etat trayaṁ khalv avaśena sevyam // 5.27 //
Nothing takes away people's beauty like aging, there is no misfortune in the world like sickness, / And no terror on earth like death. Yet these three, inevitably, shall be obeyed. // 5.27 //

snehena kaś-cin na samo 'sti pāśaḥ sroto na tṛṣṇā-samam asti hāri /
rāgāgninā nāsti samas tathāgnis tac cet trayaṁ nāsti sukhaṁ ca te 'sti // 5.28 //
There is no fetter like love, no torrent that carries one away like thirst, / And likewise no fire like the fire of passion. If not for these three, happiness would be yours. // 5.28 //

avaśya-bhāvī priya-viprayogas tasmāc ca śoko niyataṁ niṣevyaḥ /
śokena conmādam upeyivāṁso rājarṣayo 'nye 'py avaśā viceluḥ // 5.29 //
Separation from loved ones is inevitable, on which account grief is bound to be experienced. / And it is through grief that other seers who were princes have gone mad and fallen helplessly apart. // 5.29 //

prajñā-mayaṁ varma badhāna tasmān no kṣānti-nighnasya hi śoka-bāṇāḥ /
mahac ca dagdhuṁ bhava-kakṣa-jālaṁ saṁdhukṣayālpāgnim ivātma-tejaḥ // 5.30 //
So bind on the armor whose fabric is wisdom, for the arrows of grief are as naught to one steeped in patience; / And kindle the fire of your own energy to burn up the great tangled web of becoming, just as you would kindle a small fire to burn up undergrowth collected into a great heap.[12] // 5.30 //

yathauṣadhair hasta-gataiḥ savidyo na daśyate kaś-cana pannagena /
tathānapekṣo jita-loka-moho na daśyate śoka-bhujaṁgamena // 5.31 //
Just as a man concerned with science, herbs in hand, is not bitten by any snake, / So a man without concern, having overcome the folly of the world, is not bitten by the snake of grief. // 5.31 //

āsthāya yogaṁ parigamya tattvaṁ na trāsam āgacchati mṛtyu-kāle /
ābaddha-varmā sudhanuḥ kṛtāstro jigīṣayā śūra ivāhava-sthaḥ // 5.32 //
Staying with practice and fully committed to what is, at the hour of death he is not afraid – / Like a warrior-hero standing in battle, clad in armor, and equipped with a good bow, with skill in archery, and with the will to win." // 5.32 //

---

[12] *Bhava* means becoming, the tenth in the 12 links in the dependent arising of suffering (see BC Canto 14), and one of the three (or four) categories of polluting influences. *Kakṣa* means dry wood, underwood (often the lair of wild beasts), spreading creepers, tangled undergrowth. *Jāla* means a net or a web, or (at the end of a compound) a collection, multitude, mass. *Mahat... bhava-kakṣa-jālam*, then, means (metaphorically) a great tangled web of becoming; at the same time *mahat... kakṣa-jālam* means (more literally) tangled undergrowth collected into a great heap. To convey the metaphorical and literal meanings combined in the one Sanskrit phrase, I have translated it twice.

ity evam uktaḥ sa tathāgatena sarveṣu bhūteṣv anukampakena /
dhṛṣṭaṁ girāntarhṛdayena sīdaṁs tatheti nandaḥ sugataṁ babhāṣe // 5.33 //
Addressed thus by the One Thus Come, the Tathāgata, in his compassion for all living beings, / Nanda while sinking inside said boldly to the Sugata, the One Well Gone: "So be it!" // 5.33 //

atha pramādāc ca tam ujjihīrṣan matvāgamasyaiva ca pātra-bhūtam /
pravrājayānanda śamāya nandam ity abravīn maitra-manā maharṣiḥ // 5.34 //
And so wishing to lift him up out of heedlessness, and deeming him to be a vessel worthy of the living tradition, / The Great Seer, with the love of a friend in his heart, said: "Ānanda![13] Let Nanda go forth towards tranquility." // 5.34 //

nandaṁ tato 'ntarmanasā rudantam ehīti vaideha-munir jagāda /
śanais tatas taṁ samupetya nando na pravrajiṣyāmy aham ity uvāca // 5.35 //
Then the sage of Videha[14] said to Nanda, who was weeping inside: "Come!" / At this Nanda approached him meekly and said "I won't go forth." // 5.35 //

śrutvātha nandasya manīṣitaṁ tad buddhāya vaideha-muniḥ śaśaṁsa /
saṁśrutya tasmād api tasya bhāvaṁ mahā-munir nandam uvāca bhūyaḥ // 5.36 //
On hearing Nanda's idea, the Videha sage related it to the Buddha; / And so, after hearing from him also as to Nanda's actual state,[15] the Great Sage spoke to Nanda again: // 5.36 //

mayy agraje pravrajite 'jitātmane bhrātṛṣv anupravrajiteṣu cāsmān /
jñātīṁś ca dṛṣṭvā vratino gṛha-sthān saṁvinna-vit te 'sti na vāsti cetaḥ // 5.37 //
"O you who have yet to conquer yourself! Given that I, your elder brother, have gone forth, and your cousins have gone forth after me, / And seeing that our relatives who remain at home are committed to practice, are you minded to be conscious of consciousness, or are you not? // 5.37 //

rājarṣayas te viditā na nūnaṁ vanāni ye śiśriyire hasantaḥ /
niṣṭhīvya kāmān upaśānti-kāmāḥ kāmeṣu naivaṁ kṛpaṇeṣu saktāḥ // 5.38 //
Evidently the royal seers are unbeknown to you who retreated smiling into the forests; / Having spat out desires, they were desirous of tranquility and thus not stuck in lower order desires. // 5.38 //

---

[13] The bhikṣu Ānanda, a cousin of the Buddha and Nanda, is the protagonist of SN Canto 11, in which he guides Nanda to understand the folly of aspiring to a heavenly bliss which can only ever be temporary.

[14] The sage of Videha is an epithet of Ānanda. Videha corresponds to the area north of the Ganges which is now known as Tirhut, in the state of Bihar (Land of Vihāras).

[15] *Bhāva*. See notes to SN4.10 and SN6.12. Also cf. *bhava* in SN5.30.

bhūyaḥ samālokya gṛheṣu doṣān niśāmya tat-tyāga-kṛtaṁ ca śarma /
naivāsti moktuṁ matir ālayaṁ te deśaṁ mumūrṣor iva sopasargam // 5.39 //
Again, you have experienced the drawbacks of family life[16] and you have observed the relief to be had from leaving it, / And yet you, like a man in a disaster area who is resigned to his death, have no intention of giving up and leaving house and home. // 5.39 //

saṁsāra-kāntāra-parāyaṇasya śive kathaṁ te pathi nārurukṣā /
āropyamāṇasya tam eva mārgaṁ bhraṣṭasya sārthād iva sārthikasya // 5.40 //
How can you be so devoted to the wasteland of saṁsāra and so devoid of desire to take the auspicious path / When – like a desert trader who drops out from a caravan – you have been set on that very path? // 5.40 //

yaḥ sarvato veśmani dahyamāne śayīta mohān na tato vyapeyāt /
kālāgninā vyādhi-jarā-śikhena loke pradīpe sa bhavet pramattaḥ // 5.41 //
One who in a house burning on all sides, instead of getting out of there, would lie down in his folly to sleep, / Only he might be heedless, in a world burning in the fire of Time, with its flames of sickness and aging. // 5.41 //

praṇīyamānaś ca yathā vadhāya matto hasec ca pralapec ca vadhyaḥ /
mṛtyau tathā tiṣṭhati pāśa-haste śocyaḥ pramādyan viparīta-cetāḥ // 5.42 //
Again, like the condemned man being led, drunkenly laughing and babbling, to the stake, / Equally to be lamented is one whose mind is upside-down, cavorting while Death stands by, with noose in hand. // 5.42 //

yadā narendrāś ca kuṭumbinaś ca vihāya bandhūṁś ca parigrahāṁś ca /
yayuś ca yāsyanti ca yānti caiva priyeṣv anityeṣu kuto 'nurodhaḥ // 5.43 //
When kings and humble householders, leaving relations and possessions behind, / Have gone forth, will go forth, and even now are going forth, what is the point of pandering to fleeting fondnesses? // 5.43 //

kiṁ-cin na paśyāmi ratasya yatra tad-anya-bhāvena bhaven na duḥkham /
tasmāt kva-cin na kṣamate prasaktir yadi kṣamas tad-vigamān na śokaḥ // 5.44 //
I do not see any pleasure which might not, by turning into something else, become pain. / Therefore no attachment bears scrutiny – unless the grief is bearable that arises from the loss of its object. // 5.44 //

tat saumya lolaṁ parigamya lokaṁ māyopamaṁ citram ivendrajālam /
priyābhidhānaṁ tyaja moha-jālaṁ chettuṁ matis te yadi duḥkha-jālam // 5.45 //
So, my friend, knowing the human world to be fickle, a net of Indra, a web of fictions, like a gaudy magic show, / Abandon the net of delusion you call 'my love,' if you are minded to cut the net of suffering. // 5.45 //

---

[16] *Gṛheṣu doṣān* lit. means "the faults in homes" or "the faults in families."

varaṁ hitodarkam āniṣṭam annaṁ na svādu yat syād ahitānubaddham /
yasmād ahaṁ tvā viniyojayāmi śive śucau vartmani vipriye 'pi // 5.46 //
Unfancied food that does one good is better than tasty food that may do harm: / On that basis I commend you to a course which, though unpalatable, is wholesome and honest. // 5.46 //

bālasya dhātrī vinigṛhya loṣṭaṁ yathoddharatyāsya puṭa-praviṣṭam /
tathojjihīrṣuḥ khalu rāga-śalyaṁ tat tvām avocaṁ paruṣaṁ hitāya // 5.47 //
Just as a nurse keeps firm hold of an infant while taking out soil it has put in its mouth, / So, wishing to draw out the dart of passion, have I spoken to you sharply for your own good. // 5.47 //

aniṣṭam apy auṣadham āturāya dadāti vaidyaś ca yathā nigṛhya /
tadvan mayoktaṁ pratikūlam etat tubhyaṁ hitodarkam anugrahāya // 5.48 //
And just as a doctor restrains a patient then gives him bitter medicine; / So have I given you, in order to help you, this disagreeable advice with beneficial effect. // 5.48 //

tad yāvad eva kṣaṇa-saṁnipāto na mṛtyur āgacchati yāvad eva /
yāvad vayo yoga-vidhau samarthaṁ buddhiṁ kuru śreyasi tāvad eva // 5.49 //
Therefore, while you are meeting the moment of opportunity, while death has yet to come, / So long as you have the energy for practice, decide on better." // 5.49 //

ity evam uktaḥ sa vināyakena hitaiṣiṇā kāruṇikena nandaḥ /
kartāsmi sarvaṁ bhagavan vacas te tathā yathā jñāpayasīty uvāca // 5.50 //
Addressed thus by his benevolent and compassionate guide, / Nanda said, "I shall do, Glorious One, all that you say, just as you teach it." // 5.50 //

ādāya vaideha-munis tatas taṁ nināya saṁśliṣya viceṣṭamānam /
vyayojayac cāśru-pariplutākṣaṁ keśa-śriyaṁ chatra-nibhasya mūrdhnaḥ // 5.51 //
At this the sage of Videha reclaimed him, and held him close as he led him off writhing, / And then, while [Nanda's] eyes welled with tears, he separated the crowning glory of his hair from the royal umbrella of his head. // 5.51 //

atho nataṁ tasya mukhaṁ sabāṣpaṁ pravāsyamāneṣu śiro-ruheṣu /
vakrāgra-nālaṁ nalinaṁ taḍāge varṣodaka-klinnam ivābabhāse // 5.52 //
As his hair was thus being banished, his tearful downcast face / Resembled a rain-sodden lotus in a pond with the top of its stalk sagging down. // 5.52 //

nandas tatas taru-kaṣāya-virakta-vāsāś cintāvaśo nava-gṛhīta iva dvipendraḥ / pūrṇaḥ śaśī bahula-pakṣa-gataḥ kṣapānte bālātapena pariṣikta ivāvabhāse // 5.53 //
Thence, in drab garb with the dull yellow-red color of tree bark, and despondent as a newly-captured elephant, / Nanda resembled a waning full moon at night's end, sprinkled by the powdery rays of the early morning sun. // 5.53 //

saundaranande mahā-kāvye nanda-pravrājano nāma pañcama sargaḥ //5//
The 5th canto in the epic poem Handsome Nanda, titled "Nanda Is Caused to Go Forth."

Canto 6: bhāryā-vilāpaḥ
A Wife's Lament

Introduction

Bhāryā, as in the title of Canto 4, means wife, but can be read literally as carrying the hidden meanings of either "one to be borne [as a burden]" or "one to be cherished [as an object of love]." *Vilāpa*, wailing or lamenting, is from the root *vi-√lap*, to utter moaning sounds, wail, lament.

Thus, though EH Johnston translated *bhāryā-vilāpaḥ* as Sundarī's Despair, the word *vilāpa* suggests not only despair as a mental phenomenon but also the physical expression of grief, or the psycho-physical act of giving voice to suffering. In those terms, the Buddha's turning of the Dharma-wheel was a thunderous example of *vilāpa*.

The present canto, then, can be read as a study in suffering, carried out by Aśvaghoṣa with loving attention to detail, in which Sundarī is one to be cherished. Sundarī, moreover, is not the only one to be cherished. She has one friend, in particular, who at the end of the canto passes the pragmatic test of truth, by telling Sundarī what it does Sundarī good to hear - regardless of whether or not the information relayed is strictly accurate.

tato hṛte bhartari gauraveṇa prītau hṛtāyām aratau kṛtāyām /
tatraiva harmyopari vartamānā na sundarī saiva tadā babhāse // 6.1 //
And so, with her husband riven away through his respect for the Guru, bereft of her happiness, left joyless, / Though she remained at the same spot, high up in the palace, Sundarī no longer seemed to be herself. // 6.1 //

sā bhartur abhyāgamana-pratīkṣā gavākṣam ākramya payodharābhyām /
dvāronmukhī harmya-talāl lalambe mukhena tiryaṅ-nata-kuṇḍalena // 6.2 //
Anticipating her husband's approach, she leant forward, her breasts invading the bulls-eye window. / Expectantly she looked out from the palace roof towards the gateway, her earrings dangling down across her face. // 6.2 //

vilamba-hārā cala-yoktrakā sā tasmād vimānād vinatā cakāśe /
tapaḥ kṣayād apsarasāṁ vareva cyutaṁ vimānāt priyam īkṣamāṇā // 6.3 //
With her pearl necklaces hanging down, and straps dishevelled, as she bent down from the palace, / She looked like the most gorgeous of the heavenly nymphs (the *apsarases*) gazing from her celestial abode at her lover, as he falls down, having used up his ascetic credit. // 6.3 //

sā kheda-saṁsvinna-lalāṭakena niśvāsa-niṣpīta-viśeṣakeṇa /
cintā-calākṣeṇa mukhena tasthau bhartāram anyatra viśaṅkamānā // 6.4 //
With a cold sweat on her beautiful brow, her face-paint drying in her sighs, / And her eyes restless with anxious thoughts, there she stood, suspecting her husband, somewhere else. // 6.4 //

tataś cira-sthāna-pariśrameṇa sthitaiva paryaṅka-tale papāta /
tiryak ca śiśye pravikīrṇa-hārā sapādukaikārdha-vilamba-pādā // 6.5 //
Tired out by a long time standing in that state, she dropped, just where she stood, onto a couch, / And lay across it with her necklaces scattered and a slipper half hanging off her foot. // 6.5 //

athātra kā-cit pramadā sabāṣpāṁ tāṁ duḥkhitāṁ draṣṭum anīpsamānā /
prāsāda-sopāna-tala-praṇādaṁ cakāra padbhyāṁ sahasā rudantī // 6.6 //
One of her women, not wishing to see Sundarī in such tearful distress, / Was making her way down from the palace penthouse, when she burst into tears, and made a commotion with her feet on the stairs. // 6.6 //

tasyāś ca sopāna-tala-praṇādaṁ śrutvaiva tūrṇaṁ punar utpapāta /
prītyāṁ prasaktaiva ca saṁjaharṣa priyopayānaṁ pariśaṅkamānā // 6.7 //
Hearing the sound on the stairs of that woman's feet [Sundarī] quickly jumped up again; / Transfixed with joy, she bristled with excitement, believing it to be the approach of her beloved. // 6.7 //

sā trāsayantī valabhī-puṭa-sthān pārāvatān nūpura-nisvanena /
sopāna-kukṣiṁ prasasāra harṣād bhraṣṭaṁ dukūlāntam acintayantī // 6.8 //
Scaring the pigeons in their rooftop roosts with the jangling of her ankle bracelets, / She dashed to the stairwell, without worrying, in her excitement, about what extremity of her diaphonous raiments might be falling off. // 6.8 //

tām aṅganāṁ prekṣya ca vipralabdhā niśvasya bhūyaḥ śayanaṁ prapede /
vivarṇa-vaktrā na rarāja cāśu vivarṇa-candreva himāgame dyauḥ // 6.9 //
On seeing the woman she was crestfallen; she sighed, threw herself again onto the couch, / And no longer shone: with her face suddenly[1] pallid she was as grey as a pale-mooned sky in early winter. // 6.9 //

sā duḥkhitā bhartur adarśanena kāmena kopena ca dahyamānā /
kṛtvā kare vaktram upopaviṣṭā cintā-nadīṁ śoka-jalāṁ tatāra // 6.10 //
Distressed at not seeing her husband, burning with desire and fury, / She sat down with face in hand and steeped herself in the river of worries, whose water is sorrow. // 6.10 //

tasyāḥ mukhaṁ padma-sapatna-bhūtaṁ pāṇau sthitaṁ pallava-rāga-tāmre /
chāyāmayasyāmbhasi paṅkajasya babhau nataṁ padmam ivopariṣṭāt // 6.11 //
Her lotus-rivalling face, resting on the hennaed stem of her hand, / Was like a lotus above the reflection in the water of its mud-born self, drooping down. // 6.11 //

[1] EHJ notes that *āśu* is often used in epic and Buddhist Sanskrit merely to strengthen the force of the verb, like 'right' and 'straight' in English, rather than with its proper sense of 'quickly.'

sā strī-svabhāvena vicintya tat-tad dṛṣṭānurāge 'bhimukhe 'pi patyau /
dharmāśrite tattvam avindamānā saṁkalpya tat-tad vilalāpa tat-tat // 6.12 //
She considered various possibilities, in accordance with a woman's nature[2]; then, failing to see the truth that her husband had taken refuge in the dharma, while obviously still impassioned and in love with her, she constructed various scenarios and uttered various laments: // 6.12 //

eṣyāmy anāśyāna-viśeṣakāyāṁ tvayīti kṛtvā mayi taṁ pratijñām /
kasmān nu hetor dayita-pratijñaḥ so 'dya priyo me vitatha-pratijñaḥ // 6.13 //
"He promised me: 'I'll be back before your make-up is dry'; / From what cause would such a cherisher of promises as my beloved is, be now a breaker of promises? // 6.13 //

āryasya sādhoḥ karuṇātmakasya man-nitya-bhīror atidakṣiṇasya /
kuto vikāro 'yam abhūta-pūrvaḥ svenāparāgeṇa mamāpacārāt // 6.14 //
In him who was noble, good, compassionate, always in awe of me, and all too honest, / How has such an unprecedented transformation come about? Through a loss of passion on his part? From a mistake of mine? // 6.14 //

rati-priyasya priya-vartino me priyasya nūnaṁ hṛdayaṁ viraktam /
tathāpi rāgo yadi tasya hi syān mac-citta-rakṣī na sa nāgataḥ syāt // 6.15 //
The heart of my lover - lover of sexual pleasure and of me - has obviously waned in its passion, / For if he did still love me, having regard for my heart, he would not have failed to return. // 6.15 //

rūpeṇa bhāvena ca mad-viśiṣṭā priyeṇa dṛṣṭā niyataṁ tato 'nyā /
tathā hi kṛtvā mayi mogha-sāntvaṁ lagnāṁ satīṁ mām agamad vihāya // 6.16 //
Another woman, then, in beauty and in nature better than me, my beloved has surely beheld; / For, having soothed me as he did with empty words, the guy has gone and left me, attached to him as I am. // 6.16 //

bhaktiṁ sa buddhaṁ prati yām avocat tasya prayātuṁ mayi so 'padeśaḥ /
munau prasādo yadi tasya hi syān mṛtyor ivogrād anṛtād bibhīyāt // 6.17 //
As for that devotion to Buddha of which he spoke, it was just a line to me for leaving; / For if he were clearly settled on the Sage he would fear untruth no less than a grisly death. // 6.17 //

sevārtham ādarśanam anya-citto vibhūṣayantyā mama dhārayitvā /
bibharti so 'nyasya janasya taṁ cen namo 'stu tasmai cala-sauhṛdāya // 6.18 //
While I put my make-up on, he held the mirror as a service to me, and thought of another! / If he holds it now for that other so much for his fickle affection! // 6.18 //

---

[2] Or "via a woman's [non-empty conception of] self-existence." The sub-text may be to point indirectly at the original cause of the grief of a wife who objectified her husband, just as he objectified her.

necchanti yāḥ śokam avāptum evaṁ śraddhātum arhanti na tā narāṇām /
kva cānuvṛttir mayi sāsya pūrvaṁ tyāgaḥ kva cāyaṁ janavat kṣaṇena // 6.19 //
Any woman who does not wish to suffer grief like this should never trust a man. / How could he treat me before with such regard and then in a twinkling leave me like this, like anybody?" // 6.19 //

ity evam-ādi priya-viprayuktā priye 'nyad āśaṅkya ca sā jagāda /
saṁbhrāntam āruhya ca tad-vimānaṁ tāṁ strī sabāṣpā giram ity uvāca // 6.20 //
This she said and more, love-lorn, and suspecting her love of loving another. / Then the giddy weeping woman, having dizzily climbed the palace stairs, tearfully told her these words: // 6.20 //

yuvāpi tāvat priya-darśano 'pi saubhāgya-bhāgyābhijanānvito 'pi /
yas tvāṁ priyo nābhyacarat kadā-cit tam anyathā pāsyasi kātarāsi // 6.21 //
"Though he may be young, good-looking, full of noble ancestry, and filled with charm and fortune, / Never did your husband cheat on you. You are being silly, and judging him amiss. // 6.21 //

mā svāminaṁ svāmini doṣato gāḥ priyaṁ priyārhaṁ priya-kāriṇaṁ tam /
na sa tvad anyāṁ pramadām avaiti svacakravākyā iva cakravākaḥ // 6.22 //
Ma'am! Do not accuse your loving husband, a doer of loving deeds who merits your love; / He never even looks at any woman other than you, like greylag gander with kindred greylag goose. // 6.22 //

sa tu tvad-arthaṁ gṛha-vāsam īpsan jijīviṣus tvat-paritoṣa-hetoḥ /
bhrātrā kil' āryeṇa tathāgatena pravrājito netra-jalārdra-vaktraḥ // 6.23 //
For you, he wished to stay at home; for your delight, he wished to live; / But his noble brother, the Tathāgata, so they say, has banished him, his face made wet by tears, into the wandering life. // 6.23 //

śrutvā tato bhartari tāṁ pravṛttiṁ sa-vepathuḥ sā sahasotpapāta /
pragṛhya bāhū virurāva coccair hṛdīva digdhābhihatā kareṇuḥ // 6.24 //
Then, on hearing what had happened to her husband, all of a sudden, up she leapt, shaking; / She clasped her arms and screamed out loud like a she-elephant shot in the heart by a poisoned arrow. // 6.24 //

sā rodanāroṣita-rakta-dṛṣṭiḥ saṁtāpa-saṁkṣobhita-gātra-yaṣṭiḥ /
papāta śīrṇākula-hāra-yaṣṭiḥ phalātibhārād iva cūta-yaṣṭiḥ // 6.25 //
Her eyes puffed-up and reddened by tears, the slender trunk of her body trembling with anguish, / She broke and scattered strings of pearls, as down she fell, like a mango branch weighed down by too much fruit.[3] // 6.25 //

---

[3] A triple play on the word *yaṣṭiḥ* seems designed to emphasize the tenuousness of life in saṁsāra. *Yaṣṭiḥ* means a twig or branch, and by extension anything thin or slender, including in this verse Sundari's slender frame, and a string for pearls.

sā padma-rāgaṁ vasanaṁ vasānā padmānanā padma-dalāyatākṣī /
padmā vipadmā patiteva lakṣmīḥ śuśoṣa padma-srag ivātapena // 6.26 //
Wearing clothes suffused with lotus colors, with lotus face, and eyes as long as lotus petals, / She was like a Lotus-Hued Lakṣmī, who had fallen from her lotus [pedestal].[4] And she withered like a lotus-garland left in the sun. // 6.26 //

saṁcintya saṁcintya guṇāṁś ca bhartur dīrghaṁ niśaśvāsa tatāma caiva /
vibhūṣaṇa-śrī-nihite prakoṣṭhe tāmre karāgre ca vinirdudhāva // 6.27 //
She thought and thought about her husband's good points, sighing long and hard and gasping / As out she flung the arms that bore her gleaming jewels and [hennaed] hands, with reddened fingertips.[5] // 6.27 //

na bhūṣaṇārtho mama saṁpratīti sā dikṣu cikṣepa vibhūṣaṇāni /
nirbhūṣaṇā sā patitā cakāśe viśīrṇa-puṣpa-stabakā lateva // 6.28 //
"Now I don't have any need for ornaments!" she cried, as she hurled her jewels in all directions. / Unadorned and drooping, she resembled a creeper shorn of blossoms. // 6.28 //

dhṛtaḥ priyeṇāyam abhūn mameti rukma-tsaruṁ darpaṇam āliliṅge /
yatnāc ca vinyasta-tamāla-patrau ruṣṭeva dhṛṣṭaṁ pramamāja gaṇḍau // 6.29 //
She clasped the golden-handled mirror, and reflected, "My husband held this up for me." / And the tamāla paint she had applied so carefully, she rubbed aggressively off her cheeks, as if the paint had angered her. // 6.29 //

sā cakravākīva bhṛśaṁ cukūja śyenāgra-pakṣa-kṣata-cakravākā /
vispardhamāneva vimāna-saṁsthaiḥ pārāvataiḥ kūjana-lola-kaṇṭhaiḥ // 6.30 //
Like a greylag goose, when a hawk has wounding talons on the gander's wing, she hooted mightily, / As if in competition with the cooing pigeons on the palace roof, whose throats were all atremble. // 6.30 //

vicitra-mṛdvāstaraṇe 'pi suptā vaiḍūrya-vajra-pratimaṇḍite 'pi /
rukmāṅga-pāde śayane mahārhe na śarma lebhe paricesṭamānā // 6.31 //
She lay down to sleep in soft and gorgeous bedclothes, on a bed bedecked with cats-eye gems and diamonds, / But in her costly crib with golden legs, she tossed and turned, and no respite did she obtain. // 6.31 //

---

[4] *Vipadmā patitā* lit. means "fallen, being deprived of her lotus." The goddess of beauty, Lakṣmī, is portrayed in statues set on top of a lotus pedestal.

[5] EHJ translated *tamre kārāgre* as reddened fingers, LC as hennaed fingertips. Aśvaghoṣa may have had both meanings in mind, but it is noteworthy that gasping, abduction of the arms, and going red, are all symptoms of an infantile fear reflex called (after Ernst Moro, the Austrian pediatrician who identified it) "the Moro reflex."

saṁdṛśya bhartuś ca vibhūṣaṇāni vāsāṁsi vīṇā-prabhṛtīṁś ca līlāḥ /
tamo viveśābhinanāda coccaiḥ paṅkāvatīrṇeva ca saṁsasāda // 6.32 //
She eyed her husband's ornaments; his clothes, guitar and other items of amusement; / Thus she entered deeply into darkness: she raised a shriek, and then, as if descending into a mire, sank down. // 6.32 //

sā sundarī śvāsa-calodarī hi vajrāgni-saṁbhinna-darī-guheva /
śokāgninântar-hṛdi dahyamānā vibhrānta-citteva tadā babhūva // 6.33 //
Her belly trembled out of breathlessness, like a cave being rent inside by fiery thunderbolts. / As, in her innermost heart, she burned with the fire of grief, Sundarī seemed at that moment to be going out of her mind. // 6.33 //

ruroda mamlau virurāva jaglau babhrāma tasthau vilalāpa dadhyau /
cakāra roṣaṁ vicakāra mālyaṁ cakarta vaktraṁ vicakarṣa vastram // 6.34 //
She howled, then wilted, screamed, then swooned; she reeled, stood rooted, wailed then brooded. / She vented anger and rended garlands; she scratched her face and slashed her clothes. // 6.34 //

tāṁ cāru-dantīṁ prasabhaṁ rudantīṁ saṁśrutya nāryaḥ paramābhitaptāḥ /
antar-gṛhād āruruhur vimānaṁ trāsena kiṁnarya ivādri-pṛṣṭham // 6.35 //
Hearing the howling of the lovely-toothed one – for O, how lovely[6] were her teeth! - the ladies-in-waiting suffered utmost torment; / They climbed from inside the palace up to the roof, like nervous *kiṁnarīs* ascending a mountain peak. // 6.35 //

bāṣpeṇa tāḥ klinna-viṣaṇṇa-vaktrā varṣeṇa padminya ivārdra-padmāḥ /
sthānānurūpeṇa yathābhimānaṁ nililyire tām anu-dahyamānāḥ // 6.36 //
Their despondent faces wet with tears, like lotus ponds with rain-soaked lotus buds, / They settled down along with her, according to rank and as they wished, and along with her they burned in grief. // 6.36 //

tābhir vṛtā harmya-tale 'ṅganābhiś cintā-tanuḥ sā sutanur babhāse /
śata-hradābhiḥ pariveṣṭiteva śaśāṅka-lekhā śarad-abhra-madhye // 6.37 //
On the palace roof, enfolded by her women, the slender Sundarī, gaunt with worry, / Seemed like a streak of crescent moon enshrouded among the autumn clouds by a hundred rays of lightning. // 6.37 //

yā tatra tāsāṁ vacasopapannā mānyā ca tasyā vayasādhikā ca /
sā pṛṣṭhatas tāṁ tu samāliliṅge pramṛjya cāśrūṇi vacāṁsy uvāca // 6.38 //
There was one among them there, however, who was senior in years, and good with words, a well-respected woman: / Holding Sundarī from behind in a firm embrace and wiping tears away, she spoke as follows: // 6.38 //

---

[6] The original contains a play on *rudantīm*. "Howling" is *rudantīm*. "Lovely teethed-one" is *cārudantīm*.

rājarṣi-vadhvās tava nānurūpo dharmāśrite bhartari jātu śokaḥ /
ikṣvāku-vaṁśe hy abhikāṅkṣitāni dāyādya-bhūtāni tapo-vanāni // 6.39 //
"Grief does ill become you, the wife of a royal seer, when your husband has taken refuge in dharma; / For in the lineage of Ikṣvāku, an ascetic forest is a desired inheritance. // 6.39 //

prāyeṇa mokṣāya viniḥsṛtānāṁ śākya-ṛṣabhāṇāṁ viditāḥ striyas te /
tapo-vanānīva gṛhāṇi yāsāṁ sādhvī-vrataṁ kāmavad āśritānām // 6.40 //
Well you know of wives of Śākya bulls gone forth in search of freedom: / As a rule, they turn their houses almost into ascetic groves and they observe the vow of chastity, as if it were a pleasure. // 6.40 //

yady anyayā rūpa-guṇādhikatvād bhartā hṛtas te kuru bāṣpa-mokṣam /
manasvinī rūpavatī guṇāḍhyā hṛdi kṣate kātra hi nāśru muñcet // 6.41 //
If your husband had been stolen by another, due to her superior looks and qualities, then tears you should let flow; / For how could any beautiful and virtuous wife, who abounds in excellence, refrain from shedding teardrops when her heart was broken? // 6.41 //

athāpi kiṁ-cid vyasanaṁ prapanno mā caiva tad bhūt sadṛśo 'tra bāṣpaḥ /
ato viśiṣṭaṁ na hi duḥkham asti kulodgatāyāḥ pati-devatāyāḥ // 6.42 //
Or had he met with some disaster - and may no such thing ever be! - then yes, tears; / Because there is no greater sorrow for a woman of noble birth who dignifies her husband as if he were a god. // 6.42 //

atha tv idānīṁ laḍitaḥ sukhena sva-sthaḥ phala-stho vyasanāny adṛṣṭvā /
vīta-spṛho dharmam anuprapannaḥ kiṁ viklave rodiṣi harṣa-kāle // 6.43 //
But on the contrary, he now is roving happily, meeting no disasters, but enjoying a healthy and fruitful life. / Free from eager longing, he is following dharma: at a time for celebration, why are you in such a state of weeping consternation?" // 6.43 //

ity evam uktāpi bahu-prakāraṁ snehāt tayā naiva dhṛtiṁ cakāra /
athāparā tāṁ manaso 'nukūlaṁ kālopapannaṁ praṇayād uvāca // 6.44 //
Though this woman, with her [unctuous] kindness,[7] thus put forward many sorts of argument, [Sundarī] could not be satisfied at all. / Then another woman, with a sense of intimacy, said what helped her mind and fit the occasion.[8] // 6.44 //

bravīmi satyaṁ su-viniścitaṁ me prāptaṁ priyaṁ drakṣyasi śīghram eva /
tvayā vinā sthāsyati tatra nāsau sattvāśrayaś cetanayeva hīnaḥ // 6.45 //
"Truly and categorically, I am telling you that soon enough you'll see your husband back again. / Dispossessed of you, the fellow will survive out there no longer than living things survive when dispossessed of consciousness. // 6.45 //

---

[7] *Snehāt* originally means "out of oiliness" and hence both "unctuously" and "tenderly."

[8] The words of this more intimate friend, therefore, are a precursor to the words of the Buddha and Ānanda in Cantos 10 & 11, whereas the eloquent but ineffectual words of the more formal woman may be seen as a precursor to the words of the striver in Cantos 8 & 9.

aṅke 'pi lakṣmyā na sa nirvṛtaḥ syāt tvaṁ tasya pārśve yadi tatra na syāḥ /
āpatsu kṛcchrāsv api cāgatāsu tvāṁ paśyatas tasya bhaven na duḥkham // 6.46 //
Even in the lap of luxury he could not be happy, lacking you there by his side; / And even in the direst pickle, not a thing could trouble him, as long as you were in his sight. // 6.46 //

tvaṁ nirvṛtiṁ gaccha niyaccha bāṣpaṁ taptāśru-mokṣāt parirakṣa cakṣuḥ /
yas tasya bhāvas tvayi yaś ca rāgo na raṁsyate tvad-virahāt sa dharme // 6.47 //
Be happy. Don't keep crying. Spare your eyes from shedding molten tears. / The way he feels for you, and his passion, are such that he, bereft of you, will find no pleasure in the dharma. // 6.47 //

syād atra nāsau kula-sattva-yogāt kāṣāyam ādāya vihāsyatīti /
anātmanādāya gṛhonmukhasya punar vimoktuṁ ka ivāsti doṣaḥ // 6.48 //
Some might say that having worn the ochre robe, he won't relinquish it, by dint of noble birth combined with strength of character. / But, he put it on unwillingly, while looking forward to going home: what fault is there in taking it back off?" // 6.48 //

iti yuvati-janena sāntvyamānā hṛta-hṛdayā ramaṇena sundarī sā /
dramiḍam abhimukhī pureva rambhā kṣitim agamat parivāritāpsarobhiḥ // 6.49 //
Thus consoled by her little women when her husband had purloined her heart, / Sundarī came to earth, just as Rambhā,[9] with her heart turned towards Dramiḍa, came once upon a time, enfolded in the midst of sister *apsarases*. // 6.49 //

saundaranande mahā-kāvye bhāryā-vilāpo nāma ṣaṣṭhaḥ sargaḥ //6//
The 6th canto in the epic poem Handsome Nanda, titled "A Wife's Lament."

---

[9] Rambhā was reputedly the most gorgeous of all the *apsarases*, or celestial nymphs; she is also mentioned in SN7.36.

Canto 7: nanda-vilāpaḥ
Nanda's Lament

Introduction

If the hidden meaning of the previous canto title is "One to Be Cherished, Giving Voice to Suffering," then the ironic hidden meaning of the present canto title might be "Joy Expressing Suffering."

As in his description of the suffering Sundarī, Aśvaghoṣa's description of the suffering Nanda has a physical component, an emotional component (with mention of sorrow, tearful remembering, and burning desire), but especially a psychological and intellectual component in which Nanda thinks one defeatist thought after another, before arriving at a defeatist conclusion. Since Sundarī is the one who was abandoned, since her physical suffering is described more vividly, and since her emotional suffering has less of a sexual component than Nanda's does, our feelings towards Sundarī seem to be guided more in the direction of empathic distress. But there is only so much empathic distress that one can take. The desired effect on the reader in the present canto seems to be to nurture in us the wish to sweep away (a) all Nanda's defeatist thoughts, along with (b) all the tiresome cultural references with which he seeks to justify his defeatist conclusion.

liṅgaṁ tataḥ śāstṛ-vidhi-pradiṣṭaṁ gātreṇa bibhran na tu cetasā tat /
bhāryā-gatair eva mano-vitarkair jehrīyamāṇo na nananda nandaḥ // 7.1 //
Bearing the insignia, then, whose form was fixed by his teacher – bearing it with his body but not with his mind – / And being constantly carried off by thoughts of his wife, he whose name was joy was not joyful. // 7.1 //

sa puṣpa-māsasya ca puṣpa-lakṣmyā sarvābhisāreṇa ca puṣpa-ketoḥ /
yānīya-bhāvena ca yauvanasya vihāra-saṁstho na śamaṁ jagāma // 7.2 //
Amid the wealth of flowers of the month of flowers, assailed on every side by the flower-bannered god of love,[1] / And with feelings that are familiar to the young, he stayed in a *vihāra* but found no peace. // 7.2 //

sthitaḥ saḥ dīnaḥ sahakāra-vīthyām ālīna-saṁmūrcchita-ṣaṭpadāyām /
bhṛśaṁ jajṛmbhe yuga-dīrgha-bāhur dhyātvā priyāṁ cāpam ivācakarṣa // 7.3 //
Standing, distraught, by a row of mango trees amid the numbing hum of hovering insects, / He with his lengthy arms and yoke-like shoulders, thought of his beloved and forcibly stretched himself open, as if drawing a bow. // 7.3 //

sa pītaka-kṣodam iva pratīcchaṁś cūta-drumebhyas tanu-puṣpa-varṣam /
dīrghaṁ niśaśvāsa vicintya bhāryāṁ nava-graho nāga ivāvaruddhaḥ // 7.4 //
Receiving from the mango trees a rain of tiny flowers like saffron powder, / He thought of his wife and heaved long sighs, like a newly-captured elephant in a cage. // 7.4 //

---

[1] "Flower-bannered one" is an epithet of Kāma-deva, god of love.

śokasya hartā śaraṇāgatānāṁ śokasya kartā pratigarvitānām /
aśokam ālambya sa jāta-śokaḥ priyāṁ priyāśoka-vanāṁ śuśoca // 7.5 //
He had been, for those who came to him seeking refuge, an abater of sorrow, and, for the conceited, a creator of sorrow, / Now he leant against 'the tree of freedom from sorrow,' the *a-śoka* tree,[2] and he became a sorrower: he sorrowed for a lover of *a-śoka* groves, his beloved wife. // 7.5 //

priyāṁ priyāyāḥ pratanuṁ priyaṅguṁ niśāmya bhītām iva niṣpatantīm /
sasmāra tām aśru-mukhīṁ sabāṣpaḥ priyāṁ priyaṅgu-prasavāvadātām // 7.6 //
A slender *priyaṅgu* creeper, beloved of his beloved, he noticed shying away, as if afraid, / And tearfully he remembered her, his lover with her tearful face, as pale as a *priyaṅgu* flower. // 7.6 //

puṣpāvanaddhe tilaka-drumasya dṛṣṭvānya-puṣṭāṁ śikhare niviṣṭām /
saṁkalpayām āsa śikhāṁ priyāyāḥ śuklāṁśuke 'ṭṭālam apāśritāyāḥ // 7.7 //
Seeing a cuckoo resting on the flower-covered crest of a *tilaka* tree,[3] / He imagined[4] his lover leaning against the watchtower, her curls and tresses resting on her white upper garment. // 7.7 //

latāṁ praphullām atimuktakasya cūtasya pārśve parirabhya jātām /
niśāmya cintām agamat kadaivaṁ śliṣṭā bhaven mām api sundarīti // 7.8 //
A vine with 'flowers whiter than pearls,' the *ati-muktaka,* having attached itself to the side of a mango tree, was thriving: / Nanda eyed the blossoming creeper and fretted "When will Sundarī cling to me like that?" // 7.8 //

puṣpaiḥ karālā api nāga-vṛkṣā dāntaiḥ samudgair iva hema-garbhaiḥ /
kāntāra-vṛkṣā iva duḥkhitasya na cakṣur ācikṣipur asya tatra // 7.9 //
The budding teeth of yawning *nāga* trees[5] erupted there like ivory caskets filled with gold, / But they drew his anguished eye no better than desert scrub. // 7.9 //

---

[2] The Aśoka tree, which is indigenous to India, Burma and Malaya, flowers throughout the year but is especially famed for the beauty of the orange and scarlet clusters which it produces in January and February. It has some romantic connotations with female beauty – for example, the traditions that it will only flower in places where a woman's foot has trodden, and that a tree will bloom more vigorously if kicked by a beautiful young woman. Aśoka, meaning "without sorrow," is also the name of the celebrated King Aśoka.

[3] The *tilaka* tree, aka Clerodendrum phlomoides (Symplocos racemosa), as may be guessed from the context, produces clusters of white flowers.

[4] *Saṁkalpa* here evidently means imagine. The verbal root √*kḷp* originally means to produce, to arrange, to fix, or to frame; and hence to produce or frame in the mind, to invent, to imagine. See SN13.49-53.

[5] The *nāga* tree is the same ornamental tree referred to in SN4.18.

gandhaṁ vamanto 'pi ca gandhaparṇā gandharva-veśyā iva gandhapūrṇāḥ /
tasyānya-cittasya śugātmakasya ghrāṇaṁ na jahrur hṛdayaṁ pratepuḥ // 7.10 //
The *gandha-parṇa* trees emitted their fragrance like a *gandharva's* girlfriend, brimming with perfume,[6] / But for him whose mind was elsewhere, and who was sorrowful to the core, they did not win the nose: they pained the heart. // 7.10 //

saṁrakta-kaṇṭhaiś ca vinīla-kaṇṭhais tuṣṭaiḥ prahṛṣṭair api cānyapuṣṭaiḥ /
lelihyamānaiś ca madhu dvirephaiḥ svanad vanaṁ tasya mano nunoda // 7.11 //
Resounding with the throaty cries of impassioned peacocks,[7] with the satisfied celebrating of cuckoos, / And with the relentless supping of nectar by bees, the forest encroached upon his mind. // 7.11 //

sa tatra bhāryāraṇi-saṁbhavena vitarka-dhūmena tamaḥ-śikhena /
kāmāgninā̄ntar-hṛdi dahyamāno vihāya dhairyaṁ vilalāpa tat-tat // 7.12 //
As there he burned with a fire arisen from the fire board of his wife, a fire with fancies for smoke and darkest hell for flames, / As he burned in his innermost heart with a fire of desire, fortitude failed him and he uttered various laments: // 7.12 //

adyāvagacchāmi su-duṣkaraṁ te cakruḥ kariṣyanti ca kurvate ca /
tyaktvā priyām aśru-mukhīṁ tapo ye cerūś cariṣyanti caranti caiva // 7.13 //
"Now I understand what a very difficult thing those men have done, will do, and are doing / Who have walked, will walk, and are walking the way of painful asceticism, leaving behind their tearful-faced lovers. // 7.13 //

tāvad dṛḍhaṁ bandhanam asti loke na dāravaṁ tāntavam āyasaṁ vā /
yāvad dṛḍhaṁ bandhanam etad eva mukhaṁ calākṣaṁ lalitaṁ ca vākyam // 7.14 //
There is no bond in the world, whether of wood or rope or iron, / As strong as this bond: an amorous voice and a face with darting eyes. // 7.14 //

chittvā ca bhittvā ca hi yānti tāni sva-pauruṣāc caiva suhṛd-balāc ca /
jñānāc caraukṣyāc ca vinā vimoktuṁ na śakyate sneha-mayas tu pāśaḥ // 7.15 //
For having been cut or broken – by one's own initiative or by the strength of friends – those bonds cease to exist; / Whereas the fetter made of love, except through wisdom and toughness, cannot be undone. // 7.15 //

---

6 *Gandha* means perfume or smell, as in the name of the tree *gandha-parṇa* ("fragrant leaved"). In Sanskrit epic poetry the *gandharvas* are the celestial musicians who form the orchestra at the banquets of the gods; they belong, together with the *apsarases*, to Indra's heaven.

7 *Kaṇṭha* means throat, neck, or guttural sound emanating therefrom. And *vinīla-kaṇṭha*, "a blue neck," is a peacock. So the first pāda is lit. "with the blue-necks with their impassioned neck[-sound]s."

jñānaṁ na me tac ca śamāya yat syān na cāstiraukṣyaṁ karuṇātmako 'smi /
kāmātmakaś cāsmi guruś ca buddhaḥ sthito 'ntare cakra-gater ivāsmi // 7.16 //
That wisdom is not in me which might make for peace, and since I am of a kindly nature, toughness also is lacking. / I am sensual by nature and yet the Buddha is my guru: I am stuck as if inside a moving wheel. // 7.16 //

ahaṁ gṛhītvāpi hi bhikṣu-liṅgaṁ bhrātṝṣiṇā dvir-guruṇānuśiṣṭaḥ /
sarvāsv avasthāsu labhe na śāntiṁ priyā-viyogād iva cakravākaḥ // 7.17 //
For though I have adopted the bhikkhu's insignia, and am taught by one who is twice my guru, as elder brother and enlightened sage, / In every circumstance I find no peace – like a greylag gander separated from its mate. // 7.17 //

adyāpi tan me hṛdi vartate ca yad darpaṇe vyākulite mayā sā /
kṛtānṛta-krodhakam abravīn māṁ kathaṁ kṛto 'sīti śaṭhaṁ hasantī // 7.18 //
Even now it continues to run through my mind how after I clouded the mirror / She pretended to be angry and said to me, as she wickedly laughed, 'What are you doing!' // 7.18 //

yathaiṣy anāśyāna-viśeṣakāyāṁ mayīti yan mām avadac ca sāśru /
pāriplavākṣeṇa mukhena bālā tan me vaco 'dyāpi mano ruṇaddhi // 7.19 //
Again, the words she spoke to me, while her girlish eyes were swimming with tears, 'Before this paint on my face is dry, come back': those words, even now, block my mind. // 7.19 //

baddhvāsanaṁ pāda-ja-nirjharasya svastho yathā dhyāyati bhikṣur eṣaḥ /
saktaḥ kva-cin nāham ivaiṣa nūnaṁ śāntas tathā tṛpta ivopaviṣṭaḥ // 7.20 //
This bhikkhu meditating at ease, who has crossed his legs in the traditional manner, and is of the waterfall, arising out of the foot [of the hill][8]: / Surely he is not as attached as I am to anybody, since he sits so calmly, with an aura of contentment. // 7.20 //

puṁs-kokilānām avicintya ghoṣaṁ vasanta-lakṣmyām avicārya cakṣuḥ /
śāstraṁ yathābhyasyati caiṣa yuktaḥ śaṅke priyākarṣati nāsya cetaḥ // 7.21 //
Deaf to the cuckoos' chorus, his eyeballs never grazing upon the riches of spring, / This fellow concentrates so intently upon the teaching, that I suspect no lover is tugging at his heart. // 7.21 //

asmai namo 'stu sthira-niścayāya nivṛtta-kautūhala-vismayāya /
śāntātmane 'ntar-gata-mānāsāya caṅkramyamāṇāya nir-utsukāya // 7.22 //
Credit to him who is firm in his resolve, who has retreated from curiosity and pride, / Who is at peace in himself, whose mind is turned inward, who does not strive for anything, as he walks up and down. // 7.22 //

---

[8] A play may be intended on the word *pāda*, whose meanings include 1. a human foot (as placed upon the opposite thigh when assuming the traditional sitting posture under discussion) and 2. a hill at the foot of a mountain.

nirīkṣamāṇāya jalaṁ sa-padmaṁ vanaṁ ca phullaṁ parapuṣṭa-juṣṭam /
kasyāsti dhairyaṁ nava-yauvanasya māse madhau dharma-sapatna-bhūte // 7.23 //
And beholds the lotus-covered water and the flowering forest where cuckoos come calling! / What man in the prime of youth could keep such constancy in those months of spring which are, as it were, the rival of dharma? // 7.23 //

bhāvena garveṇa gatena lakṣmyā smitena kopena madena vāgbhiḥ /
jahruḥ striyo deva-nṛpa-ṛṣi-saṁghān kasmādd hi nāsmad-vidham ākṣipeyuḥ // 7.24 //
With their way of being, their pride, their way of moving, their grace; with a smile or show of indignation, with their exuberance, with their voices, / Women have captivated hosts[9] of gods and kings and seers: how then could they fail to bewilder a bloke like me? // 7.24 //

kāmābhibhūto hi hiraṇya-retāḥ svāhāṁ siṣeve maghavān ahalyām /
sattvena sargeṇa ca tena hīnaḥ strī-nirjitaḥ kiṁ bata mānuṣo 'ham // 7.25 //
Overcome by desire, the fire god Hiraṇya-retas, 'Golden Sperm,'[10] succumbed to sex with his wife 'Oblation,' Svāhā,[11] as did 'The Bountiful' Indra[12] with nymph Ahalyā; / How much easier to be overwhelmed by a woman am I, a man, who lacks the strength and resolve of the gods. // 7.25 //

sūryaḥ saraṇyūṁ prati jātarāgas tat-prītaye taṣṭa iti śrutaṁ naḥ /
yām aśva-bhūto 'śva-vadhūṁ sametya yato 'śvinau tau janayāṁ babhūva // 7.26 //
Our tradition has it that the sun god Sūrya, roused to passion for the dawn goddess Saraṇyū, let himself be diminished for the sake of pleasure with her; / He became a stallion so as to cover her as a mare, whereby she conceived the two charioteers.[13] // 7.26 //

strī-kāraṇaṁ vaira-viśakta-buddhyor vaivasvatāgnyoś calitātma-dhṛtyoḥ /
bahūni varṣāṇi babhūva yuddhaṁ kaḥ strī-nimittaṁ na caled ihānyaḥ // 7.27 //
When the mind of Vaivasvata, son of the Sun, and the mind of the fire god Agni turned to enmity, when their grip on themselves was shaken, / There was war between them for many years, because of a woman. What lesser being, here on earth, would not be caused to stray by a woman? // 7.27 //

---

[9] This is an example of Aśvaghoṣa using as a collective noun for miscellaneous beings the word *saṅgha,* which he nowhere uses in the 'Buddhist' sense given in SED – "a clerical community, congregation, church, (esp.) the whole community or collective body or brotherhood of monks (with Buddhists)."

[10] Hiraṇya-retas is an epithet of the fire-god Agni.

[11] *Svāhā* means an oblation or offering to the gods. As a proper noun, Oblation personified, Svāhā is the wife of the fire-god Agni, and is thought to preside over burnt-offerings; her body is said to consist of the four Vedas, and her limbs are the six *vedāṅgas* or limbs of the Vedas.

[12] Maghavat, "the Bountiful," is an epithet of Indra.

[13] The *Ṛg-veda* tells the tale of how the sun god and dawn goddess, taking the form of a stallion and a mare, brought into being "the two charioteers" who appear in the sky before the dawn in a golden carriage drawn by horses, or by birds.

bheje śvapākīṁ munir akṣamālāṁ kāmād vasiṣṭhaś ca sa sad-variṣṭhaḥ /
yasyāṁ vivaśvān iva bhū-jalādaḥ sutaḥ prasūto 'sya kapiñjalādaḥ // 7.28 //
And through desire the sage Vasiṣṭha,[14] who even among the upstanding was eminent, had his way with an outcaste,[15] Akṣa-mālā, 'String of Beads,'[16] / To whom was born his son Kapiñjalāda, an eater of earth and water to rival the Sun. // 7.28 //

parāśaraḥ śāpa-śaras tatha rṣiḥ kālīṁ siṣeve jhaṣa-garbha-yonim /
suto 'sya yasyāṁ suṣuve mahātmā dvaipāyano veda-vibhāga-kartā // 7.29 //
So too did the seer Parāśara, user of curses as arrows, have intercourse with Kālī,[17] who was born from the womb of a fish; / The son he conceived in her was the illustrious Dvaipāyana,[18] classifier of the Vedas. // 7.29 //

dvaipāyano dharma-parāyaṇaś ca reme samaṁ kāśiṣu veśya-vadhvā /
yayā hato 'bhūc cala-nūpureṇa pādena vidyul-latayeva meghaḥ // 7.30 //
Dvaipāyana, equally, while having dharma as his primary object, enjoyed a woman at a brothel in Kāśi;[19] / Struck by her foot, with its trembling ankle bracelet, he was like a cloud being struck by a twist of lightning. // 7.30 //

tathāṅgirā rāga-parīta-cetāḥ sarasvatīṁ brahma-sutaḥ siṣeve /
sārasvato yatra suto 'sya jajñe naṣṭasya vedasya punaḥ pravaktā // 7.31 //
So too did brahma-begotten Aṅgiras,[20] when his mind was seized by passion, have sex with Sarasvatī;[21] / To her was born his son Sārasvata, who gave voice again to missing Vedas. // 7.31 //

tathā nṛpa-rṣer dilipasya yajñe svarga-striyāṁ kāśyapa āgatāsthaḥ /
srucaṁ gṛhītvā sravad ātma-tejaś cikṣepa vahnāv asito yato 'bhūt // 7.32 //
Likewise Kāśyapa, at a sacrifice under the aegis of the royal seer Dilipa, while fixated on a celestial nymph, / Took the ceremonial ladle and cast into the fire his own streaming semen, whence was conceived Asita.[22] // 7.32 //

---

[14] Vasiṣṭha is the legendary owner of the cow of plenty. See SN1.3.
[15] *Śva-pakī* is lit. "a woman who cooks dogs."
[16] Akṣa-mālā, so called because she wore a rosary, is a name of Vasiṣṭha's wife Arundhatī.
[17] Kālī, "Black Colour," is a name of Satyavatī (see verse 41 below). According to the *Mahā-bhārata,* she and Parāśara were the mother and father of Vyāsa, author of the Vedas.
[18] Dvaipāyana, "Island-Born," so called because his birthplace was a small island in the Ganges, is a name of Vyāsa, author or compiler of the Vedas.
[19] Kaśi broadly corresponds to modern-day Varanasi. See also SN3.15.
[20] Aṅgiras is celebrated as the inspired bard/seer who authored the hymns of the *Ṛg-veda.* "Brahma-begotten" refers to the legend that Angiras was born from Brahma's mouth.
[21] Sarasvatī, "Abounding in Ponds," was the name of a river, and of a goddess associated with that river.
[22] Kāśyapa is regarded as another of the authors of the *Ṛg-veda,* and Asita (also called Asita Devala) is known as one of his male progeny.

tathāṅgado 'ntaṁ tapaso 'pi gatvā kāmābhibhūto yamunām agacchat /
dhīmattaraṁ yatra rathītaraṁ sa sāraṅga-juṣṭaṁ janayām babhūva // 7.33 //
Aṅgada,[23] equally, though he had gone to the ends of ascetic practice, went overwhelmed by desire to Yamunā[24] / And in her he begat the super-bright Rathītara, 'The Super Charioteer,' and friend of the spotted deer. // 7.33 //

niśāmya śāntāṁ nara-deva-kanyāṁ vane 'pi śānte 'pi ca vartamānaḥ /
cacāla dhairyān munir ṛṣya-śṛṅgaḥ śailo mahī-kampa ivocca-śṛṅgaḥ // 7.34 //
Again, on catching sight of the princess Śāntā, 'Tranquility,' though he had been living in tranquility in the forest, / The sage Ṛṣya-śṛṅga, 'Antelope Horn,' was moved from steadfastness, like a high-horned mountain in an earthquake. // 7.34 //

brahmarṣi-bhāvārtham apāsya rājyaṁ bheje vanaṁ yo viṣayeṣv anāsthaḥ /
sa gādhi-jaś cāpahṛto ghṛtācyā samā daśaikaṁ divasaṁ viveda // 7.35 //
And the son of Gādhin who, in order to become 'the Brahman Seer,'[25] renounced his kingdom and retired to the forest, having become indifferent to sensual objects: / He was captivated by the nymph Ghṛtācī,[26] reckoning a decade with her as a single day. // 7.35 //

tathaiva kandarpa-śarābhimṛṣṭo rambhāṁ prati sthūla-śirā mumūrcha /
yaḥ kāma-roṣātmatayānapekṣaḥ śaśāpa tām apratigṛhyamāṇaḥ // 7.36 //
So too, when hit by an arrow fired by Love, did Sthūla-śiras, 'Thick Head,' lose his senses over Rambhā.[27] / He with his libidinous and wrathful nature was reckless: when she refused him he cursed her. // 7.36 //

pramadvarāyāṁ ca ruruḥ priyāyāṁ bhujaṅgamenāpahṛtendriyāyām /
saṁdṛśya saṁdṛśya jaghāna sarpān hriyaṁ na roṣeṇa tapo rarakṣa // 7.37 //
And Ruru, after his beloved Pramadvarā had been robbed of her senses by a snake, / Exterminated snakes wherever he saw them: he failed, in his fury, to maintain his reserve or his ascetic practice. // 7.37 //

naptā śaśāṅkasya yaśo-guṇāṅko budhasya sūnur vibudha-prabhāvaḥ /
tathorvaśīm apsarasaṁ vicintya rāja-rṣir unmādam agacchad aiḍaḥ // 7.38 //
As grandson of the hare-marked moon, as son of 'The Learned' Budha and the goddess Iḍā, and as one marked by personal honor and virtue, [Purū-ravas] had the special powers of the lunar and the very learned;[28] / But thinking of the *apsaras* Urvaśī, this royal seer also went mad. // 7.38 //

---

[23] Aṇgada was a brother of Rāma.
[24] Yamunā also was originally the name of a river.
[25] Refers to Viśva-mitra "Friend of All," who was born into the warrior caste of kṣatriyas but after a requisite number of years of ascetic self-denial eventually gained the epithet "Brahman Seer," signifying a purported elevation from the kṣatriya into the brahmin caste.
[26] Ghṛtācī, "Abounding in Ghee," is the name of another notable nymph.
[27] Rambhā was reputed to be the most beautiful of all the beautiful nymphs in Indra's paradise; she is the nymph referred to at the end of SN Canto 6.
[28] The son of Budha is Purū-ravas, a royal seer of the lunar race whose love affair with the nymph

rakto girer mūrdhani menakāyāṁ kāmātmakatvāc ca sa tāla-jaṅghaḥ /
pādena viśvāvasunā sa-roṣaṁ vajreṇa hintāla ivābhijaghne // 7.39 //
And when 'Long Shanks' Tāla-jaṅgha, on top of a mountain, was reddened, in his libidinous state, with passion for the *apsaras* Menakā, / From the foot of 'All-Beneficent' Viśvā-vasu he got an angry kick, like a thunderbolt striking a *hin-tāla* palm.[29] // 7.39 //

nāśaṁ gatāyāṁ paramāṅganāyāṁ gaṅgā-jale 'naṅga-parīta-cetāḥ /
janhuś ca gaṅgāṁ nṛpatir bhujābhyāṁ rurodha maināka ivācalendraḥ // 7.40 //
When his favourite female drowned in the waters of the Ganges, King Jahnu, his mind possessed by disembodied Love,[30] / Blocked the flow of the Ganges with his arms, as if he were Mount Maināka, the paragon of non-movement.[31] // 7.40 //

nṛpaś ca gaṅgā-virahāj jughūrṇa gaṅgāmbhasā sāla ivātta-mūlaḥ /
kula-pradīpaḥ pratipasya sūnuḥ śrīmat-tanuḥ śantanur asvatantraḥ // 7.41 //
And King 'Good Body' Śan-tanu, when separated from goddess Gaṅgā, shook like a *śāla* tree whose roots the Ganges was washing away: / The son of Pratipa and light of his family, he of the body beautiful, became uncontrollable.[32] // 7.41 //

hṛtāṁ ca saunandakinānuśocan prāptām ivorvīṁ striyam urvaśīṁ tām /
sad-vṛtta-varmā kila somavarmā babhrāma cittodbhava-bhinna-varmā // 7.42 //
Again, when the avatar Saunandakin[33] took away his Urvaśī, "She of the Wide Expanse," the wife whom, like the wide earth, Soma-varman[34] had made his own, / 'Moon-Armored' Soma-varman whose armor, so they say, had been virtuous conduct, roamed about grieving, his armor pierced by mind-existent Love.[35] // 7.42 //

Urvaśī is much celebrated in Indian art and literature – most notably in Kālidāsa's drama *Vikramorvaśī* ("Urvaśī [Won] by Valour"). But the story of the love between Purū-ravas and Urvaśī is as old as the *Ṛg-veda*, one hymn of which consists of a dialogue between the two lovers. See also verse 42.

[29] Tāla-jaṅgha literally means "Having Legs as Long as a Palm Tree," and so the metaphor of lightning striking a palm tree is a play on Tāla-jaṅgha's name.

[30] The first line includes an alliterative play on the word *aṇga*, which means a limb of the body or the body itself, and sounds like *gaṇga*, "Swift Goer," the name of the river we call the Ganges. "Favorite female" is *paramāṇgana;* lit. "chief [woman] of well-rounded limbs"; and "disembodied Love" is *an-aṇga*, the Bodiless One – i.e. the god of love Kāma whom Śiva angrily disembodied when Śiva's love for Pārvatī came into conflict with his ascetic practice.

[31] Many Indian legends link the royal sage Jahnu with the River Ganges; one legend says that Jahnu drank up the waters of the Ganges. This version as described by Aśvaghoṣa seems to have more of a connotation of the kind of blocked flow, or fixity, that is liable to accompany ascetic practice.

[32] Despite his devastation when the goddess Gaṇga left him to return to the Ganges whence she came, King Śan-tanu was able to perk up again when he set eyes on Satyavatī the fisherwoman, also known as Kālī (see verse 44 below).

[33] Saunandakin means "Bearer of the Saunanda," Saunanda being the name of the club born by Bala-rāma, who was the elder brother of Kṛṣṇa and said to be the 8th avatar of Viṣṇu. Bala is mentioned again in SN10.8.

[34] Soma-varman, "Moon-Armoured" is another epithet of the protagonist of verse 39, Purū-ravas; the epithet reflects his provenance as founder of the lunar dynasty.

[35] Cittodbhava, "He whose Existence Is Mind," again means Kāma-deva, god of Love, who was rendered bodiless as a punishment for bothering Śiva.

bhāryāṁ mṛtāṁ cānumamāra rājā bhīma-prabhāvo bhuvi bhīmakaḥ saḥ /
balena senāka iti prakāśaḥ senā-patir deva ivātta-senaḥ // 7.43 //
A king who followed his departed wife in death was 'The Dreaded' Bhīmika - he who was dread power on earth; / He who was famed, because of his military might, as Senāka, 'The Missile of War'; he who was, with his war machine, like a God of War.[36] // 7.43 //

svargaṁ gate bhartari śantanau ca kālīṁ jihīrṣan jana-mejayaḥ saḥ /
avāpa bhīṣmāt samavetya mṛtyuṁ na tad-gataṁ manmatham utsasarja // 7.44 //
Again, when Kālī's husband Śan-tanu had gone to heaven, Jana-mejaya, 'Causer of Trembling among Men,' in his desire to marry Kālī, / Came up against Bhīṣma 'The Terrible,' and accepted death from him, rather than relinquish his love for her.[37] // 7.44 //

śaptaś ca pāṇḍur madanena nūnaṁ strī-saṁgame mṛtyum avāpsyasīti /
jagāma mādrīṁ na maharṣi-śāpād asevya-sevī vimamarśa mṛtyum // 7.45 //
And Pāṇḍu 'The Pale One' having been cursed by Passion to die on coupling with a woman, / Went nonetheless with Mādrī: he heeded not the death that would result from the great seer's curse, when he tasted what he was forbidden to taste.[38] // 7.45 //

evaṁ-vidhā deva-nṛpa-rṣi-saṅghāḥ strīṇāṁ vaśaṁ kāma-vaśena jagmuḥ /
dhiyā ca sāreṇa ca durbalaḥ san priyām apaśyan kim-u viklavo 'ham // 7.46 //
Hordes[39] of gods and kings and seers such as these have fallen by dint of desire into the thrall of women. / Being weak in understanding and inner strength, all the more discouraged, when I cannot see my beloved, am I. // 7.46 //

---

[36] Senā-pati, "Army Leader" or "Lord of the Lance," is an epithet of Kārttikeya. *Senā-pati-deva,* "army-leading god," therefore means Kārttikeya, the ancient Indian god of war, the son of Śiva and Pārvatī, who directs the fight against demons.

[37] Bhīṣma was the son of King Śan-tanu and his first wife Gaṇga (see verse 41). When Śan-tanu remarried the fisherwoman known as Kālī (or Satyavatī), the latter therefore became Bhīṣma's step-mother, and Bhīṣma evidently did not take kindly to Jana-mejaya's designs on her. Jana-mejaya, incidentally, like the Ruru mentioned in verse 37, had it in for snakes and set about exterminating them en masse.

[38] Pāṇḍu's mother Ambālikā, the story goes, was instructed by the Satyavatī/Kālī of the previous verse, to keep her eyes closed in childbirth so as not to bear a blind son. When Ambālikā eventually opened her eyes and saw the formidable form of her offspring, she became pale. That is how Pāṇḍu got his name, "the Pale," or, more exactly, "the [One whose mother became] Pale." When he became a king, Pāṇḍu married the princess Mādrī along with another princess named Kuntī. While out hunting in the woods Pāṇḍu had the misfortune to shoot the sage Kindama while the latter had taken the form of a deer and was mating with a doe. The wounded sage Kindama placed a curse on Pāṇḍu. Aśvaghoṣa says that the curse was placed *madanena*, which could mean "by [the sage, one of whose names was] Madana, 'Passion,'" or could mean "by [the god of] Passion," or possibly could mean "because of passion." Since Pāṇḍu had shot the sage in flagrante, the curse was that if Pāṇḍu himself had sex with any woman, he would die. Pāṇḍu then remorsefully renounced his kingdom and lived with his wives as a celibate ascetic. After 15 years of ascetic celibacy, however, when his second wife Kuntī was away, Pāṇḍu was irresistibly drawn to his first wife Mādrī. As soon as Pāṇḍu set about enjoying what he was not to enjoy, he fulfilled the sage's curse and died. Mādrī, out of repentance and grief, committed so-called '*sati*,' burning herself alive on her husband's funeral pyre.

[39] *Saṅghāḥ*. See note to verse 24.

yāsyāmi tasmād gṛham eva bhūyaḥ kāmaṁ kariṣye vidhivat sa-kāmam /
na hy anya-cittasya calendriyasya liṅgaṁ kṣamaṁ dharma-pathāc cyutasya // 7.47 //
Therefore I shall go back home again and properly make love, as I please! / For the insignia do not sit well upon a backslider from the path of dharma, whose senses are restless and whose mind is elsewhere. // 7.47 //

pāṇau kapālam avadhāya vidhāya mauṇḍyaṁ mānaṁ nidhāya vikṛtaṁ paridhāya vāsaḥ /
yasyoddhavo na dhṛtir asti na śāntir asti citra-pradīpa iva so 'sti ca nāsti caiva // 7.48 //
When a man has taken the bowl in his hand, has shaved his head, and, putting pride aside, has donned the patched-together robe,[40] / And yet he is given to pleasure and lacking in firmness and tranquility, then like a lamp in a picture, he is there and yet he is not. // 7.48 //

yo niḥsṛtaś ca na ca niḥsṛta-kāma-rāgaḥ kāṣāyam udvahati yo na ca niṣkaṣāyaḥ /
pātraṁ bibharti ca guṇair na ca pātra-bhūto liṅgaṁ vahann api sa naiva gṛhī na bhikṣuḥ // 7.49 //
When a man has gone forth, but the red taint of desire has not gone forth from him; when he wears the earth-hued robe but has not transcended dirt; / When he carries the bowl but is not a vessel for the virtues; though he bears the insignia, he is neither a householder nor a bhikkhu. // 7.49 //

na nyāyyam anvayavataḥ parigṛhya liṅgaṁ bhūyo vimoktum iti yo 'pi hi me vicāraḥ /
so 'pi praṇaśyati vicintya nṛpa-pravīrāṁs tān ye tapo-vanam apāsya gṛhāṇy atīyuḥ // 7.50 //
I had thought it improper for a man with noble connections, having adopted the insignia, to discard them again: / But even [such a scruple] fades away, when I think about those royal heroes who abandoned an ascetic grove and went home. // 7.50 //

śālvādhipo hi sa-suto 'pi tathāmbarīṣo rāmo 'ndha eva sa ca sāṁskṛti-rantidevaḥ /
cīrāṇy apāsya dadhire punar aṁśukāni chittvā jaṭāś ca kuṭilā mukuṭāni babhruḥ // 7.51 //
For the Śālva king,[41] along with his son; and likewise Ambarīṣa and Rāma and Andha,[42] and Rantideva, son of Saṁkṛti[43] / Cast off their rags and clothed themselves again in finest fabrics; they cut their twisted dreadlocks off and put their crowns back on. // 7.51 //

---

[40] The four verbs in this line are all from the root √*dhā*, to put or place, viz: *ava-√dhā*, to place down; *vi-√dhā*, to put in order; *ni-√dhā*, to put or keep down; *pari-√dhā*, to put on. Hence, a more accurate reflection of the original might be: "When a man has put the bowl in his hand, has put his head in order, and, putting pride aside, has put on the patched-together robe...."

[41] The Śālva king was a noted enemy of Viṣṇu, whose pseudonyms include "Śālva's Enemy."

[42] Ambarīṣa was a royal seer, as presumably were Rāma and Andha.

[43] Rantideva – another ancient Indian hero who was not necessarily a good role model for devotees of the Buddha – was a king of the lunar dynasty famed for spending his riches in performing grand sacrifices; the blood which issued from the bodies of the slaughtered victims was changed into a river called Charmaṇ-vatī "Containing Hides." It is the modern River Chambal.

tasmād bhikṣārthaṁ mama gurur ito yāvad eva prayātas
tyaktvā kāṣāyaṁ gṛham aham itas tāvad eva prayāsye /
pūjyaṁ liṅgaṁ hi skhalita-manaso bibhrataḥ kliṣṭa-buddher
nāmutrārthaḥ syād upahata-mater nāpy ayaṁ jīva-lokaḥ // 7.52 //

Therefore as soon as my guru has gone from here to beg for alms, I will give up the ochre robe and go from here to my home; / Because, for a man who bears the honored insignia with unsound judgement, stammering mind and weakened resolve, no ulterior purpose might exist, nor even the present world of living beings." // 7.52 //

saundaranande mahākāvye nanda-vilāpo nāma saptamaḥ sargaḥ //7//

The 7th canto in the epic poem Handsome Nanda, titled "Nanda's Lament."

Canto 8: strī-vighātaḥ
A Tirade against Women

Introduction

Strī means a woman or (at the beginning of a compound) women. *Vighāta*, like the *vighātana* of BC Canto 4, is from *vi-√han*, which means to strike, to ward off, or to hinder. Hence the meanings of the noun *vighāta* include 1. a blow, 2. warding off, 3. an impediment, an obstacle, and 4. failure.

The present canto describes a certain Buddhist striver striking a verbal blow against women in general. Hence the ostensible meaning of *strī-vighātaḥ* is (1.) A Tirade against Women or (as per Linda Covill) "The Attack on Women."

In BC Canto 4, the ostensible sense is of the Prince warding away the amorous advances of women, but the real intention may be to satirise the generalizations that an immature man makes about "women." We are prompted instead to consider case by case what each individual woman stands for. Hence, in BC Canto 4, *strī-vighātana* ostensibly means (2.) Warding Women Away, but in the hidden meaning Warding Away [Objectification of] Women.

EH Johnston translated the present canto title (3.) Woman the Obstacle. With appropriate punctuation, this title could convey the same hidden meaning – Woman, the Obstacle – in which case the real obstacle is not women but objectification of women. The Buddha called such objectification, in Pali, *papañca.* The eighth of the eight truths of a great person, as recorded in the final chapter of Shōbōgenzō, is 不戯論, which was a not very accurate or helpful rendering into Chinese of the Sanskrit *niṣprapañca*, "not objectifying anything." Nowhere in Saundarananda does Aśvaghoṣa make explicit mention of this teaching of *niṣprapañca*, but its importance is reflected in the Dedicatory Verses of MMK where Nāgārjuna speaks of the dependently arisen bliss of the ending of objectification.

Finally, the present canto title *strī-vighāta* could be translated (4.) Women – Failure, in which case the failure in question could be the striver's failure to have the influence on Nanda that he wants to have. Or else the failure could be, again, the striver's abject failure to grasp the Buddha's ultimate teaching of not objectifying anything.

In general, we know well enough by now, nothing that Aśvaghoṣa writes is to be taken at face value. This is especially true when Aśvaghoṣa is putting words in the mouth of somebody – like the immature 'Hurry Up' Udāyin in BC Canto 4 – who has pretensions of knowing a thing or two. Again, we saw in SN Canto 6 how a senior female servant, who was well respected and good with words, tried to take Sundarī firmly in hand and to tell her what was good for her. But the matronly advice she offered was too direct and it did not work. The striver in this canto acts out of similar conceit, and Aśvaghoṣa is out to satirize him, holding up his objectification of the female other as an extreme example of how, out of ignorance, we create division by reifying things and othering others.

atha nandam adhīra-locanaṁ gṛha-yānotsukam utsukotsukam /
abhigamya śivena cakṣuṣā śramaṇaḥ kaś-cid uvāca maitrayā // 8.1 //
Then, while Nanda was looking forward, with unsteady eyes and the eagerest of expectations, to going home, / A certain striver with a benevolent air approached him and said, in a friendly way: // 8.1 //

kim idaṁ mukham aśru-durdinaṁ hṛdaya-sthaṁ vivṛṇoti te tamaḥ /
dhṛtim ehi niyaccha vikriyāṁ na hi bāṣpaś ca śamaś ca śobhate // 8.2 //
"Why this face so clouded with tears, that reveals a darkness in your heart? / Come to constancy, restrain your emotion, for tears and tranquility do not sit well together. // 8.2 //

dvi-vidhā samudeti vedanā niyataṁ cetasi deha eva ca /
śruta-vidhy-upacāra-kovidā dvi-vidhā eva tayoś cikitsakāḥ // 8.3 //
Pain invariably arises in two ways: in the mind and in the body. / And for those two kinds of pain, there are healers skilled in education and in medicine. // 8.3 //

tad iyaṁ yadi kāyikī rujā bhiṣaje tūrṇam anūnam ucyatām /
viniguhya hi rogam āturo nacirāt tīvram anartham ṛcchati // 8.4 //
So if this pain is physical be quick to tell a doctor all about it, / For when a sick man conceals his illness it turns before long into something serious. // 8.4 //

atha duḥkham idaṁ mano-mayaṁ vada vakṣyāmi yad atra bheṣajam /
manaso hi rajas-tamasvino bhiṣajo 'dhyātma-vidaḥ parīkṣakāḥ // 8.5 //
But if this suffering is mental tell me, and I will tell you the cure for it; / Because, for a mind enshrouded in gloom and darkness, the healer is a seeker who knows himself.[1] // 8.5 //

nikhilena ca satyam ucyatāṁ yadi vācyaṁ mayi saumya manyase /
gatayo vividhā hi cetasāṁ bahu-guhyāni madākulāni ca // 8.6 //
Tell the whole truth, my friend, if you think it fit to be told, to me; / For minds have many ways of working and many secrets, wherein concealment is complicated by conceit."[2] // 8.6 //

iti tena sa coditas tadā vyavasāyaṁ pravivakṣur ātmanaḥ /
avalambya kare kareṇa taṁ praviveśānyatarad vanāntaram // 8.7 //
Pressed in this way by [the striver], while wanting to explain his own decision, / [Nanda] clung to him, with hand in his hand, and went into another corner of the forest. // 8.7 //

---

[1] The dramatic irony here, which we readers see but the striver himself does not see, is that the healer who knows himself is the Buddha, aided by Ānanda. The preachy striver – who understands the kind of pain of separation described in Cantos 4-7 to be either physical or else mental – is not such a person.

[2] Here *madākulāni* has been read as *madā* (conceit) + *ākula* (confused/complicated). The elements of this compound could equally literally have been read *mada* + *ākula* ("full of intoxication" or "complicated by infatuation"). The translation "complicated by conceit" hints, again, at the ironic subtext whereby, in negating Nanda's vanity, the striver only succeeds in showing his own vanity.

atha tatra śucau latā-gṛhe kusumodgāriṇi tau niṣedatuḥ /
mṛdubhir mṛdu-māruteritair upagūḍhāv iva bāla-pallavaiḥ // 8.8 //
And so there the two of them sat in a vibrant bower of flower-spewing creepers / Whose soft young shoots, stirring in a soft breeze, seemed to be hiding them away. // 8.8 //

sa jagāda tataś cikīrṣitaṁ ghana-niśvāsa-gṛhītam antarā /
śruta-vāg-viśadāya bhikṣave viduṣā pravrajitena dur-vacam // 8.9 //
Then, in between the heavy sighs that intermittently gripped him, he expressed his intention, / Which was a hard one for a man who has knowingly gone forth to express. He told it to the bhikkhu who was so adept at hearing and talking.[3] // 8.9 //

sadṛśaṁ yadi dharma-cāriṇaḥ satataṁ prāṇiṣu maitra-cetasaḥ /
adhṛtau tad iyaṁ hitaiṣitā mayi te syāt karuṇātmanaḥ sataḥ // 8.10 //
"Evidently, it befits a devotee of dharma who is always friendly towards any living being, / That the benevolence inherent in your compassionate nature might be shown to me in my inconstancy! // 8.10 //

ata eva ca me viśeṣataḥ pravivakṣā kṣama-vādini tvayi /
na hi bhāvam imaṁ calātmane kathayeyaṁ bruvate 'py asādhave // 8.11 //
And that is why I would like especially to speak to you who preach propriety; / For what I am feeling now I would not tell to a man who was out of balance in himself and who, though a good talker, was not a true person. // 8.11 //

tad idaṁ śṛṇu me samāsato na rame dharma-vidhāv ṛte priyām /
giri-sānuṣu kāminīm ṛte kṛta-retā iva kiṁnaraś caran // 8.12 //
Hear me then when I say, in short, that without my beloved I do not enjoy the practice of dharma; / I am like a *kiṁnara* without his lover roaming about, his semen ready, over mountain peaks. // 8.12 //

vana-vāsa-sukhāt parāṅ-mukhaḥ prayiyāsā gṛham eva yena me /
na hi śarma labhe tayā vinā nṛpatir hīna ivottama-śriyā // 8.13 //
I am averse to the happiness of the forest life, and simply want to go home; / For without her I obtain no comfort, like a king without his sovereignty." // 8.13 //

atha tasya niśamya tad vacaḥ priya-bhāryābhimukhasya śocataḥ /
śramaṇaḥ sa śiraḥ prakampayan nijagādātma-gataṁ śanair idam // 8.14 //
When he heard those words of Nanda who, with his mind on his beloved wife, was burning with pain, / The striver, softly, while allowing his head to shake, said to himself: // 8.14 //

---

[3] Ostensibly Aśvaghoṣa is praising the striver as one who both talked and listened well. In the ironic hidden meaning, the suggestion might be that the striver was one who talked the talk but failed to walk the walk – as demonstrated by his spectacular failure to abandon a view on "women."

kṛpaṇaṁ bata yūtha-lālaso mahato vyādha-bhayād viniḥsṛtaḥ /
pravivikṣati vāgurāṁ mṛgaś capalo gīta-raveṇa vañcitaḥ // 8.15 //
"What a pity! In its longing for the herd, a rushing stag that has escaped the mortal danger of the hunter's arrow, / Is about to enter the hunter's trap, deceived by a call that the hunter sang. // 8.15 //

vihagaḥ khalu jāla-saṁvṛto hita-kāmena janena mokṣitaḥ /
vicaran phala-puṣpa-vad vanaṁ pravivikṣuḥ svayam eva pañjaram // 8.16 //
Truly, a bird that was caught in a net and set free by a benevolent person, / Desires, as it flits about the fruiting and blossoming forest, to fly of its own volition into a cage. // 8.16 //

kalabhaḥ kariṇā khalūddhṛtoḥ bahu-paṅkād viṣamān nadī-talāt /
jala-tarṣa-vaśena tāṁ punaḥ saritaṁ grāhavatīṁ titīrṣati // 8.17 //
A baby elephant, truly, after an adult elephant has pulled it up out of the deep mud of a dangerous riverbed, / Is wishing, in its thirst for water, to enter again that crocodile-infested creek. // 8.17 //

śaraṇe sa-bhujaṅgame svapan pratibuddhena pareṇa bodhitaḥ /
taruṇaḥ khalu jāta-vibhramaḥ svayam ugraṁ bhujagaṁ jighṛkṣati // 8.18 //
In a shelter where slithers a snake, a sleeping boy, awoken by an elder who is already awake, / Has become agitated and, truly, he is about to grab the horrible reptile himself. // 8.18 //

mahatā khalu jāta-vedasā jvalitād utpatito vana-drumāt /
punar icchati nīḍa-tṛṣṇayā patituṁ tatra gata-vyatho dvijaḥ // 8.19 //
Truly, having flown up and away from a tree that is blazing in a great forest fire, / A chick in[4] its longing for the nest is wishing to fly there again, its former alarm forgotten. // 8.19 //

avaśaḥ khalu kāma-mūrcchayā priyayā śyena-bhayād vinā-kṛtaḥ /
na dhṛtiṁ samupaiti na hriyaṁ karuṇaṁ jīvati jīva-jīvakaḥ // 8.20 //
Truly, a pheasant separated from its mate through fear of a hawk, and so stupefied by desire as to be helpless, / Is lacking in resolve and lacking in reserve: the pathetic little beggar[5] is living a pitiful life. // 8.20 //

---

[4] The final word of the verse in Sanskrit is *dvi-jaḥ*, lit. "one twice born," which means 1. a bird, which is twice born in the sense of being born first in an egg laid by the mother, and then born again on hatching from the egg; and 2. a person, and especially a brahmin, who has in some sense been reborn, for example in an initiation or confirmation ceremony in the Āryan tradition. So in placing *dvi-jaḥ* as the last word of this verse, the striver might be appealing again to Nanda's sense of what is proper for an Āryan man of noble birth. This would be in keeping with the striver's stance as a preacher of propriety (*kṣama-vādin*; verse 11).

[5] *Jīva-jīvakaḥ* means 1. a particular species of bird, a kind of pheasant, and 2. what the dictionary defines as "a Buddhist ascetic."

akṛtātmatayā tṛṣānvito ghṛṇayā caiva dhiyā ca varjitaḥ /
aśanaṁ khalu vāntam ātmanā kṛpaṇaḥ śvā punar attum icchati // 8.21 //
Greedy and untrained, devoid of decency and intelligence, / Truly, a wretched dog is wishing to eat again some food that he himself has vomited." // 8.21 //

iti manmatha-śoka-karṣitaṁ tam anudhyāya muhur nirīkṣya ca /
śramaṇaḥ sa hitābhikāṅkṣayā guṇavad vākyam uvāca vipriyam // 8.22 //
So saying, the striver contemplated [Nanda] for a while, beholding him tormented by the sorrows of love. / Then in his eagerness to be of benefit, the striver spoke fine words, which were unpleasant to hear. // 8.22 //

avicārayataḥ śubhāśubhaṁ viṣayeṣv eva niviṣṭa-cetasaḥ /
upapannam alabdha-cakṣuṣo na ratiḥ śreyasi ced bhavet tava // 8.23 //
"For you who draws no distinction between good and bad, whose mind is settled on objects of the senses, / And who is without the eye of attainment, naturally, no delight could there be in being better.[6] // 8.23 //

śravaṇe grahaṇe 'tha dhāraṇe paramārthāvagame manaḥ-śame /
aviṣakta-mateś calātmano na hi dharme 'bhiratir vidhīyate // 8.24 //
Again, to him whose thinking is not firmly fixed – in the matters of hearing, grasping, retaining and understanding the supreme truth, and in the matter of mental peace – / To him who easily changes his mind,[7] joy in dharma is not apportioned. // 8.24 //

viṣayeṣu tu doṣa-darśinaḥ parituṣṭasya śucer amāninaḥ /
śama-karmasu yukta-cetasaḥ kṛta-buddher na ratir na vidyate // 8.25 //
But that joy is certainly known[8] to one who sees the faults in objects of the senses,[9] who is contented, pure, and unassuming, / Whose mind is versed in the religious acts that generate peace and whose understanding therein is formed. // 8.25 //

ramate tṛṣito dhana-śriyā ramate kāma-sukhena bāliśaḥ /
ramate praśamena saj-janaḥ paribhogān paribhūya vidyayā // 8.26 //
A covetous man delights in opulence; a fool delights in sensual pleasure; / A true person delights in tranquility, having transcended sensual enjoyments by virtue of his knowledge. // 8.26 //

---

6 *Śreyas*, as the Buddha uses the term, especially in SN Cantos 12 and 13, is the possibility that Nanda eventually comes to believe in: better, betterment, a better way – a better way, that is, than hedonism, and also a better way than striving in pursuit of illusory targets. This verse, however, can be understood as full, from beginning to end, of Aśvaghoṣa's irony, so that, unbeknownst to himself, the striver is just expressing the enlightenment of sitting buddha, which is free of conceit, and so there is no delight in being better than others (*na ratiḥ śreyasi).*

7 *Calātmanaḥ* generally has a negative connotation: e.g. fickle-minded (SN1.20), out of balance in himself (SN8.11), but here again Aśvaghoṣa's irony might be at play.

8 The emphatic double negative, *na ratir na vidyate,* has here been translated as a positive.

9 Does this include seeing a fault in women, for being objects of men's sexual desire?

api ca prathitasya dhīmataḥ kula-jasyārcita-liṅga-dhāriṇaḥ /
sadṛśī na gṛhāya cetanā praṇatir vāyu-vaśād girer iva // 8.27 //
What is more, when a man of good repute, a man of intelligence and breeding, bears the honored insignia / His consciousness inclines towards home no more than a mountain bends in the wind. // 8.27 //

spṛhayet para-saṁśritāya yaḥ paribhūyātma-vaśāṁ sva-tantratām /
upaśānti-pathe śive sthitaḥ spṛhayed doṣavate gṛhāya saḥ // 8.28 //
Only a man who aspires to dependence on another, spurning autonomy and self-reliance, / Would yearn, while he was on the auspicious path to peace, for life at home with all its faults. // 8.28 //

vyasanābhihato yathā viśet parimuktaḥ punar eva bandhanam /
samupetya vanaṁ tathā punar gṛha-saṁjñaṁ mṛgayeta bandhanam // 8.29 //
Just as a man released from prison might, when stricken by some calamity, betake himself back to prison, / So might one who has retired to the forest seek out again that bondage called home. // 8.29 //

puruṣaś ca vihāya yaḥ kaliṁ punar icchet kalim eva sevitum /
sa vihāya bhajeta bāliśaḥ kali-bhūtām ajitendriyaḥ priyām // 8.30 //
The man who has left his strife behind and yet would like nothing better than to go back again to his strife: / He is the fool who would leave behind and then return, with his senses still unconquered, to the strife that is a wife. // 8.30 //

sa-viṣā iva saṁśritā latāḥ parimṛṣṭā iva soragā guhāḥ /
vivṛtā iva cāsayo dhṛtā vyasanāntā hi bhavanti yoṣitaḥ // 8.31 //
Like poisonous clinging creepers, like swept-out caves still harboring snakes, / Like uncovered blades being held in the hand, women are calamitous in the end. // 8.31 //

pramadāḥ samadā mada-pradāḥ pramadā vīta-madā bhaya-pradāḥ /
iti doṣa-bhayāvahāś ca tāḥ katham arhanti niṣevaṇaṁ nu tāḥ // 8.32 //
Sexy members of the female gender engender sexual desire, whereas unsexy ones are fearsome.[10] / Since they bring with them either a fault or fear, in what way do they merit attention? // 8.32 //

svajanaḥ svajanena bhidyate suhṛdaś cāpi suhṛj-janena yat /
paradoṣa-vicakṣaṇāḥ śaṭhās tad anāryāḥ pracaranti yoṣitaḥ // 8.33 //
So that kinsman breaks with kinsman and friend with friend, / Women, who are good at seeing faults in others,[11] behave deceitfully and ignobly. // 8.33 //

---

[10] The word used here for woman, *pramadā*, etymologically is already sexually charged (*pra* = emphatic; *madā* = sexual desire), so that the dictionary gives *pramadā* as "a young and wanton woman, any woman." The similar-sounding word *pra-da* means engendering. The first line then, is an alliterative play on these words, and at the same time an example of misogynist ignorance.

[11] Who is the one who is seeing the fault, not in himself, but in others? Cf MMK24.15: *"Projecting your own faults onto us, you are the one, mounted high on a horse, who has forgotten that very horse."*

kula-jāḥ kṛpaṇī bhavanti yad yad ayuktaṁ pracaranti sāhasam /
praviśanti ca yac camū-mukhaṁ rabhasās tatra nimittam aṅganāḥ // 8.34 //
When men of good families fall on hard times, when they rashly do unfitting deeds, / When they recklessly enter the vanguard of an army, women in those instances are the cause. // 8.34 //

vacanena haranti valgunā niśitena praharanti cetasā /
madhu tiṣṭhati vāci yoṣitāṁ hṛdaye hālahalaṁ mahad-viṣam // 8.35 //
They beguile with lovely voices, and attack with sharpened minds: / There is honey in women's speech, and lethal venom in their hearts. // 8.35 //

pradahan dahano 'pi gṛhyate vi-śarīraḥ pavano 'pi gṛhyate /
kupito bhujago 'pi gṛhyate pramadānāṁ tu mano na gṛhyate // 8.36 //
A burning fire can be held, the bodiless wind can be caught,[12] / An angry snake can be captured, but the mind of women cannot be grasped. // 8.36 //

na vapur vimṛśanti na śriyaṁ na matiṁ nāpi kulaṁ na vikramam /
praharanty aviśeṣataḥ striyaḥ sarito grāha-kulākulā iva // 8.37 //
Without pausing to consider looks or wealth, or intelligence or breeding or valor, / Women attack no matter what, like a ragged assortment of crocodiles in a river. // 8.37 //

na vaco madhuraṁ na lālanaṁ smarati strī na ca sauhṛdaṁ kva-cit /
kalitā vanitaiva cañcalā tad ihāriṣv iva nāvalambyate // 8.38 //
No charming speech, nor soothing caresses,[13] nor any affection do women ever remember. / The female, even when cajoled, is flighty: so rely on one no more than you would your enemies in this world. // 8.38 //

adadatsu bhavanti narma-dāḥ pradadatsu praviśanti vibhramam /
praṇateṣu bhavanti garvitāḥ pramadās tṛptatarāś ca māniṣu // 8.39 //
Women flirt with men who give them nothing; with generous men, they get restless. / They look down with disdain on the humble, but towards the arrogant show simpering contentment. // 8.39 //

guṇavatsu caranti bhartṛ-vad guṇahīneṣu caranti putravat /
dhanavatsu caranti tṛṣṇayā dhanahīneṣu caranty avajñayā // 8.40 //
They lord it over men of merit, and submit like children to men who are devoid of merit. / When men with money are around, they act rapaciously; men who are short of money they treat with contempt. // 8.40 //

---

[12] For example, a fire can be held by means of a flaming torch, and the wind can be caught by a sail.
[13] As an amendment to the paper manuscript's original *na rādranaṁ,* Shastri conjectured *na lālanaṃ.* EHJ accepted this amendment but queried *na cādaraṁ,* which would give "No charming speech, nor showing of respect."

viṣayād viṣayāntaraṁ gatā pracaraty eva yathāhṛtāpi gau /
anavekṣita-pūrva-sauhṛdā ramate 'nyatra gatā tathāṅganā // 8.41 //
Just as a cow, having gone from one pasture to another pasture, keeps right on grazing, however she's restrained, / So a woman, without regard for any affection she felt before, moves on and takes her pleasure elsewhere. // 8.41 //

praviśanty api hi striyaś citām anubadhnanty api mukta-jīvitāḥ /
api bibhrati caiva yantraṇā na tu bhāvena vahanti sauhṛdam // 8.42 //
For though women ascend their husband's funeral pyre, though they follow at the cost of their own life, / Though the restraints placed upon them they can indeed bear, they are not truly capable of genuine friendship. // 8.42 //

ramayanti patīn kathaṁ-cana pramadā yāḥ pati-devatāḥ kva-cit /
cala-cittatayā sahasraśo ramayante hṛdayaṁ svam eva tāḥ // 8.43 //
Women who sometimes, in some small way please their husband, by treating him like a god, / A thousand times more, in their fickle-mindedness, please their own heart. // 8.43 //

śva-pacaṁ kila senajit-sutā cakame mīna-ripuṁ kumudvatī /
mṛga-rājam atho bṛhad-rathā pramadānām agatir na vidyate // 8.44 //
The daughter of Sena-jit the Conqueror, so they say, coupled with a cooker of dogs;[14] Kumud-vatī, 'the Lilly Pool,' paired up with Mīna-ripu, 'the Foe of Fishes'; / And Bṛhad-rathā, 'the Burly Heroine,' loved a lion: there is nothing women will not do.[15] // 8.44 //

kuru-haihaya-vṛṣṇi-vaṁśa-jā bahu-māyā-kavaco 'tha śambaraḥ /
munir ugratapāś ca gautamaḥ samavāpur vanitoddhataṁ rajaḥ // 8.45 //
Scions of the Kurus, Haihayas and Vṛṣṇis, along with Śambara whose armor was mighty magic,[16] / And the sage Ugra-tapas Gautama – 'the Gautama of Grim Austerities' – all incurred the dust of passion which a woman raises. // 8.45 //

akṛtajñam anāryam asthiraṁ vanitānām idam īdṛśaṁ manaḥ /
katham arhati tāsu paṇḍito hṛdayaṁ sañjayituṁ calātmasu // 8.46 //
Ungrateful, ignoble, unsteady: such is the mind of women. / What man of wisdom could allow his heart to be fastened onto such fickle creatures? // 8.46 //

---

[14] *Sva-paca,* lit. "a dog-cooker," means a member of a tribe said to cook dogs, an outcaste.

[15] EHJ was unable to trace the sources of these tales of female bestiality, but thought that Mīna-rupu, the Fishes' Foe (also mentioned or alluded to in SN10.53), might here have taken the form of a crocodile.

[16] Śambara is the name of a demon formerly slain by Indra; in epic and later poetry he is an enemy of Kāma-deva, the god of love.

atha sūkṣmam atidvayāśivaṁ laghu tāsāṁ hṛdayaṁ na paśyasi /
kim-u kāyam asad-gṛhaṁ sravad vanitānām aśuciṁ na paśyasi // 8.47 //
So you fail to see how pernicious, in their intense duplicity, are their little lightweight hearts? / Do you not see, at least, that the bodies of women are impure, oozing houses of foulness? // 8.47 //

yad ahany-ahani pradhāvanair vasanaiś cābharaṇaiś ca saṁskṛtam /
aśubhaṁ tamasāvṛtekṣaṇaḥ śubhato gacchasi nāvagacchasi // 8.48 //
Day after day, by means of ablutions, garments, and jewels, they prettify an ugliness / Which you, with eyes veiled by ignorance do not see as ugliness: you see it as beauty. // 8.48 //

atha vā samavaiṣi tat-tanūm aśubhāṁ tvaṁ na tu saṁvid asti te /
surabhiṁ vidadhāsi hi kriyām aśuces tat-prabhavasya śāntaye // 8.49 //
Or else you do see that their bodies are foul but intelligence is lacking in you: / For the fragrant task in which you are engaged is extinction of the impurity that originates in them.[17] // 8.49 //

anulepanam añjanaṁ srajo maṇi-muktā-tapanīyam aṁśukam /
yadi sādhu kim-atra yoṣitāṁ sahajaṁ tāsu vicīyatāṁ śuci // 8.50 //
Cosmetic paste and powder, garlands, gems and pearls, gold and fine fabric: / What have these fine things, if fine they are, got to do with women? Let us examine what inherently in women is so immaculate. // 8.50 //

malapaṅka-dharā dig-ambarā prakṛti-sthair nakha-danta-romabhiḥ /
yadi sā tava sundarī bhaven niyataṁ te 'dya na sundarī bhavet // 8.51 //
Dirty and unclothed,[18] with her nails and teeth and body-hair in their natural state: / If she were like that, your Sundarī, whose name means 'Beautiful Woman,' surely wouldn't be such a beautiful woman to you now. // 8.51 //

sravatīm aśuciṁ spṛśec ca kaḥ saghṛṇo jarjara-bhāṇḍavat striyam /
yadi kevalayā tvacāvṛtā na bhaven makṣika-pattra-mātrayā // 8.52 //
What man who was capable of disgust would touch a woman, leaking and unclean like an old bucket, / If she were not scantily clad in skin as thin as a flying insect's wing? // 8.52 //

tvaca-veṣṭitam asthi-pañjaraṁ yadi kāyaṁ samavaiṣi yoṣitām /
madanena ca kṛṣyase balād aghṛṇaḥ khalv adhṛtiś ca manmathaḥ // 8.53 //
If you see that women's bodies are bony skeletons wrapped around with skin / And yet you are forcibly drawn by passion, truly then, Love is immune to disgust and lacking in all restraint. // 8.53 //

---

[17] Cf. "Not doing any wrong, undertaking what is good, cleansing one's own mind - this is the teaching of buddhas." (*sarva-pāpasyākaraṇaṁ kuśalasyopasaṁpadaḥ / svacitta-paryavadanam etad buddhasya śāsanam* // [Udānavarga 28.1])
[18] "Unclothed" is *dig-ambarā*, lit. "clothed in sky/space."

śubhatām aśubheṣu kalpayan nakha-danta-tvaca-keśa-romasu /
avicakṣaṇa kiṁ na paśyasi prakṛtiṁ ca prabhavaṁ ca yoṣitām // 8.54 //
In nails and in teeth, in skin, and in hair, both long and short, which are not beautiful, you are inventing beauty. / Dullard! Don't you see what women originally are made of and what they originally are? // 8.54 //

tad avetya manaḥ-śarīrayor vanitā doṣavatīr viśeṣataḥ /
capalaṁ bhavanotsukaṁ manaḥ pratisaṁkhyāna-balena vāryatām // 8.55 //
So then, reckon women, in mind and in body, to be singularly implicated with faults; / And hold back, by the power of this reckoning, the mind which strains so impulsively for home. // 8.55 //

śrutavān matimān kulodgataḥ paramasya praśamasya bhājanam /
upagamya yathā tathā punar na hi bhettuṁ niyamaṁ tvam arhasi // 8.56 //
You are educated, intelligent, and well-bred – a fitting vessel for supreme tranquility; / As such, you ought not in any way to break the contract into which you have entered. // 8.56 //

abhijana-mahato manasvinaḥ priya-yaśaso bahu-mānam icchataḥ /
nidhanam api varaṁ sthirātmanaś cyuta-vinayasya na caiva jīvitam // 8.57 //
For the man of spirit and noble birth; for the man who cherishes honor and strives to earn respect; / For the man of grit – better death for him than life as a backslider. // 8.57 //

baddhvā yathā hi kavacaṁ pragṛhīta-cāpo nindyo
bhavaty apasṛtaḥ samarād ratha-sthaḥ /
bhaikṣākam abhyupagataḥ parigṛhya liṅgaṁ
nindyas tathā bhavati kāma-hṛtendriyāśvaḥ // 8.58 //
For just as he is blameworthy who, having girded his armor on and taken up a bow, then flees in his warrior's chariot away from the battle; / So he too is blameworthy who, having accepted the insignia and taken to begging, then allows the stallion of his senses to be carted away by desire. // 8.58 //

hāsyo yathā ca paramābharaṇāmbara-srag
bhaikṣaṁ caran dhṛta-dhanuś cala-citra-mauliḥ /
vairūpyam abhyupagataḥ para-piṇḍa-bhojī hāsyas
tathā gṛha-sukhābhimukhaḥ sa-tṛṣṇaḥ // 8.59 //
And just as it would be ridiculous to go begging, while bedecked in the finest ornaments, clothes and garlands, while holding an archer's bow, and with a head full of passing fancies, / So too is it ridiculous to subsist on offerings, having consented to shapelessness, while longing thirstily for the comforts of home. // 8.59 //

yathā sv-annaṁ bhuktvā parama-śayanīye 'pi śayit
varāho nirmuktaḥ punar aśuci dhāvet paricitam /
tathā śreyaḥ śrṛṇvan praśama-sukham āsvādya
guṇavad vanaṁ śāntaṁ hitvā gṛham abhilaṣet kāma-tṛṣitaḥ // 8.60 //

Just as a hog, though fed on the best of food and lain on the finest bedding, would, when set free, run back to his familiar filth; / So, having tasted the excellent pleasure of cessation while learning the better way, would a man of thirsting libido abandon the tranquil forest and yearn for home. // 8.60 //

yatholkā hasta-sthā dahati pavana-prerita-śikhā
yathā pādākrānto daśati bhujagaḥ krodha-rabhasaḥ /
yathā hanti vyāghraḥ śiśur api gṛhīto gṛha-gataḥ
tathā strī-saṁsargo bahu-vidham anarthāya bhavati // 8.61 //

Just as a flaming torch, when fanned by the wind, burns the hand that holds it, / Just as a snake, being swift to anger, bites the foot that steps on it, / Just as a tiger, though caught as a cub, mauls the one who took it in, / So too does association with women, in many ways, make for disaster. // 8.61 //

tad vijñāya manaḥ-śarīra-niyatān nārīṣu doṣān imān,
matvā kāma-sukhaṁ nadī-jala-calaṁ kleśāya śokāya ca /
dṛṣṭvā durbalam āma-pātra-sadṛśaṁ mṛtyūpasṛṣṭaṁ jagan
nirmokṣāya kuruṣva buddhim atulām utkaṇṭhituṁ nārhasi // 8.62 //

Therefore, know these faults to be mentally and physically bound up with women; / Understand how sensual pleasure, as it flows away like river water, makes for affliction and for sorrow; / See the world, in the shadow of Death, to be fragile as an unbaked pot; / And make the peerless decision that leads to release - instead of causing the neck to stiffen up through sorrowful yearning."[19] // 8.62 //

saundaranande mahākāvye strī-vighāto nāmāṣṭamaḥ sargaḥ // 8 //

The 8th canto in the epic poem Handsome Nanda, titled "A Tirade against Women."

[19] *Utkaṇṭhitum* means to lift up (*ud-*) the neck (*kaṇṭha*) - with a connotation of being eager, or being on the point of doing something - and hence to long for, or to sorrow for.

Canto 9: madāpavādaḥ
Negation of Vanity

Introduction

Apavāda means speaking ill of, blaming, denouncing, denying, negating. The compound *madāpavāda* could be 1. *mada + apavāda* or 2. *madā + apavāda*. In other words, the fault spoken ill of, could be either 1. *mada*, which means over-exuberance, intoxication, infatuation;[1] or 2. *madā*, whose meanings include a. lust, ruttishness; and b. pride, arrogance, presumption, conceit. Ostensibly, then, *madāpavāda* could mean either (1.), as per Linda Covill, "The Denunciation of Infatuation"; or (2b.), as per EH Johnston, "The Denunciation of Conceit"; or even (2a.), The Denunciation of Lust.

Verses 29 and 30, which discuss intoxication, lend support to the former reading of *mada* as (1.) intoxication. And verse 50, which compares Nanda to an elephant in rut, supports the latter reading of *madā* as (2a.) ruttishness or lust. But the main thrust of the striver's argument in the present canto is directed against (2b.) the vanity of youth. Thus in verse 7 the striver explicitly targets Nanda's conceit (*abhimāna*) in regard to physical strength and in verse 8 he addresses Nanda as "taker of pride in strength!" (*bala-dṛpta*).

The main irony of this canto, if we take *madā* as meaning vanity or conceit, is that the conceitedness which is the object of the striver's denunciations, is also the cause of his own presumptuous preachiness. Just as in BC Canto 10 (Blaming Desires), an overarching desire for liberation causes the bodhisattva to blame desires, in the present canto it seems to be the Buddhist striver's overweening vanity that causes him to negate vanity. So it might be the old story of the pot calling the kettle black – in which case the canto title "Denunciation of Conceit" or "Negation of Vanity" might equally be translated "Denunciation out of Conceit" or "Negation born of Vanity."

athaivam ukto 'pi sa tena bhikṣuṇā jagāma naivopaśamaṁ priyāṁ prati /
tathā hi tām eva tadā sa cintayan na tasya śuśrāva visaṁjña-vad vacaḥ // 9.1 //
Though the bhikkhu reproached him in such a manner, [Nanda] did not arrive at any kind of tranquility with regard to his beloved; / So much did he think about her that he failed, as if he were unconscious, to hear a word the other said. // 9.1 //

yathā hi vaidyasya cikīrṣataḥ śivaṁ vaco na gṛṇhāti mumūrṣur āturaḥ /
tathaiva matto bala-rūpa-yauvanair hitaṁ na jagrāha sa tasya tad-vacaḥ // 9.2 //
For, just as an invalid who wants to die does not accept the kind advice of a doctor who intends to do him good; / So Nanda, bubbling with strength and looks and youth, did not accept that salutary advice of the striver. // 9.2 //

---

[1] Aśvaghoṣa in fact seems elsewhere to use *mada* as synonymous with *madā* in the sense of lust. See for example SN3.14: *krodha-mada-bhaya-taraṅga-calam*, "disturbed by waves of anger, lust, and fear."

na cātra citraṁ yadi rāga-pāpmanā mano 'bhibhūyeta tamo-vṛtātmanaḥ /
narasya pāpmā hi tadā nivartate yadā bhavaty anta-gataṁ tamas tanu // 9.3 //
It is not surprising, in such a case, that one whose mind is shrouded in darkness should be overpowered by the wrongness that arises out of a tainted desire; / For a person's wrongness ceases only when the darkness of ignorance, having reached its limit, begins to diminish. // 9.3 //

tatas tathākṣiptam avekṣya taṁ tadā balena rūpeṇa ca yauvanena ca /
gṛha-prayāṇaṁ prati ca vyavasthitaṁ śaśāsa nandaṁ śramaṇaḥ sa śāntaye // 9.4 //
And so, observing Nanda to be caught up, as he was, in his own strength and looks and youth, / Seeing him all set to go home, the striver chastised Nanda, in the name of tranquility. // 9.4 //

balaṁ ca rūpaṁ ca navaṁ ca yauvanaṁ tathāvagacchāmi yathāvagacchasi /
ahaṁ tv idaṁ te trayam avyavasthitaṁ yathāvabuddho na tathāvabudhyase // 9.5 //
"Your strength and looks and youthfulness I recognize as you do; / But that these three are impermanent you do not realise as I do. // 9.5 //

idaṁ hi rogāyatanaṁ jarāvaśaṁ nadī-taṭānokaha-vac calācalam /
na vetsi dehaṁ jala-phena-durbalaṁ balasthatām ātmani yena manyase // 9.6 //
For this body is a domicile for disease and in the face of senility it teeters helplessly, like a tree[2] with its roots on a riverbank. / Because you do not know it to be as fragile as froth on water, therefore you feel there to be abiding strength in you. // 9.6 //

yad ānna-pānāsana-yāna-karmaṇām asevanād apy atisevanād api /
śarīram āsanna-vipatti dṛśyate bale 'bhimānas tava kena hetunā // 9.7 //
When, through failure to eat and drink, or sit down, or move about, and also through over-indulgence in those acts, / The body manifestly goes to ruin, what reason is there for you to have the conceit of physical strength? // 9.7 //

himātapa-vyādhi-jarā-kṣud-ādibhir yadāpy anarthair upanīyate jagat /
jalaṁ śucau māsa ivārka-raśmibhiḥ kṣayaṁ vrajan kiṁ bala-dṛpta manyase // 9.8 //
By cold and heat, by sickness and aging, and by hunger and other such adversities, the living are being reduced / Like water in the hot season by the sun's rays. In these circumstances, what are you thinking, O taker of pride in strength! as you wander towards your end? // 9.8 //

tvag-asthi-māṁsa-kṣataj-ātmakaṁ yadā śarīram āhāra-vaśena tiṣṭhati /
ajasram ārtaṁ satata-pratikriyaṁ balānvito 'smīti kathaṁ vihanyase // 9.9 //
When a body made of skin, bone, flesh and blood owes its very existence to the taking of food, / When it is always ailing, needing continuous intervention, how can you labour under an illusion like 'I am inherently strong'? // 9.9 //

---

[2] *An-oka-ha,* "not leaving its home," means a tree.

yathā ghaṭaṁ mṛn-mayam āmam āśrito naras titīrṣet kṣubhitaṁ mahārṇavam / samucchrayaṁ tadvad asāram udvahan balaṁ vyavasyed viṣayārtham udyataḥ // 9.10 //
Like a man who aspires to cross the stormy ocean in an unbaked earthen pot, / Is he who would assume the sapless accretion of his body to be strong as he carries it around, striving after an object. // 9.10 //

śarīram āmād api mṛn-mayād ghaṭād idaṁ tu niḥsāratamaṁ mataṁ mama / ciraṁ hi tiṣṭhed vidhivad dhṛto ghaṭaḥ samucchrayo 'yaṁ sudhṛto 'pi bhidyate // 9.11 //
But even more fragile than an unbaked earthen pot, in my opinion, is this body; / For a pot that is properly kept might survive for many ages whereas this accretion crumbles even if well maintained. // 9.11 //

yad āmbu-bhū-vāyv-analāś ca dhātavaḥ sadā viruddhā viṣamā ivoragāḥ / bhavanty anarthāya śarīram āśritāḥ kathaṁ balaṁ roga-vidho vyavasyasi // 9.12 //
When the elements of water, earth, wind and fire are in constant opposition, like antagonistic snakes, / When they meet in a body only to make for calamity, how can you, in your propensity to sickness, be convinced of your strength? // 9.12 //

prayānti mantraiḥ praśamaṁ bhujaṁgamā na mantra-sādhyas tu bhavanti dhātavaḥ/ kva-cic ca kaṁ-cic ca daśanti pannagāḥ sadā ca sarvaṁ ca tudanti dhātavaḥ // 9.13 //
Snakes are lulled by charms,[3] but the elements are not apt to be charmed. / Snakes bite some people some of the time; the elements strike all people all of the time. // 9.13 //

idaṁ hi śayyāsana-pāna-bhojanair guṇaiḥ śarīraṁ ciram apy avekṣitam / na marṣayaty ekam api vyatikramaṁ yato mahāśī-viṣa-vat prakupyati // 9.14 //
For this body, though long tended with good habits of sleeping and sitting, and of eating and drinking, / Does not forgive a single step too far – at which it rears up in anger, like a great venomous snake. // 9.14 //

yadā himārto jvalanaṁ niṣevate himaṁ nidāghābhihato 'bhikāṅkṣati / kṣudhānvito 'nnaṁ salilaṁ tṛṣānvito balaṁ kutaḥ kiṁ ca kathaṁ ca kasya ca // 9.15 //
Pained by cold, one turns to fire; oppressed by heat, one longs for cold; / When hungry, one longs for food; when thirsty, for water. Where then is strength? What is it? How is it? Whose is it? // 9.15 //

tad evam ājñāya śarīram āturaṁ balānvito 'smīti na mantum arhasi / asāram asvantam aniścitaṁ jagaj jagaty anitye balam avyavasthitam // 9.16 //
So see a body as ailing and do not think 'I am possessed of strength.' / The world is insubstantial, inauspicious,[4] and uncertain, and in an impermanent world, power is undependable. // 9.16 //

---

[3] *Mantraiḥ* means by charms or by mantras.

kva kārta-vīryasya balābhimāninaḥ sahasra-bāhor balam arjunasya tat /
cakarta bāhūn yudhi yasya bhārgavaḥ mahānti śrṛṅgāṇy aśanir girer iva // 9.17 //
Where is the power of Kṛta-vīrya's son, the thousand-armed Arjuna, who fancied himself to be so strong?[5] / In battle, Bhārgava, 'The Scion of the Bhṛgus,' severed his arms like a thunderbolt lopping off the lofty horns of a mountain.[6] // 9.17 //

kva tad balaṁ kaṁsa-vikarṣiṇo hares turaṅga-rājasya puṭāvabhedinaḥ /
yam eka-bāṇena nijaghnivān jarāḥ kramāgatā rūpam ivottamaṁ jarā // 9.18 //
Where is the strength of Hari Kṛṣṇa, 'The Kaṁsa-tormentor,'[7] who broke the Horse-King's jaw?[8] / With one arrow from Jaras[9] he was brought down, like utmost beauty brought down, in due order, by old age. // 9.18 //

diteḥ sutasyāmara-roṣa-kāriṇaś camū-rucer vā namuceḥ kva tad balam /
yam āhave kruddham ivāntakaṁ sthitaṁ jaghāna phenāvayavena vāsavaḥ // 9.19 //
Where is the strength of Namuci son of Diti, light of an army and provoker of the gods? / He stood his ground in battle, furious as death, but Indra[10] slew him with a spattering of foam.[11] // 9.19 //

balaṁ kurūṇāṁ kva ca tat tadābhavad yudhi jvalitvā tarasaujasā ca ye /
samit-samiddhā jvalanā ivādhvare hatāsavo bhasmani paryavasthitāḥ // 9.20 //
And where is the power once possessed by the Kurus who blazed in combat with speed and stamina / And then lay in ashes, like sacrificial fires whose firewood has burned, their life-breath snuffed out? // 9.20 //

ato viditvā bala-vīrya-māninām balānvitānām avamarditaṁ balam /
jagaj jarā-mṛtyu-vaśaṁ vicārayan bale 'bhimānaṁ na vidhātum arhasi // 9.21 //
Know, therefore, that the strength of powerful men, who fancy themselves imbued with strength and drive, is ground down; / And do not, as you survey a world in the sway of aging and death, take pride in strength. // 9.21 //

---

[4] EHJ noted that he thought that Speyer's *asvāntam* = *anātmakam* (unreal), rather than *asvantam* (inauspicious), might be the correct reading.

[5] Arjuna (son of Kuntī; see note to SN7.45) was an ambidextrous master-archer, renowned as the greatest warrior on earth. He is one of the Pāṇḍava heroes of the Mahā-bhārata. The Bhagavad Gita is addressed by Kṛṣṇa to Arjuna, on the eve of the great battle between the Pāṇḍavas and the Kurus.

[6] Bhārgava, lit. 'Belonging to the Bhṛgus,' is a name of Paraśu-rāma "Rāma with the Axe," who according to one version of Indian mythology was Arjuna's nemesis.

[7] Kaṁsa, a king of Mathurā, was a relation (uncle or cousin) of Kṛṣṇa, and became his implacable enemy; hence Kṛṣṇa's epithets include *kaṃsa-vikarṣin* (Kaṃsa-tormentor) and *kaṃsa-jit* (Kaṃsa-slayer). The Hari of Hari Kṛṣṇa is thought to derive from the root √*hṛ*, "to take away [evil]."

[8] EHJ notes that the story of how Kṛṣṇa broke the jaw of the horse Keshin is recorded in Canto 10 of the Bhāgavata Purāṇa, which focuses on devotion (*bhakti*) to various incarnations of Viṣṇu but especially to Kṛṣṇa.

[9] *Jaras* (masculine) is the name of a hunter who wounded Kṛṣṇa. *Jaras* (feminine) means old age.

[10] Vāsava, "descended from the Vasus (the Good Ones)," is a name of Indra.

[11] *Ṛg-veda* 8.14.13: "With waters' foam you tore off, O Indra!, the head of Namuci, subduing all contending hosts."

balaṁ mahad vā yadi vā na manyase kuruṣva yuddhaṁ saha tāvad indriyaiḥ /
jayaś ca te 'trāsti mahac ca te balaṁ parājayaś ced vitathaṁ ca te balam // 9.22 //
Whether or not you think your strength is great, just do battle against the senses! / If you are victorious in this, your strength is great; if you are defeated, your strength is nothing. // 9.22 //

tathā hi vīrāḥ puruṣā na te matā jayanti ye sāśva-ratha-dvipān arīn
yathā matā vīratarā manīṣiṇo jayanti lolāni ṣaḍ-indriyāṇi ye // 9.23 //
Less heroic are those men thought who conquer enemies armed with horses, chariots and elephants, / Than those heroic thinkers are thought who conquer the restless six senses. // 9.23 //

ahaṁ vapuṣmān iti yac ca manyase vicakṣaṇaṁ naitad idaṁ ca gṛhyatām /
kva tad-vapuḥ sā ca vapuṣmatī tanur gadasya śāmyasya ca sāraṇasya ca // 9.24 //
Again, that you think 'I am good looking' is not astute. Let this be grasped: / Where are the good looks, where the beautiful bodies, of Gada, Śāmba, and Sāraṇa?[12] // 9.24 //

yathā mayūraś cala-citra-candrako bibharti rūpaṁ guṇavat sva-bhāvataḥ /
śarīra-saṁskāra-guṇād ṛte tathā bibharṣi rūpaṁ yadi rūpavān asi // 9.25 //
Just as a peacock, flashing the eye in its tail, naturally carries its excellent looks, / That is how, without any distinction got from grooming the body,[13] you must carry your looks - if after all you are good-looking. // 9.25 //

yadi pratīpaṁ vṛṇuyān na vāsasā na śauca-kāle yadi saṁspṛśed apaḥ /
mṛjā-viśeṣaṁ yadi nādadīta vā vapur vapuṣman vada kīdṛśaṁ bhavet // 9.26 //
If its unpleasantness were not covered with clothes, if it never touched water after excretion, / Or if it never received a good washing, tell me, O handsome one! what might a body be like? // 9.26 //

navaṁ vayaś cātma-gataṁ niśāmya yad gṛhonmukhaṁ te viṣayāptaye manaḥ /
niyaccha tac chaila-nadīrayopamaṁ drutaṁ hi gacchaty anivarti yauvanam // 9.27 //
Again, perceiving the prime of life to be a personal belonging, your mind looks forward to going home and gaining its sensual end: / Curb that mind! for, like a river coursing down a rocky mountain, youth passes swiftly and does not return. // 9.27 //

---

[12] It has not been possible to ascertain who these three were - which in itself, in a way, supports the striver's argument.

[13] *Saṁskāra* is from the verb *saṁs-√kṛ*, lit. "to do/make/form/put (*√kṛ*) together (*sam-*)." The many meanings of *saṁs-√kṛ* thus include to put together, to compose, to form well, to fabricate; to prepare, make ready, dress; to adorn, embellish, refine, elaborate, make perfect. In the context of this verse, then, *śarīra-saṃskāra* means "adorning/grooming the body." But the phrase brings to mind the Buddha's advice in the Rāhula Sutta (MN62; see Appendix) that Rāhula should breathe out and breathe in while thinking of "dropping off the fabrication of a body" (Pali: *passambhayaṁ kāya-saṅkhāraṁ* - in Sanskrit, *praśamayan kāya-saṁskāraṁ*).

ṛtur vyatītaḥ parivartate punaḥ kṣayaṁ prayātaḥ punar eti candramāḥ /
gataṁ gataṁ naiva tu saṁnivartate jalaṁ nadīnāṁ ca nṛṇāṁ ca yauvanam // 9.28 //
A season that has passed comes around again, the moon wanes and waxes again, / But gone, gone, never to return is the water of rivers, and the youth of men. // 9.28 //

vivarṇita-śmaśru valī-vikuñcitaṁ viśīrṇa-dantaṁ śithila-bhru niṣprabham /
yadā mukhaṁ drakṣyasi jarjaraṁ tadā jarābhibhūto vimado bhaviṣyasi // 9.29 //
When you are white whiskered and wrinkled, with broken teeth and sagging brows; when you are lacking in luster; / When, humbled by age, you see your face grown old, then you will sober up. // 9.29 //

niṣevya pānaṁ madanīyam uttamaṁ niśā-vivāseṣu cirād vimādyati /
naras tu matto bala-rūpa-yauvanair na kaś-cid aprāpya jarāṁ vimādyati // 9.30 //
Having wasted nights and greeted dawns drinking the most intoxicating liquor, one finally comes around, / But drunk on strength, looks and youth, no man ever comes round – until he reaches old age. // 9.30 //

yathekṣur atyanta-rasa-prapīḍito bhuvi praviddho dahanāya śuṣyate /
tathā jarā-yantra-nipīḍitā tanur nipīta-sārā maraṇāya tiṣṭhati // 9.31 //
Just as sugar-cane, when all its juice has been squeezed out, is thrown on the ground to dry, ready for burning, / So, pressed in the vice of aging and drained of energy, does the body wait to die. // 9.31 //

yathā hi nṛbhyāṁ kara-pattram īritaṁ samucchritaṁ dāru bhinatty anekadhā /
tathocchritāṁ pātayati prajām imām ahar-niśābhyām upasaṁhitā jarā // 9.32 //
Just as a saw worked by two men cuts a tall tree into many pieces, / So old age, pushed and pulled by day and night, topples people here and now who are high and mighty. // 9.32 //

smṛteḥ pramoṣo vapuṣaḥ parābhavo rateḥ kṣayo vāc-chruti-cakṣuṣāṁ grahaḥ /
śramasya yonir bala-vīryayor vadho jarā-samo nāsti śarīriṇāṁ ripuḥ // 9.33 //
Robber of memory; destroyer of looks; ender of pleasure; seizer of speech, hearing and sight; / Birthplace of fatigue; slayer of strength and manly vigor: for those with a body, there is no enemy to rival aging. // 9.33 //

idaṁ viditvā nidhanasya daiśikaṁ jarābhidhānaṁ jagato mahad-bhayam /
ahaṁ vapuṣmān balavān yuveti vā na mānam āroḍhum anāryam arhasi // 9.34 //
Knowing this great terror of the world named 'aging' to be a pointer on the way to death, / Do not rise to the ignoble conceit of an 'I' that is beautiful, or young, or strong. // 9.34 //

ahaṁ mamety eva ca rakta-cetasaḥ śarīra-saṁjñe tava yaḥ kalau grahaḥ /
tam utsṛjaivaṁ yadi śāmyatā bhaved bhayaṁ hy ahaṁ ceti mameti cārchati // 9.35 //
With your mind tainted by 'I' and 'mine,' you are latching onto the strife called a body. / Let go of that, if peace is to come about, for 'I' and 'mine' usher in danger. // 9.35 //

yadā śarīre na vaśo 'sti kasya-cin nirasyamāne vividhair upaplavaiḥ /
kathaṁ kṣamaṁ vettum ahaṁ mameti vā śarīra-saṁjñaṁ gṛham āpadām idam // 9.36 //
When no-one has dominion over a body that is ravaged by manifold misfortunes, / How can it be right to recognize as 'I' or as 'mine' this house of calamities called a body? // 9.36 //

sa-pannage yaḥ ku-gṛhe sadāśucau rameta nityaṁ prati-saṁskṛte 'bale /
sa duṣṭa-dhātāv aśucau calācale rameta kāye viparīta-darśanaḥ // 9.37 //
One who would delight in a flimsy snake-infested hovel that was always unclean and constantly needing repair:[14] / He is the man of perverted view who would delight in a body with its corrupted elements and unclean, unstable state. // 9.37 //

yathā prajābhyaḥ ku-nṛpo balād balīn haraty aśeṣaṁ ca na cābhirakṣati /
tathaiva kāyo vasanādi-sādhanaṁ haraty aśeṣaṁ ca na cānuvartate // 9.38 //
Just as a bad king takes forcibly from his subjects his full toll of taxes, and yet does not protect; / So the body takes its full toll of provisions such as clothes and the like, and yet does not obey. // 9.38 //

yathā prarohanti tṛṇāny ayatnataḥ kṣitau prayatnāt tu bhavanti śālayaḥ /
tathaiva duḥkhāni bhavanty ayatnataḥ sukhāni yatnena bhavanti vā na vā // 9.39 //
Just as in soil, grass sprouts readily but rice is grown through sustained effort, / So too does sorrow arise readily whereas happiness is produced with effort, if at all. // 9.39 //

śarīram ārtaṁ parikarṣataś calaṁ na cāsti kiṁ-cit paramārthataḥ sukham /
sukhaṁ hi duḥkha-pratikāra-sevayā sthite ca duḥkhe tanuni vyavasyati // 9.40 //
For him who drags around a hurting, perishable body, there is no such thing, in the supreme sense, as happiness; / For what he determines to be happiness, by taking counter-measures against suffering, is only a condition wherein suffering remains minimal. // 9.40 //

yathānapekṣyāgryam apīpsitaṁ sukhaṁ prabādhate duḥkham upetam aṇv api /
tathānapekṣyātmani duḥkham āgataṁ na vidyate kiṁ-cana kasya-cit sukhaṁ // 9.41 //
Just as the intrusion of even a slight discomfort spoils enjoyment of the greatest longed-for pleasure, / In a similar way, nobody ever enjoys any happiness by disregarding suffering that is upon him. // 9.41 //

śarīram īdṛg bahu-duḥkham adhruvaṁ phalānurodhād atha nāvagacchasi /
dravat phalebhyo dhṛti-raśmibhir mano nigṛhyatāṁ gaur iva śasya-lālasā // 9.42 //
You fail to see the body as it is – full of suffering and inconstant – because of fondness for its effects: / Let the mind that chases after effects, like a cow after corn, be restrained by the reins of steadfastness. // 9.42 //

[14] This can be read as a typical expression of the Big Pharma interventionist view of human health, posture, et cetera – the opposite of promoting welfare (SN1.8) by letting happen (SN15.5).

na kāma-bhogā hi bhavanti tṛptaye havīṁṣi dīptasya vibhā-vasor iva /
yathā yathā kāma-sukheṣu vartate tathā tathecchā viṣayeṣu vardhate // 9.43 //
For sensual enjoyments, like offerings fed into a blazing fire, do not make for satisfaction; / The more one indulges in sensual pleasures, the more the desire for sensual objects grows. // 9.43 //

yathā ca kuṣṭha-vyasanena duḥkhitaḥ pratāpayan naiva śamaṁ nigacchati /
tathendriyārtheṣv ajitendriyaś caran na kāma-bhogair upaśāntim ṛcchati // 9.44 //
Again, just as a man suffering from the blight of leprosy does not obtain a cure by way of application of heat, / Similarly, one who goes among sense objects with his senses unconquered does not tend towards peace by way of sensual enjoyments. // 9.44 //

yathā hi bhaiṣajya-sukhābhikāṅkṣayā bhajeta rogān na bhajeta tat-kṣamam /
tathā śarīre bahu-duḥkha-bhājane rameta mohād viṣayābhikāṅkṣayā // 9.45 //
For just as desire for pleasure from one's medicine might cause one to accept one's infirmity instead of taking proper measures against it, / So, because of desire for one's object, might one ignorantly rejoice in that receptacle of much suffering which is a body. // 9.45 //

anartha-kāmaḥ puruṣasya yo janaḥ sa tasya śatruḥ kila tena karmaṇā /
anartha-mūlā viṣayāś ca kevalā nanu praheyā viṣamā yathārayaḥ // 9.46 //
One who wishes adversity on a man is said, because of that action, to be his enemy. / Should not sense objects, as the sole root of adversity,[15] be shunned as dangerous enemies? // 9.46 //

ihaiva bhūtvā ripavo vadhātmakāḥ prayānti kāle puruṣasya mitratāṁ /
paratra caiveha ca duḥkha-hetavo bhavanti kāmā na tu kasya-cic chivāḥ // 9.47 //
Those who were his deadly enemies in this world can in time become a man's friend; / But not benign for anybody, in this or other worlds, are the desires which are the causes of suffering. // 9.47 //

yathopayuktaṁ rasa-varṇa-gandhavad vadhāya kimpāka-phalaṁ na puṣṭaye /
niṣevyamāṇā viṣayāś calātmano bhavanty anarthāya tathā na bhūtaye // 9.48 //
Just as eating a tasty, colorful and fragrant *kiṁpāka* fruit leads to death not nourishment, / So an imbalanced person's devotion to objects makes for misfortune, and not for well-being. // 9.48 //

---

[15] The striver's words sound in places very much like the Buddha's teaching – until we investigate the two in detail. For example, in light of the Buddha's teaching of dependent arising, there is no sole root of adversity, but if there were, would it tend to lie in the object, or in thirsting for that object? Aśvaghoṣa's intention, in formulating the striver's arguments as he does, may be to stimulate us to ask such questions and to conduct such investigations – not innocently believing the striver's words just because the striver was a Buddhist monk in personal contact with the Buddha himself.

tad etad ājñāya vipāpmanātmanā vimokṣa-dharmādy-upasaṁhitaṁ hitam /
juṣasva me saj-jana-saṁmataṁ mataṁ pracakṣva vā niścayam udgiran giram // 9.49 //
As an innocent, then, heed this good advice pertaining to liberation, dharma, and so forth; / Affirm my opinion, with which the righteous[16] concur. Or else speak up and state your agenda." // 9.49 //

iti hitam api bahv apīdam uktaḥ śruta-mahatā śramaṇena tena nandaḥ /
na dhṛtim upayayau na śarma lebhe dvirada ivātimado madāndha-cetāḥ // 9.50 //
Though reproached at length in this salutary fashion by a striver so great in hearing what is heard, / Nanda neither found firmness nor took comfort: he was like a tusker in full rut, mind blinded by lust.[17] // 9.50 //

nandasya bhāvam avagamya tataḥ sa bhikṣuḥ
pāriplavaṁ gṛha-sukhābhimukhaṁ na dharme /
sattvāśayānuśaya-bhāva-parīkṣakāya
buddhāya tattva-viduṣe kathayāṁ cakāra // 9.51 //
Then, having assured himself that Nanda's being was not in the dharma but was turned unsteadily towards the comforts of home, / That bhikkhu reported back to the investigator of living creatures' dispositions, tendencies and ways of being, to the Buddha, knower of reality. // 9.51 //

saundaranande mahākāvye madāpavado nāma navamaḥ sargaḥ // 9 //
The 9th canto in the epic poem Handsome Nanda, titled "Negation of Vanity."

---

[16] As the first element in the compound, *sadjana* could refer to true people or to a true person in the singular. In the latter case, the striver might be heard as suggesting – without justification – that he is speaking on behalf of the Buddha.

[17] In this compound, *madāndha* (whether read as *madā* + *andha* or as *mada* + *andha*) evidently means blinded by sexual desire, wantonness, lust, ruttishness, or rut (as of an elephant).

Canto 10: svarga-nidarśanaḥ
A Vision of Heaven

Introduction

Svarga means heaven or paradise. *Nidarśana* is an *-na* action noun from the root *ni-√dṛś*, which is used causatively to mean "to cause to see, to indicate, to impart knowledge, to teach." So *nidarśana* means pointing to, showing, indicating, or teaching. *Nidarśana* can also mean an object indicated for the purpose of teaching, i.e. an example, illustration, or proof. Again, *nidarśana* can mean a vision, as in a dream-vision *(svapna-nidarśana)*. Thus "The Vision of Paradise" (as per EH Johnston) and "A Lesson in Heaven" (as per Linda Covill) are two of several possible translations of the canto title.

In the canto, with pragmatic helpfulness reminiscent of the female confidante who comforts Sundarī at the end of Canto 6, the Buddha presents Nanda with a vision of heaven. It is a convenient fiction, a skilful means, whereby the hitherto lack-luster Nanda is caused to mobilize his energy with his eyes on a prize. Insofar as Nanda understands the prize to be sexual union with celestial nymphs, the goal he sets himself is an illusory one. The Buddha is evidently not worried about this. Rather, as Nanda's story unfolds we understand that what was important for Nanda initially, by any means, however unconventional, was to shake off downheartedness and somehow to start directing his energy somewhere.

Such is the ostensible gist of the canto. Below the surface, meanwhile, since the vision of heaven is a fantasy, Aśvaghoṣa is given free rein to conjure apparently far-fetched images which, on closer inspection, have practical hidden meaning. This provides a deeper layer of convenient fiction, like a dream within a dream. The fantastic descriptions of trees and birds in heaven in the first half of the present canto thus have much in common with the fantastic descriptions of troops in Māra's army in Canto 13 of Buddhacarita. The fabulous visions turn out on closer investigation to be very much grounded in practical reality. Thus, as a Chinese Zen master observed, "Flowers in space open on the ground."[1]

śrutvā tataḥ sad-vratam utsisṛkṣuṁ bhāryāṁ didṛkṣuṁ bhavanaṁ vivikṣum /
nandaṁ nirānandam apeta-dhairyam abhyujjihīrṣur munir ājuhāva // 10.1 //
Thus did he hear about Nanda's desire to abandon sincere practice, to see his wife, and to go home; / And so the Sage summoned the joyless[2] and weak-willed Nanda, wishing to take him up. // 10.1 //

---

[1] See Shōbōgenzō chap. 43, *Kuge*.

[2] *Nir-ānandam* describes Nanda as without (*nir-*) joy (*ānanda*). Besides the play on the name of Nanda himself, there is a hidden connotation of describing Nanda before the intervention of Ānanda, which will be described in the next canto.

taṁ prāptam aprāpta-vimokṣa-mārgaṁ papraccha citta-skhalitaṁ sucittaḥ /
sa hrīmate hrī-vinato jagāda svaṁ niścayaṁ niścaya-kovidāya // 10.2 //
When [Nanda], having not yet arrived at liberation's path, arrived, he of the beautiful mind questioned him, whose mind was faltering. / Bowed down by humiliation, [Nanda] confessed to the one who was full of humility; he told his intention to a master intention-knower. // 10.2 //

nandaṁ viditvā sugatas tatas taṁ bhāryābhidhāne tamasi bhramantam /
pāṇau gṛhītvā viyad utpapāta maniṁ jale sādhur ivojjihīrṣuḥ // 10.3 //
And so the Sugata, the One Gone Well, seeing Nanda wandering in the darkness called "wife," / Took his hand and flew up into the sky, wishing to take him up – like an honest man in the water bearing up a pearl. // 10.3 //

kāṣāya-vastrau kanakāvadātau virejatus tau nabhasi prasanne /
anyonya-saṁśliṣṭa-vikīrṇa-pakṣau saraḥ-prakīrṇāv iva cakravākau // 10.4 //
A shining gold they shone with their ochre robes, in the clear sky, / Like a pair of greylag geese rising up from a lake, embracing one another with outstretched wings. // 10.4 //

tau devadārūttama-gandha-vantaṁ nadī-saraḥ-prasravaṇaugha-vantam /
ājagmatuḥ kāñcana-dhātu-mantaṁ devarṣi-mantaṁ hima-vantam āśu // 10.5 //
Filled with the heady fragrance of the divine deodar,[3] full of rivers and lakes, and springs and gulches, / And filled with golden ore was the Himālayan mountain full of divine seers at which the two arrived, immediately.[4] // 10.5 //

tasmin girau cāraṇa-siddha-juṣṭe śive havir dhūma-kṛtottarīye /
agamya-pārasya nirāśrayasya tau tasthatur dvīpa ivāmbarasya // 10.6 //
On that auspicious mountain – which was frequented by celestial singers and saints and blanketed in smoke from burnt offerings – / As if on an island in an unsupported sky, where no far shore is reached, the two stood.[5] // 10.6 //

śāntendriye tatra munau sthite tu sa-vismayaṁ dikṣu dadarśa nandaḥ /
darīś ca kuñjāṁś ca vanaukasaś ca vibhūṣaṇaṁ rakṣaṇam eva cādreḥ // 10.7 //
While the Sage, his sense-power stilled, remained there standing,[6] Nanda looked all around in amazement / At the caverns and bowers and forest-dwellers that were the mountain's jewels and its guardians. // 10.7 //

---

[3] The deodar tree is *deva-dāru*, lit. "god-wood" or "divine-timber." It thus carries the connotation of divinity or something spiritual.

[4] Four elements of the verse can be seen as following a fourfold dialectical progression – 1. something divine (thesis), 2. something material (antithesis), 3. a material like gold which people imbue with value and meaning (synthesis), and 4. a Himālayan mountain where great yogis have traditionally sat in full lotus (transcendent action).

[5] Similarly – 1. the spiritual presence of celestial beings; 2. the material presence of smoke from fires; 3. negation of end-gaining and affirmation of individual autonomy in action; 4. remaining upright in empty space, in what feels like a condition of zero gravity, wherein even the negation of dualism is negated.

bahv-āyate tatra site hi śṛṅge saṁkṣipta-barhaḥ śayito mayūraḥ /
bhuje balasyāyata-pīna-bāhor vaiḍūrya-keyūra ivābabhāse // 10.8 //
For there on a great long horn of white rock, lay a peacock with its tail feathers arrayed / So as to resemble, on the long and muscular arm of Bala, an armlet of cat's-eye gems.[7] // 10.8 //

manaḥśilā-dhātuśilāśrayeṇa pītā-kṛtāṁso virarāja siṁhaḥ /
saṁtapta-cāmīkara-bhakti-citraṁ rūpy-āṅgadaṁ śīrṇam ivāmbikasya // 10.9 //
A lion with shoulders made orange from contact with the orange-red ore of 'the mind-rock,' arsenic,[8] / Looked like Āmbika's[9] crumpled armband of wrought silver streaked with refined gold. // 10.9 //

vyāghraḥ klama-vyāyata-khelagāmī lāṅgūla-cakreṇa kṛtāpasavyaḥ /
babhau gireḥ prasravaṇaṁ pipāsur ditsan pitṛbhyo 'mbha ivāvatīrṇaḥ // 10.10 //
A tiger moved unhurriedly and expansively, its tail curling around its right [shoulder], / As it went to drink at a mountain spring: it looked like an offering to the ancestors, being made by somebody who has arrived at water.[10] // 10.10 //

calat-kadambe himavan-nitambe tarau pralambe camaro lalambe /
chettuṁ vilagnaṁ na śaśāka bālaṁ kulodgatāṁ prītim ivāryavṛttaḥ // 10.11 //
A yak had got stuck in a dangling *kadamba* tree swaying on the Himālayan hillside: / Unable to free its tangled tail, it was like a man of noble conduct who cannot break away from a kindness that has been shown in his House.[11] // 10.11 //

---

[6] *Tatra*, being there, is as in the description of the Buddha in the final verse of SN Canto 3. Cf. also the description in BC Canto 12 and 13 of the bodhisattva under the bodhi tree, just sitting there (*tatropaviṣṭe*; BC13.1), while Māra does his worst.

[7] Bala means Bala-rāma, the elder brother of Kṛṣṇa and third of the Rāmas, regarded as the 8th avatar of Viṣṇu. In contrast to his brother, Kṛṣṇa, who is shown as dark blue or black, Bala is generally depicted as being fair skinned (hence the comparison to a long horn of white rock), and as wearing armlets.

[8] Orange-red arsenic ore, or realgar, is *manaḥ-śilā*, lit. "mind-rock." The compound might be a clue to something that Aśvaghoṣa is intending to draw to the reader's attention in this canto, namely the material basis for even the most exotic and outlandish mental phenomena. What we imagine always has its basis in what we have experienced - flowers in space open on the ground. Therefore, investigating how a buddha imagines heaven to be, we can learn something about how a buddha experiences the world - as, for example, governed absolutely by cause and effect.

[9] The name Āmbika is a conjecture, but evidently the reference is to some mythical figure; the point might be that a lion's mane (something real, albeit imagined to exist in Indra's heaven) resembled something mythical or legendary - a flower on the ground opened in space.

[10] The tail curling around the right shoulder may allude to the traditional method of wearing a kaṣāya, with the right shoulder bare. Arriving at water might suggest the state of a tathāgata, one who has arrived at reality.

[11] In the hidden meaning, *kula* could mean e.g. the lineage of Zen patriarchs - where freedom is described, ironically, as being caught in the grip of stillness.

suvarṇa-gaurāś ca kirāta-saṁghā mayūra-pittojjvala-gātra-lekhāḥ /
śārdūla-pāta-pratimā guhābhyo niṣpetur udgāra ivācalasya // 10.12 //
Communities of golden mountain-men, the Kirātas,[12] their limbs streaked with shining peacock gall, / Rushed out from their caves like flying tigers,[13] as if spewed out of the unmoving mountain. // 10.12 //

darī-carīṇām atisundarīṇāṁ manohara-śroṇi-kucodarīṇām /
vṛndāni rejur diśi kinnarīṇāṁ puṣpotkacānām iva vallarīṇām // 10.13 //
Hanging out in nooks and crannies, and going beyond Beauty[14] with their heart-stealing hips, breasts and bellies, / Were the bevies of *kiṁnarīs* who appeared in every quarter, like creepers with flowers in their upward winding curls. // 10.13 //

nagān nagasyopari devadārūn āyāsayantaḥ kapayo viceruḥ /
tebhyaḥ phalaṁ nāpur ato 'pajagmur mogha-prasādebhya iveśvarebhyaḥ // 10.14 //
Pestering the godly deodars,[15] monkeys roved from peak to peak; / Obtaining from those trees no fruit, they went away,[16] as if from powerful masters whose favor is futile.[17] // 10.14 //

tasmāt tu yūthād alasāryamāṇāṁ niṣpīḍitālaktaka-rakta-vaktrām /
śākhā-mṛgīm eka-vipanna-dṛṣṭiṁ dṛṣṭvā munir nandam idaṁ babhāṣe // 10.15 //
But lagging behind that troop was one whose face was red as pressed red resin – / A female monkey[18] with one eye missing. Seeing her, the Sage spoke this to Nanda: // 10.15 //

kā nanda rūpeṇa ca ceṣṭayā ca saṁpaśyataś cārutarā matā te /
eṣā mṛgī vaika-vipanna-dṛṣṭiḥ sa vā jano yatra gatā taveṣṭiḥ // 10.16 //
"Which, Nanda, in beauty and in manner, is the lovelier in your eyes: / This one-eyed monkey, or the person who is the focus of your wishing?" // 10.16 //

---

[12] Kirāta mountain men were said to be golden; they were famous, or infamous, for their abandonment of all religious rites and views – and so, in the Brahmanical tradition, they were regarded as heretics. The final word of the verse, *ācala*, as an adjective, means "not moving" or "immoveable"; as a noun it means a mountain. See also SN3.7.

[13] These tigers may be contrasted with the tiger in verse 10 that moves unhurriedly. That tiger might symbolize mindful or careful practice (at the first phase). These tigers might symbolize an attitude of transcendent carelessness (in the third phase).

[14] *Ati-sundarī*, "beyond beauty" or "exceedingly beautiful," includes the hint that Nanda is on the way to getting over the Beauty who is Sundarī herself.

[15] *Deva-dāru*, as in verse 5, lit. means "divine tree." Because of its heady fragrance, the deodar tree was assigned a certain divinity, to which the behavior of greedy monkeys is here comically opposed.

[16] Going away suggests, at the third phase, action in which nothing is to be gained (see the metaphor of walking away in SN16.4).

[17] This can be read as a reminder, at the fourth phase, that praying for the Buddha's benevolence without directing one's own energy in sitting-mediation, is as useless as praying to a doctor without taking the medicine he or she has prescribed.

[18] *Śākhā-mṛgī* is the feminine form of *śākhā-mṛga*, lit. "branch creature."

ity evam uktaḥ sugatena nandaḥ kṛtvā smitaṁ kiṁ-cid idaṁ jagāda /
kva cottama-strī bhagavan vadhūs te mṛgī naga-kleśa-karī kva caiṣā // 10.17 //
Addressed thus by the One Gone Well, Nanda said, with a slight smirk: / "How can a gap be measured,[19] Glorious One!, between that most excellent of women your sister-in-law, and this tree-tormenting monkey?" // 10.17 //

tato munis tasya niśamya vākyaṁ hetv-antaraṁ kiṁ-cid avekṣamāṇaḥ /
ālambya nandaṁ prayayau tathaiva krīḍā-vanaṁ vajra-dharasya rājñaḥ // 10.18 //
Then the Sage, hearing his protestation, and having in mind a slightly unconventional means,[20] / Took hold of Nanda as before and proceeded to the pleasure-grove of the royal bearer of the thunderbolt.[21] // 10.18 //

ṛtāv-ṛtāv ākṛtim eka-eke kṣaṇe-kṣaṇe bibhrati yatra vṛkṣāḥ /
citrāṁ samastām api ke-cid anye ṣaṇṇām ṛtūnāṁ śriyam udvahanti // 10.19 //
There one by one, season by season, and moment by moment, trees convey their individual form; / While some odd ones[22] also bring out the combined manifold glory of all six seasons. // 10.19 //

puṣyanti ke-cit surabhīr udārā mālāḥ srajaś ca granthitā vicitrāḥ /
karṇānukūlān avataṁsakāṁś ca pratyarthi-bhūtān iva kuṇḍalānām // 10.20 //
Some produce garlands and wreaths[23] which are fragrant and affecting, with variously interwoven strands,[24] / And small round creations[25] suited to the ear which are akin to earrings' opponents. // 10.20 //

---

[19] *Kva... kva...* implies excessive incongruity – Where is this? Where is that? In other words, how distant is this from that?

[20] *Hetv-antaram*: "a different means," i.e. a means different from what one might expect, an unconventional means. This use of *antara* mirrors Aśvaghoṣa's frequent use of *anya* with a subtext that affirms the individual and unconventional – see note to verse 19.

[21] *Vajra-dhara*, "bearing the thunderbolt," is an epithet of Indra.

[22] *Anye* means other. At the same time it means different, odd, individual, atypical, not conforming to ideas and expectations. This use of the Sanskrit word *anya* may thus be understood as similar to the use of the Chinese/Japanese character 非 (*hi-*), non-, in the phrase 非仏 (*hi-butsu*), "non-buddha." A non-buddha, in its ironic hidden meaning, as explored in Shōbōgenzō chap. 28, is a buddha as a real individual.

[23] *Mālā* and *sraj*, wreath and garland, are the names of metres used in Sanskrit poetry.

[24] The meanings of *granthita* include 1. strung, tied together or in order; 2. artificially composed or put together (as in the plot of a play); 3. closely connected with each other, difficult to be distinguished from each other; 4. having knots, knotty. These definitions all work as descriptions of Aśvaghoṣa's poetry, with the variously interwoven strands of, for example, its recurring metaphors.

[25] *Avataṃsaka* (from the root √*taṁs*, to decorate) is a garland, a ring-shaped ornament. Below the surface, Aśvaghoṣa may be suggesting a well-constructed verse whose fourth pāda brings a sense of completion.

raktāni phullāḥ kamalāni yatra pradīpa-vṛkṣā iva bhānti vṛkṣāḥ /
praphulla-nīlotpala-rohiṇo 'nye sonmīlitākṣā iva bhānti vṛkṣāḥ // 10.21 //
Trees there that abound in red lotuses look like trees ablaze. / Different trees,[26] growing full-blown blue lotuses,[27] seem to have their eyes open. // 10.21 //

nānā-virāgāṇy atha pāṇḍarāṇi suvarṇa-bhakti-vyavabhāsitāni /
atāntavāny eka-ghanāni yatra sūkṣmāṇi vāsāṁsi phalanti vṛkṣāḥ // 10.22 //
In various colorless hues, or else white; beautifully illuminated with golden dividing lines; / Beyond the weaving together of strands, being nothing but a unity; are the exquisite robes that trees there bear as fruit.[28] // 10.22 //

hārān maṇīn uttama-kuṇḍalāni keyūra-varyāṇy atha nūpurāṇi /
evaṁ-vidhāny ābharaṇāni yatra svargānurūpāṇi phalanti vṛkṣāḥ // 10.23 //
Pearl necklaces and gemstones, supreme earrings, choicest armlets, and ankle bracelets, / Are the kinds of ornament, fit for heaven, that trees there bear as fruit.[29] // 10.23 //

vaiḍūrya-nālāni ca kāñcanāni padmāni vajrāṅkura-kesarāṇi /
sparśa-kṣamāṇy uttama-gandhavanti rohanti niṣkampa-talā nalinyaḥ // 10.24 //
There rise golden lotuses with beryl stems and diamond shoots and stamens; / Receptive to touch, they have a scent of the ultimate: still pools without ripples allow them to grow.[30] // 10.24 //

yatrāyatāṁś caiva tatāṁś ca tāṁs tān vādyasya hetūn suṣirān ghanāṁś ca /
phalanti vṛkṣā maṇi-hema-citrāḥ krīḍā-sahāyās tridaśālayānām // 10.25 //
All kinds of musical instrument, with lengthened [sinews] and widened [skins], with open tubes and solid substance, / Are born there as fruit, by the distinctively bejeweled and gilded trees which are the heaven-dwellers' playing companions.[31] // 10.25 //

---

[26] *Anye vṛkṣāḥ* again means different trees, or trees that are not what people think of as trees, as in Yakusan's famous phrase describing the practice of sitting-dhyāna as 非思量 (*hi-shiryo*), "non-thinking."

[27] Whereas blazing redness symbolizes the passions, a blue lotus, which comes into full bloom in cool pools at the height of the hot season, is a symbol of coolness and hence enlightenment.

[28] Verses 19-22 relate to things in Indra's paradise which, at the first of four phases, seem to have religious, spiritual, or holistic meaning - like poetic words, symbols of Buddhist enlightenment, and traditionally-sewn robes.

[29] The ornaments described in this verse, from a spiritual viewpoint, might be meaningless baubles. From a materialistic viewpoint, they might be worth a lot of money. The verse can thus be taken, at the second phase, to be antithetical to the previous four verses.

[30] Golden lotuses with beryl stems can be understood as symbolizing, at the third phase, what transcends the opposition between red and blue, profane and spiritual, organic and inorganic, material and immaterial, et cetera. That they grow out of stillness seems to acknowledge the practical value of yogic practices that allow body and mind to come to quiet.

[31] *Krīḍā*, play or sport, suggests enjoyment of actions - again, at the third phase - like standing, walking, lying down, and sitting.

mandāra-vṛkṣāṁś ca kuśe-śayāṁś ca puṣpānatān koka-nadāṁś ca vṛkṣān /
ākramya māhātmya-guṇair virājan rājāyate yatra sa pārijātaḥ // 10.26 //
Over *mandāra* coral trees, and over trees weighed down with water-lily and ruddy lotus blossoms, / The 'Full Grown' Coral, shining there with majestic qualities, steps up and reigns supreme.[32] // 10.26 //

kṛṣṭe tapaḥ-śīla-halair akhinnais tripiṣṭapa-kṣetra-tale prasūtāḥ /
evaṁ-vidhā yatra sadānuvṛttā divaukasāṁ bhoga-vidhāna-vṛkṣāḥ // 10.27 //
Growing there, on soil tilled in Indra's heaven[33] by unwearying ploughs of austerity and discipline, / Are such trees as these, which are always adapting to provide for sky-dwellers' enjoyment. // 10.27 //

manaḥśilābhair vadanair vihaṁgā yatrākṣibhiḥ sphāṭika-saṁnibhaiś ca /
śāvaiś ca pakṣair abhilohitāntair māñjiṣṭhakair ardha-sitaiś ca pādaiḥ // 10.28 //
Birds[34] there have bright red beaks,[35] the color of red 'mind-rock' arsenic; and crystalline eyes; / And wings[36] a deathly shade of yellow, with intensely red tips; and claws[37] as red as red dye, but half white.[38] // 10.28 //

citraiḥ suvarṇac-chadanais tathānye vaiḍurya-nīlair nayanaiḥ prasannaiḥ /
vihaṁgamāḥ śiñjirikābhidhānā rutair manaḥ-śrotra-harair bhramanti // 10.29 //
Birds which are - again - different, with distinctively golden wings and bright, beryl-blue eyes, / Birds called *śiñjirikas* fly to and fro, carrying away minds and ears with their songs.[39] // 10.29 //

raktābhir agreṣu ca vallarībhir madhyeṣu cāmīkara-piñjarābhiḥ /
vaiḍūrya-varṇābhir upānta-madhyeṣv alaṁkṛtā yatra khagāś caranti // 10.30 //
Adorned with curling feathers that are red at the tips, golden in the middle, / And the colour of beryl within borders, birds there move.[40] // 10.30 //

---

32 The *mandāra* and *pārijāta* tree are the same species of tree - the majestic coral tree. But *pārijāta* literally means "fully developed"; so it suggests something mature, fully transcendent, and ultimate - for example, a fully enlightened buddha's sitting practice, which might be both exactly the same as, and totally beyond, the sitting practice of you and me.

33 *Tri-piṣṭapa*, lit. "the third height," means the highest heaven, Indra's heaven.

34 *Vihaṁgāḥ*, lit. "sky-goers," means birds; at the same time it has connotations of acting in emptiness.

35 *Vadana*, lit. "speaking," can mean the face or the mouth - or in the case of a bird, the beak.

36 *Pakṣa* can mean wing or side.

37 *Pāda* means the foot or leg of any person or creature or inanimate thing.

38 The four colors mentioned here - 1. the red of 'mind-rock'; 2. transparency, or absence of independent color; 3. deathly yellow still tinged with red; 4. contrast or opposition between red and white - may be taken as symbolizing, in four phases, our painful struggles as ordinary, unenlightened people in the world.

39 *Anye... vihaṁgamāḥ*, "birds which are different," or "goers through the sky, being different," may once again be taken as symbols of those non-buddhas who have mastered the practice of non-thinking. On that basis they talk the talk of dharma beautifully and enchantingly, carrying away our minds and ears. The color which distinguishes them is gold, symbolizing what is most valuable, e.g. a sitting buddha's enlightenment. Verses 28 and 29 are thus antithetical to each other.

40 The double appearance of *madhyeṣu* suggests synthesis in the middle way between opposites, and

rociṣṇavo nāma patatriṇo 'nye diptāgni-varṇā jvalitair ivāsyaiḥ /
bhramanti dṛṣṭīr vapuṣākṣipantaḥ svanaiḥ śubhair apsaraso harantaḥ // 10.31 //
Winged ones of a different ilk, named *rochiṣṇus*, who have the lustre of a blazing fire, their faces seeming to be aglow, / Roam around, shaking views with their wonderful appearance, and carrying *apsarases* away with their splendid sound.[41] // 10.31 //

yatreṣṭa-ceṣṭāḥ satata-prahṛṣṭā nirartayo nirjaraso viśokāḥ /
svaiḥ karmabhir hīna-viśiṣṭa-madhyāḥ svayaṁ-prabhāḥ puṇya-kṛto ramante // 10.32 //
There, merit-makers do whatever they like; constantly erect, they are free from pain, free from aging, and beyond sorrow; / Each by his actions inferior, superior, or in the middle, each letting his own light shine, the merit-makers rejoice. // 10.32 //

nityotsavaṁ taṁ ca niśāmya lokaṁ nis-tandri-nidrārati-śoka-rogam /
nando jarā-mṛtyu-vaśaṁ sadārtaṁ mene śmaśāna-pratimaṁ nṛ-lokam // 10.33 // (EHJ: 10.34)
Seeing that world to be in a perpetually elevated state, free from tiredness, sleep, discontent, sorrow, and disease, / Nanda deemed the ever-afflicted world of men, under the sway of aging and death, to be akin to a cremation ground. // 10.33 //

aindraṁ vanaṁ tac ca dadarśa nandaḥ samantato vismaya-phulla-dṛṣṭiḥ /
harṣānvitāś cāpsarasaḥ parīyuḥ sagarvam anyonyam avekṣamāṇāḥ // 10.34 // (EHJ: 10.35)
Nanda beheld Indra's forest all around him, his eyes wide open with amazement. / And the *apsarases* surrounded him, bristling with joyous excitement, while eyeing each other haughtily. // 10.34 //

sadā yuvatyo madanaika-kāryāḥ sādhāraṇāḥ puṇya-kṛtāṁ vihārāḥ /
divyāś ca nir-doṣa-parigrahāś ca tapaḥ-phalasyāśrayaṇaṁ surāṇām // 10.35 // (EHJ: 10.36)
Eternally youthful and devoted purely to Love, the *apsarases* are zones of recreation open to all who have made merit; / They are the heavenly and innocent resort of gods, their reward for ascetic practices. // 10.35 //

tāsāṁ jagur dhīram udāttam anyāḥ padmāni kāś-cil lalitaṁ babhañjuḥ /
anyonya-harṣān nanṛtus tathānyāś citrāṅga-hārāḥ stana-bhinna-hārāḥ // 10.36 // (EHJ: 10.37)
Odd ones among those women sang, in low and in high voices; some pulled lotuses apart, playfully; / Others in the same vein danced, bristling with mutual delight, limbs making exotic gestures, breasts perturbing pearl necklaces.[42] // 10.36 //

---

khagāś caranti, "sky-goers move," emphasizes action itself.

[41] These birds, like the 'Full Grown' Coral Tree, seem to have something especially transcendent and energetic about them, which causes views to be dropped off. Cf. Nāgārjuna: *In the direction of abandoning all views, he taught the true Dharma, / Clinging to compassion - I bow to him, Gautama.//* (MMK27.30).

pūrvaṁ tapo-mūlya-parigraheṇa svarga-krayārthaṁ kṛta-niścayānām /
manāṁsi khinnāni tapo-dhanānāṁ haranti yatrāpsaraso laḍantyaḥ // 10.37 // (EHJ: 10.33)

Here, having first accepted the price in austerities and made the decision to splash out on heaven, / Ascetics rich in austerities have their weary minds enthralled by the flirting *apsarases*.[43] // 10.37 //

kāsāṁ-cid āsāṁ vadanāni rejur vanāntarebhyaś cala-kuṇḍalāni /
vyāviddha-parṇebhya ivākarebhyaḥ padmāni kādamba-vighaṭṭitāni // 10.38 //

The faces of some of these women, ear-rings atremble, peeped through chinks in the undergrowth / Like duck-dunked[44] lotuses peeping through scattered and displaced leaves. // 10.38 //

tāḥ niḥsṛtāḥ prekṣya vanāntarebhyas taḍit-patākā iva toya-debhyaḥ /
nandasya rāgeṇa tanur vivepe jale cale candramasaḥ prabheva // 10.39 //

When he saw them emerging from their forest niches like ribbons of lightning from rainclouds, / Nanda's body trembled with passion like moonlight on rippling water. // 10.39 //

vapuś ca divyaṁ lalitāś ca ceṣṭās tataḥ sa tāsāṁ manasā jahāra /
kautūhalāvarjitayā ca dṛṣṭyā saṁśleṣa-tarṣād iva jāta-rāgaḥ // 10.40 //

Their heavenly form and playful gestures he then mentally seized; / And, while his eye was appropriated by curiosity, he became impassioned, as if from a thirst for union. // 10.40 //

sa jāta-tarṣo 'psarasaḥ pipāsus tat-prāptaye 'dhiṣṭhita-viklavārtaḥ /
lolendriyāśvena mano-rathena jehrīyamāṇo na dhṛtiṁ cakāra // 10.41 //

He became thirsty, desirous of drinking up the *apsarases*, afflicted by a pervading itch to have them. / Dragged along by the mind-chariot whose horse is the restless power of the senses, he could not come to stillness. // 10.41 //

yathā manuṣyo malinaṁ hi vāsaḥ kṣāreṇa bhūyo malinī-karoti /
mala-kṣayārthaṁ na malodbhavārthaṁ rajas tathāsmai munir ācakarṣa // 10.42 //

For just as a man adds soda ash to dirty clothes and thereby makes them even dirtier / Not in order to increase dirt but in order to remove it, so the Sage had stirred the dust of passion in Nanda. // 10.42 //

---

[42] This is one of several places where Aśvaghoṣa makes a play on the many possible meanings of *hāra*, which include "bearing" (hence *aṅga-hāra*, "limb-bearing" means gesture) and "pearl necklace."

[43] EHJ expressed in his preface doubts about whether this verse might be spurious. But the verse appears as verse 37 in both the palm-leaf and paper manuscripts, whose order has been maintained here. EHJ repositioned the verse, so that it appears as verse 33 in his edition.

[44] In his Sanskrit text, EHJ amended *kādamba-vighaṭṭitāni* to *kāraṇḍava-ghaṭṭitāni*, but at the translation stage he reflected that the amendation was perhaps hardly necessary since the Indian lexica give *kāraṇḍava* (SED: a sort of duck) and *kādamba* (SED: a kind of goose with dark-grey wings) as synonymous.

doṣāṁś ca kāyād bhiṣag ujjihīrṣur bhūyo yathā kleśayituṁ yateta /
rāgaṁ tathā tasya munir jighāṁsur bhūyastaraṁ rāgam upānindruāya // 10.43 //
Again, just as a healer who wishes to draw faults from the body would endeavour to aggravate those faults, / So, wishing to kill the red taint of passion in him, the Sage brought about an even greater passion. // 10.43 //

dīpa-prabhāṁ hanti yathāndhakāre sahasra-raśmer uditasya dīptiḥ /
manuṣya-loke dyutim aṅganānām antar-dadhāty apsarasāṁ tathā śrīḥ // 10.44 //
Just as a light in the dark is extinguished by the thousand-rayed brightness of the rising sun, / So the lovely radiance of women in the human world is put in the shade by the brilliance of the celestial nymphs. // 10.44 //

mahac ca rūpaṁ svaṇu hanti rūpaṁ śabdo mahān hanti ca śabdam alpam /
gurvī rujā hanti rujāṁ ca mṛdvīṁ sarvo mahān hetur aṇor vadhāya // 10.45 //
Great beauty blots out lesser beauty, a loud noise drowns out a small noise, / And a severe pain kills a mild pain – every great stimulus tends towards the extinction of a minor one. // 10.45 //

muneḥ prabhāvāc ca śaśāka nandas tad-darśanaṁ soḍhum asahyam anyaiḥ /
avītarāgasya hi durbalasya mano dahed apsarasāṁ vapuḥ śrīḥ // 10.46 //
And Nanda was able, relying on the power of the Sage, to endure that sight unendurable to others. / For the mind of a man lacking dispassion, when he was weak, would be burned up by the *apsarases'* shining splendor. // 10.46 //

matvā tato nandam udīrṇa-rāgaṁ bhāryānurodhād apavṛtta-rāgam /
rāgeṇa rāgaṁ pratihantu-kāmo munir virāgo giram ity uvāca // 10.47 //
Deeming then that Nanda was roused to a new height of passion, his passion having turned from love of his wife, / And desiring[45] to fight passion with passion, the dispassionate Sage spoke these words: // 10.47 //

etāḥ striyaḥ paśya divaukasas tvaṁ nirīkṣya ca brūhi yathārtha-tattvam /
etāḥ kathaṁ rūpa-guṇair matāste sa vā jano yatra gataṁ manas te // 10.48 //
"Look at these women who dwell in heaven and, having observed, truly tell the truth: / Do you think more of these women with their lovely form and excellent attributes or the one upon whom your mind has been set?" // 10.48 //

---

[45] This line draws out the distinction between *rāga*, redness, passion (from the root √rañj, to be dyed), and the wider term *kāma*, desire (from the root √*kam*, to wish, desire). Again, in the Buddha's ultimate teaching of *alpecchu-saṁtuṣṭi*, wanting little and being content, *icchu* is from √*iṣ*, to seek for. The point to be clear about is that being dispassionate does not mean having no desire.

athāpsaraḥsv eva niviṣṭa-dṛṣṭī rāgāgnināntar-hṛdaye pradīptaḥ /
sa-gadgadaṁ kāma-viṣakta-cetāḥ kṛtāñjalir vākyam uvāca nandaḥ // 10.49 //
So, letting his gaze settle upon the *apsarases*, burning in his innermost heart with a fire of passion, / And stammering, with a mind stuck on objects of desire, Nanda joined his hands like a beggar and spoke. // 10.49 //

haryaṅganāsau muṣitaika-dṛṣṭir yadantare syāt tava nātha vadhvāḥ /
tad-antare 'sau kṛpaṇā vadhūs te vapuṣmatīr apsarasaḥ pratītya // 10.50 //
"Whatever difference there might be, Master, between that one-eyed she-monkey and your sister-in-law, / Is the same when your poor sister-in-law is set against[46] the lovely *apsarases*. // 10.50 //

āsthā yathā pūrvam abhūn na kā-cid anyāsu me strīṣu niśāmya bhāryām /
tasyāṁ tataḥ samprati kā-cid āsthā na me niśāmyaiva hi rūpam āsām // 10.51 //
For just as previously, when I beheld my wife, I had no interest in other women, / So now when I behold their beauty I have no interest in her. // 10.51 //

yathā pratapto mṛdunātapena dahyeta kaś-cin mahatānalena /
rāgeṇa pūrvaṁ mṛdunābhitapto rāgāgnināanena tathābhidahye // 10.52 //
Just as somebody who had been pained by mild sunshine might be consumed by a great fire, / So I who was previously toasted by a mild passion am now roasted by this blaze of passion. // 10.52 //

vāg-vāriṇāṁ māṁ pariṣiñca tasmād yāvan na dahye sa ivābja-śatruḥ /
rāgāgnir adyaiva hi māṁ didhakṣuḥ kakṣaṁ sa-vṛkṣāgram ivotthito 'gniḥ // 10.53 //
Therefore pour on me the water of your voice, before I am burned, as was The Fishes' Foe;[47] / For a fire of passion is going now to burn me up, like a fire rising up to burn both undergrowth and treetops. // 10.53 //

prasīda sīdāmi vimuñca mā mune vasundharā-dhairya na dhairyam asti me /
asūn vimokṣyāmi vimukta-mānasa prayaccha vā vāg-amṛtaṁ mumūrṣave // 10.54 //
Please,[48] O Sage firm as the earth,[49] I am sinking. Liberate me who am without firmness. / I shall give up my life, O Man of Liberated Mind,[50] unless you extend to a dying man the deathless nectar of your words.[51] // 10.54 //

---

[46] *Pratītya* is here used as the absolutive of *prati-√i*, in the sense of "to go against," i.e. to be compared to. *Pratītya* is as in *pratītya-samutpāda*, "dependent arising" (see SN17.21, but especially BC Canto 14), in which compound *pratītya* seems to mean "going back to" or "having gone back to," and hence "dependent upon" or "grounded in."

[47] *Abja-śatruḥ* lit. "the enemy of the water-born," can be understood as another name for *mīna-ripu* (The Fishes' Foe) mentioned in SN8.44.

[48] *Prasīda* (be pleased to; please!) and *sīdāmi* (I am sinking) are both from the root *√sad*, to sit or sink down, to settle.

[49] The second pāda, similarly, contains plays on words from the root *√dhṛ*, to bear or hold firm – thus the earth is *vasun-dharā* (lit. "treasure-bearer") and firm is *dhairya*.

[50] *Vimokṣyāmi* (I shall give up) and *vimukta* (liberated) are both from *vi-√muc*.

anartha-bhogena vighāta-dṛṣṭinā pramāda-daṁṣṭreṇa tamo-viṣāgninā /
ahaṁ hi daṣṭo hṛdi manmathāhinā vidhatsva tasmād agadaṁ mahā-bhiṣak // 10.55 //
For a snake whose coils are calamity, whose eyes are destruction,[52] whose fangs are madness, whose fiery venom is dark ignorance: / The snake of love has bitten me in the heart. Therefore, Great Healer, supply the antidote![53] // 10.55 //

anena daṣṭo madanāhinā hi nā na kaś-cid ātmany anavasthitaḥ sthitaḥ /
mumoha vodhyor hy acalātmano mano babhūva dhīmāṁś ca sa śantanus tanuḥ // 10.56 //
For nobody bitten by this snake of love remains anything but unsettled in himself / Bewildered was the mind of Vodhyu, whose essence had been immovability, while 'Good-Body' Śan-tanu, who had been a sensible man, grew gaunt.[54]// 10.56 //

sthite viśiṣṭe tvayi saṁśraye śraye yathā na yāmīha vasan diśaṁ diśam /
yathā ca labdhvā vyasana-kṣayaṁ kṣayaṁ vrajāmi tan me kuru śaṁsataḥ sataḥ // 10.57 //
In you who abides conspicuously in the state of refuge, I seek refuge. So that I do not wander through this world loafing in this place and that place; / So that I might come to and then go beyond that abode which is my adversity-ending end,[55] please, repeatedly I plead that you help me."[56] // 10.57 //

---

[51] *Amṛtam* (deathless [nectar]) and *mumūrṣave* (to one about to die) are both from the root √*mṛ*. Even though Nanda himself is evidently taking his own burning desire so deadly seriously, the plays on words impart a certain subversive sense of levity.

[52] *Vighāta*, "a blow, destruction, ruin," is as in the title of SN Canto 7, *strī-vighātaḥ*, A Tirade against Women.

[53] *Agada* means medicine and especially an antidote. As a rule, the antidote to sexual passion (*rāga*), as recorded in suttas like the Rāhula Sutta (MN62; see Appendix), is to come back to that aspect of practice which is unattractive or unglamorous or unsexy (*aśubha*; see e.g. SN16.60; SN17.38). This is picked up in the Buddha's description of *bhāvanā* in Canto 16. The striver's description of the repulsive aspects of the human body in Cantos 7 and 8 stems from a different understanding of the so-called "impurity meditation." The Buddha himself, in his administering of the medicine of dharma to Nanda, evidently sees the wisdom in an unconventional approach, and therefore takes an altogether more indirect route than the kind of impurity meditation the striver seems to have in mind.

[54] Śan-tanu is the king mentioned by Nanda in SN7.41 and 7.44. No reference to Vodhyu has been traced. As in verse 54, Nanda's sense of the deadly seriousness of his situation is subverted by the latitude Aśvaghoṣa exhibits in finding time for poetic wordplay, whereby the closing two syllables of each pāda are repeated|: *...hi nā hi nā; ...sthi taḥ sthi taḥ; ...ma no ma no; ...ta nus ta nuḥ.*

[55] The meanings of *kṣayam* include both ending and abode. Like the *hāra* of verse 36, *kṣaya* is one of Aśvaghoṣa's favourite words for punning.

[56] Again, the closing two syllables of each pāda are repeated: *...śraye śraye; ...diśaṃ diśam; ...kṣayaṃ kṣayam; ... sataḥ sataḥ.* The sense of the repetitiveness of Nanda's pleading is emphasized not only by the sound of *śaṁsataḥ sataḥ*, but also by the meaning of *śaṁsataḥ*, from the root √*śaṁs*, to repeat.

tato jighāṁsur hṛdi tasya tat-tamas tamo-nudo naktam ivotthitaṁ tamaḥ /
maharṣi-candro jagatas tamo-nudas tamaḥ-prahīṇo nijagāda gautamaḥ // 10.58 //
Desiring to dispel that darkness in his heart like the moon[57] dispersing the darkness that rises by night, / Then spoke the moon of great seers, the disperser of the world's darkness, the one devoid of darkness – Gautama: // 10.58 //

dhṛtiṁ pariṣvajya vidhūya vikriyāṁ nigṛhya tāvac chruta-cetasī śṛṇu /
imā yadi prārthayase tvam aṅganā vidhatsva śulkārtham ihottamaṁ tapaḥ // 10.59 //
"Embrace firmness, shake off indecision, get a grip of hearing and of heart, and listen! / If you desire these women practice now the utmost asceticism to pay their price. // 10.59 //

imā hi śakyā na balān na sevayā na saṁpradānena na rūpavattayā /
imā hriyante khalu dharma-caryayā sacet praharṣaś cara dharmam ādṛtaḥ // 10.60 //
For these women are conquered neither by force nor by service, neither by gifts nor by good looks; / They are mastered[58] just by dharma-conduct. If aroused,[59] practice dharma diligently. // 10.60 //

ihādhivāso divi daivataiḥ samaṁ vanāni ramyāṇy ajarāś ca yoṣitaḥ /
idaṁ phalaṁ svasya śubhasya karmaṇo na dattam anyena na cāpy ahetutaḥ // 10.61 //
Perching here in heaven with gods; delightful forests; ageless women – / Such is the fruit of your own pure action. It is not conferred by another; nor is it without cause. // 10.61 //

kṣitau manuṣyo dhanur-ādibhiḥ śramaiḥ striyaḥ kadā-cidd hi labheta vā na vā /
asaṁśayaṁ yat tv iha dharma-caryayā bhaveyur etā divi puṇya-karmaṇaḥ // 10.62 //
Through strenuous efforts on earth – drawing a bow and suchlike – a man may sometimes win women, or else he may not; / But what is certain is that, through his practice of dharma here and now, these women in heaven can belong[60] to a man of meritorious action. // 10.62 //

---

[57] *Tamo-nuda*, "darkness-disperser," means the sun or, as in this case, the moon.

[58] Again, the ambiguity of √*hṛ* (root of *hāra* in verse 36) is well suited to Aśvaghoṣa's ironic purposes. Ostensibly *hriyante* means they are mastered or conquered or overpowered or won over, and taken as wives or lovers; but in the hidden meaning *hriyante* might mean they are won over in the sense of being persuaded to go in the right direction; or again *hriyante* might mean they are eclipsed, or surpassed, or transcended.

[59] The first definition of *praharṣa* in SED is "erection of the male organ." But *pra-* √*hṛṣ* also means to rejoice, be glad, exult. So in the hidden meaning, *praharṣa* suggests non-sexual arousal, as in BC Canto 3, titled *saṁvegotpattiḥ*, Arising of Nervous Excitement.

[60] Ostensibly, again, the Buddha is affirming the ancient idea that celestial nymphs can belong to an ascetic practitioner in a sexual sense. The verb √*bhū*, however, is again ambiguous: *bhaveyur puṇya-karmaṇaḥ* means "can belong to" and equally "can happen for" a man of meritorious karma. So not only belonging in a sexual sense but perhaps belonging in the sense of all being on the same side; or perhaps happening – as repeatedly described in MMK – like Gandharva City.

tad apramatto niyame samudyato ramasva yady apsaraso 'bhilipsase /
ahaṁ ca te 'tra pratibhūḥ sthire vrate yathā tvam ābhir niyataṁ sameṣyasi // 10.63 //
So delight in restraint, being attentive and ready, if you desire to secure[61] the *apsarases*, / And I guarantee that, insofar as you persist in your observance, you certainly shall be one[62] with them." // 10.63 //

ataḥ-paraṁ paramam iti vyavasthitaḥ parāṁ dhṛtiṁ parama-munau cakāra saḥ /
tato muniḥ pavana ivāmbarāt patan pragṛhya taṁ punar agaman mahī-talam // 10.64 //
"From now on, I will!" he agreed. Believing intently in the supreme Sage, he had become extremely determined.[63] / Then the Sage, gliding down from the sky like the wind, brought him back down again to earth. // 10.64 //

saundaranande mahākāvye svarga-nidarśano nāma daśamaḥ sargaḥ // 10 //
The 10th canto in the epic poem Handsome Nanda, titled "A Vision of Heaven."

---

[61] *Abhilipsase* is a desiderative form of *abhi-√labh,* which ostensibly means, again, to obtain or secure in a sexual sense; but in the hidden meaning to reach, or to win over, in a transformative sense.

[62] *Sameṣyasi* is from *sam-√i,* which, again, ostensibly means to come together in sexual union, to cohabit; but which in its hidden meaning might simply mean to be together, to live harmoniously together.

[63] "From now on" is *ataḥ-param*; "'I will,' he agreed" is *paramam iti.* "Extremely determined" is *parām dhṛtim.* "In the supreme sage" is *parama-munau.* Hence a particularly poetic canto finishes with a final poetic flourish – *param, paramam, parām, paramam....*

Canto 11: svargāpavādaḥ
Negation of Heaven

Introduction

Apavāda, as in the title of SN Canto 9, means speaking ill of, blaming, denouncing, denying, negating. In Canto 9 the object negated in the canto title *madāpavādaḥ* is *mada* or *madā*. In the present canto the object negated in the canto title *svargāpavādaḥ* is *svarga*, heaven or paradise. So the two canto titles parallel each other. Moreover, Ānanda himself in the present canto, for example in verse 37, emphasizes that peace is not possible for one who thirsts after desires, thereby seeming to confirm the Buddhist striver's negation of *mada/madā* as lust.

A fundamental difference, however, is that the striver in Canto 9 fails the pragmatic test of truth - his reproaches do not have the desired effect on Nanda. Ānanda's teaching, in contrast, does have the desired effect on Nanda; it causes Nanda to see the folly of striving for a heaven whose attractions, however pleasurable, could only ever be temporary.

Another difference is that the striver's tone is wholly negative, whereas Ānanda, evidently speaking from first person experience, not only negates pursuit of a fleeting heaven but also points to the lasting enjoyment to be had from directing the mind within. Whereas the striver presents Nanda only with the stick, Ānanda shows himself also to be skilled, like the Buddha, in the use of the carrot.

tatas tā yoṣito dṛṣṭvā nando nandana-cāriṇīḥ /
babandha niyama-stambhe durdamaṁ capalaṁ manaḥ // 11.1 //
And so, having gazed upon those women who wander in the Gladdening Gardens of Nandana, / Nanda tethered the fickle and unruly[1] mind to a tethering post of restraint. // 11.1 //

so 'niṣṭa-naiṣkramya-raso mlāna-tāma-rasopamaḥ /
cacāra viraso dharmaṁ niveśyāpsaraso hṛdi // 11.2 //
Failing to relish the taste of freedom from care, sapless as a wilting lotus, / He went through the motions of dharma-practice, having installed the *apsarases* already in his heart.[2] // 11.2 //

---

[1] *Durdamam* lit. means "hard to tame."

[2] In the first pāda *raso* means taste. In the second pāda *tāma-rasopamaḥ* means like a day-lotus. In the third pāda, *vi-raso* means insipidly or saplessly, not sincerely and vigorously. In the fourth pāda, *apsaraso is* accusative plural for the *apsarases* whom Nanda has installed in his heart. In a similar way, verse 3 contains in each line the word *indriya* (or *endriya* in compound), and verse 4 contains in each line *carya* or *cārya*.

tathā lolendriyo bhūtvā dayitendriya-gocaraḥ /
indriyārtha-vaśād eva babhūva niyatendriyaḥ // 11.3 //
Thus did one whose sense-power had been restless, whose senses had grazed on the pasture of his wife, / Come, by the very power of sense-objects, to have his sense-power reined in. // 11.3 //

kāma-caryāsu kuśalo bhikṣu-caryāsu viklavaḥ /
paramācārya-viṣṭabdho brahma-caryaṁ cacāra saḥ // 11.4 //
Adept in the practices of love, confused about the practices of a bhikkhu, / Set firm by the best of practice guides,[3] Nanda did the devout practice of abstinence.[4] // 11.4 //

saṁvṛtena ca śāntena tīvreṇa madanena ca /
jalāgner iva saṁsargāc chaśāma ca śuśoṣa ca // 11.5 //
Stifling restraint and ardent love, / Like water and fire in tandem, smothered him and burned him dry. // 11.5 //

svabhāva-darśanīyo 'pi vairūpyam agamat param /
cintayāpsarasāṁ caiva niyamenāyatena ca // 11.6 //
Though naturally good-looking, he became extremely ugly, / Both from agonizing about the *apsarases* and from protracted restraint. // 11.6 //

prastāveṣv api bhāryāyāṁ priya-bhāryas tathāpi saḥ /
vītarāga ivottasthau na jaharṣa na cukṣubhe // 11.7 //
Even when mention was made of his wife, he who had been so devoted to his wife / Stood by, seemingly bereft of passion; he neither bristled nor quavered. // 11.7 //

taṁ vyavasthitam ājñāya bhāryā-rāgāt parāṅ-mukham /
abhigamyābravīn nandam ānandaḥ praṇayād idam // 11.8 //
Knowing him to be adamant, turned away from passion for his wife, / Ānanda, having come that way, said to Nanda with affection: // 11.8 //

aho sadṛśam ārabdhaṁ śrutasyābhijanasya ca /
nigṛhītendriyaḥ svastho niyame yadi saṁsthitaḥ // 11.9 //
"Ah! This is a beginning that befits an educated and well-born man – / Since you are holding back the power of your senses and, abiding in yourself, you are set on restraint! // 11.9 //

---

[3] *Ācārya* means one who knows or teaches *ācāra*, practice.

[4] *Brahma-carya*, brahma-practice. Otherwise rendered as "spiritual practice" or "spiritual growth." The concept is rooted in a tradition of celibacy that pre-dated the Buddha (see BC12.42). In MMK17.23, Nāgārjuna speaks of the fault of *abrahmacarya-vāsas*, "a life not conducive to spiritual growth."

abhiṣvaktasya kāmeṣu rāgiṇo viṣayātmanaḥ /
yad iyaṁ saṁvid utpannā neyam alpena hetunā // 11.10 //
In one entangled in desires, in a man of passion, a sensualist, / That such consciousness has arisen – this is by no small cause! // 11.10 //

vyādhir alpena yatnena mṛduḥ pratinivāryate /
prabalaḥ prabalair eva yatnair naśyati vā na vā // 11.11 //
A mild illness is warded off with little effort; / A serious illness is cured with serious efforts, or else it is not. // 11.11 //

durharo mānaso vyādhir balavāṁś ca tavābhavat /
vinivṛtto yadi sa te sarvathā dhṛtimān asi // 11.12 //
An illness of the mind is hard to remove, and yours was a powerful one. / If you are rid of it, you are in every way steadfast. // 11.12 //

duṣkaraṁ sādhv anāryeṇa māninā caiva mārdavam /
atisargaś ca lubdhena brahmacaryaṁ ca rāgiṇā // 11.13 //
For an ignoble man good is hard to do; for an arrogant man it is hard to be meek; / For a greedy man giving is hard, and hard for a man of passion is the practice of devout abstinence. // 11.13 //

ekas tu mama saṁdehas tavāsyāṁ niyame dhṛtau /
atrānunayam icchāmi vaktavyaṁ yadi manyase // 11.14 //
But I have one doubt concerning this steadfastness of yours in restraint. / I would like assurance on this matter, if you think fit to tell me. // 11.14 //

ārjavābhihitaṁ vākyaṁ na ca gantavyam anyathā /
rūkṣam apy āśaye śuddhe rukṣato naiti sajjanaḥ // 11.15 //
Straight talk should not be taken amiss: / However harsh it is, so long as its intention is pure, a good man will not retain it as harsh. // 11.15 //

apriyaṁ hi hitaṁ snigdham asnigdham ahitaṁ priyam /
durlabhaṁ tu priya-hitaṁ svādu pathyam ivauṣadham // 11.16 //
For there is disagreeable good advice, which is kind; and there is agreeable bad advice, which is not kind; / But advice that is both agreeable and good is as hard to come by as medicine that is both sweet and salutary. // 11.16 //

viśvāsaś cārtha-caryā ca sāmānyaṁ sukha-duḥkhayoḥ /
marṣaṇaṁ praṇayaś caiva mitra-vṛttir iyaṁ satām // 11.17 //
Trust, acting in the other's interest, sharing of joy and sorrow, / And tolerance, as well as affection: such, between good men, is the conduct of a friend. // 11.17 //

tad idaṁ tvā vivakṣāmi praṇayān na jighāṁsayā /
tac chreyo hi vivakṣā me yat te nārhāmy upekṣitum // 11.18 //
So now I am going to speak to you out of affection, with no wish to hurt. / For my intention is to speak of that better way for you in regard to which I ought not to be indifferent.[5] // 11.18 //

apsaro-bhṛtako dharmaṁ carasīty abhidhīyase /
kim idaṁ bhūtam āho svit parihāso 'yam īdṛśaḥ // 11.19 //
You are practicing dharma, so they say, for celestial nymphs as wages. / Is that so? Is it true? such a thing would be a joke! // 11.19 //

yadi tāvad idaṁ satyaṁ vakṣyāmy atra yad auṣadham /
auddhatyam atha vaktṝṇām abhidhāsyāmi tad rajaḥ // 11.20 //
If this really is true, I will tell you a medicine for it; / Or if it is the impertinence of chatterers, then that dust I shall expose." // 11.20 //

ślakṣṇa-pūrvam atho tena hṛdi so 'bhihatas tadā /
dhyātvā dīrghaṁ niśaśvāsa kiṁ-cic cāvāṅmukho 'bhavat // 11.21 //
Then – though it was tenderly done – [Nanda] was stricken in his heart. / After reflecting,[6] he drew in a long breath, and his face inclined slightly downward. // 11.21 //

tatas tasyeṅgitaṁ jñātvā manaḥ-saṁkalpa-sūcakam /
babhāṣe vākyam ānando madhurodarkam apriyam // 11.22 //
And so, knowing the signs that betrayed the set of Nanda's mind, / Ānanda spoke words which were disagreeable but sweet in consequence: // 11.22 //

ākāreṇāvagacchāmi tava dharma-prayojanam /
yaj jñātvā tvayi jātaṁ me hāsyaṁ kāruṇyam eva ca // 11.23 //
"I know from the look on your face what your motive is in practicing dharma.
And knowing that, there arises in me towards you laughter and at the same time pity. // 11.23 //

yathāsanārthaṁ skandhena kaś-cid gurvīṁ śilāṁ vahet /
tadvat tvam api kāmārthaṁ niyamaṁ voḍhum udyataḥ // 11.24 //
Like somebody who, with a view to sitting on it, carried around on his shoulder a heavy rock; / That is how you, with a view to sensuality, are laboring to bear restraint. // 11.24 //

---

[5] *Upekṣā*, indifference or equanimity, is a characteristic of the fourth dhyāna (see SN17.54-55) and one of the seven limbs of awakening (SN17.24). In general, then, indifference or equanimity is a virtue to be cultivated – but not, as Ānanda suggests here and as the Buddha emphasizes from SN16.57, in all circumstances.

[6] *Dhyā*, to reflect or to think of, is as in *dhyāna*, reflection or meditation. If a hidden meaning is sought, the hidden meaning might be that, in sitting practice, free and full breathing and poise of the head are not arrangements, but they tend to follow, indirectly, from healthy thinking processes.

titāḍayiṣayā dṛpto yathā meṣo 'pasarpsati /
tadvad abrahmacaryāya brahmacaryam idaṁ tava // 11.25 //
Just as, in its desire to charge, a wild ram draws back, / So, for the sake of non-abstinence, is this devout abstinence of yours![7] // 11.25 //

cikrīṣanti yathā paṇyaṁ vaṇijo lābha-lipsayā /
dharmacaryā tava tathā paṇya-bhūtā na śāntaye // 11.26 //
Just as merchants buy merchandise moved by a desire to make profit, / That is how you are practising dharma, as if it were a tradable commodity, not for the sake of peace. // 11.26 //

yathā phala-viśeṣārthaṁ bījaṁ vapati kārṣakaḥ /
tadvad viṣaya-kārpaṇyād viṣayāṁs tyaktavān asi // 11.27 //
Just as, with a particular crop in view, a ploughman scatters seed, / That is how, because of being desperate for an object, you have renounced objects. // 11.27 //

ākāṅkṣec ca yathā rogaṁ pratīkāra-sukhepsayā /
duḥkham anvicchati bhavāṁs tathā viṣaya-tṛṣṇayā // 11.28 //
Just as a man who craves some pleasurable remedy might want to be ill, / That is how in your thirst for an object you are seeking out suffering. // 11.28 //

yathā paśyati madhv eva na prapātam avekṣate /
paśyasy apsarasas tadvad bhraṁśam ante na paśyasi // 11.29 //
Just as a man sees honey and fails to notice a precipice, / That is how you are seeing the heavenly nymphs and not seeing the fall that will come in the end. // 11.29 //

hṛdi kāmāgninā dīpte kāyena vahato vratam /
kim idaṁ brahmacaryaṁ te manasābrahmacāriṇaḥ // 11.30 //
Blazing with a fire of desire in your heart, you carry out observances with your body: / What is this devout abstinence of yours, who does not practice abstinence with his mind? // 11.30 //

saṁsāre vartamānena yadā cāpsarasas tvayā /
prāptās tyaktāś ca śataśas tābhyaḥ kim iti te spṛhā // 11.31 //
Again, since in spiraling through saṁsāra you have gained celestial nymphs and left them / A hundred times over, what is this yearning of yours for those women? // 11.31 //

tṛptir nāstīndhanair agner nāmbhasā lavaṇāmbhasaḥ /
nāpi kāmaiḥ sa tṛṣṇasya tasmāt kāmā na tṛptaye // 11.32 //
A fire is not satisfied by dry brushwood, nor the salty ocean by water, / Nor a man of thirst by his desires. Desires, therefore, do not make for satisfaction. // 11.32 //

[7] In other words: "So, done for the sake of sex, is this spiritual practice of yours!"

atṛptau ca kutaḥ śāntir aśāntau ca kutaḥ sukham /
asukhe ca kutaḥ prītir aprītau ca kuto ratiḥ // 11.33 //
Without satisfaction, whence peace? Without peace, whence ease? / Without ease, whence joy? Without joy, whence enjoyment? // 11.33 //

riraṁsā yadi te tasmād adhyātme dhīyatāṁ manaḥ /
praśāntā cānavadyā ca nāsty adhyātma-samā ratiḥ // 11.34 //
Therefore if you want enjoyment, let your mind be directed within. / Tranquil and impeccable is enjoyment of the inner self and there is no enjoyment to equal it. // 11.34 //

na tatra kāryaṁ tūryais te na strībhir na vibhūṣaṇaiḥ /
ekas tvaṁ yatra-tatra-sthas tayā ratyābhiraṁsyase // 11.35 //
In it, you have no need of musical instruments, or women, or ornaments; / On your own, wherever you are, you can indulge in that enjoyment. // 11.35 //

mānasaṁ balavad duḥkhaṁ tarṣe tiṣṭhati tiṣṭhati /
taṁ tarṣaṁ chindhi duḥkhaṁ hi tṛṣṇā cāsti ca nāsti ca // 11.36 //
The mind suffers mightily as long as thirst persists. / Eradicate that thirst; for suffering co-exists with thirst, or else does not exist. // 11.36 //

saṁpattau vā vipattau vā divā vā naktam eva vā /
kāmeṣu hi sa-tṛṣṇasya na śāntir upapadyate // 11.37 //
In prosperity or in adversity, by day or by night, / For the man who thirsts after desires,[8] peace is not possible. // 11.37 //

kāmānāṁ prārthanā duḥkhā prāptau tṛptir na vidyate /
viyogān niyataḥ śoko viyogaś ca dhruvo divi // 11.38 //
The pursuit of desires is full of suffering, and attainment of them is not where satisfaction lies; / The separation from them is inevitably sorrowful; but the celestial constant is separation. // 11.38 //

kṛtvāpi duṣkaraṁ karma svargaṁ labdhvāpi durlabham /
nṛlokaṁ punar evaiti pravāsāt sva-gṛhaṁ yathā // 11.39 //
Even having done action that is hard to do, and reached a heaven that is hard to reach, / [A man] comes right back to the world of men, as if to his own house after a spell away. // 11.39 //

yadā bhraṣṭasya kuśalaṁ śiṣṭaṁ kiṁ-cin na vidyate /
tiryakṣu pitṛ-loke vā narake vopapadyate // 11.40 //
The backslider when his residual good has run out / Finds himself among the animals or in the world of the departed,[9] or else he goes to hell. // 11.40 //

---

8 The use of *kāma* in the locative plural confirms that Aśvaghoṣa used the word *kāma* to mean, depending on context, both desire itself and an object of desire. Here *kāmeṣu* means loves or desires as objects.

tasya bhuktavataḥ svarge viṣayān uttamān api /
bhraṣṭasyārtasya duḥkhena kim āsvādaḥ karoti saḥ // 11.41 //
Having enjoyed in heaven the utmost sensual objects, / He falls back, beset by suffering: what has that enjoyment done for him? // 11.41 //

śyenāya prāṇi-vātsalyāt sva-māṁsāny api dattavān /
śibhiḥ svargāt paribhraṣṭas tādṛk kṛtvāpi duṣkaram // 11.42 //
Through tender love for living creatures Śibi gave his own flesh to a hawk.[10] / He fell back from heaven, even after doing such a difficult deed. // 11.42 //

śakrasyārdhāsanaṁ gatvā pūrva-pārthiva eva yaḥ /
sa devatvaṁ gate kāle māndhātādhaḥ punar yayau // 11.43 //
Having attained half of Indra's throne as a veritable earth-lord of the old school, / Māndhātṛ when his time with the gods elapsed came back down again.[11] // 11.43 //

rājyaṁ kṛtvāpi devānāṁ papāta nahuṣo bhuvi /
prāptaḥ kila bhujaṁgatvaṁ nādyāpi parimucyate // 11.44 //
Though he ruled the gods, Nahuṣa fell to earth; / He turned into a snake, so they say, and even today has not wriggled free.[12] // 11.44 //

tathaivelivilo rājā rāja-vṛttena saṁskṛtaḥ /
svargaṁ gatvā punar bhraṣṭaḥ kūrmī-bhūtaḥ kilārṇave // 11.45 //
Likewise King Ilivila being perfect in kingly conduct, / Went to heaven and fell back down, becoming, so they say, a turtle in the ocean.[13] // 11.45 //

---

[9] *Pitṛ-loke,* "in the world of the departed," means in other words, in the world of deceased ancestors, or in the world of hungry ghosts. See BC Canto 14.

[10] Both the *Mahā-bhārata* and *Rāmāyaṇa* contain the story of how the gods tested King Śibi by taking the form of a hawk and a pigeon. Chased by the hawk, the pigeon fell into the lap of Śibi, who offered to compensate the hawk with his own flesh.

[11] Māndhātṛ, reputed to be a 19th-generation descendant of Ikṣvāku, was a famous king of the ancient city of Ayodhya in Uttar Pradesh. The history of that city records that Māndhātṛ obtained half the throne of Śakra ("the Mighty" = Indra) and conquered the whole earth in one day.

[12] Book 13 of the *Mahā-bhārata* tells the story of how King Nahuṣa became chief of the gods, knocking Indra off top spot, by assiduously performing Brahmanical rites. By his arrogance, however, Nahuṣa incurred the wrath of one of the sages whom he had charged with carrying his palanquin. This sage reacted to being booted in the head by placing a curse on Nahuṣa who duly turned into a great snake which slithered off to skulk in a Himālayan cave. Thereafter, the story goes, when a group of exiled Pāṇḍavas found the snake hiding in the cave, the Pāṇḍava leader recognized that the snake was no ordinary snake and asked it about its origin. Nahuṣa then confessed and was relieved of his curse, so that he was able to shed his snakely incarnation.

[13] Viṣṇu famously became a turtle (his second avatar, Kurma) in order to stop Mt. Mandara from sinking into the ocean. Viṣṇu is said to have had a thousand names. Ilivila, however, has not been traced as one of them.

bhūridyumno yayātiś ca te cānye ca nṛpa-rṣabhāḥ /
karmabhir dyām abhikrīya tat-kṣayāt punar atyajan // 11.46 //
Bhūri-dyumna and Yayāti and other excellent kings,[14] / Having bought heaven by their actions, gave it up again, after that karma ran out – // 11.46 //

asurāḥ pūrva-devās tu surair apahṛta-śriyaḥ /
śriyaṁ samanuśocantaḥ pātālaṁ śaraṇaṁ yayuḥ // 11.47 //
Whereas the *asuras*, who had been gods in heaven when the *suras* robbed them of their rank, / Went bemoaning their lost glory down to their Pātāla lair.[15] // 11.47 //

kiṁ ca rājarṣibhis tāvad asurair vā surādibhiḥ /
mahendrāḥ śataśaḥ petur māhātmyam api na sthiram // 11.48 //
But why such citing of royal seers, or of *asuras*, *suras*, and the like? / Mighty Indras have fallen in their hundreds! Even the most exalted position is not secure. // 11.48 //

saṁsadaṁ śobhayitvaindrīm upendraś ca tri-vikramaḥ /
kṣīṇa-karmā papātorvīṁ madhyād apsarasāṁ rasan // 11.49 //
Again, Indra's luminous sidekick,[16] he of the three strides, lit up Indra's court, / And yet when his karma waned he fell to earth from the *apsarases'* midst, screaming. // 11.49 //

hā caitraratha hā vāpi hā mandākini hā priye /
ity ārtā vilapanto 'pi gāṁ patanti divaukasaḥ // 11.50 //
'Oh, the grove of Citra-ratha![17] Oh, the pond! Oh, the heavenly Ganges! Oh, my beloved!' – / Thus lament the distressed denizens of heaven as they fall to earth. // 11.50 //

tīvraṁ hy utpadyate duḥkham iha tāvan mumūrṣatām /
kiṁ punaḥ patatāṁ svargād evānte sukha-sevinām // 11.51 //
For intense already is the pain that arises in those facing death in this world / And how much worse is it for the pleasure-addicts when they finally fall from heaven? // 11.51 //

---

[14] Bhūri-dhyumna was known for his piety. His fall from heaven, according to EHJ's notes, is documented in Book 2 of the *Rāmāyaṇa*. Yayāti is the celebrated king of the lunar race whose sons are mentioned favourably in SN1.59. When Yayāti cheated on his wife, her father put a curse on him so that he immediately became an old man, whereupon he tried to buy back youth from his sons. Eventually, however, Yayāti realized the futility of his former shallow actions, let go of his worldly ambitions and took pains to redeem himself.

[15] *Asuras* and *suras* (demons and gods) as their Sanskrit names suggest, are opposed to each other. Pātāla is one of the regions under the earth supposed to be inhabited by nāgas and demons; sometimes it is used as a general name for the lower regions or hells. The resentful attitude of the *asuras* seems to be comically contrasted with the more yielding attitude of Bhūri-dhyumna and Yayāti.

[16] Upendra, lit. "Indra's younger brother," is one of the thousand names of Viṣṇu, whose distinguishing characteristic was said to be light. Hymn 7.100 of the *Ṛg-veda* refers to the celebrated 'three steps' of Viṣṇu by which he strode over the universe and in three places planted his step.

[17] Caitra-ratha, is the name of a grove of Kubera trees (Cedrela Toona) supposed to have been cultivated by the gandharva Citra-ratha "Having a Bright Chariot," the king of the gandharvas. See also SN2.53.

rajo gṛṇhanti vāsāṁsi mlāyanti paramāḥ srajaḥ /
gātrebhyo jāyate svedo ratir bhavati nāsane // 11.52 //
Their clothes gather dust; their glorious garlands wither; / Sweat appears on their limbs; and in their sitting[18] there is no enjoyment. // 11.52 //

etāny ādau nimittāni cyutau svargād divaukasām /
aniṣṭānīva martyānām ariṣṭāni mumūrṣatām // 11.53 //
These are the first signs of the imminent fall from heaven of sky-dwellers, / Like the unwelcome but sure signs of the approaching death of those subject to dying. // 11.53 //

sukham utpadyate yac ca divi kāmān upāśnatām /
yac ca duḥkhaṁ nipatatāṁ duḥkham eva viśiṣyate // 11.54 //
When the pleasure that arises from enjoyment of desires in heaven / Is compared with the pain of falling, the pain, assuredly, is greater. // 11.54 //

tasmād asvantam atrāṇam aviśvāsyam atarpakam /
vijñāya kṣayiṇaṁ svargam apavarge matiṁ kuru // 11.55 //
Knowing heaven, therefore, to be ill-fated, precarious, unreliable, unsatisfactory, and transitory, set your heart upon immunity from that circuit.[19] // 11.55 //

aśarīraṁ bhavāgraṁ hi gatvāpi munir udrakaḥ /
karmaṇo 'nte cyutas tasmāt tiryag-yoniṁ prapatsyate // 11.56 //
For though he attained a peak experience of bodiless being, Sage Uḍraka,[20] / At the expiration of his karma, will fall from that state into the womb of an animal. // 11.56 //

maitrayā sapta-vārṣikyā brahma-lokam ito gataḥ /
sunetraḥ punar āvṛtto garbha-vāsam upeyivān // 11.57 //
Through seven years of loving kindness, Sunetra went from here to Brahma's world, / But he span around again and came back to live in a womb.[21] // 11.57 //

yadā caiśvaryavanto 'pi kṣayiṇaḥ svarga-vāsinaḥ /
ko nāma svarga-vāsāya kṣeṣṇave spṛhayed budhaḥ // 11.58 //
Since heaven-dwellers, even when all-powerful, are subject to decay, / What wise man would aspire to a decadent sojourn in heaven? // 11.58 //

---

[18] The ostensible meaning of *āsane* is at the place where they were seated or stationed. Hence EH Johnston translated "*and they find no delight in their places;*" and Linda Covill "*and they take no joy in their station.*"

[19] *Apa-varga* (from the verb *apa-√vṛj*, to turn or leave off) is given in SED as "exemption from further transmigration."

[20] In SN3.3 the Sage Uḍraka, who inclined towards quietness, is mentioned as one whom Sarvārtha-siddha visited. (See also BC12.84-88.) Even though the Buddha credited only Arāḍa, and not Uḍraka, as having been his teacher (see note to BC12.84), it seems unthinkable that Ānanda would have singled out the Uḍraka of SN3.3 as one destined for rebirth as an animal. Perhaps for that reason, EHJ considered this and the next verse to be spurious.

[21] *Su-netra* lit. means "Having Good Eyes" or "Being a Good Leader." No reference has been traced.

sūtreṇa baddho hi yathā vihaṁgo vyāvartate dūragato 'pi bhūyaḥ /
ajñāna-sūtreṇa tathāvabaddho gato 'pi dūraṁ punar eti lokaḥ // 11.59 //
For just as a bird tied to a string, though it has flown far, comes back again; / So too do people return who are tied to the string of ignorance, however far they have travelled. // 11.59 //

kṛtvā kāla-vilakṣaṇaṁ pratibhuvā mukto yathā bandhanād
bhuktvā veshma-sukhāny atītya samayaṁ bhūyo vished bandhanaṁ /
tadvad dyāṁ pratibhūvad ātma-niyamair dhyānādibhiḥ prāptavān
kāle karmasu teṣu bhukta-viṣayeṣv ākṛṣyate gāṁ punaḥ // 11.60 //
A man temporarily released from prison on bail / Enjoys home comforts and then, when his time is up, he must go back to prison; / In the same way, through restrictive practices beginning with meditation, a man gets to heaven, as if on bail, / And after enjoying those objects which were his karmic reward, he eventually is dragged back down to earth. // 11.60 //

antar-jāla-gatāḥ pramatta-manaso mīnās taḍāge yathā
jānanti vyasanaṁ na rodha-janitaṁ svasthāś caranty ambhasi /
antar-loka-gatāḥ kṛtārtha-matayas tadvad divi dhyāyino
manyante śivam acyutaṁ dhruvam iti svaṁ sthānam āvartakam // 11.61 //
Fish in a pond who have swum into a net, unwarily, / Do not know the misfortune that results from capture, but contentedly move around in the water; / In the same way, meditators in heaven (who are really of this world of men), think that they have achieved their end; / And so they assume their own position to be favorable, secure and settled - as they continue to whirl around. // 11.61 //

taj janma-vyādhi-mṛtyu-vyasana-parigataṁ matvā jagad idaṁ
saṁsāre bhrāmyamāṇaṁ divi nṛṣu narake tiryak-pitṛṣu ca /
yat trāṇaṁ nirbhayaṁ yac chivam amarajaraṁ niḥśokam amṛtaṁ
tadd-hetor brahmacaryaṁ cara jahi hi calaṁ svargaṁ prati rucim // 11.62 //
Therefore, see this world to be shot through with the calamities of birth, sickness, and death; / See it - whether in heaven, among men, in hell, or among animals or the departed - to be reeling through saṁsāra. / Seeing the world to be thus, for the sake of that fearless refuge, for that sorrowless nectar of immortality, which is benign, and beyond death and decay, / Devoutly practice abstinence, and abandon your fancy for a precarious heaven." // 11.62 //

Saundara-nanda mahākāvye svargāpavādo nāma aikādaśaḥ sargaḥ // 11 //
The 11th canto in the epic poem Handsome Nanda, titled "Negation of Heaven."

Canto 12: pratyavamarśaḥ
Gaining a Foothold

Introduction

Praty-ava-√mṛś is given in SED as 1. to touch, and 2. to reflect, to meditate. The root *√mṛś* on its own is defined, again, as 1. to touch, and 2. to touch mentally, consider, reflect. Reflecting this latter sense of touching with the mind, EH Johnston translated the canto title as "Discernment," and Linda Covill as "Comprehension."

At the same time, EHJ noted that the original meaning of *mṛś* with *praty-ava* seems to be "lay hold of."[1] That the kind of hold thus intended might be a foothold, fits with the title of SN Canto 14 *ādi-prasthānaḥ*, in which *prasthāna* carries a connotation of walking or marching out. Gaining a foothold also fits with the meta-metaphor of the noble eightfold path, which is alluded to in the title of SN Canto 16.

Verses 19 and 20 of the present canto suggest that Aśvaghoṣa had in mind both senses of *pratyavamarśa* – both the metaphorical sense of gaining a foothold, and the non-figurative sense of mental discernment or comprehension.

Either way, what the Buddha makes very clear in the present canto is the practical nature of his teaching of *śraddhā*, belief, or confidence. About a hundred years ago, however, EH Johnston translated *śraddhā* as "faith," following which, more recently, building on that somewhat shaky foundation, another university professor, the Nāgārjuna scholar David Kalupahana, has denigrated Aśvaghoṣa as having "over-emphasized the function of faith."[2]

God help us! Should we laugh or cry? The truth might be that Aśvaghoṣa, like Nāgārjuna after him, touched very lightly and indirectly on religious faith in the divine, on the grounds of the emptiness which makes everything workable without putting anything, separately, on a pedestal.

So in this canto the Buddha shows with conspicuously earthy and practical metaphors – like the water-seeker digging for water, the maker of fires twirling a firestick, and the farmer sowing seed – that what he means by *śraddhā* is evidence-based belief, or confidence.

---

[1] EHJ's footnote: "It is hard to determine the exact meaning of *pratyavamarśa*... as it does not apparently occur in any other Buddhist work, Sanskrit or Pali... The original meaning of *mṛś* with *pratyava* seems to be 'lay hold of,' which suggests that it means the first step in the path of enlightenment, consisting of laying hold of the Law by faith in the Buddha."

[2] In his book *Mūlamadhyamakakārikā of Nāgārjuna* (1986), which generally has much to commend it, the Buddhist scholar Prof. David Kalupahana wrote: "Since such sophisticated Mahāyāna sutras [as the Lotus Sutra] were not available to Nāgārjuna, he could not help moving on to the early discourses in the Nikāyas and the Āgamas in search of the Buddha's teaching, especially at a time when he realized that the problems were created not only by metaphysicians like the Sarvāstivādins and the Sautrāntikas, but also by more popular religious teachers like Aśvaghoṣa, who over-emphasized the function of 'faith' in the emerging belief in a transcendent Buddha." How wrong can a Buddhist scholar be? Did Kalupahana actually bother to read for himself what Aśvaghoṣa wrote about *śraddhā*?

apsaro-bhṛtako dharmaṁ carasīty atha coditaḥ /
ānandena tadā nandaḥ paraṁ vrīḍam upāgamat // 12.1 //
"You are practicing dharma to earn the *apsarases* as wages!" To be upbraided thus, / As Nanda then was by Ānanda, made him deeply ashamed. // 12.1 //

tasya vrīḍena mahatā pramodo hṛdi nābhavat /
aprāmodyena vimukhaṁ nāvatasthe vrate manaḥ // 12.2 //
Because of the great shame the exuberance in his heart was no more. / His mind was downcast, due to disenchantment, and did not stick with practice. // 12.2 //

kāma-rāga-pradhāno 'pi parihāsa-samo 'pi san /
paripāka-gate hetau na sa tan mamṛṣe vacaḥ // 12.3 //
Though having been fixated on sensual love, and at the same time indifferent to ridicule, / Nanda's motivation had matured to a point where neither could he disregard [Ānanda's] words. // 12.3 //

aparīkṣaka-bhāvāc ca pūrvaṁ matvā divaṁ dhruvam /
tasmāt kṣeṣṇuṁ pariśrutya bhṛśaṁ saṁvegam eyivān // 12.4 //
Being of an unquestioning nature, he had presumed heaven to be a constant; / So on learning that it was perishable he was fiercely shocked. // 12.4 //

tasya svargān nivavṛte saṁkalpāśvo mano-rathaḥ /
mahā-ratha ivonmārgād apramattasya sāratheḥ // 12.5 //
Turning back from heaven, the chariot of his mind, whose horse was willpower,[3] / Was like a great chariot turned back from a wrong road by an attentive charioteer. // 12.5 //

svarga-tarṣān nivṛttaś ca sadyaḥ svastha ivābhavat /
mṛṣṭād apathyād virato jijīviṣur ivāturaḥ // 12.6 //
After turning back from his thirst for heaven, he seemed suddenly to become well. / He had given up something sweet that was bad for him, like a sick man finding the will to live. // 12.6 //

visasmāra priyāṁ bhāryām apsaro-darśanād yathā /
tathānityatayodvignas tatyājāpsaraso 'pi saḥ // 12.7 //
Just as he forgot about his beloved wife on seeing the *apsarases*, / So also, when startled by their impermanence, did he put the *apsarases* behind him. // 12.7 //

---

[3] *Saṁkalpa* is given in the dictionary as a conception or idea or notion formed in the mind or heart; will, volition, desire, purpose. It is hard to know from this context whether Aśvaghoṣa intended *saṁkalpa* to have a negative, positive, or neutral connotation. EHJ translated *"whose steeds are the fancies."* This is as per the Buddha's usage of *saṁkalpa* in SN13.35 (*"For smeared with the poison of conceptions, are those arrows, produced from five senses..."*).

mahatām api bhūtānām āvṛttir iti cintayan /
saṁvegāc ca sa-rāgo 'pi vīta-rāga ivābhavat // 12.8 //
"Even the greatest beings are subject to return!" So he reflected, / And from his shock, though given to redness, he seemed to blanch.[4] // 12.8 //

babhūva sa hi saṁvegaḥ śreyasas tasya vṛddhaye /
dhātur edhir ivākhyāte paṭhito 'kṣara-cintakaiḥ // 12.9 //
It was for growth in him of a better way that the shock happened – / Just as the verbal root "to grow" when recited by grammarians is listed [after "to happen"].[5] // 12.9 //

na tu kāmān manas tasya kena-cij jagṛhe dhṛtiḥ /
triṣu kāleṣu sarveṣu nipāto 'stir iva smṛtaḥ // 12.10 //
It was not, on the contrary, that holding on through sensual love had somehow held fast his mind – / As when the devolved particle[6] "existing"[7] is adhered to religiously in all three tenses. // 12.10 //

khela-gāmī mahā-bāhur gajendra iva nirmadaḥ /
so 'bhyagacchad guruṁ kāle vivakṣur bhāvam ātmanaḥ // 12.11 //
Trembling went he of mighty arm, like a top bull elephant, through with rut: / At a suitable moment, he approached the Guru, wishing to communicate his intention. // 12.11 //

praṇamya ca gurau murdhnā bāṣpa-vyākula-locanaḥ /
kṛtvāñjalim uvācedaṁ hriyā kiṁ-cid avāṅmukhaḥ // 12.12 //
After bowing his head to the Guru, with eyes filled with tears, / He joined the palms of his hands and spoke as follows, his face somewhat lowered, because of shame:[8] // 12.12 //

---

[4] This line may be taken as evidence of Aśvaghoṣa's insight into the mutually antagonistic fear responses (white fear paralysis and red panic) which are at the core of human suffering. Of the two, it is fear paralysis which is deeper and more primitive; hence Aśvaghoṣa is emphasizing how deep was the shock to Nanda's system.

[5] The lexicon in question is Pāṇini's *dhātu-pāṭha*, "Recital of Verbal Roots," an ancient list of 2200 verbs, the first of which is √*bhū*, which means not only to be, but also, vitally importantly for a devotee of *bhāvana*, to happen. Second on the list is √*edh*, to increase, to grow. The beginning of the list might have been almost as familiar to pandits of Aśvaghoṣa's day as "abc" is familiar to us. (Thanks to Malcolm Markovich for clarifying this background.)

[6] *Nipāta* has primarily a pejorative sense – falling down, decay, degeneration; in grammar it means 1. irregular form, irregularity, exception, and 2. a particle. Linda Covill notes that *asti* (from root √*as*) is considered to be an example of an indeclinable particle, an irregular particle whose form is supposed to remain constant – that is, in a pejorative sense, unchanged, fixed.

[7] For the significance of *asti* (as opposed to *bhū*) in the lexicon of emptiness, see in particular MMK15.7: *'In The Instructing of Kātyāyana, both "It exists" and "It does not exist" are negated by the Glorious One, Mighty in Making Things and Non-things Happen.'* For further exploration of where √*as* and √*bhū* differ and where they overlap, see MMK ch. 8.

[8] Here again, the mental phenomena – shame – is cause, and the face being lowered is effect. (It is not a question of a practitioner arranging the angle of his head in an effort to regulate his own mind.)

apsaraḥ prāptaye yan me bhagavan pratibhūr asi /
nāpsarobhir mamārtho 'sti pratibhūtvaṁ tyajāmy aham // 12.13 //
"For my gaining of the celestial nymphs, Glorious One, you stand as guarantor. / But for the nymphs I have no need; I relinquish your guarantee. // 12.13 //

śrutvā hy āvartakaṁ svargaṁ saṁsārasya ca citratām /
na martyeṣu na deveṣu pravṛttir mama rocate // 12.14 //
For since I have heard of heaven's fleeting whirl and of the varieties of aimless wandering, / Neither among mortal beings nor among heavenly beings does doing appeal to me.[9] // 12.14 //

yadi prāpya divaṁ yatnān niyamena damena ca /
a-vitṛptāḥ patanty ante svargāya tyāgine namaḥ // 12.15 //
If, after struggling to get to heaven, through self-restriction and restraint, / [Men] fall at last, unsatisfied, then homage to the heaven-bound who give up on the way. // 12.15 //

ataś ca nikhilaṁ lokaṁ viditvā sacarācaram /
sarva-duḥkha-kṣaya-kare tvad-dharme parame rame // 12.16 //
Now that I have seen through the whole world of man, with its changeability and its fixity, / It is the eradicator of all suffering, your most excellent dharma, that I rejoice in.[10] // 12.16 //

tasmād vyāsa-samāsābhyāṁ tan me vyākhyātum arhasi /
yac chrutvā śṛṇvatāṁ śreṣṭha paramaṁ prāpnuyāṁ padam // 12.17 //
Therefore, in detail and in summary, could you please communicate it to me, / O Best of Listeners, so that through listening I might come to the ultimate step." // 12.17 //

tatas tasyāśayaṁ jñātvā vipakṣāṇīndriyāṇi ca /
śreyaś caivāmukhī-bhūtaṁ nijagāda tathāgataḥ // 12.18 //
Then, knowing from where he was coming, and that, though his senses were set against it, / A better way was now emerging, the Realized One spoke: // 12.18 //

aho pratyavamarśo 'yaṁ śreyasas te purojavaḥ /
araṇyāṁ mathyamānāyām agner dhūma ivotthitaḥ // 12.19 //
"Aha! This gaining of a foothold[11] is the harbinger of a higher good in you, / As, when a firestick is rubbed, rising smoke is the harbinger of fire. // 12.19 //

---

[9] *Pra-vṛtti* is defined as "moving or rolling onwards, advance, progress, active life." So *pra-vṛtti* expresses the kind of doing which keeps the wheel of saṁsāra rolling - as opposed to *ni-vṛtti*, non-doing. See also SN12.22 and SN16.42.

[10] Notice that in this canto Nanda does NOT, as per EH Johnston's comment and David Kalupahana's subsequent aberrant assertions, express spiritual faith in the Buddha. If Nanda here expresses belief in anything, he expresses his joyful confidence that the Buddha's most excellent dharma can be effective in eradicating suffering.

[11] Verse 20, where the Buddha tells Nanda that he has 1. set foot on a true path, with 2. clarity of vision, provides support for translating *pratyavamarśa* both as 1. "gaining a foothold," and 2. "discernment/comprehension" - i.e. touching with the mind.

ciram unmārga-vihṛto lolair indriya-vājibhiḥ /
avatīrṇo 'si panthānaṁ diṣṭyā dṛṣṭyāvimūḍhayā // 12.20 //
Long carried off course by the restless horses of the senses, / You have now set foot on a path, with a clarity of vision that, happily, will not dim. // 12.20 //

adya te sa-phalaṁ janma lābho 'dya su-mahāṁs tava /
yasya kāma-rasa-jñasya naiṣkramyāyotsukaṁ manaḥ // 12.21 //
Today your birth bears fruit; your gain today is great; / For though you know the taste of love, your mind is yearning for indifference. // 12.21 //

loke 'sminn ālayārāme nivṛttau durlabhā ratiḥ /
vyathante hy apunar-bhāvāt prapātād iva bāliśāḥ // 12.22 //
In this world which likes what is close to home, a fondness for non-doing is rare; / For men shrink from the end of becoming like the puerile from the edge of a cliff. // 12.22 //

duḥkhaṁ na syāt sukhaṁ me syād iti prayatate janaḥ /
atyanta-duḥkhoparamaṁ sukhaṁ tac ca na budhyate // 12.23 //
People think 'there might be no suffering, just happiness for me!' And as they labour under this [illusion], / Any respite from incessant suffering they sense not as such, but as happiness. // 12.23 //

ari-bhūteṣv anityeṣu satataṁ duḥkha-hetuṣu /
kāmādiṣu jagat saktaṁ na vetti sukham avyayam // 12.24 //
Upon [whims] which are transient and akin to enemies, forever causing suffering, / Upon things like love, the world is fixed. It does not know the happiness that is immune to change. // 12.24 //

sarva-duḥkhāpahaṁ tat tu hasta-stham amṛtaṁ tava /
viṣaṁ pītvā yad agadaṁ samaye pātum icchasi // 12.25 //
But that deathless nectar which prevents all suffering you have in your hands: / It is an antidote which, having drunk poison, you are going in good time to drink. // 12.25 //

anarha-saṁsāra-bhayaṁ mānārhaṁ te cikīrṣitam /
rāgāgnis tādṛśo yasya dharmonmukha parāṅ-mukhaḥ // 12.26 //
In its fear of worthless wandering your intention is worthy of respect, / For a fire of passion such as yours, O you whose face is turned to dharma, is being turned around. // 12.26 //

rāgoddāmena manasā sarvathā duṣkarā dhṛtiḥ /
sa-doṣaṁ salilaṁ dṛṣṭvā pāntheneva pipāsunā // 12.27 //
With a mind unbridled by lust it is exceedingly difficult to be steadfast – / As when a thirsty traveler sees dirty water. // 12.27 //

īdṛśī nāma buddhis te niruddhā rajasābhavat /
rajasā caṇḍa-vātena vivasvata iva prabhā // 12.28 //
Obviously, the dust of passion was blocking the consciousness that is now awakening in you, / Like the dust of a sand-storm blocking the light of the sun. // 12.28 //

sā jighāṁsus tamo hārdaṁ yā saṁprati vijṛmbhate /
tamo naiśaṁ prabhā saurī vinirgīrṇeva meruṇā // 12.29 //
But now [consciousness] is blossoming forth, seeking to dispel darkness of the heart, / Like that sunlight spewed forth from mount Meru which dispels the darkness of night. // 12.29 //

yukta-rūpam idaṁ caiva śuddha-sattvasya cetasaḥ /
yat te syān naiṣṭhike sūkṣme śreyasi śraddadhānatā // 12.30 //
And this indeed befits a soul whose essence is simplicity: / That you should have confidence in a better way which is ultimate and subtle.[12] // 12.30 //

dharma-cchandam imaṁ tasmād vivardhayitum arhasi /
sarva-dharmā hi dharmajña niyamāc chanda-hetavaḥ // 12.31 //
This wish for dharma, therefore, you should nurture; / For all dharmas, O knower of dharma, invariably have wishing as their cause. // 12.31 //

satyāṁ gamana-buddhau hi gamanāya pravartate /
śayyā-buddhau ca śayanaṁ sthāna-buddhau tathā sthitiḥ // 12.32 //
As long as the intention of moving is there, one mobilizes for the act of moving; / And with the intention of staying at rest there is an act of staying at rest; with the intention of standing, likewise, there is standing up. // 12.32 //

antar-bhūmi-gataṁ hy ambhaḥ śraddadhāti naro yadā /
arthitve sati yatnena tadā khanati gām imām // 12.33 //
When a man has confidence that there is water under the ground / And has need of water, then, with an effort of will, here the earth he digs. // 12.33 //

nārthī yady agninā vā syāc chraddadhyāt taṁ na vāraṇau /
mathnīyān nāraṇiṁ kaś-cit tad-bhāve sati mathyate // 12.34 //
If a man had no need of fire, nor confidence that fire was in a firestick, / He would never twirl the stick. Those conditions being met, he does twirl the stick. // 12.34 //

sasyotpattiṁ yadi na vā śraddadhyāt kārṣakaḥ kṣitau /
arthī sasyena vā na syād bījāni na vaped bhuvi // 12.35 //
Without the confidence that corn will grow in the soil he tills, / Or without the need for corn, the farmer would not sow seeds in the earth. // 12.35 //

---

[12] Again, from the Buddha's standpoint, there is no affirmation here of faith in Buddha. There is affirmation of confidence in a better way, or belief in betterment. Why does the Buddha describe the better way as subtle (*sūkṣma*)? Because what is pure/simple (*śuddha*) happens naturally, in which case the source is to be returned to by the indirect means of willing it and allowing it, and not by a direct ascetic assault on the senses. (See also Introduction to Canto 13.)

ataś ca hasta ity uktā mayā śraddhā viśeṣataḥ /
yasmād gṛṇhāti sad-dharmaṁ dāyaṁ hasta ivākṣataḥ // 12.36 //
And so I call this confidence the Hand, because it is this confidence, above all, / That grasps true dharma, as a hand naturally takes a gift. // 12.36 //

prādhānyād indriyam iti sthiratvād balam ity ataḥ /
guṇa-dāridrya-śamanād dhanam ity abhivarṇitā // 12.37 //
From its primacy I describe it as Sensory Power;[13] from its constancy, as Strength; / And because it relieves poverty of virtue I describe it as Wealth. // 12.37 //

rakṣaṇārthena dharmasya tatheṣīk ety udāhṛtā /
loke 'smin durlabhatvāc ca ratnam ity abhibhāṣitā // 12.38 //
For its protection of dharma, I call it the Arrow, / And from the difficulty of finding it in this world I call it the Jewel. // 12.38 //

punaś ca bījam ity uktā nimittaṁ śreyaso yadā /
pāvanārthena pāpasya nadīty abhihitā punaḥ // 12.39 //
Again, I call it the Seed since it is the cause of betterment;[14] / And for its cleansing action, in the washing away of wrong, again, I call it the River. // 12.39 //

yasmād dharmasya cotpattau śraddhā kāraṇam uttamam /
mayoktā kāryatas tasmāt tatra tatra tathā tathā // 12.40 //
Since in the arising of dharma confidence is the primary cause, / Therefore I have named it after its effects in this case like this, in that case like that. // 12.40 //

śraddhāṅkuram imaṁ tasmāt saṁvardhayitum arhasi /
tad-vṛddhau vardhate dharmo mūla-vṛddhau yathā drumaḥ // 12.41 //
This shoot of confidence, therefore, you should nurture; / When it grows dharma grows, as a tree grows with the growth of its root. // 12.41 //

vyākulaṁ darśanaṁ yasya durbalo yasya niścayaḥ /
tasya pāriplavā śraddhā na hi kṛtyāya vartate // 12.42 //
When a person's seeing is disordered, when a person's sense of purpose is weak: / The confidence of that person is unsteady, for he is not veering in the direction of what remains to be done. // 12.42 //

---

[13] *Indriya* means power, force, the quality which belongs especially to the mighty Indra (see Introduction to Canto 13). EHJ translated *indriya* here as "the Faculty."

[14] *Nimittaṃ śreyasas.* Here *nimitta* evidently means "cause." (See discussion of *nimitta* from SN16.53.)

yāvat tattvaṁ na bhavati hi dṛṣṭaṁ śrutaṁ vā
tāvac chraddhā na bhavati bala-sthā sthirā vā /
dṛṣṭe tattve niyama-paribhūtendriyasya
śraddhā-vṛkṣo bhavati sa-phalaś cāśrayaś ca // 12.43 //

So long as reality is not seen and heard happening,[15] confidence does not become[16] strong or firm; / But when, through restraint, the power of the senses is subjugated[17] and reality is witnessed, the tree of confidence endures,[18] fruitful and dependable." // 12.43 //

saundaranande mahākāvye pratyavamarśo nāma dvādaśaḥ sargaḥ // 12 //
The 12th Canto in the epic poem Handsome Nanda, titled "Gaining a Foothold."

---

[15] *Bhavati is* third person singular of the verbal root √*bhū*. Here it is used in the sense of [reality] happens.
[16] *Bhavati,* in the sense of [the tree] becomes.
[17] *Paribhūta* is the past participle of *pari-√bhū,* to overpower.
[18] *Bhavati,* in the sense of arise, stay, remain, endure or thrive.

Canto 13: śīlendriya-jayaḥ
Defeating the Power of the Senses through Good Conduct

Introduction

Far from being seen as passive receptors, the senses were seen in ancient India as powerful forces. Thus the very word *indriya* means, as an adjective, "belonging to mighty Indra," and, as a noun, "power, force, the quality which belongs especially to the mighty Indra." Secondary definitions of *indriya* are "bodily power, power of the senses," and "faculty of sense, sense, organ of sense." Reflecting this conception, in ancient Indian asceticism the word *jitendriya*, "conqueror/subjugator of the senses," was used to mean the ascetic himself.

The title of the present canto can be read as expressing a subtly different conception, in which the power of the senses (*indriya*) continues to be regarded as a dangerous or hostile force to be conquered, but in which the means of conquest (*jaya*) is indirect, via habitual good conduct, or, cultivation of good habits (*śīla;* defined as such in verse 27).

As part of this metaphor of conquest, the Buddha introduces the subsidiary metaphor of wearing the armor of thinking (*smṛti-varma*) – the protective armor, that is, of preventive thinking, of thinking what one is doing, of thinking in activity.

atha saṁrādhito nandaḥ śraddhāṁ prati maharṣiṇā /
pariṣikto 'mṛteneva yuyuje parayā mudā // 13.1 //
And so, Nanda was affirmed by the great seer, in the matter of confidence; / He felt filled with the deepest joy, as if drenched in the deathless nectar. // 13.1 //

kṛtārtham iva taṁ mene saṁbuddhaḥ śraddhayā tayā /
mene prāptam iva śreyaḥ sa ca buddhena saṁskṛtaḥ // 13.2 //
To the Fully Awakened Buddha, by virtue of that confidence, he seemed already to be a success; / And to himself, having been initiated[1] by the Buddha, he felt as though he had arrived already on the better path. // 13.2 //

ślakṣṇena vacasā kāṁś-cit kāṁś-cit paruṣayā girā /
kāṁś-cid ābhyām upāyābhyāṁ sa vininye vināyakaḥ // 13.3 //
Some in soothing tones; some with tough talk, / Some by both these means, he the trainer trained. // 13.3 //

pāṁsubhyaḥ kāñcanaṁ jātaṁ viśuddhaṁ nirmalaṁ śuci /
sthitaṁ pāṁsuṣv api yathā pāṁsu-doṣair na lipyate // 13.4 //
Just as gold born from dirt is pure, spotless, gleaming, / And while lying in the dirt is not tarnished by the dirt's impurities, // 13.4 //

---

[1] *Saṁskṛta* (from *saṁ-s-√kṛ*; see also verses 13 and 29) lit. means "put together" or "well formed." "Initiated" and "made ready" are secondary meanings. For exploration of nirvāṇa as *asaṁskṛta,* unconditioned, unconfected, uncontrived, not fabricated, see MMK ch. 25.

padma-parṇaṁ yathā caiva jale jātaṁ jale sthitam /
upariṣṭād adhastād vā na jalenopalipyate // 13.5 //
And just as a lotus-leaf is born in water and remains in water, / But neither above nor below is sullied by the water, // 13.5 //

tadval loke munir jāto lokasyānugrahaṁ caran /
kṛtitvān nirmalatvāc ca loka-dharmair na lipyate // 13.6 //
So the Sage, born in the world, and acting for the benefit of the world, / Because of his state of action, and spotlessness, is not tainted by worldly things. // 13.6 //

śleṣaṁ tyāgaṁ priyaṁ rūkṣaṁ kathāṁ ca dhyānam eva ca /
mantu-kāle cikitsārthaṁ cakre nātmānuvṛttaye // 13.7 //
Joining with others and leaving them; love and toughness; and talking, as well as meditation itself: / He used these means during his instruction for the purpose of healing, not to make a following for himself. // 13.7 //

ataś ca saṁdadhe kāyaṁ mahākaruṇayā tayā /
mocayeyaṁ kathaṁ duḥkhāt sattvānīty anukampakaḥ // 13.8 //
Thus did the benevolent one, out of his great compassion, take on a form / By which he might release fellow living beings from suffering. // 13.8 //

atha saṁharṣaṇān nandaṁ viditvā bhājanī-kṛtam /
abravīd bruvatāṁ śreṣṭhaḥ krama-jñaḥ śreyasāṁ kramam // 13.9 //
Seeing, then, that by boosting Nanda he had made a receptacle, / The best of speakers, the knower of processes, spoke of better ways as a process: // 13.9 //

ataḥ prabhṛti bhūyas tvaṁ śraddhendriya-puraḥsaraḥ /
amṛtasyāptaye saumya vṛttaṁ rakṣitum arhasi // 13.10 //
"Starting afresh from here, my friend, with the power of confidence leading you forward, / In order to get to the nectar of deathlessness you should watch the manner of your action. // 13.10 //

prayogaḥ kāya-vacasoḥ śuddho bhavati te yathā /
uttāno vivṛto gupto 'navacchidras tathā kuru // 13.11 //
So that the use of body and voice happens simply[2] for you, / Make it expansive and open, and guarded, and free from flaws[3] – // 13.11 //

---

[2] *Śuddha* means pure, firstly in the sense of being cleansed, but also in the secondary sense of being simple, genuine, true... "Let the right thing do itself!"

[3] *Anavacchidra* means free from clefts or flaws, unbroken, uninterrupted, uninjured. As an adjective, *chidra* means containing holes, leaky; as a noun, *chidra* means hole, cleft, and hence defect, fault, weak point.

uttāno bhāva-karaṇād vivṛtaś cāpy agūhanāt /
gupto rakṣaṇa-tātparyād acchidraś cānavadyataḥ // 13.12 //
Expansive by happening as a means; open from not hiding; / Guarded because aimed at prevention; and flawless in the sense of beyond reproach. // 13.12 //

śarīra-vacasoḥ śuddhau saptāṅge cāpi karmaṇi /
ājīva-samudācāraṁ śaucāt saṁskartum arhasi // 13.13 //
With regard for purity of body and voice, and with regard also for the sevenfold [prohibition on bodily and vocal] conduct,[4] / You should work to perfect a proper way of making a living, on the grounds of integrity[5] - // 13.13 //

doṣāṇāṁ kuhanādīnāṁ pañcānām aniṣevaṇāt /
tyāgāc ca jyotiṣādīnāṁ caturṇāṁ vṛtti-ghātinām // 13.14 //
On the grounds of not indulging the five faults, beginning with hypocrisy; / On the grounds of fleeing the four predators of practice, such as astrology; // 13.14 //

prāṇi-dhānya-dhanādīnāṁ varjyānām apratigrahāt /
bhaikṣāṅgānāṁ nisṛṣṭānāṁ niyatānāṁ pratigrahāt // 13.15 //
On the grounds of not accepting things to be avoided, such as valuables linked to the needless killing of living creatures;[6] / On the grounds of accepting the established rules for begging, with their definite limits; // 13.15 //

parituṣṭaḥ śucir mañjuś caukṣayā jīva-saṁpadā /
kuryā duḥkha-pratīkāraṁ yāvad eva vimuktaye // 13.16 //
As a person who is contented, pristine, and pleasant, you can, through making a living cleanly and well, / Counteract suffering all the way to liberation. // 13.16 //

karmaṇo hi yathādṛṣṭāt kāya-vāk-prabhavād api /
ājīvaḥ pṛthag evokto duḥśodhatvād ayaṁ mayā // 13.17 //
Separately from overt action - indeed, from use of the body and the voice - / I have spoken of making a living because it is so hard to make a pure one:[7] - // 13.17 //

---

[4] Of the ten precepts alluded to in SN Canto 3, there seem to be seven that specifically prohibit wrong physical and vocal conduct, namely: not inflicting needless suffering on any living being, not stealing, not chasing married women; along with not lying, not gossiping, not hurting others with smooth speech, and not slandering others (see verses 3.30–33).

[5] "On the grounds of integrity" is *śaucāt*. *Śauca* is given in the dictionary as 1. cleanness, 2. purity of mind, integrity, honesty (especially in money matters). This verse alludes to the three elements of threefold habitual good conduct (*śīla*) within the noble eightfold path. Those three elements are using the voice well, using the body well, and earning a clean living (see SN16.31).

[6] EHJ's original text has *prāṇi-dhānya-dhanādīnāṃ* (living creatures, grain, money and so on), but EHJ noted that Gawronski's *prāṇi-ghāta-dhanādīnāṃ* may well be right. *Prāṇi-ghātin* means killing living beings, so that Gawronski's amendment could mean 'such things as money [procured from needless] killing of living beings' or 'goods [whose production has involved needless] killing of living beings' or 'valuables [whose acquisition has involved needless] killing of living beings.' It is difficult to see why grain would have been avoided.

[7] *Duḥśodhatvād* is lit. "from the difficulty of cleansing."

gṛha-sthena hi duḥśodhā dṛṣṭir vividha-dṛṣṭinā /
ājīvo bhikṣuṇā caiva pareṣv āyatta-vṛttinā // 13.18 //
For hard to be washed away is the view of a householder with his many and various concerns, / And also [hard to be kept pure] is the livelihood of a bhikkhu whose subsistence depends on others.[8] // 13.18 //

etāvac chīlam ity uktam ācāro 'yaṁ samāsataḥ /
asya nāśena naiva syāt pravrajyā na gṛhasthatā // 13.19 //
Such is termed "good behavior." In sum, it is conduct; / Without it there could truly be no going forth, nor state of being at home. // 13.19 //

tasmāc cāritra-sampanno brahmacaryam idaṁ cara /
aṇumātreṣv avadyeṣu bhaya-darśī dṛḍha-vrataḥ // 13.20 //
Steeped in good conduct, therefore, lead this life of devout abstinence, / And in what is even minutely blameworthy see danger, being firm in your purpose. // 13.20 //

śīlam āsthāya vartante sarvā hi śreyasi kriyāḥ /
sthānādyānīva kāryāṇi pratiṣṭhāya vasundharām // 13.21 //
For founded on integrity unfurl all actions on the better path, / Just as events[9] like standing unfold, when [a force] resists the earth. // 13.21 //

mokṣasyopaniṣat saumya vairāgyam iti gṛhyatām /
vairāgyasyāpi saṁvedaḥ saṁvido jñāna-darśanam // 13.22 //
Let it be grasped, my friend, that release is seated in dispassion, / Dispassion in witnessing, and witnessing in knowing and seeing. // 13.22 //

jñānasyopaniṣac caiva samādhir upadhāryatām /
samādher apy upaniṣat sukhaṁ śārīra-mānasam // 13.23 //
And let it be experienced, again, that the knowing is seated in practicing stillness / And that the seat of practicing stillness is a body-mind at ease. // 13.23 //

praśrabdhiḥ kāya-manasaḥ sukhasyopaniṣat parā /
praśrabdher apy upaniṣat prītir apy avagamyatām // 13.24 //
A confidence on which sits ease of the body-mind is of the highest order, / And the confidence is seated in enjoyment. Again, let this be realized in experience. // 13.24 //

---

[8] EHJ's original Sanskrit text has *pareṣṭāyatta*, as per the paper manuscript. In the notes to his translation, however, EHJ refers to the *Abhidharma-kośa* (Abhidharma Treasury) of Aśvaghoṣa's 9th-generation descendant Vasubandhu (21st Zen patriarch in India), which quotes this verse and shows the correct reading to be *pareṣv āyatta-vṛttinā.*

[9] *Kārya* lit. means "[something] to be done." Ironically, however, the description seems to be of an act of standing which is not done, but which is allowed to do itself.

tathā prīter upaniṣat prāmodyaṁ paramaṁ matam /
prāmodyasyāpy ahṛllekhaḥ kukṛteṣv akṛteṣu vā // 13.25 //
The enjoyment is seated in a great happiness which, similarly, is understood to be of the highest order; / And the happiness is seated in a freedom from furrowing the heart over things done badly or not done. // 13.25 //

avilekhasya manasaḥ śīlaṁ tūpaniṣac chuci /
ataḥ śīlaṁ nayaty agryam iti śīlaṁ viśodhaya // 13.26 //
But the freedom of the mind from remorse is seated in pristine practice of integrity. / Therefore, [realising] that good habits come first, purify the practice of good habits. // 13.26 //

śīlanāc chīlam ity uktaṁ śīlanaṁ sevanād api /
sevanaṁ tan-nideśāc ca nideśaś ca tad-āśrayāt // 13.27 //
Habitual good conduct is so called because it comes out of repeated practice;10 repeated practice comes out of devotion to training; / Devotion to training comes out of direction in it; and direction comes out of submitting to that direction. // 13.27 //

śīlaṁ hi śaraṇaṁ saumya kāntāra iva daiśikaḥ /
mitraṁ bandhuś ca rakṣā ca dhanaṁ ca balam eva ca // 13.28 //
For good habits, my friend, are the refuge: they are like a guide in the wilderness, / They are friend, kinsman, and protector; they are wealth, and strength. // 13.28 //

yataḥ śīlam ataḥ saumya śīlaṁ saṁskartum arhasi /
etat sthānam athānyeṣu mokṣārambheṣu yoginām // 13.29 //
Since good habits are such, my friend, you should work to perfect good habits. / Among those who practice, moreover, this is the stance taken in different endeavors whose aim is freedom.[11] // 13.29 //

tataḥ smṛtim adhiṣṭhāya capalāni svabhāvataḥ /
indriyāṇīndriyārthebhyo nivārayitum arhasi // 13.30 //
On this basis, standing grounded in thinking in activity, you should naturally[12] hold back the impetuous senses from the objects of those senses. // 13.30 //

---

[10] "Repeated practice" is *śīlana*; "the discipline of integrity" is *śīla*. So *śīla,* if we call it habitual good conduct, is so called because it comes from *śīlana,* repeated practice.

[11] *Yoginām* here seems to indicate not only those who practice yoga as directed by the Buddha, for example in Canto 16 (see e.g. use of the word *yoga* in SN16.33, 16.52, 16.92), but also yogins devoted to other ways of practice whose aim is freedom. The universal principle in the background, recognized by mechanical engineers as well as by yoga adepts, might be the interdependence of freedom and restraint. The use of *yoginām* in the plural in this verse mirrors the use of *śreyasāṃ* in the plural in verse 9. The point might be that there is more than one way to liberate oneself from the slavery of habit - the way of a Thai bhikkhu, the way of a Tibetan bodhisattva, the way of a Zen practitioner devoted to just sitting, the way of a martial artist, the way of a runner or a skier or a swimmer, the way of a student of FM Alexander, or of J. Krishnamurti, or of G. I. Gurdjieff - but every way is a process, in which the universal truth holds that there is no freedom without restraint.

bhetavyaṁ na tathā śatror nāgner nāher na cāśaneḥ /
indriyebhyo yathā svebhyas tair ajasraṁ hi hanyate // 13.31 //
There is less to fear from an enemy or from fire, or from a snake, or from lightning, / Than there is from one's own senses; for through them one is forever being smitten. // 13.31 //

dviṣadbhiḥ śatrubhiḥ kaś-cit kadā-cit pīḍyate na vā /
indriyair bādhyate sarvaḥ sarvatra ca sadaiva ca // 13.32 //
Some people some of the time are beleaguered by hateful enemies – or else they are not. / Besieged through the senses are all people everywhere, all of the time. // 13.31 //

na ca prayāti narakaṁ śatru-prabhṛtibhir hataḥ /
kṛṣyate tatra nighnas tu capalair indriyair hataḥ // 13.33 //
Nor does one go to hell when smitten by the likes of an enemy; / But meekly is one pulled there when smitten through the impetuous senses. // 13.33 //

hanyamānasya tair duḥkhaṁ hārdaṁ bhavati vā na vā /
indriyair bādhyamānasya hārdaṁ śārīram eva ca // 13.34 //
The pain of being smitten by those others may occur in the heart – or else it may not. / The pain of being oppressed through one's senses is a matter of the heart and indeed of the body. // 13.34 //

saṁkalpa-viṣa-digdhā hi pañcendriya-mayāḥ śarāḥ /
cintā-puṅkhā rati-phalā viṣayākāśa-gocarāḥ // 13.35 //
For smeared with the poison of conceptions,[13] are those arrows, produced from five senses, / Whose tails are anxiety, whose tips are thrills, and whose range is the vast vacuity of objects. // 13.35 //

manuṣya-hariṇān ghnanti kāma-vyādheritā hṛdi /
vihanyante yadi na te tataḥ patanti taiḥ kṣatāḥ // 13.36 //
Fired off by Desire, the hunter, they strike human fawns in the heart; / Unless they are warded away, men wounded by them duly fall. // 13.36 //

niyamājira-saṁsthena dhairya-kārmuka-dhāriṇā /
nipatanto nivāryās te mahatā smṛti-varmaṇā // 13.37 //
Standing firm in the arena of restraint, and bearing the bow of resolve, / The mighty man, as they rain down, must fend them away, wearing the armor of thinking in activity. // 13.37 //

---

[12] *Svabhāvataḥ* could be adjectival, describing the senses as naturally impetuous. In maybe a deeper reading, *svabhāvataḥ* can also be adverbial, describing taming of the senses as effected naturally or spontaneously – not by doing but by letting happen.

[13] The meanings of *saṁkalpa* include conception or idea or notion, but also willpower (see SN12.5) or definite intention, and (as defined in SED) "an idea or expectation of any advantage." EHJ here translated *saṃkalpa-viṣa* as "the poison of fancies;" and LC as "the poison of fanciful notions."

indriyāṇām upaśamād arīṇāṁ nigrahād iva /
sukhaṁ svapiti vāste vā yatra tatra gatoddhavaḥ // 13.38 //
From ebbing of the power of the senses, as if from subjugation of enemies, / One sleeps or sits at ease, in joyful recreation, wherever one may be. // 13.38 //

teṣāṁ hi satataṁ loke viṣayān abhikāṅkṣatām /
saṁvin naivāsti kārpaṇyāc chunām āśāvatām iva // 13.39 //
For in the constant hankering of those senses after objects in the world, / There occurs out of that ignominy no more consciousness than there is in the hoping of hounds. // 13.39 //

viṣayair indriya-grāmo na tṛptim adhigacchati /
ajasraṁ pūryamāṇo 'pi samudraḥ salilair iva // 13.40 //
A cluster of sense organs is no more sated by objects, / Than is the ocean, even when constantly filled, by water. // 13.40 //

avaśyaṁ gocare sve sve vartitavyam ihendriyaiḥ /
nimittaṁ tatra na grāhyam anuvyañjanam eva ca // 13.41 //
It is necessarily through the senses, each in its own sphere, that one must function in this world. / But not to be seized upon in that realm is an objectified target[14] or any secondary sexual sign:[15] // 13.41 //

ālokya cakṣuṣā rūpaṁ dhātu-mātre vyavasthitaḥ /
strī veti puruṣo veti na kalpayitum arhasi // 13.42 //
On seeing a form with your eye [you] are contained in the sum of the elements: / The conception that 'it is a woman' or 'it is a man' you should not frame.[16] // 13.42 //

---

[14] *Nimittam* in the context the Buddha is about to explain means "a woman" or "a man" made into a target. EHJ translates *nimittam* here as "general characteristic;" and LC as "major attribute." Aśvaghoṣa seems to have in mind the kind of objectification we witnessed in the striver's tirade against women, but again he refrains from using the term *prapañca.* Is it fair to say that Aśvaghoṣa leaned more towards the indirect, inductive method, whereas Nāgāruna's teaching tended to rely more on deductive reasoning?

[15] *Anu-vyañjanam* is given in SED as a word used in Buddhist literature to mean "secondary mark or token." Meanings of *vyañjanam* include "mark of sex or gender (as the beard, breasts et cetera)," and the prefix *anu-* means following from, or secondary. In this verse, the use of *anu-vyañjanam,* in combination with *nimittam,* sheds some light on a somewhat technical meaning of *nimittam.* No such Buddhist technical meaning is given in SED, which defines *nimitta* more broadly as 1. mark, target, 2. sign, omen, 3. cause, motive, reason. The Pali-English Dictionary, being more closely based on the Pali canon, defines *nimitta* as 1. a sign or omen, 2. outward appearance, mark, characteristic, attribute, 3. mark, aim, 4. sexual organ, and 5. ground, reason. Specifically with reference to the practice of meditation, the Pali-English Dictionary adds (as part of sense 2) the technical sense of "a mental reflex [i.e. reflection] or image" and cites *nimittan gaṇhāti,* "to make something the object of a thought, to catch up a theme for reflection." Cf Canto 16 from verse 53 where *nimitta* has been understood to mean not an object of meditation but an aspect of practice that is inherent in practice when we let it happen.

[16] *Kalpayitum* (the causative infinitive from the root √*kḷp*) means to frame, form, invent, compose (as a poem et cetera), and hence to imagine.

sacet strī-puruṣa-grāhaḥ kva-cid vidyeta kaś-cana /
śubhataḥ keśa-dantādīn nānuprasthātum arhasi // 13.43 //
If a notion of woman or man does intrude at any time in relation to anyone, / Upon hair, teeth, and the rest, for their beauty, you should not dwell. // 13.43 //

nāpaneyaṁ tataḥ kiṁ-cit prakṣepyaṁ nāpi kiṁcana /
draṣṭavyaṁ bhūtato bhūtaṁ yādṛśaṁ ca yathā ca yat // 13.44 //
Nothing, then, is to be taken away and nothing is to be added: / What is happening – whatever and however it is – is to be seen as happening. // 13.44 //

evaṁ te paśyatas tattvaṁ śaśvad indriya-gocare /
bhaviṣyati pada-sthānaṁ nābhidhyā-daurmanasyayoḥ // 13.45 //
In your seeing truly, like this, always in the territory of the senses, / There will be no foothold for longing and dejection. // 13.45 //

abhidhyā priya-rūpeṇa hanti kāmātmakaṁ jagat /
arir mitra-mukheneva priya-vāk-kaluṣāśayaḥ // 13.46 //
Longing, using cherished forms, smites the sensual masses: / A foe who has a friendly face, she's[17] fair of speech and foul of heart. // 13.46 //

daurmanasyābhidhānas tu pratigho viṣayāśritaḥ /
mohād yenānuvṛttena paratreha ca hanyate // 13.47 //
Conversely, what is called dejectedness is, in connection with an object, a contrary reaction[18] / By going along with which, in one's ignorance, one is smitten hereafter, and smitten here and now. // 13.47 //

anurodha-virodhābhyāṁ śitoṣṇābhyām ivārditaḥ /
śarma nāpnoti na śreyaś calendriyam ato jagat // 13.48 //
When, by getting and not getting his way, [a man] is pained as if by cold or heat, / He finds no refuge; nor arrives on a better path: hence the unsteady sense-power of the masses. // 13.48 //

nendriyaṁ viṣaye tāvat pravṛttam api sajjate /
yāvan na manasas tatra parikalpaḥ pravartate // 13.49 //
And yet the power of the senses, though operative, need not become glued to an object, / So long as in the mind, with regard to that object, illusion is not operating.[19] // 13.49 //

---

[17] *Abhidhyā*, desire or longing, is a feminine noun.

[18] *Pratigha* (from *prati-√han*, to strike back) means 1. resistance, opposition; 2. anger, wrath, enmity, resentment. In the Rāhula Sutta (MN62; see Appendix), the Pali equivalent *paṭigha* is one of six afflictive emotions specifically discussed; its antidote is *uppekhā* (Sanskrit: *upekṣā*), which means looking on with indifference, showing equanimity or forbearance – in short, not minding.

[19] *Parikalpa* is given in SED as a word used in Buddhist literature to mean "illusion." At the same time in non-Buddhist writing, *parikalpa* = *parikalpana*: fixing, contriving, making, inventing. The primary meaning of the verb *pari-√kḷp* is to fix. "Fixing" does not seem to fit in this part as a translation of *parikalpa*. EHJ translated "imaginations," but this perhaps leans too far to the psychological. What

indhane sati vāyau ca yathā jvalati pāvakaḥ /
viṣayāt parikalpāc ca kleśāgnir jāyate tathā // 13.50 //
Just as a fire burns only where fuel and air co-exist, / So a fire of affliction arises, from an object and from illusion. // 13.50 //

abhūta-parikalpena viṣayasya hi badhyate /
tam eva viṣayaṁ paśyan bhūtataḥ parimucyate // 13.51 //
For by an illusion about what never was, one is bound to an object; / Seeing that very same object as happening, one is set free.// 13.51 //

dṛṣṭvaikaṁ rūpam anyo hi rajyate 'nyaḥ praduṣyati /
kaś-cid bhavati madhya-sthas tatraivānyo ghṛṇāyate // 13.52 //
On seeing one and the same form this man is enamored, that man is disgusted; / Somebody else remains in the middle; while yet another feels thereto a human warmth. // 13.52 //

ato na viṣayo hetur bandhāya na vimuktaye /
parikalpa-viśeṣeṇa saṁgo bhavati vā na vā // 13.53 //
Thus, an object is not the cause of bondage or of liberation; / It is due to particular illusions that attachment happens or does not happen.[20] // 13.53 //

kāryaḥ parama-yatnena tasmād indriya-saṁvaraḥ /
indriyāṇi hy agutpāni duḥkhāya ca bhavāya ca // 13.54 //
Through effort of the highest order, therefore, contain the power of the senses; / For unguarded senses make for suffering and for becoming.// 13.54 //

kāmabhoga-bhogavadbhir ātma-dṛṣṭi-dṛṣṭibhiḥ pramāda-naika-mūrdhabhiḥ praharṣa-lola-jihvaiḥ /
indriyoragair mano-bila-śrayaiḥ spṛhā-viṣaiḥ śamāgadād ṛte na daṣṭam asti yac cikitset // 13.55 //
The senses are like serpents coiled in sensual enjoyment with eyes of selfish views, their many heads are heedlessness and their flickering tongues are excitement: / The snaky senses lurk in mind-pits, their venom eager desire; and when they bite there is no cure, save the antidote of cessation.[21] //13.55 //

---

kind of *parikalpa* goes on in the brain and mind of an autistic child who cannot cope with certain auditory stimuli?

[20] Here, then, is the Buddha's explicit falsification of the striver's argument that women are to blame for the reaction to women of men who objectify and blame women.

[21] This verse was omitted by both EHJ and LC from their respective translations. The verse's meter – which EHJ had not traced elsewhere – convinced EHJ that it was an interpolation.

tasmād eṣām akuśala-karāṇām arīṇāṁ cakṣur-ghrāṇa-śravaṇa-rasana-sparśanānām / sarvāvasthāsu bhava niyamād apramatto māsminn arthe kṣaṇam api kṛthās tvaṁ pramādam // 13.56 //
Therefore, towards those mischief-making foes, seeing, smelling, hearing, tasting, and feeling, / Show in every situation a vigilance born of restraint. In this matter you are not for an instant to be heedless. // 13.56 //

saundaranande mahākāvye śīlendriya-jayo nāma trayodaśaḥ sargaḥ // 13 //
The 13th Canto in the epic poem Handsome Nanda,
titled "Defeating the Power of the Senses through Good Conduct."

Canto 14: ādi-prasthānaḥ
Stepping Into Action

Introduction

Ādi means start or beginning. *Prasthāna* is an *-na* neuter action noun from the verb *pra-√sthā*, which means to stand up or set out or march forth. So *ādi-prasthāna* suggests stepping forth in earnest on the noble path that leads in the direction of the cessation of suffering. It is in the context of such directed effort that the Buddha again praises the preventive effort of *smṛti*, thinking what we are doing, as a defense against the faults which threaten our integrity in the everyday round – when we are taking food, and when we are going to sleep; when we are standing and walking and lying down; and even, ultimately, when we are sitting in seclusion.

atha smṛti-kavāṭena pidhāyendriya-saṁvaram /
bhojane bhava mātrā-jño dhyānāyānāmayāya ca // 14.1 //
And so using the floodgate of thinking[1] to close a dam on the power of the senses, / Know the measure, in eating food, that conduces to meditation and to health. // 14.1 //

prāṇāpānau nigṛṇhāti glāni-nidre prayacchati /
kṛto hy atyartham āhāro vihanti ca parākramam // 14.2 //
For it depresses in-breath and out-breath, and brings tiredness and sleepiness, / When food is taken in excess; it also destroys enterprise.[2] // 14.2 //

yathā cātyartham āhāraḥ kṛto 'narthāya kalpate /
upayuktas tathātyalpo na sāmarthyāya kalpate // 14.3 //
And just as eating too much conduces to a dearth of value, / So eating too little makes for a lack of efficacy. // 14.3 //

ācayaṁ dyutim utsāhaṁ prayogaṁ balam eva ca /
bhojanaṁ kṛtam atyalpaṁ śarīrasyāpakarṣati // 14.4 //
Of its substance, luster, and stamina; of its usefulness and its very strength, / A meagre diet deprives the body. // 14.4 //

yathā bhāreṇa namate laghunonnamate tulā /
samā tiṣṭhati yuktena bhojyeneyaṁ tathā tanuḥ // 14.5 //
Just as a weighing scale bends down with a heavy weight, bends upwards with a light one, / And stays in balance with the right one, so does this body according to intake of food. //14.5 //

---

[1] *Smṛti* is a verbal noun most literally translated by an -ing word. Hence remembering, recollecting or thinking is more literal than awareness, mindfulness, vigilance, et cetera. In SN9.33 *smṛti* was translated as memory.

[2] *Parākrama*, enterprise or initiative, is one of the elements of the noble eightfold path – sometimes included under the heading of *prajñā*, and sometimes under *samādhi*. See SN16.32.

tasmād abhyavahartavyaṁ sva-śaktim anupaśyatā /
nātimātraṁ na cātyalpaṁ meyaṁ māna-vaśād api // 14.6 //
Therefore food is to be eaten, each reflecting on his own energy, / And none apportioning himself too much or too little under the influence of pride. // 14.6 //

atyākrānto hi kāyāgnir guruṇānnena śāmyati /
avacchanna ivālpo 'gniḥ sahasā mahatendhasā // 14.7 //
For the fire of the body is damped down when it is burdened by a heavy load of food, / Like a small blaze suddenly covered with a big heap of firewood. // 14.7 //

atyantam api saṁhāro nāhārasya praśasyate /
anāhāro hi nirvāti nirindhana ivānalaḥ // 14.8 //
Excessive fasting, also, is not recommended; / For one who does not eat is extinguished like a fire without fuel. // 14.8 //

yasmān nāsti vināhārāt sarva-prāṇabhṛtāṁ sthitiḥ /
tasmād duṣyati nāhāro vikalpo 'tra tu vāryate // 14.9 //
Since without food there is none that survives among those that bear breath, / Therefore eating food is not a sin; but being choosy, in this area, is prohibited. // 14.9 //

na hy eka-viṣaye 'nyatra sajyante prāṇinas tathā /
avijñāte yathāhāre boddhavyaṁ tatra kāraṇam // 14.10 //
For on no other single object are sentient beings so stuck / As on the heedless eating of food. To the reason for this one must be awake. // 14.10 //

cikitsārthaṁ yathā dhatte vraṇasyālepanaṁ vraṇī /
kṣud-vighātārtham āhāras tadvat sevyo mumukṣuṇā // 14.11 //
Just as one who is wounded, for the purpose of healing, puts ointment on a wound, / So does one who wills freedom, for the purpose of staving off hunger, eat food. // 14.11 //

bhārasyodvahanārthaṁ ca rathākṣo 'bhyajyate yathā /
bhojanaṁ prāṇa-yātrārthaṁ tadvad vidvān niṣevate // 14.12 //
Just as, in order to ready it for bearing a burden, one greases a wagon's axle, / So, in order to journey through life, does the wise man utilize food. // 14.12 //

samatikramaṇārthaṁ ca kāntārasya yathādhvagau /
putra-māṁsāni khādetāṁ dampatī bhṛśa-duḥkhitau // 14.13 //
And just as two travelers in order to cross a wasteland / Might feed upon the flesh of a child, though grievously pained to do so, as its mother and father, // 14.13 //

evam abhyavahartavyaṁ bhojanaṁ pratisaṁkhyayā /
na bhūṣārthaṁ na vapuṣe na madāya na dṛptaye // 14.14 //
So food should be eaten, consciously, / Neither for display, nor for appearance; neither to excite hilarity, nor to feed extravagance. // 14.14 //

dhāraṇārthaṁ śarīrasya bhojanaṁ hi vidhīyate /
upastambhaḥ pipatiṣor durbalasyeva veśmanaḥ // 14.15 //
Food is provided for the upkeep of the body / As if to prop, before it falls, a dilapidated house. // 14.15 //

plavaṁ yatnād yathā kaś-cid badhnīyād dhārayed api /
na tat-snehena yāvat tu mahaughasyottitīrṣayā // 14.16 //
Just as somebody might take pains to build and then carry a raft, / Not because he is so fond of it but because he means to cross a great flood, // 14.16 //

tathopakaraṇaiḥ kāyaṁ dhārayanti parīkṣakāḥ /
na tat-snehena yāvat tu duḥkhaughasya titīrṣayā // 14.17 //
So too, by various means, do explorers sustain the body, / Not because they are so fond of it but because they mean to cross a flood of suffering. // 14.17 //

śocatā pīḍyamānena dīyate śatrave yathā /
na bhaktyā nāpi tarṣeṇa kevalaṁ prāṇa-guptaye // 14.18 //
Just as [a king] under siege yields, in sorrow, to a rival king, / Not out of devotion, nor through thirsting, but solely to safeguard life, // 14.18 //

yogācāras tathāhāraṁ śarīrāya prayacchati /
kevalaṁ kṣud-vighātārthaṁ na rāgeṇa na bhaktaye // 14.19 //
So the devotee of practice tenders food to his body / Solely to stave off hunger, neither with passion nor as devotion. // 14.19 //

mano-dhāraṇayā caiva pariṇāmyātmavān ahaḥ /
vidhūya nidrāṁ yogena niśām apy atināmayeḥ // 14.20 //
Having passed the day self-possessed, through maintenance of the mind, / You may be able, shaking off sleep, to spend the night-time too in a state of practice. // 14.20 //

hṛdi yat saṁjñinaś caiva nidrā prādur bhavet tava /
guṇavat saṁjñitāṁ saṁjñāṁ tadā manasi mā kṛthāḥ // 14.21 //
Since even when you are conscious sleep might be holding out in your heart, / Consciousness properly revealing itself is nothing to be sure about. // 14.21 //

dhātur ārambha-dhṛtyoś ca sthāma-vikramayor api /
nityaṁ manasi kāryas te bādhyamānena nidrayā // 14.22 //
Initiative, constancy, inner strength and courage are the elements / Always to bear in mind while you are being oppressed by sleep. // 14.22 //

āmnātavyāś ca viśadaṁ te dharmā ye pariśrutāḥ /
parebhyaś copadeṣṭavyāḥ saṁcintyāḥ svayam eva ca // 14.23 //
Recite clearly those dharma-teachings that you have learnt; / Point others in their direction, and think them out for yourself. // 14.23 //

prakledyam adbhir vadanaṁ vilokyāḥ sarvato diśaḥ /
cāryā dṛṣṭiś ca tārāsu jijāgariṣuṇā sadā // 14.24 //
Wet the face with water, look around in all directions, / And glance at the stars, wanting always to be awake. // 14.24 //

antargatair acapalair vaśa-sthāyibhir indriyaiḥ /
avikṣiptena manasā caṁkramyasvāsva vā niśi // 14.25 //
By the means of inner senses[3] that are not impetuous but in a state of subjection, / By the means of a mind that is not scattered, walk up and down at night or else sit. // 14.25 //

bhaye prītau ca śoke ca nidrayā nābhibhūyate /
tasmān nidrābhiyogeṣu sevitavyam idaṁ trayam // 14.26 //
In fear, in joy and in grief, one does not succumb to sleep; / Therefore against the onslaughts of sleep resort to these three: // 14.26 //

bhayam āgamanān mṛtyoḥ prītiṁ dharma-parigrahāt /
janma-duḥkhād aparyantāc chokam āgantum arhasi // 14.27 //
Feel fear from death's approach, joy from grasping a teaching of dharma, / And from the boundless suffering inherent in a birth, feel the grief. // 14.27 //

evam-ādiḥ kramaḥ saumya kāryo jāgaraṇaṁ prati /
vandhyaṁ hi śayanād āyuḥ kaḥ prājñaḥ kartum arhati // 14.28 //
Such a step may need to be taken, my friend, in the direction of being awake; / For what wise man, out of sleep, makes a wasted life? // 14.28 //

doṣa-vyālān atikramya vyālān gṛha-gatān iva /
kṣamaṁ prājñasya na svaptuṁ nistitīrṣor mahad bhayam // 14.29 //
To neglect the reptilian faults, as if stepping over snakes in the house, / And thus to slumber on, does not befit a man of wisdom who wishes to overcome the great terror. // 14.29 //

pradīpte jīvaloke hi mṛtyu-vyādhi-jarāgnibhiḥ /
kaḥ śayīta nirudvegaḥ pradīpta iva veśmani // 14.30 //
For while the world of the living burns with the fires of death, disease and aging, / Who could lie down insensibly, any more than in a burning house? // 14.30 //

tasmāt tama iti jñātvā nidrāṁ nāveṣṭum arhasi /
apraśānteṣu doṣeṣu sa-śastreṣv iva śatruṣu // 14.31 //
Therefore, knowing it to be darkness, you should not let sleep enshroud you / While the faults remain unquieted, like sword-wielding enemies. // 14.31 //

---

[3] *Antargatair... indriyaiḥ*, "by means of internal senses," would seem to refer primarily to the vestibular and proprioceptive senses.

pūrvaṁ yāmaṁ tri-yāmāyāḥ prayogeṇātināmya tu /
sevyā śayyā śarīrasya viśrāmārthaṁ sva-tantriṇā // 14.32 //
But having spent the first of the three night-watches actively engaged in practice, / You should, as one who is pulling his own strings,[4] go to bed to rest the body. // 14.32 //

dakṣiṇena tu pārśvena sthitayāloka-saṁjñayā /
prabodhaṁ hṛdaye kṛtvā śayīthāḥ śānta-mānasaḥ // 14.33 //
On your right side, then, remaining conscious of light, / Thinking in your heart of wakefulness, you might with peace of mind fall asleep. // 14.33 //

yāme tṛtīye cotthāya carann āsīna eva vā /
bhūyo yogaṁ manaḥ-śuddhau kurvīthā niyatendriyaḥ // 14.34 //
Again, by getting up in the third watch and going into movement, or indeed just sitting, / You might renew your practice, with mind refreshed, and power of the senses curbed. // 14.34 //

athāsana-gata-sthāna-prekṣita-vyāhṛtādiṣu /
saṁprajānan kriyāḥ sarvāḥ smṛtim ādhātum arhasi // 14.35 //
And so, upon acts like sitting, moving, standing, looking, and speaking – / Distinguishing every act – you should bring thinking to bear. // 14.35 //

dvārādhyakṣa iva dvāri yasya praṇihitā smṛtiḥ /
dharṣayanti na taṁ doṣāḥ puraṁ guptam ivārayaḥ // 14.36 //
One like a gatekeeper at a gateway, whose thinking is directed,[5] / The faults do not venture to attack, any more than enemies would attack a guarded city. // 14.36 //

na tasyotpadyate kleśo yasya kāya-gatā smṛtiḥ /
cittaṁ sarvāsv avasthāsu bālaṁ dhātrīva rakṣati // 14.37 //
No affliction arises in one whose thinking pervades the body – / Guarding the mind in all situations, as a nurse protects a child. // 14.37 //

śaravyaḥ sa tu doṣāṇāṁ yo hīnaḥ smṛti-varmaṇā /
raṇa-sthaḥ pratiśatrūṇāṁ vihīna iva varmaṇā // 14.38 //
But one is a target for the faults who lacks the armor of thinking: / As for enemies is one who delights, without armor, in battle.[6] // 14.38 //

---

[4] *Sva-tantrin*, "being in possession of one's own threads," means not being amenable to manipulation by somebody else – hence (notwithstanding the truth of dependent arising) free, independent.

[5] *Praṇihitā* is past participle of *pra-ṇi-√dhā*, which means to place in front, to cause to precede.

[6] *Raṇa-sthaḥ* ostensibly means engaged/standing (*stha*) in battle (*raṇa*). The first meaning of *raṇa*, however, is delight, and thence by extension battle as an object of delight. So *raṇa-sthaḥ* in its hidden meaning could be an ironic description of naked enjoyment of, for example, just sitting, without any idea of being mindful.

anāthaṁ tan-mano jñeyaṁ yat smṛtir nābhirakṣati /
nirṇetā dṛṣṭi-rahito viṣayeṣu carann iva // 14.39 //
Know to be helpless the mind that thinking does not guard – / Like a blind man without a guide roaming among objects.[7] // 14.39 //

anartheṣu prasaktāś ca svārthebhyaś ca parāṅmukhā /
yad bhaye sati nodvignāḥ smṛti-nāśo 'tra kāraṇam // 14.40 //
When [men] attach to meaningless aims and turn away from their proper aims,[8] / Failing to shudder at the danger, thoughtlessness is the cause. // 14.40 //

sva-bhūmiṣu guṇāḥ sarve ye ca śīlādayaḥ sthitāḥ /
vikīrṇā iva gā gopaḥ smṛtis tān anugacchati // 14.41 //
Again, when each virtue, beginning with integrity, is standing on its own patch, / Thinking goes after those virtues like a herdsman rounding up his scattered cows. // 14.41 //

pranaṣṭam amṛtaṁ tasya yasya viprasṛtā smṛtiḥ /
hasta-stham amṛtaṁ tasya yasya kāya-gatā smṛtiḥ // 14.42 //
The deathless nectar is lost to him whose thinking dissipates; / The nectar exists in the hands of him for whom thinking pervades the body. // 14.42 //

āryo nyāyaḥ kutas tasya smṛtir yasya na vidyate /
yasyāryo nāsti ca nyāyaḥ pranaṣṭas tasya sat-pathaḥ // 14.43 //
Where is the noble principle of him in whom thinking is not witnessed? / And for whom no noble principle exists, to him a true path has been lost.[9] // 14.43 //

pranaṣṭo yasya sanmārgo naṣṭaṁ tasyāmṛtaṁ padam /
pranaṣṭam amṛtaṁ yasya sa duḥkhān na vimucyate // 14.44 //
He who has lost the right track has lost the deathless step. / Having lost that nectar of deathlessness, he is not exempt from suffering. // 14.44 //

tasmāc caran caro 'smīti sthito 'smīti ca dhiṣṭhitaḥ /
evam-ādiṣu kāleṣu smṛtim ādhātum arhasi // 14.45 //
Therefore walking with the awareness that "I am walking" and standing with the awareness that "I am standing" – / At times[10] such as these, you should bring thinking to bear. // 14.45 //

---

[7] Both palm-leaf and paper manuscripts have *viṣayeṣu carann,* which means "moving himself in the direction of sense objects," or "living in the realm of sensual enjoyments." Based on Gawronki's conjecture, EHJ amended to *viṣameṣu carann* (going over uneven ground).

[8] Thus, thinking in activity as the Buddha taught it is associated with directed effort.

[9] Again, (notwithstanding possible ironic hidden meaning) the Buddha is taking pains to connect his teaching of thinking in activity with directed effort on the noble eightfold path. The point is underlined in SN16.33.

[10] EHJ queried reading *kāryeṣu* for *kāleṣu.* That would give "Upon such actions as these, you should bring mindfulness to bear." Either way, this verse seems to echo the *saṁprajānan kriyāḥ sarvāḥ* of verse 35 – the point being that we should know what we are doing when we are doing it, and think what we are doing.

yogānulomaṁ vijanaṁ viśabdaṁ śayyāsanaṁ saumya tathā bhajasva /
kāyasya kṛtvā hi vivekam ādau sukho 'dhigantuṁ manaso vivekaḥ // 14.46 //
In this manner, my friend, repair to a place suited for practice, free of people and free of noise, a place for lying down and sitting; / For by first achieving seclusion of the body it is easy to obtain seclusion of the mind. // 14.46 //

alabdha-cetaḥ-praśamaḥ sa-rāgo yo na pracāraṁ bhajate viviktam /
sa kṣaṇyate hy apratilabdha-mārgaś carann ivorvyāṁ bahu-kaṇṭakāyām // 14.47 //
The man of redness, the tranquility of his mind unrealized, who does not take to a playground of solitude, / Is injured as though, unable to regain a track, he is walking on very thorny ground. // 14.47 //

adṛṣṭa-tattvena parīkṣakeṇa sthitena citre viṣaya-pracāre /
cittaṁ niṣeddhuṁ na sukhena śakyaṁ kṛṣṭādako gaur iva sasya-madhyāt // 14.48 //
For a seeker who fails to see reality but stands in the tawdry playground of objects, / It is no easier to rein in the mind than to drive a foraging bull away from corn. // 14.48 //

anīryamāṇas tu yathānilena praśāntim āgacchati citra-bhānuḥ /
alpena yatnena tathā vivikteṣv aghaṭṭitaṁ śāntim upaiti cetaḥ // 14.49 //
But just as a bright fire dies down when not fanned by the wind, / So too, in secluded places, does an unstirred mind easily come to quiet. // 14.49 //

kva-cid bhuktvā yat-tad vasanam api yat-tat parihito
vasann ātmārāmaḥ kva-cana vijane yo 'bhiramate /
kṛtārthaḥ sa jñeyaḥ śama-sukha-rasa-jñaḥ kṛta-matiḥ
pareṣāṁ saṁsargaṁ pariharati yaḥ kaṇṭakam iva // 14.50 //
One who eats anything at any place, and wears any clothes, / Who dwells in enjoyment of his own being and loves to be anywhere without people: / He is to be known as a success, a knower of the taste of peace and ease, whose mind is made up – / He avoids involvement with others like a thorn. // 14.50 //

yadi dvandvārāme jagati viṣaya-vyagra-hṛdaye
vivikte nirdvando viharati kṛtī śānta-hṛdayaḥ /
tataḥ pītvā prajñā-rasam amṛtavat tṛpta-hṛdayo
viviktaḥ saṁsaktaṁ viṣaya-kṛpaṇaṁ śocati jagat // 14.51 //
If, in a world that delights in duality and is at heart distracted by objects, / He roves in solitude, free of duality, a man of action, his heart at peace, / Then he drinks the essence of wisdom as if it were the deathless nectar and his heart is filled. / Separately he sorrows for the clinging, object-needy world. // 14.51 //

vasañ śūnyāgāre yadi satatam eko 'bhiramate
yadi kleśotpādaiḥ saha na ramate śatrubhir iva /
carann ātmārāmo yadi ca pibati prīti-salilaṁ
tato bhuṅkte śreṣṭhaṁ tridaśa-pati-rājyād api sukham // 14.52 //
If he constantly abides as a unity, in an empty abode, / If he is no fonder of arisings of affliction than he is of enemies, / And if, going rejoicing in the self, he drinks the water of joy, / Then greater than dominion over thirty gods[11] is the happiness he enjoys.// 14.52 //

saundara-nanda mahākāvya ādi-prasthāno nāma caturdaśaḥ sargaḥ// 14 //
The 14th canto of the epic poem Handsome Nanda, titled "Stepping Into Action."

[11] *Tridaśa-pati-rājya*, "the realm of the lord of the 3 x 10," means heaven, i.e. the kingdom of Indra, ruler of the 33 gods (10 being approximately equal to 11). The 33 gods are the 12 *ādityas* ("sons of the Eternal and Infinite Expanse [= the Goddess Aditi]"), 8 *vasus* ("good or bright ones"), 11 *rudras* ("howlers"; storm-gods), and the 2 *aśvins* ("charioteers").

Canto 15: vitarka-prahāṇaḥ
Abandoning Ideas

Introduction

Vitarka means thought or idea, and *prahāṇa* is an *-na* neuter action noun from *pra-√hā*, to abandon or give up. So *vitarka-prahāṇaḥ* means giving up thoughts or abandoning ideas. And the fundamental means of giving up troublesome ideas, the Buddha teaches Nanda in the present canto, is, again, *smṛti*, thinking in activity.

The gist, then, is to give up one kind of thinking by means of another kind of thinking – as if driving out a wedge that has got stuck in a log, by using another wedge.

In the preceding two cantos the Buddha has described how the armor of preventive thinking protects *śīla*, good conduct. In the present canto the Buddha's extolling of thinking in activity relates more to *samādhi* and *prajñā*, practising balance and understanding.

This practice is to be undertaken, the Buddha advises in verse 1, as he does so often in the Pali Suttas, with the legs crossed in the traditional way and the body directed up – with thinking stationed to the fore.

In this context in verse 5 the Buddha speaks for the first time in Saundarananda of using *bhāvanā*, the practice of letting happen, to extinguish what lies behind desires, like using water to put out a fire.

Again, where negative thoughts are associated with specific negative emotions like ill-will and cruelty, the Buddha in verses 12-17 advises coming back to their opposite aspects, in the friendly and kind practice of *bhāvanā*.

But the bulk of the canto is devoted to steering Nanda away from the kinds of unhelpful idea that the Buddha describes in detail through to verse 63. For the abandoning of all these unhelpful ideas, the Buddha tells Nanda in verse 64, he should master – as *bhāvanā*, as a letting happen – thinking in the activity of breathing in and out.

In the closing verses of the canto these various efforts to cleanse the mind by means of *bhāvanā*, eliminating faults in the order of their grossness, are compared to the efforts of the dirt-washing miner who causes all impurities, down to the finest particles of dirt, to come out in the wash, so that a goldsmith, in due course, may be able to do his job of producing products of pure gold.

yatra tatra vivikte tu baddhvā paryaṅkam uttamam /
ṛjuṁ kāyaṁ samādhāya smṛtyābhimukhayānvitaḥ // 15.1 //
In whatever place of solitude you are, cross the legs in the supreme manner / Align the body so that it tends straight upward,[1] and, attended by thinking turned towards... // 15.1 //

nāsāgre vā lalāṭe vā bhruvor antara eva vā /
kurvīthāś capalaṁ cittam ālambana-parāyaṇam // 15.2 //
The tip of the nose or the forehead, or the space between the eyebrows, / Let an inconstant mind be fully engaged with objective support.[2] // 15.2 //

sacet kāma-vitarkas tvāṁ dharṣayen mānaso jvaraḥ /
kṣeptavyo nādhivāsyaḥ sa vastre reṇur ivāgataḥ // 15.3 //
If some desirous idea, a fever of the mind, should venture to offend you, / Entertain no scent of it but shake it off as if pollen had landed on your robe. // 15.3 //

yady api pratisaṁkhyānāt kāmān utsṛṣṭavān asi /
tamāṁsīva prakāśena pratipakṣeṇa tāñ jahi // 15.4 //
Even if, as a result of calm consideration, you have let go of desires, / You must, as if shining light into darkness,[3] abolish them by means of opposition.[4] // 15.4 //

tiṣṭhaty anuśayas teṣāṁ channo 'gnir iva bhasmanā /
sa te bhāvanayā saumya praśāmyo 'gnir ivāmbunā // 15.5 //
Underlying those desires a tendency[5] persists, like a fire covered over with ashes; / You are to extinguish it, my friend, by the practice of letting happen,[6] as if quenching a fire with water. // 15.5 //

---

[1] *Ṛjum* is (according to SED) lit. "tending in a straight direction." See also SN17.4.

[2] *Ālambana-parāyaṇam. Ālambana* means 1. depending or resting on, and hence 2. foundation, base (but see also MMK ch. 1, where *ālambanam,* "objective support," is the second of four causes in an opponent's fourfold scheme of causality). As the second half of a compound, *parāyaṇa* means making anything one's chief object, being wholly devoted to or engaged in. EHJ took *parāyaṇam* to mean "wholly intent." Thus: "*You should make your wandering mind wholly intent on an object such as the tip of your nose or your forehead or the space between the brows.*"
With *ālambanam* translated "objective support," the verse brings to mind *parānugrāhakaṁ,* "favouring the other," in MMK17.1. Equally, the verse brings to mind the Buddha's metaphor for *samādhi*, in the Eight Truths of a Great Person, where the Buddha speaks of still water being contained by what is not water.

[3] *Tamas* (here used in the plural, *tamaṁsi*) means 1. darkness, and by extension 2. ignorance.

[4] *Pratipakṣeṇa* means "by means of [their] opposite" or "by means of opposition." The opposite of desirous ideas, or desires as thoughts – as the Buddha teaches in verses 64 and 65 – might be thinking in activity itself.

[5] Sanskrit *anuśaya* (from *anu-√śī*, to sleep with) means a dormant or underlying tendency. Seven such tendencies are listed in Pali in DN33: *kāma-rāga* (craving love), *paṭigha* (resentment), *diṭṭhi* (view), *vicikicchā* (doubt), *māna* (conceit), *bhava-rāga* (craving becoming), and *avijjā* (ignorance/unwittingness) – though as a tendency that actively persists, like fire, might *avijjā* better be translated as denial? Whether it is *avijjā* or *kāma-rāga*, the tendency the Buddha has in mind seems, in context, to be bound up with a romantic idea (*vitarka*) rooted in self-existence, upon which cold water is to be poured by thinking in activity as a letting happen.

[6] *Bhāvanā*, as causative of the verbal root *√bhū*, is usually understood to mean "bringing [something]

te hi tasmāt pravartante bhūyo bījād ivāṅkurāḥ /
tasya nāśena te na syur bīja-nāśād ivāṅkurāḥ // 15.6 //
For from that source they re-emerge, like shoots from a seed. / In its absence they would be no more – like shoots in the absence of a seed. // 15.6 //

arjanādīni kāmebhyo dṛṣṭvā duḥkhāni kāminām /
tasmāt tān mūlataś chindhi mitra-saṁjñān arīn iva // 15.7 //
See how acquisition and other troubles stem from the desires of men of desire, / And on that basis cut off at their root those troubles, which are akin to enemies calling themselves friends. // 15.7 //

anityā moṣa-dharmāṇo riktā vyasana-hetavaḥ /
bahu-sādhāraṇāḥ kāmā barhyā hy āśī-viṣā iva // 15.8 //
Fleeting desires; desires which bring privation; flighty[7] desires, which are the causes of wagging to and fro;[8] / And common desires, are to be dealt with[9] like poisonous snakes – // 15.8 //

ye mṛgyamāṇā duḥkhāya rakṣyamāṇā na śāntaye /
bhraṣṭāḥ śokāya mahate prāptāś ca na vitṛptaye // 15.9 //
The chasing of which leads to trouble, the keeping of which does not conduce to peace, / And the losing of which makes for great anguish. Securing them does not bring contentment. // 15.9 //

---

into being," and hence developing [the mind] or cultivating [wisdom] or else cultivating a specific antidote to a specific polluting influence. When it does not have an object, *bhāvanā* is sometimes translated simply as "meditation" or "practice." The causative in Sanskrit is sufficiently broad, however, that "letting be" is also a literal translation of *bhāvanā*. Not only that: the meaning of the verbal root √*bhū* is sufficiently broad that "letting happen" is also a literal translation of *bhāvanā*. "Letting be" or "letting happen" are good descriptions of the essence – just sitting – of the practice known in China and Japan as 坐禅. So it seems likely that 坐禅 – "sitting-dhyāna," "sitting-Zen," or "sitting-meditation" – is the name that ancient Chinese practitioners gave to the practice that had been called in India, in Pali and Sanskrit, *bhāvana* or (as here, in the feminine) *bhāvanā*.

[7] *Rikta* means empty, void, hollow, worthless. At the same time, in augury *rikta* is the name of one of the four wagtails which serve for omens.

[8] *Vyasana* means the wagging of a tail, or moving to and fro, and hence what does not go smoothly, a calamity or disaster.

[9] The meaning of *barhyāḥ* here is uncertain, except that the word is a gerundive, meaning "to be -ed." On a superficial reading, the suggestion is that pesky desires should simply be got rid of. Hence EHJ translated "*the passions should be killed like poisonous snakes.*" EHJ noted: "neither *barhyā* nor *varhyā* is satisfactory in d and on the strength of *Abhidharma-kośa*, IV, p. 10... I would read *vadhyā* [to be killed, destroyed]." For √*barh*, the dictionary gives various meanings including to speak, to hurt, to cover, and (possibly significant in light of verse 4) to shine. Perhaps the suggestion below the surface is that a good strategy in dealing with poisonous snakes, before rushing in to try and kill them, is to shine a light on them to see where they are hiding, and to keep a careful eye on them.

tṛptiṁ vitta-prakarṣeṇa svargāvāptyā kṛtārthatām /
kāmebhyaś ca sukhotpattiṁ yaḥ paśyati sa naśyati // 15.10 //
Satisfaction through extra-ordinary wealth; success through the gaining of paradise, / And happiness born from desires: he who sees these things comes to nothing.[10] // 15.10 //

calān apariniṣpannān asārān anavasthitān /
parikalpa-sukhān kāmān na tān smartum ihārhasi // 15.11 //
Pay no heed to the changeable, unformed, insubstantial and ungrounded desires, / Which are presumed to bring happiness; you should not, here and now, think about those desires.[11] // 15.11 //

vyāpādo vā vihiṁsā vā kṣobhayed yadi te manaḥ /
prasādyaṁ tad-vipakṣeṇa maṇinevākulaṁ jalam // 15.12 //
If hatred or cruelty should stir up your mind, / Let it be charmed by their opposite, as turbid water is by a jewel. // 15.12 //

pratipakṣas tayor jñeyo maitrī kāruṇyam eva ca /
virodho hi tayor nityaṁ prakāśa-tamasor iva // 15.13 //
Know the opposite of those two to be friendliness and compassion; / For this opposition is forever like brightness and darkness.[12] // 15.13 //

nivṛttaṁ yasya dauḥśīlyaṁ vyāpādaś ca pravartate /
hanti pāṁsubhir ātmānaṁ su-snāta iva vāraṇaḥ // 15.14 //
He in whom wrongdoing has been given up and yet hatred carries on, / Hits himself with dust like an elephant after a good bath.[13] // 15.14 //

---

[10] *Kāma*, desire, is a broad concept. In the plural, its meanings include "objects of desire" (see SN9.47; 11.37). At the same time, in the singular and in the sense of subjective volition, it may mean the same as *chanda* ("wishing") as in *dharma-cchandam*, "the wish for dharma" (SN12.31). So is the real intention of this series of verses about desires necessarily what it seems to be on the surface? For example, isn't the gift of confidence the imparting of a kind of wealth? Was not Nanda's trip to Indra's paradise instrumental in his ultimate success? And in realizing that success, did Nanda become something? Or is it truer to say that he came to nothing?

[11] The ostensible meaning is as per EHJ: "Take heed (*arhasi*) not to fix your attention (*na smartum*) in this world (*iha*) on the passions (*kāmān... tān*)." The deeper hidden teaching might be "Being here and now (*iha*), you need not (*na arhasi*) even think about (*smartum*) those desires (*kāmān... tān*)." In the hidden meaning, in other words, the Buddha might be encouraging Nanda not to worry too much about desires per se - because per se, in light of emptiness, there isn't anything to worry about.

[12] I.e. goodwill rules out ill will in the way that brightness instantly rules out darkness - brightness and darkness, symbols of wisdom and ignorance, cannot exist simultaneously.

[13] Insofar as *vyāpāda* means (as per SED) "evil intent" or "malice," this verse is probably best taken at face value. But if hidden meaning is sought here, one thinks of a metaphorical elephant like Zen Master Dōgen who in Shōbōgenzō chap. 73 expressed intense hatred towards the attitude of so-called monks in China who were mainly interested in garnering their own fame and profit.

duḥkhitebhyo hi martyebhyo vyādhi-mṛtyu-jarādibhiḥ /
āryaḥ ko duḥkham aparaṁ sa-ghṛṇo dhātum arhati // 15.15 //
Upon mortal beings who are pained by sickness, dying, aging, and the rest, / What noble person with human warmth would lay the utmost pain?[14] // 15.15 //

duṣṭena ceha manasā bādhyate vā paro na vā /
sadyas tu dahyate tāvat svaṁ mano duṣṭa-cetasaḥ // 15.16 //
Again, a tainted mind here and now may or may not trouble the other; / But instantly burned up right now is the mind of the man of tainted consciousness himself.[15] // 15.16 //

tasmāt sarveṣu bhūteṣu maitrīṁ kāruṇyameva ca /
na vyāpādaṁ vihiṁsāṁ vā vikalpayitum arhasi // 15.17 //
On this basis, towards all beings, it is friendliness and compassion, / Not hatred or cruelty, that you should opt for. // 15.17 //

yad-yad eva prasaktaṁ hi vitarkayati mānavaḥ /
abhyāsāt tena-tenāsya natir bhavati cetasaḥ // 15.18 //
For whatever a human being continually thinks, / In that direction, through habit, the mind of this person veers. // 15.18 //

tasmād akuśalaṁ tyaktvā kuśalaṁ dhyātum arhasi /
yat te syād iha cārthāya paramārthasya cāptaye // 15.19 //
Therefore disregarding what is not helpful focus on what is helpful, / Which might be valuable for you here and now and might be for the reaching of ultimate value. // 15.19 //

saṁvardhante hy akuśalā vitarkāḥ saṁbhṛtā hṛdi /
anartha-janakās tulyam ātmanaś ca parasya ca // 15.20 //
For unhelpful thoughts carried in the heart densely grow, / Producing in equal measure nothing of value for the self and for the other. // 15.20 //

śreyaso vighna-karaṇād bhavanty ātma-vipattaye /
pātrībhāvopaghātāt tu para-bhakti-vipattaye // 15.21 //
Because they make obstacles on the better path, they lead to the falling apart of the self; / And because they undermine the worthy condition, they lead to the falling apart of the other's trust. // 15.21 //

---

[14] *Duḥkham aparam* can be read (as per EHJ) as "further suffering," in which case *aparam* means "further." But *aparam* can also mean "having nothing beyond" or "having no superior" – i.e. being of the highest order, being supremely valuable. So, again, if hidden meaning is sought here, one could question whether the Buddha, for example, with utmost human warmth, laid the utmost pain on Nanda and Sundarī.

[15] Ostensibly the point is that anger, for example, is primarily damaging to the health of the angry person. The deeper meaning may be related with Nāgārjuna's teaching that saṁsāra and nirvāṇa are the same event taking place, either conditioned or not conditioned by clinging. Hence: *"Whatever is going on, due to clinging or due to conditioning, that, without the clinging and conditioning, is taught as nirvāṇa."* (MMK25.9). *"Whatever is the upper edge of nirvāṇa, is the upper edge of saṁsāra. Between the two, not the slightest gap is to be found."* (MMK25.20).

manaḥ-karmasv avikṣepam api cābhyastum arhasi /
na tv evākuśalaṁ saumya vitarkayitum arhasi // 15.22 //
Concentration during activities of the mind, you should certainly practise too. / But above all, my friend, nothing unhelpful should you think. // 15.22 //

yā tri-kāmopabhogāya cintā manasi vartate /
na ca taṁ guṇam āpnoti bandhanāya ca kalpate // 15.23 //
That anxious thought of enjoying the three desires[16] which churns in the mind / Does not meet with merit, but produces bondage. // 15.23 //

sattvānām upaghātāya parikleśāya cātmanaḥ /
mohaṁ vrajati kāluṣyaṁ narakāya ca vartate // 15.24 //
Tending to cause offence to living beings and torment for oneself, / Turbidity[17] becomes delusion and leads to hell. // 15.24 //

tad vitarkair akuśalair nātmānaṁ hantum arhasi /
suśastraṁ ratna-vikṛtaṁ mṛdd-hato gāṁ khanann iva // 15.25 //
With unhelpful thoughts, therefore, you should not mar your self / – Which is a good sword and bejeweled – as if you were digging the earth and getting spattered with mud. // 15.25 //

an-abhijño yathā jātyaṁ dahed aguru kāṣṭhavat /
a-nyāyena manuṣyatvam upahanyād idaṁ tathā // 15.26 //
Just as an ignoramus might burn as firewood the best aloes, / So, wrong-headedly, would one waste this state of being human. // 15.26 //

tyaktvā ratnaṁ yathā loṣṭaṁ ratna-dvīpāc ca saṁharet /
tyaktvā naiḥśreyasaṁ dharmaṁ cintayed aśubhaṁ tathā // 15.27 //
Again, just as he might leave the jewel and carry away from the jewel-island a clod, / So would one leave dharma that leads to happiness and think evil. // 15.27 //

himavantaṁ yathā gatvā viṣaṁ bhuñjīta nauṣadham /
manuṣyatvaṁ tathā prāpya pāpaṁ seveta no śubham // 15.28 //
Just as he might go to the Himālayas and eat not herbs but poison, / So would one arrive at being a human being and do not good but harm. // 15.28 //

tad buddhvā pratipakṣeṇa vitarkaṁ kṣeptum arhasi /
sūkṣmeṇa pratikīlena kīlaṁ dārv-antarād iva // 15.29 //
Being awake to it, you must see off an idea by means of opposition,[18] / As if using a narrow counter-wedge to drive a wedge from inside a log. // 15.29 //

---

[16] The three desires can be understood as the desire to get something, the desire to become something, and the desire to be rid of something.

[17] *Kāluṣya* (from *kaluṣa*, turbid) means 1. foulness, dirtiness, turbidness, opacity; 2. disturbance or interruption of harmony.

[18] *Pratipakṣeṇa*, as in verse 4, means "by antagonistic means" or "by means of opposition." The

vṛddhy-avṛddhyor atha bhavec cintā jñāti-janaṁ prati /
svabhāvo jīva-lokasya parīkṣyas tan-nivṛttaye // 15.30 //
And so, should there be anxiety about whether or not your family is prospering, / Investigate the nature of the world of the living[19] in order to put a stop to it. // 15.30 //

saṁsāre kṛṣyamāṇānāṁ sattvānāṁ svena karmaṇā /
ko janaḥ sva-janaḥ ko vā mohāt sakto jane janaḥ // 15.31 //
Among beings dragged by our own doing through the cycle of saṁsāra / Who are our own people, and who are other people? It is through ignorance that people attach to people. // 15.31 //

atīte 'dhvani saṁvṛttaḥ sva-jano hi janas tava /
aprāpte cādhvani janaḥ sva-janas te bhaviṣyati // 15.32 //
For one who turned on a bygone road into a relative, is a stranger to you;[20] / And a stranger, on a road to come, will become your relative. // 15.32 //

vihagānāṁ yathā sāyaṁ tatra tatra samāgamaḥ /
jātau jātau tathāśleṣo janasya sva-janasya ca // 15.33 //
Just as birds in the evening flock together at separate locations, / So is the mingling over many generations of one's own and other people. // 15.33 //

pratiśrayaṁ bahu-vidhaṁ saṁśrayanti yathādhvagāḥ /
pratiyānti punas tyaktvā tadvaj jñāti-samāgamaḥ // 15.34 //
Just as, under any old roof, travelers shelter together / And then go again their separate ways, so are relatives joined. // 15.34 //

loke prakṛti-bhinne 'smin na kaś-cit kasya-cit priyaḥ /
kārya-kāraṇa-sambaddhaṁ bālukā-muṣṭivaj jagat // 15.35 //
In this originally shattered world nobody is the beloved of anybody. / Held together by cause and effect, humankind is like sand in a clenched fist. // 15.35 //

---

opposition the Buddha seems to have in mind in the following long section is the challenging of unconscious assumptions in the first instance through conscious investigation and understanding, but in the end through thinking in the activity of breathing in and out (see verse 64, and Pali Suttas such as MN62). Hence the opposition may be understood as between two different kinds of thinking – namely, thought in the sense of the ideation (*vitarka*) that must be abandoned, and thinking in the sense of remembering (*smṛti*) what must happen.

[19] *Svabhāvo jīva-lokasya parīkṣyas* very much brings to mind MMK, each chapter of which is an investigation or exploration of some aspect of self-existence (*svabhāva*) to be explored or to be investigated (*parīkṣya*). In light of MMK, therefore, a deeper translation might be: "Investigate inherent nature [as thought to exist] in the world of the living" or "Explore the self-existence that belongs to the world of the living..."

[20] *Janas tava,* lit. "a person to you," means in other words (contrasted with *sva-jana*), just another person, a stranger.

bibharti hi sutaṁ mātā dhārayiṣyati mām iti /
mātaraṁ bhajate putro garbheṇādhatta mām iti // 15.36 //
For mother cherishes son thinking "He will keep me," / And son honours mother thinking "She bore me in her womb." // 15.36 //

anukūlaṁ pravartante jñātiṣu jñātayo yadā /
tadā snehaṁ prakurvanti riputvaṁ tu viparyayāt // 15.37 //
As long as relatives act agreeably towards each other, / They engender affection; but otherwise it is enmity. // 15.37 //

ahito dṛśyate jñātir ajñātir dṛśyate hitaḥ /
snehaṁ kāryāntarāl lokaś chinatti ca karoti ca // 15.38 //
A close relation is demonstrably unfriendly; a stranger proves to be a friend. / By the different things they do, folk break and make affection. // 15.38 //

svayam eva yathālikhya rajyec citra-karaḥ striyam /
tathā kṛtvā svayaṁ snehaṁ saṁgam eti jane janaḥ // 15.39 //
Just as an artist, all by himself, might fall in love with a woman he painted, / So, each generating attachment by himself, do people become attached to one another. // 15.39 //

yo 'bhavad bāndhava-janaḥ para-loke priyas tava /
sa te kam arthaṁ kurute tvaṁ vā tasmai karoṣi kam // 15.40 //
That relation who, in another life, was so dear to you: /
What use to you is he? What use to him are you? // 15.40 //

tasmāj jñāti-vitarkeṇa mano nāveṣṭum arhasi /
vyavasthā nāsti saṁsāre sva-janasya janasya ca // 15.41 //
With thoughts about close relatives, therefore, you should not enshroud the mind. / There is no abiding difference, in the flux of saṁsāra, between one's own people and people in general. // 15.41 //

asau kṣemo janapadaḥ subhikṣo 'sāv asau śivaḥ /
ity evam atha jāyeta vitarkas tava kaś-cana // 15.42 //
"That country is an easy place to live; that one is well-provisioned; that one is happy." / If there should arise any such idea in you, // 15.42 //

praheyaḥ sa tvayā saumya nādhivāsyaḥ kathaṁ-cana /
viditvā sarvam ādīptaṁ tais-tair doṣāgnibhir jagat // 15.43 //
You are to give it up, my friend, and not entertain it in any way, / Knowing the whole world to be ablaze with the manifold fires of the faults. // 15.43 //

ṛtu-cakra-nivartāc ca kṣut-pipāsā-klamād api /
sarvatra niyataṁ duḥkhaṁ na kva-cid vidyate śivam // 15.44 //
Again, from the turning of the circle of the seasons, and from hunger, thirst and fatigue, / Everywhere suffering is the rule. Not somewhere is happiness found. // 15.44 //

kva-cic chītaṁ kva-cid gharmaḥ kva-cid rogo bhayaṁ kva-cit /
bādhate 'bhyadhikaṁ lokaṁ tasmād aśaraṇaṁ jagat // 15.45 //
Here cold, there heat; here disease, there danger / Oppress humanity in the extreme. The world, therefore, has no place of refuge. // 15.45 //

jarā vyādhiś ca mṛtyuś ca lokasyāsya mahad bhayam /
nāsti deśaḥ sa yatrāsya tad bhayaṁ nopapadyate // 15.46 //
Aging, sickness and death are the great terror of this world. / There is no place where that terror does not arise. // 15.46 //

yatra gacchati kāyo 'yaṁ duḥkhaṁ tatrānugacchati /
nāsti kā-cid gatir loke gato yatra na bādhyate // 15.47 //
Where this body goes there suffering follows. / There is no way in the world going on which one is not afflicted. // 15.47 //

ramaṇīyo 'pi deśaḥ san su-bhikṣaḥ kṣema eva ca /
ku-deśa iti vijñeyo yatra kleśair vidahyate // 15.48 //
Even an area that is pleasant, abundant in provisions, and safe, / Should be regarded as a deprived area where burns the fire of afflictions.[21] // 15.48 //

lokasyābhyāhatasyāsya duḥkhaiḥ śārīra-mānasaiḥ /
kṣemaḥ kaś-cin na deśo 'sti svastho yatra gato bhavet // 15.49 //
In this world beset by hardships physical and mental, / There is no cozy place to which one might go and be at ease. // 15.49 //

duḥkhaṁ sarvatra sarvasya vartate sarvadā yadā /
chanda-rāgam ataḥ saumya loka-citreṣu mā kṛthāḥ // 15.50 //
While suffering, everywhere and for everyone, continues at every moment, / You are not to enthuse, my friend, over the world's shimmering images. // 15.50 //

yadā tasmān nivṛttas te chanda-rāgo bhaviṣyati /
jīva-lokaṁ tadā sarvam ādīptam iva maṁsyate // 15.51 //
When your enthusiasm is turned back from all that, / The whole living world you will deem to be, as it were, on fire. // 15.51 //

---

[21] Afflictions here can be understood as ignorance, thirsting and clinging – links no. 1, 8 and 9 in the 12-fold dependent arising of suffering. See BC Canto 14.

atha kaś-cid vitarkas te bhaved amaraṇāśrayaḥ /
yatnena sa vihantavyo vyādhir ātmagato yathā // 15.52 //
Any idea you might have, then, that has to do with not dying, / Is, with an effort of will, to be obliterated as a disorder of your whole being. // 15.52 //

muhūrtam api viśrambhaḥ kāryo na khalu jīvite /
nilīna iva hi vyāghraḥ kālo viśvasta-ghātakaḥ // 15.53 //
Not a moment of trust is to be placed in life, / For, like a tiger lying in wait, Time[22] slays the unsuspecting. // 15.53 //

balastho 'haṁ yuvā veti na te bhavitum arhati /
mṛtyuḥ sarvāsv avasthāsu hanti nāvekṣate vayaḥ // 15.54 //
That "I am young," or "I am strong," should not occur to you: / Death kills in all situations without regard for sprightliness. // 15.54 //

kṣetra-bhūtam anarthānāṁ śarīraṁ parikarṣataḥ /
svāsthy-āśā jīvitāśā vā na dṛṣṭārthasya jāyate // 15.55 //
As he drags about that field of misfortunes which is a body, / Expectations of well-being or of continuing life do not arise in one who is observant. // 15.55 //

nirvṛtaḥ ko bhavet kāyaṁ mahā-bhūtāśrayaṁ vahan /
paraspara-viruddhānām ahīnām iva bhājanam // 15.56 //
Who could be complacent carrying around a body, a receptacle for the elements, / Which is like a basket full of snakes each opposed to another? // 15.56 //

praśvasity ayam anvakṣaṁ yad ucchvasiti mānavaḥ /
avagaccha tad-āścaryam aviśvāsyaṁ hi jīvitam // 15.57 //
That this man draws breath and next time around breathes in again, / Know to be a wonder; for staying alive is nothing to breathe easy about. // 15.57 //

idam āścaryam aparaṁ yat suptaḥ pratibudhyate /
svapity utthāya vā bhūyo bahv-amitrā hi dehinaḥ // 15.58 //
Here is another wonder: that one who was asleep wakes up / Or, having been up, goes back to sleep; for many enemies has the owner of a body. // 15.58 //

garbhāt prabhṛti yo lokaṁ jighāṁsur anugacchati /
kas tasmin viśvasen mṛtyāv udyatāsāv arāv iva // 15.59 //
He who stalks humankind, from the womb onwards, with murderous intent: / Who can breathe easy about him? Death, poised like an enemy with sword upraised. // 15.59 //

---

[22] *Kāla* means Time and equally, since time is the destroyer of all things, Death.

prasūtaḥ puruṣo loke śrutavān balavān api /
na jayaty antakaṁ kaś-cin nājayan nāpi jeṣyati // 15.60 //
No man born into the world, however endowed with learning and power, / Ever defeats Death, maker of ends, nor has ever defeated him, nor ever will defeat him. // 15.60 //

sāmnā dānena bhedena daṇḍena niyamena vā /
prāpto hi rabhaso mṛtyuḥ pratihantuṁ na śakyate // 15.61 //
For cajoling, bribing, dividing, or the use of force or restraint, / When impetuous Death has arrived, are powerless to beat him back. // 15.61 //

tasmān nāyuṣi viśvāsaṁ cañcale kartum arhasi /
nityaṁ harati kālo hi sthāviryaṁ na pratīkṣate // 15.62 //
So place no trust in teetering life, / For Time is always carrying it off and does not wait for old age. // 15.62 //

niḥsāraṁ paśyato lokaṁ toya-budbuda-durbalam /
kasyāmara-vitarko hi syād anunmatta-cetasaḥ // 15.63 //
Seeing the world to be without substance, as fragile as a water-bubble, / What man of sound mind could harbour the notion of not dying? // 15.63 //

tasmād eṣāṁ vitarkāṇāṁ prahāṇārthaṁ samāsataḥ /
ānāpāna-smṛtiṁ saumya viṣayī-kartum arhasi // 15.64 //
So for the giving up, in short, of all these ideas, / Thinking in the activity of breathing in and out,[23] my friend, you should make into your own possession. // 15.64 //

ity anena prayogeṇa kāle sevitum arhasi /
pratipakṣān vitarkāṇāṁ gadānām agadān iva // 15.65 //
Using this device you should take in good time / Counter-measures against ideas, like cures for illnesses. // 15.65 //

suvarṇa-hetor api pāṁsu-dhāvako vihāya pāṁsūn bṛhato yathāditaḥ /
jahāti sūkṣmān api tad-viśuddhaye viśodhya hemāvayavān niyacchati // 15.66 //
A dirt-washer in pursuit of gold washes away first the coarse grains of dirt, / Then the finer granules, so that the [material] is cleansed; and by the cleansing he retains the rudiments of gold. // 15.66 //

---

[23] *Ānāpāna-smṛtiṃ*. *Ānāpāna* = *āna* (breathing in, from √*an*, to breath) + *apāna* (breathing out, from *apa-*√*an*). The thinking involved might be what in Chinese Zen was called 非思量, "non-thinking" – that is, thinking as a letting happen. See the conclusion of the Rāhula Sutta (MN62, Appendix) for a detailed treatment of (in Pali) *ānāpāna-satiṁ bhāvanaṁ*, "thinking in the activity of breathing in and out as a letting happen."

vimokṣa-hetor api yukta-mānaso vihāya doṣān bṛhatas tathāditaḥ /
jahāti sūkṣmān api tad-viśuddhaye viśodhya dharmāvayavān niyacchati // 15.67 //
In the same way, a man whose mind is poised, in pursuit of liberation, lets go first of the gross faults, / Then of the subtler ones, so that his [mind] is cleansed, and by the cleansing he retains the rudiments of dharma. // 15.67 //

krameṇādbhiḥ śuddhaṁ kanakam iha pāṁsu-vyavahitaṁ
yathāgnau karmāraḥ pacati bhṛśam āvartayati ca /
tathā yogācāro nipuṇam iha doṣa-vyavahitaṁ
viśodhya kleśebhyaḥ śamayati manaḥ saṁkṣipati ca // 15.68 //
Just as gold, washed with water, is separated from dirt in this world, methodically, / And just as the smith heats the gold in the fire and repeatedly turns it over, / Just so is the practitioner's mind, with delicacy and accuracy, separated from faults in this world, / And just so, after cleansing it from afflictions, does the practitioner temper the mind and collect it. // 15.68 //

yathā ca sva-cchandād upanayati karmāśraya-sukhaṁ
suvarṇaṁ karmāro bahu-vidham alaṁkāra-vidhiṣu /
manaḥ-śuddho bhikṣur vaśagatam abhijñāsv api tathā
yathecchaṁ yatrecchaṁ śamayati manaḥ prerayati ca // 15.69 //
Again, just as the smith brings gold to a state where he can work it easily / In as many ways as he likes into all kinds of ornaments, / So too a bhikkhu of cleansed mind tempers his mind, / And directs his yielding mind among the powers of knowing,[24] as he wishes and wherever he wishes. // 15.69 // //

saundaranande mahākāvye vitarka-prahāṇo nāma pañca-daśaḥ sargaḥ // 15 //
The 15th canto in the epic poem Handsome Nanda, titled "Abandoning Ideas."

---

[24] *Abhijñāsu* refers either to five or to six powers of knowing. The first five powers, listed in SN16.2, are *lokya* or *laukika* (of the world; EHJ: 'mundane'). These are practiced at the level of conventional truth. The sixth power is *lokottara* (world-transcending; EHJ: 'supramundane'). This power is practiced at the level of ultimate truth, through insight into the teaching of dependent arising, aka emptiness. It is the power of knowing how, by letting happen, by not clinging, to allow the *āsravas* – those influences that pollute the mind – to come out in the wash.

Canto 16: ārya-satya-vyākhyānaḥ
Communicating the Noble Truths

Introduction

Ārya-satya means noble truth or noble truths, and *vyākhyāna* is an *-na* neuter action noun from *vy-ā-√khyā*, which means to explain in detail, to tell in full, or to communicate. The importance of this canto is indicated by its length: at 98 verses, it is comfortably the longest canto in Saundarananda. In it the Buddha tells Nanda that the birth of a sentient creature is the birth of suffering. This suffering has its cause in faults which the Buddha associates with progressive doing (*pravṛtti*), and with thirsting (*tṛṣṇā*). To eliminate the faults which are the cause of suffering is to eliminate suffering itself. As a practical means whereby Nanda might eliminate faults, then, the Buddha teaches him a noble eightfold path based on the good conduct (*śīla*) praised in Canto 13, but including the balancing act of *samādhi* indicated in Canto 15, and also comprising the crowning accomplishment of wisdom (*prajñā*), this wisdom being primarily a function of insight into the four noble truths themselves.

While the canto thus has a practical emphasis, it also contains some especially memorable examples of Aśvaghoṣa's poetry – like for example verse 4, verse 10, verses 28-29, verse 35, verse 42-43, verse 50 and verses 97-98.

In the end the present canto is much more than a detailed explanation of the four noble truths, and much more than beautiful poetry. It is a call to action, in which the Buddha exhorts Nanda, following the example of many other individuals, energetically to clear his own path of *śīla, samādhi* and *prajñā*, for the ending of all faults, gross and subtle. The canto title *ārya-satya-vākhyāna* – like all of the other canto titles from Canto 12 onwards – is thus ultimately suggestive of sitting practice itself. In the final analysis, *ārya-satya-vākhyāna* may be understood as describing the very act of sitting in the lotus posture as the expression, or the communication, of the four noble truths.

evaṁ mano-dhāraṇayā krameṇa vyapohya kiṁ-cit samupohya kiṁ-cit /
dhyānāni catvāry adhigamya yogī prāpnoty abhijñā niyamena pañca // 16.1 //
Thus, by methodically taking possession of the mind, getting rid of something and gathering something together, / The practitioner makes the four dhyānas[1] his own, and duly acquires the five powers of knowing: // 16.1 //

ṛddhi-pravekaṁ ca bahu-prakāraṁ parasya cetaś-caritāvabodham /
atīta-janma-smaraṇaṁ ca dīrghaṁ divye viśuddhe śruti-cakṣuṣī ca // 16.2 //
The principal transcendent power,[2] taking many forms;[3] then being awake to what others are thinking; / And remembering past lives from long ago; and divine lucidity of ear; and of eye.[4] // 16.2 //

---

[1] The four stages of meditation are described from SN17.42 to 17.55. See also Arāḍa's description in BC Canto 12.

[2] *Ṛddhi-pravekam.* The meanings of *ṛddhi* include 1. increase, growth, prosperity, success; and 2. accomplishment, perfection, supernatural power [= *abhijñā*]. At the end of a compound, *praveka* means principal or chief.

ataḥ paraṁ tattva-parīkṣaṇena mano dadhāty āsrava-saṁkṣayāya /
tato hi duḥkha-prabhṛtīni samyak catvāri satyāni padāny avaiti // 16.3 //

From then on,[5] exploring what really is,[6] he applies his mind to eradicating the polluting influences,[7] / For on this basis he fully understands suffering and the rest, the four true standpoints: // 16.3 //

bādhātmakaṁ duḥkham idaṁ prasaktaṁ duḥkhasya hetuḥ prabhavātmako 'yam /
duḥkha-kṣayo niḥsaraṇātmako 'yaṃ trāṇātmako 'yaṃ praśamāya mārgaḥ // 16.4 //

This is suffering, which is constant and akin to trouble; this is the cause of suffering, akin to starting it; / This is cessation of suffering, akin to walking away. And this, akin to a refuge, is a peaceable path. // 16.4 //

ity ārya-satyāny avabudhya buddhyā catvāri samyak prativídhya caiva /
sarvāsravān bhāvanayābhibhūya na jāyate śāntim avāpya bhūyaḥ // 16.5 //

Understanding these noble truths, by a process of reasoning, while getting to know the four as one, / He prevails over all pollutants, by the practice of letting happen, and, on finding peace, is not reborn again.[8] // 16.5 //

---

[3] The first pāda has been translated in such a way as to allow the reading that "taking many forms," i.e. versatility or adaptability, is the principal transcendent power. EHJ translated "the most excellent magic powers of many kinds." Cf. SN3.22.

[4] The principal transcendent power, taking many forms (1) then being awake to what others are thinking (2) /And remembering past lives from long ago (3); and divine lucidity of ear (4); and of eye (5). These five are the worldly (EHJ: 'mundane') powers of knowing, practiced at the level of conventional truth. Power no. 6 is the world-transcending (EHJ: 'supramundane') power of ending the polluting influences, through the practice of letting happen. "World-transcending," then, means allowed to happen, in light of the teaching of dependent arising, at the level of ultimate truth.

[5] *Ataḥ param*, "from then on." As EHJ wrote in his Introduction to Buddhacarita, this seems to accord with "the view generally prevailing in the schools... that the trances [*dhyānas*] are mastered in a preliminary stage before the process of *bhāvanā* begins." The prevailing view, in other words, was that sitting-dhyāna was a mundane practice, associated with the five higher powers, but not with the sixth supramundane power, by which the pollutants are eradicated. But see note to SN17.56.

[6] *Tattva-parīkṣaṇa*, "investigating/exploring reality," may be taken as equivalent to the Pali *vipassanā* (insight; see note to SN15.69). Each chapter title of MMK ends with *-parīkṣā*. Chapter One, for example, is *pratyaya-parīkṣā* "Exploring Causes."

[7] An *āsrava* (lit. "influx") is a polluting influence, or pollutant, or taint, that is said to tie us to existence in saṁsāra. Sometimes the *āsravas* are classified three ways as *kāmāsrava* (desire), *bhavāsrava* (becoming), and *avidyāsrava* (ignorance) - see Appendix, DN16. Sometimes *dṛṣṭy-āsrava* (views) is included in a four-way classification. According to one explanation, the taint of views is ended through the supramundane path of stream-entry, the taint of desire through the supramundane path of non-returning, and the taints of becoming and ignorance through the supramundane path of arhathood. EHJ's point, then, is that, in the conventional understanding, *dhyāna* is a mundane practice, and sometimes (as in the case of Arāḍa) a non-Buddhist practice, which precedes the supramundane efforts of the four kinds of noble ones to cleanse the mind of pollutants through *bhāvanā*. EHJ queries why Aśvaghoṣa seems to go against this convention in his description of Nanda's progress in SN Canto 17. (Again, see note to SN17.56.)

[8] *Bhāvanayā* (by letting happen), *abhibhūya* (prevailing over) and *bhūyaḥ* (again) are all derived from the verbal root √*bhū*. The second line may thus be taken as a hint to look into the etymology and deeper meaning of *bhāvanā* - i.e. not only to take *bhāvanā* simply to mean meditation or practice,

abodhato hy aprativedhataś ca tattvātmakasyāsya catuṣṭasya /
bhavād bhavaṁ yāti na śantim eti saṁsāra-dolām adhiruhya lokaḥ // 16.6 //
For by failing to wake up and come round to this four, whose substance is the reality of what is, / Humankind goes from existence to existence[9] without finding peace, hoisted in the swing of saṁsāra. // 16.6 //

tasmāj jarāder vyasanasya mūlaṁ samāsato duḥkham avaihi janma /
sarvauṣadhīnām iva bhūr bhavāya sarvāpadāṁ kṣetram idaṁ hi janma // 16.7 //
Therefore, at the root of a tragedy like growing old,[10] see, in short, that birth[11] is suffering. / For, as the earth supports the life of all plants, this birth is the field of all troubles. // 16.7 //

yaj janma-rūpasya hi sendriyasya duḥkhasya tan naika-vidhasya janma /
yaḥ saṁbhavaś cāsya samucchrayasya mṛtyoś ca rogasya ca saṁbhavaḥ saḥ // 16.8 //
The birth of a sentient bodily form, again, is the birth of suffering in all its varieties; / And he who begets such an outgrowth is the begetter of death and of disease. // 16.8 //

sad vāpy asadvā viṣa-miśram annaṁ yathā vināśāya na dhāraṇāya /
loke tathā tiryag-upary-adho vā duḥkhāya sarvaṁ na sukhāya janma // 16.9 //
Good food or bad food, if mixed with poison, makes for ruin and not for sustenance. / Likewise, whether in a world on the flat or above or below, all birth makes for hardship and not for ease. // 16.9 //

jarādayo naika-vidhāḥ prajānāṁ satyāṁ pravṛttau prabhavanty anarthāḥ /
pravātsu ghoreṣv api māruteṣu na hy aprasūtās taravaś calanti // 16.10 //
The many and various disappointments of men, like old age, occur as long as their doing[12] goes on. / (For, even when violent winds blow, trees do not shake that never sprouted.) // 16.10 //

ākāśa-yoniḥ pavano yathā hi yathā śamī-garbha-śayo hutāśaḥ /
āpo yathāntar-vasudhā-śayāś ca duḥkhaṁ tathā citta-śarīra-yoni // 16.11 //
As wind is born from the air, as fire sleeps in the womb of *śamī* wood, / And as water gestates inside the earth, so does suffering spring from an expectant mind-and-body. // 16.11 //

---

but to think about what the Buddha really meant by the word, which is the causative gerund from √*bhū*.

[9] *Bhava*, existence, being, coming into being, becoming, is link no. 10 of 12 in the dependent arising of suffering. See BC Canto 14, MMK ch. 26.

[10] *Jarādi*, aging et cetera, represents link no 12 – all the sufferings of aging and death. Ibid.

[11] *Janma* or *jati*, birth or rebirth is link no 11. Ibid.

[12] *Pravṛtti*, doing, progressive doing, may be taken as representing links no. 2 (works of conditioning, fabrications) and 10 (coming into existence) The two together are classed as *karma*. Ibid.

apāṁ dravatvaṁ kaṭhinatvam urvyā vāyoś calatvaṁ dhruvam auṣṇyam agneḥ /
yathā sva-bhāvo hi tathā sva-bhāvo duḥkhaṁ śarīrasya ca cetasaś ca // 16.12 //
The fluidity of water, the solidity of earth, the motion of wind, and the constant heat of fire / Are self-existent in them; as also suffering is self-existent in a body and a mind. // 16.12 //

kāye sati vyādhi-jarādi duḥkhaṁ kṣut-tarṣa-varṣoṣṇa-himādi caiva /
rūpāśrite cetasi sānubandhe śokārati-krodha-bhayādi duḥkham // 16.13 //
Insofar as a body exists, there is the suffering of sickness, aging and so on; and also of hunger and thirst, and of the rains, and summer heat and winter cold. / Insofar as a mind is bonded, tied to phenomena, there is the suffering of grief, discontent, anger, fear and so on. // 16.13 //

pratyakṣam ālokya ca janma duḥkhaṁ duḥkhaṁ tathātītam apīti viddhi /
yathā ca tad duḥkham idaṁ ca duḥkhaṁ duḥkhaṁ tathānāgatam apy avehi // 16.14 //
Seeing now before your eyes that birth is suffering, recognize that likewise in the past it was suffering. / And just as that was suffering and this is suffering, know that likewise in the future it will be suffering. // 16.14 //

bīja-svabhāvo hi yatheha dṛṣṭo bhūto 'pi bhavyo 'pi tathānumeyaḥ /
praty-akṣataś ca jvalano yathoṣṇo bhūto 'pi bhavyo 'pi tathoṣṇa eva // 16.15 //
For just as a seed's self-existence is presumed now to be evident, it happened and will happen like that. / And in the way that the fire burning before us is [presumed to be] hot, heat did happen and will happen like that.[13]// 16.15 //

tan nāma-rūpasya guṇānurūpaṁ yatraiva nirvṛttir udāra-vṛtta /
tatraiva duḥkhaṁ na hi tad-vimuktaṁ duḥkhaṁ bhaviṣyaty abhavad bhaved vā // 16.16 //
In conformance with a peculiarity,[14] then, psycho-physicality[15] develops, wherein, O man of noble conduct, / Suffering happens, right there - for nowhere else will suffering happen or has it happened or could it happen. // 16.16 //

---

[13] This verse was translated in the first edition according to its ostensible meaning: "*For just as it is evident to us now what kind of thing a seed is, we can infer that it was so in the past and that it will be so in the future. / And just as fire burning before us is hot, so was it hot and so will it be hot.*" In light of Nāgārjuna's teaching of emptiness, what really depends on inference, or [false] presumption, might be *svabhāva*, "self-existence" itself. In that case *uṣṇa* (heat) in the second line might be a synonym for suffering. What is sure, then - what always happens - is that our presumptions based on belief in self-existence turn out to be painful.

[14] SED defines *guṇa* as a quality, peculiarity, attribute or property; a property or characteristic of all created things. The latter definition, in particular, sounds like a non-empty concept, very much tied to self-existence. So on the surface *guṇa* means a particular quality, in conformity with which an individual being grows. But below the surface a peculiar view of the world, tied to self-existence, is at the root of suffering.

[15] SED defines *nāma-rūpa* as an individual being; hence EHJ translated *nāma-rūpa* in this instance as "corporeality." But as link no. 4 in the 12 links in 12-fold dependent arising of suffering, *nāma-rūpa* can also be understood to mean the psycho-physicality (link no. 4) that arises out of divided consciousness (link no. 3), and which at the same time produces divided consciousness. On the

pravṛtti-duḥkhasya ca tasya loke tṛṣṇādayo doṣa-gaṇā nimittam /
naiveśvaro na prakṛtir na kālo nāpi svabhāvo na vidhir yadṛcchā // 16.17 //
Again this, the suffering of doing in the world, has as its cause[16] thirsting and suchlike – clusters of faults.[17] / The cause is certainly not God, nor primordial matter, nor time; and surely not self-existence, nor predestination or self-will.[18] // 16.17 //

jñātavyam etena ca kāraṇena lokasya doṣebhya iti pravṛttiḥ /
yasmān mriyante sa-rajas-tamaskā na jāyate vīta-rajas-tamaskaḥ // 16.18 //
Again, you must understand how, due to this cause, because of men's faults, the cycle of doing goes on, / So that they succumb to death who are afflicted by the dust of the passions and by darkness; but he is not reborn who is free of dust and darkness. // 16.18 //

icchā-viśeṣe sati tatra tatra yānāsanāder bhavati prayogaḥ /
yasmād atas tarṣa-vaśāt tathaiva janma prajānām iti veditavyam // 16.19 //
Insofar as the specific desire exists to do this or that, an action like going or sitting happens; / Hence, in just the same way, by the force of their thirsting living creatures are reborn – as is to be observed: // 16.19 //

sattvāny abhiṣvaṅga-vaśāni dṛṣṭvā svajātiṣu prīti-parāṇy atīva /
abhyāsa-yogād upapāditāni tair eva doṣair iti tāni viddhi // 16.20 //
See sentient beings in the grip of attachment, dead set on pleasure among their own kind; / And, from their habitual practice of faults, observe them presenting with those very faults. // 16.20 //

krodha-praharṣādibhir āśrayāṇām utpadyate ceha yathā viśeṣaḥ /
tathaiva janmasv api naika-rūpo nirvartate kleśa-kṛto viśeṣaḥ // 16.21 //
Just as the anger, lust, and so on of sufferers of those afflictions give rise in the present to a personality trait, / So too in new lives, in various manifestations, does the affliction-created trait develop: // 16.21 //

---

surface, Aśvaghoṣa is describing how an individual being takes a separate self-existent shape. Below the surface, suffering arises from that very misconception of self-existence, to which the Buddha's 12-fold teaching of dependent arising is opposed.

[16] Here (as also in 12.39-40) *nimittam* is identified with *kāraṇa*, and means cause.

[17] Again, Aśvaghoṣa must have in mind the Buddha's 12-fold teaching of the dependent arising of suffering, in which links (1) unwittingness, (8) thirsting, and (9) clinging, are classed as *kleśa*, afflictions or defilements. Afflictions give rise to (2) fabrications and (10) becoming, classed as *karma*, or doing. The remaining seven links – divided consciousness (3), psycho-physicality (4), six senses (5), contact (6), feeling (7), rebirth (11) and sufferings of aging death (12) – are classed as *duḥkha*, suffering. Here clusters of faults would seem to indicate primarily *kleśa*. "Suffering of doing" indicates *duḥkha* arising from *karma*.

[18] All of the elements of the second line may be seen as typical examples of non-empty conceptions, with *svabhāva* being the most explicitly non-empty conception of all.

roṣādhike janmani tīvra-roṣa utpadyate rāgiṇi tīvra-rāgaḥ /
mohādhike moha-balādhikaś ca tad-alpa-doṣe ca tad-alpa-doṣaḥ // 16.22 //
In a life dominated by anger arises violent anger,[19] in the lover of passion arises burning passion, / And in one dominated by ignorance arises overwhelming ignorance. In one who has a lesser fault, again, the lesser fault develops. // 16.22 //

phalaṁ hi yādk samavaiti sākṣāt tādātmyato bījam avaity atītam /
avetya bīja-prakṛtiṁ ca sākṣād anāgataṁ tat-phalam abhyupaiti // 16.23 //
Seeing what kind of fruit is before one's eyes, one knows it was that kind of seed in the past.[20] / And having identified a seed before one's eyes, one knows the fruit it may be in the future. // 16.23 //

doṣa-kṣayo jātiṣu yāsu yasya vairāgyatas tāsu na jāyate saḥ /
doṣāśayas tiṣṭhati yasya yatra tasyopapattir vivaśasya tatra // 16.24 //
In whichever realms of existence a man has ended faults, thanks to that dispassion he is not born in those realms. / Wherever he remains susceptible to a fault, that is where he pops up, whether he likes it or not. // 16.24 //

taj janmano naika-vidhasya saumya tṛṣṇādayo hetava ity avetya /
tāṁś chindhi duḥkhād yadi nirmumukṣā kārya-kṣayaḥ kāraṇa-saṁkṣayādd hi // 16.25 //
So my friend,[21] with regard to the many forms of rebirth, know their causes to be thirsting and suchlike / And cut out those causes, if you wish to be freed from suffering; for ending of the effect follows from eradication of the cause. // 16.25 //

duḥkha-kṣayo hetu-parikṣayāc ca śāntaṁ śivaṁ sākṣi-kuruṣva dharmaṁ /
tṛṣṇā-virāgaṁ layanaṁ nirodhaṁ sanātanaṁ trāṇam ahāryam āryam // 16.26 //
Again, the ending of suffering follows from the disappearance of its cause. Experience that reality for yourself as peace and well-being, / A place of rest, a cessation, an absence of the red taint of thirsting, a primeval refuge which is irremovable and noble, // 16.26 //

---

[19] EHJ followed Shastri in amending the two occurrences in the first pāda of *roṣa* (anger) to *doṣa*. EHJ took *doṣa* (a fault) to represent specifically *dveṣa*, hatred. Hartmann's later discovery of the Central Asian fragment, parts of which cover this verse, tended to confirm that the paper manuscript's original *roṣa* had been correct.

[20] Originally I followed EHJ's reading of the first word in the second pāda as *tad-āgamad*, and translated "from past knowledge of that fruit." But Hartmann's fragment of Central Asian text has *tadātmyato;* this I have amended, following the conjecture of Harunaga Isaacson, to *tādātmyato (= tādātmya* + suffix *-tas*). *Tādātmya*, lit. "the state of having that as nature," is given in SED as: "sameness or identity of nature or character with." Either way, the point is that, rather than discuss the principle of cause and effect in the abstract, here the Buddha speaks of seed and fruit. (Translation amended July 2012, after completion of the audio recording of this Saundarananda translation.)

[21] Hartmann's fragment has *samyak*. Salomon points out that since *samyak* is a key word, repeated many times in this chapter, it might have been easy for the copyist to misread *saumya* as *samyak*.

yasmin na jātir na jarā na mṛtyur na vyādhayo nāpriya-saṁprayogaḥ /
necchā-vipanna priya-viprayogaḥ kṣemaṁ padaṁ naiṣṭhikam acyutaṁ tat // 16.27 //
In which there is no being born, no aging, no dying, no illness, no being touched by unpleasantness, / No disappointment, and no separation from what is pleasant: It is an ultimate and indestructible step, in which to dwell at ease. // 16.27 //

dīpo yathā nirvṛtim abhyupeto naivāvaniṁ gacchati nāntarīkṣam /
diśaṁ na kāṁ-cid vidiśaṁ na kāṁ-cit sneha-kṣayāt kevalam eti śāntim // 16.28 //
A lamp that has gone out reaches neither to the earth nor to the sky, / Nor to any cardinal nor to any intermediate point: Because its oil is spent it reaches nothing but extinction. // 16.28 //

evaṁ kṛtī nirvṛtim abhyupeto naivāvaniṁ gacchati nāntarīkṣam /
diśaṁ na kāṁ-cid vidiśaṁ na kāṁ-cit kleśa-kṣayāt kevalam eti śāntim // 16.29 //
In the same way, a man of action who has come to quiet reaches neither to the earth nor to the sky, / Nor to any cardinal nor to any intermediate point: From the ending of his afflictions he attains nothing but extinction. // 16.29 //

asyābhyupāyo 'dhigamāya mārgaḥ prajñā-trikalpaḥ praśama-dvikalpaḥ /
sa bhāvanīyo vidhivad budhena śīle śucau tripramukhe sthitena // 16.30 //
A means for gaining that end is the path of threefold wisdom and twofold tranquillity.[22] / It is to be cultivated[23] by a wakeful person working to principle – abiding in untainted threefold integrity. // 16.30 //

vāk-karma samyak saha-kāya-karma yathāvad ājīva-nayaś ca śuddhaḥ /
idaṁ trayaṁ vṛtta-vidhau pravṛttaṁ śīlāśrayaṁ dharma-parigrahāya // 16.31 //
Using the voice well and the body well in tandem, and making a clean living in a suitable manner: / These three, pertaining to conduct, are for the mastery, based on good habits, of one's dharma-duty.[24] // 16.31 //

---

[22] At the end of this line, the fragment first identified in a 1988 paper by Jens-Ewe Hartmann has *praśamas trikalpa.* Richard Salomon (1999) notes that this should probably be amended to *praśama-trikalpa.* Either way, there is a significant difference here between the Nepalese manuscript which EHJ based his text on, and the Central Asian manuscript to which Hartmann's fragment belonged. In the Nepalese manuscript *praśama-dvikalpaḥ* indicates that tranquility is twofold; in the Central Asian manuscript *praśamas trikalpaḥ* or *praśama-trikalpaḥ* indicates that tranquility is threefold. If one accepts that tranquility is threefold, then wisdom must be twofold. Therefore, though *prajñā-dvikalpaḥ* is missing from Hartmann's original fragment, Salomon makes a case for reconstructing the verse as follows: *asyābhyupāyo dhigamāya mārgaḥ prajñā-dvikalpaḥ praśama-trikalpaḥ / tau bhāvanīyau vidhivad budhena śīle śucau tripramukhe sthitena //*

[23] In Hartmann's fragment, *tau bhāvanīyau* means these two [wisdom and tranquility] are to be cultivated. Thus: "A means for gaining that end is the path of twofold wisdom and threefold tranquility. These two are to be cultivated by a wakeful person working to principle – abiding in untainted threefold integrity." In some versions of the threefold categorization of the noble eightfold path, initiative/effort is indeed included not under the heading of wisdom (*prajñā*) but under the heading of tranquility (*samādhi*), making wisdom twofold and tranquility threefold, as per Salomon's suggested reconstruction.

[24] EHJ's preferred reading is *karma-parigrahāya*, "for the mastery of one's karma-conduct."

satyeṣu duḥkhādiṣu dṛṣṭir āryā samyag-vitarkaś ca parākramaś ca /
idaṁ trayaṁ jñāna-vidhau pravṛttaṁ prajñāśrayaṁ kleśa-parikṣayāya // 16.32 //
Noble insight into suffering and the other truths, along with thinking straight, and initiative: / These three, pertaining to understanding, are for dissolution, based on wisdom, of the afflictions.[25] // 16.32 //

nyāyena satyābhigamāya yuktā samyak smṛtiḥ samyag atho samādhiḥ /
idaṁ dvayaṁ yoga-vidhau pravṛttaṁ śamāśrayaṁ citta-parigrahāya // 16.33 //
True thinking in activity, properly harnessed so as to bring one close to the truths;[26] and true balancing: / These two, pertaining to practice, are for mastery, based on tranquility, of the mind. // 16.33 //

kleśāṅkurān na pratanoti śīlaṁ bījāṅkurān kāla ivātivṛttaḥ /
śucau hi śīle puruṣasya doṣā manaḥ sa-lajjā iva dharṣayanti // 16.34 //
Good conduct no more propagates the shoots of affliction than a bygone spring propagates shoots from seeds. / The faults, as long as a man's good conduct is untainted, venture only timidly to attack his mind. // 16.34 //

kleśāṁs tu viṣkambhayate samādhir vegān ivādrir mahato nadīnām /
sthitaṁ samādhau hi na dharṣayanti doṣā bhujaṁgā iva mantra-baddhāḥ // 16.35 //
But balance casts off the afflictions like a mountain casts off the mighty torrents of rivers. / The faults do not attack a man who is standing firm in balanced stillness: like charmed snakes, they are spellbound. // 16.35 //

prajñā tv aśeṣeṇa nihanti doṣāṁs tīra-drumān prāvṛṣi nimnageva /
dagdhā yayā na prabhavanti doṣā vajrāgninevānusṛtena vṛkṣāḥ // 16.36 //
And wisdom destroys the faults without trace, as a mountain stream in the monsoon destroys the trees on its banks. / Faults consumed by it do not stand a chance, like trees in the fiery wake of a thunderbolt.[27] // 16.36 //

---

[25] In Salomon's reconstruction, EHJ's verse 32 becomes verse 33 and reads: *satyeṣu duḥkhādiṣu dṛṣṭir āryā samyag-vitarkaś-ca ? ? ? ? ? ? / idaṃ dvayaṃ jñāna-vidhau pravṛttaṃ prajñāśrayaṃ kleśa-parikṣayāya //* "Noble insight into suffering and the other truths, along with thinking straight, * * * * : These two, pertaining to know-how, are for dissolution, based on wisdom, of the afflictions."

[26] *Nyāyena satyābhigamāya yuktā samyak smṛtiḥ.* EHJ translated "*Right attention used in accordance with the plan in order to approach the Truths.*" LC translated "*Right mindfulness conjoined to the plan for the discovery of the truth.*" Whichever of many possible translations is preferred, the point is that true *smṛti* as the Buddha taught it is not bare attention divorced from any philosophical or developmental context; thinking in activity, as a letting happen, is part of an eightfold means of growing in a certain direction.

[27] Cf Appendix, DN16.

triskandham etaṁ pravigāhya mārgaṁ praspaṣṭam aṣṭāṅgam ahāryam āryam /
duḥkhasya hetūn prajahāti doṣān prāpnoti cātyanta-śivaṁ padaṁ tat // 16.37 //
Giving oneself to this path with its three divisions and eight branches – this straightforward, irremovable, noble path – / One abandons the faults, which are the causes of suffering, and comes to that step which is total well-being. // 16.37 //

asyopacāre dhṛtir ārjavaṁ ca hrīr apramādaḥ praviviktatā ca /
alpecchatā tuṣṭir asaṁgatā ca loka-pravṛttāv aratiḥ kṣamā ca // 16.38 //
Attendant on it are constancy and straightness; modesty, attentiveness, and reclusiveness; / Wanting little, contentment, and freedom from forming attachments; no fondness for worldly activity, and forbearance. // 16.38 //

yāthātmyato vindati yo hi duḥkhaṁ tasyodbhavaṁ tasya ca yo nirodham /
āryeṇa mārgeṇa sa śāntim eti kalyāṇa-mitraiḥ saha vartamānaḥ // 16.39 //
For he who knows suffering as it really is, who knows its starting and its stopping: / It is he who reaches peace by the noble path – going along with friends in the good. // 16.39 //

yo vyādhito vyādhim avaiti samyag vyādher nidānaṁ ca tad-auṣadhaṁ ca /
ārogyam āpnoti hi so 'cireṇa mitrair abhijñair upacaryamāṇaḥ // 16.40 //
He who fully appreciates his illness, as the illness it is, who sees the cause[28] of the illness and its remedy: / It is he who wins, before long, freedom from disease – attended by friends in the know. // 16.40 //

tad vyādhi-saṁjñāṁ kuru duḥkha-satye doṣeṣv api vyādhi-nidāna-saṁjñām /
ārogya-saṁjñāṁ ca nirodha-satye bhaiṣajya-saṁjñām api mārga-satye // 16.41 //
So with regard to the truth of suffering, see suffering as an illness; with regard to the faults, see the faults as the cause of the illness; / With regard to the truth of stopping, see stopping as freedom from disease; and with regard to the truth of a path, see a path as a cure. // 16.41 //

tasmāt pravṛttiṁ parigaccha duḥkhaṁ pravartakān apy avagaccha doṣān /
nivṛttim āgaccha ca tan-nirodhaṁ nivartakaṁ cāpy avagaccha mārgam // 16.42 //
Comprehend, therefore, that suffering is doing; witness the faults impelling it forward; / Realise its stopping as non-doing; and know the path as a turning back. // 16.42 //

śirasy atho vāsasi saṁpradīpte satyāvabodhāya matir vicāryā /
dagdhaṁ jagat satya-nayaṁ hy adṛṣṭvā pradahyate saṁprati dhakṣyate ca // 16.43 //
Though your head and clothes be on fire direct your mind so as to be awake to the truths.[29] / For in failing to see the purport of the truths, the world has burned, it is burning now, and it will burn. // 16.43 //

---

[28] *Nidāna*, cause, is as in the 12 *nidāna* which form the links in 12-fold dependent arising.
[29] Cf MMK24.40: *"One who sees dependent arising sees this: suffering, its coming together, its cessation and the path itself."*

yadaiva yaḥ paśyati nāma-rūpaṁ kṣayīti tad-darśanam asya samyak /
samyak ca nirvedam upaiti paśyan nandī-kṣayāc ca kṣayam eti rāgaḥ // 16.44 //
When a man sees psycho-physicality as subject to dissolution,[30] that insight of his is accurate; / In seeing accurately he is disenchanted, and from the ending of exuberance ends the red taint of passion. // 16.44 //

tayoś ca nandī-rajasoḥ kṣayeṇa samyag vimuktaṁ pravadāmi cetaḥ /
samyag vimuktir manasaś ca tābhyāṁ na cāsya bhūyaḥ karaṇīyam asti // 16.45 //
By the ending of the duality which is exuberance and gloom, I submit, his mind is fully set free. / And when his mind is fully liberated from that duality, there is nothing further for him to do. // 16.45 //

yathā-svabhāvena hi nāma-rūpaṁ tadd-hetum evāsta-gamaṁ ca tasya /
vijānataḥ pasyata eva cāhaṁ bravīmi samyak kṣayam āsravāṇām // 16.46 //
For in him who sees psycho-physicality in terms of self-existence,[31] and who sees its origin and passing away, / From the very fact of his knowing and seeing, I predict the complete eradication of the pollutants. // 16.46 //

tasmāt paraṁ saumya vidhāya vīryaṁ śīghraṁ ghaṭasv āsrava-saṁkṣayāya /
duḥkhān anityāṁś ca nirātmakāṁś ca dhātūn viśeṣeṇa parīkṣamāṇaḥ // 16.47 //
So my friend garner your energy greatly and strive quickly to put an end to polluting influences, / Exploring, specifically, the elements - as suffering, as impermanent and as devoid of self. // 16.47 //

dhātūn hi ṣaḍ bhū-salilānalādīn sāmānyataḥ svena ca lakṣaṇena /
avaiti yo nānyam avaiti tebhyaḥ so 'tyantikaṁ mokṣam avaiti tebhyaḥ // 16.48 //
For in knowing the six elements of earth, water, fire and the rest, generically, and each as specific to itself, / He who knows nothing else but those elements, knows total release from those elements.[32] // 16.48 //

---

[30] *Nāma-rūpa*, psycho-physicality born of divided consciousness, again, is the fourth in the 12 links in the dependent arising of suffering. As such it is subject to dissolution as an empty happening, not as a self-existent thing. Thus, from the use of *nidāna* in verse 40, through to the reference to *svabhāva* in verse 46, a subtext may be discerned alluding to the centrality of the teaching of dependent arising, aka emptiness.

[31] *Yathā-svabhāvena*, translated in the first edition as "as it is." Again, in light of MMK, *svabhāvena* may be better understood with a pejorative sense - so that seeing things "as they are" (as self-existing) is, ironically, not the solution but the obstacle. The point might be, below the surface, that seeing this obstacle is the beginning of the solution. Cf MMK24.10: *"Ultimate truth is not taught without relying on the conventional. Without understanding of the ultimate truth [of freedom from self-existence], nirvāṇa is not realized."*

[32] Does Aśvaghoṣa have in mind seeing each of the elements, externally and internally, *yathā-bhūta* ("as happening"), as described in the first half of the Rāhula Sutta (MN62; see Appendix), in preparation for practice of *bhāvana*?

kleśa-prahāṇāya ca niścitena kālo 'bhyupāyaś ca parīkṣitavyaḥ /
yogo 'py akāle hy anupāyataś ca bhavaty anarthāya na tad-guṇāya // 16.49 //
One set on abandoning the afflictions, then, should attend to timing and method; / For even practice itself, done at the wrong time and relying on wrong means, makes for disappointment and not for the desired end. // 16.49 //

ajāta-vatsāṁ yadi gāṁ duhīta naivāpnuyāt kṣīram akāla-dohī /
kāle 'pi vā syān na payo labheta mohena śṛṅgād yadi gāṁ duhīta // 16.50 //
If a cow is milked before her calf is born, milking at the wrong time will yield no milk. / Or even at the right time no milk will be got if, through ignorance, a cow is milked by the horn. // 16.50 //

ārdrāc ca kāṣṭhāj jvalan-ābhikāmo naiva prayatnād api vanhim ṛcchet /
kāṣṭhāc ca śuṣkād api pātanena naivāgnim āpnoty anupāya-pūrvam // 16.51 //
Again, one who wants fire from damp wood, try as he might, will not get fire. / And even if he lays down dry wood, he won't get fire from that, with bad bushcraft. // 16.51 //

tad-deśa-kālau vidhivat parīkṣya yogasya mātrām api cābhyupāyam /
balābale cātmani saṁpradhārya kāryaḥ prayatno na tu tad-viruddhaḥ // 16.52 //
Having given due consideration to the time and place as well as to the extent and method of one's practice, / One should, reflecting on one's own strength and weakness, persist in an effort that is not inconsistent with them. // 16.52 //

pragrāhakaṁ yat tu nimittam uktam uddhanyamāne hṛdi tan na sevyam /
evaṁ hi cittaṁ praśamaṁ na yāti [viś]vāyunā vahnir iveryamāṇaḥ // 16.53 //
One should not, however, resort to that aspect of practice[33] described as garnering, when the emotions are inflamed, / For thus the mind does not come to quiet, like a fire being fanned by the wind.[34] // 16.53 //

śamāya yat syān niyataṁ nimittaṁ jātoddhave cetasi tasya kālaḥ /
evaṁ hi cittaṁ praśamaṁ niyacchet pradīpyamāno 'gnir ivodakena // 16.54 //
That aspect which might be defined as calming has its time when one's mind is excited; / For thus the mind subsides into quietness, like a blazing fire [doused] with water. // 16.54 //

---

[33] Paradoxically, *nimittam* means both 1. mark, target, object (see SN13.41 "objectified target"), and 2. cause (see SN16.17, 16.96), causal factor or stimulus (see SN16.72, 16.84). It also means 3. sign (see SN1.32; 5.10). In the series of verses from verses 53 to 67 dealing with the practice of letting happen (*bhāvanā*), leading to letting go of polluting influences, *nimitta* might best be understood (somewhere in the middle of senses 2 and 3?) as that aspect of *bhāvanā* which is naturally the antidote to a particular polluting influence.

[34] EHJ's Sanskrit text has at the beginning of the fourth pāda * * * *nā* plus the following note: "I cannot solve the restoration of *d*, Evidently a four-syllable word meaning 'wind' in the instrumental is required." *Pra-vāyunā* would fit, but SED gives no such word for wind as *pra-vāyu*. There is such a word as *viś-vayu* (air, wind), but its light 2nd syllable does not fit the metre. *Viśvāyu* with a long second syllable means not "wind" but "all people" (*viśva + āyu*). Thus the fourth pāda as rendered here is not a satisfactory solution. *Viśvāyunā vahnir iveryamāṇa* literally means "like a fire fanned by all people."

śamāvahaṁ yan niyataṁ nimittaṁ sevyaṁ na tac cetasi līyamāne /
evaṁ hi bhūyo layam eti cittam anīryamāṇo 'gnir ivālpa-sāraḥ // 16.55 //
One should not resort to that aspect defined as calming when one's mind is dormant; / For thus the mind sinks further into lifelessness, like a feeble fire left unfanned. // 16.55 //

pragrāhakaṁ yan niyataṁ nimittaṁ layaṁ gate cetasi tasya kālaḥ /
kriyā-samarthaṁ hi manas tathā syān mandāyamāno 'gnir ivendhanena // 16.56 //
That aspect defined as garnering has its time when one's mind is lifeless, / For thus the mind becomes fit for work, like a feebly-burning fire [plied] with fuel. // 16.56 //

aupekṣikaṁ nāpi nimittam iṣṭaṁ layaṁ gate cetasi soddhave vā /
evaṁ hi tīvraṁ janayed anartham upekṣito vyādhir ivāturasya // 16.57 //
Nor is the transcendent[35] aspect of practice approved when one's mind is either lifeless or excited.[36] / For that might engender severe adversity, like the neglected illness of a sick man. // 16.57 //

yat syād upekṣā niyataṁ nimittaṁ sāmyaṁ gate cetasi tasya kālaḥ /
evaṁ hi kṛtyāya bhavet prayogo ratho vidheyāśva iva prayātaḥ // 16.58 //
The aspect that might be defined as transcendence[37] has its time when one's mind is in balance; / For thus practice can happen, like a wagon setting off with docile horses, in the direction of work that remains to be done.[38] // 16.58 //

rāgoddhava-vyākulite 'pi citte maitropasaṁhāra-vidhir na kāryaḥ /
rāgātmako muhyati maitrayā hi snehaṁ kapha-kṣobha ivopayujya // 16.59 //
Again, when the mind is filled with the red joys of passion, drawing towards oneself the love of a friend[39] is not to be practiced; / For a passionate type is stupefied by love, like a sufferer from phlegm taking oil. // 16.59 //

---

[35] *Aupekṣika* is, like *upekṣā* (see note below), from *upa-√īkṣ*, which means "to look on, overlook, disregard, neglect, leave be."

[36] EHJ's original text, based on the palm-leaf manuscript, has *soddhave* (*sa* = possessive prefix + *uddhava* = sacrificial fire, festival, holiday, joy). Linda Covill has *sodbhave* (*sa* = possessive prefix + *udbhava* = springing up, growing, becoming visible). The meaning is not materially affected. EHJ translated as "excited" and LC as "over-excited."

[37] "*Let happen, Rāhula, the transcendent/forgiving practice of letting happen (uppekhaṁ bhāvanaṁ),*" the Buddha tells his son in the Rāhula Sutta (MN62; see Appendix), so that any resentment will be given up. Before that, the Buddha speaks of letting practice happen like the earth, which is never worried, or shamed, or disgusted by what is thrown upon it. The point might be that the naturally earthy practice of letting happen (what in China and Japan was called 坐禅, "sitting-meditation"), can be inherently transcendent over all negative emotions – but not when the fear reflexes are unduly excited, in the directions of hyper-activity or undue passivity.

[38] In light of the four metaphors the Buddha often used for wisdom – boat, axe, torch and medicine – work might remain to be done in the direction of ferrying, cutting, illuminating, and healing.

[39] *Maitra* (or as per verse 59 *maitrā* and verse 62 *maitrī*), since it is derived from *mitra*, friend, literally means friendliness. Other possible translations are goodwill, or benevolence.

rāgoddhate cetasi dhairyam etya niṣevitavyaṁ tv aśubhaṁ nimittam /
rāgātmako hy evam upaiti śarma kaphātmako rūkṣam ivopayujya // 16.60 //
Steadiness lies, rather, when one's mind is excited by ardor, in coming back to the unglamorous aspect of practice;[40] / For thus a passionate type obtains relief, like a phlegmatic type taking an astringent. // 16.60 //

vyāpāda-doṣeṇa manasy udīrṇe na sevitavyaṁ tv aśubhaṁ nimittam /
dveṣātmakasya hy aśubhā vadhāya pittātmanas tīkṣṇa ivopacāraḥ // 16.61 //
When the mind is wound up, however, with the fault of malice, the unglamorous aspect is not to be dwelt upon, / For the unglamorous[41] is destructive to a hating type, as acid treatment is to a man of bilious nature. // 16.61 //

vyāpāda-doṣa-kṣubhite tu citte sevyā sva-pakṣopanayena maitrī /
dveṣātmano hi praśamāya maitrī pittātmanaḥ śīta ivopacāraḥ // 16.62 //
When the mind is agitated by the fault of malice, one should, as one on one's own side,[42] come back to friendliness, bringing love near. / For the love of a friend[43] is calming to a hate-afflicted soul, as cooling treatment is to the man of bilious nature. // 16.62 //

mohānubaddhe manasaḥ pracāre maitrāśubhā caiva bhavaty ayogaḥ /
tābhyāṁ hi saṁmoham upaiti bhūyo vāyv-ātmako rūkṣam ivopanīya // 16.63 //
When there is wandering of the mind, tied to delusion, both the loving and the unglamorous are unsuitable, / For a deluded man is further deluded by these two, like a windy type given an astringent. // 16.63 //

mohātmikāyāṁ manasaḥ pravṛttau sevyas tv idam pratyayatā-vihāraḥ /
mūḍhe manasy eṣa hi śānti-mārgo vāyv-ātmake snigdha ivopacāraḥ // 16.64 //
But when working of the mind is delusory, here one should come back to an appreciation of causality;[44] / For this is a path to peace when the mind is bewildered, like treating a wind condition with oil. // 16.64 //

---

[40] *Aśubhaṃ nimittam*, has been understood here, in light of daily reciting of MN62, as "the unglamorous/unsexy/unattractive aspect [of practice]." *Aśubhaṃ nimittam* is generally understood, however, to refer to the so-called impurity meditation whereby some unattractive or repulsive aspect of a human body is conjured up in the mind and contemplated. This is what the striver seems to have in mind in Canto 8. But one of the aims of Saundarananda might have been to contrast the way the striver objectified and blamed women, which did not help Nanda at all, and the way that in Canto 10 the Buddha intuited what might really help Nanda. What turned out to be effective was not, as the striver understood, meditation on the repulsive aspects of an objectified female body. On the contrary, what really worked for Nanda was a plan that began with a kind of fantasy, or thought experiment, involving the most attractive of women in Indra's paradise.

[41] The use of *aśubhā* as a nominative feminine noun ("the unsexy female," "an ugly one"?) looks unusual here, but EHJ did not see it as calling for comment. EHJ translated as "that meditation," referring back to the *aśubhaṁ nimittam* of the previous line.

[42] *Sva-pakṣa*, means "one's own wings" and by extension, somebody on one's side, a friend.

[43] *Maitrī* (from *mitra*, friend) means "that of a friend;" i.e. friendliness, love, benevolence, goodwill. The Pali equivalent is *metta*. Cf. Rāhula Sutta (MN62; see Appendix): *"Let happen, Rāhula, the friendly practice of letting happen (mettaṁ Rāhula bhāvanaṁ bhāvehi)..."*

[44] *Sevyas... pratyayatā-vihāraḥ* is lit. "taking-delight-in-causality is to be practiced," or "the pleasure-

ulkā-mukha-sthaṁ hi yathā suvarṇaṁ suvarṇa-kāro dhamatīha kāle /
kāle pariprokṣayate jalena krameṇa kāle samupekṣate ca // 16.65 //
Holding gold in the mouth of a furnace, a goldsmith in this world blows it at the proper time, / Douses it with water at the proper time, and gradually, at the proper time, he leaves it be. // 16.65 //

dahet suvarṇaṁ hi dhamann akāle jale kṣipan saṁśameyed akāle /
na cāpi samyak paripākam enaṁ nayed akāle samupekṣamāṇaḥ // 16.66 //
For he might burn the gold by blowing at the wrong time, he might make it unworkable by plunging it into water at the wrong time, / And he would not bring it to full perfection if at the wrong time he were just to leave it be. // 16.66 //

saṁpragrahasya praśamasya caiva tathaiva kāle samupekṣaṇasya /
samyaṅ nimittaṁ manasā tv avekṣyaṁ nāśo hi yatno 'py anupāya-pūrvaḥ // 16.67 //
Likewise, for garnering as also for calming, as also when appropriate for leaving well alone, / One should readily attend to the appropriate aspect; because even diligence is destructive when accompanied by a wrong approach." // 16.67 //

ity evam anyāya-nivartanaṁ ca nyāyaṁ ca tasmai sugato babhāṣe /
bhūyaś ca tat-tac caritaṁ viditvā vitarka-hānāya vidhīn uvāca // 16.68 //
Thus, on retreat from muddling through, and on the principle to come back to, the One Who Went Well spoke to [Nanda]; / And knowing the varieties of behavior, he detailed further the directions for abandoning ideas.[45] // 16.68 //

yathā bhiṣak pitta-kaphānilānāṁ ya eva kopaṁ samupaiti doṣaḥ /
śamāya tasyaiva vidhiṁ vidhatte vyadhatta doṣeṣu tathaiva buddhaḥ // 16.69 //
Just as, for a disorder of bile, phlegm, or wind – for whatever disorder of the humors has manifested the symptoms of disease – / A doctor prescribes a course of treatment to cure that very disorder; so did the Buddha prescribe for the faults: // 16.69 //

ekena kalpena sacen na hanyāt sv-abhyasta bhāvād asubhān vitarkān /
tato dvitīyaṁ kramam ārabheta na tv eva heyo guṇavān prayogaḥ // 16.70 //
"It may not be possible, following a single method, to kill off bad ideas that habit has so deeply entrenched; / In that case, one should commit to a second course but never give up the good work. // 16.70 //

---

ground of causality is to be resorted to." EHJ translated "the subject of reflection should be causality." Aśvaghoṣa's phrasing brings to mind the words of the sixth patriarch in China that when our minds are enlightened we turn the Flower of Dharma, and when our minds are deluded the Flower of Dharma turns.

[45] That is, the Buddha expanded further on *ānāpāna-smṛti*, thinking in the activity of breathing in and out. (SN15.64.)

anādi-kālopacitātmakatvād balīyasaḥ kleśa-gaṇasya caiva /
samyak prayogasya ca duṣkaratvāc chettuṁ na śakyāḥ sahasā hi doṣāḥ // 16.71 //
Because of the instinct-led accumulation,[46] from time without beginning, of the powerful mass of afflictions, / And because true practice is so difficult to do, the faults cannot be cut off all at once. // 16.71 //

aṇvyā yathāṇyā vipulāṇir anyā nirvāhyate tad-viduṣā nareṇa /
tadvat tad evākuśalaṁ nimittaṁ kṣipen nimittāntara-sevanena // 16.72 //
Just as a deep splinter, by means of the point of another sharp object, is removed by a man skilled in that task, / Likewise an unhelpful stimulus may be dispensed with through deployment of a different stimulus.[47] // 16.72 //

tavātha vādhyātma-nava-grahatvān naivopaśāmyed aśubho vitarkaḥ /
heyaḥ sa tad-doṣa-parīkṣaṇena sa-śvāpado mārga ivādhvagena // 16.73 //
There again, because of your personal inexperience, a bad idea might not give way. / You should abandon it by investigating what fault is in it, as a traveller abandons a path on which there is a wild beast. // 16.73 //

yathā kṣudh-ārto 'pi viśeṇa pṛktaṁ jijīviṣur necchati bhoktum annam /
tathaiva doṣāvaham ity avetya jahāti vidvān aśubhaṁ nimittam // 16.74 //
A man who wishes to live, even when starving, declines to eat poisoned food. / Likewise, observing that it brings with it a fault, a wise person leaves alone a bad stimulus.[48] // 16.74 //

na doṣataḥ paśyati yo hi doṣaṁ kas taṁ tato vārayituṁ samarthaḥ /
guṇaṁ guṇe paśyati yaś ca yatra sa vāryamāṇo 'pi tataḥ prayāti // 16.75 //
When a man does not see a fault as a fault, who is able to restrain him from it? / But when a man sees the good in what is good, he goes towards it despite being restrained.[49] // 16.75 //

---

[46] *Anādi-kālopacitātmakatvād* = *anādi* (without beginning) + *kāla* (time) + *upacita* (heaped up) + *ātmaka* (inherently consisting of) + *tvāt* (ablative of the suffix *tva*, indicating state or condition). So *ātmakatvāt* more literally means something like "because of the being inherent." Incidentally, *upacitam* (heaped up, accumulated, abundant) might conceivably be considered as a candidate for amending the closing words of SN Canto 18 – see note to SN18.64 on *upakaram*.

[47] In this particular context *nimitta* seems to invite the translation "stimulus."

[48] *Jahāti vidvān aśubhaṃ nimittam* means "the wise one leaves the *aśubhaṃ nimittam*." Ostensibly this means that in particular circumstances, for example, when the mind is agitated by ill will (as in verse 61), the wise practitioner does not opt for "the impurity meditation." Hence, EHJ: "the wise man abandons an impure meditation." Below the surface, it may be that Aśvaghoṣa is circumspectly calling into question – not only in this verse, but in the way he tells Nanda's whole story – how the Buddha's words *aśubhaṃ nimittam* had been misunderstood, not least by monks like the striver who seemed in Cantos 8 and 9 to epitomize the objectification of women.

[49] Again, the subtext might be that Aśvaghoṣa was aware that practice of "impurity meditation" – not as the Buddha had originally taught it (as in verse 60) – was being practiced with faulty understanding. Aśvaghoṣa's response, evidently, was not to target the pernicious misunderstanding directly, but rather to focus on the genuine merits of a beneficial practice like thinking in activity as a letting happen. "Direction is the truest form of inhibition."

vyapatrapante hi kula-prasūtā manaḥ-pracārair aśubhaiḥ pravṛtaiḥ /
kaṇṭhe manasvīva yuvā vapuṣmān acākṣuṣair aprayatair viṣaktaiḥ // 16.76 //
For those born into a noble house are ashamed of unpleasant occurrences going on in the mind, / As one who is bright, young and good-looking is ashamed of unsightly, ill-arranged [objects] hanging around his neck. // 16.76 //

nirdhūyamānās tv atha leśato 'pi tiṣṭheyur evākuśalā vitarkāḥ /
kāryāntarair adhyayana-kriyādyaiḥ sevyo vidhir vismaraṇāya teṣām // 16.77 //
If, though they are being shaken off, a trace persists of unhelpful thoughts, / One should resort to different tasks, such as study or physical work, as a means of consigning those thoughts to oblivion. // 16.77 //

svaptavyam apy eva vicakṣaṇena kāya-klamo vāpi niṣevitavyaḥ /
na tv eva saṁcintyam asan-nimittaṁ yatrāvasaktasya bhaved anarthaḥ // 16.78 //
A clear-sighted person should even sleep or resort to physical exhaustion, / But should never dwell on a bad stimulus, tied to which an adverse reaction might happen. // 16.78 //

yathā hi bhīto niśi taskarebhyo dvāraṁ priyebhyo 'pi na dātum icchet /
prājñas tathā saṁharati prayogaṁ samaṁ śubhasyāpy aśubhasya doṣaiḥ // 16.79 //
For just as a man afraid of thieves in the night would not open his door even to friends, / So does a wise man withhold consent equally to the doing of anything bad or anything good that involves the faults. // 16.79 //

evaṁ-prakārair api yady upāyair nivāryamāṇā na parāṅmukhāḥ syuḥ /
tato yathā-sthūla-nibarhaṇena suvarṇa-doṣā iva te praheyāḥ // 16.80 //
If, though fended off by such means, [faults] do not turn back, / Then, eliminated in order of their grossness, they must be driven out like impurities[50] from gold. // 16.80 //

druta-prayāṇa-prabhṛtīṁś ca tīkṣṇāt kāma-prayogāt parikhidyamānaḥ /
yathā naraḥ saṁśrayate tathaiva prājñena doṣeṣv api vartitavyam // 16.81 //
Just as a man who feels depressed following a torrid love affair takes refuge in activities like quick marching, so should a wise person proceed with regard to the faults. // 16.81 //

te ced alabdha-pratipakṣa-bhāvān naivopaśāmyeyur asad-vitarkāḥ /
muhūrtam apy aprativadhyamānā gṛhe bhujaṁgā iva nādhivāsyāḥ // 16.82 //
If their counteragent cannot be found and unreal fancies do not subside, / They must not for a moment be left unchecked: no whiff of them should be tolerated, as if they were snakes in the house. // 16.82 //

---

[50] The meanings of *doṣāḥ* include 1. faults like ignorance & clinging, and greed & anger; and 2. impurities in metal; as well as 3. diseases associated with imbalance of the humors, as alluded to from verse 59.

dante 'pi dantaṁ praṇidhāya kāmaṁ tālv agram utpīḍya ca jivhayāpi /
cittena cittaṁ parigṛhya cāpi kāryaḥ prayatno na tu te 'nuvartyāḥ // 16.83 //
Grit tooth against tooth, if you will, press the tongue forward and up against the palate, / And grip the mind with the mind – make an effort, but do not yield to them. // 16.83 //

kim-atra citraṁ yadi vīta-moho vanaṁ gataḥ svastha-manā na muhyet /
ākṣipyamāṇo hṛdi tan-nimittair na kṣobhyate yaḥ sa kṛtī sa dhīraḥ // 16.84 //
Is it any wonder that a man without any delusions should not become deluded when he has contentedly repaired to the forest? / [But] a man who is not shaken when challenged to the core by the stimuli of the aforementioned [ideas, thoughts, and fancies]:[51] he is a man of action; he is a steadfast man. // 16.84 //

tad ārya-satyādhigamāya pūrvaṁ viśodhayānena nayena mārgam /
yātrā-gataḥ śatru-vinigrahārthaṁ rājeva lakṣmīm ajitāṁ jigīṣan // 16.85 //
So, in order to make the noble truths your own, first clear a path according to this plan of action, / Like a king going on campaign to subdue his foes, wishing to conquer unconquered dominions. // 16.85 //

etāny araṇyāny abhitaḥ śivāni yogānukūlāny ajaneritāni /
kāyasya kṛtvā praviveka-mātraṁ kleśa-prahāṇāya bhajasva mārgam // 16.86 //
These salubrious wilds that surround us are suited to practice and not thronged with people. / Furnishing the body with ample solitude, cut a path for abandoning the afflictions. // 16.86 //

kauṇḍinya-nanda-kṛmilāniruddhās tiṣyopasenau vimalo 'tha rādhaḥ /
bāṣpottarau dhautaki-moharājau kātyāyana-dravya-pilindavatsāḥ // 16.87 //
Kauṇḍinya,[52] Nanda,[53] Kṛmila, Aniruddha, Tiṣya, Upasena, Vimala, Rādha, / Vāśpa, Uttara, Dhautaki, Moha-rāja, Kātyāyana, Dravya, Pilinda-vatsa, // 16.87 //

bhaddāli-bhadrāyaṇa-sarpadāsa-subhūti-godatta-sujāta-vatsāḥ /
saṁgrāmajid-bhadrajid-aśvajic ca śroṇaś ca śoṇaś ca sa-koṭikarṇaḥ // 16.88 //
Bhaddāli,[54] Bhadrāyaṇa, Sarpa-dāsa, Subhūti,[55] Go-datta, Sujāta, Vatsa, / Saṁgrāmajit, Bhadrajit, Aśvajit, Śrona and Śona Koṭikarna, // 16.88 //

---

[51] Again Aśvaghoṣa seems to be playing with the multiplicity of possible meanings of *nimitta*, which cannot mean the same here as in the series of verses from 16.53. The evident difficulty of dealing with the ambiguity of *nimitta* caused LC to amend *tan-nimittair* to *tad-vitarkair* ("by such thoughts"). EHJ retained *tan-nimittair*, translating "before the onslaught of such ideas." From 16.53, in contrast, EHJ translated *nimitta* as "subject of meditation."

[52] Kauṇḍinya (mentioned in SN3.13) was celebrated as one of the Buddha's ten great disciples, as were Aniruddha and Kātyāyana.

[53] This Nanda – not the protagonist of Saundarananda– was formerly a cowherd.

[54] A record of the Buddha's teaching addressed to Baddhāli is preserved in Pali in the Baddhāli Sutta.

[55] Subhūti was another of the Buddha's ten great disciples.

kṣemājito nandaka-nanda-mātāv upāli-vāgīśa-yaśo-yaśodāḥ /
mahāhvayo valkali-rāṣṭrapālau sudarśana-svāgata-meghikāś ca // 16.89 //
Kṣemā, Ajita, the mothers of Nandaka and Nanda, Upāli,[56] Vāgīśa, Yaśas, Yaśoda, / Mahāhvaya, Valkalin, Rāṣṭra-pāla, Sudarśana, Svāgata and Meghika, // 16.89 //

sa kapphinaḥ kāśyapa auruvilvo mahā-mahākāśyapa-tiṣya-nandāḥ /
pūrṇaś ca pūrṇaś ca sa pūrṇakaś ca śonāparāntaś ca sa pūrṇa eva // 16.90 //
Kapphina, Kāśyapa of Uruvilvā, the great Mahā-kāśyapa,[57] Tiṣya, Nanda, / Pūrṇa and Pūrṇa[58] as well as Pūrṇaka and Pūrṇa Śonāparānta, // 16.90 //

śāradvatīputra-subāhu-cundāḥ kondeya-kāpya-bhṛgu-kuṇṭhadhānāḥ /
sa-śaivalau revata-kauṣṭhilau ca maudgalya-gotraś ca gavāṁpatiś ca // 16.91 //
The son of Śāradvatī, Subāhu, Cunda, Kondeya, Kāpya, Bhṛgu, Kuṇṭha-dhāna, / Plus Śaivala, Revata and Kauṣṭhila, and he of the Maudgalya clan[59] and Gavām-pati // 16.91 //

yaṁ vikramaṁ yoga-vidhāv akurvaṁs tam eva śīghraṁ vidhivat kuruṣva /
tataḥ padaṁ prāpsyasi tair avāptaṁ [sukhāvṛtais] tvaṁ niyataṁ yaśaś ca // 16.92 //
Be quick to show the courage that they have shown in their practice, working to principle. / Then you will assuredly take the step that they took and will realise the splendor that they realized.[60] // 16.92 //

dravyaṁ yathā syat kaṭukaṁ rasena tac copayuktaṁ madhuraṁ vipāke /
tathaiva vīryaṁ kaṭukaṁ śrameṇa tasyārtha-siddhau madhuro vipākaḥ // 16.93 //
Just as a fruit may have flesh that is bitter to the taste and yet is sweet when eaten ripe, / So heroic effort,[61] through the struggle it involves, is bitter and yet, in accomplishment of the aim, its mature fruit is sweet. // 16.93 //

---

[56] Upāli was another of the Buddha's ten great disciples.

[57] The repetition of the *mahā* (great) underlines the importance of Mahā-kāśyapa, whose pre-eminence even among the ten great disciples, at the time of the Buddha's death, is described in the final canto of Buddhacarita (i.e. BC Canto 28, extant only in Tibetan and Chinese, not in Sanskrit).

[58] One of these two Pūrṇas is included in the list of the Buddha's ten great disciples.

[59] Maudgalyāyana (he of the Maudgalya clan) was another of the Buddha's ten great disciples. The two of the ten great disciples not mentioned on this list of 62 excellent individuals are Śāriputra and Ānanda.

[60] For the first five syllables of the fourth pāda, the palm-leaf manuscript has something like *sakhācattais tvaṃ* and the paper manuscript has *sakhvācattais tva*. EHJ admits that his restoration to *sukhāvṛtais tvaṃ* is little more than a stopgap. *Taiḥ... sukhāvṛtaiḥ* (= *sukha* + *avṛtaiḥ*) means something like "by those ease/happiness-filled ones." EHJ noted "In any case it must, I think, be a four-syllable compound in the instrumental plural, of which the first member is probably *sukha, sakhya, saṁkhya* ('reasoning power') or *satya*." At the translation stage, EHJ decided to omit the word altogether, the correct reading being "entirely uncertain."

[61] The meanings of *vīrya*, one of the six transcendent accomplishments (*pāramitā*), include manliness, valor, energy, and heroism. From here to the end of Canto 16, *vīrya* has been translated "directed energy."

vīryaṁ paraṁ kārya-kṛtau hi mūlaṁ vīryād-ṛte kā-cana nāsti siddhiḥ /
udeti vīryād iha sarva-saṁpan nirvīryatā cet sakalaś ca pāpmā // 16.94 //
Directed energy is paramount: for, in doing what needs to be done, it is the foundation; without directed energy there is no accomplishment at all; / All success in this world arises from directed energy - and in the absence of directed energy wrongdoing is rampant. // 16.94 //

alabdhasyālābho niyatam upalabdhasya vigamaḥ
tathaivātmāvajñā kṛpaṇam adhikebhyaḥ paribhavaḥ /
tamo nis-tejastvaṁ śruti-niyama-tuṣṭi-vyuparamo
nṛṇāṁ nir-vīryāṇāṁ bhavati vinipātaś ca bhavati // 16.95 //
No gaining of what is yet to be gained, and certain loss of what has been gained, / Along with low self-esteem, wretchedness, the scorn of superiors, / Darkness, lack of spirit, and the breakdown of learning, restraint and contentment: / For men without directed energy a great fall awaits. // 16.95 //

nayaṁ śrutvā śakto yad ayam abhivṛddhiṁ na labhate
paraṁ dharmaṁ jñātvā yad upari nivāsaṁ na labhate /
gṛhaṁ tyaktvā muktau yad ayam upaśāntiṁ na labhate
nimittaṁ kausīdyaṁ bhavati puruṣasyātra na ripuḥ // 16.96 //
When a capable person hears the guiding principle but realizes no growth, / When he knows the most excellent method but realizes no upward repose, / When he leaves home but in freedom realizes no peace: / The cause is the laziness in him and not an enemy. // 16.96 //

anikṣiptotsāho yadi khanati gāṁ vāri labhate /
prasaktaṁ vyāmathnan jvalanam araṇibhyāṁ janayati /
prayuktā yoge tu dhruvam upalabhante śrama-phalaṁ
drutaṁ nityaṁ yāntyo girim api hi bhindanti saritaḥ // 16.97 //
A man obtains water if he digs the ground with unflagging exertion, / And produces fire from fire-sticks by continuous twirling. / But those are sure to reap the fruit of their effort whose energies are harnessed to practice, / For rivers that flow swiftly and constantly cut through even a mountain. // 16.97 //

kṛṣṭvā gāṁ paripālya ca śrama-śatair aśnoti sasya-śriyaṁ
yatnena pravigāhya sāgara-jalaṁ ratna-śriyā krīḍati /
śatrūṇām avadhūya vīryam iṣubhir bhuṅkte narendra-śriyaṁ
tad vīryaṁ kuru śāntaye viniyataṁ vīrye hi sarva-rddhayaḥ // 16.98 //

After ploughing and protecting the soil with great pains, [a farmer] gains a bounteous crop of corn; / After striving to plumb the ocean's waters, [a diver] revels in a bounty of coral and pearls; / After seeing off with arrows the endeavor[62] of rival kings, [a king] enjoys royal dominion. / So direct your energy in pursuit of peace, for in directed energy, undoubtedly, lies all growth." // 16.98 //

saundaranande mahākāvya ārya-satya-vyākhyāno nāma ṣoḍaśaḥ sargaḥ // 16 //

The 16th Canto in the epic poem Handsome Nanda,
titled "Communicating the Noble Truths."[63]

[62] *Vīryam*, means endeavor or, again, directed energy. A successful king uses his own *vīryam* to see off the *vīryam* of a rival.

[63] The title of each of the last seven cantos of Saundarananda is suggestive of sitting practice itself. Hence *ārya-satya-vākhyāna* may be understood as describing sitting practice itself as "expressing/communicating the noble truths."

Canto 17: amṛtādhigamaḥ
Obtaining the Deathless Nectar

Introduction

Amṛta means undying, immortal; and hence, as a noun, the nectar of immortality - the sweet elixir which the denizens of heaven aspire to drink (SN3.8). *Adhi-√gam* means to find, discover, obtain; and so *adhigama* means obtaining, realizing, making one's own.

The deathless nectar has been mentioned already in several cantos of Saundarananda as a symbol of the eternal truth that the Buddha taught (SN3.10), like a prescription that saves a dying man (SN10.54), like a fearless refuge beyond aging and death (SN11.62), like an antidote that prevents all suffering (SN12.55), and again as exemption from suffering (SN14.44). In this canto, then, *amṛtādhigama*, "obtaining the deathless nectar," describes Nanda's success in winning the four fruits of dharma and making his own the Buddha's teaching of a remedy to end all suffering.

The philosophical appeal of the deathless nectar, in its deathless aspect, emerges in connection with the teaching of emptiness - viz. whatever happens via dependent arising is empty of its own self-existence. As such, what happens cannot be said to have a beginning or an end. Only after the penny of this teaching drops (in verse 21) is Nanda able, abandoning views grounded in self-existence, to get on the noble path towards winning the first fruit.

The other, more sensually appealing aspect of *amṛta* is that, as the heavenly nectar, its taste is so sweet that it is like pure liquid joy (SN13.1). That being so, Nanda's obtaining of the nectar represents the fulfilment of the Buddha's promises (SN12.25, SN16.93) that Nanda's bitter struggles, if he sticks to principle, will - as sure as night follows day - eventually bring the sweet taste of success.

Through the course of the canto, without referring to the ten fetters explicitly, Aśvaghoṣa describes how Nanda cuts through these ten fetters one by one, and thereby obtains the four noble fruits. The present canto thus seems to assume on the part of the reader familiarity with teachings like the ten fetters and four fruits, plus the seven limbs of awakening, the seven latent tendencies, and so on. To clarify these allusions and references to the ten, the fours and the sevens, along with the implicit distinction between conventional and world-transcending powers of knowing, pedantic and repetitive footnotes have been duly provided.

But what strikes one on reflection is that Aśvaghoṣa, while acknowledging the ten fetters and seven latent tendencies in his own description of Nanda's practice, does not record the Buddha setting forth these particular enumerations. Neither is the Buddha quoted as making the distinction between "conventional" or "world-transcending" - vital though the distinction evidently is between effort grounded or not grounded in emptiness. What Aśvaghoṣa puts into the mouth of the Buddha is primarily the four noble truths, with their eightfold practical path of *śīla*, *samādhi* and *prajñā*. In this light, I think, is the riddle of verse 60 solved.

athaivam ādeśita-tattva-mārgo nandas tadā prāpta-vimokṣa-mārgaḥ /
sarveṇa bhāvena gurau praṇamya kleśa-prahāṇāya vanaṁ jagāma // 17.1 //
Having thus had pointed out to him the path of what is, Nanda took that path of liberation.[1] / He bowed with his whole being before the Guru and, with a view to abandoning the afflictions, he made for the forest. // 17.1 //

tatrāvakāśaṁ mṛdu-nīla-śaṣpaṁ dadarśa śāntaṁ taru-ṣaṇḍa-vantam /
niḥśabdayā nimnagayopagūḍhaṁ vaiḍūrya-nīlodakayā vahantyā // 17.2 //
There he saw a clearing, a quiet glade, of soft deep-green grass, / Kept secret by a silent stream bearing water blue as beryl. // 17.2 //

sa pādayos tatra vidhāya śaucaṁ śucau śive śrīmati vṛkṣa-mūle /
mokṣāya baddhvā vyavasāya-kakṣāṁ paryaṅkam aṅkāvahitaṁ babandha // 17.3 //
Having washed his feet there, Nanda, by a clean, auspicious, and splendid tree-root, / Girded on the intention to come undone, and sat with legs fully crossed. // 17.3 //

ṛjuṁ samagraṁ praṇidhāya kāyaṁ kāye smṛtiṁ cābhimukhīṁ vidhāya /
sarvendriyāṇy ātmani saṁnidhāya sa tatra yogaṁ prayataḥ prapede // 17.4 //
Directing the whole body up, keeping thinking turned towards the body, / Integrating in his person all the senses, there he threw himself all-out into practice.[2] // 17.4 //

tataḥ sa tattvaṁ nikhilaṁ cikīrṣur mokṣānukūlāṁś ca vidhīṁś cikīrṣan /
jñānena lokyena śamena caiva cacāra cetaḥ-parikarma-bhūmau // 17.5 //
Wishing to practice, on that basis, the truth that has no gaps, and wishing to perform practices that would be favorable to release, / He moved, using conventional understanding[3] and stillness,[4] into the stage of readying of consciousness. // 17.5 //

---

[1] *Tattva-mārga*, the path of what is, or *vimokṣa-mārga*, the path of liberation, means the noble eightfold path, described by the Buddha in Canto 16 under the three headings of *śīla* (integrity), *prajñā* (wisdom), and *śama* (peace). This canto describes Nanda's progressing on that path all the way to the fourth fruit of dharma, the worthy state of the arhat.

[2] *Pra-ṇi-dhāya... vidhāya.... saṁ-ṇi-dhāya...* Putting in front (directing)... putting in order (keeping)... putting together (integrating)... The verb in each of the first three pādas is thus an absolutive form from √*dhā*, to put or place.

[3] *Jñānena lokyena.* EHJ noted that *lokya* is equivalent to *laukika* (of the world, mundane, ordinary, conventional; see verse 17), which in turn is eqivalent to *sāsrava* (still being possessed of the polluting influences, by which one is attached to saṁsāra). *Lokottara* ('world-transcending'; see verse 22) is equivalent to *anāsrava* (being free of pollutants). Describing *jñāna* as *lokya*, then, distinguishes such worldly knowing – or understanding at the level of conventional truth – from the sixth of the six transcendent powers of knowing (*abhijñāḥ*), which is the power to free the mind of polluting influences. Cf MMK24.8: *"The buddhas' teaching of dharma rests on two truths: the truth of the convenient fictions of the world [loka-saṃvṛti-satyaṃ], and ultimate truth."*

[4] EHJ noted further that possibly *śīlena* is to be understood here, since *śīla* also – like *prajñā* and *samādhi* – can be either *laukika* (worldly, i.e. practiced at the level of conventional truth) or *lokottara* (world-transcending, i.e. practiced at the level of ultimate truth). What also might be implicit, then, is that, before the penny of emptiness drops in verse 21, Nanda's threefold practice of *śīla, samādhi* and *prajñā* is able to progress only on the basis of conventional understanding. Cf MMK24.10: *"Ultimate truth is not taught without relying on the conventional. Without understanding of the ultimate truth, nirvāṇa* is not realized."

saṁdhāya dhairyaṁ praṇidhāya vīryaṁ vyapohya saktiṁ parigṛhya śaktim /
praśānta-cetā niyama-stha-cetāḥ svasthas tatobhūd viṣayeṣv anāsthaḥ // 17.6 //
By holding firm, keeping direction of energy to the fore, by cutting out clinging and garnering his energy, / With consciousness that was calmed and contained, he came back to himself and was not concerned about ends. // 17.6 //

ātapta-buddheḥ prahitātmano 'pi sv-abhyasta-bhāvād atha kāma-saṁjñā /
paryākulaṁ tasya manaś cakāra prāvṛṭsu vidyuj jalam āgateva // 17.7 //
Though his judgement had been tempered and his soul inspired, now a vestige of desire, arising out of habit, / Made his mind turbid – like lightning striking water in a monsoon. // 17.7 //

sa paryavasthānam avetya sadyaś cikṣepa tāṁ dharma-vighāta-kartrīm /
priyām api krodha-parīta-cetā nārīm ivodvṛtta-guṇāṁ manasvī // 17.8 //
Being instantly aware of incompatibilities, he saw off that authoress of the dharma's downfall, / As a man whose mind is seized by anger shoos away a loved but excitable woman, when he is trying to concentrate.[5] // 17.8 //

ārabdha-vīryasya manaḥ-śamāya bhūyas tu tasyākuśalo vitarkaḥ /
vyādhi-praṇāśāya niviṣṭa-buddher upadravo ghora ivājagāma // 17.9 //
Nanda re-directed his energy in order to still his mind, but as he did so an unhelpful thought reasserted itself, / As when, in a man intent on curing an illness, an acute symptom suddenly reappears. // 17.9 //

sa tad-vighātāya nimittam anyad yogānukūlaṁ kuśalaṁ prapede /
ārtāyanaṁ kṣīṇa-balo bala-sthaṁ nirasyamāno balināriṇeva // 17.10 //
To fend against that he turned skillfully to a different aspect, one favourable to his practice, / Like an enfeebled [prince] who seeks out a powerful protector when being overthrown by a mighty rival. // 17.10 //

puraṁ vidhāyānuvidhāya daṇḍaṁ mitrāṇi saṁgṛhya ripūn vigṛhya /
rājā yathāpnoti hi gām apūrvāṁ nītir mumukṣor api saiva yoge // 17.11 //
For just as, by laying out fortifications and laying down the rod of the law, by banding with friends and disbanding foes, / A king gains hitherto ungained land, that is the very policy towards practice of one who desires release. // 17.11 //

vimokṣa-kāmasya hi yogino 'pi manaḥ puraṁ jñāna-vidhiś ca daṇḍaḥ /
guṇāś ca mitrāṇy arayaś ca doṣā bhūmir vimuktir yatate yad artham // 17.12 //
Because, for a practitioner whose desire is release, the mind is his fortress, understanding is his rod, / The virtues are his friends, the faults are his foes; and liberation is the territory he endeavours to reach. // 17.12 //

---

[5] In SN16.76 Aśvaghoṣa uses *manasvin* in its primary sense of being full of mind, bright, intelligent. As a secondary sense, however, the dictionary gives "fixing the mind, attentive."

sa duḥkha-jālān mahato mumukṣur vimokṣa-mārgādhigame vivikṣuḥ /
panthānam āryaṁ paramaṁ didṛkṣuḥ śamaṁ yayau kiṁ-cid upātta-cakṣuḥ // 17.13 //
Desiring release from the great net of suffering; desiring to enter into possession of the pathways of release, / Desiring to experience the supreme noble path; he got a bit of the Eye,[6] and came to quiet. // 17.13 //

yaḥ syān niketas tamaso 'niketaḥ śrutvāpi tattvaṁ sa bhavet pramattaḥ /
yasmāt tu mokṣāya sa pātra-bhūtas tasmān manaḥ sv-ātmani saṁjahāra // 17.14 //
Heedless would be the unhoused man who, despite hearing the truth, housed the darkness of ignorance; / But since [Nanda] was a man of the bowl, a receptacle for liberation, he had collected his mind into himself. // 17.14 //

sambhārataḥ pratyayataḥ svabhāvād āsvādato doṣa-viśeṣataś ca /
athātmavān niḥsaraṇātmataś ca dharmeṣu cakre vidhivat parīkṣām // 17.15 //
On the grounds of their being held together, their causality, and their inherent nature, on the grounds of their flavor and their concrete imperfection, / And on the grounds of their tendency to spread out,[7] he who was now contained in himself,[8] carried out a methodical investigation into things.[9] // 17.15 //

sa rūpiṇaṁ kṛtsnam arūpiṇaṁ ca sāraṁ didṛkṣur vicikāya kāyam /
athāśuciṁ duḥkham anityam asvaṁ nirātmakaṁ caiva cikāya kāyam // 17.16 //
Desiring to examine its total material and immaterial substance, he investigated the body, / And he perceived the body to be impure, full of suffering, impermanent, without an owner, and again, devoid of self. // 17.16 //

anityatas tatra hi śūnyataś ca nirātmato duḥkhata eva cāpi /
mārga-pravekeṇa sa laukikena kleśa-drumaṁ saṁcalayāṁ cakāra // 17.17 //
For, on those grounds, on the grounds of impermanence and of emptiness, on the grounds of absence of self,[10] and of suffering, / He, by the most excellent among conventional paths,[11] caused the tree of afflictions to shake. // 17.17 //

---

[6] In general, the Dharma-Eye does not mean an organ of sight so much as it means an instrument of seeing, or means of realizing, the truth of the Buddha's dharma (see also verse 32).

[7] *Niḥsaraṇātmataś* (*niḥsaraṇātman* = tending to terminate / spread out + ablative suffix *taḥ*) can be understood as a description of impermanence, at the level of conventional truth – that is, at the level of the second law of thermodynamics (see MMK ch. 10 Exploring Fire & Fuel). EHJ, accepting Gawronski's conjecture, translated *niḥsaraṇātmakaś* (*niḥ-saraṇa* = going out, escaping + *ātmakaḥ* = being devoted to) so that the phrase described Nanda as "devoted to escape from being."

[8] The merit of being *ātmavān*, in possession of oneself, is referred to repeatedly in BC Canto 11. A hint of irony may be intended, however, in the suggestion that Nanda isn't yet at the stage of totally losing himself (cf. verses 20-21).

[9] The terminology here, especially the reference to inherent nature or self-existence (*svabhāva*), again, hints at effort on the basis of conventional truth, at which level things are studied as impermanent. At the level of ultimate truth, as Nāgārjuna will later clarify in detail, an empty happening cannot be said to have a starting point or an end, and so is neither permanent nor impermanent. *Dharmas*, in light of emptiness, are better translated as empty "happenings." But at the level of conventional truth, *dharmas* are still understood as impermanent "things."

[10] Is the suggestion that Nanda at this preparatory stage was still perceiving "things" like the body to

yasmād abhūtvā bhavatīha sarvaṁ bhutvā ca bhūyo na bhavaty avaśyam /
sa-hetukaṁ ca kṣayi-hetumac ca tasmād anityaṁ jagad ity avindat // 17.18 //
On the grounds that everything, not having happened, is now happening, and after happening it never happens again; / And the world is causal, and has waning as a cause, he understood on those grounds that the world is not permanent.[12] // 17.18 //

yataḥ prasūtasya ca karmayogaḥ prasajyate bandha-vighāta-hetuḥ /
duḥkha-pratīkāra-vidhau sukhākhye tato bhavaṁ duḥkham iti vyapaśyat // 17.19 //
Insofar as a creature's industry, motivated by bond-making or bond-breaking impulse, / Is dependent on a prescription, named "pleasure," for counteracting pain, he saw, on those grounds,[13] that existence is suffering. // 17.19 //

yataś ca saṁskāra-gataṁ viviktaṁ na kārakaḥ kaś-cana vedako vā /
samagryataḥ saṁbhavati pravṛttiḥ śūnyaṁ tato lokam imaṁ dadarśa // 17.20 //
Then, on the grounds that separateness comes from fabricating,[14] there being no doer or knower, / And the activity done happens holistically,[15] he realized, on those grounds, that this world is empty.[16] // 17.20 //

---

be empty, in theory, as opposed to witnessing as empty what was actually happening, as described in Verse 21?

[11] By EHJ's analysis, the meaning here of *laukika*, opposed to *lokottara* in verse 22, is that these efforts of Nanda's were prior to his winning the stage of a stream-enterer. *Laukika*, according to EHJ, is synonymous with *sāsrava*, being under the influence of unwittingness and other pollutants. Cf again MMK24.8-10 for Nāgārjuna's distinction between two truths, the conventional truth of the world (*loka-saṃvṛti-satyaṃ*) and ultimate truth (*satyaṃ ca paramārthataḥ*).

[12] The terminology in this verse is ambiguous, the ambiguity hinging on whether *bhavatīha* means existing now or happening now. Again, *anityaṁ jagad* could mean, at the level of conventional truth, "the world is impermanent," or could mean, in light of emptiness, "the world is beyond permanence [and impermanence]." If we didn't yet give Nanda the benefit of the doubt, the translation might be (as per the first edition): "*On the grounds that everything, after not existing, now exists, and after existing it never exists again; / And the world is causal, and has disappearance as a cause, he understood on those grounds that the world is impermanent.*"

[13] Does "on those grounds" (*tatas*) mean still on somewhat reductionist grounds, not on the grounds of emptiness?

[14] *Saṁskāra-gatam*. In BC Canto 14, Aśvaghoṣa describes the Buddha discovering that fabrications (*saṁskārāḥ*) born of ignorance are the causal grounds of divided consciousness, which in turn is both cause and effect of psycho-physicality. In this sense, separation (*viviktam*) comes from fabricating fabrications.

[15] EHJ notes that *samagrya* stands here for *sāmagrī* ("totality" [from *sam-agra*]) "which is the regular word for the complex of causes and conditions in the teaching of dependent arising." *Sāmagrī-parīkṣa*, "Exploring Totality," is, in some editions, the title of MMK ch. 20, where Nāgārjuna refutes the view of a totality of causes and conditions, on the grounds of emptiness. In this verse, however, *samagryataḥ* is used as an adverb – Nanda is not seeing anything as a non-empty "totality." It sounds like he is getting there.

[16] Bingo?

yasmān nirīhaṁ jagad asvatantraṁ naiśvaryam ekaḥ kurute kriyāsu /
tat-tat-pratītya prabhavanti bhāvā nirātmakaṁ tena viveda lokam // 17.21 //
Since the throng of humanity is passive, not autonomous, and no one exercises direct control over the workings of the body, / But happenings happen, dependent on this and that, he witnessed, in that way, that the world is devoid of self.[17]// 17.21 //

tataḥ sa vātaṁ vyajanād ivoṣṇe kāṣṭhāśritaṁ nirmathanād ivāgnim /
antaḥ-kṣiti-sthaṁ khananād ivāmbho lokottaraṁ vartma durāpam āpa // 17.22 //
Then, like air in the hot season, got from fanning; like fire latent in wood, got from rubbing; / And like water under the ground, got from digging, that world-transcending[18] path which is hard to reach, he reached: // 17.22 //

saj-jñāna-cāpaḥ smṛti-varma baddhvā viśuddha-śīla-vrata-vāhana-sthaḥ /
kleśāribhiś citta-raṇājira-sthaiḥ sārdhaṁ yuyutsur vijayāya tasthau // 17.23 //
As a bow of true knowledge, clad in the armour of thinking in activity, standing up in a chariot of pure conduct and vows of practice,[19] / He took his stance for victory, ready to engage in battle his enemies, the afflictions, who were ranged on the battlefield of his mind. // 17.23 //

tataḥ sa bodhy-aṅga-śitātta-śastraḥ samyak-pradhānottama-vāhana-sthaḥ /
mārgāṅga-mātaṅga-vatā balena śanaiḥ śanaiḥ kleśa-camūṁ jagāhe // 17.24 //
Then, unsheathing a sword that the limbs of awakening[20] had honed, standing in the supreme chariot of true motivation, / With an army containing the elephants of the branches of the path,[21] he gradually penetrated the ranks of the afflictions. // 17.24 //

---

[17] Bingo! This is the gist of the teaching of *pratītya-samutpāda*, for the clarification of which Nāgārjuna wrote his *mūla-madhyamaka-kārikā*. The wording here seems to suggest a phase change – such that "non-self" is no longer just a doctrine, the penny of emptiness having dropped.

[18] *Lokottara* (*loka + uttara*) is given in SED as "excelling or surpassing the world, beyond what is common or general, unusual, extraordinary." Here the world-transcending path in question is the first of the four world-transcending paths, viz: 1. the path to the fruit of the stream-enterer; 2. the path to the fruit of the once-returner; 3. the path to the fruit of not returning; 4. the path to the fruit of arhathood. What is significant, in light of Nāgārjuna's extolling of the practical implications of emptiness, is that Nanda is here able to get on the world-transcending path precisely by dint of those practical implications of emptiness (*śūnyatārthaṃ*; MMK24.7). What Nāgārjuna will later make explicit, particularly via the distinction in MMK ch. 24 between conventional and ultimate truth, seems to be implicit here.

[19] The three elements in the first half of the verse, again, represent the noble eightfold path's three sub-categories of 1. *prajñā* and 2. *samādhi*, based in 3. *śīla*. Cf Appendix DN16.

[20] The seven limbs of awakening are 1. *dharma-pravicaya,* investigation of happenings, 2. *vīrya*, manly endeavor, directed energy, 3. *prīti*, joy, 4 *praśrabdhi*, confidence, 5. *upekṣā*, equanimity, 6. *samādhi,* balanced stillness, 7. *smṛti,* thinking in activity.

[21] The eight branches of the path, as enumerated by the Buddha in SN16.30-37, are 1. *samyag-vāk-karma*, using the voice well, 2. *samyak-kāya-karma*, using the body well 3. *samyag-ājiva*, making one's living well, 4. *samyag-dṛṣṭi*, seeing straight, proper insight (into the four noble truths), 5. *samyag-vitarka*, thinking straight, 6. *samyag-parākrama*, fully taking initiative, 7. *samyak-smṛti*, true thinking in activity, 8. *samyak-samādhi*, true practice of balanced stillness.

sa smṛty-upasthāna-mayaiḥ pṛṣatkaiḥ śatrūn viparyāsa-mayān kṣaṇena /
duḥkhasya hetūṁś caturaś caturbhiḥ svaiḥ-svaiḥ pracārāyatanair dadāra // 17.25 //
With arrows made from abodes of thinking in activity,[22] instantly he shot those enemies whose substance is upside-down-ness: / He split apart four enemies, four causes of suffering, with four arrows, each having its own range. // 17.25 //

āryair balaiḥ pañcabhir eva pañca cetaḥ-khilāny apratimair babhañja /
mithyāṅga-nāgāṁś ca tathāṅga-nāgair vinirdudhāvāṣṭabhir eva so 'ṣṭau // 17.26 //
With the five incomparable noble powers,[23] he broke five uncultivated areas of mental ground;[24] / And with the eight true[25] elephants which are the branches of the path, he drove away eight elephants of fakery. // 17.26 //

athātma-dṛṣṭiṁ sakalāṁ vidhūya caturṣu satyeṣv akathaṁkathaḥ san /
viśuddha-śīla-vrata-dṛṣṭa-dharmo dharmasya pūrvāṁ phala-bhūmim āpa // 17.27 //
And so, having shaken off every vestige of the personality view, being free of doubt in regard to the four truths, / And knowing the score in regard to pure conduct and vows of practice, he attained the first fruit of dharma.[26] // 17.27 //

---

[22] *Smṛty-upasthāna. Upasthāna* (from *upa-√sthā*, to stand or place one's self near, to be present) means 1. the act of placing one's self near to, coming into the presence of, waiting on, attendance; 2. abiding, and hence a place of abiding, an abode. In Chinese (see Shōbōgenzō chap. 73) *smṛty-upasthāna* was rendered 念住, "thought-abode" – hence 四念住 "the four thought-abodes." In Sanskrit the four abodes of thinking are 1. *kāya-smṛtyupasthāna*, 2. *vedanā-smṛtyupasthāna*, 3. *citta-smṛtyupasthāna*, and 4. *dharma-smṛtyupasthāna* – body, feeling, mind, and happenings as an abode of thinking. In the Pali Mahā-sati-paṭṭhāna-suttaṁ (DN 22), the section on the body describes a monk who dwells reflecting on the body in the body (*kāye kāyānupassī viharati*), and similarly for feelings, for the mind, and for happenings – so that the body, feelings, mind and happenings are the object not of thinking but rather of reflecting (*anupassī*). Thinking (*sati*) is mentioned primarily in connection with directing the body up (*ujuṁ kāyaṁ paṇidhāya*), having placed thinking to the fore (*parimukhaṁ satiṁ upaṭṭhapetvā*).

[23] *Pañca balāḥ*, the five powers, are 1. *ṣraddhā*, confidence, 2. *vīrya*, manly endeavor, directed energy, 3. *smṛti*, awareness/vigilance/mindfulness, 4, *samādhi*, practicing stillness, 5. *prajñā*, understanding.

[24] *Pañca cetaḥ-khilāni*, "the five obstructions of the mind" [EHJ] or "the five barren places of the mind" [LC], are, according to a note by LC, four kinds of doubt, concerning 1. Buddha, 2. Dharma, 3. Saṁgha, and 4. Vinaya; and 5. anger. *Khila* means a piece of waste or uncultivated land situated between cultivated fields, bare soil.

[25] EHJ comments that Aśvaghoṣa is here using *tathā* as an adjective, as in Pali.

[26] Ten fetters – five lower fetters and five upper fetters – are said to tie us to the wheel of saṁsāra and impede our progress on the four world-transcending paths of the stream-enterer, once-returner, no-returner and arhat. Attainment of stream-entry is associated with the cutting of three of the five lower fetters, namely: 1. the personality view, 2. doubting, and 3. clinging to good habits and vows of practice. The three elements of this verse describe cutting of those three lower fetters. Hence *viśuddha-śīla-vrata-dṛṣṭa-dharma* is opposed to *śīla-vratopadanna*, clinging to good conduct (*śīla*) and vows of practice (*vrata*).

sa darśanād ārya-catuṣṭayasya kleśaika-deśasya ca viprayogāt /
pratyātmikāc cāpi viśeṣa-lābhāt pratyakṣato jñāni-sukhasya caiva // 17.28 //
By glimpsing the noble foursome, and by being released from one portion of the afflictions; / By realising for himself what was specific to him as well as by witnessing the ease of the sages; // 17.28 //

dārḍhyāt prasādasya dhṛteḥ sthiratvāt satyeṣv asaṁmūḍhatayā caturṣu /
śīlasya cācchidratayottamasya niḥsaṁśayo dharma-vidhau babhūva // 17.29 //
Through the stability of his stillness and the constancy of his steadiness; through not being altogether bewildered about the four truths; / And through not being full of holes in the supreme practice of integrity, he became free of doubt in the truth of dharma.[27] // 17.29 //

ku-dṛṣṭi-jālena sa viprayukto lokaṁ tathā-bhūtam avekṣamāṇaḥ /
jñānāśrayāṁ prītim upājagāma bhūyaḥ prasādaṁ ca gurāv iyāya // 17.30 //
Released from the net of a pernicious view, seeing the world as it happened, / He attained a joy pregnant with understanding and his quiet certainty in the Guru deepened all the more. // 17.30 //

yo hi pravṛttiṁ niyatām avaiti naivānya-hetor iha nāpy ahetoḥ /
pratītya tat-tat samavaiti tat-tat sa naiṣṭhikaṁ paśyati dharmam āryam // 17.31 //
For he who understands that the doing in this world is determined neither by any outside cause nor by no cause, / And who appreciates everything depending on everything: he sees the ultimate noble dharma. // 17.31 //

śāntaṁ śivaṁ nir-jarasaṁ virāgaṁ niḥśreyasaṁ paśyati yaś ca dharmam /
tasyopadeṣṭāram athārya-varyaṁ sa prekṣate buddham avāpta-cakṣuḥ // 17.32 //
And he who sees as the greatest good the dharma that is peaceful, salutary, ageless, and free of the red taint of passion, / And who sees its teacher as the noblest of the noble: he, as one who has got the Eye, is meeting Buddha. // 17.32 //

yathopadeśena śivena mukto rogād arogo bhiṣajaṁ kṛta-jñaḥ /
anusmaran paśyati citta-dṛṣṭyā maitryā ca śāstra-jñatayā ca tuṣṭaḥ // 17.33 //
When a healthy man has been freed from illness by salutary instruction, and he is aware of his debt of gratitude, / Just as he sees his healer in his mind's eye, gratefully acknowledging his benevolence and knowledge of his subject, // 17.33 //

āryeṇa mārgeṇa tathaiva muktas tathāgataṁ tattva-vid ārya-tattvaḥ /
anusmaran paśyati kāya-sākṣī maitryā ca sarva-jñatayā ca tuṣṭaḥ // 17.34 //
Exactly so is a witness to reality who, set free by the noble path, is the reality of what is noble: / His body being a seeing Eye,[28] he sees the Realized One, gratefully acknowledging his benevolence and all-knowingness. // 17.34 //

---

[27] Again, the suggestion is of real effort on the noble eightfold path under its three headings of *samādhi*, *prajñā* and *śīla*. Nanda's cutting of fetter no. 2, the fetter of doubt, was more than an effort of intellectual understanding or a gaining of book knowledge.

sa nāśakair dṛṣṭi-gatair vimuktaḥ paryantam ālokya punar-bhavasya /
bhaktvā ghṛṇāṁ kleśa-vijṛmbhiteṣu mṛtyor na tatrāsa na dur-gatibhyaḥ // 17.35 //
Sprung free from pernicious theories, seeing an end to becoming, / And feeling horror for the consequences of affliction, [Nanda] trembled not at death or hellish realms. // 17.35 //

tvak-snāyu-medo-rudhirāsthi-māṁsa-keśādināmedhya-gaṇena pūrṇam /
tataḥ sa kāyaṁ samavekṣamāṇaḥ sāraṁ vicintyāṇv api nopalebhe // 17.36 //
As full of skin, sinew, fat, blood, bone, and flesh; as full of hair and a mass of other such unholy stuff, / [Nanda] then observed the body to be; he looked into its essential reality, and found not even an atom. // 17.36 //

sa kāmarāga-pratighau sthirātmā tenaiva yogena tanū cakāra /
kṛtvā mahoraska-tanus tanū tau prāpa dvitīyaṁ phalam ārya-dharme // 17.37 //
By the yoke of that same practice,[29] he, firm in himself, minimized the duality of love and hate; / Being himself big across the chest, he made those two small, and so obtained the second fruit in the noble dharma.[30] // 17.37 //

sa lobha-cāpaṁ parikalpa-bāṇaṁ rāgaṁ mahā-vairiṇam alpa-śeṣam /
kāya-svabhāvādhigatair bibheda yogāyudhāstrair aśubhā-pṛṣatkaiḥ // 17.38 //
A small vestige of the great enemy, red passion, whose straining bow is impatient desire and whose arrow is a fixed conception, / He destroyed using darts of the unglamorous, weapons from the armory of practice mastered via the self-existence of bodies. // 17.38 //

dveṣāyudhaṁ krodha-vikīrṇa-bāṇaṁ vyāpādam antaḥ-prasavaṁ sapatnam /
maitrī-pṛṣatkair dhṛti-tūṇa-saṁsthaiḥ kṣamā-dhanurjyā-visṛtair jaghāna // 17.39 //
That gestating love-rival, malice, whose weapon is hatred and whose errant arrow is anger, / He slayed with the arrows of friendliness, which are contained in a quiver of constancy and released from the bow-string of patience. // 17.39 //

---

[28] *Kāya-sākṣī. Sākṣin* is defined as "seeing with the eyes, witnessing." So the emphasis here, again, is practical. Nanda's getting on the noble path by cutting the first fetter – "self-view" or egotism – was a matter not of intellectual recognition but of realization in practice.

[29] *Tenaiva yogena* means "by that very/same *yoga*." *Yoga* means practice and at the same time a yoke as a device that causes two to be one. Does "that same practice," then, refer to the fact that Nanda is still just sitting in lotus, letting it happen? Does letting sitting happen like this include all eight branches of the path, compared in verses 24 & 26 to war elephants? And is the implicit suggestion that when this sitting is fully informed with the teaching of dependent arising, only then can emptiness make workable the cutting of the fetters of love and hate? (Cf MMK24.14: "*For whom emptiness is workable, everything is workable.*")

[30] The fourth and fifth of the lower five fetters that bind a person to the nether regions of saṁsāra are 4. desire for sensual pleasure and 5. ill will. One who has cut the first three fetters and reduced sense desire and ill will to a minimum is said to have attained the second fruit, thus being subject to only one more return to the lower realms of saṁsāra. One who has completely cut all five lower fetters is said to have attained the third fruit of the dharma, as a non-returner. So this verse again accords with the ancient teaching of four fruits and ten fetters, saying that Nanda had reduced love and hate to manageable proportions, but that – like the citizens of Kapilavāstu described in SN3.39 – he had not yet completely cut lower fetters no. 4 and 5.

mūlāny atha trīṇy aśubhasya vīras tribhir vimokṣāyatanaiś cakarta /
camū-mukha-sthān dhṛta-kārmukāṁs trīn arīn ivāris tribhir āyasāgraiḥ // 17.40 //
And so the hero cut the three roots of sin[31] using three seats of release, / As if three rival princes, bearing bows in the van of their armies, had been cut down by one prince using three metal points.[32]// 17.40 //

sa kāma-dhātoḥ samatikramāya pārṣṇi-grahāṁs tān abhibhūya śatrūn /
yogād anāgāmi-phalaṁ prapadya dvārīva nirvāṇa-purasya tasthau // 17.41 //
In order to go entirely beyond the sphere of desire, he overpowered those enemies that grab the heel, / So that he attained, because of practice, the fruit of not returning,[33] and stood as if at the gateway to the citadel of nirvāṇa. // 17.41 //

kāmair viviktaṁ malinaiś ca dharmair vitarkavac cāpi vicāravac ca /
viveka-jaṁ prīti-sukhopapannaṁ dhyānaṁ tataḥ sa prathamaṁ prapede // 17.42 //
Distanced from desires and tainted happenings, containing ideas and containing thoughts, / Born of seclusion and possessed of joy and ease, is the first stage of meditation, which he then entered.[34] // 17.42 //

kāmāgni-dāhena sa vipramukto hlādaṁ paraṁ dhyāna-sukhād avāpa /
sukhaṁ vigāhyāpsv iva gharma-khinnaḥ prāpyeva cārthaṁ vipulaṁ daridraḥ // 17.43 //
Released from the burning of the bonfire of desires, he derived great gladness from ease in the act of meditating – / Ease like a heat-exhausted man diving into water. Or like a pauper coming into great wealth. // 17.43 //

tatrāpi tad-dharma-gatān vitarkān guṇāguṇe ca prasṛtān vicārān /
buddhvā manaḥ-kṣobha-karān aśāntāṁs tad-viprayogāya matiṁ cakāra // 17.44 //
Even in that, he realized, ideas about aforesaid happenings, and thoughts about what is or is not good, / Are something not quieted, causing disturbance in the mind, and so he decided to cut them out. // 17.44 //

---

[31] *Tri-mulāni aśubhasya,* the three roots of sin, are greed, hatred and delusion.

[32] As investigated in BC Canto 13, *āyasa* means made of iron or of metal. In that canto, the metal in question, since it is described as fire-colored, might be gold. If similar hidden meaning is sought in this verse, the three points might be the base of the pyramid in which one person's golden sitting is contained. (Nanda, after all, was described back in verse 3 as sitting in the full lotus posture, and there has been no mention so far of him breaking that posture.)

[33] He attained the third of the four fruits of dharma, the stage of the non-returner, synonymous with complete freedom from fetters 1-5.

[34] Cf Arāḍa in BC12.49: *"Then he arrives at a stage secluded from desires, and also from things like malice; / He reaches the stage born of seclusion – the first dhyāna, in which there is thinking." //SN12.49//* In general, the following description of the four dhyānas corresponds closely to the description which Aśvaghoṣa attributes to the sage Arāḍa in BC Canto 12.

kṣobhaṁ prakurvanti yathormayo hi dhīra-prasannāmbu-vahasya sindhoḥ /
ekāgra-bhūtasya tathormi-bhūtāś cittāmbhasaḥ kṣobha-karā vitarkāḥ // 17.45 //
For, just as waves produce disturbance in a river bearing a steady flow of tranquil water, / So ideas, like waves of thought, disturb the water of the one-pointed mind. // 17.45 //

khinnasya suptasya ca nirvṛtasya bādhaṁ yathā saṁjanayanti śabdāḥ /
adyātmam aikāgryam upāgatasya bhavanti bādhāya tathā vitarkāḥ // 17.46 //
And just as noises are a source of bother to one who is weary, and fallen fast asleep, / So do ideas become bothersome to one who has come to inner one-pointedness. // 17.46 //

athāvitarkaṁ kramaśo 'vicāram ekāgra-bhāvān manasaḥ prasannam /
samādhi-jaṁ prīti-sukhaṁ dvitīyaṁ dhyānaṁ tad-ādhyātma-śivaṁ sa dadhyau // 17.47 //
And so gradually bereft of idea and thought, his mind tranquil from one-pointedness, / He realized the joy and ease born of balanced stillness – that inner wellbeing which is the second stage of meditation. // 17.47 //

tad-dhyānam āgamya ca citta-maunaṁ lebhe parāṁ prītim alabdha-pūrvām /
prītau tu tatrāpi sa doṣa-darśī yathā vitarkeṣv abhavat tathaiva // 17.48 //
And on reaching that stage, in which the mind is silent,[35] he experienced an intense joy that he had never experienced before. / But here too he found a fault, in joy, just as he had in ideas. // 17.48 //

prītiḥ parā vastuni yatra yasya viparyayāt tasya hi tatra duḥkham /
prītāv ataḥ prekṣya sa tatra doṣān prīti-kṣaye yogam upāruroha // 17.49 //
For when a man finds intense joy in anything, paradoxically, suffering for him is right there. / Hence, seeing the faults there in joy, he kept going up, into practice that goes beyond joy. // 17.49 //

prīter virāgāt sukham ārya-juṣṭaṁ kāyena vindann atha saṁprajānan /
upekṣakaḥ sa smṛti-mān vyahārṣid dhyānaṁ tṛtīyaṁ pratilabhya dhīraḥ // 17.50 //
And so experiencing the ease enjoyed by the noble ones, from non-attachment to joy, knowing it totally, with his body, / He remained indifferent, fully aware, and, having realized the third stage of meditation, steady. // 17.50 //

yasmāt paraṁ tatra sukhaṁ sukhebhyas tataḥ paraṁ nāsti sukha-pravṛttiḥ /
tasmād babhāṣe śubha-kṛtsna-bhūmiṁ parāpara-jñaḥ parameti maitryā // 17.51 //
Since the ease here is beyond any ease, and there is no progression of ease beyond it, / Therefore, as a knower of higher and lower, he realized it as a condition of resplendent wholeness[36] which he deemed – in a friendly way – to be superlative. // 17.51 //

---

[35] EHJ notes that *citta-mauna* seems to be the equivalent of Pāḷi *mano-moneyya.*

[36] In BC12.55, the sage Arāḍa describes the third dhyāna as a condition of ease experienced as one with Śubha-kṛtsna deities *(śubha-kṛtsnaiḥ... daivataiḥ)*, the Gods of Resplendent Wholeness.

dhyāne 'pi tatrātha dadarśa doṣaṁ mene paraṁ śāntam aniñjam eva /
ābhogato 'pīñjayati sma tasya cittaṁ pravṛttaṁ sukham ity asram // 17.52 //
Then, even in that stage of meditation, he found a fault: he saw it as better to be quiet, not excited, / Whereas his mind was fluctuating tirelessly because of ease circulating. // 17.52 //

yatreñjitaṁ spanditam asti tatra yatrāsti ca spanditam asti duḥkham /
yasmād atas tat-sukham iñjakatvāt praśānti-kāmā yatayas tyajanti // 17.53 //
In excitement there is interference, and where there is interference there is suffering, / Which is why, insofar as ease is excitatory, devotees who are desirous of quiet give up that ease. // 17.53 //

atha prahāṇāt sukha-duḥkhayoś ca mano-vikārasya ca pūrvam eva /
dadhyāv upekṣā-smṛtimad viśuddhaṁ dhyānaṁ tathāduḥkha-sukhaṁ caturtham // 17.54 //
Then, having let go already of ease and suffering, and emotional reactivity,[37] / He realized the lucidity in which there is transcendence and full awareness: thus, beyond suffering and ease, is the fourth stage of meditation. // 17.54 //

yasmāt tu tasmin na sukhaṁ na duḥkhaṁ jñānaṁ ca tatrāsti tad-artha-cāri /
tasmād upekṣā-smṛti-pāriśuddhir nirucyate dhyāna-vidhau caturthe // 17.55 //
Since in this there is neither ease nor suffering, and the act of knowing abides here, being its own object, / Therefore utter lucidity through transcendence and awareness is specified in the protocol for the fourth stage of meditation. // 17.55 //

dhyānaṁ sa niśritya tataś caturtham arhattva-lābhāya matiṁ cakāra /
saṁdhāya mitraṁ balavantam āryaṁ rājeva deśān ajitān jigīṣuḥ // 17.56 //
Consequently, relying on the fourth stage of meditation, he made up his mind to win the worthy state,[38] / Like a king joining forces with a strong and noble ally and then aspiring to conquer unconquered lands.[39] // 17.56 //

---

[37] *Mano-vikāra* is translated by EHJ as "alteration of mind." The meanings of *vikāra* include change of form [as in the contorted postures of the women in BC Canto 5], alteration or deviation from any natural state, change (especially for the worse) of bodily or mental condition, disease, emotion, agitation.

[38] *Arhattva*, "the worthy state," means the fourth fruit, arhathood.

[39] EHJ wrote (in the Introduction to his translation of Buddhacarita) that he found it puzzling that Aśvaghoṣa elevated dhyāna into the area of 'supramundane' (or world-transcending) practice in the stage of the third fruit of the dharma, immediately prior to attainment of arhatship: *"In Canto 17, after the aspirant has reached the supramundane path, he acquires successively the three stages of the srotāpanna, sakṛdāgāmin and anāgāmin, and it is only thereafter that the four trances are described and they are said to be the immediate precursors of Arhatship. But [SN16.1], in accordance with the view generally prevailing in the schools, shows that the trances are mastered in a preliminary stage before the process of bhāvanā begins; and that they are even accessible to non-Buddhists is the regular belief, which Buddhacarita Canto 12 shows Aśvaghoṣa to share."* If what EHJ describes as "the view generally prevailing in the schools" had prevailed in Aśvaghoṣa's time, Aśvaghoṣa certainly would not have felt bound by that view. He might have felt a duty to falsify such a view, perhaps on the grounds that what in the view of scholars is linear and neatly arranged is in practice circular, or spirallic, or cyclical, and not neatly arranged at all but rather (like Aśvaghoṣa's poetry) full of *variously*

ciccheda kārtsnyena tataḥ sa pañca prajñāsinā bhāvanayeritena /
ūrdhvaṁ gamāny uttama-bandhanāni saṁyojanāny uttama-bandhanāni // 17.57 //
Then he cut the five upper fetters: with the sword of wisdom which is wielded by letting it happen, / He completely severed the five aspirational fetters, which are bound up with superiority, and tied to the first person.[40] // 17.57 //

bodhy-aṅga-nāgair api saptabhiḥ sa saptaiva cittānuśayān mamarda /
dvipān ivopasthita-vipraṇāśān kālo grahaiḥ saptabhir eva sapta // 17.58 //
Again, with the seven elephants of the limbs of awakening[41] he crushed the seven underlying tendencies[42] of the mind, / Like Time, when their destruction is due, crushing the seven continents by means of the seven planets. // 17.58 //

---

interwoven strands (SN10.20). So that in the end there might be no hard and fast dividing line between meditating (i.e. progressing through the dhyānas that EHJ calls "the trances") and letting happen (*bhāvanā*). That said, the point might be implicit in this canto that the effectiveness of non-doing practice of letting happen ultimately depends on, or follows from, the wisdom of emptiness. In that sense, is it the case that *dhyāna* can be practised grounded or not grounded in emptiness, whereas *bhāvana* – as a letting happen – can only really work with understanding of emptiness? What is for sure is that a misconstrued difference between *dhyāna* and *bhāvana* remained a source of confusion for me even after the first edition of this translation was published. I continued to associate *dhyāna* with the practice called in China 坐禅, sitting-dhyāna, that is, just sitting. *Bhāvana* seemed to refer to a different practice involving cultivation of positive emotions such that monks trained in Tibet like Mathieu Ricard were able at will to produce gamma waves that went off the charts. It was only after I studied MMK and the Rāhula Sutta that the penny dropped that *bhāvana*, when understood to mean letting happen, was just what the ancient Chinese masters transmitted as the non-doing practice of 坐禅. Though the 禅 of 坐禅 represents phonetically Sanskrit *dhyāna*, insofar as 坐禅 was the practice of just sitting – i.e. simply letting sitting happen – the ancient Chinese masters must have meant by 坐禅 no practice other than *bhāvana*, in which joy was inherent, even without being cultivated.

[40] An arhat or worthy one is one who has cut the ten fetters, the lower five of which bind the ordinary person, the stream-enterer and the once-returner to lower worlds, and the upper five of which bind the more advanced spiritual aspirant to more elevated realms. To recap, the five lower fetters are 1. personality view, 2. doubting, and 3. clinging to good conduct and vows of practice, along with 4. sensual desire, and 5. ill-will. The stream-enterer is free of fetters 1-3; the once-returner is also free of fetters 4-5 in their grosser form; the non-returner is fully free of all five of the lower fetters. Aśvaghoṣa in this verse refers to the five upper (or aspirational) fetters *(pañca ūrdhvaṁ gamāni saṃyojanāni)*, which remain for the would-be arhat to cut. They are namely: 6. undue interest in outward forms/appearances *(rūpa-rāga;* i.e. material ambition), 7. undue interest in what does not have form (*arūpa-rāga;* i.e. spiritual ambition, end-gaining desire for higher consciousness, knowledge etc.), 8. conceit, 9. restlessness, and 10. ignorance/unwittingness. In describing these five upper fetters, Aśvaghoṣa repeats the phrase *uttama-bandhanāni,* and this repetition led EHJ to think that the text might be suspect. But perhaps Aśvaghoṣa was playing with the ambiguity of *uttama*, which as an adjective means uppermost or highest, and as a noun means "the last person" – i.e. the first person singular. Relevant here is the cautionary tale that Dōgen quotes in Shōbōgenzō of the bhikṣu who, having realized the fourth dhyāna, was tripped up by conceit. See Shōbōgenzō chap. 90, *Shizen-biku*, "The Monk who Mistook the Fourth Dhyāna."
[ERRATA: In the first edition, translating *bhāvanayeritena* in the 1st line as "raised aloft by cultivation of the mind" rather blotted out this suggestion of the need for humility. Translating *bhāvanayā* "by letting it happen" helps to bring out this meaning, because, as has been said, in the work of allowing, as opposed to doing it ourselves, "humility has to be our middle name."]

[41] The seven limbs of awakening are as per verse 24. To recap, they are: investigation of happenings, energy, joy, confidence, equanimity/transcendence, balanced stillness, and thinking in activity.

agni-drumājyāmbuṣu yā hi vṛttiḥ kavandha-vāyv-agni-divākarāṇām /
doṣeṣu tāṁ vṛttim iyāya nando nirvāpaṇotpāṭana-dāha-śoṣaiḥ // 17.59 //
The action which on fire, trees, ghee and water is exerted by rainclouds, wind, a flame and the sun, / Nanda exerted that action on the faults, quenching, uprooting, burning, and drying them up. // 17.59 //

iti tri-vegaṁ tri-jhaṣaṁ tri-vicam ekāmbhasaṁ pañca-rayaṁ dvi-kūlam /
dvi-grāham aṣṭāṅgavatā plavena duḥkhārṇavaṁ dus-taram uttatāra // 17.60 //
Thus he overcame three surges, three sharks, three swells, the unity of water, five currents, two shores, / And two crocodiles: in his eight-piece raft, he crossed the flood of suffering which is so hard to cross.[43] // 17.60 //

arhattvam āsādya sa sat-kriyārho nirutsuko niṣpraṇayo nirāśaḥ /
vibhīr viśug vītamado virāgaḥ sa eva dhṛtyānya ivābabhāse // 17.61 //
Having attained to the seat of arhathood, he was worthy of being served. Without ambition, without partiality, without expectation; / Without fear, sorrow, pride, or passion; while being nothing but himself, he seemed in his constancy to be different. // 17.61 //

bhrātuś ca śāstuś ca tayānuśiṣṭyā nandas tataḥ svena ca vikrameṇa /
praśānta-cetāḥ paripūrṇa-kāryo vāṇīm imām ātmagatāṁ jagāda // 17.62 //
And so Nanda, who, through the instruction of his brother and teacher and through his own valiant effort, / Had quieted his mind and fulfilled his task, spoke to himself these words: // 17.62 //

namo 'stu tasmai sugatāya yena hitaiṣiṇā me karuṇātmakena /
bahūni duḥkhāny apavartitāni sukhāni bhūyāṁsy upasaṁhṛtāni // 17.63 //
"Praise be to him, the Sugata, the One Gone Well, through whose compassionate pursuit of my welfare, / Great agonies were turned away and greater comforts conferred. // 17.63 //

ahaṁ hy anāryeṇa śarīra-jena duḥkhātmake vartmani kṛṣyamāṇaḥ /
nivartitas tad-vacanāṅkuśena darpānvito nāga ivāṅkuśena // 17.64 //
For while being dragged, by ignoble physicality, down a path pregnant with suffering, / I was turned back by the hook of his words, like an elephant in musk by a driver's hook. // 17.64 //

---

[42] *Anuśaya* is as per SN15.5 – "*An underlying tendency persists in those [desires], like a fire covered over with ashes.*" To recap, the seven tendencies are: craving for love, resentment, holding views, doubt, conceit, craving for becoming and ignorance/denial.

[43] The point might be that the eightfold path is a means for overcoming any number and all kinds of obstacles, including both all-smothering religious oneness (the water), and dualism (the crocodiles). At the same time, the verse brings to mind the teaching of Zen Master Dōgen, who in Shōbōgenzō chap. 73 *Sanjushichi-bon-bodai-bunbo*, "The 37 Things On the Side of Bodhi," went through the seven limbs, eight branches, four abodes, five powers, and so on, one by one, and then concluded the chapter by saying that we should consign all of them to oblivion, by just sitting.

tasyājñayā kāruṇikasya śāstur hṛdi-stham utpāṭya hi rāga-śalyam /
adyaiva tāvat su-mahat sukhaṁ me sarva-kṣaye kiṁ-bata nirvṛtasya // 17.65 //
For through the liberating knowledge[44] of the compassionate teacher who extracted a dart of passion that was lodged in my heart, / Now such abundant ease is mine – Oh! how happy I am in the loss of everything! // 17.65 //

nirvāpya kāmāgnim ahaṁ hi dīptaṁ dhṛty-ambunā pāvakam ambuneva /
hlādaṁ paraṁ sāṁpratam āgato 'smi śītaṁ hradaṁ gharma ivāvatīrṇaḥ // 17.66 //
For, by putting out the burning fire of desires, using the water of constancy, as if using water to put out a blaze, / I have now come to a state of supreme refreshment, like a hot person descending into a cool pool. // 17.66 //

na me priyaṁ kiṁ-cana nāpriyaṁ me na me 'nurodho 'sti kuto virodhaḥ /
tayor abhāvāt sukhito 'smi sadyo himātapābhyām iva viprayuktaḥ // 17.67 //
Nothing is dear to me, nor offensive to me. There is no liking in me, much less disliking. / From those two not happening, I am enjoying the moment, like one immune to cold and heat. // 17.67 //

mahā-bhayāt kṣemam ivopalabhya mahāvarodhād iva vipramokṣam /
mahārṇavāt pāram ivāplavaḥ san bhīmāndhakārād iva ca prakāśam // 17.68 //
Like gaining safety after great danger; like gaining release after long imprisonment; / Like having no boat and yet gaining the far shore, after a mighty deluge; and like gaining clarity, after fearful darkness; // 17.68 //

rogād ivārogyam asahya-rūpād ṛṇād ivānṛṇyam ananta-saṁkhyāt /
dviṣat-sakāśād iva cāpayānaṁ durbhikṣa-yogāc ca yathā subhikṣam // 17.69 //
Like gaining health out of incurable illness, relief from immeasurable debt, / Or escape from an enemy presence; or like gaining, after a famine, plentiful food: // 17.69 //

tadvat parāṁ śāntim upāgato 'haṁ yasyānubhāvena vināyakasya /
karomi bhūyaḥ punar uktam asmai namo namo 'rhāya tathāgatāya // 17.70 //
Thus have I come to utmost quiet, through the majesty of the teacher. / Again and repeatedly I do homage to him: Homage, homage to the Worthy One, the Realised One! // 17.70 //

yenāhaṁ girim upanīya rūkma-śṛṅgaṁ svargaṁ ca plavaga-vadhū-nidarśanena /
kāmātmā tridiva-carībhir aṅganābhir niṣkṛṣṭo yuvati-maye kalau nimagnaḥ // 17.71 //
By him I was taken to the golden-peaked mountain, and to heaven, where, with the example of the she-monkey, / And by means of the women who wander the triple heaven, I who was a slave to love, sunk in girl-filled strife, was lifted up and out. // 17.71 //

---

[44] The metaphor of the surgeon who is able to remove a deeply-lodged dart or splinter seems to point to the primary sense of *ājñā* as deep knowledge or liberating knowledge. *Ājñā* can also mean order, command, or unlimited power, full autonomy.

tasmāc ca vyasana-parād anartha-paṅkād utkṛṣya krama-śithilaḥ karīva paṅkāt / śānte 'smin virajasi vijvare viśoke saddharme vitamasi naiṣṭhike vimuktaḥ // 17.72 //
From that extreme predicament, from that worthless mire, up he dragged me, like a feeble-footed elephant from the mud, / To be released into this quieted, dustless, feverless, sorrowless, ultimate true reality, which is free from darkness.[45] // 17.72 //

taṁ vande param anukampakaṁ maharṣim
mūrdhnāhaṁ prakṛti-guṇa-jñam āśaya-jñam /
saṁbuddhaṁ daśa-balinaṁ bhiṣak-pradhānaṁ
trātāraṁ punar api cāsmi saṁnatas tam // 17.73 //
I salute the great supremely compassionate Seer, bowing my head to him, the knower of types, the knower of hearts, / The fully awakened one, the holder of the ten powers, the best of healers, the deliverer: again, I bow to him. // 17.73 //

mahākāvye saundaranande 'mṛtādhigamo nāma saptadaśaḥ sargaḥ // 17 //
The 17th Canto in the epic poem Handsome Nanda, titled "Obtaining the Deathless Nectar."

---

[45] The darkness of ignorance, or unwittingness, is listed as the final fetter in the list of ten fetters. In Aśvaghoṣa's account of the Buddha's enlightenment, also, in BC Canto 14, full awakening is described as synonymous with the ending of ignorance.

Canto 18: ājñā-vyākaraṇaḥ
Knowing & Affirming

Introduction

Ājñā means 1. the highest knowledge, the deepest knowledge, knowledge of liberation; and 2. order, command, authority, unlimited power. *Vyākaraṇa* is an *-na* neuter action noun from *vy-ā-√kṛ,* which means 1. to expound, explain, declare, and 2. to predict or prophesy. Related to this latter definition, *vyākaraṇa* is one of the nine divisions of the teaching. This category of *vyākaraṇa* is generally understood to contain the Buddha's predictions of the future enlightenment of his followers. In Chinese, however, *vyākaraṇa* was rendered as 授記 (*juki*); and in Shōbōgenzō Dōgen explains these two characters not in terms of future time but as a real event. Hence, rather than Giving a Prophecy, 授記 is better translated in Shōbōgenzō as Giving Affirmation. Following this line of thinking, then, the canto title *ājñā-vyākaraṇaḥ* might be translated "Giving Affirmation of Deep Knowledge" or, in short, "Affirming of Knowing."

In EH Johnston's canto title "The Declaration of Insight," however, the reading of *vyākaraṇa* mirrors the usage of *vyākaraṇa* in verse 21, where Nanda does indeed declare his own insight. Again, Linda Covill's translation "His Instructions Revealed" reflects the conventional understanding of *vyākaraṇa* in which the Buddha himself is the one who does the revealing.

Thus, in view of the ambiguity of both *ājñā* and *vyākaraṇa*, it seems likely that, as in so many previous cantos, a two-word compound was chosen that might save us from the sin of certainty. "Knowing/Affirming" might come closer to conveying the real cloud of un-knowing that, ironically, Aśvaghoṣa may have had it in mind to suggest.

atha dvijo bāla ivāpta-vedaḥ kṣipraṁ vaṇik prāpta ivāpta-lābhaḥ /
jitvā ca rājanya ivārisainyaṁ nandaḥ kṛtārtho gurum abhyagacchat // 18.1 //
And so like a young initiate who mastered the Vedas, like a trader who turned a quick profit, / Or like a royal warrior who conquered a hostile army, a success, Nanda approached the Guru. // 18.1 //

draṣṭuṁ sukhaṁ jñāna-samāpti-kāle gurur hi śiṣyasya guroś ca śiṣyaḥ/
pariśramas te saphalo mayīti yato didṛkṣāsya munau babhūva // 18.2 //
For it is pleasant, at a time when wisdom has been fully realized, for teacher to see student, and for student to see teacher, / [Each thinking], "Your toil has rewarded me"; for which same reason the wish to see [Nanda] arose in the Sage. // 18.2 //

yato hi yenādhigato viśeṣas tasyottamāṅge 'rhati kartum iḍyām /
āryaḥ sarāgo 'pi kṛtajña-bhāvāt prakṣīṇamānaḥ kim-u vītarāgaḥ // 18.3 //
Thus is a noble person obliged to pay respect,[1] to his face,[2] to the one through whom he has acquired distinction. / Even a noble person who retains the taint of redness is so obliged, out of gratitude: How much more is one with no red taint, all pride having perished? // 18.3 //

---

[1] EHJ notes that *iḍyām* is a corruption here for *ijyām*, which occurs occasionally in Buddhist works in the sense of *pūjā* (honor, worship, respect).

yasyārtha-kāma-prabhavā hi bhaktis tato 'sya sā tiṣṭhati rūḍha-mūlā /
dharmānvayo yasya tu bhakti-rāgas tasya prasādo hṛdayāvagāḍhaḥ // 18.4 //
For when devotion springs from an agenda or desire, there it remains rooted; / But when a person has love and devotion for dharma, that person is steeped to the core in tranquility. // 18.4 //

kāṣāya-vāsāḥ kanakāvadātas tataḥ sa mūrdhnā gurave praṇeme/
vāteritaḥ pallava-tāmra-rāgaḥ puṣpojjvala-śrīr iva karṇikāraḥ // 18.5 //
And so, a glowing gold in his yellow-red robe, he bowed his head to the Guru / Like a *karnikāra* tree, with an outburst of ruddy shoots, and a glorious blaze of flowers, nodding in the wind. // 18.5 //

athātmanaḥ śiṣya-guṇasya caiva mahā-muneḥ śāstṛ-guṇasya caiva /
saṁdarśanārthaṁ sa na māna-hetoḥ svāṁ kārya-siddhiṁ kathayām babhūva // 18.6 //
Then, as a manifestation of his individual merit as a student and, indeed, of the great Sage's merit as a teacher, / And not out of pride, he described his own accomplishment of the work that has to be done: // 18.6 //

yo dṛṣṭi-śalyo hṛdayāvagāḍhaḥ prabho bhṛśaṁ mām atudat su-tīkṣṇaḥ /
tvad-vākya-saṁdaṁśa-mukhena me sa samuddhṛtaḥ śalya-hṛteva śalyaḥ // 18.7 //
"The splinter of a view,[3] that had penetrated to my core, O Mighty One, was paining me intensely, being very sharp; / Via the jaws of the pincers of your words - by means of a means and by way of a mouth[4] - it was pulled out of me, as a splinter is removed by a surgeon. // 18.7 //

kathaṁkathā-bhāva-gatosmi yena chinnaḥ sa niḥsaṁśaya saṁśayo me/
tvac-chāsanāt satpatham āgato 'smi sudeśikasyeva pathi pranaṣṭaḥ // 18.8 //
A doubt,[5] by which I fell into a state of hesitant questioning, O One Beyond Doubt, has been eradicated in me - / Through your teaching I have arrived at a true path like a straggler, under a good guide, getting on the road.[6] // 18.8 //

---

[2] *Uttamāṅge* (fr. *uttama* + *aṅga*) is lit. "to the highest part of the body."

[3] The cutting of ten fetters which was implicit in Aśvaghoṣa's account of Nanda's progress in Canto 17, is also implicit in Nanda's own account of his progress. The ten fetters, to recap, are: 1. personality view, 2. doubting, 3. clinging to virtue and vows; 4. sensual desire, 5. ill will, 6. concern for outward appearances, 7. concern for spiritual advancement, 8. conceit, 9. restlessness, and 10. ignorance. In this verse, then, Nanda describes the cutting in him of the first fetter, a view grounded in self.

[4] A play seems to be intended on the word *mukhena*: the meanings of *mukha* include 1. mouth, 2. tip (i.e. the jaw of a pincer) and 3. means.

[5] Describes cutting of fetter no. 2, doubting.

[6] Cutting of the fetter no. 3, clinging to virtue and vows, appears either to be understood, or else to be implicit in entry onto a true path.

yat pītam āsvāda-vaśendriyeṇa darpeṇa kandarpa-viṣaṁ mayāsīt /
tan me hataṁ tvad-vacanāgadena viṣaṁ vināśīva mahāgadena // 18.9 //
With senses ruled by relishing, I madly drank the drug of love;[7] / Its action was blocked in me by the antidote of your words, as a deadly poison is by a great remedy. // 18.9 //

kṣayaṁ gataṁ janma nirasta-janman saddharma-caryām uṣito 'smi samyak /
kṛtsnaṁ kṛtaṁ me kṛta-kārya kāryaṁ lokeṣu bhūto 'smi na loka-dharmā // 18.10 //
Rebirth is over, O Refuter of Rebirth! I am dwelling as one with observance of true dharma. / What was for me to do, O Doer of the Necessary! is totally done. I am happening in the world[8] without being of the world. // 18.10 //

maitrī-stanīṁ vyañjana-cāru-sāsnāṁ saddharma-dugdhāṁ pratibhāna-śṛṅgām /
tavāsmi gāṁ sādhu nipīya tṛptas tṛṣeva gām uttama vatsa-varṇaḥ // 18.11 //
Having drunk from the milk-cow of your voice, whose udder is the love of a friend, whose lovely dewlap is figures of speech, who is milked for true dharma, and whose horns are boldness of expression, / I am properly satisfied, O Most Excellent One, like a little calf that, because of thirst, has drunk milk.[9] // 18.11 //

yat paśyataś cādhigamo mamāyaṁ tan me samāsena mune nibodha /
sarva-jña kāmaṁ viditaṁ tavaitat svaṁ tūpacāraṁ pravivakṣur asmi // 18.12 //
And so, O Sage, hear from me in brief what, through seeing, I have made my own. / Though you know it anyway, O All-knowing One, still I wish to mention how I have worked on myself. // 18.12 //

anye 'pi santo vimumukṣavo hi śrutvā vimokṣāya nayaṁ parasya /
muktasya rogād iva rogavantas tenaiva mārgeṇa sukhaṁ ghaṭante // 18.13 //
For true freedom-loving people (however individual they are) when they hear of another person's plan that led to freedom / Will happily work at [freedom] via that same path, like sick men [hearing the plan] of one who became free from a disease. // 18.13 //

urvyādikān janmani vedmi dhātūn nātmānam urvyādiṣu teṣu kiṁ-cit /
yasmād atas teṣu na me 'sti saktir bahiś ca kāyena samā matir me // 18.14 //
In a birth, I perceive earth and the other elements, but in earth and those other elements, I perceive no self at all. / On that basis, there is no attachment in me to those elements; my orientation is equal with regard to my body and outside. // 18.14 //

---

[7] This verse can be read as relating to fetter no. 4, namely desire for sensual pleasure. Cutting of the fetter no. 5, ill will, is understood.

[8] *Lokeṣu* is locative plural. Therefore, more literally, "I am happening among the inhabitants of the world."

[9] This verse can be read as expressing freedom from fetters no. 6 and 7, which are manifestations, in material and spiritual spheres, of residual craving (*rāga*) or thirst (*tṛṣṇā*).

skandhāṁś ca rūpa-prabhṛtīn daśārdhān paśyāmi yasmāc capalān asārān /
anātmakāṁś caiva vadhātmakāṁś ca tasmād vimukto 'smy aśivebhya ebhyaḥ // 18.15 //
Again, the five constituents,[10] beginning with physicality, I see to be inconstant and without substance, / As well as unreal and life-negating; therefore I am free from those pernicious [constructs]. // 18.15 //

yasmāc ca paśyāmy udayaṁ vyayaṁ ca sarvāsv avasthāsv aham indriyāṇāṁ /
tasmād anityeṣu nirātmakeṣu duḥkheṣu me teṣv api nāsti saṁgaḥ // 18.16 //
Since I see for myself an arising and a vanishing in all situations in the realms of the senses, / Therefore, again, there is in me no clinging to those [aforementioned elements] which are impermanent, impersonal, and unsatisfactory. // 18.16 //

yataś ca lokaṁ sama-janma-niṣṭhaṁ paśyāmi niḥsāram asac ca sarvaṁ /
ato dhiyā me manasā vibaddham asmīti me neñjitam asti yena // 18.17 //
Again, on the grounds that I see the whole world as birth synonymous with death, as having no essential meaning and not being as it ought to be, / On these grounds, because of meditation, [the world] is bound fast by my mind in such a way that there is no flicker in me of 'I am.'[11] // 18.17 //

catur-vidhe naikavidha-prasaṁge yato 'ham āhāra-vidhāv asaktaḥ /
amūrcchitaś cāgrathitaś ca tatra tribhyo vimukto 'smi tato bhavebhyaḥ // 18.18 //
There is all manner of indulging in the four sorts of food, but since I am not attached to how I take food, / Since when it comes to food[12] I am not congealed or trussed up, I am free, on that score, from three kinds of becoming.[13] // 18.18 //

aniścitaś cāpratibaddha-citto dṛṣṭa-śrutādau vyavahāra-dharme /
yasmāt samātmānugataś ca tatra tasmād visaṁyoga-gato 'smi muktaḥ // 18.19 //
In the daily round of dharma-practice since I am neither certain about nor bound in mind to visual, auditory and other kinds of perception, / And since through that [dharma-round] I am graced by trailing equanimity, on that account I am detached and am free."[14] // 18.19 //

---

[10] *Skandha* means shoulder and hence part or (as in SN16.37) division. The five skandhas are *rūpa*, material form, physicality, or (as per SED) "the organized body"; *vedanā*, feeling; *saṁjñās*, perceptions; *saṁskārās*, fabrications, works of conditioning; *vijñāna*, consciousness. In agreement with the realization expressed here by Nanda, Nāgārjuna (MMK26.8) asserts that the five skandhas are just becoming.

[11] A series of verses in which Nanda seems to describe what is seen by the Dharma-Eye referred to in Canto 17, thus culminates with the association of seeing and sitting-meditation. Nanda sees what he sees because of meditating *(dhiyā)*. This verse can thus be seen as mirroring SN17.34. At the same time, it can be seen as expressing freedom from fetter no. 8, when that fetter is understood as "I am" conceit.

[12] *Tatra*, in that regard, i.e. in regard to food.

[13] Three kinds of becoming might mean three forms of fetter no. 9, which is restlessness or agitation. In the context of taking food in everyday life, the fetter might mean for example 1. the restlessness of impatient desire for food that is available, 2. the restlessness of dissatisfaction with food that is available, 3. the restlessness of envy for food that is not available.

[14] This seems to be an expression – again in terms of action in everyday life – of freedom from denial;

ity evam uktvā guru-bāhumānyāt sarveṇa kāyena sa gāṁ nipannaḥ /
praverito lohita-candanākto haimo mahā-stambha ivābabhāse // 18.20 //
After speaking thus, he prostrated himself on the ground with his whole body, out of deep appreciation for the Guru; / He looked like a great fallen column of gold tinged with red sandalwood. // 18.20 //

tataḥ pramādāt prasṛtasya pūrvaṁ śrutvā dhṛtiṁ vyākaraṇaṁ ca tasya /
dharmānvayaṁ cānugataṁ prasādaṁ meghasvaras taṁ munir ābabhāṣe // 18.21 //
Then, after listening to him who had emerged already out of heedlessness, after hearing his firmness and his testimony[15] / And a clarity consistent with the gist of dharma, the Sage boomed at him like a thundercloud: // 18.21 //

uttiṣṭha dharme sthita śiṣya-juṣṭe kiṁ pādayor me patito 'si murdhnā /
abhyarcanaṁ me na tathā praṇāmo dharme yathaiṣā pratipattir eva // 18.22 //
"You who stands firm in the dharma which is loved by those who study it, stand up! Why are you fallen with your head at my feet? / The prostration does not honor me so much as this surefootedness in the dharma. // 18.22 //

adyāsi su-pravrajito jitātmann aiśvaryam apy ātmani yena labdham /
jitātmanaḥ pravrajanaṁ hi sādhu calātmano na tv ajitendriyasya // 18.23 //
Today, conqueror of yourself, you have truly gone forth, since you have thereby gained sovereignty over yourself. / For in a person who has conquered himself, going forth has worked; whereas in an impulsive person whose senses remain unconquered, it has not. // 18.23 //

adyāsi śaucena pareṇa yukto vāk-kāya-cetāṁsi śucīni yat te /
ataḥ punaś cāprayatāṁ asaumyāṁ yat saumya no vekṣyasi garbha-śayyām // 18.24 //
Today you are possessed of purity of the highest order, in that your voice, body, and mind are untainted, / And in that, henceforward, my gentle friend, you will not again be confined in the ungentle womb of unready slumber.[16] // 18.24 //

---

in other words, from fetter no. 10, ignorance. In BC Canto 14, the Buddha's own full awakening is described as the ending of ignorance/unwittingness/denial.

[15] *Vyākaraṇam* is as per the canto title. But the usage of *vyākaraṇa* in this verse, to express Nanda's "detailed description" [SED], or testimony, is different from the conventional usage in which the Buddha is the agent of "prediction" or "prophecy" [SED], or affirmation.

[16] The palm-leaf manuscript has *garbha-śaryyāṁ*, which EHJ amended based on Shastri's conjecture, noting: "*Garbha-śayyā* ['abode/bed of the womb'] is so regular a phrase that I have not dared to keep the manuscript's interesting *garbha-śaryāṁ* with *śaryā* in the sense of 'night' and a possible pun of 'moonless' in *asaumyāṁ*." An alternative translation, then, is: *Today you are possessed of purity of the highest order, in that your voice, body, and mind are untainted, / And in that, henceforward, my moon-like friend, you will not again be confined in the womb of moonless night. //*

adyārthavat te śrutavac chrutaṁ tac chrutānurūpaṁ pratipadya dharmaṁ /
kṛta-śruto vipratipadyamāno nindyo hi nirvīrya ivāttaśastraḥ // 18.25 //
Listening [ears open] to the [truth] which is replete with listening, and with purpose, today you stand surefooted in the dharma, in a manner that befits the listening tradition. / For a man equipped with listening [ears] who is wavering is like a swordsman lacking valor: he is worthy of blame. // 18.25 //

aho dhṛtis te 'viṣayātmakasya yat tvaṁ matiṁ mokṣa-vidhāv akārṣīḥ /
yāsyāmi niṣṭhām iti bāliśo hi janma-kṣayāt trāsam ihābhyupaiti // 18.26 //
Ah! What firmness in you, who is a slave to objects no more, in that you have willed the means of liberation. / For, facing the end of existence in this world and thinking 'I will be finished,' it is a fool who gives in to a state of quivering anxiety. // 18.26 //

diṣṭyā durāpaḥ kṣaṇa-saṁnipāto nāyaṁ kṛto moha-vaśena moghaḥ /
udeti duḥkhena gato hy adhastāt kūrmo yugacchidra ivārṇavasthaḥ // 18.27 //
Happily, this meeting with the moment of opportunity, which is so hard to come by, is not being wasted under the sway of ignorance. / For a man who has been down goes up with difficulty, like a turtle to a hole in a yoke, in the foaming sea. // 18.27 //

nirjitya māraṁ yudhi durnivāram adyāsi loke raṇa-śīrṣa-śūraḥ /
śūro 'py aśūraḥ sa hi veditavyo doṣair amitrair iva hanyate yaḥ // 18.28 //
Having conquered Māra, who is so hard to stop in battle, today, at the forefront of the fight, you are a hero among men. / For even a hero is not recognized as a hero who is beaten by the foe-like faults. // 18.28 //

nirvāpya rāgāgnim udīrṇam adya diṣṭyā sukhaṁ svapsyasi vītadāhaḥ /
duḥkhaṁ hi śete śayane 'py udāre kleśāgninā cetasi dahyamānaḥ // 18.29 //
Today, having extinguished the flaming fire of redness, happily, you will sleep well, free of fever. / For even on a fabulous bed he sleeps badly who is being burned in his mind by the fire of afflictions. // 18.29 //

abhyucchrito dravya-madena pūrvam adyāsi tṛṣṇoparamāt samṛddhaḥ /
yāvat satarṣaḥ puruṣo hi loke tāvat samṛddho 'pi sadā daridraḥ // 18.30 //
You used markedly to be mad about possessions; today, because you have stopped thirsting, you are rich. / For as long as a man in the world thirsts, however rich he may be, he is always deprived. // 18.30 //

adyāpadeṣṭuṁ tava yukta-rūpaṁ śuddhodano me nṛ-patiḥ piteti /
bhraṣṭasya dharmāt pitṛbhir nipātād aślāghanīyo hi kulāpadeśaḥ // 18.31 //
Today you may fittingly proclaim that King Śuddhodana is your father. / For it is not commendable for a backslider, after falling from the dharma alighted on by ancestors, to proclaim his lineage. // 18.31 //

diṣṭyāsi śāntiṁ paramām upeto nistīrṇa-kāntāra ivāpta-sāraḥ /
sarvo hi saṁsāra-gato bhayārto yathaiva kāntāra-gatas tathaiva // 18.32 //
How great it is that you have reached the deepest tranquility, like a man making it through a wasteland and gaining possession of treasure. / For everybody in the flux of saṁsāra is afflicted by fear, just like a man in a wasteland. // 18.32 //

āraṇyakaṁ bhaikṣa-caraṁ vinītaṁ drakṣyāmi nandaṁ nibhṛtaṁ kadeti /
āsīt purastāt tvayi me didṛkṣā tathāsi diṣṭyā mama darśanīyaḥ // 18.33 //
'When shall I see Nanda settled, given over to the living of a forest bhikkhu's life?,' / So thinking, I had harbored from the start the desire to see you thus. What a wonderful sight you are for me to behold! // 18.33 //

bhavaty arūpo 'pi hi darśanīyaḥ sv-alaṁkṛtaḥ śreṣṭhatamai-guṇaiḥ svaiḥ /
doṣaiḥ parīto malinī-karais tu sudarśanīyo 'pi virūpa eva //18.34 //
For even an unlovely sort is a sight to behold when he is well-adorned with his own best features. / But a man who is full of the befouling faults, strikingly beautiful man though he may be, is truly ugly. //18.34 //

adya prakṛṣṭā tava buddhimattā kṛtsnaṁ yayā te kṛtam ātmakāryam /
śrutonnatasyāpi hi nāsti buddhir notpadyate śreyasi yasya buddhiḥ // 18.35 //
Developed in you today is the real wisdom by which you have done, totally, the work you had to do on yourself. / For even a highly educated man lacks wisdom, if wisdom fails to show in his practice of a better way. // 18.35 //

unmīlitasyāpi janasya madhye nimīlitasyāpi tathaiva cakṣuḥ /
prajñā-mayaṁ yasya hi nāsti cakṣuś cakṣur na tasyāsti sacakṣuṣo 'pi // 18.36 //
So it is with seeing, among people with eyes open and with eyes closed. / For when a man lacks sight that is packed with intuition, though he has eyes, the Eye is not present in him. // 18.36 //

duḥkha-pratīkāra-nimittam ārtaḥ kṛṣyādibhiḥ khedam upaiti lokaḥ /
ajasram āgacchati tac ca bhūyo jñānena yasyādya kṛtas tvayāntaḥ // 18.37 //
Struck by calamity, stung to do something to combat suffering, the world exhausts itself with work like ploughing; / And yet it is ceaselessly revisited by that [suffering], to which, using what you know, you today have put an end. // 18.37 //

duḥkhaṁ na me syāt sukham eva me syād iti pravṛttaḥ satataṁ hi lokaḥ /
na vetti tac caiva tathā yathā syāt prāptaṁ tvayādyāsulabhaṁ yathāvat // 18.38 //
People in the world are impelled ever forward by thinking 'There might be for me no hardship, just happiness....' / And yet [the world] does not know a means whereby that [happiness] might come to be – that rarely attained [happiness] which you today have properly realized." // 18.38 //

ity evam ādi sthira-buddhi-cittas tathāgatenābhihito hitāya /
staveṣu nindāsu ca nir-vyapekṣaḥ kṛtāñjalir vākyam uvāca nandaḥ // 18.39 //
While the Tathāgata told him this and more for his benefit Nanda remained firm in his judgement and thinking / And was indifferent to plaudits or criticisms. With hands joined, he spoke these words: // 18.39 //

aho viśeṣeṇa viśeṣa-darśiṁs tvayānukampā mayi darśiteyaṁ /
yat kāmapaṅke bhagavan nimagnas trāto 'smi saṁsāra-bhayād akāmaḥ //18.40 //
"Oh, how particular, O Seer of Particularities, is this compassion that you have shown to me! / Since I who was sunk, Glorious One, in the mire of love have been a reluctant refugee from the terror of saṁsāra. //18.40 //

bhrātrā tvayā śreyasi daiśikena pitrā phala-sthena tathaiva mātrā /
hato 'bhaviṣyaṁ yadi na vyamokṣyaṁ sārthāt paribhraṣṭa ivākṛtārthaḥ // 18.41 //
If not set free by you, a brother, a guide along a better way, a fruitful[17] father, and equally a mother, / I would be done for; like a straggler[18] dropped from a caravan, I would not have made it.[19] // 18.41 //

śāntasya tuṣṭasya sukho viveko vijñāta-tattvasya parīkṣakasya /
prahīṇa-mānasya ca nir-madasya sukhaṁ virāgatvam asakta-buddheḥ // 18.42 //
Seclusion is sweet for one who is pacified and contented, for an explorer who has discovered what is. / Again, for one who is sober and shorn of conceits, for one who is detached in his decision-making, dispassion is a pleasure.[20] // 18.42 //

ato hi tattvaṁ parigamya samyaṅ nirdhūya doṣān adhigamya śāntim /
svaṁ nāśramaṁ samprati cintayāmi na taṁ janaṁ nāpsaraso na devān // 18.43 //
And so, through squarely realising what is, through shaking off faults and coming to quiet, / I worry now neither about my own place, nor about the person there, nor about *apsarases*, nor about gods. // 18.43 //

idaṁ hi bhuktvā śuci śāmikaṁ sukhaṁ na me manaḥ kāṁkṣati kāmajaṁ sukham /
mahārham apy annam adaivatāhṛtaṁ divaukaso bhuktavataḥ sudhām iva // 18.44 //
For now that I have tasted this pure, peaceful happiness, my mind no longer hankers after happiness born of desires – / Just as the costliest earthly fare [cannot entice] a god who has supped the heavenly nectar. // 18.44 //

---

[17] *Phala-sthena* is also used in the sense of "fruitful" in SN6.43.
[18] *Akṛtārthaḥ* lit. means "one who was not successful."
[19] *Na vyamokṣyam* lit. means "I would not be set free."
[20] Nanda had freed his mind from the taint of unwittingness (*avidyāsrava*).

aho 'ndha-vijñāna-nimīlitaṁ jagat paṭāntare paśyati nottamaṁ sukham /
sudhīram adhyātma-sukhaṁ vyapāsya hi śramaṁ tathā kāma-sukhārtham ṛcchati // 18.45 //
Alas, the world has its eyes closed by blind unconsciousness; it does not see utmost happiness in a different robe. / Flinging away lasting inner happiness, it exhausts itself so, in pursuit of sensual happiness. // 18.45 //

yathā hi ratnākaram etya durmatir vihāya ratnāny asato maṇīn haret /
apāsya saṁbodhi-sukhaṁ tathottamaṁ śramaṁ vrajet kāma-sukhopalabdhaye // 18.46 //
For just as a fool, having made it to a jewel mine, might leave the jewels and carry off inferior crystals, / So would one reject the highest happiness of full awakening and struggle to gain sensual gratification.[21] // 18.46 //

aho hi sattveṣv atimaitra-cetasas tathāgatasyānujighṛkṣutā parā /
apāsya yad dhyāna-sukhaṁ mune paraṁ parasya duḥkhoparamāya khidyase // 18.47 //
Oh! high indeed, then, is the order of that desire to favour living beings which the Tathāgata has, overflowing with benevolence: / Since, O Sage, you throw away the highest-order happiness of meditation and are consumed by your effort to stop others suffering. //18.47 //

mayā nu śakyaṁ pratikartum adya kiṁ gurau hitaiṣiṇy anukampake tvayi /
samuddhṛto yena bhavārṇavād ahaṁ mahārṇavāc cūrṇita-naur ivormibhiḥ // 18.48 //
How today could I possibly repay you, my compassionate Guru whose desire is others' welfare, / By whom I was taken totally up and out of the foaming sea of becoming, like a man out of a great ocean when his boat is being battered by waves?"[22] // 18.48 //

tato munis tasya niśamya hetumat prahīṇa-sarvāsrava-sūcakaṁ vacaḥ /
idaṁ babhāṣe vadatām anuttamo yad arhati śrīghana eva bhāṣituṁ // 18.49 //
Then the Sage, hearing his well-founded words which signified the removal of all pollutants, / Voiced, as the Very Best of Speakers, these lines that none but a buddha, being 'Sheer Radiance,'[23] should voice: // 18.49 //

idaṁ kṛtārthaḥ paramārthavit kṛtī tvam eva dhīmann abhidhātum arhasi /
atītya kāntāram avāpta-sādhanaḥ su-daiśikasyeva kṛtaṁ mahāvaṇik // 18.50 //
"As a man of action who accomplished a task and who knows the ultimate task,[24] none but you, O crafty man!, should express this affirmation – / Like a great trader, having crossed a wasteland and got the goods, who affirms the work of a good guide. // 18.50 //

---

[21] Nanda had freed his mind from the taint of sensual desire (*kāmāsrava*).
[22] Nanda had freed his mind from the taint of becoming (*bhavāsrava*).
[23] EHJ noted that *śrīghana* was a very rare appellation for the Buddha and translated "spoke these words which were such as a Buddha Śrīghana should speak." The implicit principle is as expressed in Dōgen's favorite line from the Lotus Sutra 唯仏与仏乃能究尽諸法実相 "None but a buddha, together with a buddha, is able perfectly to realize that all happenings are reality."

avaiti buddhaṁ nara-damya-sārathiṁ kṛtī yathārhann upaśānta-mānasaḥ /
na dṛṣṭa-satyo 'pi tathāvabudhyate pṛthag-janaḥ kiṁ-bata buddhimān api // 18.51 //
An arhat, a man of action whose mind has come to quiet, knows the Buddha as a charioteer of human steeds who needed taming: / Not even a truth-seer appreciates the Buddha in this manner: how much less does an ordinary person, however intelligent he may be? // 18.51 //

rajas-tamobhyāṁ parimukta-cetasas tavaiva ceyaṁ sadṛśī kṛtajñatā /
rajaḥ-prakarṣeṇa jagaty avasthite kṛtajña-bhāvo hi kṛtajña durlabhaḥ // 18.52 //
This gratitude is fitting, again, in none but you whose mind has been liberated from the dust of the passions and from darkness. / For while dust prevails in the world, O man of gratitude! It is hard to find gratitude happening. // 18.52 //

sa-dharma dharmānvayato yataś ca te mayi prasādo 'dhigame ca kauśalam /
ato 'sti bhūyas tvayi me vivakṣitaṁ nato hi bhaktaś ca niyogam arhasi // 18.53 //
O possessor of dharma! Since, because of abiding by dharma, you have skill in making it your own and quiet confidence in me, / I have something else to say to you. For you are surrendered and devoted, and up to the task. // 18.53 //

avāpta-kāryo 'si paraṁ gatiṁ gato na te 'sti kiṁ-cit karaṇīyam aṇv api /
ataḥ paraṁ saumya carānukampayā vimokṣayan kṛcchra-gatān parān api // 18.54 //
Walking the transcendent walk, you have done the work that needed to be done: in you, there is not the slightest thing left to work on. / From now on, my friend, go with compassion, freeing up others who are pulled down into their troubles. // 18.54 //

ihārtham evārabhate naro 'dhamo vimadhyamas tūbhaya-laukikīṁ kriyām /
kriyām amutraiva phalāya madhyamo viśiṣṭa-dharmā punar apravṛttaye // 18.55 //
The lowest sort of man only ever sets to work for an object in this world. But a man in the middle does work both for this world and for the world to come. / A man in the middle, I repeat, works for a result in the future. The superior type, however, tends towards abstention from positive action. // 18.55 //

ihottamebhyo 'pi mataḥ sa tūttamo ya uttamaṁ dharmam avāpya naiṣṭhikam /
acintayitvātma-gataṁ pariśramaṁ śamaṁ parebhyo 'py upadeṣṭum icchati // 18.56 //
But deemed to be higher than the highest in this world is he who, having realized the supreme ultimate dharma, / Desires, without worrying about the trouble to himself, to teach tranquility to others. // 18.56 //

---

[24] *Paramārtha* is as in *paramārthataḥ*, the word that Nāgārjuna uses in distinguishing between conventional truth (*loka-saṃvṛti-satyam*) and ultimate truth (*satyaṃ ca paramārthataḥ*). In this verse, however, the Buddha's emphasis seems to be more practical than philosophical.

vihāya tasmād iha kāryam ātmanaḥ kuru sthirātman para-kāryam apy atho /
bhramatsu sattveṣu tamo-vṛtātmasu śruta-pradīpo niśi dhāryatām ayam // 18.57 //
Therefore forgetting the work that needs to be done in this world on the self, do now, stout soul, what can be done for others. / Among beings who are wandering in the night, their minds shrouded in darkness, let the lamp of this transmission be carried. // 18.57 //

bravītu tāvat puri vismito janas tvayi sthite kurvati dharma-deśanāḥ /
aho batāścaryam idaṁ vimuktaye karoti rāgī yad ayaṁ kathām iti // 18.58 //
Just let the astonished people in the city say, while you are standing firm, voicing dharma-directions, / 'Well! What a wonder this is, that he who was a man of passion is preaching liberation!' // 18.58 //

dhruvaṁ hi saṁśrutya tava sthiraṁ mano nivṛtta-nānā-viṣayair mano-rathaiḥ /
vadhūr gṛhe sāpi tavānukurvatī kariṣyate strīṣu virāgiṇīḥ kathāḥ // 18.59 //
Then, surely, when she hears of your steadfast mind with its chariots turned back from sundry objects, / Your wife following your example will also talk, to women at home, the talk of dispassion. // 18.59 //

tvayi parama-dhṛtau niviṣṭa-tattve bhavana-gatā na hi raṁsyate dhruvaṁ sā /
manasi śama-damātmake vivikte matir iva kāma-sukhaiḥ parīkṣakasya // 18.60 //
For, with you showing constancy of the highest order, getting to the bottom of what is, she surely will not enjoy life in the palace, / Just as the mind of an explorer does not enjoy sensual pleasures, when his mental state is tranquil and controlled, and his thinking is detached and distinct." // 18.60 //

ity arhataḥ parama-kāruṇikasya śāstur
mūrdhnā vacaś ca caraṇau ca samaṁ gṛhītvā /
svasthaḥ praśānta-hṛdayo vinivṛtta-kāryaḥ
pārśvān muneḥ pratiyayau vimadaḥ karīva // 18.61 //
Thus spoke the Worthy One, the instructor whose compassion was of the highest order, / Whose words and equally whose feet [Nanda] had accepted, using his head; / Then, at ease in himself, his heart at peace, his task ended, / He left the Sage's side like an elephant free of rut. // 18.61 //

bhikṣārthaṁ samaye viveśa sa puraṁ dṛṣṭīr janasyākṣipan
lābhālābha-sukhāsukhādiṣu samaḥ svasthendriyo nispṛhaḥ /
nirmokṣāya cakāra tatra ca kathāṁ kāle janāyārthine
naivonmārga-gatān parān paribhavann ātmānam utkarṣayan // 18.62 //
When the occasion arose he entered the town for begging and attracted the citizens' gaze; / Being impartial towards gain, loss, comfort, discomfort, and the like and with his senses composed, he was free of longing; / And being there, in the moment, he talked of liberation to people so inclined – / Never putting down others on a wrong path or raising himself up. // 18.62 //

ity eṣā vyupaśāntaye na rataye mokṣārtha-garbhā kṛtiḥ
śrotṛṇāṁ grahaṇārtham anya-manasāṁ kāvyopacārāt kṛtā /
yan mokṣāt kṛtam anyad atra hi mayā tat kāvya-dharmāt kṛtaṁ
pātuṁ tiktam ivauṣadhaṁ madhu-yutaṁ hṛdyaṁ kathaṁ syād iti // 18.63 //

This work is pregnant with the purpose of release: it is for cessation, not for titillation; / It is wrought out of the figurative expression of kāvya poetry in order to capture an audience whose minds are on other things – / For what I have written here not pertaining to liberation, I have written in accordance with the conventions of kāvya poetry. / This is through asking myself how the bitter pill might be made pleasant to swallow, like bitter medicine mixed with something sweet. // 18.63 //

prāyeṇālokya lokaṁ viṣaya-rati-paraṁ mokṣāt pratihataṁ
kāvya-vyājena tattvaṁ kathitam iha mayā mokṣaḥ param iti /
tad buddhvā śāmikaṁ yat tad avahitam ito grāhyaṁ na lalitaṁ
pāṁsubhyo dhātu-jebhyo niyatam upacitaṁ cāmīkaram iti // 18.64 //

Seeing, in general, that the world is moved primarily by fondness for objects and is repelled by liberation, / I for whom liberation is paramount have told it here like it is, using a *kāvya* poem as a pretext. / Being aware of the deceit, take from this [verb-rooted dust][25] what pertains to peace and not to idle pleasure. / Then elemental dust, assuredly, shall yield up abundant[26] gold. // 18.64 //

saundaranande mahākāvya ājñā-vyākaraṇo nāmaṣṭādaśaḥ sargaḥ //18//
The 18th canto in the epic poem Handsome Nanda, titled "Knowing & Affirming."

ārya-suvarṇākṣī-putrasya sāketakasya bhikṣor ācārya-bhadantāśvaghoṣasya
mahā-kaver mahā-vādinaḥ kṛtir iyam //

This is the work of a bhikkhu, the respected teacher Aśvaghoṣa of Saketa,
son of the noble Suvarṇākṣī, crafter of epic poetry and talker of the great talk.

---

[25] *Pāṃsubhyo dhātu-jebhyaḥ* in the fourth pāda – "*dhātu*-born dust" – contains a play on the word *dhātu*, which means "element" both in the sense of a primary element of the earth and also in the sense of a grammatical element, i.e. a verbal root or stem.

[26] EHJ notes that *upakara*, as per the original manuscript, is not met with elsewhere, nor is there any obvious amendment. The noun *upakāra* (from *upa-√kṛ*, to serve) means benefit, service, favour, use, advantage, and *upakāraṇa* means "doing a service." Hence LC translated *upakaraṃ cāmīkaram* as "serviceable gold." The shortening of a vowel to fit a verse's metre is very common in works that pre-dated Aśvaghoṣa, such as *Udāna-varga*, written in what is known as Buddhist Hybrid Sanskrit. But Aśvaghoṣa was the first known author to express the Buddha's teaching in pure classical Sanskrit, and such vowel shortening is not characteristic of his poetry. One possible amendment (possible in the sense that it fits the meter) is *upacitaṁ* (see BC2.56, SN16.71), which means "heaped up," "furnished in abundance," or in short "abundant."

Appendix 1
Mahā-Rāhulovāda-suttaṁ (MN 62)
The Long Discourse Giving Advice to Rāhula

Evaṁ me sutaṁ.
Thus have I heard:

Ekaṁ samayaṁ Bhagavā Sāvatthiyaṁ viharati
At one time the Glorious One was dwelling near Sāvatthī
Jeta-vane Anāthapiṇḍikassa ārāme.
at Anāthapiṇḍika's grounds in Jeta's Wood.
Atha kho Bhagavā pubbanha-samayaṁ nivāsetvā,
Then the Glorious One, having dressed in the morning time,
patta-cīvaraṁ ādāya Sāvatthiṁ piṇḍāya pāvisi.
and picked up his bowl and robe, entered Sāvatthī for alms.
Āyasmā pi kho Rāhulo pubbanha-samayaṁ nivāsetvā,
Venerable Rāhula also, having dressed in the morning time,
patta-cīvaraṁ ādāya Bhagavantaṁ piṭṭhito piṭṭhito anubandhi.
and picked up his bowl and robe, followed along close behind the Glorious One.

[Seeing What Happens, As Happening]

Atha kho Bhagavā apaloketvā āyasmantaṁ Rāhulaṁ āmantesi:
Then the Glorious One, looking back, addressed venerable Rāhula, saying:
"Yaṁ kiñci Rāhula rūpaṁ atītānāgata-paccuppannaṁ,
"Whatever physicality there is, Rāhula – past, yet to come, or now happening;
ajjhattaṁ vā bahiddhā vā, oḷārikaṁ vā sukhumaṁ vā,
inside or outside; gross or subtle;
hīnaṁ vā paṇītaṁ vā, yaṁ dūre santike vā sabbaṁ rūpaṁ:
base or excellent; far or near – all physicality that there is:
"Netaṁ mama, nesoham asmi, na meso attā" ti,
"It does not belong to a me. This doesn't mean I am. A self of mine, this is not."
evam etaṁ yathā-bhūtaṁ sammappaññāya daṭṭhabban"-ti.
It should be seen like this, with true wisdom, as happening."

"Rūpam eva nu kho Bhagavā? Rūpam eva nu kho Sugatā" ti.
"Only physicality, Glorious One? Only physicality, One Going Well?"

"Rūpam pi Rāhula, vedanā pi Rāhula, saññā pi Rāhula,
"Physicality, Rāhula; and feelings, Rāhula; and perceptions, Rāhula;
saṅkhārā pi Rāhula, viññāṇam pi Rāhulā" ti,
and fabrications, Rāhula; and consciousness, Rāhula."

Atha kho āyasmā Rāhulo: "ko najja
Then venerable Rāhula thinks: "Who today,
Bhagavatā sammukhā ovādena ovadito
when given face-to-face advice by the Glorious One,
gāmaṁ piṇḍāya pavisissatī?" ti
would enter a village for alms?"

Tato paṭinivattitvā aññatarasmiṁ rukkha-mūle nisīdi.
Therefore he turned back and sat at the root of a certain tree.
Pallaṅkaṁ ābhujitvā,
With legs folded crosswise,
ujuṁ kāyaṁ paṇidhāya, parimukhaṁ satiṁ upaṭṭhapetvā,
he directed his body up, having stationed thinking to the fore;
addasā kho āyasmā Sāriputto āyasmantaṁ Rāhulaṁ
and then venerable Sāriputta saw venerable Rāhula
aññatarasmiṁ rukkha-mūle nisinnaṁ pallaṅkaṁ ābhujitvā,
sitting at the root of a certain tree, legs folded crosswise,
ujuṁ kāyaṁ paṇidhāya parimukhaṁ satiṁ upaṭṭhapetvā,
directing his body up, with thinking stationed to the fore;
disvāna āyasmantaṁ Rāhulaṁ āmantesi,
and having seen venerable Rāhula, he addressed him, saying:

"Ānāpāna-satiṁ Rāhula bhāvanaṁ bhāvehi.
"Let happen, Rāhula, as a letting happen, thinking in the activity of breathing in & out.
Ānāpāna-sati Rāhula
Thinking in the activity of breathing in & out, Rāhula,
bhāvitā bahulī-katā
when allowed to happen, when made much of,
mahapphalā hoti mahāni-saṁsā" ti.
happens enormously fruitfully, with great benefits."

Atha kho āyasmā Rāhulo sāyanha-samayaṁ patisallānā vuṭṭhito
Then venerable Rāhula rising from seclusion in the evening time
yena Bhagavā tenupasaṅkami,
approached the Glorious One,
upasaṅkamitvā Bhagavantaṁ abhivādetvā ekam antaṁ nisīdi.
and after approaching and greeting the Glorious One, he sat to one side.
Ekam antaṁ nisinno kho āyasmā Rāhulo Bhagavantaṁ etad avoca:
While sitting to one side, venerable Rāhula said this to the Glorious One:
"Kathaṁ bhāvitā nu kho bhante ānāpāna-sati
"How, Sir, when thinking in the activity of breathing in & out is allowed to happen,
kathaṁ bahulī-katā
how when it is made much of,

mahapphalā hoti mahāni-saṁsā" ti.
does it happen enormously fruitfully, with great benefits?"

[The Elements]

"Yaṁ kiñci Rāhula ajjhattaṁ paccattaṁ
"Whatever there is, Rāhula, inside, of an individual,
kakkhalaṁ khari-gataṁ upādinnaṁ, seyyathīdaṁ:
that is taken hold of as hard, as solid - such as
kesā, lomā, nakhā, dantā, taco,
head hairs, body hairs, nails, teeth, skin,
maṁsaṁ, nahārū, aṭṭhī, aṭṭhimiñjā, vakkaṁ,
flesh, sinews, bones, bone-marrow, kidneys,
hadayaṁ, yakanaṁ, kilomakaṁ, pihakaṁ, papphāsaṁ,
heart, liver, pleura, spleen, lungs,
antaṁ, antaguṇaṁ, udariyaṁ, karīsaṁ
intestines, mesentery, undigested food, excrement -
yaṁ vā panaññam pi kiñci ajjhattaṁ paccattaṁ
or whatever else there is inside, of an individual,
kakkhalaṁ khari-gataṁ upādinnaṁ,
that is taken hold of as hard, as solid:
ayaṁ vuccati Rāhula ajjhattikā paṭhavī-dhātu.
this, Rāhula, is called the internal earth element.
Yā ceva kho pana ajjhattikā paṭhavī-dhātu,
Now, whatsoever is the internal earth element,
yā ca bāhirā paṭhavī-dhātu, paṭhavī-dhātur evesā.
and whatever is the external earth element, that is the same earth element.
Taṁ "netaṁ mama, nesoham asmi, na meso attā" ti,
Regarding that: "It does not belong to a me. This doesn't mean I am. A self of mine, this is not."
evam etaṁ yathā-bhūtaṁ sammappaññāya daṭṭhabbaṁ.
It should be seen like this, with true wisdom, as happening.
Evam etaṁ yathā-bhūtaṁ sammappaññāya disvā,
Having seen it like this, with true wisdom, as happening,
paṭhavī-dhātuyā nibbindati,
one loses interest in the earth element,
paṭhavī-dhātuyā cittaṁ virājeti.
one frees the mind from the red taint of desire for the earth element.
Katamā ca Rāhula āpo-dhātu?
And what, Rāhula, is the water-element?
Āpo-dhātu siyā ajjhattikā siyā bāhirā.
The water element may be internal or may be external.
Katamā ca Rāhula ajjhattikā āpo-dhātu?
And what, Rāhula, is the internal water element?

Yaṁ ajjhattaṁ paccattaṁ āpo āpo-gataṁ upādinnaṁ, seyyathīdaṁ:
Whatever there is inside, of an individual, that is taken hold of as water, as wet - such as
pittaṁ, semhaṁ, pubbo, lohitaṁ, sedo, medo,
bile, phlegm, pus, blood, sweat, oil,
assu, vasā, khelo, siṅghānikā, lasikā, muttaṁ,
tears, grease, spit, mucus, synovial fluid, urine,
yaṁ vā panaññam pi kiñci ajjhattaṁ paccattaṁ
or whatever else there is that is inside, of an individual,
āpo āpogataṁ upādinnaṁ,
that is taken hold of as water, as wet:
ayaṁ vuccati Rāhula ajjhattikā āpo-dhātu.
that, Rāhula, is called the internal water element.
Yā ceva kho pana ajjhattikā āpo-dhātu,
Now, whatsoever is the internal water element,
yā ca bāhirā āpo-dhātu, āpo-dhātur evesā.
and whatever is the external water element, that is the same water element.
Taṁ "netaṁ mama, nesoham asmi, na meso attā" ti,
Regarding that: "It does not belong to a me. This doesn't mean I am. A self of mine, this is not."
evam etaṁ yathā-bhūtaṁ sammappaññāya daṭṭhabbaṁ.
It should be seen like this, with true wisdom, as happening.
Evam etaṁ yathā-bhūtaṁ sammappaññāya disvā,
Having seen it like this, with true wisdom, as happening,
āpo-dhātuyā nibbindati,
one loses interest in the water element,
āpo-dhātuyā cittaṁ virājeti.
one frees the mind from the red taint of desire for the water element.

Katamā ca Rāhula tejo-dhātu?
And what, Rāhula, is the fire element?
Tejo-dhātu siyā ajjhattikā siyā bāhirā.
The fire element may be internal or may be external.
Katamā ca Rāhula ajjhattikā tejo-dhātu?
And what, Rāhula, is the internal fire element?
Yaṁ ajjhattaṁ paccattaṁ tejo tejo-gataṁ upādinnaṁ, seyyathīdaṁ:
Whatever there is inside, of an individual, that is taken hold of as fire, as fiery - such as
yena ca santappati, yena ca jīrīyati, yena ca pariḍayhati,
that by which one warms up, by which one grows old, by which one is consumed,
yena ca asita-pīta-khāyita-sāyitaṁ sammā pariṇāmaṁ gacchati,
and that by which what is eaten, drunk, chewed, and tasted, gets completely digested -
yaṁ vā panaññam-pi kiñci ajjhattaṁ paccattaṁ
or whatever else there is inside, of an individual,
tejo tejo-gataṁ upādinnaṁ,
that is taken hold of as fire, as fiery:

ayaṁ vuccati Rāhula ajjhattikā tejo-dhātu.
that, Rāhula, is called the internal fire element.
Yā ceva kho pana ajjhattikā tejo-dhātu,
Now, whatsoever is the internal fire element,
yā ca bāhirā tejo-dhātu, tejo-dhātur evesā.
and whatever is the external fire element, that is the same fire element.
Taṁ "netaṁ mama, nesoham asmi, na meso attā" ti,
Regarding that: "It does not belong to a me. This doesn't mean I am. A self of mine, this is not."
evam etaṁ yathā-bhūtaṁ sammappaññāya daṭṭhabbaṁ.
It should be seen like this, with true wisdom, as happening.
Evam etaṁ yathā-bhūtaṁ sammappaññāya disvā,
Having seen it like this, with true wisdom, as happening,
tejo-dhātuyā nibbindati,
one loses interest in the fire element,
tejo-dhātuyā cittaṁ virājeti.
one frees the mind from the red taint of desire for the fire element.

Katamā ca Rāhula vāyo-dhātu?
And what, Rāhula, is the wind element?
Vāyo-dhātu siyā ajjhattikā siyā bāhirā.
The wind element may be internal or may be external.
Katamā ca Rāhula ajjhattikā vāyo-dhātu?
And what, Rāhula, is the internal wind element?
Yaṁ ajjhattaṁ paccattaṁ vāyo vāyo-gataṁ upādinnaṁ, seyyathīdaṁ:
Whatever is inside, of an individual, that is taken hold of as wind, as windy – such as
uddhaṅgamā vātā, adhogamā vātā, kucchisayā vātā,
winds that go up, winds that go down, winds in the bowels,
koṭṭhasayā vātā, aṅgamaṅgānusārino vātā, assāso, passāso iti -
winds in the belly, winds that go through the limbs, in-breath, out-breath -
yaṁ vā panaññam-pi kiñci ajjhattaṁ paccattaṁ
or whatever else there is inside, of an individual,
vāyo vāyogataṁ upādinnaṁ,
that is taken hold of as wind, as windy:
ayaṁ vuccati Rāhula ajjhattikā vāyo-dhātu.
that, Rāhula, is called the internal wind element.
Yā ceva kho pana ajjhattikā vāyo-dhātu,
Now, whatsoever is the internal wind element,
yā ca bāhirā vāyo-dhātu, vāyo-dhātur evesā.
and whatever is the external wind element, that is the same wind element.
Taṁ "netaṁ mama, nesoham asmi, na meso attā" ti,
Regarding that: "It does not belong to a me. This doesn't mean I am. A self of mine, this is not."
evam etaṁ yathā-bhūtaṁ sammappaññāya daṭṭhabbaṁ.
It should be seen like this, with true wisdom, as happening.

Evam etaṁ yathā-bhūtaṁ sammappaññāya disvā,
Having seen it like this, with true wisdom, as happening,
vāyo-dhātuyā nibbindati,
one loses interest in the wind element,
vāyo-dhātuyā cittaṁ virājeti.
one frees the mind from the red taint of desire for the wind element.

Katamā ca Rāhula ākāsa-dhātu?
And what, Rāhula, is the space element?
Ākāsa-dhātu siyā ajjhattikā siyā bāhirā.
The space element may be internal or may be external.
Katamā ca Rāhula ajjhattikā ākāsa-dhātu?
And what, Rāhula, is the internal space element?
Yaṁ ajjhattaṁ paccattaṁ ākāsaṁ ākāsa-gataṁ upādinnaṁ seyyathīdaṁ:
Whatever is inside, of an individual, that is taken hold of as space, as spacious – such as
kaṇṇa-cchiddaṁ, nāsa-cchiddaṁ, mukha-dvāraṁ,
ear-holes, nose-holes, the door of the mouth,
yena ca asita-pīta-khāyita-sāyitaṁ ajjhoharati,
and the means by which what is eaten, drunk, chewed, and tasted is swallowed,
yattha ca asita-pīta-khāyita-sāyitaṁ santiṭṭhati,
and the place where what is eaten, drunk, chewed, and tasted settles,
yena ca asita-pīta-khāyita-sāyitaṁ adho-bhāgā nikkhamati,
and the lower part by which that which is eaten, drunk, chewed, and tasted goes out,
yaṁ vā panaññam pi kiñci ajjhattaṁ paccattaṁ
or whatever else is inside, of an individual,
ākāsa ākāsa-gataṁ upādinnaṁ,
that is taken hold of as space, as spacious:
ayaṁ vuccati Rāhula ajjhattikā ākāsa-dhātu.
that, Rāhula, is called the internal space element.
Yā ceva kho pana ajjhattikā ākāsa-dhātu,
Now, whatsoever is the internal space element,
yā ca bāhirā ākāsa-dhātu, ākāsa-dhātur evesā.
and whatever is the external space element, that is the same space element.
Taṁ "netaṁ mama, nesoham asmi, na meso attā" ti,
Regarding that: "It does not belong to a me. This doesn't mean I am. A self of mine, this is not."
evam etaṁ yathā-bhūtaṁ sammappaññāya daṭṭhabbaṁ.
It should be seen like this, with true wisdom, as happening.
Evam etaṁ yathā-bhūtaṁ sammappaññāya disvā,
Having seen it like this, with true wisdom, as happening,
ākāsa-dhātuyā nibbindati,
one loses interest in the space element,
ākāsa-dhātuyā cittaṁ virājeti.
one frees the mind from the red taint of desire for the space element.

[Letting Letting-Happen Happen, Like the Elements]

Paṭhavī-samaṁ Rāhula bhāvanaṁ bhāvehi,
Let happen like the earth, Rāhula, the practice of letting happen,
paṭhavī-samaṁ hi te Rāhula bhāvanaṁ bhāvayato
for from letting happen like the earth, Rāhula, the practice of letting happen,
uppannā manāpāmanāpā phassā cittaṁ na pariyādāya ṭhassanti.
pleasant and unpleasant contacts that have arisen will not maintain a hold over the mind.
Seyyathā pi Rāhula paṭhaviyā sucim pi nikkhipanti,
Just as, Rāhula, they throw on the earth what is clean,
asucim pi nikkhipanti, gūtha-gatam pi nikkhipanti,
and they throw what is unclean, and they throw what is shitty,
mutta-gatam pi nikkhipanti, khela-gatam pi nikkhipanti,
and they throw what is covered in piss, and they throw what is covered in spit,
pubba-gatam pi nikkhipanti, lohita-gatam pi nikkhipanti,
and they throw what is covered in pus, and they throw what is bloody,
na ca tena paṭhavī aṭṭīyati vā harāyati vā jigucchati vā,
but the earth is not worried, or ashamed, or disgusted by it,
evam eva kho tvaṁ Rāhula paṭhavī-samaṁ bhāvanaṁ bhāvehi,
just like that, Rāhula, let happen like the earth the practice of letting happen,
paṭhavī-samaṁ hi te Rāhula bhāvanaṁ bhāvayato
for from letting happen like the earth, Rāhula, the practice of letting happen,
uppannā manāpāmanāpā phassā cittaṁ na pariyādāya ṭhassanti.
pleasant and unpleasant contacts that have arisen will not maintain a hold over the mind.

Āpo-samaṁ Rāhula bhāvanaṁ bhāvehi,
Let happen like water, Rāhula, the practice of letting happen,
āpo-samaṁ hi te Rāhula bhāvanaṁ bhāvayato
for from letting happen like water, Rāhula, the practice of letting happen,
uppannā manāpāmanāpā phassā cittaṁ na pariyādāya ṭhassanti.
pleasant and unpleasant contacts that have arisen will not maintain a hold over the mind.
Seyyathā pi Rāhula āpasmiṁ sucim pi dovanti,
Just as, Rāhula, they wash in water what is clean,
asucim pi dovanti, gūtha-gatam pi dovanti,
and they wash what is unclean, and they wash what is shitty,
mutta-gatam pi dovanti, khela-gatam pi dovanti,
and they wash what is covered in piss, and they wash what is covered in spit,
pubba-gatam pi dovanti, lohita-gatam pi dovanti,
and they wash what is covered in pus, and they wash what is bloody,
na ca tena āpo aṭṭīyati vā harāyati vā jigucchati vā,
but the water is not worried, or ashamed, or disgusted by it,

evam eva kho tvaṁ Rāhula āpo-samaṁ bhāvanaṁ bhāvehi,
just like that, Rāhula, let happen like water the practice of letting happen,
āpo-samaṁ hi te Rāhula bhāvanaṁ bhāvayato
for from letting happen like water, Rāhula, the practice of letting happen,
uppannā manāpāmanāpā phassā cittaṁ na pariyādāya ṭhassanti.
pleasant and unpleasant contacts that have arisen will not maintain a hold over the mind.

Tejo-samaṁ Rāhula bhāvanaṁ bhāvehi,
Let happen like fire, Rāhula, the practice of letting happen,
tejo-samaṁ hi te Rāhula bhāvanaṁ bhāvayato
for from letting happen like fire, Rāhula, the practice of letting happen,
uppannā manāpāmanāpā phassā cittaṁ na pariyādāya ṭhassanti.
pleasant and unpleasant contacts that have arisen will not maintain a hold over the mind.
Seyyathā pi Rāhula tejo sucim pi ḍahati
Just as, Rāhula, fire burns what is clean,
asucim pi ḍahati, gūtha-gatam pi ḍahati,
and burns what is unclean, and burns what is shitty,
mutta-gatam pi ḍahati, khela-gatam pi ḍahati,
and burns what is covered in piss, and burns what is covered in spit,
pubba-gatam pi ḍahati, lohita-gatam pi ḍahati,
and burns what is covered in pus, and burns what is bloody,
na ca tena tejo aṭṭīyati vā harāyati vā jigucchati vā,
but the fire is not worried, or ashamed, or disgusted by it,
evam eva kho tvaṁ Rāhula tejo-samaṁ bhāvanaṁ bhāvehi,
just like that, Rāhula, let happen like fire the practice of letting happen,
tejo-samaṁ hi te Rāhula bhāvanaṁ bhāvayato
for from letting happen like fire, Rāhula, the practice of letting happen,
uppannā manāpāmanāpā phassā cittaṁ na pariyādāya ṭhassanti.
pleasant and unpleasant contacts that have arisen will not maintain a hold over the mind.

Vāyo-samaṁ Rāhula bhāvanaṁ bhāvehi,
Let happen like the wind, Rāhula, the practice of letting happen,
vāyo-samaṁ hi te Rāhula bhāvanaṁ bhāvayato
for from letting happen like the wind, Rāhula, the practice of letting happen,
uppannā manāpāmanāpā phassā cittaṁ na pariyādāya ṭhassanti.
pleasant and unpleasant contacts that have arisen will not maintain a hold over the mind.
Seyyathā pi Rāhula vāyo sucim pi upavāyati
Just as, Rāhula, wind blows on what is clean,
asucim pi upavāyati, gūtha-gatam pi upavāyati,
and blows on what is unclean, and blows on what is shitty,
mutta-gatam pi upavāyati, khela-gatam pi upavāyati,
and blows on what is covered in piss, and blows on what is covered in spit,

pubba-gatam pi upavāyati, lohita-gatam pi upavāyati,
and blows on what is covered in pus, and blows on what is bloody,
na ca tena vāyo aṭṭīyati vā harāyati vā jigucchati vā,
but the wind is not worried, or ashamed, or disgusted by it,
evam eva kho tvaṁ Rāhula vāyo-samaṁ bhāvanaṁ bhāvehi,
just like that, Rāhula, let happen like the wind the practice of letting happen,
vāyo-samaṁ hi te Rāhula bhāvanaṁ bhāvayato
for from letting happen like the wind, Rāhula, the practice of letting happen,
uppannā manāpāmanāpā phassā cittaṁ na pariyādāya ṭhassanti.
pleasant and unpleasant contacts that have arisen will not maintain a hold over the mind.

Ākāsa-samaṁ Rāhula bhāvanaṁ bhāvehi,
Let happen like space, Rāhula, the practice of letting happen,
ākāsa-samaṁ hi te Rāhula bhāvanaṁ bhāvayato
for from letting happen like space, Rāhula, the practice of letting happen,
uppannā manāpāmanāpā phassā cittaṁ na pariyādāya ṭhassanti.
pleasant and unpleasant contacts that have arisen will not maintain a hold over the mind.
Seyyathā pi Rāhula ākāso na kattha-ci patiṭṭhito
Just as space, Rāhula, is not fixed anywhere,
evam eva kho tvaṁ Rāhula ākāsa-samaṁ bhāvanaṁ bhāvehi,
just like that, Rāhula, let happen like space the practice of letting happen,
ākāsa-samaṁ hi te Rāhula bhāvanaṁ bhāvayato
for from letting happen like space, Rāhula, the practice of letting happen,
uppannā manāpāmanāpā phassā cittaṁ na pariyādāya ṭhassanti.
pleasant and unpleasant contacts that have arisen will not maintain a hold over the mind.

[Letting Letting-Happen Happen, As Letting Go of Afflictions]

Mettaṁ Rāhula bhāvanaṁ bhāvehi,
Let happen, Rāhula, the friendly practice of letting happen,
mettaṁ hi te Rāhula bhāvanaṁ bhāvayato
for from letting happen, Rāhula, the friendliness of letting happen,
yo vyāpādo so pahīyissati.
any unfriendliness will be let go.

Karuṇaṁ Rāhula bhāvanaṁ bhāvehi,
Let happen, Rāhula, the kindly practice of letting happen,
karuṇaṁ hi te Rāhula bhāvanaṁ bhāvayato
for from letting happen, Rāhula, the kindness of letting happen
yā vihesā sā pahīyissati.
any aggression will be let go.

Muditaṁ Rāhula bhāvanaṁ bhāvehi,
Let happen, Rāhula, the joyful practice of letting happen,
muditaṁ hi te Rāhula bhāvanaṁ bhāvayato
for from letting happen, Rāhula, the joy of letting happen,
yā arati sā pahīyissati.
any unhappiness will be let go.

Uppekhaṁ Rāhula bhāvanaṁ bhāvehi,
Let happen, Rāhula, the transcendent practice of letting happen,
uppekhaṁ hi te Rāhula bhāvanaṁ bhāvayato
for from letting happen, Rāhula, the transcendence of letting happen,
yo paṭigho so pahīyissati.
any resentment will be let go.

Asubhaṁ Rāhula bhāvanaṁ bhāvehi,
Let happen, Rāhula, the unglamorous practice of letting happen,
asubhaṁ hi te Rāhula bhāvanaṁ bhāvayato
for from letting happen, Rāhula, the unglamorousness of letting happen,
yo rāgo so pahīyissati.
any redness of desire will be let go.

Anicca-saññaṁ Rāhula bhāvanaṁ bhāvehi,
Let happen, Rāhula, the practice of letting happen that is conscious of impermanence,
anicca-saññaṁ hi te Rāhula bhāvanaṁ bhāvayato
for from letting happen, Rāhula, practice that is conscious of impermanence,
yo asmi-māno so pahīyissati.
any "I am" conceit will be let go.

[Letting Thinking Happen]

Ānāpāna-satiṁ Rāhula bhāvanaṁ bhāvehi.
Let happen, Rāhula, as a letting happen, thinking in the activity of breathing in & out.

Ānāpāna-sati Rāhula
Thinking in the activity of breathing in & out, Rāhula,
bhāvitā bahulī-katā
when allowed to happen, when made much of,
mahapphalā hoti mahāni-saṁsā.
happens enormously fruitfully, with great benefits.

Kathaṁ bhāvitā ca Rāhula
And how when it is allowed to happen, Rāhula,

ānāpāna-sati kathaṁ bahulī-katā
how when it is made much of, does thinking in the activity of breathing in & out
mahapphalā hoti mahāni-saṁsā?
happen enormously fruitfully, with great benefits?

Idha Rāhula bhikkhu arañña-gato vā, rukkha-mūla-gato vā,
Here, Rāhula, as a bhikkhu gone to the forest, or gone to the root of a tree,
suññāgāra-gato vā, nisīdati.
or gone to an empty place, one sits.

Pallaṅkaṁ ābhujitvā,
With legs folded crosswise,
ujuṁ kāyaṁ paṇidhāya,
directing the body up,
parimukhaṁ satiṁ upaṭṭhapetvā,
having stationed thinking to the fore,
so sato va assasati, sato passasati.
one breathes out - yes! - thinking, and breathes in, thinking.

Dīghaṁ vā assasanto "dīghaṁ assasāmī" ti pajānāti.
Breathing out long, one knows "I am breathing out long."
Dīghaṁ vā passasanto "dīghaṁ passasāmī" ti pajānāti.
Or, breathing in long, one knows "I am breathing in long."

Rassaṁ vā assasanto "rassaṁ assasāmī" ti pajānāti.
Breathing out short, one knows "I am breathing out short."
Rassaṁ vā passasanto "rassaṁ passasāmī" ti pajānāti.
Or, breathing in short, one knows "I am breathing in short."

Sabba-kāya-paṭisaṁvedī assasissāmī ti sikkhati.
One trains like this: witnessing the whole body I will breathe out.
Sabba-kāya-paṭisaṁvedī passasissāmī ti sikkhati.
One trains like this: witnessing the whole body I will breathe in.

Passambhayaṁ kāya-saṅkhāraṁ assasissāmī ti sikkhati.
One trains like this: dropping off the fabrication of a body I will breathe out.
Passambhayaṁ kāya-saṅkhāraṁ passasissāmī ti sikkhati.
One trains like this: dropping off the fabrication of a body I will breathe in.

Pīti-paṭisaṁvedī assasissāmī ti sikkhati.
One trains like this: witnessing grace I will breathe out.
Pīti-paṭisaṁvedī passasissāmī ti sikkhati.
One trains like this: witnessing grace I will breathe in.

Sukha-paṭisaṁvedī assasissāmī ti sikkhati.
One trains like this: witnessing ease I will breathe out.
Sukha-paṭisaṁvedī passasissāmī ti sikkhati.
One trains like this: witnessing ease I will breathe in.

Citta-saṅkhāra-paṭisaṁvedī assasissāmī ti sikkhati.
One trains like this: witnessing the fabricating of a mind I will breathe out.
Citta-saṅkhāra-paṭisaṁvedī passasissāmī ti sikkhati.
One trains like this: witnessing the fabricating of a mind I will breathe in.

Passambhayaṁ citta-saṅkhāraṁ assasissāmī ti sikkhati.
One trains like this: dropping off the fabrication of a mind I will breathe out.
Passambhayaṁ citta-saṅkhāraṁ passasissāmī ti sikkhati.
One trains like this: dropping off the fabrication of a mind I will breathe in.

Citta-paṭisaṁvedī assasissāmī ti sikkhati.
One trains like this: witnessing the mind I will breathe out.
Citta-paṭisaṁvedī passasissāmī ti sikkhati.
One trains like this: witnessing the mind I will breathe in.

Abhippamodayaṁ cittaṁ assasissāmī ti sikkhati.
One trains like this: gladdening the mind I will breathe out.
Abhippamodayaṁ cittaṁ passasissāmī ti sikkhati.
One trains like this: gladdening the mind I will breathe in.

Samādahaṁ cittaṁ assasissāmī ti sikkhati.
One trains like this: composing the mind I will breathe out.
Samādahaṁ cittaṁ passasissāmī ti sikkhati.
One trains like this: composing the mind I will breathe in.

Vimocayaṁ cittaṁ assasissāmī ti sikkhati.
One trains like this: freeing the mind I will breathe out.
Vimocayaṁ cittaṁ passasissāmī ti sikkhati.
One trains like this: freeing the mind I will breathe in.

Aniccānupassī assasissāmī ti sikkhati.
One trains like this: reflecting on impermance I will breathe out.
Aniccānupassī passasissāmī ti sikkhati.
One trains like this: reflecting on the impermanent I will breathe in.

Virāgānupassī assasissāmī ti sikkhati.
One trains like this: reflecting on dispassion I will breathe out.
Virāgānupassī passasissāmī ti sikkhati.
One trains like this: reflecting on the dispassionate I will breathe in.

Nirodhānupassī assasissāmī ti sikkhati.
One trains like this: reflecting on stopping I will breathe out.
Nirodhānupassī passasissāmī ti sikkhati.
One trains like this: reflecting on stopping I will breathe in.

Paṭinissaggānupassī assasissāmī ti sikkhati.
One trains like this: reflecting on allowing I will breathe out.
Paṭinissaggānupassī passasissāmī ti sikkhati.
One trains like this: reflecting on allowing I will breathe in.

Evaṁ bhāvitā kho Rāhula
When allowed to happen like this, Rāhula,
ānāpāna-sati evaṁ bahulī-katā
thinking in the activity of breathing in & out, when made much of like this,
mahapphalā hoti mahāni-saṁsā.
happens enormously fruitfully, with great benefits.

Evaṁ bhāvitāya kho Rāhula ānāpāna-satiyā,
Through thinking in the activity of breathing in & out, Rāhula,
when allowed to happen like this,
evaṁ bahulī-katāya
when made much of like this,
ye pi te carimakā assāsa-passāsā
whatever last out-breaths and in-breaths are breathed,
te pi viditā va nirujjhanti no aviditā" ti.
they also are witnessed even as they cease; they do not go unwitnessed."

Idam avoca Bhagavā,
The Glorious One said this,
attamano āyasmā Rāhulo
and venerable Rāhula was transported,
Bhagavato bhāsitaṁ abhinandī ti.
rejoicing in what was said by the Glorious One.

Pali text drawn from
https://www.ancient-buddhist-texts.net/Texts-and-Translations/Short-Pieces/MahaRahulovadasuttam.htm.

With acknowledgement and thanks to Ven Ānandajoti Bhikkhu.

Appendix 2
[On Freeing the Mind from Polluting Influences]

Mahā-parinibbāna-suttaṁ (DN 16)

Tatra pi sudaṁ Bhagavā Ambalaṭṭhikāyaṁ viharanto Rājāgārake,
There also the Glorious One,
while living in Ambalaṭṭhikā in the King's Rest House,

etad eva bahulaṁ bhikkhūnaṁ Dhammiṁ kathaṁ karoti:
often spoke to the monks of the Truth of What Must Happen:

"Iti sīlaṁ, iti samādhi, iti paññā,
"Such is practicing good habits, such is practicing stillness, such is understanding.

sīla-paribhāvito samādhi mahapphalo hoti mahāni-saṁso,
Practicing stillness, when good habits are allowed fully to take effect, is abundantly fruitful and greatly advantageous;

samādhi-paribhāvitā paññā mahapphalā hoti mahānisaṁsā,
understanding, when practicing stillness is allowed fully to take effect, is abundantly fruitful and greatly advantageous;

paññā-paribhāvitaṁ cittaṁ sammad eva āsavehi vimuccati,
the mind, when understanding is allowed fully to take effect, is well and truly freed from the polluting influences -

seyyathīdaṁ: kāmāsavā bhavāsavā avijjāsavā" ti
that is, for instance, the influence of sensual desire, the influence of becoming, the influence of unwittingness."

Anicca-suttaṁ (SamN 22.45)

Yad anattā taṁ:
What is without self:
Netaṁ mama, nesoham-asmi, na meso attā ti,
It does not belong to a me, this doesn't mean I am, a self of mine this is not.
evam etaṁ yathā-bhūtaṁ sammappaññāya daṭṭhabbaṁ.
It is to be seen like this, with true wisdom, as happening.
Evam etaṁ yathā-bhūtaṁ sammappaññāya passato
Seeing it like this, with true wisdom, as happening,
cittaṁ virajjati, vimuccati anupādāya āsavehi.
the mind detaches itself and is freed from polluting influences by not clinging.

Printed in Great Britain
by Amazon

28152220R10245